Fiji

AFRO Z
9915699

**Robyn Jones
Leonardo Pinheiro**

D0108948

LONELY PLANET PUBLICATIONS
Melbourne • Oakland • London • Paris

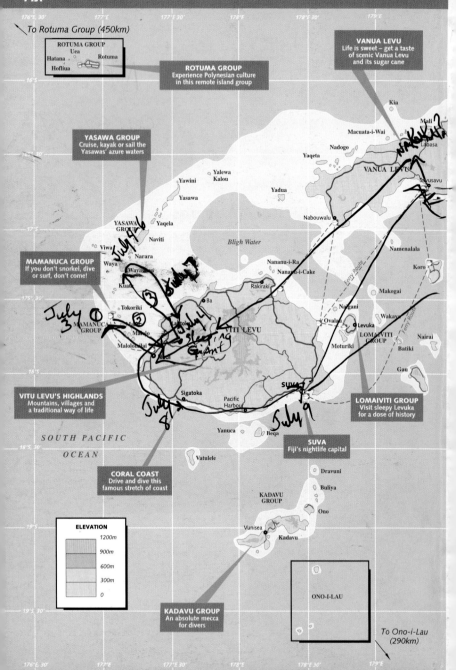

To Rotuma Group (450km)

ROTUMA GROUP
Uea
Hatana   Rotuma
Hofliua

ROTUMA GROUP
Experience Polynesian culture
in this remote island group

VANUA LEVU
Life is sweet – get a taste
of scenic Vanua Levu
and its sugar cane

Kia

Macuata-i-Wai   Mali
Nadogo   Labasa
Yaqeta
VANUA LEVU
Savusavu

YASAWA GROUP
Cruise, kayak or sail the
Yasawas' azure waters

Yawini
Yalewa
Kalou
Yawa   Yadua
Yasawa

Nabouwalu   Namenalala

YASAWA
GROUP   Yaqela   *Bligh Water*   Koro

Viwa   Naviti   Makogai
Narara   Nananu-i-Ra
MAMANUCA GROUP   Waya Wayasewa   Nananu-i-Cake   Naigani   Wakaya
If you don't snorkel, dive   Kuata   Rakiraki   Ovalau   Levuka   Nairai
or surf, don't come!   LOMAIVITI
Tokoriki   Ba   Natovi   GROUP   Batiki

July   MAMANUCA   Tovoko   VITI LEVU   Moturiki   Gau
3   GROUP   Malolo
Sleeping
Malololailai   Giant
Lomai

Sigatoka   SUVA
VITU LEVU'S HIGHLANDS   Pacific   **LOMAIVITI GROUP**
Mountains, villages and   July   Harbour   Visit sleepy Levuka
a traditional way of life   8   for a dose of history
Yanuca   Beqa   July 9
SOUTH PACIFIC
SUVA
OCEAN   Fiji's nightlife capital

Vatulele
CORAL COAST   Dravuni
Drive and dive this
famous stretch of coast   Buliya

KADAVU   Ono
GROUP

ELEVATION   Vunisea
1200m   Kadavu
900m
600m
300m
0

ONO-I-LAU

KADAVU GROUP
An absolute mecca
for divers   To Ono-i-Lau
(290km)

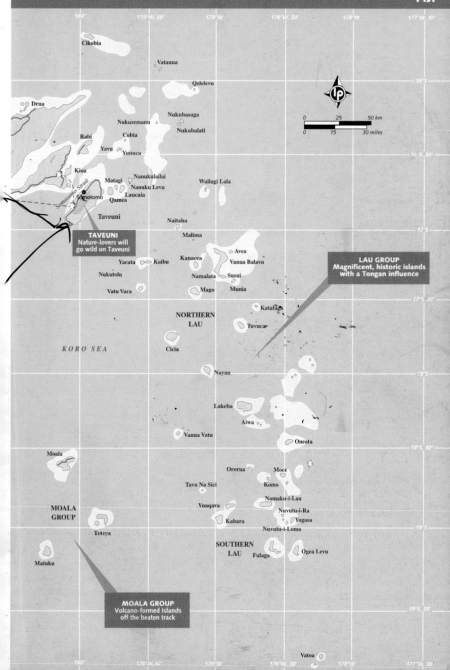

Cikobia

Vatauua

Qelelevu

Drua

Nukubasaga

Nukusemanu

Nukubalati

Rabi

Cobia

Yavu

Yunuca

Kioa

Nanukulailai

Matagi

Nanuku Levu

Wailagi Lala

Laucaia

Qamea

Somosomo

Somosomo Strait

Taveuni

TAVEUNI
Nature-lovers will
go wild on Taveuni

Naitaba

Malima

Kanacea

Avea

Yacata

Kaibu

Vanua Balavu

Nukutolu

Namalata

Susui

LAU GROUP
Magnificent, historic islands
with a Tongan influence

Vatu Vara

Mago

Munia

Katafaga

**NORTHERN
LAU**

Tuvuca

KORO SEA

Cicia

Nayau

Lakeba

Aiwa

Vanua Vatu

Oneata

Moala

Ororua

Moce

Tavu Na Sici

Komo

Namaku-i-Lau

**MOALA
GROUP**

Vuaqava

Nuvutu-i-Ra

Kabara

Yogasa

Nuvutu-i-Loma

Totoya

**SOUTHERN
LAU**

Ogea Levu

Matuku

Fulaga

MOALA GROUP
Volcano-formed islands
off the beaten track

Vatoa

0   25   50 km
0   15   30 miles

Fiji
5th edition – June 2000
First published – March 1986

Six-monthly upgrades of this title available free on
www.lonelyplanet.com/upgrades

Published by
Lonely Planet Publications Pty Ltd ABN 36 005 607 983
90 Maribyrnong St, Footscray, Victoria 3011, Australia

Lonely Planet Offices
Australia Locked Bag 1, Footscray, Victoria 3011
USA 150 Linden St, Oakland, CA 94607
UK 10a Spring Place, London NW5 3BH
France 1 rue du Dahomey, 75011 Paris

Photographs
Many of the images in this guide are available for licensing from
Lonely Planet Images.
Web site: www.lonelyplanetimages.com

Front cover photograph
Palm trees at dusk, Fiji (S Achernar, Image Bank)

ISBN 0 86442 679 8

text & maps © Lonely Planet Publications Pty Ltd 2000
photos © photographers as indicated 2000

Printed through Colorcraft Ltd, Hong Kong
Printed in China

Contents – Text

2 Contents – Text

Contents – Maps

MAP INDEX

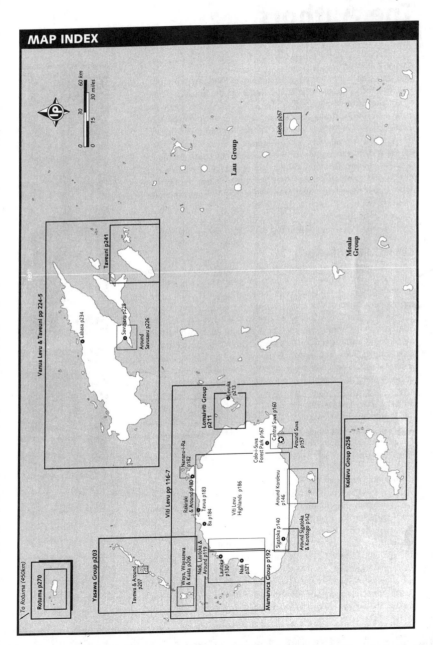

To Rotuma (450km)

Rotuma p270

Yasawa Group p203

Tavewa & Around p207

Wava, Wayasewa & Kuata p206

Nadi, Lautoka & Around p119

Lautoka p130

Nadi p121

Mamanuca Group p192

Vanua Levu & Taveuni pp 224–5

Labasa p234

Savusavu p228

Around Savusavu p226

Taveuni p241

Viti Levu pp 116–7

Rakiraki & Around p180

Nananu-i-Ra p182

Ba p184

Tavua p183

Viti Levu Highlands p186

Around Korolevu p146

Sigatoka p140

Around Sigatoka & Korotogo p142

Colo-i-Suva Forest Park p167

Lomaiviti Group p211

Levuka p213

Central Suva p160

Around Suva p157

Kadavu Group p258

Lau Group

Lakeba p267

Moala Group

0   30   60 km
0   15   30 miles

The Authors

Robyn Jones

As a teenager Robyn traded her quiet life on the farm in Victoria, Australia, for a year as an exchange student in the Brazilian mega-city of São Paulo. While studying for a degree in architecture she tripped around Australia and Europe, and later returned to Brazil, to get to know her future in-laws. She has worked on editions of Lonely Planet's *Brazil* and *South America,* and co-wrote *Fiji* and the Fiji and Tuvalu chapters of the 1st edition of *South Pacific.* In between travels Robyn works as an architect in Melbourne. Robyn and Leonardo's son, Alex (pictured below right), now makes their travelling much more interesting! He accompanied them on the entire research trip for this book – it was his job to check the bounciness of the beds and that the taps, fans and lights were all working, and to test hotel staff for friendliness.

Leonardo Pinheiro

Leonardo was born and raised in Rio de Janeiro, Brazil. At 15, curious to roam farther than Rio city, he jumped on a bus to the north-east coast. From then on he travelled as much as his pocket money and time would allow throughout Brazil. After tertiary studies in agricultural science he came to Sydney to do a master's degree in biotechnology and to check out the Australian surf. He met Robyn, and moved to Melbourne where they now live with their toddler, Alex. Leonardo has also worked on Lonely Planet's *Brazil, South America* and *Fiji,* and the Fiji and Tuvalu chapters of *South Pacific.* He is studying for his PhD in biochemistry.

From the Authors

We would like to thank the following people: Bob for getting us around Kadavu; the Bulou family in Navala; Leslie and Bruce from Suva for helping us recover from our travels on several occasions; John for agreeing to our crazy schedule in the Mamanucas; baby Georgia for letting Alex have her helicopter – it was a very useful distraction!; Abe from the FVB in Nadi for his great help and consistently friendly smile; Abdul in Nadi; Tups from the FVB in Suva for again providing helpful tips; Professor Firth at USP; Mike in Ovalau; Helen for dive tips; Michelle in Korotogo; Travis, Kitty, Bruce and friends for the fun and help in the Yasawas; Peter and David in Nadi; Noreen in Waiyevo; Al for proofing the history on the last edition; Ian, Peter and Jack for the last-minute computer use and babysitting; and Mum for again paying our bills while we were away! A special *vinaka vakalevu* (thank you very much) to all the people who gave Alex lots of attention along the way. Lastly, thanks to Alex, for coping so well with the travel and having his cheeks squeezed so often.

This Book

This Edition

The first three editions of *Fiji* were written by Robert Kay. The 4th edition was totally rewritten by Robyn and Leonardo. The 5th edition was updated by Robyn and Leonardo.

From the Publisher

This fifth edition of *Fiji* was produced at Lonely Planet's Melbourne office. Joanne Newell coordinated the editing and Hilary Ericksen and Cherry Prior provided editorial and proofing assistance. Kusnandar coordinated the mapping, design and layout. The groovy cover was designed by Maria Vallianos and Andrew Weatherill. Illustrations were drawn by Martin Harris, Dorothy Natsikas, Kate Nolan and Mick Weldon.

Thanks to Vince Patton for casting an eye over the health section, Quentin Frayne for checking the language section, Tim Uden and Jenny Jones for providing technical assistance and to Linda Suttie for her house style guidance. Our appreciation also goes to Professor Patrick Nunn of the University of the South Pacific for providing global warming information.

THANKS
Many thanks to the travellers who used the last edition and wrote to us with helpful hints, advice and interesting anecdotes. Your names appear in the back of this book.

Foreword

ABOUT LONELY PLANET GUIDEBOOKS

The story begins with a classic travel adventure: Tony and Maureen Wheeler's 1972 journey across Europe and Asia to Australia. Useful information about the overland trail did not exist at that time, so Tony and Maureen published the first Lonely Planet guidebook to meet a growing need.

From a kitchen table, then from a tiny office in Melbourne (Australia), Lonely Planet has become the largest independent travel publisher in the world, an international company with offices in Melbourne, Oakland (USA), London (UK) and Paris (France).

Today Lonely Planet guidebooks cover the globe. There is an ever-growing list of books and there's information in a variety of forms and media. Some things haven't changed. The main aim is still to help make it possible for adventurous travellers to get out there – to explore and better understand the world.

At Lonely Planet we believe travellers can make a positive contribution to the countries they visit – if they respect their host communities and spend their money wisely. Since 1986 a percentage of the income from each book has been donated to aid projects and human rights campaigns.

Updates Lonely Planet thoroughly updates each guidebook as often as possible. This usually means there are around two years between editions, although for more unusual or more stable destinations the gap can be longer. Check the imprint page (following the colour map at the beginning of the book) for publication dates.

Between editions up-to-date information is available in two free newsletters – the paper *Planet Talk* and email *Comet* (to subscribe, contact any Lonely Planet office) – and on our Web site at www.lonelyplanet.com. The *Upgrades* section of the Web site covers a number of important and volatile destinations and is regularly updated by Lonely Planet authors. *Scoop* covers news and current affairs relevant to travellers. And, lastly, the *Thorn Tree* bulletin board and *Postcards* section of the site carry unverified, but fascinating, reports from travellers.

Correspondence The process of creating new editions begins with the letters, postcards and emails received from travellers. This correspondence often includes suggestions, criticisms and comments about the current editions. Interesting excerpts are immediately passed on via newsletters and the Web site, and everything goes to our authors to be verified when they're researching on the road. We're keen to get more feedback from organisations or individuals who represent communities visited by travellers.

Lonely Planet gathers information for everyone who's curious about the planet – and especially for those who explore it first-hand. Through guidebooks, phrasebooks, activity guides, maps, literature, newsletters, image library, TV series and Web site we act as an information exchange for a worldwide community of travellers.

Research Authors aim to gather sufficient practical information to enable travellers to make informed choices and to make the mechanics of a journey run smoothly. They also research historical and cultural background to help enrich the travel experience and allow travellers to understand and respond appropriately to cultural and environmental issues.

Authors don't stay in every hotel because that would mean spending a couple of months in each medium-sized city and, no, they don't eat at every restaurant because that would mean stretching belts beyond capacity. They do visit hotels and restaurants to check standards and prices, but feedback based on readers' direct experiences can be very helpful.

Many of our authors work undercover, others aren't so secretive. None of them accept freebies in exchange for positive write-ups. And none of our guidebooks contain any advertising.

Production Authors submit their raw manuscripts and maps to offices in Australia, USA, UK or France. Editors and cartographers – all experienced travellers themselves – then begin the process of assembling the pieces. When the book finally hits the shops, some things are already out of date, we start getting feedback from readers and the process begins again …

WARNING & REQUEST

Things change – prices go up, schedules change, good places go bad and bad places go bankrupt – nothing stays the same. So, if you find things better or worse, recently opened or long since closed, please tell us and help make the next edition even more accurate and useful. We genuinely value all the feedback we receive. A well travelled team that reads and acknowledges every letter, postcard and email and ensures that every morsel of information finds its way to the appropriate authors, editors and cartographers for verification.

Everyone who writes to us will find their name in the next edition of the appropriate guidebook. They will also receive the latest issue of *Planet Talk*, our quarterly printed newsletter, or *Comet*, our monthly email newsletter. Subscriptions to both newsletters are free. The very best contributions will be rewarded with a free guidebook.

Excerpts from your correspondence may appear in new editions of Lonely Planet guidebooks, the Lonely Planet Web site, *Planet Talk* or *Comet*, so please let us know if you *don't* want your letter published or your name acknowledged.

Send all correspondence to the Lonely Planet office closest to you:

Australia: Locked Bag 1, Footscray, Victoria 3011
USA: 150 Linden St, Oakland, CA 94607
UK: 10A Spring Place, London NW5 3BH
France: 1 rue du Dahomey, 75011 Paris

Or email us at: talk2us@lonelyplanet.com.au

For news, views and updates see our Web site: www.lonelyplanet.com

HOW TO USE A LONELY PLANET GUIDEBOOK

The best way to use a Lonely Planet guidebook is any way you choose. At Lonely Planet we believe the most memorable travel experiences are often those that are unexpected, and the finest discoveries are those you make yourself. Guidebooks are not intended to be used as if they provide a detailed set of infallible instructions!

Contents All Lonely Planet guidebooks follow roughly the same format. The Facts about the Destination chapters or sections give background information ranging from history to weather. Facts for the Visitor gives practical information on issues like visas and health. Getting There & Away gives a brief starting point for researching travel to and from the destination. Getting Around gives an overview of the transport options when you arrive.

The peculiar demands of each destination determine how subsequent chapters are broken up, but some things remain constant. We always start with background, then proceed to sights, places to stay, places to eat, entertainment, getting there and away, and getting around information – in that order.

Heading Hierarchy Lonely Planet headings are used in a strict hierarchical structure that can be visualised as a set of Russian dolls. Each heading (and its following text) is encompassed by any preceding heading that is higher on the hierarchical ladder.

Entry Points We do not assume guidebooks will be read from beginning to end, but that people will dip into them. The traditional entry points are the list of contents and the index. In addition, however, some books have a complete list of maps and an index map illustrating map coverage.

There may also be a colour map that shows highlights. These highlights are dealt with in greater detail in the Facts for the Visitor chapter, along with planning questions and suggested itineraries. Each chapter covering a geographical region usually begins with a locator map and another list of highlights. Once you find something of interest in a list of highlights, turn to the index.

Maps Maps play a crucial role in Lonely Planet guidebooks and include a huge amount of information. A legend is printed on the back page. We seek to have complete consistency between maps and text, and to have every important place in the text captured on a map. Map key numbers usually start in the top left corner.

Although inclusion in a guidebook usually implies a recommendation we cannot list every good place. Exclusion does not necessarily imply criticism. In fact there are a number of reasons why we might exclude a place – sometimes it is simply inappropriate to encourage an influx of travellers.

Introduction

The Fiji archipelago has over 300 islands, of which only about one-third are populated. The country's central position in the south-west Pacific and relatively large land area has favoured its development as one of the most important nations of the region.

When most people think of Fiji they imagine beautiful white-sand beaches, coral islets, azure waters and tropical resorts. Fiji has all of this and much more. The larger islands are of volcanic origin and have rugged highland interiors with striking landscapes and remote villages. Travellers can snorkel and dive in the clear warm waters, explore gorgeous coral reefs teeming with underwater life, trek to waterfalls and through tropical forests, see historical and archaeological sites, and visit Fiji villages for the traditional welcoming *kava* ceremony.

Fiji has an interesting blend of various cultures, namely Melanesian, Polynesian, Indian, European and Chinese. This mix is reflected in Fiji's food, language and architecture. Food includes Fiji *lovo* (feasts in which food is cooked in a pit oven), Indian curries, European steak and chips and Chinese stir-fry. While the common language is English, the universal greeting is a warm *bula!* Most people also speak one of the many Fijian dialects or Fiji Hindi or Urdu. Hindu temples, Islamic mosques, Christian churches and *bure* (traditional Fijian houses) contrast with modern buildings.

While Fiji once had a fearsome reputation as the 'Cannibal Isles', paradoxically it is now renowned for its easy-going and friendly people. In the 19th century, Fiji was the trade centre of the South Pacific and in 1874 the islands became a British colony. The British brought Indian indentured labourers to work for them on the sugar plantations, and their descendants are now fourth-generation Fiji Indians. Fiji remained a British colony for almost 100 years, gaining independence in 1970.

Unlike many countries, the indigenous people of Fiji have not lost their traditional

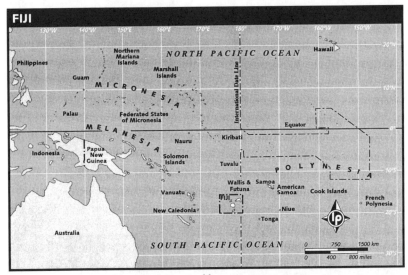

land rights, and retain ownership of 83% of the country. Access to land and political rights for all of Fiji's ethnic groups are currently controversial topics.

Despite the influence of Western values, the indigenous Fijian culture and social structure have remained strong. Many rural people live a semisubsistence village lifestyle under the authority of a local chief. Traditional values and culture are maintained through *meke* (dance performances telling stories and legends), kava ceremonies, bure construction and crafts such as bark-cloth making and pottery. However, many Fijian customs, such as elaborate hairdressing and body painting, as well as the old religion, disappeared when Christianity was introduced by missionaries in the 19th century.

Fiji is a relatively easy country in which to travel: It has a pleasant tropical climate, it's malaria free, it has a wide range of options for activities and accommodation, and has an extensive transportation network of buses, ferries and small planes. You can have a great time discovering Fiji, both above and under water, regardless of whether you are on a tight budget or indulging at an exclusive island resort. You can travel solo or in a group, use local transport, hire a car or take an organised tour or cruise. While Fiji is suitable for a short trip, it's great to spend a month or two exploring some of its many islands.

Facts about Fiji

HISTORY
Vitian Culture

Fiji, the name given to the island group after the arrival of the Christian missionaries and European colonisation, comes from the Tongan name for the islands. Before the arrival of Europeans, the inhabitants called their home Viti.

Vitian culture was a complex blend of influences, shaped by Polynesian, Melanesian and, to a lesser extent, Micronesian peoples who came and went over 35 centuries. Archaeological evidence from pottery remains indicates that Fiji experienced various periods of significant cultural change before the arrival of Europeans.

The Lapita people first settled the Fiji islands about 1500 BC. Linguistic studies suggest that they came from Vanuatu or the eastern Solomons. These people, coastal dwellers who relied on fishing, are thought to have lived in relative peace. However, from about 2500 years ago, a shift towards agriculture occurred, along with an expansion of population. This led to an increase in intertribal feuding. Cannibalism became common and in times of war villages moved to fortified sites.

About 1000 years ago Tongans and Samoans invaded from the east, prompting larger scale, more organised wars. More Tongans invaded in the 18th century and villagers again sought refuge in fortified sites. While there were also extended periods of peace, Viti was undergoing intense social upheaval at the time of first European settlement. By the early 19th century, local skirmishes between tribes were verging on civil wars. This led the Europeans to believe that the islands were in a constant state of war.

No Vitian community was completely self-sufficient. Some villages produced specialised products that were traded through networks operating throughout the islands. Trade even extended to Tonga and Samoa. Viti was, however, never politically unified and there were local variations in culture.

Portrait of a Fijian Man – engraving by JD MacDonald, 19th century

Vitian society centred around *mataqali* (extended family groups), which were headed by a *turaga-ni-koro* (hereditary village chief), who was usually male. The chief's everyday role was to chat and solve problems while the men of the village worked in the fields and the women fished, cooked and made crafts. Ownership was collective but the chiefs controlled the allocation of land and labour. A chief's immense power over the community was reinforced by the belief that he or she was *tabu* (sacred), and their *mana* (spiritual power) was derived from a special relationship with an ancestral god.

Chiefs were polygamous and intermarriage led to complex interrelationships between mataqali. Villages were also grouped under a paramount chief. Normally, the position of chief passed through a generation of half-brothers before passing to their sons, but the appointment was often hotly debated by village elders. Rivalry and power struggles were common, resulting in fighting and occasionally all-out war between close neighbours, who were invariably related. To further complicate matters, a chiefly woman's sons could claim ownership over property of her brothers from other villages. This was known as the *vasu* system.

A startling array of vicious weapons, including barbed spears, javelins, bows and arrows, slinging stones, throwing clubs and skull-piercing battle hammers and clubs, can be seen at the Fiji Museum in Suva.

European Explorers

During the 17th and 18th centuries, Europeans crossed the south-west Pacific searching for *terra australis incognita*, or the 'unknown southern land'.

The first-known European to visit Fijian waters was Abel Tasman, who, on his way to Indonesia on a voyage for the Dutch East India Company, sailed past the group in 1643. He negotiated the reefs north-west of Vanua Levu and Taveuni. His descriptions of the treacherous reef system kept mariners out of Fijian waters for the next 130 years.

After claiming Australia for Britain, the English navigator James Cook visited Tonga (then known as the Friendly Islands). There he learnt of the Fijians' reputation as formidable warriors and ferocious cannibals. Despite this, Cook stopped at Vatoa in the southern Lau Group in 1774. However, the notoriety Fiji gained as the 'Cannibal Isles' deterred sailors from visiting the islands for some time.

After the famous mutiny on the *Bounty* in 1789, Captain William Bligh and 18 others were cast adrift near Tonga. In their small open boat, with only a few provisions and navigation instruments, they sailed for Timor in the Dutch East Indies, a 6000km trip that lasted 41 days. They passed through southern Lau, across the Koro Sea and between Vanua Levu and Viti Levu (through a channel now known as Bligh Water). Almost clearing the Cannibal Isles without incident, they were chased by two Fijian war canoes near the Yasawas. Bligh managed to make rudimentary charts along the way and during another voyage in 1792 added to these charts, sailing through the Lau Group, the Koro Sea and past Kadavu.

Traders & Beachcombers

Tongans had long been trading with the Lau Group and other more distant Fiji islands. Colourful *kula*-bird feathers, which were highly valued for their use in ceremonial dress, *masi* (printed bark cloth) and weapons were all traded. From the early 19th century, European traders also began to visit Fiji waters. Whalers and sandalwood and bêche-de-mer (sea cucumber) traders had a significant and disruptive impact on the local population, introducing arms and foreign capitalist values. Some chiefs even sold land for guns to use in warfare.

Sandalwood Trade The fragrant sandalwood timber was highly valued in Asia. Initially Tongans obtained sandalwood from the Fijian chiefs of Bua Bay on Vanua Levu, and sold it on to the Europeans. However, when Oliver Slater, a survivor of the shipwrecked *Argo,* discovered the location of the supply, he spread the news of its whereabouts. Europeans began to trade directly with Fijians in 1805.

The sandalwood trade was a high-risk, high-profit business for the traders. Early on the timber was bartered for metal tools, tobacco, cloth, muskets and powder, to be sold for an average profit of 400% to 600%. The chiefs, however, began to drive harder bargains, and often demanded assistance in wars against other chiefs. By 1813 the accessible supply of sandalwood was exhausted.

The timber was a source of wealth and advantage for the chiefs of Bua (Vanua Levu) and Bau (south-east Viti Levu), and this led to jealousy and conflict with others. The introduction of firearms and the resulting increase in violent tribal warfare were a lasting consequence of the trade.

Bêche-de-Mer Trade Asia was also a lucrative market for bêche-de-mer, where people consider it a delicacy. As with sandalwood, this trade was short-lived due to overexploitation, only lasting from 1830 to 1835 and 1844 to 1850.

Fijian labour was used in the intensive process, which involved collection from the reefs, cleaning, boiling, cutting wood, drying, smoking and packaging. Hundreds of workers were required for a bêche-de-mer station. Some chiefs sent their villagers to work on the trade to boost their own wealth and power, and this affected the lifestyle and economies of communities. The chief of Bau received 5000 muskets and 600 kegs of powder in return for helping suppress objections to the trade.

Beachcombers During the 17th and 18th centuries, beachcombers lived with Fijian villagers. They were mainly deserting and shipwrecked sailors or escaped convicts from the British penal settlements in Australia. Some didn't survive long before being eaten, others though, were recruited into Fijian society and given special treatment for helping the chiefs in warfare. The wise beachcombers made themselves useful in order to increase their chances of survival, serving as interpreters and go-betweens, carpenters, arms-owners and marksmen.

Charles Savage was an especially influential beachcomber. After being shipwrecked on the *Eliza* in 1808, the Swede retrieved muskets and ammunition from the wreck. Savage helped Bau to become one of the most powerful chiefdoms in Fiji. In return for war service he received a privileged position and many wives, and survived about five years before being killed in battle. His skull was preserved as a kava bowl. Paddy Connel played a similar role in neighbouring Rewa.

Many of these beachcombers adopted Fijian dress, hairstyles and body painting, either for convenience or at the insistence of their hosts and protectors. It was unwise to be a conspicuous white man in battle.

Expanding Chiefdoms

By 1829 the chiefdom of Bau controlled Lomaiviti and the coastal areas of northern and eastern Viti Levu, where trade with Europeans had been most intense. For reasons

Suva's statue of the influential Bauan chief Ratu Cakobau

of intermarriage, Bau's chiefly family exerted influence over Rewa and Cakaudrove, as well as over much of northern Lau, Ovalau and Moturiki. It had accumulated wealth, tools, weapons and influence from dealings with traders and beachcombers. From Bau's strategic location, enormous canoes were used to carry out raids, intervene in disputes and otherwise assert the chief's power.

The competing chiefs of the regions of Bau, Rewa and Verata in the south-east involved their people in vicious power struggles, and war was the norm from the late 1840s to the early 1850s. Bauan chief Ratu Seru Cakobau, who succeeded his father Chief Tanoa, was at the height of his influence by 1850. He was known to foreigners as Tui Viti (King of Fiji), despite having no real claim over most of Fiji. His former Fijian allies eventually turned against him for the unreasonable demands he placed on local custom.

Tongan Influence

In the early and mid-19th century, Tonga began to have more influence on Fijian affairs. The chiefdoms of Bau, Rewa and Cakaudrove became dependent on Tongan canoe building and seafaring skills, and Bau received Tongan military support.

In 1848 Tongan noble Enele Ma'afu led an armada of war canoes to capture the island of Vanua Balavu in the Lau Group. His ultimate goal was to conquer all of Fiji, annex it to Tonga, and convert the people to Christianity along the way. In 1853 his cousin, the King of Tonga, made him governor of all Tongans in Lau. By 1854 Ma'afu had become a serious threat to Cakobau's power, especially in the Lau Group. In the late 1850s much of Fiji was taking sides with Cakobau or Ma'afu, resulting in the Tongans becoming the controlling force in eastern Fiji. Local chiefs, however, still presided over much of western Viti Levu and other remote areas.

Missionaries

Missionaries were drawn to Fiji to find converts for Christianity and to preach against cannibalism. They first entered the eastern islands via the Lau Group, from Tahiti and Tonga. In the 1830s the London Missionary Society (LMS) sent Tahitian pastors to Oneata, and Wesleyan Methodist missionaries David Cargill and William Cross set up in Lakeba. Cross and Cargill developed and taught a language system using a single letter to represent each Fijian sound (**b** for 'mb', **c** for 'th', **d** for 'nd', **g** for 'ng' and **q** for 'ngg').

The Tongan population of Lau converted fairly easily, but Fijians were not very interested in giving up their own gods. Progress was slow for the missionaries due to Fiji's lack of political unification. They realised that in order to convert the Fijian people it was necessary to convert the chiefs first, especially the powerful chiefs of eastern Viti Levu. Bau and Rewa were warring intensely at the time and it was not until 1839 that the missionaries' first real victory was achieved. The high chief of Viwa (3km from Bau) converted to the new religion, setting a precedent for his villagers and for other chiefs under his influence.

Cakobau reluctantly adopted Christianity in 1854, on the threat of withdrawal of Tongan military support. The Methodist Church saw his conversion as a triumph. There was a setback, however, when Reverend Baker, attempting to spread the Gospel in the western highlands in 1867, was killed and eaten by locals who resisted the imposition of ideas associated with Bau. See the 'Reverend Baker' boxed text in the Suva section of the Viti Levu chapter.

Some chiefs endured the presence of missionaries in their village for the trade opportunities this brought. Others converted because they were impressed by the new god's power, as demonstrated by the machines, guns and warships of its followers. Missionaries and Fijian ministers gradually displaced the priests of the old religion and assumed their privileged positions. The concept of holiness was accepted for its similarity to the existing beliefs of tabu and mana. The influence of missionaries and Europeans on traditional culture and everyday life was all pervasive: dress and once-elaborate body decoration and hairdressing became conservative; rituals such as initiation tattooing were discouraged; tribal warfare was suppressed; and Bauan was promoted over other dialects as the written language. Many Fijians, however, adopted Christianity while continuing to worship their own gods and ancestor spirits. The kava ceremony and *tabua* (whales' teeth) still hold symbolic meaning.

European Settlement & Levuka

By the 1830s a small whaling and beachcomber settlement was established at Levuka, on Ovalau. Foreigners married local women and Levuka became one of the main ports of call in the South Pacific for traders and warships. A US expedition, led by Commandant Charles Wilkes, arrived in Fiji in 1840 with the purpose of exploring the Pacific. Wilkes' team, including scientists, artists and a language expert, produced the first reasonably complete chart of the Fijian islands. While surveying the islands, Wilkes negotiated with the powerful Chief Tanoa of Bau and created a port-regulation treaty. The chiefdom was paid in return for protection of foreign ships and the supply of provisions.

In 1846 John Brown Williams was appointed as the American commercial agent.

In 1858 the British, fearful that America or France might try to annex the group, sent WT Pritchard to Levuka to act as their consul.

The chiefs of Bau and the early foreign settlers of Levuka had a mutually beneficial relationship. But relations deteriorated when the settlement was razed by fires in 1841 and Cakobau was suspected of being behind it. During the 1849 American Independence Day celebrations, the home of Williams, on the island of Nukulau, was accidentally destroyed by fire and locals helped themselves to his possessions. Williams held Cakobau, as King of Fiji, responsible for the actions of his people and sent him a substantial damages bill. This set a precedent and claims against Cakobau for compensation for the loss of American property rose to an inflated amount of US$45,000.

Cakobau came under increasing pressure from all sides. In 1862, claiming to have power over the whole of Fiji, he proposed to Pritchard that he would cede the islands to Britain in return for the payment of his debts. The offer was not seriously considered at the time, but representatives were sent to investigate the attractiveness of the proposition. Rumours and speculation caused a large influx of British settlers via Australia and New Zealand. Settlers bickered between themselves and disputes erupted with Fijians over land. Levuka town had become a lawless, greedy outpost bordering on anarchy and racial war.

Cakobau's debt was not cleared until 1868 when the Polynesia Company agreed to pay it in exchange for land (see the Suva section of the Viti Levu chapter). Various attempts to form a local Fijian government met with limited success. In 1865 a council of chiefs was established but it only lasted a couple of years, after which regional governments were formed in Bau (headed by Cakobau), in Lau (headed by Ma'afu), and also in Bua. Finally, in 1871 Cakobau formed a Fiji-wide government based at Levuka. It only survived for two years, however, as Cakobau's opponents accused his government of extravagance, ineptness and corruption.

Blackbirding

Europeans brought other Pacific Islanders to labour on cotton, copra and sugar plantations in Fiji. The American Civil War indirectly stimulated the trade in labourers by prompting a worldwide cotton shortage that resulted in a cotton boom in Fiji.

Levuka was a centre of the trade, and planters paid recruiters up front to secure labour. Initially, people were coaxed into agreeing to work for three years in return for minimal wages, food, clothing and return passage. Later, chiefs were bribed and men and women traded for ammunition.

Most labourers were islanders from the south-west Pacific, especially the Solomons and New Hebrides (now Vanuatu), but Fijians were also coerced. For a short time the chiefs of Ra province, in northern Viti Levu, traded their people for guns to use in defence against raiding war parties from the hills. In 1871 Cakobau sold the Lovoni people of the interior of Ovalau into virtual slavery on the plantations (see the boxed text 'The Enslavement of the People of Lovoni' in the Lomaiviti Group chapter for more information).

By the 1860s and 1870s blackbirding had developed into an organised system of kidnapping. Stories of atrocities and abuses by recruiters resulted in pressure on Britain to stop the trade. In 1872 the Imperial Kidnapping Act was passed, but this had limited success in regulating the traffic as Britain had no power to enforce it.

Cession to Britain

Cakobau's government was unable to maintain peace, and in 1873 JB Thurston, the acting British consul, again requested that Fiji be annexed by Britain. This time Britain was interested, citing blackbirding as its principal justification. Cakobau felt that internal instability was placing Fiji in a vulnerable position. He saw annexation by Britain as preferable to annexation by other European powers, such as France and Germany, who were increasing their presence in the Pacific.

Fiji was pronounced a British Crown colony on 10 October 1874 at Levuka. The islands of Fiji were in effect given to

Queen Victoria, her heirs and successors. Signatories to the Deed of Cession were Cakobau ('King of Fiji and warlord'), Ma'afu (then chief of Lau, Taveuni and much of Vanua Levu) and 11 other chiefs. It is significant that all but one of the high chiefs who signed the deed were from eastern Fiji: cession was not universally accepted by Fiji's chiefs.

The Colonial Period

Colonial Government Sir Hercules Robinson, the then governor of NSW, was sent to determine the terms of the cession contract and was then instated as provisional governor of the new colony. His replacement, Sir Arthur Gordon, arrived in the new colony in June 1875 and stayed for five years.

Along with the end of the American Civil War came a slump in the world cotton market. The local economy was depressed and unrest and epidemics followed. Cholera and the common cold took their toll and an outbreak of measles wiped out about a third of the indigenous Fijian population.

The recent Maori-Pakeha wars in New Zealand were fresh in people's memories. The fact that Europeans were greatly outnumbered prompted fears that racial war could also break out in Fiji. Like the missionaries before it, the colonial government appreciated the influence of the chiefs. They knew that if the chiefs could be persuaded to collaborate then Fiji would be more easily, cheaply and peacefully governed.

The last significant conflict in Fiji was the Kai Colo Uprising of 1875–76. This involved the highlanders of western Viti Levu, who had no part in the cession of their land to Britain and were unhappy with the imposition of new foreign laws. This posed a threat to the viability of the colonial administration. Gordon used the strategy of pitting Fijians against Fijians in order to quash the 'rebellion'. See the 'Kai Kolo Uprising' boxed text in the Queens Road section of the Viti Levu chapter.

Christianity was an effective form of social control. It helped the colonial government enforce and protect its new capitalist economic order. To reinforce the chiefs' traditional support, Gordon introduced a system of administration that incorporated the existing Fijian hierarchy. Fijian institutions were developed to provide a line of authority extending from the village chief to the governor.

Levuka's geography hindered expansion, so the administrative capital was officially moved to Suva in 1882. The early 1880s saw a considerable infusion of capital from New Zealand and Australia.

A land commission was set up to determine whether Europeans who had obtained land prior to cession had acquired it honestly and at a fair price. All tribal land was to be retained by traditional owners and the remainder of the land designated Crown or government land. It was the policy of the colonial government to protect Fijian land rights by forbidding sales to foreigners. Between 1905 and 1909, however, the rules of inalienability of land, as agreed upon in the Deed of Cession, were temporarily waived to attract investors. The system was successful in retaining land rights for the indigenous owners, and 83% of the land is still owned by Fijian communities.

Fijian Labour Governor Gordon was apparently keen to protect Fijians from being exploited, and he prohibited their employment as labourers on the plantations. This was largely calculated to maintain good relations between the new colonial government and indigenous Fijians. Fijian labour had been exploited in the harvesting of sandalwood, in the processing of bêche-de-mer and in cotton and copra production, and this had proved disruptive to village life. Fijians were becoming increasingly reluctant to take full-time wage work, preferring subsistence work, which satisfied their village obligations and was less regimented. Fijian labour, however, did generate wealth for the colony as village agricultural produce was appropriated by the government as a form of tax.

The colonial government was placed under increasing pressure from Britain to make the Fijian economy self-sufficient.

Plantation crops, such as cotton, copra and sugar cane, were a potential solution, but these demanded large pools of cheap labour. Slavery had been abolished, blackbirding was under control, Gordon was opposed to using Fijian labour, and Fijians were unwilling to leave their communal lands to work on the plantations anyway. Having served in Mauritius and Trinidad, where he had experienced an indentured-labour system using Indian workers, Gordon set about establishing a similar system in Fiji.

Indentured Labour In 1878, negotiations were made with the Indian government for people to come to work in Fiji. The contracts were for five years, after which the labourers, or *girmitiyas*, were free to return to India at their own expense. If they stayed for another five years the return passage would be paid.

Some Indians saw the system as a way to escape poverty, conflict with family or with authorities, or as a chance to start a new life. Others were recruited by trickery and deceit. Many were reluctant to join because the journey would involve loss of caste and mean extensive purification ceremonies upon their return. *Arkatis* (agents under commission) misled many by promising fine prospects or by failing to explain the penalty clauses of the contract. Most girmitiyas were transported from the ports of Calcutta in northeast India and Madras in the south.

The girmitiyas soon discovered the reality of life on the plantations. It was in the overseers' and foremen's interest to overload the workers; they often received a bonus from their employers for work done quickly and cheaply. Heavy work allocations were given and food was strictly rationed; if the girmitiyas failed to complete the daily tasks, wages were withheld and they could be prosecuted. Corporal punishment and human rights' abuses by the overseers were rife, checks were rare and there was little or no recourse to legal aid. In this high-pressure situation, crime, suicide, sickness and disease were common.

About 80% of the labourers were Hindu, 14% Muslim, and the remainder mostly Sikhs and Christians. Caste rules governed all aspects of a Hindu's life, dictating eating habits, dress, marriage and the level of personal physical purity. Overcrowded accommodation gave little privacy, and people of different caste and religion were forced to mix. The overseers were not sympathetic to these matters and the result was a breaking down of the caste system.

The Indian government initially insisted that there be a ratio of 10 men to every four women, but this was not enforced. Women were fought over and rape and adultery were common. Girls married and became mothers at a young age, and remarriage became widespread, though illegal under traditional law. The social and religious structures were crumbling; there was a lack of traditional leadership, very little knowledge of correct religious rituals and no education for children other than in Christian missionary schools.

Even though they may have been through great hardship, even *narak* (hell), the vast majority of Indians decided to stay in Fiji once they had served their contract. Many brought their families across from India. Some people of lower caste had much greater prospects if they stayed in Fiji, as those who returned were usually given the social standing of outcastes or untouchables, the lowest status in India.

By the early 1900s the Indian government was being pressured to abolish the indenture system. The missionary CF Andrews highlighted the plight of the girmitiyas, and others, including Mahatma Ghandi, denounced the civil and human rights' abuses that were occurring on the plantations. The Indian lawyer Manilal Maganlal Doctor from Mauritius, who arrived in Fiji in 1912, helped give focus and political direction to the Indian labourers. However, strikes by Indians against low wages, the 12-hour working day, rising prices and unfair taxes had little immediate effect. Recruiting stopped in 1916 and indenture ended officially in January 1919. About 2000 Indians had been transported each year from 1879 to 1916, a total of 60,537 people.

Power Play Interaction between Indians and Fijians was discouraged by the colonial government. Indians, restricted from buying land from indigenous Fijians by the colonial administration, moved instead into small business, trade and bureaucracy, or took out long-term leases as independent farmers. Differences in wealth began to emerge between northern and southern Indians. The former, who arrived earlier, tended to be more prosperous.

Up until 1904 the Legislative Council had been all-European and nominated by the governor. The constitution was subsequently amended to include six elected Europeans and two Fijians to be nominated by the Great Council of Chiefs. It was not until 1916 that the governor nominated one Indian member, and 1929 that the first Indian members were elected to the government. The 1920s saw the first major struggle for better conditions for Indians.

By the mid-1930s Australian dominance in the Fijian economy had extended beyond the sugar sector into gold-mining. The working classes were becoming more assertive and many indigenous Fijians laboured in mining. Occupational and geographical concentrations of labour developed along broadly racial lines as did labour organisations. The government resisted the introduction of fairer labour laws and instead promoted further racial fragmentation of the trade union movement in order to 'divide and conquer'. Working Fijians viewed themselves principally as Fijians, rather than as members of a social class.

Meddling, stirring and manipulation by a section of the local European community aimed to protect that community's capital and to quell labour troubles occurring within the Indian-dominated workforce. By taking sides with the Fijians they diverted attention from their monopoly on freehold land and their power and influence in the civil service. It was convenient to blame all problems on the Indian community and to exacerbate fears that the Indian population would surpass that of indigenous Fijians.

In the 1940s Britain allocated money to Fijian development funds. Europeans involved in the planning process diverted money to strengthen their own interests, principally to infrastructure that favoured the growth of tourism.

World Wars Fiji had only a minor involvement in WWI. Being distant from the conflict, the war was of little relevance, except that Britain was involved. Even so, about 700 of Fiji's European residents and about 100 Fijians were sent to serve in Europe.

The conflict in the Pacific during WWII was much closer to home. Around 8000 Fijians were recruited into the Fiji Military Force (FMF) and trained by American and New Zealand forces, and from 1942 to 1943 Fijians fought against the Japanese in the Solomon Islands. While there was no armed combat in Fiji, air-raid shelters and batteries were built in Suva and cannons placed at the strategic spots of Vuda Point near Nadi and Momi Bay.

Understandably, after the racism and exploitation experienced in the cane fields during and since the indenture period, Indians did not rush to enlist. The Fijian and European leaders chose to see this action, together with the cane farmers' strike of 1943, as cowardly and unpatriotic.

The aftereffects of WWII included additional exposure to Western ways, increased control by Fijian citizens over their own affairs, growth in the FMF, and greater links with the New Zealand government, who assisted in the administration and training of the FMF. Traditional divisions and local prejudices were partially broken down during the war. Fijian officers commanded groups of Fijians who were thrown together from different regions.

Fijian troops, who had gained a reputation for jungle fighting in WWII, served again in the 1952 Malaya conflict against communism. Malaysia, with its indigenous Malay population and Chinese immigrants, was later to serve as a role model for some economic and political development. Since 1978 the FMF has served in the Middle East and Zimbabwe as part of the United Nations' peacekeeping forces.

Independence

After WWII, Fijians became more conscious of the need for democratically elected government and the importance of forming organisations such as trade unions. The 1960s saw the formation of ministerial government, voting rights for women, the establishment of political parties, constitutional changes and a movement towards self-government. Increasingly, more members of the government were elected by the people rather than nominated by the governor.

Political parties were divided along racial lines. The National Federation Party, led by AD Patel, represented Fiji Indians and wanted independence from Britain and the introduction of a common electoral roll. The Alliance Party, led Sir Ratu Sir Kamisese Mara, represented indigenous Fijians and other races. It was interested in keeping a link with the British Crown and in introducing a racially divided voting roll. By purporting to embrace multiracialism and make peace with sections of the Indian community they hoped to weaken support for a common electoral roll. The Alliance gained the majority in the 1966 elections and a ministerial system was created, with Ratu Mara as the chief minister.

In 1963 the Legislative Council consisted of 38 members, divided equally between Fijian, Indian and European groups, with each racial community voting from separate rolls. In 1966 a new constitution expanded the Legislative Council to 40 members, changed the racial balance of the council by reducing the proportion of seats reserved for Europeans, and incorporated a system of cross-voting in which all voters also elected members from the different racial groups.

Fiji became independent on 10 October 1970, after 96 years of colonial administration. The 1970 constitution followed the British model of two houses with a Senate, comprised of Fijian chiefs, and a House of Representatives, comprised of 22 Fijians, 22 Indians and eight general members (Europeans, part-Fijians and Chinese).

In the rush towards independence, important problems, such as land ownership and leases; how to protect the interests of a racially divided country; the voting system; and appropriate development, were not resolved. The long history of segregation in Fiji was continued in the division of political seats and with parties being separated along racial lines.

Postindependence Fiji

In the immediate postindependence years, Fiji experienced a period of prosperous economic development. The road system and airstrips were upgraded, hydroelectricity was introduced, building, commerce, tourism, sugar-cane and pine plantations expanded and urbanisation increased. The high growth rate lasted for most of the 1970s. It fell during the early 1980s with a decline in the price of sugar, the country's main source of wealth. Along with the perceived benefits derived from foreign investment came foreign debt.

Fiji's first postindependence election was won by the Alliance Party, led by Ratu Mara. Although the Alliance promoted itself as pro-multiculturalism, the results in the polls showed a clear racial division of voting. The following year Ratu George Cakobau, the paramount chief of indigenous Fijians, became the new governor general. Ironically, he was a descendant of the great chief Cakobau, who had ceded Fiji to Britain almost one hundred years before!

Ethnic Tensions

In the first few years after independence, Fijians, especially town and urban dwellers, were optimistic, and people of different races generally got along well. There were, however, underlying tensions that became more apparent as the economy worsened. In 1975 there was a rise in nationalism led by Mr Sakesai Butadroka, who called a parliamentary motion to repatriate the entire Indian community, despite the fact that most were fourth-generation Fiji Indians. The motion was rejected by both the National Federation Party (NFP) and the Alliance Party, but many Fijians agreed with the idea. The following elections in 1977 saw Butadroka's Fijian Nationalist Party (FNP) divide Alliance voters, allowing the Indian

NFP to win. Its victory was short lived, however, as the governor general called for a new election, and the Alliance regained its majority.

In both urban and rural areas, most retail outlets and transport services were (and still are) run by Indian families. A racial stereotype developed portraying Indians as obsessed with making money. The vast majority of Indians, like the vast majority of Fijians, belonged, in fact, to the poorer working classes.

Meanwhile the economic aspirations of indigenous Fijians were changing: while some wanted to preserve their traditional ways, others sought to modernise their values and practices. In the subsistence economy of the villages Fijians were, and still are, relatively self-sufficient. In a cash economy, however, traditional obligations and a communal way of thinking are a definite disadvantage; instead, individualism, entrepreneurship and access to capital are required.

Prior to independence there had been an anti-Fijian bias in lending policies, and the economic boom had not directly benefited most indigenous Fijians. They were mostly employed in agriculture, the unskilled workforce and in the tightly controlled gold-mining industry. Efforts were made by the government to encourage Fijians to enter business through a 'soft loan scheme' developed by the Fiji Development Bank. However, many new businesses failed because they attempted to move into already competitive areas. Competition in business, education and employment tended to be seen in purely racial terms.

The Alliance Party was perceived to be failing indigenous Fijians in their hopes for economic advancement, and Fiji Indians were tired of the fighting between the Hindu and Muslim factions within the NFP. Greater unity among the working classes led to a shifting of loyalties and the formation of the Fiji Labour Party (FLP) in 1985, led by Dr Timoci Bavadra.

In the April 1987 elections an FLP-NFP coalition defeated the Alliance Party by winning 28 of the 52 house of representative seats; 19 of the elected FLP-NFP members were Fiji Indians. Despite having a Fijian prime minister and a cabinet comprised of an indigenous-Fijian majority, the new government was labelled 'Indian dominated'.

Military Coups

The victory of the coalition immediately raised racial tensions in the country. The extremist Taukei movement, supported by the eastern chiefs and the Fijian elite, launched a deliberate destabilisation campaign. In a demonstration in Suva, 5000 Fijians marched in protest against the new government.

Taukei leaders played on Fijian fears of losing their land rights and of Fiji-Indian political and economic domination. They suggested that development would result in the loss of Fijian culture, and pointed to the suppression of Maori and Australian Aboriginal cultures as examples.

In the following weeks there were violent incidents against Fiji-Indian businesses around the country and petrol bombs were thrown into the government offices in Suva. On 14 May 1987, only a month after the elections, there was a surprise invasion of parliament by armed soldiers led by Lieutenant Colonel Sitiveni Rabuka. He took over the elected government in a bloodless coup and placed Dr Bavadra and his cabinet under arrest.

General Rabuka, leader of the May 1987 military coup

A state of emergency was declared by Governor General Ratu Penaia Ganilau; however, he was unable to reverse the situation. Rabuka formed a civil interim government, comprised mostly of members of the previous Alliance government, with himself as military member directing a council of ministers. His 'government' was supported by the Great Council of Chiefs. In the face of international condemnation, Rabuka attempted to legitimise his government. He negotiated a deal with Governor General Ganilau to head the council of ministers, with himself heading the security forces and home affairs.

Talks were held between the self-imposed government and the opposition parties. They discussed amending the constitution and preparing for new elections. Taukei extremists, however, were radically opposed to any ideas of unification or compromise, and staged a series of violent protests. In September 1987, when the government was about to announce that elections would be held, Rabuka again intervened with military force. The 1970 constitution was invalidated and Fiji declared a republic. Rabuka proclaimed himself head of state and appointed a new council of ministers, which included leaders of the Taukei movement and army officers. Arrests of community leaders and academics followed, a curfew was imposed in urban centres, newspapers closed and all political activities were restricted.

In October 1987, Ratu Ganilau resigned as governor general and Fiji was dismissed from the Commonwealth. By December, Rabuka had nominated Ratu Mara as the prime minister, and Ratu Ganilau returned as the president of the new republic.

Background to the Coups There are many different theories as to what motivated the coups.

Many believe that the nationalist movement within the Methodist Church was behind the coups. The majority of indigenous Fijians are Methodist and were supporters of the deposed Alliance Party. Church leaders took part in the racist Taukei movement, and postcoup, Sunday observances, which included a ban on Sunday trading, were imposed on the whole country by the military government.

Another theory is that the CIA was involved to protect US interests in the South Pacific nuclear-weapons testing ground. The FLP-NFP coalition was opposed to nuclear testing.

There were underlying tensions and some jealousy on the part of Fijians against the Fiji Indians, but these racial differences were deliberately exaggerated by the Fijian elite who stood to lose by the Alliance Party's defeat. The FLP-NFP coalition, with its western Fijian and Fiji-Indian members, threatened the political power of the traditional hierarchy of the Great Council of Chiefs, which was dominated by the eastern chiefs.

The coups, which were supposed to benefit all indigenous Fijians, in fact caused immense hardship and benefited only a minority. When the Fiji-Indian element was effectively removed, tensions within the Fijian community itself were exposed. Clear examples of this are the conflicts and contradictions between chiefs from eastern and western Fiji; between paramount chiefs and village chiefs; between urban and rural dwellers; and within the church and trade-union movement.

Interim Government

The economic consequences of the coups were drastic. By the end of 1987, Fiji experienced negative growth in GDP, a devalued dollar, inflation, price increases and wage cuts. The economy's two main sources of income were seriously affected: Fiji-Indian sugar farmers refused to harvest their crops, and tourism declined significantly. Aid from Australia and New Zealand was temporarily suspended and large numbers of people, including thousands of Fiji Indians, skilled tradespeople and professionals, began emigrating.

Although there were a number of interruptions in sugar-cane harvesting and crushing while the interim government was in power, Fiji managed to largely recover from the economic effects of the coups. The government created a tax-free zone for export business, and loans were offered to start new businesses in tourism, timber and construction.

In 1989 the government relaxed the Sunday observance rules. In protest, the Methodist Church fundamentalist leader, Manasa Lasaro, organised demonstrations and roadblocks in Labasa, resulting in his arrest and that of 57 others. Methodist Church groups also firebombed and destroyed three Hindu temples.

Ratu Mara, the interim government's prime minister, became antagonistic towards Rabuka for his incompatibility with the old cabinet's traditions and political interests, and suggested he return to the military forces. In late 1989, Rabuka resigned from his position in the cabinet and took command of the army as major-general.

The 1990 Constitution

Early in 1990 diplomatic problems between Fiji and India resulted in the closure of the Indian High Commission in Suva.

On 25 July 1990 a new constitution was proclaimed by President Ratu Ganilau. The constitution increased the political power of the Great Council of Chiefs, giving them the right to appoint the president and a majority of senators, as well as authority over legislation relating to land ownership and common rights. The Native Lands Trust Board was one of the public bodies excluded from the jurisdiction of the courts. The president was given the right to appoint the prime minister from indigenous-Fijian members of the House of Representatives. Two seats in cabinet were reserved for the army, and the military was given ultimate responsibility for the welfare of the country. The constitution also granted the military, including Rabuka, police and prison forces, special immunity from legal prosecution in relation to the coups d'etat of 1987.

The constitution reserved a majority of seats in the House of Representatives for indigenous Fijians. Of the 70 seats, 37 were reserved for Fijians, 27 for Indians, one for Rotumans (Polynesians) and five for general electors. An electoral gerrymander meant that people who did not support the regime

were discriminated against. Compulsory Sunday observance was legislated, imposing Christian religious values on the population.

Fiji-Indian political leaders immediately opposed the constitution, claiming it was racist and undemocratic and that it condemned Fiji Indians to perpetual minority status. In protest a group of academics ceremonially burnt a copy of the constitution. A University of the South Pacific (USP) lecturer, Dr Sigh, was kidnapped and tortured while being questioned about the protest. The soldiers involved in the kidnapping were merely fined and then set free under suspended jail sentences.

The Postcoup Years

As 1991 advanced and the election approached, anticipation of change grew. The Great Council of Chiefs disbanded the multicultural Alliance Party in March 1991 and in its place they formed the Soqosoqo-ni-Vakavulewa-ni Taukei (Party of Policy Makers for Indigenous Fijians; SVT). The General Voters Party (GVP) was formed to represent Europeans, part-Fijians and Chinese. The Fiji-Indian NFP and the FLP considered boycotting the election, but in the end decided to participate. Differences between the two parties ruled out the possibility of a coalition.

Rabuka gave up his military career to pursue full-time politics and in November 1991 he was elected president and party leader of the SVT. Rabuka's position as army commander was taken over by the president's (and ex-governor general's) son, Brigadier Ratu Epeli Ganilau.

There was industrial unrest by trade unions after the introduction of new anti-labour legislation. Strikes occurred at the Emperor Gold Mine in Vatukoula, in garment factories and in the public service.

To suit his political ambitions, Rabuka changed his hardline approach and became increasingly populist. Prior to the 1992 elections he promised to repeal labour laws affecting trade unions, to review the constitution and to extend Fiji-Indian farmers' land leases. The SVT won the first postcoup general election, held in May 1992, but failed to obtain a clear majority in the lower house and had to seek coalition partners. Amazingly, in order to gain a majority and be appointed prime minister, Rabuka secured the support of the Fiji-Indian members of the House of Representatives, who had belonged to the same parties that he had expelled in the 1987 coup. Soon after the election, the GVP agreed to form a coalition with the SVT, thereby strengthening the new government's position. However, the postelection promises made to the FLP by the SVT – constitutional change, labour reform, land tenure and the scrapping of a value-added tax (VAT) – were not fulfilled.

The new government faced a faltering economy, with growing unemployment and crime and increasing urbanisation of the population. To promote indigenous-Fijians in business, companies with more than 50% indigenous-Fijian ownership were offered a 20-year tax exemption.

The concept of a government representing the interests of all groups in society was discussed in parliament, but, predictably, chiefs and members of the Taukei movement condemned the idea. FLP members eventually walked out of parliament in protest against the delay in revising the constitution and Rabuka's failure to keep promises.

To add to the poor economic situation Hurricane Kina hit at the start of 1993, causing widespread damage. Later in the year the government presented a budget with a large deficit. The proposed budget was defeated when seven members of the SVT-GVP coalition voted against it and formed a new political party, the Fijian Association Party (FAP). Parliament was dissolved and a new general election called. During the election campaign the president, Ratu Penaia Ganilau, died and the Great Council of Chiefs elected Ratu Mara in his place.

In the 1994 election, the SVT was re-elected. It won 31 of the 37 seats reserved for indigenous Fijians, a one-seat increase. The new FAP won two seats in the Lau province. Fiji-Indian allegiance shifted, with the FLP losing seven seats and the

NFP increasing its tally from 13 to 20. Rabuka was reappointed as prime minister and continued as leader of the SVT-GVP coalition. The previously defeated budget remained unchanged and was approved by parliament.

1995 began with revelations that the Public Trustee's Office had been borrowing funds for nonexistent developments. The revelations resulted in criminal charges being laid. But the main scandal of the year was the confirmation that the National Bank of Fiji was bankrupt. World Bank figures revealed debts mounting to F$150 million. As a rescue effort, the government considered bringing 28,000 paying Chinese migrants from Hong Kong to boost the economy by hundreds of millions of dollars. The idea, however, was not pursued.

On a positive note, 1995 saw the lifting of the Sunday observance decree and the ban on Sunday trading, although to a large extent this is still followed.

In 1996 France, the UK and the USA signed a comprehensive test-ban treaty at the South Pacific Forum (SPF) headquarters in Suva (see Ecology & Environment later in this chapter). Prime Minister Sitiveni Rabuka declared it a day of joy and celebration for the people of the South Pacific.

The 1997 Constitution

Rabuka came under increasing pressure to review the 1990 constitution. There had been a provision in the constitution that it be reviewed within seven years; Rabuka had become prime minister in 1992 by promising a review, and it was politically important because the constitution had been so controversial and divisive. The Constitutional Review Commission (CRC) was established in 1995. The SVT's submission to the commission called for continued political dominance by indigenous Fijians and the retention of the 1990 constitution because 'Fijians don't trust Indians politically'.

In response, a multiracial, multi-interest group called the Citizens' Constitutional Forum (CCF) submitted a report to the CRC. It proposed a move beyond ethnic issues to a national perspective, in nonracial and secular terms. It argued that the 1990 constitution perpetuated racial differences; was undemocratic and divisive; was weak on accountability; lumped all indigenous-Fijian interests together; and was contributing to economic and social decline.

In 1996 the CRC presented its findings. The 800-page report called for a return to a multiethnic democracy and a move away from communally based elections towards open noncommunal seats where all Fiji citizens could vote and stand for election. While accepting that the position of president be reserved for an indigenous Fijian, it proposed no provision of ethnicity for the prime minister. Nationalists publicly spat on, burnt and destroyed copies of the report in acts of symbolic defiance.

Public expectations of reform and a fairer electoral system were high. There was a widespread lack of confidence in the political system and a lack of national identity. The government acted on most of the CRC's recommendations and a new constitution was declared in 1997. Seats were still reserved for ethnic groups. After negotiations, the end result was that the 71 seats of the House of Representatives were broken down as follows: 23 Fijians (the CRC recommended an allocation of 12), 19 Indians (10 recommended), one Rotuman, three from other races (two recommended) and 25 open seats (45 recommended). Contrary to CRC recommendations, the Great Council of Chiefs retained the power to appoint the president, the Senate is by appointment not election, and it is compulsory to have a multiparty government; any party with more than 10% of the seats is entitled to join the government in a power-sharing arrangement.

The new constitution includes a Bill of Rights that outlaws racial discrimination, guarantees freedom of speech and association, the independence of the judiciary and the right of equality before the law.

Recent Events

In 1997 Rabuka apologised to Queen Elizabeth for the 1987 military coups, which ended her position as head of state.

He presented her with a tabua as a gesture of atonement. The following month Fiji was readmitted to the Commonwealth.

In 1998 the Fiji dollar was devalued. Fiji had been badly affected by the Asian economic crisis, with tourist numbers from South Korea and Japan plunging. The prolonged drought, the worst in Fiji's recorded history, had had a devastating effect on the sugar-cane industry. Uncertainty continued as Fiji-Indian farmers' land leases began to expire. The outflow of professional and skilled workers continued, the vast majority being Fiji Indians.

In an apparent aboutface, Rabuka recommended that all of Fiji's citizens, regardless of race, religion or country of origin, be called 'Fijian', to promote oneness and national unity into the new millennium.

Under the new constitution voting became compulsory and a record number of political parties joined the competition for seats, dividing voters' traditional preferences. Female candidates held a joint campaign rally in Suva and called for women voters to vote for female candidates, rather than along party lines.

In the May 1999 elections, Fijian voters rejected Rabuka and the SVT. The FLP, led by Mahendra Chaudhry, won the majority of seats and formed a coalition with the FAP. The NFP, led by former opposition leader Jai Ram Reddy, had expected to join the SVT in a coalition government, but fared poorly in the election. Chaudhry, a Fiji Indian, became Fiji's prime minister. Many feared that another coup would be staged. There was an organised demonstration in the weeks that followed, and in August a series of explosions in Suva.

Rabuka has since become chairman of the Great Council of Chiefs. It is widely believed he will make a comeback for the next elections, using his new position to reunite the Fijian political movement.

Prior to the elections, Rabuka had invited India to restore diplomatic relations with Fiji. An Indian high commissioner arrived in Fiji after the elections, following a nine-year diplomatic stand-off between countries.

GEOGRAPHY

The Fiji islands are in the south-west Pacific Ocean, south of the equator and north of the tropic of Capricorn. Australia lies 3160km to the south-west, and New Zealand 2120km to the south. Nearby Pacific islands include Tonga, 770km to the east, and Vanuatu, 1100km to the west.

Fiji's territorial limits cover an area of over 1.3 million sq km, but less than 1.5% of this is dry land. The total land area is about 18,300 sq km. The islands lie between latitudes 12° and 21° south of the equator, and between longitudes 177° east and 175° west. The 180° meridian cuts across the group at Taveuni, but the International Date Line doglegs eastward so all islands fall within the same time zone – 12 hours ahead of Greenwich Mean Time.

The archipelago comprises 300 islands, or many more, depending on how you apply the definition of island. Island sizes vary from tiny patches of land a few metres in diameter, to Viti Levu ('big Fiji'), which is 10,390 sq km. The second-largest island is Vanua Levu ('big land'), with an area of 5538 sq km. Only about one-third of the islands are inhabited, mainly due to isolation or lack of fresh water.

Viti Levu has Fiji's highest peak, Mt Tomanivi (Mt Victoria) at 1323m. It is near the northern end of the dividing range that separates east from west. Suva, the country's capital, is in south-eastern Viti Levu. Both Nadi, home to the country's main international airport, and Lautoka, the second most important port after Suva, are on the western side. Viti Levu has the country's largest rivers and most extensive transport and communication systems. The Kings Road and Queens Road join to form a main road around the island's perimeter.

Vanua Levu, north-east of Viti Levu, is of irregular shape with a deeply indented coast and many bays of various shapes and sizes. The huge Natewa Bay between the Natewa Peninsula and the remainder of the island is about 70km long by 15km wide. Like Viti Levu, the main part of the island is divided by a mountain range. Nasorolevu (1032m) is the highest peak. Most roads are unsealed, but a sealed stretch links the two main towns: Savusavu, in the south, and Labasa, in the north.

Taveuni, the third-largest island, is separated from Vanua Levu by the Somosomo Strait. It is rugged with rich volcanic soil and luxuriant vegetation, and is known as 'Fiji's garden island'. Its mountainous backbone of volcanic cones includes Uluigalau (1241m), the second-highest summit in Fiji.

The Kadavu Group is south of Viti Levu. It includes Kadavu, of similar size to Taveuni, Ono and a number of small islands, all within the Astrolabe Reef. The main island is three irregularly shaped, rugged land masses linked by isthmuses. Like Taveuni, Kadavu is very scenic, with beautiful reef lagoons, mountains, waterfalls and dense vegetation.

The remainder of Fiji's islands are relatively small and are classified in groups: Lomaiviti, Lau, Moala, Yasawa, Mamanuca and Rotuma. Beqa, Yanuca and Vatulele are small islands off southern Viti Levu. Refer to individual chapters for the geography of specific islands.

GEOLOGY

Apart from Kadavu and the islands of the Koro Sea, all of the Fijian islands belong to one massive horse-shoe-shaped submarine platform. The largest land masses, Viti Levu and Vanua Levu, are situated on the broader and higher north-west end of the platform. The eastern arm of the platform extends almost 500km to the southern end of the Lau Group. The whole platform is tilted to the south-east, resulting in deeper waters at the narrower south-eastern end. The waters of the Koro Sea almost cut the platform in two at Nanuku Passage, the north-east shipping gateway to the Fijian islands.

About 300 million years ago Fiji was part of a large Melanesian continent that included eastern Australia, New Zealand and South-East Asia; it extended as far north as the Philippines and as far east as Fiji. A complex series of geological events built and shaped the archipelago over a long period of time, with volcanic material and sediments being deposited on the ancient platform.

Types of Islands & Coral Reefs

The Fijian islands are of three different types: coral, limestone or, most commonly, volcanic.

Volcanic Islands These are generally of high relief with a series of conical hills rising to a central summit. Sharp pinnacles indicate the sites of old volcanoes, and crystallised lava flows often reach the coast as ridges to form cliffs or bluffs. Between these ridges are green valleys, and on the coast are beaches and mangrove communities. Flat land is only found in the river valleys of the larger islands. The sides of the islands facing the prevailing winds get more rain and support thriving perennial forest vegetation. The leeward hills are home to grasslands with only a sparse covering of trees.

While there are no active volcanoes in Fiji, live volcanic vents have recently been discovered on Taveuni. There is plenty of geothermal activity on Vanua Levu, and in Savusavu some locals use the hot springs to do their cooking! Viti Levu and Kadavu are also volcanic islands.

Limestone Islands These are characteristically rocky land masses that have uplifted from the sea. They have cliffs undercut by the sea, with shrubs and trees growing on the top. Generally, there is a central depression forming a basin, with fertile undulating hills. Volcanic materials also thrust up through the limestone mass. Vanua Balavu in the Lau Group is an example of a limestone island.

Coral Islands These are small low islands without many topographic variations. Generally, they are situated in areas protected by barrier reefs, so don't get washed away by the sea. Surface levels raise only to the height at which waves and winds can deposit sand and coral fragments. These islands support simple yet luxuriant vegetation, mostly overhanging palms, broad-leafed trees, shrubs, vines and grasses. The coast has bright, white-sand beaches and mangroves in the shallows of lagoons. Examples of coral islands are Beachcomber Island and Treasure Island, in the Mamanuca Group, and Leleuvia and Caqelai, in the Lomaiviti Group.

Fringing Reefs These are usually narrow stretches of reef linked to the shore and extending seaward. Sometimes they can extend up to 5km out from the shore. During low tide the reefs are exposed. Often the bigger fringing reefs have higher sections at the open-sea edge and drainage channels on the inside, which remain filled with water and are navigable by canoes and small boats. Rivers and streams break the reefs, the fresh water preventing coral growth. The Coral Coast, on southern Viti Levu, is an example of an extensive fringing reef. Most islands in Fiji have sections of fringing reefs somewhere along their coast.

Barrier Reefs These are strips of continuous reef, broken only by occasional channels some distance from the coastline. They sometimes encircle islands and often occur in combination with fringing reefs. The biggest barrier reef in Fiji is the Great Sea Reef, which extends about 500km from the coast of south-western Viti Levu to the northernmost point of Vanua Levu. A section of this barrier is unbroken for more than 150km, and lies between 15 and 30km off the coast of Vanua Levu. Other smaller well-known barrier reefs include the one encircling Beqa Lagoon, and the Astrolabe Reef of Kadavu.

Atolls These are small islands, rising just above sea level, sitting on a ring of coral reef enclosing a lagoon. An atoll where the land forms a complete circle is rare, and is invariably small when it does occur.

Despite the idyllic representation of atolls in tales of the South Pacific, most have inhospitable environments. The porous soil derived from dead coral, sand and driftwood retains little water, and unless the atoll is situated within a rain belt it is subject to droughts. The vegetation is usually small and hardy, with species such as pandanus and coconut palms, shrubs and coarse grasses. Fiji has only a few islands that can be classified as atolls. The most well-known is Wailagi Lala, east of Nanuku Passage in the Lau Group. There are, however, a number of 'looping' barrier reefs that encircle islands.

Viti Levu is believed to be the oldest of the Fijian islands. Its characteristic volcanic mountains were formed by upthrusts of masses of magma from below the platform. Around 150 million years ago, four long periods of volcanic activity began and uplifts resulted in the formation of sediments and limestone deposits.

Erosion over about 35 million years formed river deltas such as the Rewa near Suva, and the sand hills of Kulukulu, near Sigatoka.

CLIMATE

Fiji has a mild and mostly stable tropical maritime climate throughout the year. The main reason for this stability is the large expanse of ocean surrounding the islands. Unlike land masses that can change temperature in just a few hours, causing local atmospheric disturbances, the sea surface heats and cools slowly.

There are, however, local variations, from hot and dry to warm and wet. The prevailing winds are the easterly and the south-east trade winds. All the large islands have mountain ranges lying across the path of these prevailing winds, resulting in frequent cloud and greater rainfall on the windward eastern sides. The leeward sides are drier, with clear sky for most of the year and more variable temperatures and wind direction. Smaller islands tend to have dry and sunny microclimates.

Suva is notorious for its cloudy, wet weather. Fiji's resorts, however, are concentrated in areas of abundant sunshine, especially on the south-western side of Viti Levu and in the Mamanuca Group.

Fiji's 'wet season' is from November to April, and the 'dry season' from May to October, but rainfall occurs throughout the year. Suva, which is in a typical windward locality, has an average rainfall of around 3100mm per year. In comparison, Nadi, on the leeward side of Viti Levu, gets just under 2000mm. The heaviest rains fall from December to mid-April, and during this period the leeward side can get wetter than the windward sides. Strong thunderstorms can occur at any time during the year, but are

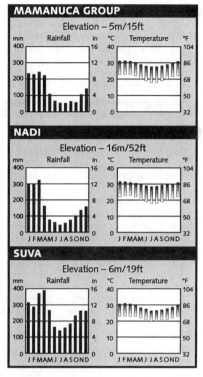

more frequent around March and are rare in July and August.

Fiji has mild average temperatures of around 25°C, however, hot summer days can reach 30°C. During the coolest months, July and August, temperatures can drop to 18°C. It can be much cooler in the mountainous interiors of the main islands, especially at night. Temperatures on the smaller islands tend to be more stable. Fiji's warm tropical waters are great for snorkelling and diving, with temperatures averaging 25°C to 28°C year-round.

Humidity is high, with averages ranging from 60% to 80% in Suva and 60% to 70% in Lautoka. Hot, windless, summer days with humidity levels of up to 90% can become oppressive. Most of the year, however, the humidity is offset by pleasant sea breezes.

Tropical Cyclones

Tropical cyclones, or hurricanes, are most likely to occur between November and April, the so-called 'hurricane season'. Cyclones originate from low-pressure centres near the equator and travel to higher latitudes, accelerating along a curving path. They often reach their full power at latitudes such as Fiji's.

Strong, destructive cyclones are, however, a fairly rare phenomenon in Fiji. The country has been hit by an average of 10 to 12 cyclones per decade, with two or three of these being very severe. Of the 52 storms

Global Warming

Since the Industrial Revolution in the 18th century, the concentration of greenhouse gases in the earth's atmosphere has risen dramatically – particularly carbon dioxide from burning fossil fuels. These gases increase the earth's natural greenhouse effect, reducing the loss of heat to space and raising the earth's temperature. The predicted increase in average temperature may seem small – about 4°C (6°F) in the next 100 years – but this rate of increase is vastly faster than any change in the last 10,000 years.

One of the most obvious effects of global warming will be a rise in sea level from thermal expansion of the oceans and the melting of polar icecaps – estimated at a 0.5 to 1m increase in the next 100 years. Although sea levels have been rising and falling over thousands of years due to periodic ice ages, the enhanced greenhouse effect is likely to accelerate the levels that have been rising by about 1.5mm per year over the past century. Other important effects are an increase in the severity of storms in some regions, an increase in the frequency of droughts in other areas and coral bleaching (where water temperature increases and causes coral to expel the colourful symbiotic algae that live within it, resulting in colourless, dead coral).

Rising sea levels will eventually cause devastating sea flooding and coastal erosion in many Pacific countries, most disastrously on low-lying coral atolls. However, even on 'high' islands most agriculture, population centres and infrastructure are in low-lying coastal areas. As well as the loss of land, higher seas will increase the effects of storms and cyclones, and the rising seawater table will poison crops and reduce the available fresh groundwater.

According to Professor Patrick Nunn of the University of the South Pacific, some of the Fijian islands most likely to be at risk in the future include Beachcomber and Treasure islands in the Mamanuca Group, and within the next 30 years, Leleuvia and Caqelai (near Ovalau). These are low islands made of unconsolidated materials such as sand and gravel. Some islands have already been affected by sea-level rise, including the island of Gau in the Lomaiviti Group, part of which has lost 200m of coast. Other sites affected include the village of Tokou, on Ovalau, and villages in southern Viti Levu, including Culanuku and Toguvu (near Navua).

An increase in the number of cyclones has also occurred in recent years (from three in the 1940s to 15 in the 1990s). Professor Nunn believes this may be due to warming, as tropical cyclones only develop where ocean temperatures exceed 27°C.

Although it is extremely difficult to accurately predict the effect of global warming, there is no longer any doubt that it is occurring. A measured increase in global temperatures and the break-up of polar ice are accepted. Other claims related to a measured increase in storm severity, the cause of coral bleaching events, and already-rising sea levels, are hotly debated.

There are people who express doubt about the whole issue of global warming – and they're not *all* groups with vested interests, such as oil companies. Some doubters claim the risks are being exaggerated by extreme 'green' movements. However, these dire predictions are sourced from the United Nations Environment Program, the Inter-Governmental Panel on Climate Change, and the South Pacific Regional Environment Programme – hardly the lunatic left!

recorded between 1940 and 1980, only 12 were considered severe. On the other hand, in 1985, four cyclones hit Fiji within four months, including Eric and Nigel, which caused deaths and millions of dollars worth of damage to towns, agriculture and the tourism industry. Cyclone Kina, early in 1993, caused severe flooding, completely destroying the bridge over the Ba River in the north-west of Viti Levu.

More recently, in 1997, Hurricane Gavin devastated areas of the Yasawas and the Mamanucas.

ECOLOGY & ENVIRONMENT

In the past the population limited itself through warfare, disease, famine, sexual abstinence and infanticide. About 2500 years ago the population began to increase and move inland. The burning of forests and clearing of land for agriculture resulted in widespread erosion. With the arrival of Europeans, the concept of individual wealth began to influence traditional communal and subsistence land use, leading to more intensive practices and environmental damage.

Since the 1960s more than 100,000 hectares (between 11% and 16%) of Fiji's forests have been cleared. Most of the deforestation is in drier lowland forests and whole coastal forest ecosystems have disappeared completely. Forests in the interiors of the large islands have been cut more sparingly. Logging practices are poor and have been one of the main causes of land degradation. In recent years some villages have turned to ecotourism as an alternative income source to logging their land. Mangroves are being replanted in the Korotogo area.

Unsustainable agricultural practices, such as steep-land sugar-cane and ginger farming, have increased natural erosion. This has increasingly led to large areas of land becoming unproductive as fertile topsoil is washed away. Landowners seeking short-term gain, through extensive and uncontrolled commercial agriculture, is the principal cause of deforestation. Fiji has a pine-plantation reforestation program on dry and degraded lands.

As more and more rural people head for the cities in search of employment, there is increasing pressure on the infrastructure and services of the towns – urban development is largely unplanned. This increased urbanisation is creating pressure on resources, infrastructure and services, and even prompting racial tensions.

Fiji's plentiful freshwater resources are not well managed, even in areas where water shortages can be a problem. In urban centres water quality is generally good, but supply and quality in many rural areas is poor. The water supply in Rakiraki has been deemed unfit for human consumption. In 1998 Fiji had its worst drought on record and water restrictions were applied in many areas.

The waters around Suva are quite severely polluted, and in certain areas fish consumption is a health hazard. Despite previous 'boom and bust' exploitation of bêche-de-mer and clams, over-fishing continues around the most populated areas. Destructive fishing techniques, such as the use of poisons and explosives, are commonly employed in Fiji without much control. However, the use of drift nets for fishing is officially opposed. Coral harvesting for the aquarium industry is becoming common.

Waste management is a national problem. Many villages dispose of their garbage as they always did, as if it were still biodegradable. Discarded plastic Coke bottles are a common site. In urban areas, such as Suva, only 60% of sewage goes into a sewerage system and it isn't always processed before being discharged into the sea. There are a number of industries using a variety of toxic chemicals and materials, with little or no data on the pollution generated. Oil spills are a problem in Suva's Walu Bay.

There is a high prevalence of asthma near the gold mine at Vatukoula. The asthma is thought to be a result of sulphur releases.

The World Wide Fund for Nature (WWF) has community-based projects in Fiji that aim to protect biodiversity and encourage the conservation of medicinal and cultural plants. It has a project with some local communities on Vanua Levu, together with the Women's Association for Natural Medicinal Therapy (Wainimate). It involves *kuta,* a water plant used for traditional weaving.

It hopes to conserve the plant by helping local women to restore its habitat, re-learn its cultural significance and hopefully derive an income from the woven products. The local conservation group, South Pacific Action Committee for Human Ecology and Environment (Spachee), has an Ecowoman project that promotes sustainable use of resources and links village women with women in science and technology through community-based projects.

The government departments of environment, agriculture, tourism and forestry are working in association with the Foundation for the Peoples of the South Pacific (FSP/Fiji), USP, Fiji Museum, National Archives, and National Lands Trust Board (NLTB) to revise environmental legislation. They are also working together on specific projects, including investigating the choice between logging and ecotourism.

Landowners are being encouraged to become involved in activities based on ecotourism. The potential for low-impact tourism exists, but it also has problems, especially in remote areas. While benefiting from the cash infusion, villages are faced with additional pollution and rapid cultural change. When visiting remote areas, including the ocean, take your rubbish away with you, especially batteries, disposable nappies and plastic. Avoid bumping against or walking on coral reefs and consider whether you really need that shell as a souvenir. Ecotourism projects include Bouma and Lavena, on Taveuni, and in Koroyanitu National Heritage Park in the Viti Levu Highlands. Some resorts and tours are more environmentally aware than others. In areas of intense tourism, such as the Mamanucas, the resorts are being pressured to clean up their acts and implement environmentally sustainable waste practices. See Responsible Tourism in the Facts for the Visitor chapter.

The following conservation groups are based in Fiji:

Greenpeace (Pacific region office ☎ 312 861, fax 312 784) upstairs, Old Town Hall, Suva
Spachee (☎ 312 371, fax 303 053) on the corner of Ratu Cakobau and Domain Rds, Suva

WWF (Pacific region office ☎ 315 533, 315 410, ✆ wwfspp@is.com.fj)

South Pacific Forum

Founded in 1971, the 16 members of the SPF are the heads of state of all the independent Pacific island countries, plus Australia and New Zealand.

Headquartered in Suva, the SPF meets annually to address issues of mutual interest, including environmental and social concerns, emergency relief and the status of Pacific territories remaining under colonial administration. Forum leaders signed the Treaty of Rarotonga in 1986, establishing the South Pacific Nuclear-Free Zone. Since the late 1980s the SPF has been lobbying the world's governments on the hazard posed to Pacific nations by global warming.

Fiji has received money from the SPF's Regional Natural Disaster Relief Fund to help people affected by heavy flooding.

In late 2000 the SPF will be renamed the Pacific Islands Forum, to recognise its north and central Pacific member countries.

FLORA & FAUNA

Much of Fiji's indigenous flora and fauna is related to that of Indonesia and Malaysia. Plant and animal species are thought to have migrated to the islands on the prevailing winds and sea currents. Another theory for the dispersal of species in the South Pacific is that during prior ice ages, parts of South-East Asia, Australia, New Zealand and the South Pacific were linked as one large Australasian continent.

Flora

Fiji has over 3000 identified plant species, with one-third of these endemic. Much of the native flora is used for food, medicine, implements and building materials.

Rainforest Plants There are hundreds of different species of fern in Fiji, a number of which are edible and are known as *ota*. *Balabala* (tree ferns) are similar to those found in Australia and New Zealand. Tree fern trunks, traditionally used on the gable ends of *bure* (traditional houses), are now used

Fiji-Indian dancers in traditional dress

Fijian girl, Leluvia, Lomaiviti Group

Government House guard, Suva

Smiling children on Waya in the Yasawas

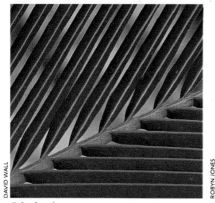
Palm frond

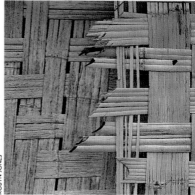
Woven bamboo wall cladding

Parrot fish

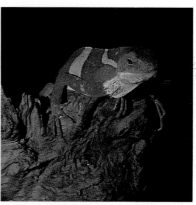
The iguana, an early inhabitant of Fiji

Produce from the Sigatoka market

Breadfruit, which is boiled or baked in a *lovo*

for orchid stands and carved garden warriors! Some *wakalou* (climbing fern) species were used to secure thatched roofing and to demarcate the chief's house and temples.

Forest giants include valuable timbers such as *dakua* (Fijian kauri) and *yaka*. These very hard, durable timbers have a beautiful grain and are used for furniture making. However, due to unrestricted logging and the absence of an efficient planting program, these trees are becoming less common in Fiji.

Degeneria vitienses is a primitive flowering plant found only in Fiji. It is related to the ornamental magnolia. The leaves, known as *masiratu*, were used in the past as sandpaper for wood carving.

Fiji has various species of pandanus and at least two of these are endemic. They are cultivated around villages and the leaves provide the raw material for roof thatching and weaving baskets and mats.

Fiji's national flower is the *tagimaucia* or *Medinilla waterhousei*. This flower only grows at high altitudes on the island of Taveuni and on one mountain of Vanua Levu. Its petals are white and its branches bright red. See the boxed text 'The Legend of the Tagimaucia Flower' in the Taveuni chapter.

Orchids are abundant in Fiji's rainforests. Vanilla is a common orchid and there is a renewed commercial interest in its cultivation for use as a natural flavouring by the food industry.

Edible Plants The Fijian root crops *tavioka* and *dalo* are the country's food staples. Tavioka, also known as cassava, is a shrub with starchy tuberous roots that grows up to three metres high. The leaves are also edible but are usually only eaten by people from the Lau Group. Dalo, also known as taro, has a high protein content and is more nutritious than cassava. Its leaves are often used in traditional Fijian dishes. Fijians distinguish 80 different varieties of dalo.

Breadfruit, still an important staple in many villages, is obtained from the breadfruit tree, which grows up to 18 metres tall. The fruit, up to 25cm in diameter, can be eaten boiled, roasted or fried, or it can be

The *tavioka* (cassava) plant, a Fijian root crop

fermented underground to produce a type of edible sourdough. In the past its wood was used to make canoes. The jackfruit is another large tree. Its seeds are used by Fiji Indians in curries, and when ripe the flesh of the fruit can be eaten (if you can cope with the unpleasant smell). Bananas are common, as are pawpaw and mangoes.

Piper methysticum, or kava, a plant belonging to the pepper family, is widely cultivated in Fiji. The roots are dried, ground and then mixed with water to make *yaqona,* a beverage with relaxing properties, drunk socially and in yaqona ceremonies.

Garden Plants Many of Fiji's common garden plants were introduced by JB Thurston in the 19th century. The hibiscus, introduced from Africa, is Fiji's most common and well-known garden plant and is used for decoration, food, dye and medicine. The bougainvillea and the allemanda are both common plants, both introduced from Brazil. The latter produces large yellow flowers all year round. *Bua,* or frangipani, with its scented white flowers, is also an introduced species.

Coastal & River Plants The most distinctive plant communities found along coastlines are mangrove forests. They cover large areas around river deltas and are important for the protection of sea shores against damage by sea and wind. The aerial roots, sulphurous mud and saline water of mangrove forests provide breeding grounds for various fish species. Mangrove hardwood is used for firewood and for building houses, and this has led to the destruction of many mangrove areas.

Casuarina, also known as ironwood or *nokonoko*, grows on sandy beaches and atolls. As its name suggests, the timber is heavy and strong and was used to make war clubs and parts of canoes.

The coconut palm has played an important role in the history of human occupation of the Pacific. The nuts provide food and drink, the shells are used for making cups and charcoal, the leaves for baskets and mats, the oil for cooking and lighting and as body and hair lotion.

Other common coastal plants include the beach morning glory, with its purple or lavender flowers, and wild passionfruit and the *vau*, or beach hibiscus. The latter has large yellow flowers and its light wood was once used for canoe building.

Aquatic Plants Plants are integral to the structure and energy balance of reefs. The most common is the variety of algae that grows as a film over dead coral. *Nama*, or grape weed, is an algae that looks like miniature green grapes and is often found in lagoons; Fijians consider it a delicacy. Large submerged meadows of sea grass grow in lagoons.

Fauna

Over 3500 years ago the first settlers introduced poultry and probably also dogs and pigs. This coincided with the extinction of at least three bird species (two megapodes, or mound-building birds, and a giant fruit pigeon).

Mammals Due to its distance from other land masses, Fiji has relatively few native mammals. Six species of bats are the only native terrestrial mammals. The most common are the large fruit bats, also known as *beka* or flying foxes, which roost in large

numbers in tall forest trees. Two species of insectivorous bats are cave dwellers and therefore seldom seen. They are the free-tailed bat and the smaller *bekabeka,* or sheath-tailed bat.

All other land-dwelling mammals have been introduced. Perhaps the most common wild animal on Viti Levu and Vanua Levu is the small Indian mongoose, often seen scurrying across the roads. It was introduced in 1883 to control rats in the sugar-cane plantations. It succeeded, but it also ate native snakes, toads, frogs, birds and birds' eggs. Although mongooses are often blamed for the depletion of banded iguanas, it is more likely that feral cats and habitat destruction are the cause. Domestic animals that have turned feral include the pig, introduced by the Polynesians, and goat, brought by missionaries. Both damage the native vegetation.

Three species of rat have also been introduced. In the 19th century, Europeans inadvertently brought with them the brown-and-black rat and the house mouse. The Polynesian rat came to Fiji much earlier, probably as a food source.

Dolphins, pilot whales and the occasional sperm whale visit Fijian waters.

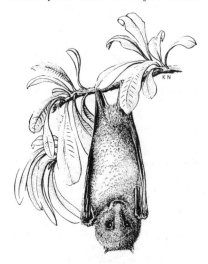

Fruit bats roost in Fiji's tall forest trees.

Baleen whales pass by on their annual migration to escape the Antarctic winter. Tabua, the teeth of sperm whales, have a special ceremonial value for Fijians. They are still used as negotiating tokens and they symbolise esteem or atonement. See the boxed text 'Tabua' in the Lomaiviti Group chapter.

Reptiles Fiji has 20 species of land-dwelling reptiles, four species of turtle and four species of sea snake.

Fiji's crested iguana, which was only identified in 1979, is found on Yadua Taba (a small island off Bua, Vanua Levu) and on the Yasawas. It can reach one metre in length. Since there are no other species of crested iguana found in South-East Asia, its ancestors are thought to have floated to Fiji on vegetation from South America. The banded iguana is found here as well as on other Pacific islands, including Wallis, Futuna and Tonga. Iguanas have been bred in captivity at the Orchid Island Cultural Centre near Suva.

Fiji has about seven types of gecko. The smallest grows to a mere 8cm, while the giant forest gecko, which yaps like a dog and changes colour, can reach 30cm. Various types of skink (slim, quick lizards) are also common, some growing to 25cm.

Two types of terrestrial snakes are found in Fiji. The Pacific boa constrictor reaches two metres in length. The burrowing snake *Ogmodon vitianus,* recognisable by a cream chevron on the top of its head, is venomous but seldom seen. Under the old religion, Pacific boas were considered sacred snakes. They were raised in rubble-filled pits or around the stone plinth of a spirithouse. Chiefs and priests would eat them during religious rituals, and their vertebrae were threaded for necklaces.

There are four sea snakes in Fiji, two of which are semiterrestrial. You are likely to see Fiji's most common snake, the *dadakulaci* or banded sea krait, while snorkelling or diving. Occasionally they enter freshwater inlets to mate and lay eggs on land. They are placid, and locals may tell you that they cannot open their jaws wide enough to bite humans, but don't risk it: The sea krait's

Despite restrictions on their capture, turtles can still be found in Fijian markets.

venom is three times more potent than the venom of the Indian cobra. The yellow-bellied sea snake, however, can be aggressive. It is able to remain submerged for up to two hours and is found throughout the Pacific. Another aquatic snake is *Hydrophis melanocephalus.*

Four turtle species are found in Fijian waters: the hawksbill, the loggerhead (which visits but does not breed in Fiji), the green turtle (named after the colour of its fat) and the leatherback. The leatherback is the largest, growing up to two metres, and is under strict protection to prevent its extinction. As in many other parts of the world its meat, as well as its eggs, are considered a delicacy here. Taking eggs is now banned in Fiji and it is illegal to catch adults with a shell length under 46cm. However, doesn't make much sense as the turtles only reach breeding age at sizes considerably larger than this! Unfortunately turtle meat is still sold at the Suva market. The shells, especially of the endangered hawksbill turtle, can still be found in shops and markets even though most countries prohibit its importation.

Amphibians The cane toad was introduced from Hawaii in 1936 to control insects in the cane plantations. It has now become a pest itself, competing with the native ground frog in coastal and lowland regions. The tree frog and ground frog have retreated deep into the forests and are rarely seen.

Birds Fiji has around 100 bird species, and about 23 of these are endemic. Fijian names imitate the birds' sounds; 'kaka' for parrots, 'ga' for ducks, 'kikau' for honeyeaters. Despite the relatively short distance between islands, some species, such as the Kadavu parrot or the Taveuni dove, are found on one island only.

Introduced species are common around densely populated areas like Suva. Aggressive species, such as Indian mynahs and bulbuls, have taken over and forced native birds into the forest. Taveuni and Cicia have imported the Australian magpie.

Fiji has seven species of nectar-eating parrot, three lory, eight species each of pigeon and dove (including the Malay turtle-dove), as well as ducks and wild fowls,

cuckoos and warblers. Tropical sea birds include the kingfisher, the frigate bird and the booby. The Fiji petrel, pink-billed parrot finch, red-throated lorikeet, and long-legged warbler are either rare or endangered species. *Birds of the Fiji Bush,* by Fergus Clunie, is a good reference for bird-watchers. Taveuni, eastern Vanua Levu, Kadavu and near Waidroka Bay Resort, on southern Viti Levu, are the best areas for bird-watching.

Insects Fiji, like other islands in the Pacific, is a paradise for insects, and there are many thousands of species here. Isolation initially hindered colonisation, but along with each human movement came a number of insect species, some of which have evolved into new species, unique to Fiji. Most of Fiji's insects haven't yet been described and catalogued. There are plenty of mosquitoes, but fortunately there's no malaria. There are, however, occasional outbreaks of dengue fever.

Marine Life Fiji's richest diversity of fauna is underwater, especially within the reefs and protected lagoons. There are hundreds of species of hard coral, soft coral, sea fan and sea sponge, which are often intensely colourful and form fantastic shapes.

Coral needs sunlight and oxygen to survive, and is restricted to depths less than 50m. Wave-breaks on shallow reefs are a major source of oxygen. Corals on a reef-break are generally densely packed and able to resist the force of the surf. Fewer corals grow in lagoons, where the water is quieter, but more fragile corals such as staghorn can be found in these places. Reefs near populated areas can be damaged by alluvial run off, sewage, chemicals, reef-walking, and the use of dynamite to kill fish. Infestations of the crown-of-thorns starfish also kill reefs.

There is a seemingly infinite variety of exquisite tropical fish. Many have descriptive names, for example, soldier fish, surgeon fish, trumpet fish, red lizard fish, goat fish, bat fish, butterfly fish and parrot fish. The ribbon or leaf-nose eel has an interesting

The Feather Trade

Vibrant-coloured parrot feathers of the endemic *kula* lory and *kaka*, or red-breasted musk parrot, were a symbol of chiefly and priestly status in Fiji as well as Polynesia. Priests and chiefs wore headbands made of a strip of pandanus leaf to which red, and sometimes green and blue, feathers were glued. A trade in parrot feathers persisted between Fiji, Tonga and Samoa until the 20th century, when it was banned by the colonial government for reasons of nature conservation. Seafaring Tongans would come to Fiji to obtain the feathers and then trade them with Samoans for fine mat kilts bordered with the feathers. The demand was so high that Tongans were even willing to fight for them. The Tongans initially could trade them for as little as a few nails, but after the sandalwood era the Fijians became more demanding. According to Thomas Williams, who lived on Taveuni in 1844, they were traded for 'European ironware, *yaqona* bowls, or use of their wives, sisters and daughters for a night or two'.

life cycle: from a young black male it changes to a brilliant blue male or bright yellow female. The territorial anemone fish, or clown fish, lives in a symbiotic relationship with the sea anemone, having developed an immunity to its poisonous sting. Some of the most beautiful fish and marine creatures, such as the scorpion fish and lionfish, are also highly venomous. If in doubt, don't touch!

Species such as the barracuda, jackfish, sting ray, small reef shark and large parrot fish are found cruising along channels and the edges of reefs. In open sea and deeper waters, larger fish are common, including tuna, bonito, sword fish, rays and sharks. Large sharks, however, normally stay away from the coast. The grey reef shark is most often seen on steeper outer-reef drops. It has a reputation for being aggressive, but it feeds primarily on small fish. Large manta and devil rays feed on zooplankton and small fish. Sting rays are most often found near swamp areas and among mangroves.

For an insight into the lives of molluscs, crustaceans, sea slugs, feather stars, starfish, Christmas-tree worms and other marine life, pick up a copy of Paddy Ryan's *The Snorkeller's Guide to the Coral Reef*.

National Parks & Protected Areas

Fiji's potential for land and sea reserves is excellent. There are a number of places of outstanding natural beauty, with interesting landscapes and vegetation, and rare or unique animals and birds. Archaeological and historical sites have great potential for tourism.

Since 1971, environmental policies and national development plans have been proposed by government. Implementation, however, has been slow and Fiji still has few legally protected conservation areas. The few areas selected as 'nature reserves' by Fiji's Department of Forestry have not had their ecological attributes fully evaluated. The existing legislation is adequate, but due to a lack of resources and commitment to conservation, preservation of sites is not being enforced.

The increased popularity of ecotourism has led to the development of a few forest parks and reserves. The Bouma National Heritage Park now protects over 80% of Taveuni's land area. The Lavena Coastal Walk, Vidawa Forest Walk and Tavoro Falls are attractions for travellers. The Koroyanitu National Heritage Park in the Mount Evans Range, near Lautoka in the Viti Levu Highlands, is also well established. Other sites of significance include the Sigatoka Sand Dunes on Viti Levu's Coral Coast; the Sovi Basin and Colo-i-Suva Park in Naitasiri province near Suva; and Tunuloa Silktail Reserve in the Cakaudrove district on Vanua Levu. Refer to the respective chapters for more information.

GOVERNMENT & POLITICS

The SVT-GVP coalition led by Sitiveni Rabuka, leader of the two military coups d'etat of 1987, was ousted in the 1999 elections. The Republic of Fiji is presently governed by the FLP-FAP coalition, led by Prime Minister Mahendra Chaudhry, a Fiji Indian. Of the new multiracial cabinet, four ministers are women. A joint campaign fund was set up by the National Council of Women. The president of Fiji is Ratu Sir Kamisese Mara, who has been prominent in the Fijian political scene since the 1960s.

The government is divided into 16 ministries. For administrative purposes the country has four political divisions: Western, Northern, Eastern and Central. Local government includes city, town and municipal councils.

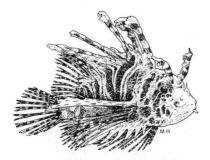

Avoid the beautiful yet venomous lionfish

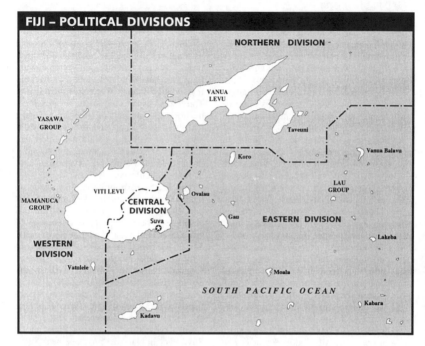

FIJI – POLITICAL DIVISIONS

NORTHERN DIVISION

VANUA LEVU

YASAWA GROUP

Taveuni

Vanua Balavu

Koro

LAU GROUP

VITI LEVU

Ovalau

MAMANUCA GROUP

CENTRAL DIVISION

Suva

Gau

EASTERN DIVISION

Lakeba

WESTERN DIVISION

Vatulele

Moala

SOUTH PACIFIC OCEAN

Kabara

Kadavu

Parliament & the Judiciary

The 1990 constitution was seen by many as racist and detrimental to the country. In 1997 it was replaced by a fairer constitution that would encourage multiethnic governments.

The constitution provides for a parliament consisting of a president, a House of Representatives and a Senate.

The president has executive authority and serves for a period of five years. The position is reserved for an indigenous Fijian appointed by the Great Council of Chiefs and requires support from a majority in the House of Representatives.

The Senate (upper house) consists of 32 members appointed by the president. Of these, the majority are appointed on the advice of the Great Council of Chiefs, one on the advice of the Rotuman Island Council and the remainder on the advice of other communities. The role of the Senate is to revise bills and debate issues.

The House of Representatives (lower house) consists of 71 members. Of these seats 23 are reserved for indigenous Fijians, 19 for Indians, one for a Rotuman, three for members of other races and 25 are open seats.

The position of prime minister is no longer reserved for an indigenous Fijian.

The judiciary is comprised of three courts: a high court, court of appeal and supreme court.

Political Parties

After a long history of segregation, Fiji's political parties remain largely separated along racial lines. A record number of parties registered for the May 1999 elections. The country's political parties include:

Soqosoqo-ni-Vakavulewa-ni Taukei (SVT)
Dubbed the chief's party, the SVT is a Fijian nationalist group sponsored by the Great Council of Chiefs and supported by the Taukei movement.
National Federation Party (NFP) Comprised mostly of Fiji Indians. It was part of the NFP-

FLP coalition, which won the 1987 election and was then deposed in the first coup.

Fiji Labour Party (FLP) Comprised of Fijian and Fiji-Indian trade-union members.

Fijian Association An ultranationalist party intent on preserving traditional chiefly power.

General Voters Party (GVP) Comprised of European, part-Fijian, Chinese and other Pacific Islanders.

Fijian Nationalist United Front (FNUF) A Fijian ultranationalist party in favour of rule by indigenous-Fijians.

Christian Democratic Party (Veitokani ni Lewenivanua Lotu Vakarisito) Backed by the Methodist Church, this is the country's largest Christian denomination.

Great Council of Chiefs

Parallel to and intertwined with government administration is the traditional chiefly system. Chiefs make decisions at a local level as well as being extremely influential at a national level through the Bose Levu Vakaturaga or Great Council of Chiefs. The former prime minister and coup leader, Sitiveni Rabuka, is now chairman of the council.

The basic unit of Fijian administration is the *koro* (village) headed by the *turaga-ni-koro* (a hereditary chief), who is appointed by the village elders. Several koro are linked as a *tikina*, and several tikina form a *yasana* or province. Fiji is divided into 14 provinces, and each has a high chief.

The Great Council of Chiefs includes members of the lower house as well as nominated chiefs from the provincial councils. The council was originally created to strengthen the position of the ruling Fijian elite, and gained great power after the military coups and the introduction of the 1990 constitution. The council appoints the president, who in turn is responsible for appointing judges, in consultation with the Judicial & Legal Services Commission. It also has authority over any legislation related to land ownership and common rights.

ECONOMY

Tourism and sugar are Fiji's main earners and together employ about 80,000 people. Fiji also exports molasses, gold, timber, fish, copra and coconut oil, and clothing.

National Symbols

Although Fiji is a republic, and since the coups is no longer a member of the Commonwealth, British influence is still retained in the national symbols and the national anthem – *God Bless Fiji*. Queen Elizabeth II still figures on all currency.

The Fijian coat of arms features two warriors with war club and spear, a *takia* (Fijian canoe) and a shield. The shield bears a heraldic lion clasping a cocoa pod, sugar cane, coconut palm, bananas and a dove of peace. The words *Revevaka na Kalou ka doka na Tui*, meaning 'fear God and honour the queen', also appeared on the flag of the Cakobau 'government' before cession.

The Fijian Flag has the British Union Jack on a light-blue background, and the shield from the coat of arms.

Recent years have seen diversification, with the exportation of forest wood chips and sawn timber, and an expansion in manufacturing to include products such as leather and furniture.

Fiji is facing many economic problems. The population is increasing and people's expectations are rising. Poverty and inequality are growing, along with unemployment and increasing urbanisation, with a shift away from subsistence farming.

Unemployment is especially high among youth. The semisubsistence village economy is no longer able to absorb large numbers of young people. Cash is required for clothing, school fees, church levies, imported goods and community projects. Urban children lead a different life, away from the discipline and structure of village life. Theft in the cities and towns is increasing.

The traditional Fijian and modern economic systems have different and often contradictory requirements. Traditional economic systems rely on kinship and village structure to sustain them. With the global push for internationalisation of production and trade, Fiji is becoming more export orientated and open to increased competition.

The former SVT government's policies included downsizing the public sector, tax reform, encouragement of overseas investment and increased indigenous-Fijian participation in business. The public sector accounts for about 40% of all formal employment. The size of both the armed forces and parliament increased in 1987. The new government reversed some of the SVT's decisions. One of its election promises was to reinstate Nadi airport workers who had lost their jobs as part of the rationalisation and reform of the country's airports.

Fiji has long been reliant on overseas aid from Australia and New Zealand, and, more recently, Japan.

Economic growth is needed to service Fiji's massive loans. In 1994 foreign debt stood at F$190 million and internal debt at F$800 million, and in 1995 it was confirmed that the National Bank of Fiji was bankrupt. Growth was hindered by the public's reluctance to invest and make long-term commitments. This was due to racial tensions and uncertainty over the constitution. The uncertainty over the renewal of Fiji-Indian farmers' land leases is still a problem. After the coups many skilled and educated workers, especially Fiji Indians, left, and are continuing to leave, Fiji in search of greater security.

Tourism

Fiji receives about 360,000 visitors every year. Since 1989, earnings from tourism have amounted to about 17% of GDP, surpassing sugar as primary source of foreign-exchange earnings. Most visitors are from Australia and New Zealand, followed by the USA, the UK and Japan. The industry is promoted by the Fiji Visitors Bureau (FVB) and the Tourism Council of the South Pacific (TCSP).

Travellers should be aware that there is a 10% VAT on all goods and services. It is a competitive industry and the resorts often have good deals on offer, especially in the low season.

Agriculture

Agriculture is the largest sector of the economy. Only about 16% of Fiji's land is suitable for agriculture, and this is mainly along the coastal plains and river valleys and deltas of the two main islands. The principal cane-growing areas are western Viti Levu and western Vanua Levu, with mills at Lautoka, Ba, Rakiraki and Labasa. Dairy farming is concentrated in the Rewa Delta, near Suva. Other produce includes molasses, copra, coconut oil, cocoa, ginger, rice, vanilla, fruit and vegetables.

The sugar industry was the mainstay of the economy for most of the 20th century, and it currently provides employment for almost a third of the population. The prosperity of the industry is therefore extremely important to the economy, providing taxes to the government and rent from leased land to landowners. To counteract the problem of falling markets, there is a need for greater productivity, investment in technology and long-term planning. In 1998 the economy was badly affected by the sharp fall in sugar production (reduced by 50% in 1998), a result of the extended drought.

Due to historical and constitutional reasons, the industry is compartmentalised along racial lines. Most cane is grown by Fiji-Indian farmers on land leased from indigenous landowners. Indigenous Fijians own 83% of the total land area, and, due to rules of ownership, Fiji Indians cannot own this land. Long-term land leases began expiring in 1997 and anxious farmers are avoiding long-term planning and investment.

Other Industries

The fisheries industry produces canned tuna, bêche-de-mer, shark fin, trochus shell and trochus-shell buttons.

Pine plantations are common on the western sides of Viti Levu and Vanua Levu. Most forest is on communally owned native land, and has been planted by Fiji Pine Limited.

Gold is being mined at Vatukoula, near Tavua in northern Viti Levu, and until recently at Mt Kasi, in Vanua Levu.

Fiji's manufacturing sector produces clothing, some footwear, cigarettes, food and beverages. Aluminium and plastic products, agricultural equipment, boats, cement, furniture, and handicrafts are also manufactured here.

Trade Agreements

In 1994 Fiji became a signatory to the General Agreement on Tariffs and Trade (GATT). The South Pacific Regional Trade and Economic Cooperation Agreement (Sparteca) provides for duty and quota-free access to New Zealand and Australian markets, and this has benefited Fiji. However, Australia is now removing its trade protection. The Lome Convention gives Fiji preferential access to the European Union, and the Generalised System of Preferences does the same in the USA and Japan. Fiji is also pursuing trade links with the markets of South-East Asia.

Standard of Living

Life expectancy is 61.4 years for men and 65.2 for women. Food is relatively plentiful and many rural people live a semisubsistence village lifestyle. The urban poor are less well off, and support networks and extended families are less intact. About 70% of the population has access to a piped water supply. Many rural villages and settlements in the interior and outer islands rely on diesel generators or have no electricity. About 8% of households have an annual income of less than F$3000. The government provides some housing assistance for low-income earners. About 21% of women have jobs outside the home.

POPULATION & PEOPLE

Fiji has a total population of 775,077, according to the 1996 census. About half of the population is under the age of 20 and about two-thirds under 30. Youths aged between 15 and 24, who comprise 20% of the total population, are facing high unemployment.

The most populated island is Viti Levu, with 75% of the overall population, followed by Vanua Levu, with 18%. The remaining 7% is spread over 100-odd islands. About 39% of the population are urban dwellers. The highest densities occur in the major urban centres of Suva, Nadi, Lautoka and in the sugar-cane growing areas of Rewa and Ba.

Fiji's population is the most multiracial of the South Pacific countries. Due to historical factors, such as indenture, some areas have a higher proportion of particular races. The Fijian administration categorises people according to their racial origins and this promotes a lack of national identity. The term 'Fijian' is used for indigenous Fijians only, even if a person's family has lived in Fiji for generations. Fiji Indians are referred to as 'Indians', and the naming system for 'Chinese' and other Pacific Islanders is similar. People of Australian, New Zealand, American or European descent are all labelled 'Europeans'. Those people with a mixed descent of European and indigenous Fijian are known as 'part-Europeans'. There is, however, relatively little marriage between racial groups.

Fijians also use the following terms: *kaiviti* for indigenous Fijian, *kaihidi* for Fiji Indians, and *kaivelagi,* or literally 'people from far away', for Europeans. The term 'pre-mix' is occasionally used informally to describe people of mixed race.

From the late 1940s until the military coups of 1987, indigenous Fijians were outnumbered by Fiji Indians. Indigenous Fijians presently account for about 50% of the population and Fiji Indians for about 45%. A large number of Fiji Indians immigrated after the coup and the trend is still continuing. Some other Pacific countries, including Tonga, refused to let Fiji Indians into their country.

Indigenous Fijians

Indigenous Fijians are predominantly of Melanesian origin, but with strong Polynesian influences. These influences, both physical and cultural, are especially evident in the Lau Group due to its proximity to Tonga. Melanesian features (such as darker skin and frizzy hair) mix with Polynesian features (lighter skin tone and straight hair).

Fiji Indians

Most Fiji Indians are descendants of indentured labourers. Initially, most of the Indians came from the states of Bengal (Bangladesh), Bihar and Uttar Pradesh in north-eastern India. Later, large groups of southern Indians arrived. The great diversity of languages, religions, customs and subcultures has merged to a certain extent over the years.

Other Indians, mostly Punjabis and Gujeratis, voluntarily came to Fiji soon after the end of the indenture system. These groups are prominent in Fiji's business elite.

Other Groups

There are about 4500 so-called 'Europeans' (see earlier in this section) who were born in Fiji, and over 10,000 'part-Europeans' living in Fiji. Some of these families established themselves at Levuka during the early 19th century as traders and shipbuilders or on the copra plantations of Vanua Levu, Lomaiviti and Lau. Europeans tend to work in agriculture, business, tourism and in the public sector.

The 8600 Fijians from Rotuma are of Polynesian origin. Most of them live and work in Suva, far away from their remote island. Among the other 9000 Pacific Islanders in Fiji are Tongans and Samoans and 3000 Banabans – Micronesians whose own island was stripped by phosphate mining, and who were resettled on Rabi after WWII. There are also more than 8000 descendants of blackbirder labourers from the Solomon Islands, most living in communities near Suva and on Ovalau.

About 0.7% of the population (5000 people) is of Chinese or part-Chinese origin. The majority of their ancestors arrived early in the 20th century to open general stores and other small businesses. More Chinese have migrated to Fiji in the past decade. Most are living in urban centres and tend to work in restaurants and commerce. The first Chinese settlers married Fijian women, but today the Chinese tend to form their own groups within the community.

EDUCATION

Fiji has a relatively good education system, and is considered the educational centre of the South Pacific. While education is not compulsory, primary and lower secondary education are accessible almost country wide, and the country's literacy rate is high (around 87%).

About 25% of the population is school-aged. Almost 100% of children attend primary school and most complete lower secondary education. There are incentives for poor rural children in the form of free tuition for primary and secondary students, and per capita grants. The government has also been trying to reduce the disparity between rural and urban schools by upgrading teacher quality and student assessments. At some stage during their education, nearly all rural Fijian children move away from their home villages to attend boarding school or to live with relatives in towns.

Education is not officially segregated, but schools are run by the major religions. Normally, Fiji-Indian children attend Hindu or Muslim schools while indigenous Fijians attend Christian schools. English is the official language taught in all Fijian schools, however, in recent years students have been encouraged to learn either Fijian or Hindi to increase the interaction between different communities. The former Rabuka government made special provisions for scholarships and education facilities for indigenous Fijians, in an effort to increase their representation in higher education. Under the new constitution, students of all races are to be given equal opportunity for government scholarships.

The University of the South Pacific was established in 1968 as a regional university for 12 Pacific island countries. Its main campus is in Suva, but it has another campus in Western Samoa and centres in the other member countries. The Fiji School of Medicine opened in 1985 to provide medical training in the region. The Fiji College of Agriculture, in conjunction with the USP, offers training in tropical agriculture and receives students from other South Pacific countries. The main centre for technical education is Suva's Fiji Institute of Technology (FIT). The FIT runs 10 different programs, some in association with local industry, and also has offices in Labasa and Lautoka.

ARTS

Fijian villagers still practise traditional arts, crafts, dance and music. While some arts remain an integral part of the culture, others are practised solely to satisfy tourist demand. Other cultural groups also retain some of their traditional arts.

Recent movements include fashion and, though not common, painting and photography. The paintings of Debora Veli, which feature on postcards, are stylised, almost naive scenes mainly of the forest and mythology. There are local fashion designers, and Viti Levu has a textile and clothing industry. A theatre group in Suva showcases local playwrights, and drama is taught at the university.

Dance

Visitors are often welcomed at resorts and hotels with a *meke,* a dance performance that enacts local stories and legends. While performances for tourists may seem staged, the meke is an ongoing tradition. The arrangement of the group and every subtle movement has significance. Important guests and onlookers are honoured with the best seating positions.

In the past, Fijian meke were accompanied by chanting by a chorus or by 'spiritually possessed seers', and usually rhythmic clapping, the thumping and stamping of bamboo clacking sticks, the beating of slit drums, and dancing. They were held purely for entertainment, for welcoming visitors, or on important religious and social occasions: births, deaths, marriages and property exchanges between villages. Chants included laments at funerals, war incitement dirges and animal impersonations. Meke were handed down through generations and new routines were composed for special events.

Men, women and children participated in meke. Men performed club and spear dances and the women performed fan dances. In times of war, men performed the *cibi,* or death dance, and women the *dele,* or *wate,* a dance in which they sexually humiliated enemy corpses and captives. Paddles were used as dance props in areas of Tongan influence. Dancing often took place by moonlight or torch light, with the performers in costume, and with bodies oiled and faces painted and combs and flowers decorating their hair.

Traditional Chinese dancing is still practised, and Indian classical dance, including Bharat Natyam and *kathak,* is taught at Indian cultural centres.

Music

While in Fiji, try to attend at least one meke and a church service to witness fantastic choir singing. Guitar is now the most commonly used instrument. Popular local musicians include Seru Serevi, the Black Roses, Danny Costello, Michelle Rounds, the Freelancers, Karuna Gopalan, Laisa Vulakoro, Soumini Vuatalevu, and the more mellow Serau Kei Mataniselala. Reggae has been influential and is very popular, and there are jazz bands in Suva. Tapes of local bands can be found in music shops such as SPR and Morris Hedstrom.

Music from 'Bollywood' films (Indian melodramas) is popular among Fiji Indians. Dr Bombay's Indian dance music is also a hit. Local bands do covers of Indian songs. Vocal/harmonium, tabla (percussion) and sitar lessons are given at Indian cultural centres.

Pottery

Fiji's best-known potters are Diana Tugea of Nakabuta, in the Sigatoka Valley, and Taraivini Wati of Nasilai, on the Rewa River near Nausori. The pottery-making tradition in these villages has been handed

Traditional Musical Instruments

Traditional nose flutes were once quite common in the Pacific but have now almost, if not completely, disappeared in Fiji. The instrument was typically a single section of bamboo about 70cm long, closed at each end by a node, and carved with intricate patterns. The musician lay on a pandanus mat, with his or her head resting on a bamboo pillow. Small panpipes, made of two to 12 hollow cane barrels, were also used. They were usually worn around the neck.

Wind instruments were played by both men and women while serenading, and the flute was supposed to have the power to attract the opposite sex.

Other instruments such as shell trumpets and whistles were used for communication. *Lali,* large slit drums made of resonant timbers, are audible over large distances and are still used to beckon people to the chief's *bure* (thatched dwelling) or to church. Portable war drums were used as warnings and for communicating tactics on the battlefield.

down through the centuries. Different areas had, and still have, different techniques and styles. Both villages receive visitors.

Tugea's clay pots are smooth with a wide belly, open neck and outward curving lip. They are used for cooking. The food is wrapped in banana or *rourou* (taro leaves) and the pot is sealed with coiled leaves.

Wati's pots are highly decorated. This style was traditionally used for water storage and was once reserved for use by high chiefs only. Most of her pots have a smooth outer belly with a raised pattern of triangular spikes and a narrow neck and lip with patterned incisions. The raised spikes are a traditional motif and are thought to represent a type of war fence that was used to defend ring-ditch villages in the Rewa Delta. She also makes replicas of elaborately designed 19th-century drinking vessels.

Wooden paddles of various shapes and sizes are used to beat the pots into shape, while the form is held from within using a pebble anvil. Coil and slab-building techniques are also used. Once dried they are then fired outdoors in an open blaze on coconut husks. Pots are often sealed with resin varnish from the *dakua* tree.

Wati displays her work at the Fiji Museum in Suva each Thursday and Friday, and the two potters give joint demonstrations on the first Thursday of each month, also at the Fiji Museum. Refer to the Viti Levu chapter – the Sigatoka entry in the Queens Road section and the Nausori & the Rewa Delta entry in the Kings Road section.

Wood Carving

Traditional wood-carving skills are being kept alive by the tourist trade, which provides a ready market for war clubs, spears and chiefs' and priests' cannibal forks. *Tanoa,* or yaqona drinking bowls, are still part of everyday life. In areas of Tongan influence, wooden articles are inlaid with ivory, shell and bone. Traditional designs are still made by the Lemaki people of Kabara, southern Lau (descendants of Tongan and Samoan wood carvers and canoe builders who settled in Viti in the 18th and

War club

Vitian Pottery

Pottery remains serve as one of the main archaeological records of Vitian culture, showing how Vitian people and culture has varied greatly over time. Shards of Lapita pottery (named after the Lapita people, the early inhabitants of the islands) have been found in the Sigatoka area that date back to 1290 BC, and to 1030 BC on nearby Yanuca. These pots, decorated with intricate, paddle-impressed geometric patterns, are thought to be ceremonial and suggest an involved social structure. Other impressed pottery found on Yanuca dates back to 710 BC.

Simple, functional pots replaced the more sophisticated Lapita pottery, at the time of a population explosion and increase in agriculture 2500 years ago. People were moving inland and there was intertribal warring; cannibalism and the use of defensive forts also increased. About 2000 years ago there was another abrupt change in pottery, which is thought to have been caused by further influxes of Melanesians. Vitian pottery of 100 BC to AD 1000 is characterised by a chequered decoration. A later plain-pottery phase lasted from 1250 AD to European arrival.

Cooking pots were usually perched on the hearth on three hollow earthenware stands. Drinking vessels ranged widely in shape and form. In the 19th century, bizarre-shaped drinking vessels were made for the chiefs of Bau and south-eastern Viti Levu. Some were in the shape of *tabua* (whales' teeth), turtles, canoe hulls or even groups of citrus fruit.

Pot making seems to have generally been the work of women from seafaring *mataqali* (extended family groups), who traded these items for agricultural and land produce.

19th centuries). Religious objects, such as yaqona vessels, were traditionally made of *vesi*, which was considered a sacred timber. Carvings in human and animal forms were generally restricted to such objects. Yaqona bowls shaped like turtles are thought to have derived from turtle-shaped *ibuburau* (vessels used in indigenous Vitian yaqona rites).

The Fiji Museum is the best place to see authentic traditional wood carvings. Beware that many of the artefacts for sale at handicraft centres are not genuinely Fijian. Quality varies greatly and much is now mass-produced by machine.

Bark Cloth & Traditional Textiles

Masi, also known as *malo* or *tapa*, is bark cloth with black and rust-coloured printed designs. Masi played an important role in Vitian culture and its motifs had symbolic meaning and to a certain extent still do. It is used for special occasions – in 1996 the Tui Cakau wore masi ceremonial attire at his installation as paramount chief of the Cakaudrove region. The beautiful tapa panels that now hang in parliament house are perhaps a symbolic link to the ancestor spirits. However, Fijian masi is now mostly made for tourists and is used for postcards, wall hangings and other decorative items. Textile designers are now incorporating traditional masi motifs in their fabrics.

Masi's status and symbolic worth was of similar importance to yaqona and tabua. It has long been associated with the marking of special occasions and was worn by men in the form of snowy white male loincloths during initiation rituals, for renaming ceremonies

Masi, once an important item of exchange

following killings and as an adornment in dance, festivity and war. The finest sheet tissue was worn as sashes, waistbands, trains and turbans by priests and chiefs. It was also used to wrap the cord with which a man's widows were strangled for burial with him, so that they would accompany him into the afterlife. Masi was an important exchange item and was used in bonding ceremonies between related tribes. Chiefs would dance swathed in a huge puffball of masi cloth, and then give it to members of the other tribe, who then clad themselves in it. Local motifs and patterns were sometimes used to signify allegiance to a particular tribe.

While men wore the masi, production was traditionally a woman's role. The cloth is made from the inner bark of the paper mulberry bush. The bark is peeled and the inner white bark is stripped, soaked in water, scraped clean and stored in rolls. The bark is then beaten and widened and felted together for hours, until it has a fine even texture. Large sheets of 2m by 2.2m are not uncommon. Rich, oily, brown cloth is made by soaking the material in coconut oil and smoking it over burning leaves. Intricately painted designs are done by hand or stencil. In areas of Tongan influence patterns are obtained by rubbing the cloth over a tablet made of raised leaf strips. Rusty-coloured paints are traditionally made from an infusion of candlenut and mangrove bark; pinker browns are made from red clays; and blacks are made from the soot of burnt dakua resin

and charred candlenuts. Modern paints and glues are now used as shortcuts.

It is difficult for visitors to see masi being made. Most Fijian masi is made on the island of Vatulele, which has one exclusive resort, on Namuk and Moce in the southern Lau Group, and on Taveuni.

Mat & Basket Weaving

Most Fijian homes use woven pandanus-leaf mats for floor coverings, dining mats and as finer sleeping mats. They are much in demand as wedding presents and for baptisms, funerals and presentations to chiefs.

Most village girls learn the craft; traditionally it was the hereditary role of the women of certain tribes. The pandanus leaves are cut and laid outdoors to cure, then stripped of the spiny edges and boiled and dried. The traditional method for blackening the leaves for contrasting patterns is to bury them in mud for days and then boil them with special leaves. The dried pandanus leaves, made flexible by scraping with shells, are split into strips of about 1 to 2cm. Mat borders are now decorated in brightly coloured wools instead of parrot feathers.

Literature

The indigenous-Fijian oral tradition of telling tall stories, myths and legends around the kava bowl is still strong, both as entertainment and for passing on history. English is the principal written means of expression. *Myths & Legends of Fiji & Rotuma* by AW Reed & Inez Hames is an interesting collection of these stories.

Fiji has a small but strong community of poets, playwrights and other writers. Contemporary literature includes works by Joseph Veramu, the author of the short-story collection *The Black Messiah* and the novel *Moving Through the Streets,* which is about urban teenagers in Suva. Jo Nacola's work includes the play *I Native No More.* The Fiji Writers Association has published *Trapped: A Collection of Writings From Fiji.* The Fiji issue of *Mana* (vol 9, no 1), a South Pacific journal of language and literature, has a selection of local poetry, short stories and critiques of Fijian literature by male and female writers. Other notable authors are short-story writer Marjorie Crocombe and Rotuman playwright Vilsoni Hereniko. The poet Teresia Kieuea Teaiwa, who grew up in Fiji, explores her black American and Pacific Islander identity in *Searching for Nei Nim'anoa* (1995).

Fiji Indians continue writing poetry in Hindi, but since the 1970s some, principally USP academics, began to write poetry in English. Writers of note include Subramani, Satendra Nandan, Raymond Pillai, Prem Banfal and poet Mohit Prasad (*The Eyes of the Mask*, 1998). The theme of the injustice of the indenture experience rates highly in Fiji-Indian literature and the natural environment is often portrayed as harsh and alien. As a body of work it often dwells on a sense of hopelessness and is not necessarily representative of the contemporary or historical Fiji-Indian identity. Prem Banfal's work is from a female perspective.

Architecture

Traditional The most beautiful example of a traditional village is Navala, nestled in the Viti Levu highlands. It is the only village remaining where every home is a bure. Bure are cheap, relatively quick to build and use local materials. Young rural men still sometimes build themselves a bure if they need a home. Bure building is a skilled trade passed from father to son, although the whole community helps when a bure is under construction, and most village people would know how to maintain the walls and roof of their bure. Skills are also kept alive for the tourist industry with its demand for authentic-looking buildings. Most villagers, however, now live in simple rectangular, pitched-roof houses made from industrialised materials that require less maintenance. While a bure's structure is generally able to withstand cyclones, the government offers incentives to build concrete cyclone-proof houses.

Most traditional bure are rectangular in plan, with a hipped or gabled roof. However, in areas of Tongan and Samoan influence such as Lau, round-ended plans are common.

Bure have one large room, usually with a sleeping compartment behind a curtain at one end. With few windows, the interior space is normally quite dark. Pandanus mats cover a packed-earth floor. Cooking is now normally done in a separate bure.

Colonial Levuka, the old European trader settlement and former capital of Fiji, has been declared an historic town and has been nominated for World Heritage listing. A number of buildings date from its boom period of the late 19th century, and the main streetscape is surprisingly intact, giving the impression that the town has stopped in time.

The British influence on Suva is reflected in its many colonial buildings, including Government House, Suva City Library, Grand Pacific Hotel and government buildings.

Modern Some modern architecture combines traditional Fijian aesthetics, knowledge and materials with modern technology. Notable buildings include the new parliament complex, the USP campus in Suva, and the *bure bose* (meeting house) at Somosomo on Taveuni.

Many of the resorts have fairly predictable designs in tropical style. Those whose architecture stands out are the upmarket Vatulele Island Resort (combining American Santa Fe style with traditional design); Namale Resort near Savusavu, Vanua Levu; and the smaller Natadola Beach Resort. Young architects with new ideas for tropical architecture are also making an impact on the commercial and resort scene.

SOCIETY & CONDUCT
Traditional Culture

Indigenous Fijians Many features of Viti's rich culture were suppressed along with the old religion in the mid to late 19th century. Pre-Christian costume, hairdressing and body decoration were far removed from today's conservative dress style. However, despite the changing influences and pressures, many aspects of the communal way of life are still strong. Throughout the colonial era the chiefly system and village structure remained intact, partly due to the laws protecting Fijian land rights and prohibiting Fijian labour on the plantations.

Most indigenous Fijians live in villages in mataqali (extended family groups) and acknowledge a hereditary chief who is usually male. Each mataqali owns land, and wider groups have a paramount chief. Each family is allocated land for farming by the chief.

Clans gather for births, deaths, marriages, meke, *lovo* feasts (where food is cooked in a pit oven) and to exchange gifts. Yaqona drinking is still an important social ceremony. Communal obligations also have to be met, including farming for the chief, preparing for special ceremonies and feasts, fishing, building and village maintenance. Village life is now only semisubsistent; cash is needed for school fees, community projects and imported goods.

Village life, based on interdependence, is supportive and provides a strong group identity. It is conservative; independent thinking is not encouraged and being different or too ambitious is seen to threaten the stability of a village. Conflict arises between those who want change and those

who resist it. Profits from any additional business are normally expected to be shared with the whole village. Concepts such as *kerekere* and *sevusevu* are still strong, especially in remote areas. Kerekere is where someone, especially a friend or relative, asks for something: You cannot refuse as property is considered communal. This can put employees of businesses in difficult situations, as it is especially difficult to say no if the person is of higher rank! Sevusevu is the presentation of a gift such as yaqona or, more powerfully, a tabua in exchange for certain favours. The receiver is obligated to honour your request. In remote areas the role of men and women is clearly demarcated. The hill villagers still adhere to a strong hierarchy and customs. For example, a man is not supposed to speak directly to his sister-in-law.

Fiji is also becoming increasingly urbanised and traditional values and the wisdom of elders are less respected in urban areas. Regional cultural and social differences that were noticeable in the past are quickly disappearing as Fijians travel more. Villages are no longer self-sufficient and

Traditional Fijian Face & Body Painting

Face painting reached its artistic peak in the mid-19th century. The indigenous palette of red, yellow, black and white was joined by the vermilion and blue introduced by traders. Vermilion became 'equal to gold' and was traded with the Europeans for baskets of bêche-de-mer. Black pigment was obtained from the soot of burnt candlenut or kauri resin, or from charcoal or fungus spores, then mixed with coconut and other oils. Yellow was obtained from a type of ginger root as well as from turmeric.

Before painting, the skin was oiled and scented with coconut oil. An endless variety of creative designs was used fairly informally for everyday cosmetic decoration. Faces could be striped, zigzagged, spotted, bisected or plain black except for a red nose. There were special rules for war and certain festive occasions. Face painting was perhaps a convenient disguise in wars against close neighbours, although warriors generally wished to gain glory and notoriety. The bodies of dead or dying women were adorned with turmeric or vermilion paint. Turmeric was also used to paint babies, and women for the first three months of pregnancy and after the birth until the baby was weaned. During this time a woman was under sexual *tabu* (taboo) and males were ridiculed if they were found smudged with yellow paint. Young men were also covered in turmeric for *buli yaca* (puberty) ceremonies, or renaming ceremonies celebrating their first enemy kill. Men mostly used red and black (associated with war and death) on their faces and sometimes chests. Women favoured yellow, saffron, pink and red. Fine black circles drawn around the eyes were considered beautiful.

The tradition of face painting was phased out along with the old religion.

Traditional Fijian Hairdressing

Prior to European contact a Fijian's head was considered sacred, and hairdressing in Viti was an art form. Early Europeans were astonished by the variety of elaborate styles and the custom was deliberately suppressed by missionaries, who regarded it as a 'flagrant symbol of paganism', not suitable for the 'neat and industrious Christian convert'.

Before initiation girls wore either a cascade of bleached or reddened corkscrew ringlets, or had their heads shaven except for two ringlets, which sometimes reached their hips. These ringlets, known as *tobe,* represented the prawns they were destined to fish in later life. Once married, the tobe were removed and often the entire head was shorn. Women kept their crown shaved or close-cropped in uniform length, sometimes ringed by a ruff of hair dyed rusty brown or yellow. Their hairstyle had to be more understated than their husband's, with the exception of female chiefs who could wear huge regal hair-dos.

Until initiation boys were bald except for one or two upstanding tufts. A man's hair, however, was a symbol of his masculinity, vanity and social standing. Men grew flamboyant, extravagant, fantastic and often massive hair-dos. Styles ranged from the relatively conventional giant puffball (up to 30cm tall) to shaggy or geometric shapes with variations of ringlets, tufts and ruffs. Ringlet style was better suited to those with Polynesian ancestry who had wavier, less frizzy hair. Hair was dyed black, grey, sky blue, rust, orange, yellow, white or multicoloured. Before the introduction of the razor and mirror by traders, beards and moustaches were also grown long.

Hairdressers were employed to prick up the hair, stiffen it with burnt lime, and have it teased and singed into a sculpted form. People slept on uncomfortable-looking raised wooden pillows to keep their coiffure from being spoilt. The head was especially dressed for festive occasions. Accessories included hair scratchers (practical for lice), ornamental combs, scarlet feathers, wreaths of small flowers and vines, larger flowers at the ears and grated sandalwood as a perfume.

Shaving one's head was a profound sacrifice for a man. There were special wigs for balding men or for those who had sacrificed their hair in mourning or to appease a wrathful ancestral spirit. Tobe ringlets (the long ones could take 10 years to grow) were popular war trophies.

A chief's head was considered *tabu* (taboo) and required the attention of a special hairdresser. The work could take two days to complete. The circumference of a chief's hair could reach more than 1.5m. Huge turbans of fine *masi* (bark cloth) were often worn, but would be removed in the presence of a superior as a token of submission and respect.

many young people travel to the cities for education, employment or to escape the restrictions of village life. For those who have grown up in the relative security and disciplined structure of a village, adapting to urban life is not easy. Together with increased freedom comes competition for jobs and a less supportive social structure. The Bauan dialect is now being used widely for business purposes. Television, only introduced in the last decade, presents opposing values and contradictory messages.

Indigenous Fijians own about 83% of the land, some of which is leased to others for farming and tourism. In addition to agriculture, mining and the public service, many indigenous Fijians are employed in the tourism industry, so there is some pressure placed on Fijians to retain the more exotic aspects of their culture. While most of the larger resorts are foreign-owned, there are some smaller-scale projects that directly benefit villagers.

Fiji Indians Most Fiji Indians are descendants of indentured labourers and many families have been living in Fiji for four or five generations. The majority of the labourers were young, illiterate farmers from communal villages. Traditional social structures and cultural traditions have been partially broken down through the experience of indentured labour and some intermarriage over the years. Fiji Indians of different religions and diverse cultural backgrounds were, and still are, stereotyped as a single group.

Extended families often live in the same house, but the trend is towards nuclear families. Females generally have a stricter upbringing than boys. In rural areas it is common for girls to marry at a young age and marriages are often arranged. Once married, Hindu women wear a red spot between the brows, while girls often wear decorative, coloured *bindi* spots. While dress codes are more cosmopolitan in Suva, Hindu women throughout Fiji usually wear saris and Muslims wear traditional robes and head coverings.

Fiji Indians tend to be involved in commerce, transportation and farming on leasehold land. Most Gujeratis (from the region north of Bombay) and Punjabis (mostly Sikhs from north of Delhi) arrived as free settlers, traders and merchants, and their descendants now run shops and businesses. Gujeratis and Punjabis have stronger social networks and links with India.

The Fiji-Indian community shares an interest in soccer and 'Bollywood' movies – escapist melodramas with lots of romance, violence and music, which are made by India's equivalent of the Hollywood film industry. Although cut off from mainstream Indian traditions for a long period, there has been a recent movement to maintain and preserve cultural values. Fiji-Indian cultural centres run lectures and language classes, and theatre, music and dance lessons. The four centres are at Ba (☎ 676 800), Suva (☎ 300 050), Labasa (☎ 814 433) and Nadi (☎ 703 144).

Dos & Don'ts

Indigenous Fijians have quite complex codes of behaviour. While Fijians are pretty tolerant of travellers, it is ideal to be aware of local customs to both understand what is going on and to show the appropriate respect. If you are unsure of what's expected, just ask. If you are travelling with children, try to get them to be quiet when indoors, and to be obedient and respectful of their elders! When choosing tours consider those that are conservation-oriented, and support local people and services. Expect to pay a fair price.

Staying with a Family Should you be invited to stay with a Fijian family, prepare yourself for a novel and heart-warming experience. Fijians are masters at entertaining and go out of their way to make guests feel as comfortable as possible.

When you visit an indigenous-Fijian family, bring some yaqona with you. This is for your sevusevu – a formal presentation, comparable to bringing a bottle of wine when you visit friends back home.

Fiji Indians are also very hospitable. If you're invited to someone's house, you'll certainly be offered a cup of tea and usually a delicious meal. In rural areas, men and women socialise and eat separately. Many Fiji-Indian men enjoy drinking yaqona as much as the Fijians. But it isn't the custom for guests to bring yaqona with them to a Fiji-Indian house. If you want to bring something, sweets for the kids are usually appreciated. Some men also drink alcohol, often following yaqona (called 'washdown'). Women tourists who feel like drinking can be considered honorary men for the occasion.

Note that the custom throughout Fiji is to finish drinking yaqona and/or alcohol before the meal. This can mean some very late dinners.

Village Visits Try not to show up at a village uninvited, or, if you do, ask the first person you meet if it is possible to visit their village. They will probably take you to see the chief. Never wander around unaccompanied: gardens, backyards and bure are someone's private realm. Even in remote areas the land, beaches and reefs are usually owned by a mataqali.

Fijian culture demands that visitors be treated as honoured guests. It is common for villagers to invite visitors into their home and offer food, even if they are very poor. It is polite to accept, and also a good chance to chat with locals. Try to reciprocate hospitality by leaving some basic groceries such as sugar, tea or tinned meat, which you can buy at the village shop. If you intend to travel outside the main tourist areas, consider taking some extra clothes to give away in return for villagers' kindness. Second-hand clothes are OK, especially for kids.

Always take a sevusevu when visiting a village. About 500g of *taga yaqona*, (pounded kava, which costs about F$14 per kilogram) is acceptable. Even better, take a bundle of *waka* (kava roots). You'll find kava at markets, service stations and some shops. Don't bring alcohol; some villages ban it. In most villages yaqona is drunk every day, but some villages abstain completely, so ask the person taking you on the visit. Request to present the yaqona to the turaga-ni-koro (hereditary chief), who will welcome you in a small ceremony on behalf of the village. This may develop into a friendly *talanoa* (gossip session) around the yaqona bowl, where you will have to recount your life story.

Gunusede

A *gunusede*, literally, 'drink money', is a village fundraising activity. You may be invited to attend one, and it is considered offensive to refuse. You will need to take some money, and if you are on a tight budget, don't take more than you can afford to give away! You should spend every cent you take to a gunusede. If you participate, even to a small extent, it will be appreciated. At a gunusede, people buy drinks, usually *yaqona*, for themselves and others. The price is usually a token 10 cents. If someone buys a drink for you and you can't stand another drop (this happens with yaqona) you can get out of it by bidding a higher price for someone else to drink it. Otherwise you must drink what is bought for you. These fundraising parties are used to pay for things such as school fees for the village children. It is an example of how the community works together, and it is usually a fun get-together.

Emma Hegarty

When visiting a bure leave your shoes outside. Stoop when entering (doorways are often low anyway), and quietly sit cross-legged on the pandanus mat. If you are in the presence of someone of high social rank, such as the chief and his family, it is polite to keep your head at a lower level than theirs. Fijians consider the head private, even sacred, so never touch a person's head or hair.

Do not question the authority of a *ratu* (male chief), *adi* (female chief) or *tui* (king). It is considered rude to speak badly of anyone or to criticise people personally. It is also impolite to push people to talk about contentious topics such as politics.

It is unusual for villagers to use a tourist unreasonably as a source of money, but it can happen. However, tourists sometimes take advantage of Fijian hospitality. If you do stay in a village, contribute food or money (about F$10 per day to cover your costs). Don't camp outside if you have been offered a place to sleep inside a home; it can embarrass the hosts if they think their bure is not good enough. When taken somewhere by private boat always offer to pay your share to cover fuel costs. As a rule Fijians are exceptionally polite and will not ask you for money, and will let you know if you are behaving in an insensitive manner or have overstayed your welcome.

Because of the custom of kerekere, or shared property, children or even adults may ask you for your shoes, jewellery or other travelling gear. If you don't want to give the item away, you can usually get out of awkward situations by saying that you can't do without it. Try not to flash around expensive items that are beyond the reach of villagers.

Many locals think that all tourists are wealthy and that the standard of living is much higher in other countries. Travellers are often asked to become a pen pal or even to sponsor someone to migrate. If you are not keen, a polite refusal should be OK.

Sunday is considered a day of rest when families spend time together and attend church. Visits by travellers may not be appreciated by the chief.

Yaqona Drinking Yaqona, otherwise known as kava, is an infusion prepared from the root of *Piper methysticum,* a type of pepper plant. It is extremely important in Fijian culture – in the time of the 'old religion' it was used ceremonially by chiefs and priests only. Today yaqona is part of daily life, not only in villages but across the different races and in urban areas. 'Having a grog' is used for welcoming and bonding with visitors, for storytelling sessions or merely for passing time.

Certainly soon after your arrival in Fiji you will be offered a drink of kava. When visiting a village you will usually be welcomed with a short ceremony, and it is good manners to bring a bunch of kava or powdered root to present to the chief.

There are certain protocols to be followed at a kava ceremony and in some remote villages it is still a semireligious experience. Sit cross-legged, facing the chief and the *tanoa,* or large wooden bowl. Women usually sit behind the men and won't get offered the first drink unless they are the guest of honour. Never walk across the circle of participants, turn your back to the tanoa or step over the cord that leads from the tanoa to a white cowry (it represents a link with the spirits).

The drink is prepared in the tanoa. The dried and powdered root, wrapped in a piece of cloth, is mixed with water and the resulting concoction looks (and tastes) like muddy water. You will then be offered a drink from a *bilo* (half a coconut shell).

The Yaqona Ritual

A daily *burau* (a ceremonial *yaqona*-drinking ritual) was an integral part of the old Fijian religion. In ancient times the priest knelt or lay on the floor to drink the liquid from a *tanoa* bowl, an earthenware vessel or an elegant, shallow dish made of *vesi,* which was considered a sacred timber. For *tabu* (taboo) reasons priests were not meant to touch either food or drink with their hands, and to this end a straw was sometimes used.

In the past yaqona drinking was the prerogative of chiefs, priests and important male elders, and often happened inside spirithouses. Late in the 18th century, Tongan contact saw the introduction of a different way of drinking yaqona. Yaqona started to be served using coconut-shell cups and deep, wooden tanoa bowls. Tongans also introduced the kava circle ritual, which was a less religious yaqona ceremony, and the habit of chewing the kava root. Youths of both sexes were employed to chew the root prior to preparing the infusion. By the mid-19th century, these rituals were widespread in Fiji.

The long plaited cords on kava bowls, studded with egg-cowry (a symbol of divine fertility), are a relatively recent innovation. The cord is extended towards the principal chief to form a link with the spirits. It was believed that if the cord was crossed, death would result. After drinking from the bowl the participant in the formal ritual would clap and say 'mana, yaqona', thanking the god.

The original Fijian yaqona ceremony was an essential part of the old religion, and therefore condemned by the missionaries. The more Tongan kava ceremonies were tolerated and remain to the present. Yaqona is still an extremely important part of the culture and is ritually served on important occasions. Remote villages still practise quasi-religious ceremonies around the kava bowl. Galvanised or plastic buckets are now often used for informal social drinking.

Grab a *bilo* and get a taste of Fiji at a *yaqona* ceremony.

Clap once, accept the bilo, and say '*bula*' (meaning 'cheers' or, literally, 'life'), before drinking it all in one go (best to get it over with quickly anyway!). Clap three times in gratification and try not to grimace. The drink will be shared until the tanoa is empty. You are not obligated to drink every bilo offered to you, but it is polite to drink at least the first.

Yaqona is a mild narcotic and has been used as a diuretic and stress reliever for pharmaceutical purposes. After a few drinks you may feel a slight numbness of the lips. Long sessions, however, with stronger mixes will probably make you drowsy. Some heavy drinkers develop *kanikani,* or scaly skin, and excessive use can lead to impotence.

Dress Precolonial Fijians wore very little. Children ran around naked. Girls from about seven to puberty used a skimpy apron, and afterwards the short *liku,* the skirt of womanhood (made out of grass or strips of pandanus leaves). Men wore just the *malo,* a loincloth. The missionaries, however, imposed a puritanical dress code. Today, indigenous-Fijian women generally wear long dresses with sleeves and underskirts, and men wear shirts and *sulu* (skirts to below the knees), or long pants. Similarly, most Fiji-Indian women cover up in long saris. The dress code in the urban centres is not so strict, with a mix of traditional and Western styles.

Men and women are expected to dress modestly. You will rarely see adult Fijians swimming and when they do they cover up with a T-shirt and sulu. Western-style bathers are fine at the resorts, otherwise avoid offence by using a sulu to below the knee and a T-shirt to cover the shoulders. This applies to both men and women. Don't swim or sunbathe naked or topless, unless at an exclusive or remote resort. See Women Travellers in the Facts for the Visitor chapter.

When you're in a village be careful not to offend the chief. Don't wear a hat or cap – if you want protection from the sun, use sunblock, look for a tree for shade or use an umbrella. It's also rude to wear sunglasses, especially when meeting people. Cameras and carry bags should be carried in the hands, not over the shoulder. To respect traditions shoulders should be covered and women should wear knee-length dresses or skirts rather than long trousers or shorts. Men are better received if they are clean shaven and neatly dressed.

Socialising It is rare to see public displays of affection between men and women. So curtail your passions in public to avoid embarrassing or offending locals.

A tip for disco-goers: if a woman refuses to dance with a man, she must then refuse every other man who asks.

Fiji-Indian Temples Refrain from eating meat on the day you intend visiting a Hindu temple and remove your shoes before you enter.

Photography Ask permission before taking photos of people, although Fijians usually enjoy having their photo taken (or are too polite to say no anyway). Consider sending photos as a thank-you present for villagers' hospitality. You will normally have to wait until after the formal ritual of a yaqona ceremony before taking a photo; check first.

Cruelty to Animals According to an opinion poll held in Fiji in 1996, 57% of those polled said cruelty to animals was a big problem in Fiji. Fijians and Fiji Indians generally view animals in terms of their practical use. Working animals such as horses and bullocks are sometimes badly nourished, and are often whipped as they work. Dairy cattle often founder in the wet pastures. Village animals are rarely treated for worms and parasites and travellers will notice that animals used for horse riding are not always well tended. Cockfighting is practised for entertainment, though in secret. Many resorts and tours promote game fishing.

Turtle is banned from restaurants but is sometimes found at markets. Turtle meat and eggs are considered a delicacy and are still eaten by some villagers, as are bats and giant clams.

RELIGION

Religion is extremely influential in all aspects of Fijian society, affecting politics, government, education and interaction within and between different races. Only 0.4% of the population is nonreligious. Together the different Christian denominations command the largest following (52.9% of the population), followed by Hindus (38.1%), Muslims (7.8%), Sikhs (0.7%) and other religions (0.1%).

Traditional Fijian Religion

The old Fijian religion was based on ancestor worship. The souls of outstanding ancestors were made into local deities so there were many gods and spirits. A hero in battle could become a war god, or an outstanding farmer could become a god of plenty. Appeasing and thanking the gods shaped all aspects of life in Viti, including medicine and mythology. Spirithouses were built for each significant god.

Initiation Ceremonies

After having proven their skill at fishing and crafts, girls traditionally underwent a prolonged and painful initiation into adulthood. This normally took place between about seven years and puberty. The *veiqia* rite involved elaborate tattooing of the pubic area and in some cases this was extended as a band around the hips so that it resembled 'dark, skin-tight, intricately patterned shorts'. Girls were told that it would enhance their beauty and sex drive.

Each village had a female *duabati* (hereditary tattoo specialist), who had a special hut on the outskirts of the village or often a more distant hide-out. Often a few girls were operated on at once, taking turns to hold each other down. The ritual was carried out during the day when men were out, so they wouldn't hear the screaming. It was extremely painful, taking weeks, months, even up to a year to complete. Many could not endure the whole procedure. The blue-black (soot mixed with oil) designs were tapped into the flesh with a special spiked pick and light mallet, and lines were made with bamboo slivers or sharp shells.

A celebratory feast was held on the fourth day after completion of the operation and the young woman was then entitled to wear the *liku* (skirt of womanhood) and to marry.

Designs were similar to those found on *masi* (bark cloth), woodcarving, pottery and nose flutes. The patterns represented everyday items such as net sinkers and floats, and special designs were reserved for chiefly women. To signify that a woman had undergone initiation, a pair of dots or crescents were tattooed at the corners of her mouth. In some regions, if a woman had her whole hips tattooed then her mouth was surrounded in a spotted or chequered pattern, although this was also sometimes done just to hide wrinkles.

It was believed that untattooed women would be persecuted by the ancestor spirits in the afterlife – slashed about the pubic region or pounded to a pulp and fed to the gods. This was a dreaded fate and girls were loath to defy the custom.

Even into the 20th century, fake tattoos were sometimes painted on dead girls in an attempt to bluff the gods.

Church authorities regarded tattooing, with its religious and sexual significance, as a symbol of paganism and were intent on its suppression. In some regions it was still practised into the 1930s, for sexual rather than religious motives. Other cosmetic tattoos were and still are common on the faces and limbs of both sexes.

Boys had to endure the less painful initiation ritual of circumcision. After having his bravado tested for four nights, a boy was entitled to use the loincloth of manhood, grow his hair and move to the men's bure. Boys were trained from infancy in the use of arms and in how to dodge missiles, and were only granted a real man's name once they had killed an enemy.

Ear-lobe piercing and expansion to accept ornamental plugs was obligatory for all, otherwise the soul would suffer persecution in the afterlife.

Hereditary chiefs and priests were the representatives of the gods, and the priest served as a medium through which a god spoke to its descendants. Relics and idols kept in the temple were also mediums. Images were carved from sacred vesi wood or whales' teeth and sometimes took human form. Food, yaqona roots or tabua were given as offerings.

The gods demanded that the people carry out mutilative rituals, mourning sacrifices and initiation ceremonies. Mourning sacrifices included amputation of the little finger at the joint and self-induced burns. Shaving one's head was the ultimate religious or mourning sacrifice for a man. For a woman the equivalent was being strangled to accompany her husband to the afterlife! In initiation rituals women were tattooed and men circumcised. It was believed that the demon guardians of the spirit path would ambush and inspect each ghost to see if it had been properly tattooed or circumcised and that its ear lobes had been plugged and little fingers lopped. Concerned friends and family would often try to trick priests and spirits by painting on designs or chopping off a person's fingers after they had died. Belief in the afterlife was a strong incentive for all actions in life.

The early missionaries abhorred the worship of idols and 'heathen' deities and translated the Fijian word for gods, *tevoro*, as devil. The tevoro were not necessarily evil, but the label stuck. Many Vitian beliefs and practices were wiped out or at least suppressed, but traces and attitudes remain and some have fused with Christianity.

Christianity

Most indigenous Fijians adhere to one of the Christian sects and invariably each village and settlement has at least one church. Church attendance is high and spiritual leaders are very influential. In small villages that retain their hierarchical society, people generally follow the religion of the chief. Some villages have a number of religions, occasionally leading to jealousy and conflict. Only about 2% of Fiji Indians are Christians.

Of the all the Christian denominations, the Methodist Church is the most powerful. Extremist factions of the church were supporters of the nationalist movement and the military coups, and played a role in the Sunday ban on business activities. Other denominations include Catholic, Seventh-Day Adventist, Anglican and Presbyterian, and more recently there has been a growth in numbers of Assembly of God followers, Mormons and Jehovah's Witnesses.

Even if you are not at all religious, try to attend a church service in a Fijian village. The singing is amazing and visitors are welcome. Leave a small donation to help with community projects.

Indian Religions

There are many tiny, beautiful temples and green-and-white mosques scattered around Fiji's countryside, especially in the cane-growing areas of Viti Levu and Vanua Levu. Indentured labourers established temples to pursue their own faith and boost their sense of security in the new alien country. There were, however, a lack of spiritual leaders, and knowledge of the philosophy behind the religions was partly lost. After generations of separation from their homeland, Fiji Indians are generally less orthodox in terms of caste and religion, and tolerance of religious differences is greater than in India. Most are Hindus or Muslims, and Sikhism (combining Hindu and Islamic beliefs) is practised by some descendants of north-west Indians. Hare Krishnas also have a small following. They have a temple in Lautoka and run good vegetarian restaurants both there and in Suva.

Islam Muslims believe in peace and submission to Allah (God), and following the teachings of the prophet Mohammed and the holy book the Koran. Religious festivals include Ramadan (30-day, dawn-to-dusk fasting), the Eid festival to celebrate the end of fasting, and Mohammed's birthday.

Hinduism Hindus believe in reincarnation and that the consequence of all past deeds will be faced – thus the importance of leading a moral life. Most Hindu homes in Fiji have small shrines for family worship. High-caste Hindus who are more secure economically tend to be less devoted to their religious activities.

Hindus worship one supreme power, Brahman, who assumes many forms and names in order to be better understood. The characteristic Hindu form of God is the Great Mother. She is the personification of nature, which gives life, meaning and purpose to all things. The greatest goddess is Maya Devi. She is all powerful, all knowing, all pervading. All energy is believed to come from her and she is symbolised by water (the life giver) and fire (the purifier or destroyer). She shows compassion to those who surrender to her, and punishes those who disobey. Devotees see every woman as the personified essence of the Divine Mother. The green goddess Parvati symbolises nature, the dark blue Kali represents time, and the red Lakshmi, wealth. Other goddess forms include Durga, Maari and Shakti.

Descendants of southern Indians perform a fire-walking ritual in July or August at many temples, including the Mariamma temple in Suva. A group of orthodox Hindus, of north-Indian origin, perform Durga Gram Puja each August at Wailekutu, near Suva. The goddess Durga is worshipped by undergoing ordeals including whipping, having the tongue and body pierced with metal instruments, the hands immersed in boiling ghee (clarified butter), and dancing on upturned knife blades. Important Hindu festivals include Holi (Festival of Colours), Diwali (Festival of Lights) and the Birth of Lord Krishna. Refer to the Public Holidays & Special Events section in the Facts for the Visitor chapter for festival dates and more information.

LANGUAGE

English is the official language of Fiji. Only young children in remote areas may not speak it. Most Fijians are multilingual, and speak their vernacular Fijian or Hindi. See the Language chapter later in this book for more information, and for more tips, refer to Lonely Planet's *Fiji phrasebook* or *South Pacific phrasebook*.

Facts for the Visitor

HIGHLIGHTS

- Snorkel or dive Fiji's fantastic coral reefs.
- Learn about Fiji's cannibal history – visit the Fiji Museum, the Tavuni Hill Fort and the Naihehe cave.
- Go kayaking or rafting through the gorges and wilderness of the Namosi Highlands.
- Walk Taveuni's beautiful Lavena coastal track and through the Vidawa Forest.
- Cruise, sail or kayak the azure waters of the Yasawas.
- Admire the traditional architecture of the highland village of Navala.
- Visit Levuka, the wild and lawless capital of the 19th century.
- Enjoy spectacular views from the mountains of Koroyanitu National Heritage Park.
- Wander along the windswept Sigatoka Sand Dunes.
- Explore rugged and remote Kadavu.

SUGGESTED ITINERARIES

Even if you have a few months you will only be able to visit a small number of Fiji's 300 islands. If you are after swimming beaches, it's best to head for one of the smaller offshore coral islands. High volcanic islands such as Viti Levu, Vanua Levu and Taveuni have few good beaches. Rugged Taveuni and Kadavu should be a high priority for nature lovers. Just about all of the islands have access to good snorkelling and diving. Note that the eastern sides of the larger islands have wetter climates.

Depending on the time available, your pace and budget, consider the following itineraries:

Day Trips & Organised Tours from Nadi

- Cruise or fly to the Mamanucas for swimming, snorkelling or diving.
- Visit Koroyanitu National Heritage Park.
- Take an organised tour to the Nausori Highlands for a village visit.
- Go rafting on the Navua River in the Namosi Highlands.

- Take an organised tour to a waterfall near Biausevu or inland to Naihehe cave.
- Drive or bus along the Queens Road (visit the Sigatoka Sand Dunes and Tavuni Hill Fort).
- Combine the Coral Coast Scenic Railway, Natadola Beach and the island of Likuri.

One Week

Take a bus, or hire a car or 4WD, and explore Viti Levu for at least four days. Include Natadola beach, Sigatoka (Tavuni Hill Fort and the Sigatoka Sand Dunes), the Coral Coast, Suva, the Kings Road and Rakiraki. Head up to Navala and the Nausori Highlands (4WD or bus), then return to Nadi. Spend a couple of days on offshore islands, such as the Mamanucas or Nananu-i-Ra for water sports. Alternatively, combine day trips from Nadi with either a flight to Taveuni (four days minimum, see the Tavoro Falls at Bouma and hike the Lavena Coastal Walk), or a cruise to the Yasawas.

Two Weeks

Spend one week exploring Viti Levu as above, including day trips to offshore islands and the highlands. Spend the second week on Taveuni, the Yasawas, Kadavu or Ovalau (visiting the historic town of Levuka and hiking to Lovoni).

One Month & Over

Combine some of the above, and add eastern Vanua Levu. Western Vanua Levu is not a high priority, but if you have the funds, Vanua Levu is interesting to explore by 4WD. Travel around Viti Levu, the Nausori Highlands and offshore islands including Ovalau for about two weeks. Fly or ferry to Taveuni and take a trip to the Yasawas.

PLANNING
When to Go

The best time to visit is during the so-called 'Fijian winter' or 'dry season', from May to October. This time of year has lower rainfall and humidity, milder temperatures, and less risk of tropical cyclones. Fiji can be enjoyed year-round, however, and is a great place to escape either southern or northern hemisphere winters.

The end of the year is often busy, coinciding with school holidays in both Australia and New Zealand, and people visiting relatives. February and March, however, are quiet months for tourism in Fiji, with accommodation discounts and vacancies more likely. See also Climate in the Facts about Fiji chapter and Public Holidays & Special Events later in this chapter.

What Kind of Trip

Fiji is one of the South Pacific's major transit hubs. Even if you are just passing through, it would be a shame to spend only a couple of days in the country. The Fiji archipelago is an excellent place for the independent traveller to explore, either solo or with friends or family. You could either try to cover as many islands as possible in a mad dash; stay in one or two spots and pursue special interests such as diving or trekking; or choose one special place for your entire stay. There are accommodation options and resorts for every budget as well as many tours on offer. Try to include the beach and water sports, a jaunt to the mountains, and at least some contact with the local culture.

Maps

The best place to buy maps of the towns and Fiji islands is the Lands and Surveys Department (☎ 211 395, fax 304 037) in Suva. There are 1:50,000 scale topographical maps of most areas, useful if you are going trekking, for under F$5. Aerial photographs of some islands are available. Inquire at Room 10, Records and Reprographic Subsection, Government Buildings, Suva. The office is open from 9 am to 3.30 pm Monday to Thursday and 9 am to 3 pm Fridays, closed from 1 to 2 pm for lunch. Orders can also be made from overseas.

Bookshops sometimes stock town maps, and some tourist brochures also have simple town maps. At the Fiji Visitors Bureau, or specialist book and map shops overseas,

you can purchase the latest Hema map of Fiji (F$8). It is a topographical map with an index for islands, towns and some resorts, plus general visitor information and town maps on the back.

Specialist marine charts are expensive in Fiji, so its best to buy them overseas. Failing this, inquire at the Suva Yacht Club.

What to Bring

Pack as little as possible – less to lug around, less to lose. Backpacks should ideally be the fold-away type (compact, comfortable, waterproof) and have double zips that can be padlocked. A chain is handy for locking gear to a fixture in shared rooms, or in a hotel's safe-deposit room. Carry cash, important documents and some travellers cheques in a moneybelt. You will need a day pack, and waterproof bags are handy for carrying stationery (notebook, addresses etc), photocopies of important documents (see Photocopies under Visas & Documents later in this chapter) and camera gear on boat trips.

Lightweight, cotton casual clothes are best for Fiji's tropical climate. Bathers, shorts and singlet tops are OK for the resorts, however, you will need to respect local traditions when outside the main tourist areas. Below-the-knee dresses or skirts are fine for women. T-shirts that cover the shoulders and a *sulu* (a length of material wrapped around as a skirt) are appropriate for both sexes. Pack low-fuss, wash-and-wear items. Take a light jumper as it can get cool in the highlands and elsewhere in the winter months, especially between May and August. Include a light raincoat or compact umbrella, sunglasses, a malleable hat and a lightweight towel or chamois. Refer also to the Women Travellers section later in this chapter.

Make sure that shoes are worn-in before travelling; the last thing you want is blisters that can lead to infections. You can pretty much live in a good pair of walking sandals and will only need walking boots if you are going hiking in muddy conditions. An old pair of sneakers or reef walking shoes may be useful (make sure you only walk over sand and dead coral!). The dress code for Suva or Nadi's night spots requires neat shoes.

Pack toiletries in small containers to reduce bulk and weight. Take resealable plastic bags to avoid those disastrous leaks. Pharmacies and large supermarkets in the main towns stock condoms, tampons and baby items, such as disposable nappies, formula and sterilising solution. Nappies, however, are expensive in Fiji. Most resorts have a shop with basic toiletries. If you are going directly to a remote island, bring your personal needs from home. It's also advisable to carry an emergency supply of toilet paper when travelling. Include a good insect repellent containing plenty of DEET; vitamins if you will be on the road for an extended period; prescription medicines (with a copy of scripts); and spare glasses or contact lenses (disposables are handy). Refer to the medical kit check list in the Health section later in this chapter.

Keen snorkellers should consider taking their own mask, snorkel and fins. Divers should remember to bring their scuba certification card. While equipment can be hired at most resorts and dive shops, you may prefer to take your own gear. A lycra suit for summer or a 3mm wetsuit for winter is recommended.

Consider how you will be travelling when choosing photographic equipment, and bring plenty of film (see Photography & Video later in this chapter). Photos make great thank-you gifts.

Other equipment could include a Swiss army knife, torch, compass, travel alarm, calculator or electronic organiser (if you're addicted to technology) and spare batteries (you should be able to get them there, but bring some to avoid the hassle of searching). A needle and thread, laundry soap and traveller's clothesline are all handy.

Most accommodation places provide mosquito nets or screened windows. Campers and self-caterers should take a lightweight waterproof tent, a plastic plate, a cup, utensils, matches and possibly a camping stove (kerosene is readily available in Fiji).

RESPONSIBLE TOURISM

Tourism is one of the country's main money-spinners and employs a large percentage of the population. Many of the up-market resorts have foreign owners but some money also flows on to local communities. Ecotourism projects are also beginning to take off where money directly benefits local villages. Be conscious of your contribution to waste problems in these remote areas.

There are many cultural issues that the traveller to Fiji should be aware of and respect. For example, you cannot just hike or camp anywhere – you need the permission of the local landowners. See Hiking in the Activities section and Camping in the Accommodation section later in this chapter.

Travellers can minimise their impact by choosing resorts, tours and activities that support local services and people and that are environmentally and culturally aware. Expect to pay a fair price. See the Ecology & Environment, Society & Conduct sections in the Facts about Fiji chapter and the Diving section later in this chapter.

The United Nations has reported that child-sex tourists have now begun travelling to Fiji and other South Pacific nations as well as South-East Asia. Fiji now has legislation against such crimes and foreigners have begun to be prosecuted.

The responsible traveller should not bring in or take out shells, coral or turtle products, even if legal (see the Customs section later in this chapter).

TOURIST OFFICES

The Fiji Visitors Bureau (FVB) is the primary tourist information body in Fiji. It has many overseas representatives (see the office details later). The head office is in Suva, but your first encounter is likely to be at Nadi International Airport. If you arrive here by plane you will be greeted by an FVB representative. The office is on the left, just past the ANZ bank as you come out of arrivals. There will be many other faces smiling at you, including travel agents or representatives of resorts and other accommodation. The FVB has a 24-hour, toll-free helpline for complaints or emergencies – ring from anywhere in Fiji (☎ 0800 721 721).

The Tourism Council of the South Pacific (TCSP; ☎ 304 177, fax 301 995, ☻ spice@is.com.fj) has an office on the corner of Loftus St and Victoria Parade (on the 3rd floor, above Dolphin Plaza Food Court) in Suva. It promotes cooperation between the South Pacific island nations for the development of tourism in the region. It is funded by the European Union (EU) but aims to become self-sufficient by selling its services. It has an interesting service on the Internet (www.tcsp.com), in the format of a travel directory for the Pacific countries.

Other useful sources of information include the following publications:

Affordable Fiji A brochure published by the FVB specifically for the budget traveller (costs F$5).
Fiji Islands Travel Guide An annual magazine published by the FVB.
Fiji Magic (☎ 313 944, fax 302 852) An OK source of information for the independent traveller. It has details and prices of accommodation, restaurants, activities and tours and is free and widely available (try the FVB, hotels and airline offices). Although issued monthly, the information is not always up-to-date.
Fiji Today and *Fiji Facts and Figures* The Ministry of Information (☎ 211 218), Government Buildings, Suva, produces these brochures. The government Web site is at www.fiji.gov.fj.
The Yacht Help Booklet, Fiji This booklet has useful information for yachties, including tide tables and clearance formalities (available from marinas).

The Fiji Hotel Association (☎ 302 980, fax 300 331), at 42 Gorrie St, Suva, produces a pamphlet that summarises the facilities of its member hotels. Most of the country's mid-range and top-end hotels and resorts are members of this organisation.

Local Tourist Offices

The FVB has offices in Suva and Nadi:

Suva (☎ 302 433, fax 300 970, ☻ infodesk@ fijifvb.gov.fj) Thomas St, GPO Box 92
Web site: www.bulafiji.com
Nadi (☎ 722 433, 0800 721 721, fax 720 141, ☻ fvbnadi@is.com.fj) Nadi Airport Concourse, Box 9217, Nadi International Airport

Tourist Offices Abroad

The FVB also has offices in the following countries:

Australia (☎ 02-9264 3399, 1800 25 1715, fax 9264 3060) Level 12, St Martins Tower, 31 Market St, Sydney 2000
Canada (☎ 1800 932 3454, fiji@primenet.com)
Japan (☎ 03-3587 2038, fax 3587 2563) 14th floor, NOA Building, 3–5, 2 Chome Azabudai, Minato-Ku, Tokyo 106
New Zealand (☎ 09-373 2133, fax 309 4720) 5th floor, 48 High St, Auckland, PO Box 1179
USA (☎ 310-568 1616, 1800 932 3454, fax 670 2318) 5777 West Century Blvd, Suite 220, Los Angeles, CA 90045

It also has representatives in:

Germany (☎ 30-4225 6026, fax 4225 6287, ☻ 100762.3614@compuserve.com) Petersburger Strasse 94, 10247 Berlin
UK (☎ 020-7584 3661, fax 7584 2838, ☻ fijirepuk@compuserve.com) 34 Hyde Park Gate, London SW7 5BN

VISAS & DOCUMENTS
Passport & Visas

Tourist visas of four months are granted on arrival to citizens of most countries, including: most countries belonging to the British Commonwealth, North America, Western Europe, Antigua, Argentina, Barbuda, Belize, Bolivia, Brazil, Chile, Colombia, Ecuador, Federated States of Micronesia, Iceland, India, Indonesia, Israel, Japan, Marshall Islands, Mexico, Nauru, Papua New Guinea, Paraguay, Peru, Philippines, Russia, Samoa, Solomon Islands, South Korea, Tanzania, Tonga, Tuvalu, Tunisia, Turkey, Uruguay, Vanuatu and Venezuela. There is no charge for the initial visa. Nationalities from excluded countries will have to apply for visas through a Fijian embassy prior to arrival.

Those entering Fiji by boat are subject to the same visa requirements as those arriving by plane. Yachts can only enter through the designated ports of Suva, Lautoka, Savusavu and Levuka. Yachts have to be cleared by immigration, health and customs, and are prohibited from visiting any outer islands before doing so. Yachties need to apply for special written authorisation to visit the Lau Group (see Travel Permits later in this section).

Visitors cannot partake in political activity or study, and work permits are needed if you intend to live and work in Fiji for more than six months. Foreign journalists will require a permit if they spend more than 14 days in Fiji (see the Work section later in this chapter).

Visa Extensions Visa extensions (F$55 fee) will be granted for up to two months pending the following: a passport valid for three months after the expected date of departure from Fiji; an onward or return ticket; and proof of sufficient funds. Vaccinations for yellow fever and cholera may be required if you are coming directly from an infected area.

Apply at the Immigration Department: Nadi International Airport (☎ 722 263, fax 721 720); Nausori International Airport (☎ 478 785); Lautoka (☎ 661 706, fax 668 120, Namoli Ave); or Suva (☎ 312 672, fax 301 653, Gohil Building, Toorak). You can also apply through police stations in Ba, Tavua, Taveuni, Savusavu, Labasa and Levuka, but allow at least two weeks for the paperwork. If you wish to stay longer than four months you'll have to leave and then re-enter the country. Those wishing to work will need to apply through a Fijian high commission prior to arrival.

Travel Permits
Yachties intending to sail to the outer islands, such as the Lau Group, will require a customs permit and a permit to cruise the islands, obtained from the Ministry of Foreign Affairs (☎ 211 458) at 61 Carnarvon St in Suva, or from the commissioner's office in Lautoka, Savusavu or Levuka. They will ask to see customs papers and details of all crew members. Seek advice from a yachting agent or yacht club in Fiji before applying for the permit.

Travel Insurance
A travel insurance policy to cover theft, loss and medical problems is a good idea.

There are many policies available and your travel agent will be able to recommend one. The policies handled by STA Travel and other student travel organisations are usually good value. Some policies offer lower and higher medical-expense options but the higher ones are mainly for countries such as the USA, which have extremely high medical costs. Check the small print:

- Some policies specifically exclude 'dangerous activities', which can include diving, motorcycling and even hiking. If such activities are on your agenda you don't want that sort of policy. A locally acquired motorcycle licence may not be valid under your policy.
- You may prefer a policy that pays doctors or hospitals direct rather than you having to pay on the spot and claim later. If you have to claim later make sure you keep all documentation. Some policies ask you to call back (reverse charges) to a centre in your home country where an immediate assessment of your problem is made.
- Check that the policy covers ambulances and an emergency flight home. If you have to stretch out you will need two seats and somebody has to pay for them!

Driving Licence & Permits
If you hold a current driving licence from an English-speaking country you are entitled to drive in Fiji. Otherwise you will need an international driving permit, which should be obtained in your home country before travelling.

Hostel Cards
The Cathay chain, which has accommodation on Viti Levu at Lautoka, Saweni Beach, Korotogo and Suva, gives small discounts for those with Hostelling International (HI), VIP or Australian Nomads Dreamtime cards.

Student & Youth Cards
STA Travel gives discounts on international air fares to full-time students who have an International Student Identity Card (ISIC). Application forms are available at STA Travel offices. Have the completed form stamped at the registry office of your school

or university, and return it to the STA office. Upon payment of about A$10 your card will be issued on the spot. Student discounts are occasionally given for entry fees, restaurants and accommodation in Fiji. You can also use the student health service at the University of the South Pacific (USP) in Suva.

Photocopies

Keep photocopies of vital documents and an emergency stash of about F$50 hidden in your luggage. Include a copy of the following: your passport's data pages, your birth certificate, credit cards, airline tickets, travel insurance, driving licence, and, if you are going to work in Fiji, your employment documents and education qualifications. Also include the serial numbers of your travellers cheques, your vaccination details and prescriptions. Remember to leave a copy of all these things with someone at home.

It's also a good idea to store details of your vital travel documents in Lonely Planet's free online Travel Vault in case you lose the photocopies or can't be bothered with them. Your password-protected Travel Vault is accessible online anywhere in the world – you can create it at www.ekno.lonelyplanet.com.

EMBASSIES
Fijian Embassies Abroad

Fiji has diplomatic representation in the following countries:

Australia (☎ 06-239 6872, fax 295 3283) 9 Beagle St, Red Hill, Canberra, ACT 2600; PO Box E159, Queen Victoria Terrace
Belgium (☎ 02-736 9050, fax 736 1458) 66 Avenue de Corteberg, 1000 Brussels; Boîte Postale 7
Japan (☎ 03-3587 2038, fax 3587 2563) 10th floor, Noa Building, 3-5, 2 Chome Azabudai, Minato-Ku, Tokyo 106
Malaysia (☎ 03-264 8422, fax 262 5636) 2nd floor, Suite 203, Wisma Equity, 150 Jalan Ampang, 50450, Kuala Lumpur
New Zealand (☎ 04-473 5401, fax 499 1011) 31 Pipitea St, Thorndon, Wellington; PO Box 3940
Papua New Guinea (☎ 211 914, fax 217 220) 4th floor, Defense House, Champion Parade, Port Moresby, NCD; PO Box 6117
UK (☎ 020-7584 3661, fax 7584 2838) 34 Hyde Park Gate, London SW7 5BN
USA (☎ 202-337 8320, fax 337 1966) 2233 Wisconsin Avenue, NW, Suite 240, Washington, DC 20007

Foreign Embassies in Fiji

The following countries have diplomatic representation in Fiji:

Australia (☎ 382 211, fax 382 065, @ austembassy@is.com.fj) 37 Princes Rd, Tamavua, Suva, PO Box 214
China (☎ 300 251, fax 300 950) 147 Queen Elizabeth Drive, Suva
European Union (☎ 313 633, fax 300 370) 4th Floor, Fiji Development Bank Centre, Victoria Parade, Suva
Federated States of Micronesia (☎ 304 566, fax 304 081) 37 Loftus St, Suva

Your Own Embassy

It's important to realise what your own embassy – the embassy of the country of which you are a citizen – can and can't do to help you if you get into trouble. Generally speaking, it won't be much help in emergencies if the trouble you're in is remotely your own fault. Remember that you are bound by the laws of the country you are in. Your embassy will not be sympathetic if you end up in jail after committing a crime locally, even if such actions are legal in your own country.

In genuine emergencies you might get some assistance, but only if other channels have been exhausted. For example, if you need to get home urgently, a free ticket home is exceedingly unlikely – the embassy would expect you to have insurance. If you have all your money and documents stolen, it might assist with getting a new passport, but a loan for onward travel is out of the question.

Some embassies used to keep letters for travellers or have a small reading room with home newspapers, but these days the mail holding service has usually been stopped and even newspapers tend to be out of date.

France (☎ 312 233, fax 301 894) 7th floor, Dominion House, Thomson St, Suva

Japan (☎ 302 122, fax 301 452) 2nd floor, Dominion House, Thomson St, Suva

Korea (☎ 300 977, fax 303 410) 8th floor, Vanua House, Victoria Parade, Suva

Malaysia (☎ 312 166, fax 303 350) 5th floor, Air Pacific House, Butt St, Suva, PO Box 356

Marshall Islands (☎ 387 899, fax 387 115) 41 Borron Rd, Samabula, Government Buildings, Suva, PO Box 2038

Nauru (☎ 313 566, fax 302 861) 7th floor, Ratu Sukuna House, Government Buildings, Suva, PO Box 2420

New Zealand (☎ 311 422, fax 300 842, @ nzhc@is.org.fj) 10th floor, Reserve Bank Building, Pratt St, Suva, PO Box 1378

Papua New Guinea (☎ 302 244, fax 300 178) 3rd floor Credit Corp Building, Gordon St, Suva, PO Box 2447

Tuvalu (☎ 301 355, fax 301 023) 16 Gorrie St, Suva, PO Box 14449

UK (☎ 311 033, fax 301 046, @ ukinfo@ bhc.org.fj) Victoria House, 47 Gladstone Rd, Suva, PO Box 1355

USA (☎ 314 466, fax 300 081) 31 Loftus St, Suva, PO Box 218

CUSTOMS

If you are travelling with expensive camera or computer equipment, carry a receipt to avoid hassles when returning home.

Visitors can leave Fiji without paying duty or value-added tax (VAT) on the following: up to F$400 per passenger of duty-assessed goods; two litres of liqueur or spirits, or four litres of wine or beer; 500 cigarettes or 500g of cigars/tobacco, or all three under a total of 500g; and personal effects. Pottery shards, turtle shells, coral and trochus and giant clam shells cannot be taken out of the country without a permit.

Quarantine

Importation of vegetable matter, seeds, animals, meat or dairy produce is prohibited without a licence from the Ministry of Agriculture & Fisheries. Domestic pets require a permit to enter Fiji and will be kept in quarantine in Suva, usually for a week.

MONEY

It's a good idea to have a couple of options for accessing money – take a credit card, some travellers cheques and a small amount of cash.

Currency

The local currency is the Fiji dollar (F$). The dollar is broken down into 100 cents. All prices quoted herein are in Fiji dollars unless otherwise specified.

The Fiji dollar is fairly stable, although it suffered a devaluation in 1998. As a result, many of the resorts that charge in US dollars have significantly increased prices. The currency has been fairly stable relative to the Australian and New Zealand dollars.

Bank notes come in denominations of F$50, F$20, F$10, F$5 and F$2. There are coins to the value of F$1, F$0.50, F$0.20, F$0.10, F$0.05, F$0.02 and F$0.01. Even though Fiji is now a republic, notes and coins still have a picture of England's Queen Elizabeth II on one side.

Exchange Rates

At the time of writing the exchange rates were as follows:

country	unit		conversion
Australia	A$1	=	F$1.29
Canada	C$1	=	F$1.35
euro	€1	=	F$1.96
France	1FF	=	F$2.99
Germany	DM1	=	F$1.00
Japan	¥100	=	F$1.86
New Zealand	NZ$1	=	F$0.99
UK	UK£1	=	F$3.21
USA	US$1	=	F$1.95
Vanuatu	VT100	=	F$1.52

Exchanging Money

The best currencies to carry are Australian, New Zealand or US dollars.

The commercial banks operating in Fiji include Fiji Westpac, ANZ, National Bank (previously the government-owned National Bank of Fiji), Bank of Hawaii, Bank of Baroda and Habib Bank. Bank hours are 9.30 am to 3 pm Monday to Thursday, 9.30 to 4 pm Fridays. The ANZ at Nadi airport provides 24-hour service. While banks in larger towns keep standard business hours, branches in smaller towns may not open every day.

Exchange houses include:

American Express
  Nadi: (☎ 722 325) Nadi Airport Concourse
  Suva: (☎ 302 333, fax 302 0480) 25 Victoria
  Parade. It has a good reputation for quick re-
  placement of lost or stolen cards or cheques.
Diners Club International
  (☎ 300 552, fax 301 312) 5th floor, ANZ
  House, Victoria Parade
Thomas Cook
  Suva: (☎ 301 603, fax 300 304) 30 Thomson St
  Nadi: (☎ 703 110, fax 703 877) on the corner
  of Main and Sukuna Sts

Travellers Cheques Travellers cheques
can be changed in most banks and exchange
houses, and at larger hotels and duty-free
shops. However, it is best to change plenty
of money before travelling to outer islands
or remote areas. It's a good idea to take
travellers cheques in both small and large
denominations to avoid being stuck with
lots of cash when leaving.

The 24-hour ANZ bank at Nadi International Airport charges F$2 on each transac-
tion. Other banks and exchange bureaus
don't normally charge a fee. Some small
branches will not exchange travellers
cheques. In a small branch you may have
trouble exchanging your money if it is a
public holiday in your home country, as it
will not be able to access the latest exchange rate.

Credit Cards Restaurants, shops, mid to
upper-range hotels, car rental agencies, tour
and travel agents will usually accept all of
the major credit cards. Visa, American Express, Diners Club and MasterCard are
widely used. Some resorts, though, will
charge an additional 5% for payment by
credit card.

Cash advances are available through
credit cards at most banks, but always confirm this before travelling to a remote area
as some of the smaller branches will not
handle credit card transactions.

ATMs The ANZ has an ATM at Nadi International Airport and the Bank of Hawaii
has one in downtown Suva.

Black Market There is no obvious black
market in Fiji, but you may occasionally
get people on the street wanting to buy US
dollars.

Security

While it is relatively uncommon for travellers to be robbed in Fiji, it does happen.
Avoid becoming suddenly destitute by
splitting money in secret stashes. Use hidden pouches rather than keeping your wallet in a back pocket.

Costs

Travelling independently in Fiji is good
value compared to many Pacific countries.
However, since the whole country is so
heavily geared to tourism, it can also be
very easy to spend a lot of money, especially at the upmarket resorts. To give an
idea of overall expenses: a local phone call
by cardphone costs F$0.20; the *Fiji Times*
costs F$0.70; one litre of long-life milk is
F$1.20; and a glass of beer costs from F$2.
See also the Accommodation and Food sections later in this chapter. Following are
some money-saving hints:

• If you are on a tight budget, follow the locals to
  the cheaper restaurants and avoid trendy joints
  aimed at tourists. Self-catering may be a good
  idea; try the local market for fresh fruit and vegetables.
• Carry lots of small notes and coins, essential for
  bargaining or when taking taxis, which are often
  without change.
• Be careful with transport; a bit of planning can
  save a lot of money. Inter-island hopping and
  fuel for boats is fairly expensive.
• When looking for a taxi, try for a 'return taxi'
  (one on its way back to base). Refer to the Getting Around chapter.
• We don't recommend hitching, but the locals
  hitch all the time in Fiji. It is courteous to pay
  the equivalent of the bus fare.
• Accommodation prices vary enormously in
  Fiji, from backpacker beds from F$8 to F$10
  and cheap hotel rooms for F$35, to luxury re-
  sorts for F$1000 per person per night. Some of
  the budget and mid-range places give access to
  the same activities and sites as the resorts, for
  a fraction of the price. Some resorts offer package deals. Inquire about local rates if you are
  living in Fiji.

Hard coral garden, the 'Cabbage Patch'

ASTRID WITTE & CASEY MAHANEY

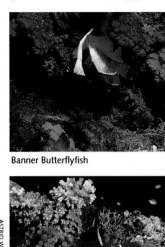

Banner Butterflyfish

ASTRID WITTE & CASEY MAHANEY

Anemonefish and *Amphirion frenatus*

ASTRID WITTE & CASEY MAHANEY

Soft coral, Somosomo Strait

ASTRID WITTE & CASEY MAHANEY

Sea fans and soft corals

ASTRID WITTE & CASEY MAHANEY

ROBYN JONES

Working in the rice field, western Viti Levu

DAVID WALL

Sugar-cane train, Lautoka

DAVID WALL

Suva Municipal Market

DAVID WALL

Building a new *bure* (traditional thatched house), Viti Levu

ROBYN JONES

Drying kava roots, which are used to make an intoxicating drink

JOHN BORTHWICK

Traditional feast

Tipping & Bargaining

Tipping is not expected or encouraged in Fiji; however, many of the resorts have a Staff Christmas Fund to which you may choose to contribute.

Indigenous Fijians generally do not like to bargain, but always expect to do so in Fiji-Indian stores, especially in Nadi. It is considered bad luck for a shop owner or taxi driver to lose their first customer of the day, so arrive first thing to drive an especially hard bargain!

Taxes & Refunds

Always confirm whether prices of accommodation, food or transport etc are being quoted with or without VAT, a 10% sales tax on goods and services introduced in July 1992. Prices quoted in the book include VAT. Travellers and locals alike have to pay this tax.

POST & COMMUNICATIONS

Fiji Posts & Telecommunications Ltd provides a wide range of services throughout the islands, and since Nadi International Airport is a major flight hub, international deliveries are usually quite efficient. Post offices are open from 8 am to 4 pm weekdays and from 9 am to noon Saturdays.

Postal Rates

To mail a postcard or standard letter (under 15g) from Fiji costs F$0.13 within the country, F$0.31 to New Zealand, F$0.44 to Australia, F$0.63 to the USA and F$0.81 to Europe.

Sending Mail

Sending mail is straightforward. An international express mail service is available through the main post offices. Use surface mail if your items are too heavy and expensive to send by air mail, and if you don't mind a long delivery time.

Receiving Mail

It is possible to receive mail at all major post offices through general deliveries. Mail is held for up to two months. It is also possible to receive faxes from Fintel (Fiji International Telecommunications) and the major post offices (see Fax later in this section).

Telephone

The majority of mid-range and top-end hotel rooms have telephones. However, hotels usually add hefty surcharges so the cheapest and most convenient way to make international calls is by direct dial from public cardphone. The cards are also a good way to limit costs. Most post offices have public phones, although not always functioning. Phonecards can be purchased at post offices, newsagents and some pharmacies. It's a good idea to buy a few at the airport when you arrive (at the shops near departures). The plastic phonecards come in denominations of F$3, F$5, F$10, F$20 and F$50, and have interesting designs. However, avoid buying the large denomination cards as phonecards are very easy to leave behind! Fintel, in downtown Suva, also provides an international phone service.

There are no area codes within Fiji. Be aware that national calls are charged according to time. Rates on public phones are F$0.20 per three minutes for a local call; around F$0.20 per 45 seconds between neighbouring towns; and F$0.20 for each 15 seconds for more distant calls (eg, Nadi to Suva or between islands). Collect calls are more expensive, and when using operator assistance the minimum charge is three minutes and a surcharge of F$1.10 applies. If you want to charge calls to your home telephone, using a Telecom Calling Card or Telecom Credit Card, call the operator for assistance.

Most towns have automatic telephone exchanges, however, some remote areas have a manual exchange service. Islands are linked by cable and satellite to worldwide networks. Calls to radio phones may have to go through the operator: dial ☎ 013.

Vodaphone (☎ 312 000, fax 312 007), the local cellular service provider, operates a GSM digital mobile communication service. Mobile phones can be rented from some car rental agencies. You can arrange to bring your mobile phone from home but this may mean you pay international rates for local calls – check it out beforehand!

Useful numbers include:

Emergency	☎ 000
International collect calls	☎ 031 + number
International directory inquiries	☎ 022
International operator assistance, bookings	☎ 012
Local collect calls	☎ 030 + number
Local directory inquiries	☎ 011
Operator assistance and reminder calls	☎ 010

The international dial-in code for Fiji is ☎ 679 followed by the local number. There are no area codes.

To use International Direct Dial (IDD), dial ☎ 05 plus the country code given below. The following rates are for three minutes minimum:

country	code	rate
Australia	☎ 61	F$4.74
France	☎ 33	F$8.01
French Polynesia	☎ 689	F$5.04
Germany	☎ 49	F$8.01
Japan	☎ 81	F$8.01
New Zealand	☎ 64	F$4.74
Tonga	☎ 676	F$4.74
USA	☎ 598	F$8.01
Vanuatu	☎ 678	F$5.04

Fax

In Suva you have a choice of using the services of the post office or Fintel (☎ 301 655, fax 301 025). Fintel deals with international services only (telephone calls, faxes and telegrams), and has booths and sells phonecards for this purpose. The Fintel fax service is cheaper if you wish to send multiple pages. If you are expecting incoming faxes, ring Fintel to inquire. The office is open from 8 am to 8 pm Monday to Saturday, but is closed on Sunday and public holidays.

At post offices, fax charges per page are as follows:

Incoming faxes – F$1.10
Local – F$2.20 plus F$0.55 handling fee

Pacific countries – F$5.50 plus F$3.30 handling fee
Other countries – F$7.70 plus F$3.30 handling fee

Post offices offering fax services include:

Labasa	fax 813 666
Lautoka	fax 664 666
Nadi International Airport	fax 720 467
Savusavu	fax 880 359
Suva (GPO)	fax 306 088
Waiyevo, Taveuni	fax 880 459

Email & Internet Access

Use of email is now popular in Fiji. Nadi, Lautoka and Suva all have cybercafes (see the Nadi, Lautoka & Around and Suva sections of the Viti Levu chapter). Expect to pay about F$0.22 per minute.

Fintel in Suva will allow those with their own notebook computer and modem to hook up to an overseas server. It charges the regular international time fee for phone calls. For information on Telecom Fiji's Internet services, contact ☎ 300 100, fax 307 237 or ✉ info@is.com.fj. Check out its Web site at www.is.com.fj. Resorts and larger hotels will often let you use their facilities. Note that some exclusive resorts, such as Vatulele Island Resort, discourage the use of personal computers, telephones and faxes, as they believe it interferes with your holiday!

INTERNET RESOURCES

The World Wide Web is a rich resource for travellers. You can research your trip, hunt down bargain air fares, book hotels, check on weather conditions or chat with locals and other travellers about the best places to visit (or avoid!).

There's no better place to start your Web explorations than the Lonely Planet Web site (www.lonelyplanet.com). Here you'll find succinct summaries on travelling to most places on earth, postcards from other travellers and the Thorn Tree bulletin board, where you can ask questions before you go or dispense advice when you get back. You can also find travel news and updates to many of our most popular guide-books, and the subWWWay section links you to the most useful travel resources elsewhere on the Web.

Try the following Web sites for useful information on Fiji:

Fiji Village Has news and excellent links to local events, including music, movies and sport.
www.fijivillage.com
Fiji Visitors Bureau Has information on accommodation, activities and getting around, with links and an email directory.
www.bulafiji.com
Internet Fiji Has many links and newsbytes from the *Fiji Times*
www.internetfiji.com
Pacific Islands Report An excellent place to get news summaries covering Pacific events.
pidp.ewc.hawaii.edu/pireport/
Tourism Council of the South Pacific In the form of a travel directory, and includes Fiji, Cook Islands, Kiribati, New Caledonia, Niue, Papua New Guinea, Solomon Islands, Tahiti, Tonga, Tuvalu, Vanuatu and Western Samoa.
www.tcsp.com

BOOKS

Most books are published in different editions by different publishers in different countries. As a result, a book might be a hardcover rarity in one country while it's readily available in paperback in another. Fortunately, bookshops and libraries search by title or author, so your local bookshop or library is best placed to advise you on the availability of the following recommendations. Many of these books can be ordered through the Institute of Pacific Studies (☎ 313 900, fax 301 594, ✉ ips@usp.ac.fj). Others can be purchased at the Fiji Museum in Suva.

Lonely Planet

Also published by Lonely Planet are *Diving & Snorkeling Guide to Fiji,* the *Fijian phrasebook,* by Paul Geraghty, an excellent aid to talking with locals, the *South Pacific phrasebook,* the new *South Pacific* guidebook and *Travel with Children,* by Maureen Wheeler, which is packed with useful information for family travel and has an account of travelling in Fiji.

History & Politics

Books that cover precolonial history include:

Yalo i Viti by Fergus Clunie, published by the Fiji Museum (1986), is recommended. It explains the significance of the Fijian artefacts you will see in the museum.
Matanitu – The Struggle for Power in Early Fiji by David Routledge, 1985.
Fiji and the Fijians – The Islands and Their Inhabitants, Vol 1 (1858) by Wesleyan minister Rev Thomas Williams. A 1982 reprint of the original book is available at the Fiji Museum.
Journals of Baron Anatole von Hugel by Jane Roth & Steven Hooper is published by the Fiji Museum. It is an interesting account of the baron's experiences in Fiji between 1875 and 1879.
The Fiji and New Caledonia Journals of Mary Wallis, 1851–1853, edited by David Routledge, 1994.
My Twenty-One Years in the Fiji Islands, by Totaram Sanadhya, is an interesting first-hand account of the indenture system. Written in the 1910s, a new edition (1991) is available at the Fiji Museum.

Other general history books include:

Fiji in the Pacific – A History and Geography of Fiji by Donnelly, Quanchi & Kerr, 1994, was designed as a school textbook but is nevertheless a good introduction to Fiji.
Fiji Times – A History of Fiji by Kim Gravelle, 1979.
Plantation to Politics, Studies on Fiji Indians by Ahmed Ali, 1980.
Beyond the Politics of Race, an Alternative History of Fiji to 1992 by William Sutherland.
Broken Waves – A History of the Fiji Islands in the Twentieth Century by Brij V Lal, 1992.

The titles below deal specifically with the military coup and postcoup era:

Power and Prejudice – The Making of the Fiji Crisis by Brij V Lal, 1988.
More Letters From Fiji, 1990–1994 – First Years Under a Post-coup Constitution by Len Usher.
Fiji – The Politics of Illusion by Deryck Scarr, 1988.
Rabuka – No Other Way by Eddie Dean & Stan Ritova, 1988.

Fiji – Shattered Coups by RT Robertson & AT Amanisau, 1988.

Biographies

He Served – A Biography of Macu Salato by Robyet C. Kiste, 1998, covers the life of an indigenous Fijian who was born as a commoner in Lau and became a doctor and a member of the Great Council of Chiefs. He served as mayor of Suva and as the acting High Commissioner to the UK.

Beyond the Black Waters – A Memoir of Sir Sathi Narain by Satya Colpani, 1996, is about the life of a man who emigrated from southern India and became a prominent Fiji Indian in industry and business.

Life in Feejee, or, Five Years Among the Cannibals by A Lady (Mary Davis Wallis), 1851, reprinted 1983, is the memoirs of the wife of a Yankee trading captain. It can be purchased at the Fiji Museum shop.

Fiction

Fiji by Daryl Tarte, 1988, is the ultimate trashy Fijian novel, a sprawling saga following over a century of Fijian history through the experiences of a plantation family. It's based on the Tarte family of Taveuni, whose old colonial farm is now a backpacker and dive resort (Susie's Plantation). It's easy to read and covers a wide range of historical topics.

Refer to Literature in the Arts section of the Facts about Fiji chapter for more information. For those who have a specific interest in contemporary Fijian literature, *South Pacific Literature: From Myth to Fabulation,* published by the Institute of Pacific Studies, 1992, is a survey of Pacific Islanders and their work. It has an extensive bibliography.

Traditional Culture

Traditional Sailing Canoes in Lau by Gillett, Ianelli, Waqaratoqu & Qaica, 1993, has photos and construction details of the vessels.

Myths and Legends of Fiji and Rotuma by AW Reed & Inez Hames, 1967, includes stories about the powerful shark-god Dakuwaqa and the great snake-god Degei.

Vaka i Taukei, the Fijian Way of Life by Asesela Ravuvu, 1983.

Secrets of Fijian Medicine by MA Weiner, published by the University of California, will give you an insight into the traditional uses of plants.

Nai Vola ni Wai Vakaviti by Wainimate, 1997, is another book on this subject, published only in Fijian.

Traditional Handicrafts of Fiji by Tabualevu, Uluinaceva & Raimua, 1997.

Photography

Children of the Sun by Glen Craig, with poetry by Bryan McDonald, 1996, has stunning photography of smiling locals with perfect teeth as well as spectacular landscapes. The book has a humorous and interesting design and has photos taken over an eight-year period on Craig's many visits to Fiji. You should be able to purchase a copy at the FVB (F$44).

Fiji, the Uncharted Sea by Frederico Busonero has great underwater photography. It is available at the FVB (F$44).

Rotuma, Fiji's Hidden Paradise by Ian Osborn, 1996, has beautiful photos that will inspire visitors to visit this remote island group.

Environment

Fiji – Beneath the Surface by Professor Patrick Nunn, 2000, is a compilation of 52 articles about the Fiji environment and its mysteries. The articles appeared as weekly columns in the *Fiji Times.* The book is published by the University of the South Pacific.

The Snorkeller's Guide to the Coral Reef by Paddy Ryan, 1994, is recommended. It has photographs by the author and by Peter Atkinson.

Fiji's Natural Heritage, also by Paddy Ryan, 1988, covers Fiji's amazing flora, fauna and environment.

FILMS

Both the original 1948 *Blue Lagoon,* starring Jean Simmons, and the 1979 remake with Brooke Shields were shot in the Yasawa islands. *Return to the Blue Lagoon* was filmed on Taveuni in 1991.

The FVB has various videos promoting the Fiji islands.

NEWSPAPERS & MAGAZINES

The *Fiji Times,* founded in Levuka in 1869, is the oldest media organisation in the country. Now owned by Rupert Murdoch, it has a circulation of 38,000. Its slogan is 'the first newspaper published in the world today', due to its proximity to the International Date Line. The *Fiji Times* also pub-

Freedom of the Press

The concept of a free press is still in its infancy in Fiji. There are opposing views regarding media freedom. Journalists and academics are strong promoters of media freedom, advocating the right of every citizen to have access to information, especially government information. Others oppose the application of 'Western concepts', arguing that media freedom is disruptive to traditional institutions and endangers the harmony of Fijian customs, values and hierarchical systems of authority.

The former Rabuka government at one moment assumed a position of commitment to openness and at another introduced media legislation to secure confidentiality and privacy for certain citizens. Rabuka, however, was quick to defend the public's voice when Chaudhry, the new prime minister, criticised the media and threatened to establish a media tribunal.

Under the 1997 constitution, Fiji is to adopt freedom of information legislation.

lishes the newspapers *Nai Lalaki,* in Fijian, and *Shanti Dut,* in Hindi. The *Daily Post,* established in 1987, has a circulation of about 16,000, and also publishes *Nai Volasiga* in Fijian. Magazines include *Pacific Islands Monthly* and *Island Business,* which cover regional issues, and the *Review,* which is Fiji-oriented.

Australian newspapers (at least a few days old) are available at some Suva newsagents for an inflated price. The *Sydney Morning Herald* costs F$8.75 and the *Australian* F$8. Alternatively, try the embassy reading rooms.

Refer to the Tourist Offices section earlier in this chapter for details of magazines that contain useful information for travellers to Fiji.

RADIO & TV

The government-sponsored Fiji Broadcasting Commission has two stations in English (Radio Fiji 3 and FM 104), one in Fijian (Radio Fiji 1) and two in Hindi (Radio Fiji 2 and 98 FM).

Running since 1990, FM 104 has music programs, including the World Chart Show, Take 40 Australia, Roots Rhythm, UK Top 10 and dance and reggae shows. The station plays 10% local content: listen for Seru Serevi, Danny Costello, Michelle Rounds, Karuana Gopalan, The Freelancers and The Black Roses.

The independent commercial station FM 96 began as Communications Fiji Limited in 1985. It has 24-hour broadcasting with music, sports and community information in English and Hindi.

Radio Pacific (FM 88.8), managed by the USP Student Association, began broadcasting in May 1996. Student volunteers host programs with music and information from different Pacific countries, as well as some academic programs. The government licence binds them to avoid political and religious topics.

Fiji received its first TV transmission in October 1991, when Television New Zealand played a live telecast of World Cup rugby matches. The Fiji Television Company received its licence in August 1993. There is just one station – Fiji One. Check the *Fiji Times* or the fortnightly *TV Guide* magazine for programming. Cable TV was introduced in 1996.

VIDEO SYSTEMS

The various video systems – PAL, NTSC and Secam – are incompatible. The system used in Fiji is PAL G, as in Australia and New Zealand. When buying video recordings ensure they are compatible with the system in your home country.

PHOTOGRAPHY & VIDEO
Film & Equipment

Film and photography equipment is readily available in Fiji, although it is best to buy film before leaving your country. Always check expiry dates and, if intending to take lots of shots, buy 36-exposure film, which will be less bulky to carry. While for most conditions 100 ASA will be OK, also take some 400 ASA film for darker, forest conditions. There are labs with same-day processing services in Nadi, Lautoka and Suva.

For travel photography (portraits, landscapes, architecture, wildlife and macro shots) it is best to have equipment that gives you flexibility. An SLR camera with a combination wide angle and zoom lens is great. However, weight and simplicity of operation are also of prime importance. Make sure your equipment and flash are working well, take spare batteries and consider bringing a polariser.

Don't leave your camera gear exposed to the sun, heat, humidity or salty sea air. Fungal growth on camera lenses can be a problem. If you plan to stay in Fiji or the tropics for more than a few weeks, it may be a good idea to keep equipment in airtight containers with activated silica gel (available at pharmacies). If travelling around in small boats, store your camera and film in a waterproof bag or container.

Photography

Make sure you are familiar with how to operate your camera equipment before you leave home.

Avoid flat shots of landscapes with no foreground: they may look gorgeous in real life, but are often boring as a photo. Experiment with a variety of subjects, taking into consideration composition (framing, balance, centre of interest and position of horizon) and modelling (direction and intensity of light on the subject). Fiji's midday sun can be bright and harsh, leading to overexposed photos, so you'll need to adjust your camera settings accordingly. The best light conditions are generally in the early morning and late afternoon. Be careful that dark-skinned people don't turn out as silhouettes on bright backgrounds. In this situation it might be best to overexpose your photos, or, if your camera has one, to employ the contrast-adjustment setting. A flash can also be used to highlight the foreground.

Underwater Photography Novelty cameras are a fun introduction to underwater photography. Some resorts and dive centres offer underwater cameras for hire, with tuition and sometimes processing facilities. Special underwater cameras are an expensive investment. Alternatively, standard cameras can be used with special waterproof housings and an underwater strobe flash, or, on sunny days, with underwater slide film. As a general rule, close-up shots will be more successful. Give preference to high shutter speeds to avoid camera shake and blurred fish. Water absorbs certain wavelengths, and red filters can be used to reduce the exaggerated blue. If you are bringing your own equipment, make sure your lights can be charged on 240V, or bring a converter.

Video

Make sure you are familiar with your camera and its limitations. For a successful travel video, consider light conditions and avoid glare, panning too quickly and camera shudder. Give a running commentary to entertain the viewers, and avoid filming in the wind, as it can cause noise distortion. As with any photography, try to take creative shots with variety, humour and plenty of close-ups. Protect your gear from humidity, heat and sea air.

Restrictions

At a *yaqona* ceremony you will normally have to wait until after the formal ritual before taking photos; check first. Don't wander around villages photographing and filming people's private space, unless invited. Try not to flash expensive gear around.

Photographing People

Fijians usually enjoy having their photo taken, but always ask permission first and ask if they would like copies sent to them.

Airport Security

Repetitive exposure to airport X-ray machines can damage film, especially those of high speed. Carry films in a lead-lined bag, or in a clear plastic bag and ask for them to be checked by hand.

TIME

The concept of time in Fiji is fairly flexible ('Fiji time'), so don't get too stressed if people are not punctual for appointments or if transport is running late; just go with the flow.

Although the 180° meridian passes through the Fiji archipelago, the International Date Line doglegs so that all Fiji islands lie to the west of it. Fiji is 12 hours ahead of GMT/UTC. Daylight is from about 6 am to 6 pm. Fiji recently introduced daylight saving (summer time, starting in November), in part to be in the running to be the first country to see in the new millennium! There was intense rivalry between competing countries, which include Tonga and Kiribati, and arguments over whether the Date Line or the 180° meridian should decide it.

When it's noon in Suva, corresponding times elsewhere are as follows:

Same day

Sydney	10 am
New Caledonia & Vanuatu	11 am
Auckland	noon
Tonga	1 pm

Previous day

London	midnight
Samoa	1 pm
San Francisco	4 pm
New York	7 pm

Subtract one hour from these times if the other country does not have daylight saving in place.

ELECTRICITY

Electricity in Fiji is supplied at 240V, 50 Hz AC, as in Australia. Many remote areas and island resorts rely on solar and generator power. It is best to buy adaptors prior to leaving home, but they are also available in duty-free shops. Many of the resorts and hotels have universal outlets for 240V or 110V shavers and hair dryers. Outlets are of the three-pin type and use flat two- or three-pin plugs of the Australian type.

WEIGHTS & MEASURES

Fiji follows the metric system, hence distance is measured in kilometres, goods bought in kilograms or litres, and temperature registered in degrees Celsius. Refer to the conversion chart on this book's inside back cover.

LAUNDRY

Most resorts and hotels will do your laundry for a small fee. A load is normally about F$5, although some places will charge by item, which can become costly. People travelling away from cities, towns and resorts may wish to carry laundry soap and a scrubbing brush, although village stores usually stock these items. In rural areas women sit down in the creeks or rivers fully clothed to do their washing. Same-day laundry and dry-cleaning services are available in Nadi and Suva. Consult the telephone directory (Fiji's *Yellow Pages*).

TOILETS

Toilets are the sit-down type. Fiji has public toilets in cities and larger towns, hotels and resorts, and sometimes near small groups of shops on country roads. Toilets in restaurants and in resort and hotel foyers are usually cleaner than those outside. It's a good idea to carry an emergency supply of toilet paper.

Most remote villages don't have toilets and the local creek is used for washing clothes and bodies. Ask about the local bathing customs, don't just strip off near the village. For a toilet, make do with the bush or the beach, making sure you are a suitable distance from any creeks or rivers, and bury your toilet paper.

HEALTH

Travel health depends on your predeparture preparations, your daily health care while travelling and how you handle any medical problem that does develop. While the potential dangers can seem quite frightening, in reality few travellers experience anything more than upset stomachs.

Those arriving directly from a temperate climate may initially find the tropical heat and humidity a bit overwhelming. Fiji is malaria-free, though some neighbouring countries, such as Vanuatu, have the disease. Obtain a doctor's advice about

Medical Kit Check List

Following is a list of items you should consider including in your medical kit – consult your pharmacist for brands available in your country.

☐ **Aspirin or paracetamol (acetaminophen in the USA)** – for pain or fever

☐ **Antihistamine** – for allergies, eg, hay fever; to ease the itch from insect bites or stings; and to prevent motion sickness

☐ **Cold and flu tablets, throat lozenges and nasal decongestant**

☐ **Multivitamins** – consider for long trips, when dietary vitamin intake may be inadequate

☐ **Antibiotics** – consider including these if you're travelling well off the beaten track; see your doctor, as they must be prescribed, and carry the prescription with you

☐ **Loperamide or diphenoxylate** –'blockers' for diarrhoea

☐ **Prochlorperazine or metaclopramide** – for nausea and vomiting

☐ **Rehydration mixture** – to prevent dehydration, which may occur, for example, during bouts of diarrhoea; particularly important when travelling with children

☐ **Insect repellent, sunscreen, lip balm and eye drops**

☐ **Calamine lotion, sting relief spray or aloe vera** – to ease irritation from sunburn and insect bites or stings

☐ **Antifungal cream or powder** – for fungal skin infections and thrush

☐ **Antiseptic (such as povidone-iodine)** – for cuts and grazes

☐ **Bandages, Band-Aids (plasters) and other wound dressings**

☐ **Water purification tablets or iodine**

☐ **Scissors, tweezers and a thermometer** – note that mercury thermometers are prohibited by airlines

☐ **Syringes and needles** – in case you need injections in a country with medical hygiene problems; ask your doctor for a note explaining why you have them

antimalarials if you also plan to visit such countries. There are occasional outbreaks of dengue fever and filariasis in Fiji (both are mosquito-transmitted diseases). Hepatitis A and B also occur in Fiji.

Predeparture Planning

Immunisations No jabs are required for travel to Fiji, unless you have been travelling in a part of the world where yellow fever may be prevalent. Ensure that your normal childhood vaccinations (polio, tetanus, diptheria) are up-to-date. Plan ahead for getting vaccinations; some of them require more than one injection, while some vaccinations should not be given together, during pregnancy or to people with allergies – discuss with your doctor.

Hepatitis A vaccine (eg, Avaxim, Havrix 1440 or VAQTA) provides long-term immunity (possibly more than 10 years) after an initial injection and a booster at six to 12 months.

Alternatively, an injection of gamma globulin can provide short-term protection against hepatitis A – two to six months, depending on the dose given. It is not a vaccine, but is a ready-made antibody collected from blood donations. It is reasonably effective and, unlike the vaccine, it is protective immediately, but because it is a blood product, there are current concerns about its long-term safety.

Hepatitis A vaccine is also available in a combined form, Twinrix, with hepatitis B vaccine. Three injections over a six-month period are required, the first two providing substantial protection against hepatitis A.

The risk of tuberculosis (TB) to travellers is usually very low, unless you will be living with or closely associated with local people in Fiji. Vaccination against TB (the BCG vaccine) is recommended for children and young adults living in these areas for three months or more.

Health Insurance Make sure that you have adequate health insurance, especially if you plan to go diving. See Travel Insurance under Visas & Documents earlier in this chapter for details.

Travel Health Guides Lonely Planet's *Healthy Travel Australia, New Zealand & the Pacific* is a handy pocket-sized book and is packed with useful information including pretrip planning, emergency first aid, immunisation and disease information and what to do if you get sick on the road. *Travel with Children,* from Lonely Planet, also includes advice on travel health for younger children.

Other Preparations Make sure you're healthy before you start travelling. If you are going on a long trip make sure your teeth are OK. If you wear glasses take a spare pair and your prescription.

If you require a particular medication take an adequate supply, as it may not be available locally. Take part of the packaging showing the generic name rather than the brand, which will make getting replacements easier. It's a good idea to have a legible prescription or letter from your doctor to show that you legally use the medication to avoid any problems.

Basic Rules
Food Vegetables and fruit should be washed with purified water or peeled where possible. Beware of ice cream that is sold in the street or anywhere else it might have been melted and refrozen; if there's any doubt (eg, a power cut in the last day or two), steer well clear. Shellfish such as mussels, oysters and clams should be avoided, as should undercooked meat, particularly in the form of mince. Steaming does not make shellfish safe for eating.

Ciguatera This is a type of food poisoning caused by eating tropical and subtropical fish that have accumulated certain toxins through their diet. The toxins are contained in algae, which is eaten by smaller reef fish, which are in turn the prey of larger fish. It is best to avoid eating big reef predators such as snapper, barracuda and grouper. Ocean fish such as tuna, wahoo and Spanish mackerel are generally safe to eat, and small reef fish that the locals eat and recommend should be OK.

The symptoms of ciguatera poisoning include nausea, vomiting, diarrhoea and stomach cramps, alternating fevers and chills, and tingling in the skin and mouth. A feeling of weak muscles and joints and aching pain in the fingers and feet may sometimes last weeks or even months. Hot may feel cold and vice versa. According to Peter Dunn-Rankin, in *Fishing the Reefs,* Mannitol, an intravenous medication, has been used to successfully treat the poisoning.

Water The water in Fiji's major towns, hotels and resorts is generally safe to drink, but the same cannot be said of all villages and islands. The water supply in the Rakiraki area in northern Viti Levu has been deemed unsafe. Many of the resort islands of the Mamanucas pipe or barge their water from the mainland.

The number one rule is *be careful of the water* and especially ice. If you don't know for certain that the water is safe, assume the worst. Take care with fruit juice, particularly if water may have been added. Milk should be treated with suspicion as it is often unpasteurised, though boiled milk is fine if it is kept hygienically. Tea or coffee should also be OK, as the water should have been boiled.

Water Purification The simplest way of purifying water is to boil it thoroughly.

For a long trip, consider purchasing a water filter. There are two main kinds of filter. Total filters take out all parasites, bacteria and viruses and make water safe to drink. They are often expensive, but they can be more cost effective than buying bottled water. Remember also that to operate effectively, a water filter must be regularly maintained; a poorly maintained filter can be a breeding ground for germs. Simple filters (which can even be a nylon mesh bag) take out dirt and larger foreign bodies from the water so that chemical solutions work much more effectively; if water is dirty, chemical solutions may not work at all. It's very important when buying a filter to read the specifications, so that you know exactly what it removes from the water and what it doesn't. Simple filtering will not remove all dangerous organisms, so if you cannot boil water it should be treated chemically. Chlorine tablets (Puritabs, Steritabs or other brands) will kill many pathogens, but not some parasites like giardia and amoebic cysts. Iodine is more effective in purifying water and is available in tablet form (such as Potable Aqua). Follow the directions carefully and remember that too much iodine can be harmful.

Environmental Hazards

Heat Exhaustion Dehydration and salt deficiency can cause heat exhaustion. Take time to acclimatise to high temperatures and make sure you drink sufficient liquids – don't rely on feeling thirsty to indicate when you should drink. Not needing to urinate or dark yellow urine is a danger sign. Remember to always carry a water bottle with you on long trips.

Salt deficiency is characterised by fatigue, lethargy, headaches, giddiness and muscle cramps; salt tablets may help, but adding a little extra salt to your food is better.

Heatstroke This serious, occasionally fatal, condition can occur if the body's heat-regulating mechanism breaks down and body temperature rises to dangerous levels. Long, continuous periods of exposure to high temperatures and insufficient fluids can leave you vulnerable to heatstroke.

The symptoms are feeling unwell, not sweating very much (or at all) and a high body temperature (39° to 41°C or 102° to 106°F). Where sweating has ceased, the skin becomes flushed and red.

Severe, throbbing headaches and lack of coordination will also occur, and the sufferer may be confused or aggressive. Eventually the victim will become delirious or convulse. Hospitalisation is essential, but in the interim get victims out of the sun, remove their clothing, cover them with a wet sheet or towel and then fan continually. Give fluids if they are conscious.

Motion Sickness Eating lightly before and during a trip will reduce the chances of motion sickness. If you are prone to motion sickness try to find a place that minimises movement – near the wing on aircraft, close to midships on boats, near the centre on buses. Fresh air usually helps; reading and cigarette smoke don't. Commercial motion-sickness preparations, which can cause drowsiness, have to be taken before the trip commences. Ginger (available in capsule form) and peppermint (including mint-flavoured sweets) are natural preventatives.

Prickly Heat Prickly heat is an itchy rash caused by excessive perspiration trapped under the skin. It usually strikes people who have just arrived in a hot climate. Keeping cool, bathing often, drying the skin and using a mild talcum or prickly heat powder or resorting to air-conditioning may help.

Sunburn You can get sunburnt surprisingly quickly, even through cloud. Use sunscreen, a hat, and barrier cream for your nose and lips. Calamine lotion or Stingose are good for relieving mild sunburn. Protect your eyes with good-quality sunglasses, particularly if you will be near water, sand or snow.

Infectious Diseases

Diarrhoea Simple things like a change of water, food or climate can all cause a mild bout of diarrhoea, but a few rushed toilet trips with no other symptoms is not indicative of a major problem.

Dehydration is the main danger with any diarrhoea, particularly in children or the elderly. Under all circumstances, *fluid replacement* (at least equal to the volume being lost) is the most important thing to remember. Weak black tea with a little sugar; soda water; or soft drinks allowed to go flat and diluted 50% with clean water are all good. With severe diarrhoea a rehydrating solution is preferable to replace minerals and salts lost. Commercially available oral rehydration salts (ORS) are very useful; add them to boiled or bottled water. In an emergency you can make up a solution of six teaspoons of sugar and a half teaspoon of salt to a litre of boiled or bottled water.

Keep drinking small amounts often. And stick to a bland diet as you recover.

Seek medical help urgently if you experience any of the following: diarrhoea with blood or mucus (dysentry), any diarrhoea with fever, profuse watery diarrhoea, or severe or persistent diarrhoea.

Fungal Infections Fungal infections occur more commonly in hot weather and are usually found on the scalp, between the toes (athlete's foot) or fingers, in the groin and on the body (ringworm). You get ringworm (which is a fungal infection, not a worm) from infected animals or other people. Moisture encourages these infections.

To prevent fungal infections, wear loose, comfortable clothes, avoid artificial fibres, wash frequently and dry yourself carefully. If you do get an infection, wash the infected area at least daily with a disinfectant or medicated soap and water, and rinse and dry well. Apply an antifungal cream or powder like tolnaftate (Tinaderm). Try to expose the infected area to air or sunlight as much as possible and wash all towels and underwear in hot water, change them often and let them dry in the sun.

Hepatitis Hepatitis is a general term for inflammation of the liver. It is a common disease worldwide. There are several different viruses that cause hepatitis, and they differ in the way that they are transmitted. The symptoms are similar in all forms of the illness, and include fever, chills, headache, fatigue, feelings of weakness and aches and pains, followed by loss of appetite, nausea, vomiting, abdominal pain, dark urine, light-coloured faeces, jaundiced (yellow) skin and yellowing of the whites of the eyes. People who have had hepatitis should avoid alcohol for some time after the illness, as the liver needs time to recover.

Hepatitis A This is transmitted by contaminated food and drinking water. You should seek medical advice, but there is not much you can do apart from resting, drinking lots of fluids, eating lightly and avoiding fatty foods.

Hepatitis B This is spread through contact with infected blood, blood products or body fluids, for example through sexual contact, unsterilised needles and blood transfusions, or contact with blood via small breaks in the skin. Other risk situations include having a tattoo, body piercing or a shave with contaminated equipment. Early symptoms of hepatitis B may be more severe than type A and the disease can lead to long-term problems such as chronic liver damage, liver cancer or a long-term carrier state.

HIV & AIDS Infection with the human immunodeficiency virus (HIV) may lead to acquired immune deficiency syndrome (AIDS), which is a fatal disease. Exposure to blood, blood products or body fluids may put the individual at risk. The disease is often transmitted through sexual contact or dirty needles – vaccinations, acupuncture, tattooing and body piercing can be potentially as dangerous as intravenous drug use. HIV/AIDS can also be spread through infected blood transfusions.

Fear of HIV infection, however, should never preclude treatment for serious medical conditions.

Sexually Transmitted Infections (STIs) HIV/AIDS and hepatitis can be transmitted through sexual contact – see the relevant entries earlier in this section. Other STIs include: gonorrhoea, herpes and syphilis. Sores, blisters or rashes around the genitals and discharges or pain when urinating are common symptoms. In some STIs, such as wart virus or chlamydia, symptoms may be less marked or not observed at all, especially in women. Syphilis symptoms eventually disappear completely but the disease continues and can cause severe problems in later years. While abstinence from sexual contact is the only 100% effective prevention, using condoms is also effective. The treatment of gonorrhoea and syphilis is with antibiotics. The different sexually transmitted diseases each require specific antibiotics. There is no cure for either HIV or herpes.

Fiji, like many other Pacific island countries, has high STI rates compared with

Australia and New Zealand. The human papilloma virus, an STI associated with cervical cancer, is almost epidemic in Fiji.

Diphtheria Cases of diphtheria do occur in Fiji, although most people are vaccinated against the disease. Diphtheria is an acute bacterial infection that usually affects the nose, throat or skin. It can be prevented by vaccination.

Cuts, Bites & Stings

Bedbugs & Lice Bedbugs live in various places, but particularly in dirty mattresses and bedding, evidenced by spots of blood on bedclothes or on the wall. Bedbugs leave itchy bites in neat rows. Calamine lotion or Stingose spray may help.

All lice cause itching and discomfort. They make themselves at home in your hair (head lice), your clothing (body lice) or in your pubic hair (crabs). You catch lice through direct contact with infected people or by sharing combs, clothing and the like. Powder or shampoo treatment will kill the lice, and infected clothing should then be washed in very hot, soapy water and left in the sun to dry.

Bites & Stings Bee and wasp stings are usually painful rather than dangerous. However, for people who are allergic to them, severe breathing difficulties may occur and require urgent medical care. Calamine lotion or Stingose spray will give relief and ice packs will reduce the pain and swelling.

The sting of certain cone shells can be dangerous or even fatal. There are various fish and other sea creatures that have harmful stings or bites or are toxic to eat – seek local advice.

Cuts & Scratches Skin punctures can easily become infected in hot climates and may be difficult to heal. Wash well and treat any cut with an antiseptic such as povidone-iodine. Where possible avoid bandages and Band-Aids, which can keep wounds wet. If the sore is not healing and starts spreading, consult a doctor as antibiotics may be needed. Coral cuts are notoriously slow to

heal and if they are not adequately cleaned, small pieces of coral are likely to remain embedded in the wound.

Insect-Borne Diseases

While malaria is not a significant risk in Fiji, several other potentially serious mosquito-borne diseases do occur. Travellers are advised to avoid mosquito bites at all times. The main messages are:

- Wear light-coloured clothing.
- Wear long trousers and long-sleeved shirts.
- Use mosquito repellents containing the compound DEET on exposed areas of your body (prolonged overuse of DEET may be harmful, especially to children, but its use is considered preferable to being bitten by mosquitoes that transmit diseases).
- Avoid perfumes or aftershave.
- Use a mosquito net impregnated with mosquito repellent (permethrin) – it may be worth taking your own.
- Impregnate clothes with permethrin, which effectively deters mosquitoes and other insects.

Dengue Fever This viral disease is transmitted by mosquitoes. Generally, there is only a small risk to travellers except during epidemics, which are usually seasonal (during and just after the rainy season). With unstable weather patterns thought to be responsible for large outbreaks in the Pacific, travellers to Fiji may be especially at risk of infection.

The *Aedes aegypti* mosquito, which transmits the dengue virus, is most active during the day, unlike the malaria mosquito, and is found mainly in urban areas, in and around human dwellings.

Signs and symptoms of dengue fever include a sudden onset of high fever, headache, joint and muscle pains (hence its old name, 'breakbone fever') and nausea and vomiting. A rash of small red spots appears three to four days after the onset of fever. Dengue is commonly mistaken for other infectious diseases, including malaria and influenza.

You should seek prompt medical attention if you think you may be infected. A blood test can exclude malaria and indicate the possibility of dengue fever. There is no specific treatment for dengue. Aspirin should be avoided, as it increases the risk of haemorrhaging. Recovery may be prolonged, with tiredness lasting for several weeks. Severe complications are rare in travellers but include dengue haemorrhagic fever (DHF), which can be fatal without prompt medical treatment. DHF is thought to be a result of secondary infection due to a different strain (there are four major strains) and usually affects residents of the country rather than travellers.

There is no vaccine against dengue fever. The best prevention is to avoid mosquito bites at all times.

Filariasis This is a mosquito-transmitted parasitic infection that is found in many parts of the world. In Fiji the disease is prevalent in the wet south-east coastal areas of the larger islands, as well as in some small island communities. There is a range of possible manifestations of the infection, depending on which filarial parasite species has caused the infection. These include fever; pain and swelling of the lymph glands; inflammation of lymph drainage areas; swelling of a limb or the scrotum; skin rashes and blindness. Treatment is available to eliminate the parasites from the body, but some of the damage they cause may not be reversible. Medical advice should be obtained promptly if the infection is suspected.

Intestinal Worms These parasites are most common in rural, tropical areas. The different worms have different ways of infecting people. Some may be ingested on food such as undercooked meat (eg, tapeworms) and some enter through the skin (eg, hookworms). Infestations may not show up for some time, and although they are generally not serious, if left untreated some can cause severe health problems later. Consider having a stool test when you return home to check for these and determine the appropriate treatment.

Snakes Fiji's most common snake is the *dadakulaci,* or banded sea krait, and you are likely to see it when snorkelling or diving. Although placid, its venom is three times more potent than that of the Indian cobra. The yellow-bellied sea snake can be aggressive, and the burrowing snake is venomous but seldom seen. To minimise your chances of being bitten do not approach any sea snake, and wear boots, socks and long trousers when walking through undergrowth where snakes may be present. Don't put your hands into holes and crevices, and be careful when collecting firewood.

Snake bites do not cause instantaneous death, and antivenenes are usually available. Keep the victim calm and still, wrap the bitten limb tightly, as you would for a sprained ankle, and then attach a splint to immobilise it. Then seek medical help. Tourniquets and sucking out the poison are now comprehensively discredited.

Jellyfish Heeding local advice is the best way to avoid contact with these sea creatures, which have stinging tentacles. Stings from most jellyfish are rather painful. Dousing in vinegar will de-activate any stingers that have not 'fired'. Calamine lotion, antihistamines and analgesics may reduce the reaction and relieve the pain.

Women's Health

Gynaecological Problems Antibiotic use, synthetic underwear, sweating and contraceptive pills can lead to fungal vaginal infections, especially when travelling in hot climates. Fungal infections are characterised by a rash, itch and discharge and can be treated with a vinegar or lemon-juice douche, or with yoghurt. Nystatin, miconazole or clotrimazole pessaries or vaginal cream are the usual treatment. Maintaining good personal hygiene and wearing loose-fitting clothes and cotton underwear may help prevent these infections.

Sexually transmitted infections are a major cause of vaginal problems. Symptoms include a smelly discharge, painful intercourse and sometimes a burning sensation when urinating. Medical attention should be sought and male sexual partners must also be treated. Remember also that HIV and hepatitis B may also be contracted through sexual contact. Besides abstinence, the best thing is to practise safe sex using condoms.

Pregnancy Consult your doctor if you are planning to travel while pregnant, as some vaccinations normally used to prevent serious diseases are not advisable during pregnancy. Also, some diseases are much more serious during pregnancy (and may increase the risk of a stillborn child).

Most miscarriages occur during the first three months of pregnancy. Miscarriage is not uncommon and can occasionally lead to severe bleeding. The last three months should also be spent within reasonable distance of good medical care. A baby born as early as 24 weeks stands a chance of survival, but only in a good modern hospital. Pregnant women should avoid all unnecessary medication, but vaccinations and malarial prophylactics should still be taken where needed. Talk to your doctor about what vaccinations are safe during pregnancy. Additional care should be taken to prevent illness and particular attention should be paid to diet and nutrition. Alcohol and nicotine, for example, should be avoided.

WOMEN TRAVELLERS
Attitudes Towards Women

Domestic violence is quite a problem in Fiji. There has been a campaign to curb this situation and you will see 'real men don't hit women' and 'women's rights are human rights' stickers in public areas and buses. It occurs in both the Fiji-Indian and indigenous Fijian communities.

In general, though, female travellers will find Fijian men friendly and helpful, especially if you are travelling with a male partner. You'll find you will be treated with more respect if you follow the local dress codes (see the Dos & Don'ts section in the Facts about Fiji chapter). Calls of 'Hello' and 'Where are you from?' are usually pretty innocent. Unfortunately though, some men will assume lone females are fair game; several female readers have complained of being annoyed, harassed or ripped off. One found Suva 'a complete hellhole', as she couldn't walk on her own after dark without being grabbed at. You may even strike the opposite problem of being totally ignored, especially by Indian men. If you get a blank response when trying to get information or buy a ticket, seek help from someone who does acknowledge your existence.

If you become uncomfortable or bored in a male-dominated situation, such as an evening around the yaqona bowl, seek the company of Fijian women instead, and you will see another side of village life.

Fiji is very difficult for a single, white woman. I was harassed by men, constantly. The Fijian men wanted to talk to me, to know where I was from and what I thought of Fiji. The Indian men wanted me to marry them, go to the beach with them etc. One man told me he would meet me in my hotel room. Fortunately, by this time I had learned to lie and was very rude to him...I was never physically touched by the men...cab drivers, store clerks and even minibus drivers lied to me, always telling me I had to pay more. I realise that this is part of their culture, but it gets extremely annoying. I felt like I had to be on the defensive all the time.

A Whittier

Safety Precautions

Ask local women for practical advice if you are unsure of how to act, or if any male behaviour towards you is making you uncomfortable. Here are a few tips:

- Don't hitchhike alone.
- Avoid walking at night through dimly lit streets, especially in Nadi and Suva.
- Don't go drinking with Fijian men, however friendly they are to begin with. It's rare but the friendliness may be false and you could end up losing your wallet. Unfortunately the likelihood of a Fijian man becoming violent rises dramatically if he is drunk.
- Wearing a wedding ring may deter unwelcome comments or advances.
- Draw the curtains! There are 'window shoppers' or peeping toms in some rural areas. If a man is interested in a woman he may come to her window at night. Evidently there is no need to be distressed, but it can give a fright! Just tell him to go away.

What to Wear

The Fijian dress code is conservative, especially in the rural areas. A woman in a short skirt, brief shorts or sleeveless top is unusual and will attract lots of attention. Such dress is considered inappropriate except for resorts. Indian women generally wear long saris and Fiji women wear big floral caftans down to the ankles. In Suva the code is slightly more liberal. To avoid hassles, respect the local dress code and cover your knees and shoulders. Refer to the Dos & Don'ts in the Facts about Fiji chapter for local attitudes to dress and behaviour.

Organisations

There are several women's organisations where you can meet local women, including:

Fiji WIP Project – National Council of Women
(☎ 311 880) Stinson Parade, Suva
Fiji Women's Crisis Centre
Suva: (☎ 313 300) 88 Gordon St
Labasa: (☎ 814 609)
Lautoka: (☎ 650 500)
Fiji Women's Rights Movement
(☎ 313 156) 88 Narseys Building, Renwick Rd, Suva. This prominent community organisation deals with issues such as domestic violence, women in trade unions and women's legal rights. It also assists rape victims.
International Women's Association
PO Box 15880, Suva. Its booklet, *Settling in Suva,* is a useful guide for expat families.
Women's Action for Change
(☎ 314 363) 350 Waimanu Rd, Suva
Young Women's Christian Association
(☎ 304 829) Suva

GAY & LESBIAN TRAVELLERS

While homosexuality is outlawed in Fiji, socially it is tolerated as long as it's kept private. There are words for male and female homosexuality in Fijian, suggesting that it may not have been an issue until the missionaries came along. Some of the bars in Suva are gay-friendly. There are some resorts that are decidedly gay-unfriendly.

Organisations

For pretrip planning advice consult the latest *Spartacus International Gay Guide,* *Outrage* magazine, and the ALSO Foundation, or check out www.qrd.org and www.planetout.com on the Internet.

DISABLED TRAVELLERS

In Pacific countries disabled people are simply part of the community, looked after by family where necessary, but still expected to play some useful role. In some cities there are schools for disabled children. Access facilities, such as ramps, lifts and braille, are rare. Airports and some hotels and resorts have reasonable access. Before booking a particular resort, check if it suits your needs. Some of the mid-range and top-end resorts have better wheelchair access than others, however, most are designed with multiple levels and lots of stairs and many of the island resorts have sandy paths.

Alicia Close, a reader who travelled to Fiji with a group of people with various disabilities, highly recommends Hideaway Resort on the Coral Coast, Viti Levu, for catering to their special needs:

The staff at our hotel...came with us wherever we went to help carry (literally) the people in wheelchairs up stairs, over curbs, into and out of (wheelchair-inaccessible) buses, inter-island ferries etc!

Organisations

For pretrip planning advice try the Internet and disabled people's associations in your home country. The Fiji Disabled People's Association (☎ 311 203), 355 Waimanu Rd, Suva, may also be able to provide advice.

SENIOR TRAVELLERS

Fiji is a good place for senior travellers. It is relatively disease-free and has many options for transport and accommodation. You can choose to stay at resorts, take tours, travel in groups or roam around independently. It is easy to hire vehicles and explore the larger islands. Some travel agents offer discounts for groups or those with a seniors' card. For pretrip planning advice, try the Internet and senior-traveller associations in your home country.

TRAVEL WITH CHILDREN

Fiji is a major family destination and is very child-friendly. Some resorts cater specifically for children, with baby-sitting and child-minding services, cots and high chairs, organised activities and children's pools. However, many smaller exclusive resorts ban children or relegate them to a specific period during the year. Some resorts have lots of levels and sand paths, which make using prams and strollers difficult. Larger resorts that are well set up for kids include Shangri-La's Fijian Resort on Viti Levu's Coral Coast, Plantation Island Resort in the Mamanucas and Jean-Michel Cousteau Fiji Islands Resort on Vanua Levu. Tokatoka Resort Hotel near Nadi International Airport is good for those awaiting flights. For those who want to avoid children there are many smaller hotels and resorts.

Travelling around is fairly easy. Some car-rental companies will provide baby seats. If you intend to take public transport, a backpack for transporting young children is a good idea. Long-life milk is readily available, as is bottled spring water and fruit juice. Nappies, formula and sterilising solution are available in pharmacies and supermarkets in the main cities and towns, but if you are travelling to remote areas or islands, take your own supplies. Consider using cloth nappies wherever you can.

Children are valued in Fiji, and childcare is seen as the responsibility of the extended family and the community. Everyone will want to talk with your kids and invite them to join activities or visit homes. Babies and toddlers are especially popular – they may tire of having their cheeks squeezed! Fijian men play a large role in caring for children and babies, so don't be surprised if they pay a lot of attention to kids. Fijian children are expected to be obedient and happy and spend lots of time playing outdoors. Backchat and showing off is seen as disruptive to the fabric of the community, so when visiting a village, try to curb any crying, tantrums and noisy behaviour.

Lonely Planet's *Travel with Children* has useful advice on family travel, and has a section on Fiji.

DANGERS & ANNOYANCES

Fiji is still a pretty safe place for travellers, however, crime is on the increase. Be careful when walking around at night, even as a couple, as travellers have been robbed in Nadi. Don't hitchhike alone. (See the Women Travellers section earlier in this chapter). As a precaution, use a moneybelt and keep your valuables in a safe place. It's rare but travellers may be asked if they want marijuana (see Legal Matters later in this chapter).

Sword sellers are not as common as they used to be, since the FVB has tried to curtail the practice. If anyone becomes overly friendly, wants to know your life story and begins carving your name on a long piece of wood, just walk away, even if they pursue you claiming that you have to pay for the rubbishy item.

If you are unlucky enough to be caught in a natural disaster such as a cyclone or flood, ask locals for advice on where to seek protection from the elements.

Developing tropical ulcers from something as simple as a mosquito bite or scratch can be a hazard (see Health earlier in this chapter).

If you are travelling for an extended period you may tire of being asked 'Where are you from?', followed by 'Where are you staying?'. While this is often just innocent conversation, it is also a way of judging how much you are paying or are willing to pay.

In some areas during the peak season, the sheer number of tourists may be a nuisance.

Swimming

Contrary to Fiji's image promoted overseas, many beaches, especially on the large islands, aren't that great for swimming. The fringing coral reefs usually become too shallow at low tide. Avoid swimming or snorkelling alone and be very careful of currents and tidal changes. Always seek local advice on conditions. Sea lice or stingers can be annoying at some places at different times of the year.

Some of the most beautiful sea creatures such as the scorpion fish and lionfish are also highly venomous. So avoid the temptation and keep your hands to yourself! Sea urchins, crown-of-thorns starfish and stonefish can be poisonous or cause infections. Barracuda eels, which hide in coral crevices, may bite. Some sea snakes are venomous (see Flora & Fauna in the Facts about Fiji chapter). Jellyfish and fire coral can cause nasty stings, and cone shells often have a tiny venomous harpoon.

Shark attacks on divers and snorkellers are rare in Fiji. Reef sharks don't normally attack humans for food, but they can be territorial. We did hear of a shark attack on a spearfisher who was carrying the day's catch around his waist! Avoid swimming near waste-water outlets, the mouths of rivers or murky waters. If you are lucky enough to see a shark, just move away calmly.

LEGAL MATTERS
The only drug you are likely to come across is marijuana. Don't seek it out or buy it – the risk is too high. It is not uncommon for drug users in Fiji to be imprisoned in the psychiatric hospital! It is illegal to drink and drive. Refer also to the Customs and Gay & Lesbian Travellers sections earlier in this chapter for information on legal restrictions.

BUSINESS HOURS
Fijians are not known for their punctuality and usually adhere to 'Fiji time'. However, most businesses open from 8 am to 5 pm weekdays, and from 8 am to 1 pm some Saturdays. Government offices are open from 8 am to 4.30 pm Monday to Thursday, 8 am to 4 pm Fridays. Many places close for lunch from 1 to 2 pm. Although the post-coup Sunday observance's ban on trading has now been lifted, little happens on Sunday. For indigenous Fijians it is a day for church, rest and spending time with family. Activities may be restricted at the resorts.

PUBLIC HOLIDAYS & SPECIAL EVENTS
Fijians celebrate a variety of holidays and festivals. New Year's Day is celebrated all over Fiji. In villages, festivities can last a week or even the whole month of January.

There is also a day commemorating the man considered Fiji's greatest statesman, Ratu Sir Lala Sukuna. Annual holidays include:

New Year's Day	1 January
National Youth Day	March
Easter (Good Friday and Easter Monday)	March/April
Ratu Sir Lala Sukuna Day	May
Queen's Birthday	June
Constitution Day	July
Mohammed's Birthday	July
Birth of Lord Krishna	August/September
Fiji Day (Independence Day)	early October
Christmas Day	25 December
Boxing Day	26 December

Fijian festivals include:

February or March
Hindu Holi (Festival of Colours) People squirt coloured water at each other; it is best observed in Lautoka.

March or April
Ram Naumi (Birth of Lord Rama) A Hindu religious festival and party on the shores of Suva Bay. Worshippers wade into the water and throw flowers.

August
Hibiscus Festival Held in Suva, it has lots of floats and processions.
Hindu Ritual Fire Walking Performed by southern Indians in many of their temples (try the Maha Devi Temple, Howell Rd, Suva).

September
Lautoka's Sugar Festival

October or November
Diwali Festival holidays (Festival of Lights) Hindus worship Lakshmi (goddess of wealth and prosperity) – houses are decorated and business settled.

Refer to Religion in the Facts about Fiji chapter for information on Indian festivals.

ACTIVITIES
On your trip to Fiji you can either 'pack in' lots of different activities or laze around and do very little.

Village Visits

Avoid visiting villages on Sunday, as it is considered a day for church and rest. Most tours will include a village visit with the obligatory *kava* presentation. Navala, in Viti Levu's highlands, with its beautiful traditional architecture, is Fiji's most picturesque village. Refer to the Dos & Don'ts section under Society & Conduct in the Facts about Fiji chapter.

Archaeological Sites

Fiji has a number of fascinating archaeological sites. The Tavuni Hill Fort and the Sigatoka Sand Dunes, both near Sigatoka, are the only sites set up for visitors. There are many ring-ditch sites in the Sigatoka Valley and Rewa Delta. Labasa has a ceremonial *naga* site (a stone enclosure where religious rites were carried out), and Nukubolu near Savusavu has the remains of an extensive village and pools with hot spring water. On Taveuni, the old Vuda village defensive site is partly on Vatuwiri Farm Resort land.

Bird-Watching

The best places for bird-watching are Taveuni and Kadavu. Taveuni has a better infrastructure than Kadavu, and is cheaper and easier to travel around. Vanua Levu's Tunuloa Peninsula also has some good spots and the Tunuloa Silktail Rainforest Retreat is specially for bird-watchers. On Viti Levu, Colo-i-Suva Forest Park near Suva and the area near Waidroka Bay Resort on the Queens Road are also good spots. Pick up a copy of *Birds of the Fiji Bush,* by Fergus Clunie & Pauline Morse, Fiji Museum, 1984.

Cycling

Cycling is a good way to explore Viti Levu, Vanua Levu (the Hibiscus Hwy) and parts of Ovalau and Taveuni. With the exception of Kings and Queens Roads, most roads, especially inland, are rough, hilly and unsealed, so mountain bikes are the best option. Consider taking a carrier (a small truck) up to Abaca and riding back down to Lautoka. It can be hot and dusty so make

sure you carry plenty of water to avoid dehydration. Also, especially on the main roads, watch out for mad drivers! The best time to go is the 'drier' season, and note that the eastern sides of the larger island receive higher rainfall. Take waterproof gear and a repair kit to be self-sufficient, as it is difficult to get bike parts in Fiji. Maps are available from the Department of Lands & Survey in Suva. If you wish to take a bike on a domestic flight, make sure it is a demountable type.

Some resorts have bikes for hire. Expect to pay F$10 to F$15 for a half day. Independent Tours, in Korovou near Sigatoka, runs guided mountain-bike tours on Viti Levu, including half/full day tours for F$49/79. Three-day/two-night trips to the highlands are F$299. Mountain bikes provided are 21-speed and there is a 15% discount if you bring your own. Food and drinks are carried in a support truck. Refer to Korotogo & Around in the Queens Road & Coral Coast section of the Viti Levu chapter for details.

Hiking

It is culturally offensive to simply hike anywhere – you need to ask permission, be invited or take a tour. For more details see the Society & Conduct section in the Facts about Fiji chapter, or Camping under Accommodation later in this chapter. You should ask local villagers or hotel staff to organise permission and a guide. It is best to go hiking in the dry season when it won't be so muddy. Make sure others know where you are heading in case you get lost or have an accident. Good boots are essential and carry plenty of water, good maps, a compass, a warm jumper and a waterproof coat.

Viti Levu and Taveuni are the best islands for hiking. Kadavu is more isolated but equally beautiful.s Colo-i-Suva Forest Park on Viti Levu and the Lavena Coastal Walk and the Tavoro Falls at Bouma on Taveuni have marked trails and don't require guides. The Vidawa Forest Walk is a full-day guided tour. Other good places for hiking are Taveuni's Lake Tagimaucia (difficult), Mt Tomanivi on Viti Levu near Nadarivatu, and Koroyanitu National Heritage Park and Mt Koroyanitu near Lautoka. For an easy but scenic walk, follow the Coral Coast Scenic Railway from the Shangri-La's Fijian Resort to the beautiful Natadola beach. If you will be in Fiji for a while, consider contacting the Rucksack Club in Suva (see the Suva section of the Viti Levu chapter for details). It organises regular walks and excursions.

A few companies organise hiking to Viti Levu's highlands, including Rosie Tours, and Peni's Inland Adventures. On the Suva side of Viti Levu, Discover Fiji Tours also has one-day and three-day hikes. The tours offer different standards of service, but expect to pay about F$60 for a day trip, and up to F$100 a day for longer trips of four to six days. Refer to the Taveuni chapter and the Viti Levu Highlands section of the Viti Levu chapter.

Horse Riding

There are a couple of places in Fiji where horse riding is an organised activity. Ratuva's, near Sigatoka on Viti Levu's Coral Coast, charges F$15 to F$20 per hour. At Vatuwiri Farm in southern Taveuni horse riding is F$30/35 per day for guests/nonguests.

Surfing

It is believed that surfing has existed in Fiji for hundreds of years. Surfing reefs over warm, crystal-clear, turquoise-blue water is a very special experience. Most of Fiji's coral reefs, however, are not suitable for surfing. The majority of rideable breaks are on offshore reefs that require boat trips. When choosing accommodation, also consider the price of getting to the surf. The best surf spots are in barrier-reef passages – where powerful swells from the open ocean break onto the reefs – along southern Viti Levu (Frigate Passage south of Yanuca island near Beqa Lagoon) and along western Viti Levu (Malolo and Wilkes Passages in the southern Mamanuca Group). Winter is the best time to go due to low pressures bringing in big surf.

Accommodation near the southern Mamanuca breaks is at Tavarua Island Resort, Namotu Island Resort, and on the mainland at the budget Seashell Surf and Dive Resort near Momi Bay. Riding these dangerous reef-breaks should only be attempted by experienced surfers. If you want to stay at the popular surf resorts on Tavarua and Namotu, book well in advance. It is also possible to charter a yacht from Musket Cove Marina on Malololailai (Plantation Island) to access the breaks – it can be an OK deal for a group. However, some breaks are likely to be out of bounds unless you are staying at the resorts.

There are a few places on mainland Viti Levu where you can paddle out to the surf, including the beach-break at the Sigatoka River mouth, near the budget Club Masa, and the reef-break near the more upmarket Hideaway Resort on the Coral Coast. Natadola Beach sometimes has small surf that can be good for beginners and there is better surf offshore (requiring a boat). Waidroka Bay Resort on the Coral Coast has a couple of offshore breaks. From here it is a half-hour boat trip to Frigate Passage. You can also get to Frigate Passage from Pacific Harbour and there are two surf camps on Yanuca. Suva has a reef-break at the lighthouse – you need a boat to get there.

Kadavu's Cape Washington has good surf but no place to stay, and there are breaks on the passages near Matava, Astrolabe Hideaway resort on Kadavu. Lavena Point on Taveuni also has rideable though inconsistent waves.

You should be aware that Fijian villages usually have fishing rights to, and basically own, adjacent reefs. Some resorts pay the villages for exclusive surfing rights, which has led to disputes between competing surfing and diving operations. If you would like to explore lesser-known areas you will need to respect local traditions and seek permission of the local villagers.

Surfboards can be hired in Nadi at Viti Surf Legend (F$30 per day for a long board). It can arrange trips to the beach-breaks at Natadola and Sigatoka (F$50 for guide and transport). If you are a keen surfer, bring your own board (ideally, three boards, with two over 2m). It is fairly easy to lose or snap a board. In winter take a light wetsuit or vest; surfing booties and a helmet are also a good idea.

If you are staying in Fiji for an extended period, contact Ian Muller (☎/fax 721 866) of Viti Surf Legend in Nadi or Ed Lovell (☎ 361 358) in Suva from the Surf Rider's Association. You can join the association for F$20 per year, entitling you to enter surf contests and receive its newsletter.

Windsurfing

Many of the resorts have windsurfers for guests. Wave jumpers should consider the surf-break off the Namotu Island Resort on Namotu (Magic Island) in the Mamanucas (refer to the Mamanuca Group chapter). You will have to take your own board though.

Another option is to use your sailboard as a means of transportation! We received a letter from a couple who spent seven months travelling through Fiji by sailboard, visiting 40 different islands, and camping and staying at budget accommodation along the way.

They sailed from southern Lau to Taveuni, across to Vanua Levu, down to Ovalau, around northern Viti Levu to the Mamanucas and along the Yasawas. Obviously, only experienced windsurfers should try something like this. You should have a permit to visit the Lau Group (see Travel Permits under Visas & Documents earlier in this chapter). Refer also to the Climate section in the Facts about Fiji chapter.

Boat Chartering & Fishing

Villages have rights over the reefs and fishing so you cannot just drop a line anywhere; seek permission first. Many of the more expensive resorts offer game-fishing tours and boat chartering. Matangi Island Resort, in the Taveuni island group, specialises in saltwater fly fishing. The smaller resorts will also arrange for local boats to take you fishing. Consider the south-east trade winds when choosing the best spot – the leeward sides of the islands are generally calmer.

For boat chartering in the Mamanucas, handline fishing and night fishing in Nadi Bay, contact Bay Cruises (☎ 722 696, fax 720 288, ✉ baycruises@is.com.fj) or South Sea Cruises (☎ 750 500, fax 750 501, ✉ southsea@is.com.fj), both operating out of Port Denarau. Also refer to the *Fiji Magic* magazine.

Peter Dunn-Rankin, author of *Fishing the Reefs,* 1994, a guide to top-water spinning in Hawaii and the South Pacific, rates Fiji as the most promising area in the South Pacific for sports fishing. He promotes the 'catch and release' motto, especially for large breeding-age fish.

River Trips

Bilibili (bamboo rafting) and kayaking trips can be made on the Navua River in Namosi Highlands (see Viti Levu Highlands in the Viti Levu chapter). Day trips with Rivers Fiji start at F$160 per person. The 'Shotover Jet' through the mangroves at Denarau Island near Nadi is a quick but expensive thrill (F$55).

Sailing

Yachties are often looking for extra crew and people to share costs. Approach the marinas, ask around and look on the notice boards.

Fiji's marinas include the Suva Yacht Club, Vuda Point Marina between Nadi and Lautoka, Levuka Marina on Ovalau, Savusavu Marina on Vanua Levu, and Musket Cove Marina on Malololailai (Plantation Island) in the Mamanucas. The designated ports of entry are Suva, Levuka, Lautoka and Savusavu. Refer to the Visas & Documents section earlier in the chapter.

The main yachting season is June, July and August, but there are races and regattas throughout the year. Fiji Regatta Week and the Musket Cove to Port Vila Regatta are held in September. Obviously the Fijian reefs require good charts and crews with sailing experience.

For organised cruises and charters, refer to the individual island chapters. Musket Cove Marina (☎/fax 666 710) has a range of vessels for hire for sailing around the

Mamanucas and Yasawas. Fully crewed boats with skipper and cook are available. There are surfing and diving safaris, sailing lessons and 10-day sailing safaris to the Yasawas aboard the 17m *Gallivant* for three couples or two families. Flotilla Yachts (contact the marina) has four-berth 20-foot yachts for hire for F$300 for day-sailing or F$1,000 for five nights/six days. You don't need a lot of experience as you follow the lead of the yacht skipper. Try old-style sailing on the double-hulled canoe *Tabu Tabu Soro* (contact the marina for details).

Contact individual yacht clubs for further information, and pick up a copy of the *Yacht Help Booklet, Fiji*. *Landfalls of Paradise – The Guide to Pacific Islands,* by Earl R Hinz, University of Hawaii Press, 1979, and Michael Calder's *Yachtsman's Fiji* are popular references.

Sea & Dive Kayaking

Sea and dive kayaking is becoming increasingly popular in Fiji. It is a great way of exploring the coast at a gentle pace. Dive kayaks, which can carry lunch, snorkelling gear and scuba gear, can be double the fun.

The islands of Taveuni, Vanua Levu, Yasawa and Kadavu are great for kayaking. Some keen kayakers paddle Taveuni's rugged Ravilevu Coast, but generally the western sides of the islands are preferred as they are sheltered from the south-east trade winds.

Many of the resorts have kayaks for guest use, or for hire at about F$20/30 for a half/full day. There are also special kayaking tours available during the drier months between May and November. Some combine paddling with hiking into rainforests, snorkelling, fishing and village visits, and have support boats that carry camping gear and food. They don't necessarily require that you have previous experience.

On Taveuni, Garden Island Resort and Beverly Beach Camping & Aquaventure rent out kayaks. Ringgold Reef Kayaking conducts seasonal kayaking/camping tours. On Vanua Levu, Eco Divers-Tours hires kayaks and has trips around Savusavu Bay. Southern Sea Ventures runs 11-day trips to the Yasawas. On Kadavu, Dive Kadavu at the Matava, Astrolabe Hideaway resort has diving kayaks for hire and professional instruction is available. Tamarillo Sea Kayaking has trips around northern Kadavu. Refer to individual island chapters for details.

Independent travellers planning extended trips should check weather forecasts, watch the tides and currents, and wear a life jacket, hat and plenty of sunscreen. Ideally, take a signalling device or even a mobile phone or radio and always let someone know of your plans.

Diving

Fiji's warm, clear waters and abundance of reef life and its well-established dive industry make the islands a magnet for divers. Visibility regularly exceeds 30m, though this is reduced on stormy days or when there is a heavy plankton bloom. The drier months of April to November have more reliable visibility.

The beauty of Fiji is that you can have great access to diving regardless of whether your accommodation funds extend to budget or luxury. When choosing a place to stay, decide whether the sole purpose of your trip is diving or whether you also want to pursue other activities. Some resorts specialise in diving, and exclusive resorts often include diving in the daily tariff. Prices for a two-tank dive range from F$85 to F$180. Some places, including Subsurface in the Mamanucas, have half-price dive specials from mid-January to the end of March. Most operators rent out equipment (in varying states of maintenance) if you don't want to lug around your own gear. You may prefer to bring your own buoyancy control jacket, regulator, mask, snorkel and fins. Refer to individual island chapters for specific information on dive operators and resorts.

Many travellers take the opportunity to learn scuba diving while in Fiji, and most operators offer courses for beginners as well as certification and advanced courses. Open-water certification courses, either by the Professional Association of Diving Instructors (PADI) or less commonly by the National Association of Underwater

Considerations for Responsible Diving

The popularity of diving is placing immense pressure on many sites. Please consider the following tips when diving and help preserve the ecology and beauty of reefs:

• Do not use anchors on the reef, and take care not to ground boats on coral. Encourage dive operators and regulatory bodies to establish permanent moorings at popular dive sites.
• Avoid touching living marine organisms with your body or dragging equipment across the reef. Polyps can be damaged by even the gentlest contact. Never stand on corals, even if they look solid and robust. If you must hold on to the reef, only touch exposed rock or dead coral.
• Be conscious of your fins. Even without contact the surge from heavy fin strokes near the reef can damage delicate organisms. When treading water in shallow reef areas, take care not to kick up clouds of sand. Settling sand can easily smother the delicate organisms of the reef.
• Practise and maintain proper buoyancy control. Major damage can be done by divers descending too fast and colliding with the reef. Make sure you are correctly weighted and that your weight belt is positioned so that you stay horizontal. If you have not dived for a while, have a practice dive in a pool before taking to the reef. Be aware that buoyancy can change over the period of an extended trip: initially you may breathe harder and need more weight; a few days later you may breathe more easily and need less weight.
• Take great care in underwater caves. Spend as little time in them as possible as your air bubbles may be caught within the roof and thereby leave previously submerged organisms high and dry. Taking turns to inspect the interior of a small cave will lessen the chances of damaging contact.
• Resist the temptation to collect or buy corals or shells. Aside from the ecological implications, taking home marine souvenirs depletes the beauty of a site and spoils the enjoyment of others. The same goes for marine archaeological sites (mainly shipwrecks). Respect their integrity; some sites are even protected from looting by law.
• Ensure that you take home all your rubbish and any litter you may find as well. Plastics in particular are a serious threat to marine life. Turtles can mistake plastic for jellyfish and eat it.
• Resist the temptation to feed fish. You may feed them food that is detrimental to their health; disturb their normal eating habits; or encourage aggressive behaviour.
• Minimise your disturbance of marine animals. In particular, do not ride on the backs of turtles as this causes them great anxiety.

Instructors (NAUI) take four to five days to complete and cost between F$350 and F$600. There are other specialised courses. Equipment rental is about F$30 per day. Make sure your instructor is qualified and that your travel insurance covers scuba diving and emergency treatment. If you need an air transfer and stint in a recompression chamber you will be glad to have insurance! Some dive operators offer courses in languages other than English. Mana, in the Mamanuca Group, has instruction in Japanese, and Vuna Reef Divers on Taveuni and Action Diving on Nananu-i-Ra in German. Check with the Fiji Dive Operators Association (FDOA) or the FVB.

The bends, or decompression sickness, occurs in divers when, having descended into the water to a substantial depth, not enough time is allowed while rising to the surface to let the body's tissues expel the gases. It's the forming of these bubbles in the brain, spinal cord or peripheral nerves that results in the bends, the symptoms of which include numbness, difficulties with muscle coordination, nausea, speech defects, paralysis and convulsions, as well as personality changes. Small nitrogen bubbles trapped under the skin can cause a red rash and an itching sensation known as diver's itch, but these symptoms usually pass in 10 to 20 minutes. Other symptoms include excessive coughing and difficulty in breathing, chest pain, a burning sensation while breathing and severe shock.

It is important to get a diver suffering from the bends to a recompression chamber as quickly as possible to avoid permanent tissue damage – be assertive if you or other divers experience symptoms. There is a recompression chamber in Suva (☎ 850 630, 305 154, or 362 172 for 24-hour service) and a medevac system that transfers dive accident victims to the chamber. Most operators belong to the FDOA, which requires its members to abide by international diving standards, a code of practice and a code of ethics, and to support the Fiji Recompression Chamber Facility. Other operators may offer cheaper diving, but perhaps less reliable instruction, equipment and safety procedures.

For further information on diving in Fiji, contact the FDOA (☎ 850 620, fax 850 344, ✉ seafijidive@is.com.fj), PO Box 264, Savusavu. The FVB publishes an annual glossy *Fiji Islands Dive Guide*. Also try the Internet and diving magazines. Lonely Planet's Pisces *Diving and Snorkeling Guide to Fiji* and Paddy Ryan's *The Snorkeller's Guide to the Coral Reef* are recommended, and you may like to pick up a laminated Fiji fish identification card (available from dive shops).

See the Photography & Video section earlier in this chapter for advice on underwater photography, and the Sea & Dive Kayaking entry earlier in this section.

Dive Sites Fiji has vast unexplored regions as well as many dive sites of world renown. The soft corals of the Rainbow Reef and the Great White Wall of the Somosomo Strait near Taveuni, the Beqa Lagoon off southern Viti Levu and the Astrolabe Reef off Kadavu are all famous.

However, there is no such thing as the best diving site, especially in Fiji. Each dive site has something special or unique. Sites range from the safe and easy, to wall dives in fast currents, to dives with reef sharks.

Mamanuca Group The Mamanucas have a variety of dive sites, which are easily ac-

cessed from the Nadi/Lautoka area. The Malolo Barrier Reef protects the group, and the currents through its passages provide nutrients, promoting soft and hard coral growth. Inside the barrier reef the waters are generally calm with many coral reefs and abundant fish life. There are exciting dive sites outside the barrier reef at the Namotu and Malolo Passages, where you can see large pelagic fish, manta rays and turtles. It often gets rough here and should therefore only be attempted by experienced, adventurous divers. The Supermarket shark dive is popular.

Despite the large number of tourist resorts in the Mamanucas, the coral ecosystems are still good. Most of the resorts have their own dive operations. Day-trippers to resorts such as Beachcomber Island Resort or Musket Cove Resort may be able to arrange a dive. Inner Space, based at Newtown Beach, and Dive Tropex, based at the Sheraton on Denarau Island, both take diving trips from Nadi. It is also possible to charter a yacht from Musket Cove Marina for diving in the Mamanucas.

Yasawa Group The Yasawas have plenty of spectacular reefs with vibrant corals, walls and underwater caves. There are plenty of unexplored areas. Diving activity has been fairly low as most tourists visit the islands by cruise ship. The upmarket Yasawa Island Lodge and Turtle Island Resort offer diving for their guests and there is also a diving operation run by locals at the budget Wayalailai Resort on Wayasewa. Westside Watersports has a dive operation on Tavewa, which caters for backpackers as well as Blue Lagoon cruise passengers.

Viti Levu Dive sites off Viti Levu include the Mamanucas (see the earlier Mamanuca Group entry), the Coral Coast, Beqa Lagoon and Nananu-i-Ra.

The main advantage of diving on the Coral Coast is the proximity of sites to the coast, and the wide range of accommodation available. The inside reefs can be reached by small boat, currents are usually moderate and you will see reasonably good coral and small reef fish. To see bigger pelagic fish and more spectacular coral you have to dive the outer reefs and passages. Sea Sports at Shangri-La's Fiji Resort caters for the Coral Coast resorts as most don't have their own diving operations. Waidroka Bay Resort has dives east of Korolevu.

The large barrier reef surrounding the islands of Beqa and Yanuca forms Beqa Lagoon – one of the world's top diving locations. The reef and its various passages have a number of excellent sites, with coral heads, walls, tunnels, undercuts, abundant soft coral and large fish. Pacific Harbour dive operators take trips to the lagoon, and Marlin Bay Resort on Beqa has diving for its guests.

There are many dive sites and unexplored areas around Nananu-i-Ra, which is just off the northernmost point of Viti Levu. Divers can expect to see soft and hard corals, black coral, walls, caves, large fish, dolphins, turtles and the occasional whale cruising through Bligh Water.

Lomaiviti Group This is still a relatively unexplored area. Ovalau Watersports is based in Levuka. Most of the island resorts have their own operations: the backpacker resort on Leluvia; the mid-range Naigani; the more expensive Namenalala; and the exclusive Wakaya.

Kadavu Kadavu's diving reputation was established on the Astrolabe and Soso Reefs during the 1980s. The reefs north of the island are also beautiful and are sheltered from the south-west trade winds. The most spectacular dives are the passages between the lagoons and the open sea and on the outside face of the barrier reefs. Expect to find abundant soft and hard corals, vertical walls and lots of fish.

Kadavu is a remote and rugged island away from the mainstream tourist destinations, and remains a relatively new frontier for diving in Fiji. There is lots of scope for exploratory diving, and there is a small range of resorts and diving operators to choose from for various budgets. Dive Kadavu Resort is easily accessible, has very good facilities with mid-range to upmarket

accommodation. It is also the dive operator for the budget Jona's Paradise Resort and Waisalima Beach Resort. The Matava, Astrolabe Hideaway resort and Albert's Place have their own set-ups.

Taveuni & Vanua Levu Fiji's northern region has developed a reputation as one the best areas for diving in Fiji. The vast number of reefs offer all that the diver could wish for: lots of soft coral; huge walls, overhangs and caves; reef; and pelagic fish.

The best sites, including Rainbow Reef and Great White Wall, are on the outer barrier reefs in the Somosomo Strait, between the islands of Vanua Levu and Taveuni. Somosomo Strait dive sites often have strong currents and involve drift diving.

Taveuni dive operations include Aquaventure and Swiss Fiji Divers based in Matei and Vuna Reef Divers in the south. Taveuni Island Resort, Garden Island Resort and the upmarket offshore island resorts of Matangi, Laucala and Qamea each have their own dive operations.

Vanua Levu operations include Eco Divers-Tours and L'Aventure Jean-Michel Cousteau, in the Savusavu area. Nukubati Island Resort dives the Great Sea Reef off northern Vanua Levu. The famous Rainbow Reef is off the south-eastern coast. Buca Bay Resort dives this site and Rainbow Reef Resort arranges diving with Aquaventure on Taveuni.

Lau Group Due to its distance from the rest of Fiji, the Lau Group is still relatively unexplored in terms of diving. The upmarket Lomaloma Resort near Vanua Balavu and Kaimbu Island Resort, both in northern Lau, have their own dive operations. There is reportedly great potential in the area, with dive sites as good as or better than the best found in the rest of the country.

Live-Aboard Operators Due to the number of readily accessible dive sites in Fiji, live-aboards are not as popular as in some dive localities. They are, however, a good option for exploring reefs where the usual operators don't go.

Sink or Swim: Choosing a Dive School or Operation

In general, diving in Fiji is very safe, with a high standard of staff training and good equipment maintenance. However, as with anywhere in the world, some operations are more professional than others, and it is often difficult, especially for inexperienced or beginner divers, to select the best operation for their needs. Here are a few tips to help you select a well set-up and safety-conscious dive shop:

1. Is it a member of the FDOA? The Fiji Dive Operators Association is made up of dive centres that meet certain safety and staff training standards. A list of members is available by contacting the FDOA president, Curly Carswell (☎ 850 620, fax 850 344), PO Box 264, Savusavu.

2. Are its staff fully trained and qualified? Ask to see certificates or certification cards – no reputable shop will be offended by this request. Guides must reach 'full instructor' level (the minimum certification level) to be able to teach *any* diving course. To guide certified divers on a reef dive, guides must hold at least 'rescue diver' or preferably 'dive master' qualifications. Take note that a dive master cannot teach – only fully qualified instructors can do that. A school that allows uncertified divers to go out with a dive master is breaking all the safety rules.

3. Does it have safety equipment on the boat? Legally, a dive boat must carry oxygen and a first-aid kit, radio and flares. An easy way to check this is to ask what kind of oxygen equipment they carry, and see if they can show it to you. Do not dive with any operator not carrying oxygen.

4. Is its equipment OK and its air clean? This is often the hardest thing for the new diver to judge. A few guidelines are:

   a. Smell the air – open a tank valve a small way and breathe in. Smelling dry or slightly rubbery is OK. Smelling of oil or car exhaust tells you they do not filter the air correctly. Go somewhere else.

   b. When the equipment is put together, are there any big air leaks? All dive centres get some small leaks at some time, and usually will explain that a tiny bit of air loss is unimportant. This is true, and not a reason to reject a dive shop. However, if you get a *big* hiss of air coming out of any piece of equipment, ask to have it replaced. Usually that solves the problem. If you have three or more equipment failures, seek another dive shop.

5. Is it conservation-oriented? Most good dive shops explain that you should not touch corals or take shells from the reef. If any dive guide suggests that they might to spearfish or collect clams during the dive, please report the guide to the FDOA.

Diving in Fiji is wonderful and varied. Some areas are more suitable for experienced divers, some for beginners. In general terms, if you want to learn to dive, or are relatively inexperienced, the best areas are the Mamanucas, the north-west Coral Coast, and the north of Viti Levu. For more experienced divers, the most spectacular reefs are off the western Coral Coast, Kadavu, Vanua Levu and Taveuni, and off dive live-aboard vessels. All divers are recommended to ensure their travel insurance covers them for *scuba* diving. There is a recompression chamber in Suva, contactable in an emergency on ☎ 362 172.

Helen Sykes

Fiji Aggressor (☎ 504-385 2628, 504-384 0817 USA, 998 820 vessel cellular, ✉ divboat@compuserve.com) is based in Savusavu. *Nai'a* (☎ *450 382, fax 450 566*, ✉ *naia@is.com.fj*) has cruises to Beqa, the Lomaiviti Group, the Namena Barrier Reef near the island of Namenalala, and even Lau by special charter.

Snorkelling

Snorkelling in Fiji's warm waters is a definite highlight. There are beautiful reefs teeming with amazing life, often very close to the coast, making it a relatively inexpensive and easy pastime compared to diving. Many snorkellers get a taste for the underwater experience and use it as a stepping stone to diving, while others are content without the fuss of all that heavy equipment. All you need is a mask, snorkel and fins. Ideally wear a T-shirt and waterproof sunscreen as it is easy to become absorbed by the spectacle, lose sense of time and scorch your back and legs.

If you have not snorkelled before or are not a confident swimmer, familiarise yourself with the equipment in a pool or shallow water. Learn how to clear your snorkel, so that you don't panic, tread over the fragile coral or drown! Keep to the surface if you feel more comfortable there and never dive too deep. It is best to swim with a partner, to always use fins and to ask locals about currents. Some operators who take snorkellers on their dive trips may just dump you overboard with a buoy, on a barrier reef, far from land. If you are not confident, ask for a life jacket. It is common to see reef sharks but don't panic, they are probably more scared of you. The most beautiful creatures can be poisonous so avoid touching anything. Also avoid being washed against the reef as coral cuts can turn into nasty infections.

You are likely to see brilliant soft and hard corals, multitudes of colourful fish of various shapes and sizes, sponges, sea cucumbers, urchins, starfish, Christmas-tree worms and molluscs. Crustaceans are more difficult to spot and many only come out at night. Night snorkelling is a fantastic experience if you can overcome your fear of the unknown!

Snorkelling becomes even more enjoyable if you can recognise different species. See the previous Diving section for details of books that can help you make the most of Fiji's underwater world.

Snorkelling Sites Most resorts offer snorkelling and/or diving and have equipment for hire. However, always check first when going to a remote budget resort – it can be frustrating if you are in a gorgeous location without any equipment. If you are a keen snorkeller it may be worth having your own equipment for greater flexibility. Dive operations usually take snorkellers to outer reefs if there is room on the boat, although some prefer to keep the activities separate and have special snorkelling trips.

In many places you can snorkel off the shore, however, often you can only swim at high tide and channels can be dangerous. The best sites on Viti Levu are at Natadola Beach (watch the current here though), Nananu-i-Ra and Beqa Lagoon. Viti Levu's Coral Coast is not that great for snorkelling as it is usually a fair way to the drop, much of the reef is dead and swimming is mostly tidal.

The best snorkelling sites are on the outer islands. Notable sites include: the Mamanucas and Yasawas (superb reefs with mostly hard coral); Vanua Levu's rocky coastline, especially near Mumu's Resort; Taveuni's Vuna Reef; Kadavu, offshore of the Matava, Astrolabe Hideaway resort and Jona's Paradise Resort on Ono; and the Lomaiviti Group's Caqelai and Leleuvia.

COURSES

The USP in Suva runs some informal courses on different subjects. Also check the *Fiji Times* diary page, which sometimes advertises classes. Indian cultural centres have three-month programs, including *kathak* (classical dance), vocal/harmonium, tabla, sitar, yoga and Hindi language. While classes are mostly for local children, you may be able to negotiate something.

WORK

Those travelling to Fiji for reasons other than a holiday must declare this on their arrival card. They will be given a visa for 14 days and will have to apply for subsequent extensions. Those wishing to live or work in Fiji for more than six months will require a working visa (see Visas & Documents earlier in this chapter). These can be difficult to get and need to be organised at least two months prior to travelling to Fiji.

Application forms can be obtained from any Fijian embassy and must be completed and sent by the applicant to the immigration authorities in Fiji. Your application will normally only be approved if supported by a prospective employer and if your skills cannot be found locally. If you want to conduct business in Fiji, contact the Fiji Trade and Investment Board (☎ 315 988, fax 301 783, @ ftibinfo@ftib.org.fj), 6th floor, Civic Tower, Victoria Parade, Government Buildings, Suva (PO Box 2303).

Volunteer Work

Volunteers are required to apply for a work permit.

There are two types of volunteer work available to foreigners in Fiji. One is through an overseas aid organisation such as Australian Volunteers Abroad, British Voluntary Service Overseas and GAP Activity Projects (☎ 0118-959 4914; fax 957 6634 UK). Responsible organisations will only go where invited, pay their people local wages, and teach volunteers the local language and respect for traditional culture and customs. The other option, usually taken up by expats, is to help a Fijian charitable or community organisation, such as the Fiji Women's Rights Movement (refer to the Women Travellers section earlier in this chapter). However, there have been problems in the past when volunteers with good intentions imposed their unconscious political agendas in culturally insensitive ways. The Fiji Museum in Suva is always looking for volunteers (see the Suva section in the Viti Levu chapter). Greenpeace, the World Wide Fund for Nature (WWF), National Trust for Fiji and South Pacific Action Committee for Human Ecology and Environment (Spachee) also have offices in Suva. (See the Ecology & Environment section in the Facts about Fiji chapter for contact details.)

ACCOMMODATION

Tourism is one of Fiji's main industries. There is no shortage of accommodation options, ranging from dorm beds at very low prices (about F$10 per night) to world-class luxury resorts charging up to F$1000 per person per night! Accommodation prices are subject to 10% VAT. Always check if this tax is included in the price quoted before signing in. Prices quoted throughout this guide are VAT-inclusive. Rates often vary between high season and low season (February and March). There are also lower 'local rates' for residents of Fiji. There are a few homestays and B&B-type places and many hostels, hotels and resorts.

The Nadi/Lautoka area has a large range of places to stay. While Nadi itself is nothing special, it is a good base from which to plan your trip, organise tours or cruises and seek up-to-date advice from other travellers.

Reservations

If after a short stay in one place, consider prebooking hotel or resort accommodation as a package deal. Book well in advance for popular resorts. You may get cheap deals in the low season. Hardly anyone pays the quoted 'rack rate' (normal room rate without discounts). Expect to get about 25% off for packages or if you just turn up ('walk-in' rates).

While it is handy to have somewhere to crash on the first night, the independent traveller should adopt a flexible approach – avoid paying too much in advance and keep your options open. There are many places to choose from so if you are not happy for some reason, just move on. However, places do tend to get booked out in the busy months.

Remote islands, such as Kadavu, have few places to stay and the main form of transportation is by small boat. In this case, avoid being left stranded without a vacancy in your price range by prebooking – this will also ensure you'll be met at the airport or ferry.

Camping

Don't just set up camp anywhere without permission. Most of Fiji's land, even in seemingly remote areas, is owned by the indigenous population, by *mataqali* (extended families) or villages. If you are invited to camp in villages, avoid setting up next to someone's *bure* (thatched dwelling). Doing so can be misinterpreted as implying that you feel the house is not good enough for you to stay in. Camping is not very common in Fiji, however, there are a couple of camping areas on Viti Levu, Vanua Levu and Taveuni. Expect to pay F$5 to F$10 per person per night. For details of the location of camping areas refer to the individual island chapters.

Hostels

The Cathay chain has budget accommodation at Lautoka, Saweni Beach, the Coral Coast and Suva. It gives discounts for HI and Nomad card holders. The Suva YWCA has a few beds for women. There are many cheap hotels with dormitory accommodation and some low-end hotels claiming to be youth hostels.

Guesthouses

Guesthouses are normally cheap hotels. Sometimes though, the term is used for hotels rented by the hour by local prostitutes. There are also government guesthouses in remote areas. They are mostly used by government workers, but travellers are usually accepted if there is a vacancy.

Hotels

Fiji has many budget hotels, especially in the Nadi/Lautoka area, the Coral Coast and Suva on Viti Levu. Spartan rooms are available for around F$30 to F$50 a double. Many budget hotels have dormitories for about F$8 to F$10 a night – a good option for solo travellers who want to meet other like souls. Some have communal cooking facilities.

There are also lots of mid-range hotels. Prices vary between F$70 and F$150 for doubles; discounts may apply if the hotel is not busy. Amenities usually include air-con, tea- and coffee-making facilities, and a restaurant, bar and pool.

Resorts

The term 'resort' is used very loosely in Fiji and can refer to any accommodation anywhere near the sea, ranging from backpacker-style to exclusive luxury. If you are prepared to put up with rudimentary facilities and services you can find an inexpensive piece of paradise. There are some beautiful

coral islands where you can stay cheaply in simple thatched-roof bure in idyllic settings.

Wailoaloa and Newtown beaches near Nadi have a concentration of 'backpacker resorts'. Although the black-sand beaches aren't that great and it's pretty isolated, it is an OK place to stay while deciding where to go or while waiting for a flight. There are many backpacker resorts on the offshore islands, including the Yasawas, on Mana in the Mamanucas, Kadavu, Nananu-i-Ra, and Leluvia and Caqelai near Ovalau. Normally they ask for payment up front, so before embarking try to get information from travellers who have just been there. Popular places can become overcrowded. Transport is usually by small open boat, which can be risky in rough weather.

For those who are happy to spend up to a few hundred dollars per day for extra comfort, services and activities, there are many popular resorts in the Mamanucas and on Viti Levu's Coral Coast, as well as on more remote islands. Mainland resorts have the advantage of more options for tours, entertainment and shopping, however, with the exception of beautiful Natadola Beach, offshore islands usually have better beaches. If you are just looking for water sports or a relaxing time on the beach, choose an offshore island. There is a trend towards small, exclusive and expensive resorts such as Natadola Beach Resort on Viti Levu, Namale Resort and Nukubati Island Resort on Vanua Levu, Kaimbu Island Resort in the Lau Group and Vatulele Island Resort off southern Viti Levu. These are best suited to couples with a very healthy bank balance or on a honeymoon spree.

Rental Accommodation

Most of the long-term rental accommodation is in Suva and Pacific Harbour, and to a lesser extent in Nadi. Renting apartments or rooms with weekly rates may be a cheap option if you are looking for a fixed base from which to take day trips. Normally apartments have cooking facilities, and if you are in a small group, a joint effort to buy groceries, fresh fruit and vegetables from the local market can save a fair bit of money.

FOOD
Local Food
Fiji is the multicultural hub of the Pacific, and its food is a blend of indigenous Fijian, Polynesian, Indian, Chinese and Western influences. Traditional Fijian foods include *tavioka* (cassava) and *dalo* (taro) roots, boiled or baked fish, and seafood in *lolo* (coconut cream). Meat (pork or beef) is fried and accompanied with the dalo roots and *rourou* (boiled dalo leaves) in lolo. Kokoda is a popular traditional dish made of raw fish marinated in coconut cream and lime juice. Seasonal tropical fruits include guava, pineapple and mango. Fiji-Indian dishes tend to be heavily spiced. A typical meal is a meat curry with rice, lentil soup and roti (a type of flat bread). Chinese stir-fries, fried rice, chop suey or 'Chinese curries' are widely eaten, and some restaurants have bêche-de-mer on the menu.

If you are invited to share a meal with a Fijian or Fiji-Indian family you will experience authentic Fijian food. At home, Fijians generally eat with their hands and sit on woven mats. In Indian homes there may be a strict protocol for eating, using a particular hand etc. Ask your hosts for advice. You will be provided with plenty of food, whether they can afford it or not. Some hosts will even wait for you to have your fill before they start eating – if that is the case, leave enough for everybody. Try to reciprocate by buying some groceries for the family.

You may get to taste Fijian 'bush food' while hiking in the highlands. Your guides might catch some freshwater prawns and cook them on the spot. Tavioka and prawns are roasted on a small open fire, and water, salt, lime juice and chillies are mixed together in a bowl made from banana leaves. You then dip the baked tavioka and prawns into the mixture and eat!

Although turtles are an endangered species and there are strict controls on their capture and eating, turtle meat can still be found in markets. If villagers offer you *vonu* (turtle), politely refuse. An adult female is about 20 to 50 years old before she can lay eggs.

Village children catch the crabs that swarm along beaches under a full moon, and then hold a feast. Fishing for flounder is also popular by moonlight. It involves wading into shallow water to spear or net the fish.

Avoid eating large predatory reef fish such as snapper, barracuda and groupers, as these sometimes carry the ciguatera toxin (refer to the Health section earlier in this chapter).

Fast Food
Fijians are facing nutritional problems as they forgo traditional foods for Western-style tinned and packaged foods. Diabetes is on the increase. The number of fast-food outlets is growing quickly in the main towns. Pizzas are now fairly popular, as are takeaways of fried, greasy Indian or Chinese food. McDonald's opened in Nadi in early 1996 and followed shortly after in Suva.

Restaurants
Fiji's main towns, especially Nadi and Suva, have a good variety of restaurants ranging from cheap cafes to fine dining. Most have a combination of adapted Chinese, Indian and Western dishes. Cheap restaurants charge between F$5 and F$10 for main meals. If you are on a long trip and a tight budget, restaurant and cafe food may become monotonous. Many restaurants serve imported beef, as local beef can be of poor quality.

Suva has one good Fijian restaurant (the Old Mill Cottage). In general, though, it is difficult to find traditionals. Many resort restaurants do have *lovo* nights, which are often accompanied by a *meke* (dance performance that enacts stories and legends). Lovo are traditional Fijian banquets in which the food is prepared in an underground oven.

Boiled Bat
Beka (bat) was once a popular food, but now tends to be eaten only by older people. The smell of boiling bat is disgusting and it tastes foul. Fortunately it is not considered rude to refuse an offer to eat it.

Traditional Fijian Recipes

Here are some traditional Fijian recipes that are quite simple to prepare:

Palusami
12 *dalo* (taro) leaves
250g ground corned beef or smoked chicken, or pumpkin/sweet potato (for vegetarians)
1 onion, diced
1 tomato, diced
1 tin *lolo* (coconut cream)
seasoning to taste

Mix the meat, onion and tomato with the seasoning. Divide the mixture into 12 portions and wrap each in a dalo leaf. Place in a baking dish and add the lolo. Cover with foil or a lid and bake in an oven for one hour at 200°C. Serve with *tavioka* (cassava) and sweet potato.

Kokoda
500g very fresh white fish (Fijians usually use *walu*, Spanish mackerel)
1 cup freshly squeezed lemon or lime juice
¼ cup of *lolo* (coconut cream)
2 tbspns white or spring onions, chopped very finely
2 tbsp of ripe tomatoes, chopped finely
chilli, freshly chopped (to your taste)
salt (to your taste)

Cut the fish into cubes. Marinate in lemon juice overnight or for at least two hours. Drain the juice and set aside. Add lolo, onions, tomatoes, chilli and salt, and some of the juice to taste (it should be tangy). Serve chilled and garnished with spring onions, a wedge of lemon or lime and a chilli – ideally, in a half coconut or clam shell. Kokoda is good as an entree.

Nama
Nama, or grapeweed, is a seaweed that looks like miniature green grapes. During the summer it can be found floating on the water's surface above reefs and lagoons. Nama should be served fresh, on the same day that it is collected. You will see it sold at the markets, typically on a bed of green leaves to keep it cool and fresh, and sold along with a packet of *kora,* or fermented coconut, which Fijians like to eat with nama.

250g nama
lolo
2 small tomatoes, diced
chilli, freshly chopped (to your taste)
lemon or lime juice (to your taste)

Make a thick lolo by scraping out the meat of a few coconuts and squeezing it. Dice the tomatoes, chillies and the lemon or lime juice and add this to the lolo. Pour this mixture on top of the nama and serve as a wet and juicy salad.

A hole is dug in the ground and stones are put inside and heated by an open fire. The food, wrapped in banana leaves and cooked slowly on top of the hot stones.

Vegetarian Food
The Hare Krishna restaurants in Lautoka and Suva are the best places for vegetarian fare. Most Indian and pizza restaurants have

some vegetarian dishes and McDonald's has vegetarian burgers.

Self-Catering

Every large town in Fiji has a fresh fruit-and-vegetable market and at least one supermarket where you can get basic groceries. Most villages have a small shop, but the range of food items is normally very limited as villagers grow their own fresh produce. Some backpacker places have cooking facilities and also sell basic groceries. If you are a guest in a village it is a good idea to buy some goods at the local shop for your host family.

Useful Fijian food words include:

bele – green leafy vegetable, served boiled

bu – green coconut

bulumakau – beef

dalo – taro, the starchy root, usually boiled

luve ni toa – chicken

ika – fish

ivi – nut of the *ivi* tree, a type of chestnut

kokoda – raw fish marinated in lime juice, served with chilli and onions

lolo – coconut milk

lovo – food cooked in a underground oven on hot stones

nama – seaweed that looks like miniature green grapes

niu – brown coconut

palusami – corned beef, onions and lolo wrapped in dalo leaves and baked in a lovo

rourou – boiled dalo leaves (similar taste to spinach)

tavioka – cassava

ura – freshwater prawns

uto – breadfruit – boiled or baked in lovo

vakalolo – a pudding of mashed starchy roots like cassava and dalo, and fruit such as breadfruit. In the old days vast quantities of this delicacy were made for traditional feasts. The pudding is made with a sweet sauce of caramelised sugar-cane juice mixed and boiled with lolo, kneaded and rolled into balls, coated with more sweet sauce and wrapped in leaves.

DRINKS
Nonalcoholic Drinks

Both local and imported mineral water and soft drinks are available in Fiji. Most of the milk available is long-life. Fresh local fruit juices are great, but don't be misled by 'juice' on a menu – it often means cordial. One of the local soft drinks is a sickly sweet banana flavour. The water from chilled green coconuts is much more refreshing.

Alcoholic Drinks

Most restaurants and bars stock a variety of local and imported spirits and beer. Fiji Bitter and Fiji Gold are locally brewed beers. Most of the wines available are from Australia or New Zealand. Expect to pay about F$2 for a glass of beer, although the upmarket resorts will charge more. A 750ml bottle of Fiji Rum is about F$20.

Yaqona

Yaqona is the national drink, and is an integral part of Fijian life. It is mildly narcotic, looks like muddy water and you won't escape trying it! Refer to the Society & Conduct section in the Facts about Fiji chapter.

ENTERTAINMENT

Little happens on Sunday, so it's a good idea to organise activities in advance or attend a Fijian church service to hear some great singing. Nadi has minimal nightlife, although the larger mainland resort hotels have discos, live bands, meke, lovo nights and fire-walking performances. Beachcomber Island Resort in the Mamanucas has a reputation as being fun for young travellers. Suva, with its cosmopolitan and student population, is the nightlife capital. Here there are lots of bars, an 'Irish pub', nightclubs (with recorded or live music), a country-music venue and a jazz club. Restaurants normally close early – don't expect to find many places open after 10 pm.

Cinemas

Every major town has at least one cinema. Suva has a Village cinema complex and another is being built in Lautoka. Screenings include fairly up-to-date, mainstream English-language productions and Indian 'Bollywood' films. Admission is a mere F$3 or so. Check the entertainment section in the *Fiji Times* for what's showing.

SPECTATOR SPORTS

Rugby union and soccer are Fiji's major competitive sports. Rugby, especially popular with indigenous Fijians, is the one sport that has continually put Fiji on the world sporting scene. Consider seeing a local rugby match on Viti Levu – even if you don't like rugby it is interesting watching the crowd. Every village has a rugby field, and interested visitors may be invited to join an informal game. Soccer is especially strong with Fiji Indians, and Gujeratis have their own competition.

The British brought the golfing habit to Fiji. There are golf courses on Denarau Island and along Viti Levu's Coral Coast and also at Pacific Harbour and Suva. Other popular sports include cricket, basketball, netball, volleyball, squash, badminton, tennis, lawn bowls, surfing, chess, athletics and boxing.

Refer to the sports pages of the *Fiji Times* for venues and events.

SHOPPING

The main tourist centres of Nadi, the Coral Coast and Suva have lots of handicraft shops. Lautoka is quieter and the salespeople are less pushy. You can also buy interesting handicrafts direct from villages or on outer islands such as Taveuni. Watch out for sword sellers on the streets who will try to sell you a piece of rubbish with your name carved on it (refer to Dangers & Annoyances earlier in this chapter).

In Suva, the Government Crafts Centre has better quality goods than most of the articles at the Curio & Handicraft Centre, where many of the artefacts are not even genuinely Fijian. The centre is interesting for a stroll. There are lots of desperate stall holders who will try to entice you to buy their goods, which are usually the same as those in the next stall. Occasionally one has better quality items or a better deal. Beware: if there is a cruise ship in port, prices will skyrocket.

Fiji was once a duty-free mecca, but now there is nothing particularly special about the shopping. When buying duty-free electrical equipment check that the voltage and cycle are compatible with those of your home country.

Traditional artefacts, such as war clubs, spears and chiefly cannibal forks, are popular souvenirs. So too are yaqona bowls of various sizes (miniature ones for salt and pepper), woven pandanus mats, baskets from Kioa, shell buttons, sandalwood/coconut soap and *tapa* cloth (*masi* – bark cloth in the form of wall hangings, covered books, postcards). Pottery can be a good buy – if you can get it home in one piece. Don't buy any products derived from endangered species such as turtle shell.

Clothing shops in Suva and Nadi have bula shirts (in colourful tropical prints) and fashion by local designers. There are also vibrant saris and Indian jewellery. Fijian ceramic jewellery is sold in the Government Crafts Centre in Suva.

The Fiji Museum shop in Suva has some interesting books, posters and postcards. Posters include the Fiji Natural Heritage series. There are several beautiful photography books, including *Children of the Sun,* available in the major souvenir shops.

Getting There & Away

Most visitors to Fiji arrive at Nadi International Airport, though a few flights from Sydney and nearby Pacific countries also land at Nausori airport near Suva. Centrally situated in the South Pacific, Fiji is one of the main airline hubs of the Pacific region (Hawaii is the other). Many travellers visit Fiji on round-the-world (RTW) tickets or on a stopover between Australia, New Zealand and the USA.

AIR
Airports & Airlines

Nadi International Airport is Fiji's main airport. It is 9km north of central Nadi (about F$8 by taxi). There are frequent local buses to town (F$0.45) and the bus stop is just outside the Queens Road entrance.

The arrivals and customs area has a board displaying the names and rates of hotels in the Nadi area that are members of the Fiji

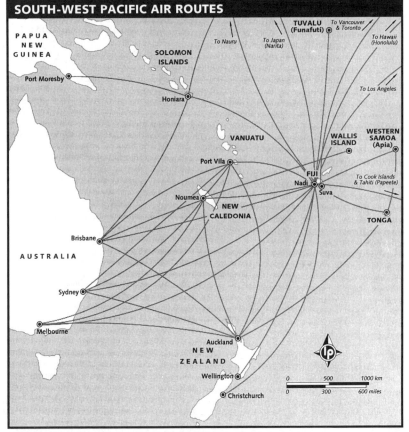

SOUTH-WEST PACIFIC AIR ROUTES

PAPUA NEW GUINEA

Port Moresby

SOLOMON ISLANDS

To Nauru

To Japan (Narita)

TUVALU (Funafuti)

To Vancouver & Toronto

To Hawaii (Honolulu)

Honiara

To Los Angeles

VANUATU

WALLIS ISLAND

WESTERN SAMOA (Apia)

Port Vila

FIJI

Nadi   Suva

To Cook Islands & Tahiti (Papeete)

Noumea

NEW CALEDONIA

TONGA

Brisbane

AUSTRALIA

Sydney

Melbourne

Auckland

NEW ZEALAND

Wellington

Christchurch

0   500   1000 km
0   300   600 miles

Hotels Association. The best source of information, however, is the Fiji Visitors Bureau (FVB) office. It is on the left as you exit the customs area. As you enter arrivals you will be greeted by a sea of smiling faces and guitar serenading. Most of these people will be representatives of local accommodation and the many travel agencies on the ground floor and first floor concourse of the airport. Usually representatives of the FVB will be there to help you, and it's worth escaping the crowd and going to their office to get an update on available accommodation and activities.

The airport has a 24-hour ANZ bank with currency exchange (F$2 commission fee per transaction) just next to the FVB office. There are many travel agencies, airline offices and car-rental offices in the arrivals area, as well as a post office, cafeteria, restaurant, duty-free shop, newsagency and luggage storage area. Luggage storage costs F$3 to F$6 per day.

Airlines with direct services to Nadi include Fiji's Air Pacific, Qantas Airways, Air New Zealand, Aircalin, Air Nauru and Solomon Airlines.

Nausori International Airport, 23km north-east of downtown Suva, is Fiji's second airport. Air Fiji has flights to Tuvalu and Tonga, and Royal Tongan Airlines also has flights to Tonga. Air Pacific now has a direct route from Sydney. Otherwise the airport is mostly used for domestic purposes: The premises are small and low key but include an ANZ bank.

Taxis to/from Suva cost about F$17. There is no direct bus service to/from Suva, but there is a bus service connecting the Centra hotel in Suva that anyone can use (F$2.10). Another way to get from the airport to town is to take a taxi to the Nausori bus station (about F$2.50, 4km) and then catch one of the frequent local buses to Suva for about F$0.80.

The following international airlines have representatives in Fiji:

Aircalin (General sales agents for Air France)
(☎ 722 145) Nadi; (☎ 303 133) Suva
Web site: www.aircalin.nc

Air Fiji (General sales agents for Air India)
(☎ 722 521, fax 720 555) Nadi; (☎ 313 666, fax 300 771, @ airfiji@is.com.fj) Suva
Air Nauru
(☎ 722 795) Nadi; (☎ 312 377, fax 302 861) Suva
Web site: www.airnauru.com.au
Air New Zealand
(☎ 722 955, 722 472, fax 721 450) Nadi; (☎ 313 100, fax 302 294) Suva
Web site: www.airnz.co.nz
Air Pacific (General sales agents for Air Canada, British Airways, Cathay Pacific Airways and Malaysia Airlines)
(☎ 720 777, 722 272, fax 720 126, @ airpacific@is.com.fj) Nadi; (☎ 304 388, fax 304 153, @ airpacific@is.com.fj) Suva
Web site: www.airpacific.com.au
Air Vanuatu
(☎ 722 521, fax 720 555) Nadi; (☎ 315 055, fax 300 771) Suva
Ansett Airlines International
(☎ 722 870, fax 720 351) Nadi; (☎ 301 671, fax 302 294) Suva
Web site: www.ansett.com.au
Canadian Airlines International
(☎ 722 400, fax 722 523) Nadi; (☎ 313 830) Suva
Polynesian Airlines
(☎ 722 521, fax 720 555) Nadi; (☎ 315 055, fax 300 771) Suva
Web site: www.polynesianairlines.co.nz
Qantas Airways
(☎ 722 880, fax 720 444) Nadi; (☎ 313 888, fax 304 795) Suva
Web site: www.qantas.com.au
Royal Tongan Airlines
(☎ 724 355, fax 724 810) Nadi; (☎ 315 755) Suva
Web site: kalianet.to/rta
Solomon Airlines
(☎ 722 831) Nadi; (☎ 315 889, fax 315 992) Suva
Web site: www.solomonairlines.com.au

Buying Tickets

A plane ticket will probably be the single most expensive item in your budget, and buying it can be an intimidating business. There is likely to be a multitude of airlines and travel agents hoping to separate you from your money, so it is always worth putting aside a few hours to research the current state of the market. Start early: Some of the cheapest tickets have to be

Air Travel Glossary

Cancellation Penalties If you have to cancel or change a discounted ticket, there are often heavy penalties involved; insurance can sometimes be taken out against these penalties. Some airlines impose penalties on regular tickets as well, particularly against 'no-show' passengers.

Courier Fares Businesses often need to send urgent documents or freight securely and quickly. Courier companies hire people to accompany the package through customs and, in return, offer a discount ticket which is sometimes a phenomenal bargain. However, you may have to surrender all your baggage allowance and take only carry-on luggage.

Full Fares Airlines traditionally offer 1st class (coded F), business class (coded J) and economy class (coded Y) tickets. These days there are so many promotional and discounted fares available that few passengers pay full economy fare.

Lost Tickets If you lose your airline ticket an airline will usually treat it like a travellers cheque and, after inquiries, issue you with another one. Legally, however, an airline is entitled to treat it like cash and if you lose it then it's gone forever. Take good care of your tickets.

Onward Tickets An entry requirement for many countries is that you have a ticket out of the country. If you're unsure of your next move, the easiest solution is to buy the cheapest onward ticket to a neighbouring country or a ticket from a reliable airline which can later be refunded if you do not use it.

Open-Jaw Tickets These are return tickets where you fly out to one place but return from another. If available, this can save you backtracking to your arrival point.

Overbooking Since every flight has some passengers who fail to show up, airlines often book more passengers than they have seats. Usually excess passengers make up for the no-shows, but occasionally somebody gets 'bumped' onto the next available flight. Guess who it is most likely to be? The passengers who check in late.

Promotional Fares These are officially discounted fares, available from travel agencies or direct from the airline.

Reconfirmation If you don't reconfirm your flight at least 72 hours prior to departure, the airline may delete your name from the passenger list. Ring to find out if your airline requires reconfirmation.

Restrictions Discounted tickets often have various restrictions on them – such as needing to be paid for in advance and incurring a penalty to be altered. Others are restrictions on the minimum and maximum period you must be away.

Round-the-World Tickets RTW tickets give you a limited period (usually a year) in which to circumnavigate the globe. You can go anywhere the carrying airlines go, as long as you don't backtrack. The number of stopovers or total number of separate flights is decided before you set off and they usually cost a bit more than a basic return flight.

Transferred Tickets Airline tickets cannot be transferred from one person to another. Travellers sometimes try to sell the return half of their ticket, but officials can ask you to prove that you are the person named on the ticket. On an international flight tickets are compared with passports.

Travel Periods Ticket prices vary with the time of year. There is a low (off-peak) season and a high (peak) season, and often a low-shoulder season and a high-shoulder season as well. Usually the fare depends on your outward flight – if you depart in the high season and return in the low season, you pay the high-season fare.

bought months in advance and some popular flights sell out early. Talk to other recent travellers – they may be able to stop you making some of the same old mistakes. Look at the ads in newspapers and magazines, consult reference books and watch for special offers – then phone travel agents for bargains. (Airlines are useful for supplying information on routes and timetables; however, except at times of airline ticketing wars, they do not supply the cheapest tickets.) Find out the fare, the route, the duration of the journey and any restrictions on the ticket. Then sit back and decide which ticket is best for you.

You may discover that those impossibly cheap flights are 'fully booked, but we have another one that costs a bit more...'; or the flight is on an airline notorious for its poor safety standards and leaves you in the world's worst airport mid-journey for 14 hours; or the airline claims to have the last two seats available for that country for the whole of July, which it will hold for you for a maximum of two hours: Don't panic – keep ringing around. Use the fares quoted in this book as a guide only. They are approximate and based on the rates advertised by travel agents at the time of going to press. Quoted air fares do not necessarily constitute a recommendation for the carrier.

If you are travelling from the UK or the USA, you will probably find that the cheapest flights are being advertised by obscure bucket (discount) shops whose names haven't yet reached the telephone directory. Many such firms are honest and solvent, but there are a few rogues who will take your money and disappear, to reopen elsewhere a month or two later under a new name. If you feel suspicious about a firm, don't give them all the money at once – leave a deposit of 20% or so and pay the balance when you get the ticket. If they insist on cash in advance, go somewhere else. Once you have the ticket, ring the airline to confirm that you are actually booked onto the flight.

You may decide to pay more than the rock-bottom fare and opt for the safety of a better-known travel agent. Firms such as STA Travel, which has offices worldwide,

Council Travel in the USA or Travel CUTS in Canada are not going to disappear overnight, leaving you clutching a receipt for a nonexistent ticket, and they offer good prices to most destinations.

Once you have your ticket, write down its number, the flight number and other details, and keep the information somewhere separate. If the ticket is lost or stolen, this will help you get a replacement. It's sensible to buy travel insurance as early as possible. If you buy it the week before you fly, you may find, for example, that you're not covered for delays to your flight caused by industrial action.

Round-the-World Tickets & Circle Pacific Fares RTW tickets are often real bargains. One that takes in the Pacific will be about US$1600. They are usually put together by a combination of two or more airlines and permit you to fly anywhere you want on their route systems so long as you do not backtrack. There may be restrictions on how many stops you are permitted and usually the tickets are valid for 90 days up to one year. An alternative type of RTW ticket is one put together by a travel agent using a combination of discounted tickets.

Circle Pacific tickets use a combination of airlines to circle the Pacific – combining Australia, New Zealand, the USA and Asia. As with RTW tickets, there are advance purchase restrictions and limits to how many stopovers you can take. These fares are likely to be about 15% cheaper than RTW tickets.

Air Passes Intercountry flights in the Pacific can be prohibitively expensive. The only really workable way to travel to more than a handful of countries is by using an air pass. Conditions apply and seating can be limited, so book early.

Australia's east coast and New Zealand are both included in the Polynesian Airlines Polypass, which can be a cheap option for visiting Fiji, Samoa and Tonga. It costs US$999 for (almost) unlimited travel within 45 days, excluding the Christmas period. Linking with Hawaii/Los Angeles costs US$150/450 extra.

There are also Circle the South West Pacific passes, which include flights with five airlines. Travel must start and finish in Australia, must be completed within 28 days, and there's a minimum stay per destination of five nights. It costs A$650 to A$1035 (depending on which countries you visit) for travel to two of the Solomon Islands, Vanuatu, Fiji or New Caledonia, and A$130 to A$400 for an extra country.

Air Pacific's Triangle Fare links Fiji, Vanuatu and the Solomon Islands for US$600. The fare is only available from the USA and South America, and travel must be completed within 30 days.

The Pacifica pass uses a number of airlines, and must be combined with an Air New Zealand or United Airlines ticket. It is not available to residents of Australia, New Zealand or Fiji. For US$1048/1298 in the low/high season you can fly Los Angeles-Auckland return with one stopover in the Pacific; additional stopovers can be made for US$150 each. Six-month and one-year tickets are also available.

The Visit the South Pacific pass combines many airlines and countries and costs US$115 to US$210 per sector (minimum of two sectors, maximum of eight). The pass must be bought in conjunction with an air or sea ticket from outside the region.

The Pacific pass allows for travel (within 30 days) with Air Pacific between Fiji, Samoa, Tonga and Vanuatu for US$462. It is available only in the USA, South America, Africa and Europe.

Air Nauru's Pacific Explorer is a 30-day ticket linking the Philippines, Guam, Pohnpei, Nauru, Kiribati, Fiji and Australia. It costs from US$450 for the first three flights and US$75 for each additional leg (maximum of eight flights).

The Circle Excursion is a multi-airline pass for travel between Fiji-Australia-New Zealand, Fiji-Australia-Vanuatu, Fiji-Tonga-Samoa or Fiji-Vanuatu-New Caledonia. It costs US$741.

The Boomerang pass is only available in connection with air or sea travel to/from Australia, New Zealand or Fiji from outside the region; it is not available to residents of

these countries. It costs US$394 (for two countries) to US$1183 (for six countries). It covers Fiji, Vanuatu, Tonga, Western Samoa, New Caledonia and the Solomon Islands on Air Pacific, Qantas Airways and Ansett.

Travellers with Special Needs

If you have special needs of any sort – you've broken a leg, are vegetarian, travelling in a wheelchair, taking the baby, terrified of flying – let the airline know as soon as possible so that it can make arrangements accordingly. You should remind it when you reconfirm your booking (at least 72 hours before departure) and again when you check in at the airport. It may also be worth ringing airlines before you make your booking to find out how they can handle your particular needs.

Airports and airlines can be surprisingly helpful, but they do need advance warning. Most international airports will provide escorts from check-in desk to plane where needed, and there should be ramps, lifts, accessible toilets and phones. Aircraft toilets, however, are likely to present a problem; travellers should discuss this with the airline at an early stage and, if necessary, with their doctors. Guide dogs for the blind often have to travel in pressurised baggage compartments with other animals, away from their owners. They are subject to the same quarantine laws (six months in isolation etc) as any other animal when entering or returning to countries currently free of rabies, such as Britain or Australia. Deaf travellers can ask for airport and in-flight announcements to be written down for them.

Children under two travel for 10% of the standard fare (or free, on some airlines) as long as they don't occupy a seat. They don't get a baggage allowance either. 'Skycots' should be provided by the airline if requested in advance; these will take a child weighing up to about 10kg. Children aged two to 12 can usually occupy a seat for half to two-thirds of the full fare and get a baggage allowance. Push chairs can often be taken as hand luggage.

Bicycles can travel by plane. You can take them to pieces and put them in a bike bag or box, but it's much easier to wheel your bike to the check-in desk, where it should be treated as a piece of baggage. You may have to remove the pedals and turn the handlebars sideways so that it takes up less space in the aircraft's hold; check all this with the airline well in advance, preferably before you pay for your ticket.

Departure Taxes

An international departure tax of F$20 applies to all visitors over 12 years old.

The USA

Fiji is a major stopover between west-coast USA and Australia and New Zealand. Fiji is about six hours from Hawaii and 12 hours from west-coast USA. Fares from the USA vary greatly in price depending on season and ticket restrictions. Los Angeles-Nadi with Air New Zealand is about US$1348/1518 for low/high season.

The *New York Times*, the *Los Angeles Times*, the *Chicago Tribune* and the *San Francisco Examiner* all produce weekly travel sections. Council Travel, the USA's largest student travel organisation, has around 60 offices in the USA; its head office (☎ 800-226 8624) is at 205 E 42 St, New York, NY 10017. Call it for the office nearest you or visit its Web site at www.ciee.org. STA Travel (☎ 800-777 0112) has offices in Boston, Chicago, Miami, New York, Philadelphia, San Francisco and other major cities. Call the toll-free 800 number for office locations or visit its Web site at www.statravel.com.

Canada

Fiji is a popular stopover between Canada and Australia and New Zealand, and for travellers on RTW tickets. Canadian Airlines International code shares with Air Pacific on this route. Fares for Vancouver-Nadi via Honolulu start at about C$1964/2264 for low/high season. From Ottawa or Toronto flights are generally via Chicago and Los Angeles; fares to Nadi are around C$1963/2400. The airline Canada 3000 (☎ 02-9567 9631) has better fares (C$1399 Vancouver-Nadi, low season).

Toronto's *Globe & Mail*, the *Montreal Gazette,* the *Toronto Sun* and the *Vancouver Sun* are good places to look for cheap fares.

Travel CUTS (☎ 800 667 2887, toll-free in Canada) is Canada's national student travel agency and has offices in all major cities. Its Web site is www.travelcuts.com.

Australia

Air Pacific is the main carrier between Australia and Fiji, and Qantas Airways tickets to Fiji are usually seats on Air Pacific planes. The flight time is about 3¾ hours from Sydney and about 4½ hours from Melbourne.

Excursion fares from Sydney or Brisbane are typically A$739/839 return for low/high (school holidays) season for a minimum five days and a maximum 120 days. Advance purchase fares are cheaper, but less flexible. You will need to pay 14 days in advance, no changes are permitted and cancellation penalties apply. These are about A$740/840 for low/high season. Add A$50 to the above fares from Melbourne. Children pay 67% of the adult fare.

With Air New Zealand, a return economy fare (low season with a six-month validity) from Sydney to west-coast USA with a stopover in Fiji, costs around A$1630.

It is possible to get better deals so you should shop around. STA and Flight Centre are major dealers in cheap air fares. Check the *Yellow Pages* and ring around.

New Zealand

Air Pacific operates Nadi-Auckland, Nadi-Wellington and Nadi-Christchurch services. Air New Zealand also flies Nadi-Auckland and has shared services on the other routes. At the time of writing, Air New Zealand's subsidiary, Freedom Air, had announced plans for a twice weekly Palmerston North-Nadi flight. From Auckland to Fiji (three hours) costs about NZ$822/983 for low/high season, though Freedom Air was advertising its initial flights for NZ$499/599. Flights from Wellington are about NZ$338 extra and from Christchurch NZ$450 extra. It is possible to get better deals so you should shop around. Air New Zealand flies

Auckland-Los Angeles with a stopover in Fiji. Return fares cost about NZ$1999 for a seven-day advance purchase, six-month validity, low-season ticket. With Air New Zealand, Fiji can also be a stopover from Auckland on the way to Japan, Korea, Singapore and Canada.

As in Australia, STA and Flight Centre are popular travel agents in New Zealand.

Other Pacific Countries

There are many airline connections between Fiji and other Pacific countries: Air Nauru flies Nadi-Nauru and Suva-Nauru; Air Fiji flies Suva-Funafuti (Tuvalu) and has recently started a Suva-Tonga service; Aircalin flies Nadi-Noumea (New Caledonia) and Nadi-Papeete (Tahiti); Solomon Airlines flies Nadi-Honiara (Solomon Islands); Royal Tongan Airlines flies Nausori-Fua'amotu (Tongatapu, Tonga) and Nausori-Lupepau'u (Vava'u, Tonga); Air Pacific flies Nadi-Honiara, Nadi-Apia (Western Samoa), Nadi-Port Vila (Vanuatu), and Nadi-Fua'amotu.

Flights within the Pacific can be expensive, so to cover a number of countries, consider an air pass (see the Air Passes section earlier in this chapter).

The UK

Airline ticket discounters are known as bucket shops in the UK, and many advertise in the travel pages of the weekend broadsheets, such as the *Independent* on Saturday and the *Sunday Times*. Look out for the free magazines, such as *TNT,* which are widely available in London – start by looking outside the main railway and underground stations.

Recommended travel agencies in the UK include STA Travel (☎ 020-7361 6161), Usit Campus (☎ 020-7730 3402), Trailfinders (☎ 020-7938 3939), Bridge the World (☎ 020-7734 7447) and Flightbookers (☎ 020-7757 2000).

A return ticket from London to Nadi costs about £700/1000 in the low/high season.

Continental Europe

London is the travel discount capital of Europe, but there are several other cities in which you will find a range of good deals. Generally there is not much variation in air fare prices for departures from the main European cities, but good deals can be had, so shop around.

Across Europe many travel agencies have ties with STA Travel, where cheap tickets can be purchased and STA-issued tickets can be altered. Outlets in major cities include: Voyages Wasteels (☎ 08 03 88 70 04 – this number can only be dialled from within France, fax 01 43 25 46 25) Paris; STA Travel (☎ 030-311 0950, fax 313 0948) Berlin; Passaggi (☎ 06-474 0923, fax 482 7436) Rome; and ISYTS (☎ 01-322 1267, fax 323 3767) Athens.

Isa Lei, a Fijian Farewell Song

The traditional Fijian farewell song *Isa Lei* is often played for leaving travellers.

Isa Isa Vulagi lasa dina
Isa Isa you are my only treasure
Nomu lako au na rarawa kina
Must you leave me so lonely and forsaken
Cava beka ko a mai cakava
As the roses will miss the sun at dawning
Nomu lako au na sega ni lasa
Every moment my heart for you is yearning

Isa lei, na noqu rarawa
Isa Lei the purple shadows fall
Ni ko sa na gole e na mataka
Sad the morrow will dawn upon my sorrow
Bau nanuma na nodatou lasa
Oh forget not when you are far away
Mai Viti nanuma tiko ga
Precious moments from Fiji

Vanua rogo na nomuni vanua
Isa Isa my heart was filled with pleasure
Kena ca ni levu tu na ua
From the moment I heard your tender greeting
Lomaqu voli me'u bau butuka
Mid the sunshine we spent the hours together
Tovolea ke balavu na bua
Now so swiftly those happy hours are fleeting

France has a network of student travel agencies that can supply discount tickets to travellers of all ages. OTU Voyages (☎ 01 44 41 38 50) has 43 offices, including one in Paris. Acceuil des Jeunes en France (☎ 01 42 77 87 80) is another popular discount travel agency. Good general travel agencies in Paris are Nouvelles Frontières (☎ 08 03 33 33 33) and Voyageurs du Monde (☎ 01 42 86 16 00).

Belgium, the Netherlands and Greece are also good places for buying discount tickets. Acotra Student Travel Agency (☎ 02-512 86 07) in Brussels, WATS Reizen (☎ 03-226 16 26) in Antwerp, SSR Voyages (☎ 01-297 11 11) throughout Switzerland, and NBBS Reizen (☎ 020-624 09 89) and Malibu Travel (☎ 020-626 32 30) in Amsterdam are worth trying. In Athens, check the many travel agencies in the backstreets between Syntagma and Omonia Squares or try Magic Bus (☎ 01-323 7471, fax 322 0219).

Africa

Some RTW tickets include Africa and the Pacific in their itinerary options. Otherwise take a Johannesburg-Nadi ticket via Melbourne, joining up with Qantas Airways and Air Pacific.

Asia

There are direct flights from Japan to Fiji. Air Pacific flies Nadi-Narita for ¥96,277 return for a 21-day ticket. Direct flights from South Korea were suspended following the Asian economic crisis.

Most flights to/from South-East Asia go via Australia or New Zealand. Hong Kong is the discount plane-ticket capital of the region. Its bucket shops are at least as unreliable as those of other cities. Ask the advice of other travellers before buying a ticket. STA, which is reliable, has branches in Hong Kong, Tokyo, Singapore, Bangkok and Kuala Lumpur.

South America

LanChile flies from Santiago to Papeete (a two-month return ticket costs US$1549/1728 in the low/high season). From here you can fly with Air New Zealand to Nadi.

A full economy Papeete-Nadi return ticket costs about F$2870, however, there are 23-day tickets for F$1326 return.

SEA

Travelling to Fiji by sea is now difficult unless you're on a cruise ship or yacht. Few of the shipping companies will take passengers on cargo ships and those that do will usually charge hefty rates. It is virtually impossible to leave Fiji by cargo ship unless passage has been prearranged. However, you could try asking your local shipping agents, or go to the docks and personally approach the captains. Shipping companies include:

Burns Philp (☎ 313 068, fax 301 127) Suva
Carpenters Shipping (☎ 312 244, fax 301 572) Suva
Pacific Forum Line (☎ 315 444, fax 302 754) Suva. This is the agent for the Tuvalu government's cargo/passenger ship the MV *Nivaga II*. It does trips from Suva to Funafuti, Tuvalu, every three months or so (about A$57.40/172.20 or US$38/113 for deck/double cabin, without meals, five days). You have to pay the return fare regardless.
Williams & Goslings (☎ 312 633) Suva

Cruise Ship

Some cruise ships have Fiji on their itineraries, but usually stop only for one or two nights in Suva. From Australia, P&O's *Fair Princess* has a 14-night cruise starting in Sydney and stopping at six ports for between A$1635 (US$1073; no porthole) to A$3700 (US$2428) per person for a twin cabin. In Fiji it visits Suva and the Yasawas. The Norwegian Capricorn Line also has cruises that depart Sydney and include Lautoka in the itinerary. Fares start at A$3690 (US$2421) per person for a twin cabin with ocean views.

Yacht

Fiji's islands are a popular destination and stopover for yachts cruising the Pacific. Yachts need to head for the designated ports of entry at Suva, Lautoka, Levuka or Savusavu. Other marinas include Vuda Point Marina (between Nadi and Lautoka), Port Denarau, Savusavu Yacht Club on Vanua Levu and Musket Cove Marina on

Malololailai (Plantation Island) in the Mamanucas. Yachties are often looking for extra crew and people to share day-to-day costs. If you are interested, ask around the marinas and look on the noticeboards. For more details see the Activities section in the Facts for the Visitor chapter.

On reaching Fijian waters, yachts must first call at a designated port of entry to be cleared by customs, immigration and quarantine: Present a certificate of clearance from the previous port of call, a crew list and passports. Yachties intending to visit outer islands within the Fiji group must have the approval of the Department of Fijian Affairs, 61 Carnarvon Street, Suva. If in Lautoka, Savusavu or Levuka, approval can be obtained from the Commissioner's Department at the district offices.

Before departing, you'll again need to complete clearance formalities (within 24 hours), providing inbound clearance papers, your vessel's details and your next port of call. Customs must be cleared before immigration, and you must have paid all port dues and health fees.

Yacht Help (☎ 668 969, fax 668 814, ☺ yachthelp@mail.is.com.fj), PO Box 4799, Lautoka, publishes the booklet *Yacht Help, Mariners Guide to the Fiji Islands*. It has general information about services for yachties and up-to-date clearance formalities. Pacific Marine Yacht Consultants (☎ 668 969, fax 668 814, ☺ yachthelp@is.com.fj), Vuda Point Marina, offers services to help sort out paperwork, cruising arrangements and obtaining parts not available in Fiji. The Royal Suva Yacht Club (☎ 312 921/304 201, fax 304 433, ☺ rsyc@is.com.fj) is also a good place to get the latest information and to meet local yachties.

The best time to sail is in the 'winter' from late April to early November when the south-easterly trade winds are blowing. During the summer months winds change

> ### Warning
>
> The information in this chapter is particularly vulnerable to change: Prices for international travel are volatile, routes are introduced and cancelled, schedules change, special deals come and go, and rules and visa requirements are amended. Airlines and governments seem to take a perverse pleasure in making price structures and regulations as complicated as possible. You should check directly with the airline or a travel agent to make sure you understand how a fare (and ticket you may buy) works. In addition, the travel industry is highly competitive and there are many lurks and perks.
>
> The upshot of this is that you should get opinions, quotes and advice from as many airlines and travel agents as possible before you part with your hard-earned cash. The details given in this chapter should be regarded as pointers and are not a substitute for your own careful, up-to-date research.

direction more often and the chance of striking storms and hurricanes is greater.

ORGANISED TOURS

While travelling independently is easy in Fiji, many visitors pre-arrange some type of package tour. It may be the ideal option if you have limited time, prefer an upfront, all-inclusive price, wish to stay in a particular resort, or have special interests and activities, such as diving. Most travel agents will be able to organise this type of trip and can often arrange cheap deals. There are many options, and prices depend on the season, type of accommodation and length of the trip. Alternatively, some Pacific cruises such as P&O's *Fair Princess* include Fiji on their itinerary (see the Cruise Ship section earlier in this chapter).

Getting Around

By using local buses, carriers and ferries you can get around Fiji's main islands relatively cheaply and easily. If you'd like more comfort or are short on time you can use air-conditioned express buses, rental vehicles, charter boats and small planes.

AIR
Domestic Air Services

Fiji is well serviced by internal airlines, which have frequent and generally reliable flights. Some may find the light planes scary, especially if it's windy or turbulent, but the views of the islands, coral reefs and lagoons are fantastic.

The international airports on Viti Levu, at Nadi and Nausori (near Suva), are also the main domestic hubs. Other domestic airports include Savusavu and Labasa on

Vanua Levu, Matei on Taveuni, Vunisea on Kadavu, Bureta on Ovalau and, in the Mamanucas, Malololailai and Mana. Many other small islands also have airstrips. There are flights to outer islands where there is no accommodation for tourists and an invitation is needed to visit – in some cases it is illegal to turn up uninvited. Rotuma, Gau, Koro, Moala and Vanua Balavu, and Lakeba in Lau have airstrips but receive few visitors, while other islands such as Vatulele, Yasawa and Wakaya have their own airstrips to serve the upmarket resorts.

Air Fiji and Sunflower Airlines have regular inter-island flights by light plane. Most of Air Fiji's services operate out of Nausori, while Sunflower Airlines' base and major hub is Nadi; prices on shared routes are almost identical. Their contact details are as follows:

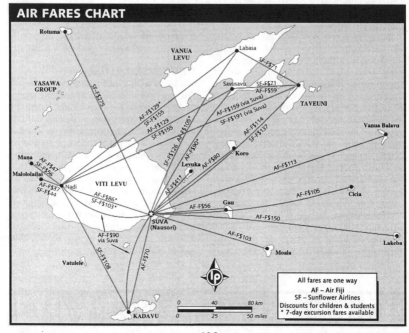

AIR FARES CHART

All fares are one way
AF – Air Fiji
SF – Sunflower Airlines
Discounts for children & students
* 7-day excursion fares available

Air Fiji (☎ 722 521, fax 720 555) Nadi; (☎ 313 666, fax 300 771, ✉ airfiji@is.com.fj) Suva; (☎ 478 077) Nausori airport and (☎ 811 188, fax 813 819) Labasa. The airline has a fleet of Bandits, Twin Otters, Harbins, Britten Norman Islanders and Bandeirantes. From Suva, there are daily flights to Labasa, Levuka, Nadi, Savusavu, Taveuni and Kadavu. From Nadi, there are daily flights to Suva, Savusavu, Malololailai, Mana, Labasa, Taveuni and Kadavu via Suva. Seven-day excursion fares (minimum one day, maximum seven) are available for Nadi-Suva, Nadi-Labasa, Suva-Labasa, Suva-Savusavu and Suva-Levuka routes for about 20% of the normal return fare. Air Fiji's Web site is www.airfiji.net

Sunflower Airlines (☎ 723 016, fax 723 611, ✉ sunair@is.com.fj) Nadi airport; (☎ 315 755, fax 305 027) Suva; (☎ 477 310) Nausori airport; (☎ 811 454, fax 281 9542) Labasa. For overseas reservations contact:(☎ 02-9236 3322, fax 9235 3488) Australia; (☎ 09-428 1025, fax 428 1035) New Zealand and (☎ 800 224 0220, fax 909 659 5830) USA/Canada. Sunflower Airlines' fleet of small planes includes Britten Norman Islanders, Twin Otters and Shorts 330 aircraft. Sunflower Airlines has daily services to major tourist destinations (except Ovalau), including Suva, Labasa, Savusavu, Taveuni, Kadavu, Malololailai (Plantation Island Resort and Musket Cove Resort) and Mana. Seven-day excursion fares (minimum one day, maximum seven) are available for the Nadi-Suva, Nadi-Labasa and Suva-Labasa routes for about 20% less than the normal return fare.

Air Passes

Air Fiji has a 30-day Discover Fiji Pass for F$472 (US$236). It is sold only outside Fiji in conjunction with an international air fare. There is a choice of three set itineraries, including: Nadi-Taveuni-Suva-Kadavu-Nadi; Nadi-Taveuni-Suva-Levuka-Suva-Nadi; and Nadi-Savusavu-Suva-Kadavu-Nadi-Malololailai-Nadi. It's best to book your seats, as the small planes often fill up quickly. Children under 12 pay 50% of the full fare, infants are charged 10%. There is a US$50 predeparture cancellation fee, and reimbursement is minimal once in Fiji. If you change your mind it will cost US$70 per flight to reroute. If you are a student, a 25% discount applies to regular air fares, which may be more economical than the air pass.

Charter Services & Joyflights

Charter services and joyflights are available with:

Island Hoppers (☎ 720 410, fax 720 172, ✉ islandhopper@is.com.fj) Nadi airport. Island Hoppers operates helicopter flight-seeing tours departing from Denarau Island. It also transfers guests to island resorts, such as Vomo and Tokoriki. A 20-minute flight costs F$133 per person, 35 minutes is F$224 per person.

Turtle Airways (☎ 721 888, fax 720 095, ✉ southseaturtle@is.com.fj) Newtown Beach, Nadi. Turtle has a fleet of Cessna seaplanes that can carry up to four passengers. As well as flight seeing, it provides transfer services to the Mamanucas, the Fijian Resort (on the Queens Road), Pacific Harbour, Suva, Toberua Island Resort and other islands as required. A flight to Malololailai by seaplane costs F$198 return (compared with F$74 by Air Fiji). The charter service costs F$890 per flying hour.

BUS

Fiji's larger islands have an extensive and inexpensive bus network. Catching the local buses is a cheap and fun way to get around, assuming you have the time. While they can be fairly noisy and smoky, they are perfect for the tropics, with unglazed windows and pull-down tarpaulins for when it rains. There are bus stops but you can often just hail buses, especially in rural areas.

Viti Levu's main bus stations are at Lautoka, Nadi and Suva, and express buses operate along the Queens Road and the Kings Road. There are also many bus companies operating on a local level. Even remote inland villages, such as Nadarivatu in Viti Levu's highlands, have regular (though less frequent) services. These trips might take a while, stopping in many villages along the way, but it is an opportunity to mix with the locals. Before heading to an isolated area, make sure you check to see if there is a return bus so that you don't get stranded without any accommodation – often the last bus of the day stays at the final village.

Queens Road Services

The Queens Road has many regular and express services, with some picking up or dropping off at Coral Coast hotels.

Fiji Holiday Connections (☎ 720 977) Suite 8, arrival concourse, Nadi airport. This company operates a minibus shuttle between Nadi and Suva (about 3½ hours) along the Queens Road, and will pick up and drop off travellers at hotels along the Coral Coast. There is also an express service that takes about half an hour less. It has early morning departures from Nadi and departs from Suva in the early afternoon. Book a day in advance. It also has minibuses for hire within Viti Levu.

Pacific Transport Limited (☎ 700 044) Nadi; (☎ 660 499) Lautoka; (☎ 500 088) Sigatoka; (☎ 304 366) Suva and (☎ 880278) Taveuni. Regular buses service Lautoka-Suva (about F$9, six/five hours for regular/express) via the Coral Coast on the Queens Road. The first bus leaves Lautoka at 6.30 am, the last about 5.30 pm. If you are not in a hurry, it's good to have a break along the way and catch another bus an hour or two later. It is generally OK to turn up at the bus station, but you can book in advance for an extra F$0.50. Pacific Transport Limited also runs the Taveuni bus service.

Sunbeam Transport Limited (☎ 662 822) Lautoka and (☎ 382 122) Suva. It has Lautoka-Suva express services via the Queens Road (F$9.70, five hours).

United Touring Fiji (UTC; ☎ 722 811, fax 720 389) Nadi airport and (☎ 312 287) Suva. UTC has a daily express air-con coach service between Nadi and Suva (about F$27, 4½ hours) along the Queens Road, stopping at Nadi airport and the larger hotels along the way. It has daily departures from Nadi about midday, and from Suva around 7.30 am. From Nadi airport to Korolevu costs F$19.

Kings Road Services

The Kings Road route is scenic, especially around Rakiraki and the unsealed section to Korovou.

PVV Tours (☎ 700 600, fax 701 541). PVV provides transport for some of the budget resorts on Nananu-i-Ra (see Rakiraki & Around in the Kings Road section of the Viti Levu chapter).

Sunbeam Transport Limited (☎ 662 822) Lautoka and (☎ 382 122) Suva. It has Lautoka-Suva express services via the Kings Road (F$11, about six hours).

Reservations

Reservations are not necessary for local buses. If you are on a tight schedule or have

an appointment, however, it may be a good idea to buy your ticket in advance, especially for coach trips and tours over longer distances (eg, Suva to Nadi). Pacific Transport and Sunbeam issue timetables, but for most local buses just ask around the bus stations.

CARRIERS & MINIBUSES

Many locals drive small trucks (known as carriers) with a tarpaulin-covered frame on the back. These often have passenger seating and some run trips between Nadi and Suva. You can pick up a ride in main street Nadi. They leave when full and are quicker than taking the bus. Similarly, Viti Minibuses shuttle along the Queens Road between Lautoka (pick up near the bus station) and Suva (pick up near the market), and charge F$10. However, the drivers are notorious for speeding.

TRAIN

The only passenger train is on Viti Levu's Coral Coast between the Fijian Resort and Natadola Beach. It is a scenic jaunt for tourists. For details, see Yanuca & Around in the Queens Road & Coral Coast section of the Viti Levu chapter.

CAR & MOTORCYCLE

Ninety percent of Fiji's 5100km of roads are on Viti Levu and Vanua Levu, of which about one-fifth are sealed. Both of these islands are fun to explore by car.

Road Rules

Driving is on the left-hand side of the road, as in Australia and New Zealand. If you have a licence from an English-speaking country that will suffice, otherwise, you'll need an International Driving Permit. The speed limit is 80km/h and 50km/h in towns. Many villages have speed humps to force drivers to respect the village pace. Seat belts are compulsory for front-seat passengers. Should you pick up a parking fine in Suva it's likely to be only F$2 or so.

As a rule, local drivers are maniacs, often speeding, stopping suddenly and overtaking on blind corners, so take care, especially on gravel roads. Buses also stop where and when they please. There are lots of potholes, and sometimes the roads are too narrow for two vehicles to pass, so be aware of oncoming traffic. Avoid driving at night as there are many pedestrians and wandering animals, especially along the south-east coast of Viti Levu. Watch for sugar trains in the cane-cutting season, as they have right of way. Inquire at the Fiji Visitors Bureau (FVB, see Tourist Offices in the Facts for the Visitor chapter) for further information.

Rental

Rental cars are relatively expensive in Fiji. However, it is a good way to explore the larger islands, especially if you can split the cost with others. Rental motorcycles are uncommon. The perimeter of Viti Levu is easy to get to know by car: The Queens Road and most of the Kings Road are sealed. Most other roads are unsealed and are better for 4WD vehicles.

Some rental agencies will not allow their cars to be driven on unpaved roads, which limits exploration of the highlands. It is possible to take vehicles on roll-on, roll-off ferries to Vanua Levu or Taveuni, but again, some companies do not allow this. It is pretty expensive and vehicles are available on both these islands anyway. If you do take a car on a ferry to Vanua Levu, it's best if it's a 4WD.

The shorter the hire period, the higher the rate. Delivery and collection charges usually apply. Avis Rent A Car rates for three to six days with unlimited travel are F\$99/132 per day for a small car/4WD with air-conditioning. Thrifty Car Rental has cheaper rates for slightly older cars. Some companies will hire at an hourly rate or per half-day, while some have a minimum hire of three days. It's usual to pay a deposit by credit card, although some companies require a minimum cash payment per day as well as a passport-size photograph. Some will give discounts for advance bookings.

A valid overseas or international driving licence is required. Third party insurance is compulsory and personal accident insurance is highly recommended if you are not already covered by travel insurance.

The minimum-age requirement is 21, or in some cases 25.

Ask the FVB about the various companies. Generally, the larger, well-known companies have better cars and support, but are more expensive. The cheaper companies are notorious for providing faulty cars that conk out. Often, when you add up the hidden costs, the price may not be that cheap anyway. Consider what's appropriate for you, including how inconvenienced you might be if the car breaks down, what support services are provided, the likely travel distance, insurance, if value-added tax (VAT) is included and the excess or excess waiver amount (what you pay to waiver paying the excess). Avis has an excess of F\$500 – other companies can be up to F\$1500. Common exclusions, or problems that won't be paid for by the insurance company, include tyre damage, underbody and overhead damage, and theft of the vehicle. Check brakes, water, and tyre pressure and condition before heading off.

The main towns have service stations but fill up the tank before heading inland. If you do run out of fuel, it might be available in village shops. Fuel costs between F\$0.90 and F\$1 per litre.

The easiest place to rent vehicles is on Viti Levu. Most rental agencies have offices at Nadi International Airport; the established companies also have offices in other towns and rental desks at larger hotels.

Car-rental agencies on Viti Levu include:

Avis Rent A Car
Nadi airport: (☎ 722 688, fax 720 482, ✆ aviscarsfj@is.com.fj)
Nausori airport: (☎ 478 963)
Budget Rent a Car
Nadi airport: (☎ 722 735, fax 722 053)
Nausori airport: (☎ 479 299)
Central Rent-a-Car
Nadi airport: (☎ 722 771)
Suva: (☎ 311 866)
Dove Rent a Car
Suva: (☎ 311 755, fax 311 755)
Hertz
Nadi: (☎ 723 466, fax 723 650)
Suva: (☎ 302 186)
Kenns rent-a-car
Nadi airport: (☎ 724 845)
Suva: (☎ 305 429)

Khans Rental Cars
Nadi airport: (☎ 723 506, fax 702 159)
Suva: (☎ 385 033)
Satellite Rentals
Nadi airport: (☎ 721 957)
Nadi: (☎/fax 701 911)
Sharmas Rent-A-Car
Nadi airport: (☎ 721 908)
Nadi: (☎ 701 055, fax 702 038)
Suva: (☎ 314 365)
Thrifty Car Rental
Nadi airport: (☎ 722 755, fax 722 607,
✉ rosiefiji@is.com.fj)
Suva: (☎ 314 436)

Car-rental agencies on Vanua Levu have mostly 4WDs due to the island's rough roads.

Avis Rent A Car
Savusavu: (☎ 850 195, fax 850 430,
✉ aviscarsfj@is.com.fj) Hot Springs Hotel
Budget Rent a Car
Savusavu: (☎ 850 799)
Labasa: (☎ 811 999)

Taveuni has 4WD vehicles available through:

Budget Rent a Car
(☎ 880 297) Naqara

BICYCLE
Fiji's larger islands have good potential for cycling, although some areas are too hilly and rugged. Viti Levu has long, flat stretches of sealed road along the scenic Coral Coast, and it is possible to cycle around the perimeter of the island by the Kings Road and the Queens Road. Take a carrier up to a highland location such as Abaca and ride back down. You could also cycle along Vanua Levu's unsealed roads from Savusavu along Natewa Bay (no accommodation around here) and along the Hibiscus Hwy from Buca Bay, where you can take the ferry over to Taveuni. Ovalau also has a scenic unsealed (mainly flat) coastal road.

The best time to go would be in the 'drier' season. If you intend to do a lot of cycling bring your own bicycle and repair kit. Mountain bikes are best for exploring

the interior. Bicycles can be rented on the Coral Coast, Taveuni and Ovalau, and Independent Tours near Sigatoka runs mountain-bike tours. Rental bikes can be in pretty poor condition, so test the brakes and gears beforehand.

The biggest hazard is the unpredictable traffic – Fijian drivers can be pretty manic. Avoid riding in the evening when visibility is low. Travel light but carry plenty of water – it can be hot and dusty. You can usually buy coconuts and bananas from villages along the way. Storage at Nadi airport is relatively expensive; the cheapest place to store bikes is at backpacker hostels. For more information see Cycling under Activities in the Facts for the Visitor chapter.

HITCHING
Hitching is never entirely safe in any country, and we don't recommend it. Travellers who decide to hitch should understand that they are taking a small but potentially serious risk.

Hitching in Fiji, however, is common. Locals do it all the time, especially with carriers. It is customary to pay the equivalent of the bus fare to the driver. Hitchhikers will be safer if they travel in pairs and let someone know where they are planning to go. Crime is more prevalent around Suva, although there have been cases of hitchhickers being mugged around Nadi.

BOAT
With the exception of the upmarket resort islands, often the only means of transport to and between the islands is by small local boats, especially for the backpacker resorts. Life jackets are rarely provided and usually the boats have no radio-phones. If the weather looks ominous or the boat is overcrowded, consider postponing the trip!

Inter-island trips for sightseeing and catamaran transfers are available in the Mamanucas, and the Yasawas have organised cruises: see these chapters for more details. In most areas, however, it is difficult to explore and hop from island to island unless you have a charter boat or yacht. In Kadavu, for example, transport is mostly by small village or resort boats.

Apart from the Suva-Kadavu ferry, there is no organised transport here and most resorts have their own boats. Similarly, in the Yasawas it is expensive to hop around the islands unless you're on an organised cruise. The backpacker resorts on Waya, Wayasewa and Tavewa transport their guests from Lautoka by small boats.

Ferry

Regular ferry services link Viti Levu to Vanua Levu and Taveuni, and also Viti Levu to Ovalau. See the Fiji map at the beginning of this book for ferry routes. The Patterson Brothers, Beachcomber Cruises and Consort Shipping boats are large roll-on, roll-off ferries, carrying passengers, vehicles and cargo. They have canteens where you can buy drinks, snacks and light meals. Ferry timetables are notorious for changing frequently. Boats sometimes leave at odd hours and there is often a long waiting period at stopovers. The worst thing about the long trips is that the toilets can become disgusting (take your own toilet paper). There are irregular boats that take passengers from Suva to Lau, Rotuma and Kadavu.

Ferry operators include:

Beachcomber Cruises
Lautoka: (☎ 661 500, fax 664 496)
Savusavu: (☎ 850 266, fax 850 499)
Suva: (☎ 307 889, fax 307 359) Taina's Travel Service, Suite 8, Epworth Arcade
Taveuni: (☎ 880 216, fax 880 202) Raj's Tyre Repair, Naqara
Consort Shipping
Savusavu: (☎ 850 279, fax 850 442)
Suva: (☎ 302 877, fax 303 389) Dominion House Arcade, Thomson St
Taveuni: Waiyevo market
Emosi's Shipping
Levuka: (☎ 440 057, 440 013)
Suva: (☎ 313 366) 35 Gordon St
Kadavu Shipping
Suva: (☎ 312 428, 311 766) Rona Street, Walu Bay
Patterson Brothers Shipping
Labasa: (☎ 812 444)
Lautoka: (☎ 661 173)
Levuka: (☎ 440 125)
Savusavu: (☎ 850 161)
Suva: (☎ 315 644, fax 301 652) Suites 1 & 2, Epworth Arcade, Nina St

Taveuni: (☎ 880 382) Lesuma Holdings, Waiyevo
South Sea Cruises
(☎ 750 500, fax 750 501, ☎ southsea@is.com.fj)
The *Yabula*
Taveuni: (☎ 880 134)

Nadi (Denarau Marina)-Mamanucas

South Sea Cruises has a fast catamaran shuttle between Denarau Marina and some of the Mamanuca islands. There is also a catamaran connection to Musket Cove Marina on Malololailai. Refer to Getting Around in the Mamanuca chapter for information on both these services.

Suva-Savusavu-Taveuni Consort Shipping's MV *Spirit of Free Enterprise (SOFE)* does weekly voyages Suva-Koro-Savusavu (F$34/60 for economy/cabin, 13 hours) and Suva-Koro-Savusavu-Taveuni (F$37/70 for economy/cabin, about six hours). The stop at Koro is about one hour and the Suva-Taveuni trip involves a 13-hour stopover in Savusavu.

Beachcomber Cruises' 500-passenger ship the *Adi Savusavu* (previously known as *Dana Star*) has better facilities than the *SOFE* and has Suva-Savusavu voyages three times weekly (F$28/47 for economy/first class, taking about 11 hours). Once a week the ferry continues Savusavu-Taveuni (F$20/28, or F$43/50 from Suva, an extra five hours).

Patterson Brothers also has a once or twice daily (except Sunday) service Savusavu-Buca Bay-Taveuni (F$5.50), involving 1½ hours by bus to Natuvu, Buca Bay, and 1¾ hours by ferry to Waiyevo. There are bus connections to Labasa.

There are also daily (except Sunday) Taveuni-Buca Bay-Savusavu services (F$7) across the Somosomo Strait aboard the *Yabula*, and then by bus (F$2.95). The *Yabula* also does weekly Taveuni-Rabi trips.

Lautoka-Ellington Wharf-Nabouwalu-Labasa Patterson Brothers plies this route three times a week (F$43.10). It involves a bus ride (3½ hours) from Lautoka, a trip on the *Ashika* ferry (3¾ hours) and a trip on another bus to Labasa (four hours).

Suva-Natovi-Nabouwalu-Labasa Patterson Brothers plies this route daily, except Sunday (F$43.00). It involves a bus ride (1½ hours) from Suva, a ferry trip (4½ hours) and another bus to Labasa (four hours).

Suva-Natovi-Buresala-Levuka This Patterson Brothers service (F$23.60), daily except Sunday, involves a bus ride (1½ hours) from Suva to Natovi Landing, followed by a ferry to Buresala Landing (one hour) and another bus to Levuka (one hour).

Suva-Bau Landing-Leleuvia-Levuka Emosi's Shipping has a daily (except Sunday) minibus/small boat service from Suva to Leleuvia via Bau Landing (F$20/40 one way/return). Three times a week the boat continues to Levuka (F$25/50 one way/return).

Suva-Kadavu Kadavu Shipping has irregular passenger services on the MV *Bulou-ni-Ceva* (F$42 one way).

Suva-Rotuma Kadavu Shipping has irregular passenger services on the MV *Bulou-ni-Ceva* (F$90/130 for deck/saloon).

Suva-Lau Group There are several cargo/passenger boats that visit the Lau Group. Vanua Balavu and Lakeba both have budget accommodation, otherwise you need to be invited to stay by a local.

Ika Corporation (☎ 308 169, fax 312 827), Yatulau Arcade, Rodwell Road, Suva. Ika has fortnightly trips from Suva to Cicia, Vanua Balavu, Lakeba, Nayau, Tuvuca and Mago (F$55 one way, excluding meals).
Saliabasaga Shipping (☎ 303 403), GPO Box 14470, Walu Bay, Suva. Saliabasaga has fortnightly trips aboard the MV *Tunatuki* from Narain's Wharf, Walu Bay, to Lakeba, Nayau, Cicia, Tuvuca, Vanua Balavu and occasionally Moce and Oneata (F$66 one way, including meals).
Taikabara Shipping (☎ 302 258, fax 320 251), based at the Muaiwalu Complex, Old Millers wharf, Rona Street, Walu Bay, Suva. Taikabara has fortnightly trips aboard the *Taikabara* to the southern Lau Group. It visits Lakeba, Vanua-vatu, Komo, Kabara, Moce, Fulaga, Namuka, Vatoa, Ogea Levu and Ono-i-Lau (F$66/77 one way for deck/cabin, including meals). It costs an extra F$10 to visit the far south of the group (Vatoa and Ono-i-Lau).

Suva-Moala Group There is no accommodation on the Moala islands – you would need to be invited to stay by a local. Khans Shipping (☎/fax 308 786), PO Box 367, Suva, has almost weekly trips aboard the cargo/passenger boats, the *Te Maori* and *Cagidonu*. They visit Moala, Matuku and Totoya in the Moala Group and Gau and Nairai in the Lomaiviti Group. A one-way fare is F$55, or F$80 for a VIP room.

Yacht
Yachting is a great way to explore the Fiji archipelago. It is possible to charter boats or hitch a ride on cruising vessels. See the Sea section of the Getting There & Away chapter or Activities in the Facts for the Visitor chapter.

LOCAL TRANSPORT
Taxi
You will find taxis on Viti Levu, Vanua Levu, Taveuni and Ovalau. The bus stations in the main towns usually have taxi depots and there is often an oversupply of taxis, with drivers competing for business. There are some good cabs, but most are rickety old dinosaurs bound for or retrieved from the wrecker. Most taxi drivers are Fiji Indians who are keen to discuss life and local politics. They invariably have relatives in Australia, New Zealand or Canada.

Unlike in Suva, taxi drivers in Nadi, Lautoka and most rural areas don't use their meters. First ask locals what is the acceptable rate for a trip. If there is no meter, confirm an approximate price with the driver beforehand. Cabs can be shared for long trips. For touring around areas with limited public transport such as Taveuni, forming a group and negotiating a taxi fee for a half-day or day may be an option.

Always ask if the taxi is a return cab (a taxi returning to its base). If so, you can expect to pay F$1 per person or less (confirm the going rate with locals) as long as the taxi doesn't have to go out of its way. To make up for the low fare, the driver will usually pick up extra passengers from bus stops. You can usually recognise a return cab, as most taxis have the name of their home depot on the bumper bar.

ORGANISED TOURS

Fiji has many companies providing tours within the country, including trekking, cycling, kayaking, diving, bus or 4WD tours. Cruises to the outer islands such as the Mamanucas and Yasawas are popular. Viti Levu has the most tours, and Ovalau, Taveuni and Vanua Levu also have a few. For more information, see Activities in the Facts for the Visitor chapter.

Viti Levu

Viti Levu (Great Fiji) is Fiji's largest island. Approximately 75% of Fiji's total population live here and it is the political, administrative and industrial centre of the archipelago. Viti Levu also has the most extensive transport and communication system of the group.

Geography

The island has an area of approximately 10,400 sq km and is roughly oval in shape, measuring about 146km from east to west and 106km from north to south. The main geographical feature is the mountain range that runs north-south. The highest Fijian peak, Tomanivi (Mt Victoria, 1323m), is near the northern end of the range. On either side of this backbone there are rugged ranges and hills sloping steeply towards the lowland coastal areas. Different areas of the highlands have their own drainage systems: the Colo East Plateau has the Rewa River; the Navua Plateau, to the south, has the Navua River; the Colo West Plateau has the Sigatoka River; and the Navosa Plateau has the Ba River.

Climate

The central highlands lie in the path of the prevailing south-east trade winds, resulting in higher rainfall on the eastern side of the range: Slopes here are predominantly covered by lush vegetation and rainforest. In contrast, the western slopes are mostly open grasslands, which turn light yellow to brown according to the season. See the Facts about Fiji chapter for more information about climate.

Orientation

The country's capital, largest city and main port is Suva on the eastern, wetter side of Viti Levu. The main international airport, however, is on the western, drier side at Nadi, with the city of Lautoka nearby. Nadi and Suva are linked by the sealed Queens Road, along the southern perimeter of Viti

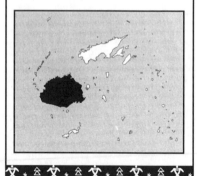

Levu (221km), and Kings Road (mostly sealed), around the northern side of the island (265km). Expect to find lots of people and animals walking on the edge of the roads both day and night. There are regular buses along the Kings and Queens Roads.

There are many minor roads leading to isolated coastal areas or into the Viti Levu highland. Most are unsealed and often too rough for non-4WD vehicles. Sometimes, especially during the wetter season, these roads can become muddy and flooded. Refer to the Viti Levu Highlands section later in this chapter for details.

Nadi and Lautoka are 33km apart on the western coast of Viti Levu. Nadi International Airport is 9km north of Nadi and 24km south of Lautoka. There are a few places of interest in between. Sugar cane, well suited to the hot and relatively dry climate of western Viti Levu, is grown extensively. There is a high proportion of Fiji Indians in the area, who are mostly fourth-generation descendants of indentured labourers brought to Fiji to work in the cane fields (see The Colonial Period under History in the Facts about Fiji chapter).

South of Nadi, the Queens Road winds through cane fields with a few interesting detours, including Momi Bay, Natadola Beach and the Sigatoka Sand Dunes. The Sigatoka River is Fiji's second-largest river and the Sigatoka Valley, which extends into the highlands, is known as Fiji's 'salad bowl'. The Queens Road passes Korotogo and Korolevu along a beautiful stretch of coast. This area is known as the Coral Coast because of its wide fringing reef, broken only by passages adjacent to rivers and streams. Past Korolevu, the Queens Road turns away from the shore and climbs up over the southern end of the main mountain range that divides east and west Viti Levu. Deuba and Pacific Harbour have the last OK beaches before Suva. The islands of Beqa and Yanuca and the Beqa Lagoon are directly offshore.

Heading north from Suva, the Kings Road passes Nausori on the margin of the Rewa River and then heads to Korovou and inland. Another route follows the coast past Natovi Landing, rejoining the Kings Road farther north near Viti Levu Bay, but as this road is unsealed, it's best suited to 4WD. The Kings Road is mostly sealed except for a section of about 56km between Korovou and Dama, but is usually well maintained and suitable for any type of car. We somehow managed to get stuck in a rut though! This stretch passes through more isolated Fijian villages. From Dama the newly sealed road heads down through the hills to Viti Levu Bay and along the coast to Rakiraki, with some spectacular views of the mountains, coast and offshore islands, including Nananu-i-Ra. Just before Tavua is the turn-off to Nadarivatu and Tomanivi. Beyond Tavua the Kings Road becomes less scenic, passing through Ba and sugarcane country and finishing at Lautoka.

Accommodation

On arrival at Nadi airport you will be bombarded with a huge range of accommodation options in the Nadi/Lautoka area. If you haven't already decided where to go, we recommend staying a night or two in Nadi to assess your options and hear other travellers' tales. In Nadi you can either stay downtown, at the 'beach' or close to the airport for convenience while awaiting connections. The town has good restaurants and infrastructure for travellers. Lautoka is quieter and easier to get around. There is also accommodation between the two towns at Vuda Point.

There are also plenty of places to stay along the Queens Road (Coral Coast), and in Fiji's capital, Suva. Along the Kings Road accommodation is relatively sparse. See the respective sections later in this chapter. With the exception of beautiful Natadola Beach and the OK beaches of the Coral Coast, you will have to pay extra for a boat or plane to the offshore and outer islands to find idyllic beaches and peace and quiet.

Getting There & Away

Most travellers arrive in Fiji at Nadi International Airport. Refer to the Getting There & Away chapter for details on airports and airline offices, and for prices of fares. From Nadi there are domestic flights to most other islands. Refer to the Getting Around chapter and individual island chapters for information on inter-island flights and ferry services.

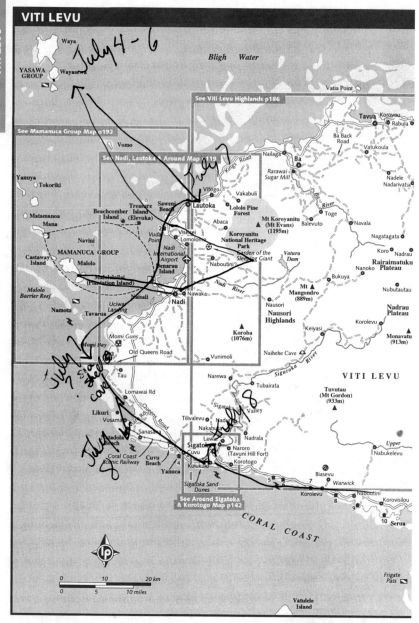

VITI LEVU

Handwritten annotations on map:
July 4 - 6
July 7
July 7 Sleeping Giant cave
July 8

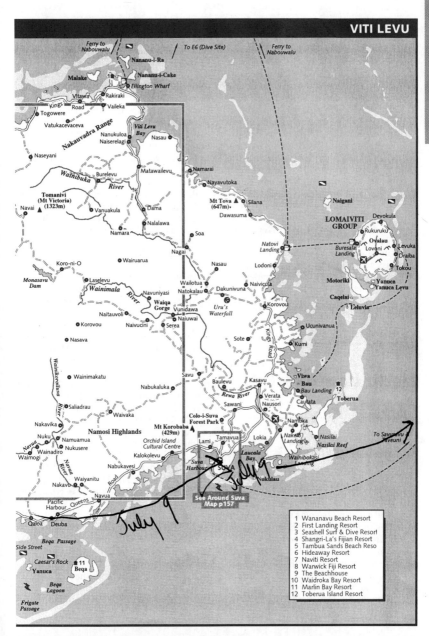

VITI LEVU

1 Wananavu Beach Resort
2 First Landing Resort
3 Seashell Surf & Dive Resort
4 Shangri-La's Fijian Resort
5 Tambua Sands Beach Reso
6 Hideaway Resort
7 Naviti Resort
8 Warwick Fiji Resort
9 The Beachhouse
10 Waidroka Bay Resort
11 Marlin Bay Resort
12 Toberua Island Resort

Getting Around

There are regular domestic flights by light plane between Nadi and Suva, costing from F$86 to F$103. To get to and from Nadi International Airport, see under Air in the Getting There & Away chapter earlier in this book. Local buses are a cheap and are an interesting way to get around the islands, and Viti Levu has a good bus network with many different bus companies operating on a local level. Express buses link the main centres along the Queens and Kings Roads. The main bus stations are at Lautoka, Nadi and Suva. There are also minibuses and carriers (small trucks carrying passengers) shuttling at regular intervals along the Queens Road. Taxis are plentiful, but drivers don't always use meters, so always remember to confirm the price in advance. Viti Levu is also easy to explore by car, but be careful of local drivers, as they can drive rather erratically at times. You may find it preferable to travel by bus, as this means you get to mix with the locals. See the Getting Around chapter for a list of car-rental and bus companies and for details of the road rules.

Nadi, Lautoka & Around

NADI
pop 30,884

Nadi (pronounced **nan**-di) is Fiji's third-largest city and is the country's tourism hub. While not all that appealing, it is a convenient base to organise your trip around Viti Levu or to the islands. There are organised day trips that pick up participants from Nadi hotels. Nadi has heaps of places to stay, from budget dorms to luxury resort hotels on Denarau Island. Its main street is packed with restaurants and duty-free and souvenir shops. The Swami Temple at the southern end of the main street is worth a visit, as is the produce market. To the east lie the beautiful Nausori Highlands and to the north the Sabeto mountain range.

Orientation

The Queens Road heads south from Lautoka into Nadi, passing Nadi airport (9km north of Nadi town) and crossing the Nadi River. The road becomes Nadi's main street. Turn right at the T-junction and the Queens Road continues to Suva, while to the left the Nadi Back Rd bypasses the busy centre and rejoins the Queens Road back near the airport. The road to the Nausori Highlands leads off into the mountains from the Nadi Back Rd.

The market, bus station, post office and telephone exchange are downtown to the east of the main street.

Between the mosque and the Nadi River bridge, just north of town, Narewa Rd leads west to Denarau Island, 6km off the Queens Road. The 255-hectare island is reclaimed mangrove swamp and has dark-sand beaches, which may be disappointing for some. It has Nadi's two most upmarket resorts and the Denarau Golf & Racquet Club (see Activities later in this section). Most tours and boat services to the Mamanuca islands depart from Denarau Marina.

Wailoaloa Rd also turns west off the Queens Road (to the right if you are coming from the airport) near West's Motor Inn. Wailoaloa Beach is about 1.75km from the highway. To get to Newtown Beach turn right off Wailoaloa Rd after 1.25km and continue for another 1.25km. Here there are several budget places to stay, a golf course and the Turtle Airways seaplane base. You can also get to Wailoaloa Beach along Enamanu Rd.

Information

Tourist Offices The Fiji Visitors Bureau (FVB; ☎ 722 433, fax 720 141, ✉ fvbnadi@is.com.fj) is a good information source for travellers. The office is at Nadi airport. It is open to meet all international flights and is a great source of information. The office has an heaps of brochures but if you tell the staff what you are after you are more likely to obtain useful information. Take a look at the visitors' comments book. Places other than the FVB claiming to be 'tourist information centres' are actually travel agents.

Money The ANZ bank at the airport is open 24 hours daily. It charges F$2 per transaction to change foreign currency and travellers cheques. The ANZ, Westpac, Bank of Hawaii and National Bank are on the Main St in Nadi and do not charge transaction fees. There is a Thomas Cook money exchange bureau on the main street (near the Mobil petrol station), which is open from 9 am to 5 pm weekdays and from 8.30 am to noon Saturdays. Many hotels exchange cash and travellers cheques, but often they pay a little less than the banks.

Post & Communications The post office and the telephone exchange are in downtown Nadi near the market. There is also a post office at Nadi airport, across the car park from the arrivals area near the cargo sheds. Public cardphones are not usually too hard to find. See Post & Communications in the Facts for the Visitor chapter for phonecard information.

Email & Internet Access Bedarra House Booking Office (☎ 725 130, fax 725 131, @ bedarra@is.com.fj), on Queens Rd in Martinar next to the Bounty restaurant, has

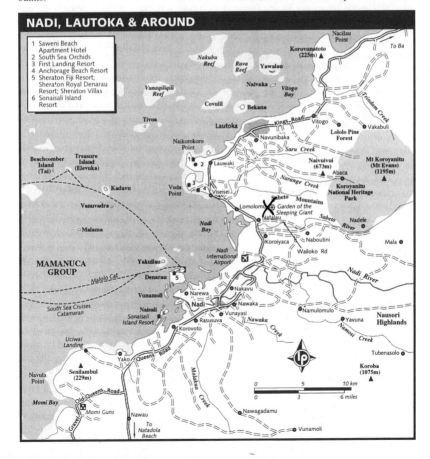

NADI, LAUTOKA & AROUND

1 Saweni Beach
  Apartment Hotel
2 South Sea Orchids
3 First Landing Resort
4 Anchorage Beach Resort
5 Sheraton Fiji Resort;
  Sheraton Royal Denarau
  Resort; Sheraton Villas
6 Sonaisali Island
  Resort

VITI LEVU

email and Internet access. It is open from 9am to 5pm. The West Coast Cafe, across the road, also has email and Internet services and stays open until 10 pm.

Travel Agencies Nadi has a plethora of travel agencies. Most are at the Nadi International Airport arrivals area on the ground and 1st floors. It is a good idea to have a look at the FVB, an independent organisation, before booking anything with the agents, who receive commissions from different places. Some specialise in budget accommodation and offer good deals, but be careful with the arrangements and forms of payment. Avoid paying too much money upfront for your trip or tour, and get information on details such as: the safety of the transport, especially if it includes small-boat trips; the cleanliness and facilities; the type and price of food available; and any hidden costs. If possible, quiz other travellers or browse through the FVB comments book to get the current picture of a place.

Agents include:

Margaret Travel Service
   (☎ 721 988, fax 721 992) Nadi airport concourse
Rosie, The Travel Service
   Fiji: (☎ 722 935, fax 722 607) Nadi airport concourse
   Australia: (☎ 02-9389 3666, fax 9369 1129) East Towers, 9 Bronte Rd, Bondi Junction, Sydney, NSW 2022
Tourist Information Centre
   (☎ 700 243, fax 702 746) on the corner of Market Rd and Main St, Nadi. Note that this is *not* independent tourist information!

Bookshops Nadi has few bookshops. Your best option is the handicraft shops at the airport, downtown and the hotels. Paper Power in the Town Council Arcade (Civic Centre) also has a limited selection.

Medical Services For medical treatment, contact:

Dr Ram Raju Surgical Clinic (☎ 700 240, 976 333) 2 Lodhia St, Nadi
Nadi Hospital (☎ 701 128) Market Rd, Nadi

Namaka Medical Centre (☎ 722 288) on the corner of Queens Road and Namaka Lane, Namaka

Emergency Emergency phone numbers include:

Emergency	(☎ 000)
Fiji Visitors Bureau emergency hotline	(☎ 0800 721 721)
Police	(☎ 700 222)
Ambulance	(☎ 701 128)

Dangers & Annoyances The only annoyance in Nadi is the sporadic pestering by souvenir and duty-free vendors. You may also come across sword sellers. Fiji is a relatively safe place to travel, however, there are occasional muggings and thefts in the Nadi area, even during daylight. These incidents are not limited to lone travellers. Avoid walking along quiet roads such as Wailoaloa Rd or even the road to Denarau Island, as well as the stretch along the Queens Road from downtown Nadi north to Kennedy Ave. Leave valuables at your hotel and if you are carrying a pack it may be best to take a bus or taxi.

Sri Siva Subramaniya Swami Temple

At the southern end of Nadi's main street, set against a beautiful mountain backdrop, is a large, elaborate and colourful Hindu temple (☎ 700 016, fax 703 777). Before it was built, devotees worshipped at this site in a small *bure* (thatched dwelling).

The Hindu Lord Shiva takes on various forms, all incarnations being manifestations of the One Supreme Lord. This is a Murugan temple and worship of Lord Murugan is equivalent to the worship of nature. He is the guardian deity of the seasonal rains.

Visitors are welcome but are requested to wear neat and modest dress, and to have consumed no alcohol or nonvegetarian food that day. The temple is open 5 am to 8 pm daily, though it is closed from 1 to 3.30 pm weekdays. There is a devotees' lunch on Sunday. Annual festivals such as Karthingai Puja (23 March), Panguni Uthiram

NADI

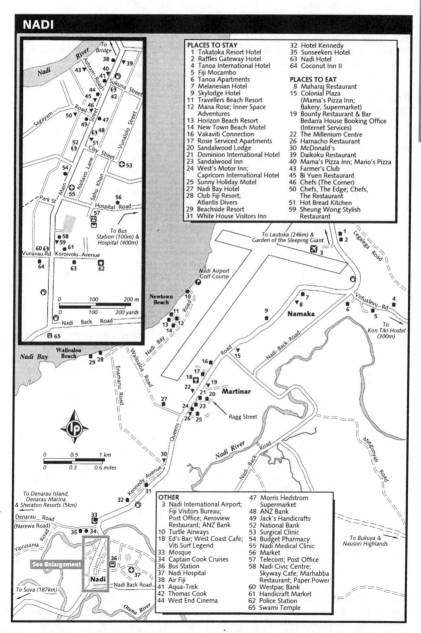

PLACES TO STAY
1 Tokatoka Resort Hotel
2 Raffles Gateway Hotel
4 Tanoa International Hotel
5 Fiji Mocambo
6 Tanoa Apartments
7 Melanesian Hotel
9 Skylodge Hotel
11 Travellers Beach Resort
12 Mana Rose; Inner Space
    Adventures
13 Horizon Beach Resort
14 New Town Beach Motel
16 Vakaviti Connection
17 Rosie Serviced Apartments
20 Sandalwood Lodge
21 Dominion International Hotel
23 Sandalwood Inn
24 West's Motor Inn;
    Capricorn International Hotel
25 Sunny Holiday Motel
27 Nadi Bay Hotel
28 Club Fiji Resort;
    Atlantis Divers
29 Beachside Resort
31 White House Visitors Inn

32 Hotel Kennedy
35 Sunseekers Hotel
63 Nadi Hotel
64 Coconut Inn II

PLACES TO EAT
8 Maharaj Restaurant
15 Colonial Plaza
    (Mama's Pizza Inn;
    Bakery, Supermarket)
19 Bounty Restaurant & Bar
    Bedarra House Booking Office
    (Internet Services)
22 The Millenium Centre
26 Hamacho Restaurant
30 McDonald's
39 Daikoku Restaurant
40 Mama's Pizza Inn; Mario's Pizza
43 Farmer's Club
45 Bi Yuen Restaurant
46 Chefs (The Corner)
50 Chefs, The Edge; Chefs,
    The Restaurant
51 Hot Bread Kitchen
59 Sheung Wong Stylish
    Restaurant

OTHER
3 Nadi International Airport;
   Fiji Visitors Bureau;
   Post Office; Aeroview
   Restaurant; ANZ Bank
18 Ed's Bar; West Coast Cafe;
    Viti Surf Legend
33 Mosque
34 Captain Cook Cruises
36 Bus Station
37 Nadi Hospital
38 Air Fiji
41 Aqua-Trek
42 Thomas Cook
44 West End Cinema

47 Morris Hedstrom
    Supermarket
48 ANZ Bank
49 Jack's Handicrafts
52 National Bank
53 Surgical Clinic
54 Budget Pharmacy
55 Nadi Medical Clinic
56 Market
57 Telecom; Post Office
58 Nadi Civic Centre;
    Skyway Cafe; Marhabba
    Restaurant; Paper Power
60 Westpac Bank
61 Handicraft Market
62 Police Station
65 Swami Temple

To Lautoka (24km) &
Garden of the Sleeping Giant

Nadi Airport
Golf Course

Newtown
Beach

Namaka

To
Kon Tiki Hostel
(300m)

Nadi Bay

Wailoaloa
Beach

Nadi Bay

Martinar

Ragg Street

Nadi River

To Bukuya &
Nausori Highlands

To Denarau Island,
Denarau Marina
& Sheraton Resorts (5km)

Denarau
(Narewa Road)

Yavusania

See Enlargement

Nadi

Nadi Back Road

To Suva (187km)

Otuna River

To Bus
Station (100m) &
Hospital (400m)

Vunavau Rd   Koroivolu   Avenue

To
Bridge

River

Nadi

Adiram Road

Sukuna Street

Vunatolo Street

Sagayam   Road   Street

Clay Street

Main   Naitavo Lane

Sahu Khan

Park St

Hospital Road

Nadi   Back   Road

Thiru-naal (1 to 3 April) and Thai Pusam attract devotees from around the world. The temple has four full-time priests who perform eight pujas (prayers) daily and, for a fee, are available for home and vehicle blessings.

Activities

Diving Inner Space Adventures (☎/fax 723 883) near the Travellers Beach Resort offers good-value budget dive trips to the Mamanuca sites. It charges F$85 for a two-tank dive trip, which includes all gear, lunch and a transfer from hotels in the Nadi area. Open-water certification costs F$320.

Atlantis Divers (☎ 702 704, fax 702 921) at Wailoaloa Beach in the Club Fiji Resort also picks up guests from Nadi hotels for dive trips to the Mamanucas. It charges F$99 for two-tank dive trips and F$420 for open-water courses.

Alternatively, Dive Tropex (☎ 701 888), based at Sheraton Fiji Resort on Denarau Island, has better and faster boats and covers a wider range of dive sites in the Mamanucas. A two-tank dive trip costs F$141, F$614 for open-water certification.

Aqua-Trek (☎ 702 413, fax 702 4120), one the largest dive operations in Fiji, has a shop at 465 Main St, Nadi, but it does not have organised diving excursions from Nadi.

River Rafting Rivers Fiji is based at Pacific Harbour, but does pick up from Nadi hotels. It offers interesting river-rafting trips to the Namosi Highlands. See under Namosi Highlands in the Viti Levu Highlands section later in this chapter.

Jet-Boat Trips The New Zealand company Shotover Jet Fiji (☎ 750 400, fax 750 666) has a noisy, hair-raising jet-boat trip (F$59/25 per adult/child, half hour) of the Nadi River mangroves. The jet boats carry 12 passengers, are powered by 8L V8 engines and are designed to speed on as little as 10 cm of water. The drivers are trained to perform 360° spins and frighteningly close shaves. A similar trip operates in Queenstown, New Zealand. It departs from Denarau Marina and there's a courtesy minibus for transfers from hotels.

Mountain Biking If you feel like a day trip from Nadi, Independent Tours (☎/fax 520 678), based in Korotogo, near Sigatoka, has guided bike tours for groups of two to six people, as well as bike hire. See Korotogo & Around in the Queens Road & Coral Coast section of the Viti Levu chapter for more information.

Golf & Tennis The Denarau Golf & Racquet Club (☎ 750 477, fax 750 484) caters mainly for guests of the Sheraton hotels. It has an 18-hole golf course with bunkers in the shape of sea creatures. Green fees are F$81 for 18 holes and F$49 for nine holes. The all-weather and grass tennis courts fees are F$18 per hour and racket hire is F$8 per person.

A much cheaper alternative is the Nadi Airport Golf Club (☎ 722 148), which is open daily during daylight hours. It is near Turtle Airways at Newtown Beach. Green fees here are F$15 for 18 holes. It is F$20 to rent a full set of clubs and F$5 for a pull-cart.

Organised Tours

Cruises to the Mamanucas & Yasawas

Cruises to the stunning Mamanuca and Yasawa islands are very popular. Most leave from Nadi's Denarau Marina or Lautoka's Queens Wharf. Half- and full-day cruises are available to the Mamanucas: operators include Beachcomber Cruises, South Seas Cruises, Captain Cook Cruises and the Whale's Tale. Longer cruises to the Yasawas are offered by Blue Lagoon Cruises and Captain Cook Cruises. See the Yasawa Group and Mamanuca Group chapters for more information. Malololailai, Mana and Castaway islands take day-trippers.

Scenic Flights Most domestic flights are scenic, especially on a clear day. Easy day trips include Nadi to Malololailai and Mana in the Mamanucas with Air Fiji or Sunflower Airlines. The islands, coral reefs and depths of blues and greens are gorgeous from above – snorkellers and divers will drool at the sight. Flights over the Nausori Highlands and the Sigatoka Valley are also spectacular.

Turtle Airways (☎ 721 888, fax 720 095, ℮ southseaturtle@is.com.fj), based at Newtown Beach, Nadi, has a fleet of Cessna seaplanes, which can carry up to four passengers (departing from Newtown Beach or the resorts on Denarau). It also provides scenic flights as well as transfers. The charter service is F$890 per flying hour.

Island Hoppers (☎ 720 410, fax 720 172, ℮ islandhoppers@is.com.fj) has an office at Nadi airport and offers helicopter flights departing from Denarau Island. A 20-minute flight over the Sabeto mountain range and the gorges of Mt Evans, east of Lautoka, costs F$133 per person. The 'Islands & Highlands' trip is F$224 per person (for a trip lasting 35 minutes). A 'Tag-a-Long Tour' joins transfer guests to one of the offshore islands and costs F$35 (40 to 60 minutes).

Motorcycle Touring Motor Bike Tours Fiji (☎ 722 900, fax 722 983, ℮ mihajoltd@is.com.fj) offers a half-day off-road ride into the interior from Nadi for F$249, including lunch. It also has a four-day bike-and-dive package for F$1999, which includes a ride to Natovi landing via the Queens Road, ferry trip to Ovalau with the bikes, rides and two days diving in Ovalau, ferry trip back to Natovi landing and return ride to Nadi via Viti Levu's Kings Road.

Visiting the Interior See the Viti Levu Highlands section later in this chapter for information on visiting the mountains independently. Koroyanitu National Heritage Park is an easy day trip from Lautoka. Organised tours can also be an OK way to have a look at the high country and visit interior villages. Rivers Fiji has rafting on the Navua River (see Namosi Highlands in the Viti Levu Highlands section of this chapter). Adventures in Paradise offers 'Cannibal Cave and Waterfall' day tours on the Coral Coast, where it is based, and often collect guests from Nadi hotels. Independent Tours has guided bike tours to the highlands (see Korotogo & Around in the Queens Road & Coral Coast section later in this chapter). Rosie Tours (also known as Adventure Tours, ☎ 722 755, fax 722 607) has daily (except Sunday) full-day trekking to the Nausori Highlands from Nadi for F$58 including lunch. It also offers more expensive six-day, five-night tours to the central highlands.

Traditional Vale & Bure

A traditional family house was called a *vale*, while men's houses were known as *bure*.

These buildings were dark and smoky inside, with no windows and usually only one low door. Vale had hearth pits where the women cooked, and the earth floor was covered with grass or fern

leaves and then pandanus leaf or coarse coconut-leaf mats. Sleeping compartments were at one end, behind a bark-cloth curtain. People slept on finely woven mats and wooden headrests. Coconut-fibre string was used for lashing and decorating the timber roof structure.

Bure and vale were mostly rectangular, but in western Viti Levu some were round or, later, square with conical roofs supported on a central post (thought to be a New Caledonian influence). In eastern Fiji, rounded gables were a Tongan influence.

Most villages still have some traditional houses; however, the majority of Fijians now live in simple, rectangular houses built with industrialised materials.

Traditional *bure* near the town of Cuata on Viti Levu

CHRIS MELLOR

Places to Stay – Budget

Consider whether you want the convenience of staying close to downtown (where there are lots of places to eat), at the black-sand Wailoaloa Beach (fairly isolated but peaceful) or along the Queens Road between the airport and downtown Nadi. Proximity to the airport will affect the level of aircraft noise. The only place that allows camping is Sunny Holiday Motel.

Note that some places get a commission for selling travellers certain tours. Most places have free airport transfers.

Along the Highway The Martinar suburb, halfway between Nadi and the airport along the Queens Road, is becoming a good area to stay, with a number of services close by.

There are two budget places to stay on Kennedy Ave, parallel to the Queens Road. Both of these hotels are within a 15-minute walk from downtown; however, there have been muggings along this stretch in the past so avoid walking in the dark by yourself, especially if carrying packs. Consider catching the bus or a taxi: The ride should cost around F$2.

White House Visitor's Inn (☎ 700 022, fax 702 822, 40 Kennedy Ave) is recommended as it is reasonably clean and has a friendly atmosphere. Small four- or five-bed fan-cooled dorms cost F$11 per bed. Fan-cooled rooms with en suite cost F$33/44 for singles/doubles, air-con double rooms cost F$49.50. A twin room with shared toilet and bathroom costs F$25. A simple breakfast (toast and coffee) is included in the price and there is a communal kitchen. There is also a small swimming pool and the restaurant serves Chinese meals for F$6 to F$14.

Hotel Kennedy (☎ 702 360, fax 702 218), on Kennedy Ave, is a 10-minute walk from downtown. It is clean and reasonably maintained but in need of some redecoration. Fan-cooled standard rooms are F$35 single or double and deluxe air-con rooms cost F$50/55. An apartment with two bedrooms and cooking facilities costs F$99. Dorm beds cost F$12 each, or three people can share a room for F$25. There is a restaurant and karaoke bar, a gym and swimming pool.

The budget rooms at *West's Motor Inn* on the Queens Road and *Raffles Gateway Hotel* opposite the airport can be good options (see Places to Stay – Mid-Range later in this section). Next door, the *Sandalwood Inn* (☎ 722 044, fax 720 103, ✉ sandalwood@is.com.fj), on the corner of Ragg St, was once a nice little hotel but is now getting a bit shabby. Nevertheless, it still has a Fijian atmosphere, a reasonable restaurant, and a swimming pool. Fan-cooled rooms with shared bathroom cost F$28.60/35.20. Rooms with en suite, fans and fridge cost F$35.20/41.80, while air-con rooms are F$55/62. All rooms have tea- and coffee-making facilities.

Sandalwood Lodge, 200m farther down Ragg St, is better maintained with good-value self-contained units with small kitchen, TV, phone, private balcony and a cute swimming pool for F$70/77/83 for singles/doubles/triples. The family room is spacious with one double and four single beds.

Sunny Holiday Motel (☎ 722 158, fax 701 541), on Northern Press Rd, near the Hamacho Restaurant, is a bit of a dump and best avoided unless you are camping, in which case you can use its front lawn for F$2.50. Dorm beds are F$6; the downstairs dorm is stuffy with no external window, but the upstairs room is a bit better. Although it describes itself as a youth hostel it is not affiliated with Hostelling International. Rooms with share facilities cost F$15/20, or with private facilities F$22/27. A self-contained apartment with cooking facilities is F$35.

Nadi Bay Hotel (☎ 723 599, fax 720 092, ✉ nadibay@is.com.fj), on Wailoaloa Rd about 400m off the Queens Road, is a good option for budget accommodation. Dorm beds are F$12 in a 10-bed room; try the one upstairs, which may get more light and breezes. Rooms with shared facilities are F$35/45, with private bathroom F$56/68. Two-bedroom air-con apartments cost F$68/82. Rooms are reasonably clean and have fans but no cooking facilities. The hotel has a pleasant outdoor sitting area, a swimming pool and a reasonably priced restaurant. Credit cards are accepted.

Melanesian Hotel (☎ 722 438, fax 720 425), on the Queens Road in Namaka, is about three-minutes' drive (F$3 taxi) or a short bus ride east of the airport. It has OK three- or four- bed dorms for F$14 per bed, with a small breakfast. Standard rooms have three beds and a fan for F$33/40, or with air-con and TV for F$43/50. There is a swimming pool, and a small restaurant with meals for about F$8.50.

Kon Tiki (☎ 722 836) is a backpacker hostel near Nadi airport. Turn off the Queens Road at the first roundabout south of the airport, continue along Votualevu Rd for 1.3km and then turn right and travel for 100m. It is pretty hidden, on the hill to the right. A dorm bed here costs F$8 (no fan). Rooms with en suites for F$20/27.50 are clean and OK value. There is a grotty communal kitchen and meals can be provided. The main drawback here is that it is quite a long way to restaurants and supermarkets. It has free transfers to international flights and daily transfers to Kon Tiki Lodge on Nananu-i-Ra.

A new budget option is *Vakaviti Connection (☎ 724 505, @ bulavakaviti@is.com.fj)* on the Queens Road in Martinar opposite St Mary's School. It has one double room for F$30 as well as two four-bed dorms costing F$12 per bed upstairs in a double-storey house near the road. Accommodation is very simple, but is clean and airy with a large kitchen.

Rosie Serviced Apartments (☎ 722 755, fax 722 607), on the Queens Road, look fairly unattractive from the outside but can be a cheap way to stay in Nadi if you are in a small group or family. It's on the roadside and the self-contained apartments are up two flights of stairs. They are spacious (sleeping four) with cooking facilities and dated decor.

At the Beach There are six budget places to stay at Newtown and Wailoaloa beaches on Nadi Bay. It is an alternative to staying in the bustling town, however, the Nadi Bay beaches are fairly unattractive: Dark sand, no coral and shallow waters for swimming. Another disadvantage of staying here is that food and transport are limited. Ring ahead

to check availability of accommodation. To get to town you can catch a local bus (F$0.50) or taxi for about F$3 (although they will try to charge F$5). A taxi to the airport costs F$7 but normally the resorts have free airport transfers. Buses depart from Wailoaloa Beach for town every hour till 11.30 am and less frequently in the afternoon until the last one at 4.30 pm. Boats leave from here to the backpacker 'resorts' on Mana in the Mamanucas.

Horizon Beach Resort (☎ 722 832, fax 720 662, 10 Wasawasa Rd) has friendly staff and a small swimming pool. Dorm rooms cost F$10 per person and can get crowded, but are usually clean and have hot showers. Fan-cooled rooms are F$28/30 for singles/doubles, but seaview air-con rooms are bigger and better value for F$37/40. There are no cooking facilities, and meals cost around F$6/9 for lunch/dinner. You can use its washing machine for F$5 per load.

New Town Beach Motel (☎ 723 339, fax 720 087, 5 Wasawasa Rd) is quieter and more homey. Its fan-cooled, five-bed dorm costs F$13.70 per person, and double rooms cost F$38. Meals are F$6/8 for lunch/dinner. It has a swimming pool and deck in the back garden.

Mana Rose (☎ 721 959) is a double-storey house with a six-bed dorm for F$11 per person. A fan-cooled double room with en suite is F$33. Prices include breakfast. There are pleasant communal sitting areas and a balcony, and a kitchen and laundry for guests' use. Airport transfers are included.

Travellers Beach Resort (☎ 723 322, fax 720 026) is the largest place in this area but it has the least atmosphere. The dorm rooms are OK and sleep a maximum of four for F$11 per person. Standard rooms with fans cost F$33/38.50 or F$38.50/49.50 with air-con, but it is possible to bargain. There are also kitchenette villas with fans, microwave and TV, which sleep four people, for F$66. The hotel has a restaurant, a small pool and a deck on the beach. It accepts Visa and MasterCard.

Club Fiji Resort (☎ 702 189, fax 720 350) on Wailoaloa Beach is farther south.

It has more of a resort feel, but it's a bit misplaced on this stretch of dark sand on the edge of the mangroves. It's not a destination in itself, however, it's not a bad stopover while awaiting a flight. There are 24 fan-cooled bure; you pay extra for the sea breeze. Prices are F$85.80/66/42.90 for beachfront/oceanview/garden bure. The newer beachfront rooms in a double-storey block at the south end of the resort are good. Here you'll get a fan, fridge, balcony and bay views for F$132 a double. Dorm beds are F$11/14.85 per person without/with breakfast. The resort has a tour desk, a large bar-restaurant bure (meals F$9 to F$20), a small pool and a diving operation. There is a daily shuttle bus to downtown Nadi at 10 am, returning at 1 pm, or a taxi ride costs F$5.

Also on Wailoaloa Beach is the newer **Beachside Resort** (✆ 703 488, 703 688, ✉ beachsideresort@is.com.fj). It is 80m back from the beach and offers 15 air-con rooms in a double-storey building next to the swimming pool, and three family bure with two bedrooms each. Air-con rooms with balconies cost F$88/98 a double/triple per night (an extra rollaway bed can be supplied for a second child) and up to two children under 12 years are free. Meals cost F$10 for breakfast, or a meal package including breakfast and a two-course dinner costs F$40/25 per adult/child.

Downtown Nadi *Sunseekers Hotel* (✆ 700 400) is conveniently located near the north end of town on the Narewa Rd to Denarau. While not strictly downtown, it is only a few minutes' walk away, over the bridge. The hotel houses up to 100 guests, but is reasonably clean and organised and a good option for budget travellers. Dorm beds cost F$8.80 a night. Fan-cooled private rooms are F$27 to F$38.50. Some rooms have a private toilet and shower. There is also a small shop, tourist information, a bar, an outdoor deck with tables, a swimming pool and a small restaurant serving snacks all day (F$5 for dinner).

Coconut Inn II in Vunavau Rd has little atmosphere. It charges F$11 per person in the dorm or F$25/40 for fan cooled singles/doubles with no external window. There are better air-con rooms on the roof terrace, which have more light, for F$30 a double.

Nadi Hotel (✆ 700 000, fax 700 280), on Koroivolu Ave, is right in town near the post office, market and bus station. It offers budget accommodation in a double-storey building with a garden and swimming pool. The male and female dorms are on opposite sides of the pool and are not bad for F$15. Standard fan-cooled rooms are OK but a bit musty; they cost F$35/40. Dingy air-con rooms in the old building are F$45/50. Pay a bit more (F$50/60) for the deluxe versions in the newer building, though it can be noisy with the disco next door. The restaurant, also open for outsiders, has sandwiches for F$4.50 and a grill of the day for F$6.50.

Places to Stay – Mid-Range

Most of the mid-range hotels are located on the Queens Road near the airport, an important consideration given the early morning departure times of many international flights. Most have courtesy airport transfers. The disadvantage is their distance from most restaurants and entertainment. If they don't appear busy, ask about reduced 'walk-in rates'. Day rooms (for those awaiting night-time flights) are usually about half-price.

Raffles Gateway Hotel (✆ 722 444, fax 720 620), directly opposite the airport, is convenient and good value with a pleasant garden and a pool-side bar. Standard air-con budget rooms are F$44 for doubles (rooms upstairs are better). There are also more spacious deluxe rooms for F$116.60. Up to two children under 16 years can share with parents for free. Day rooms cost F$50 for a maximum of six hours between 6 am and 6 pm. Restaurant meals cost around F$15.

Tokatoka Resort Hotel (✆ 720 222, fax 720 400, ✉ tokatokaresort@is.com.fj) has 74 villa-style units, ranging from studios and villa studios for F$137/151 for doubles/up to four people, better-value villa apartments for F$193 (up to four) and full villas (up to seven) for F$307. All units have cooking facilities. The atmosphere and facilities are good for families and it has a great swimming pool with water slide, a pleasant garden, a small supermarket and conference facilities. The pool-side restaurant-bar has lunch for around F$12 and dinner for F$19 to F$24. Child-minding is F$3.50 per hour. It has good disabled and pram access.

Skylodge Hotel (☎ 722 200, fax 724 330) has been renovated and now belongs to the Tanoa group of hotels. It has pitch-and-putt golf, minitennis and a swimming pool. Air-con rooms in the building near reception start at F$104 (up to four people). They are quite comfortable with TV, fridge and en suite; some have kitchens. Cottages are spaced around the garden. Self-contained units are F$131 each and are available for long-term rental. Security may be a problem as there is no check at the gate and reception is at the end of the road, although there is a guard at night.

Dominion International Hotel (☎ 722 255, fax 720 187, *@ dominionint@is.com.fj*) is on the Queens Road about 4.5km from Nadi airport. Standard air-con rooms (called superior) cost F$110/115/125 for singles/doubles/triples, but deluxe versions are better value at F$130/135/145. Children under 12 years occupying a separate room are half-price. Amenities include a swimming pool and tennis courts, and there is a *meke* (dance performance that enacts stories and legends) on Saturday night. Meals at the restaurant cost F$6 to F$12 for lunch and F$12.50 to F$29.50 for dinner.

West's Motor Inn (☎ 720 044, fax 720 071, *@ westsmotorin@is.com.fj*), on the Queens Road and previously known as the Westin Plaza Hotel, has been refurbished recently and is friendly and good value. Standard rooms with air-con, ceiling fan, tea- and coffee-making facilities and a fridge cost F$55 for singles or doubles. The more spacious deluxe versions around the swimming pool and courtyard have TV and cost F$99. Discounted walk-in rates may apply. The hotel has a bar and restaurant offering OK meals (dinner mains F$14 to F$19.50).

Capricorn International Hotel (☎ 720 088, fax 720 522), just south of West's Motor Inn on the Queens Road, offers OK-value mid-range accommodation and has nice gardens. Rooms cost F$85 to F$135. It has a shop, dining room and bar and a garden.

Places to Stay – Top End
Near the Airport There are two expensive hotels near the airport, both offering pretty standard rooms without much character. Both also have swimming pools and 24-hour cafes.

The 128-room *Fiji Mocambo* (☎ 722 000, fax 720 324, *@ mocambo@is.com.fj*) is managed by Shangri-la Hotels, but don't expect the same standards here. It is in the Namaka Hills, a few minutes' drive south-east of the airport. Rooms have air-con, TV and refrigerator, most with mountain views. Standard (called superior) rooms cost F$186/198 for singles/doubles. There are also corporate rates. The hotel has a nine-hole golf course, tennis courts, and live bands Wednesday to Saturday nights.

Tanoa International Hotel (☎ 720 277, fax 720 191, *@ tanoahotels@is.com.fj*) used to be a Travelodge but is now locally owned. Air-con studio (superior) rooms are F$180/200 for doubles/deluxe rooms. Interconnecting rooms are available. The restaurant has dinner for F$16 to F$32 and lunches for F$9 to F$16. Amenities include a fitness centre and a convention centre.

Tanoa Apartments (☎ 723 685, fax 721 193, *@ tanoahotels@is.com.fj*), on the hill above the roundabout just south of the airport, has 23 self-contained and serviced apartments. It has great mountain views and a swimming pool. Rates are F$164 for a deluxe bedroom or F$220 for an apartment with three bedrooms. Some units accommodate up to six people. Weekly and non-serviced long-term rates are negotiable.

Denarau Island *Sheraton Royal Denarau Resort* (☎ 750 000, fax 750 259), previously the Regent Fiji, was Fiji's first luxury hotel. It has 273 rooms in spacious grounds. Prices start at F$402 for garden-view rooms to F$633 for beachfront rooms.

Sheraton Fiji Resort (☎ 750 777, fax 750 818) has 292 rooms, all with ocean views, from F$534 to F$727 for singles or doubles. While Sheraton Royal has a traditional feel with buildings blending in with luxuriant gardens, Sheraton Fiji has more of a modern Mediterranean style. Prices quoted are rack rates (normal prices without discounts): there are seasonal price variations and most people arrange some sort of package deal or discount.

The new *Sheraton Villas (☎ 750 777, fax 750 818)*, part of the Sheraton resorts, are a very good option if you prefer a self-contained apartment. There are nice new villas with two and three bedrooms. Prices per night range from F$450 to F$1400.

Denarau Island is a reclaimed mangrove area and the beach has dark-grey sand, which may be disappointing for some. It is an up-market world in itself, with many restaurants, bars, shops, a golf and tennis club, archery and lawn-bowling facilities, fitness centres, water aerobics and beach masseurs. There are snorkelling and fishing trips, windsurfing, sailing and cruises from the marina. Motorised water activities cost extra. Diving is with Dive Tropex, based at the Sheraton Fiji Resort. The Sheraton resorts cater well for young families, with a daily entertainment program for children and a baby-sitting service. Denarau Island is about 6km from the Queens Road turn-off and it is not pleasant to walk. There are no local bus services to Denarau; a taxi ride from Nadi town costs F$6.60 and from the airport F$18.

Places to Eat

Nadi has a good variety of restaurants and eating places. Most places serve a mixture of Fijian, Indian, Chinese and Western dishes, and there are lots of cheap lunchtime eateries downtown.

Restaurants There is a huge variety of restaurants in Nadi, featuring a range of cuisines.

Fijian It seems bizarre, but it is quite difficult to get traditional Fijian-style food in restaurants. Most restaurants and cafes, however, have a Fijian dish or two and the resorts have special *lovo* nights, where food is cooked in a pit oven.

Italian For pizza and pasta, a good inexpensive option is *Mama's Pizza Inn*, downtown or at the Colonial Plaza in Namaka on the Queens Road. The large pizza is huge and costs F$13 to F$22, or try the yummy vegetarian bolognaise spaghetti for F$6. *Mario's Pizza (☎ 703 903)* a few doors up has OK medium-sized pizza and pasta for around F$10.

Indian *Maharaj (☎ 722 962)* on the Queens Road near the airport serves quite good Indian food. It does takeaway but is not conveniently located. Prices range from F$6 to F$15 per dish. *Farmer's Club* in downtown Nadi on Ashram Rd has OK curries and welcomes visitors.

Chinese *Bi Yuen Restaurant (☎ 703 771)* has quick, friendly service and is reasonably cheap: F$5 to F$8 for meals that include unlimited rice, a pickled appetiser and ice cream. *Sheung Wong Stylish Restaurant (☎ 703 245)*, near the Civic Centre in the main street, has cheap chow mein and chop suey, and Sichuan dishes and seafood for F$6 to F$18. It also has Indian curries.

Japanese Nadi has two good Japanese restaurants. *Hamacho (☎ 720 252)*, on the Queens Road near the Capricorn Hotel, is good value and has comfortable bar seating. It has excellent miso soup, sushi, nori rolls and yaki-tori (skewers) for F$2 to F$5, but the serves are small. A la carte meals cost from F$5 to F$12. *Daikoku Restaurant (☎ 703 622)*, downtown near the bridge, is best avoided by those who are hungry and on a budget. It has a la carte meals for F$18 to F$29 and teppanyaki for F$22 to F$48. It can be reasonable for lunch if you stick to miso soup, sushi (F$5 to F$7) or noodles (F$12 to F$18). This spacious restaurant has air-con.

Other Cuisines 'Chefs' has three different places to eat, all on Sagayam Rd, just off the main street in Nadi. All have air-con:

Sunset, Denarau Island (west of Nadi)

Horse riding on the Coral Coast, Viti Levu

A taste of beautiful scenery along the Kings Road, north-east Viti Levu

Navala village, Nausori Highlands on Viti Levu

Walk for miles along Vatulele island's beach (off southern Viti Levu)

Chefs (the Corner) has good-value meals, including curries, cakes, coconut pies, coffee and ice cream. It opens 8 am to 10 pm (closed Sunday). *Chefs, the Edge* is a medium-priced restaurant and is open 10 am to 10 pm, while *Chefs, the Restaurant* (☎ 703 131) is one of the most expensive restaurants in Nadi, offering international cuisine and candlelit dinners. It is open 10 am to 2 pm and 6 to 10 pm (closed Sunday).

Aeroview restaurant and bar, upstairs at Nadi airport, has OK food (soups for F$3 and mains from F$6.50 to F$24), air-con and accepts credit cards.

If you crave seafood or a good steak and are prepared to spend a bit more on food and taxis, try the *Wet Mongoose Bar & Grill* (☎ 750 900) at the Denarau Marina. Mains are in the F$12 to F$29 range. The upmarket resorts on Denarau also have fine-dining restaurants that are open to visitors.

The Sheraton Royal Denarau has fine dining, offering a mixed international menu at *Garden View* and *Ocean Terrace* or fish and grills at the *Steak House*. At the Sheraton Fiji Resort, the *Beachside Terrace* restaurant is pleasant in the evening and the *Ports of Call* restaurant is more expensive.

There is a new fine-dining European-style and seafood restaurant and bar opening in the new *Millennium Centre* on the Queens Road in Martinar, opposite Dominion International Hotel.

Bounty Restaurant & Bar (☎ 720 840), also in Martinar on the Queens Road, serves OK-value breakfast, lunch and dinner and has a friendly bar with icy beer.

Cafes *West Coast Cafe* is on the Queens Road in Martinar, across from the Bounty restaurant. It serves snacks, pies and sandwiches and has email and Internet services.

Fast Food Try the small cafes, such as *Skyway,* around the Nadi Civic Centre – while not particularly clean, they often have good, cheap food and are popular with locals. *Marhabba Restaurant* on the courtyard has *tavioka* (cassava), Indian snacks, curries and chop suey for under F$4.

McDonald's, about 2km north of town on the corner of the Queens Road and Enamanu Rd, is very popular with locals and has vegetarian burgers.

Self-Catering Nadi has a large produce *market*, which sells lots of fresh fruit and vegetables. Good-quality meat, however, is fairly difficult to come by. There are several large *supermarkets* and *bakeries* downtown as well as along the Queens Road at the Colonial Plaza and at Namaka.

Entertainment

Nadi has nowhere near the variety of nightlife of Suva; however, the upmarket hotels usually have something happening at weekends. *Fiji Mocambo Hotel* has live bands Wednesday to Saturday nights. There is a cover charge, a dress code and cars often wait in line to get into the grounds. The *Sheraton* hotels on Denarau have bars and night-time performances including fire-walking and meke. *Ed's Bar* on Queen's Road in Martinar is a good place for a drink.

There are a few cinemas downtown that show a mix of Hollywood and Indian 'Bollywood' movies (admission is about F$3). The *West End Cinema* on Ashram Rd has four screenings daily except Sunday. Check the *Fiji Times* for information on what's showing.

Shopping

Nadi's Main St is largely devoted to souvenir and duty-free shops. Jack's Handicrafts sells crafts, clothing and jewellery and has a small art gallery. Both Sogo and Nad's Handicrafts sell similar items. There is an outdoor handicraft market near the Civic Centre, where you can bargain. Check if the items are hand- or machine-made. There are also many stores selling Indian clothing. The Pacific Art Shop at the Sheraton Fiji Resort on Denarau has quality arts and handicrafts.

Popular souvenirs include *masi* (bark cloth), *tanoa* (*kava* bowls) ranging from miniature to huge, war clubs, Fijian combs, *sulu* (a skirt or wrapped cloth worn to below the knees), *bula* shirts (in colourful tropical

VITI LEVU

prints), woven baskets and mats, and local pottery. Some shops also sell handicrafts from other Pacific islands, such as face masks from Papua New Guinea and canoe prows from the Solomon Islands. Also see the Shopping section in the Facts for the Visitor chapter.

Getting There & Away
See the Getting There & Away chapter for information on Nadi International Airport and the Getting Around chapter for car rental and inter-island air and boat services. Most trips to the Mamanucas depart from Denarau Marina.

Getting Around
There are regular local and express buses that travel the Queens Road. There are local buses to Newtown Beach but not to Denarau. Taxis are plentiful in Nadi but do not use meters, so prices should be confirmed in advance.

LAUTOKA
pop 43,274
Lautoka, the administrative centre of the Western Division, is Fiji's second port and is the largest city after Suva. It has the beautiful Mt Evans Range (Koroyanitu Range) as a backdrop. While it is not an especially interesting city, if you want to avoid the tourist hype of Nadi, it is a much simpler place to get around on foot and is a good base for taking trips to the Mamanuca and Yasawa Groups. The main street is lined with royal palms. There is a large produce and handicraft market and a reasonably organised bus station. Buses travel from Lautoka to Suva via the Kings Road to the north and via the Queens Road to the south (see Bus in the Getting Around chapter).

The local economy revolves around sugar-cane growing and the large Lautoka Sugar Mill has been operating here since 1903. You will see lots of little sugar trains shuttling the cane to the mill during cutting

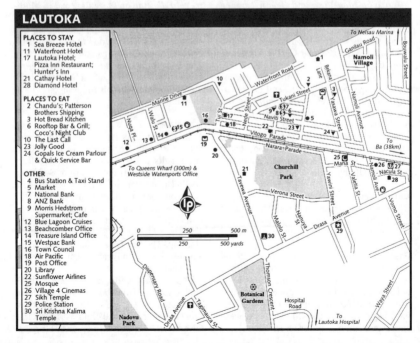

LAUTOKA

PLACES TO STAY
1 Sea Breeze Hotel
11 Waterfront Hotel
17 Lautoka Hotel;
   Pizza Inn Restaurant;
   Hunter's Inn
21 Cathay Hotel
28 Diamond Hotel

PLACES TO EAT
2 Chandu's; Patterson
   Brothers Shipping
3 Hot Bread Kitchen
6 Rooftop Bar & Grill;
   Coco's Night Club
10 The Last Call
23 Jolly Good
24 Gopals Ice Cream Parlour
   & Quick Service Bar

OTHER
4 Bus Station & Taxi Stand
5 Market
7 National Bank
8 ANZ Bank
9 Morris Hedstrom
   Supermarket; Cafe
12 Blue Lagoon Cruises
13 Beachcomber Office
14 Treasure Island Office
15 Westpac Bank
16 Town Council
18 Air Pacific
19 Post Office
20 Library
22 Sunflower Airlines
25 Mosque
26 Village 4 Cinemas
27 Sikh Temple
29 Police Station
30 Sri Krishna Kalima
   Temple

VITI LEVU

A Sweet Success Turned Sour

The sugar industry was the mainstay of the colonial capitalist economy, and the Australian-owned Colonial Sugar Refining Company (CSR) gained phenomenal power in Fiji. In the early 1880s CSR established mills on the banks of the Rewa River (at present day Nausori), on the Ba River at Rarawai, at Lautoka, and at Labasa on Vanua Levu. Another mill at Rakiraki, northern Viti Levu, was taken over by CSR in 1926.

The colonial government was keen to attract foreign investment and facilitated the purchase of land. It arranged for cheap labour through the indenture system. CSR initially developed its own plantations, but later shifted the burden of heavy production costs to others by subcontracting the sugar-growing work. In 1894 the company began leasing land to ex-indentured Indians, a minority of whom became rich cane farmers, leading to resentment among white plantation owners. CSR profits hinged on long working hours (a 50-hour week) and heavy workloads. During the period 1914 to 1924, CSR reaped the best profits in its history. However, after the abolition of indenture and the resulting labour shortage, company land was divided and rented to small tenant farmers.

There was industrial trouble from 1942 to 1960. Mill owners, workers and growers disputed over wages, cane prices and conditions, leading to the establishment of the Sugar Advisory Board & Advisory Council. CSR finally pulled out of Fiji in 1972 due to reduced profits, and the plant and its freehold land were nationalised.

Today, the Fijian government is still a major shareholder in the sugar industry. It suffers from outdated infrastructure and has been experiencing serious financial problems, only exacerbated by the recent drought. Many believe that privatisation is the way to rehabilitate the industry.

and crushing season in the latter half of the year. Wood-chip export is another major industry. There is a high proportion of Fiji Indians in the area, mostly descendants of indentured labourers. They now tend to farm leased land or to work in their own businesses.

Koroyanitu National Heritage Park, in the mountains east of Lautoka, is a fantastic place for hiking and has budget accommodation and village stays (see Koroyanitu National Heritage Park in the Viti Levu Highlands section later in this chapter). About 9km north of Lautoka on the Kings Road is a turn-off to the right that leads to the Lololo Pine Plantation and to the Drasa Timber Mill, which is about 8km inland.

Information

Money There are several banks downtown that will change money and travellers cheques. The Cathay Hotel will also change money at bank rates.

Post & Communications The post office is on the corner of Vitogo Parade and Tavewa Ave, where there are a few public telephones.

Email & Internet Access Lautoka has a cybercafe with email and Internet services – The Last Call (see Places to Eat later in this section).

Travel Agencies The following travel agencies are in Lautoka:

Air Pacific (☎ 664 022) 159 Vitogo Parade
Beachcomber Cruises/Ferries/Resort office (☎ 661 500, fax 664 496) 1 Walu St
Blue Lagoon Cruises (☎ 661 662, fax 664 098) Vitogo Parade
Patterson Brothers Shipping (☎ 866 1173) 15 Tukani St
Sunflower Airlines (☎ 664 753) Vidilo St

Medical Services For medical treatment, contact:

Lautoka Hospital (☎ 660 399) Thomson Crescent
Vakabale St Medical Centre (☎ 661 961) Vakabale St

Emergency In an emergency, contact:

Emergency	(☎ 000)
FVB emergency hotline	(☎ 0800 721 721)
Police	(☎ 660 222)
Ambulance	(☎ 660 399)

Places to Stay

Lautoka has two very cheap hotels. *Diamond Hotel* (☎ *661 920, 8 Nacula St*) is a small building with a bar downstairs. It has simple rooms for F$18.60/24.80 for singles/doubles and a five-bed dorm for F$7.60 per person. *Mon Repo Hotel* (☎ *661 595*) on the corner of Vitogo Parade and Yasawa St, is also cheap but is apparently used for short-term business by prostitutes. There are much better budget options. There are also *camping* and *dorms* at Saweni Beach, south of town.

Lautoka Hotel (☎ *660 388, fax 660 201, 2–12 Naviti St*) is popular with both locals and travellers. The old wing has grungy but spacious budget rooms for F$16.50/22 with a sink but shared bathroom. There are also rooms with air-con and private bathrooms for F$39.60 for singles or doubles. Dorms (maximum eight people) are F$8.80/11 per person with fan/air-con. Most rooms don't have external windows and it seems like it could be a bit of a fire trap. The new wing has good air-con motel rooms with private bathroom, fridge and telephone for F$55 singles or doubles. There is a swimming pool, a reasonably good restaurant, a bar and a TV lounge.

Cathay Hotel (☎ *660 566, fax 660 136,* @ *cathay@fiji4less.com),* at Tavewa Ave up from the post office roundabout, is a good place to meet other budget travellers. It has a swimming pool, bar, a TV lounge, and a restaurant that serves OK meals for F$4 to F$7. The fruit smoothies are good. Rooms with bathrooms cost F$29/38.50 with fans or F$40/47 with air-con. There are various dorms (up to four people in each) for F$9.50 a bed. The reception will help arrange trips to Koroyanitu National Heritage Park and the Yasawas.

Sea Breeze Hotel (☎ *660 717)* is at the end of Bekana Lane on the waterfront, in a quiet cul-de-sac close to the market and bus station. Air-con rooms with sea view cost F$37/44/47 for singles/doubles/triples. Others without the view are cheaper. Fan-cooled rooms are F$30/35 for singles/doubles, but these are often booked out. There is also a family room; it costs F$53 for four people. All rooms have en suites. While a bit expensive for some budget travellers, it is a good place for getting over jet lag before heading inland or to the Yasawas. It has a breakfast room upstairs, a quiet bar and TV lounge downstairs, and a swimming pool.

Waterfront Hotel (☎ *664 777, fax 665 870,* @ *tanoahotels@is.com.fj)* is the only upmarket hotel in Lautoka, catering mainly to local business travellers. Its 47 rooms are in a modern double-storey building on Marine Dr. It has a spacious lounge and bar, an outdoor deck, a swimming pool, conference facilities and a good restaurant (see the following Places to Eat section). Rooms are not bad value at F$111 for 'superior' rooms or F$128 for spacious suites.

Places to Eat

Lautoka has far fewer restaurants than Nadi or Suva. There are, however, various cheap restaurants near the bus station that serve Indian, Chinese and Fijian fare for lunch. *Chandu's,* upstairs at 15 Tukani St opposite the station, has quite good meals for around F$6 for both lunch and dinner. *Jolly Good*, at the corner of Naviti and Vakabale Sts, is a popular outdoor venue for snacks and New Zealand ice cream. Inexpensive Indian, Chinese and Fijian fast food is under F$4, while burgers and hot dogs are under F$2.50. The *cafe* at the Morris Hedstrom supermarket has good-value fast food. Self-caterers should try Lautoka's produce *market*.

Gopals Ice Cream Parlour and Quick Service Bar is a Hare Krishna restaurant serving vegetarian meals. It is on the corner of Naviti and Yasawa Sts near the bus station and market. Prices range from F$1.50 for simple dishes and soups to F$6.50 for a fruit juice and a thali food platter with assorted curries, relish and rice or naan. It also has lots of brightly coloured sweets.

The Last Call (☎ 650 525, 21 Tui St) is a trendy Italian restaurant/cybercafe on the waterfront and quite a contrast with the outside surroundings. It serves pasta, snacks, salads, coffee and cakes. Some of the dishes are a bit pricey, but generally the food is quite good.

Rooftop Bar & Grill (☎ 668 988, 21 Naviti St) is open seven days a week for lunch and dinner. It is a pleasant place with a licensed bar and live music Thursday to Saturday nights, and a daily happy hour from 5 to 7.30 pm. The restaurant serves good steak dishes at reasonable prices.

The restaurant at the *Lautoka Hotel* offers OK main meals from F$7 to F$12, and pizzas at the *Pizza Inn* next door are reasonable. The *Old Mill Restaurant* at the Waterfront Hotel serves light meals all day from F$7 to F$11.50 and main meals from F$13.50 to F$21.50. The hotel also has a bar and nice views out to the harbour.

Entertainment

Lautoka has a Village 4 cinema complex on Namoli Ave, just south of Vitogo Parade. On Thursday to Saturday nights the *Rooftop Bar & Grill* on Naviti St has live music (see Places to Eat earlier in this section). For more of a nightclub scene on Friday and Saturday nights, try *Coco's Night Club* below the Rooftop Bar, or the *Hunter's Inn*, around the corner from the Lautoka Hotel on Tui St.

Getting There & Away

Lautoka is 33km north of Nadi and 24km north of Nadi airport. Local buses shuttle between the two towns every 15 minutes during the day and less frequently in the evening. There are also regular express buses along the Kings and Queens Roads (see Bus in the Getting Around chapter), as well as carriers (small trucks) and Viti minibuses to Suva. Both Sunbeam and Pacific Transport have offices in Yasawa St opposite the market.

Getting Around

It is easy to get around Lautoka on foot. Taxis are plentiful and short rides are relatively cheap.

AROUND LAUTOKA
Koroyanitu National Heritage Park

This park is in the mountains about 10km east of Lautoka. The area has beautiful nature and trekking trails through native rainforest, waterfalls, archaeological sites and natural swimming pools. There is budget accommodation at Nase Lodge. See Koroyanitu National Heritage Park in the Viti Levu Highlands section later in this chapter for details.

Saweni Beach

While littered and fairly unattractive, this is one of the few beaches between Nadi and Lautoka. It is popular with locals for weekend picnics. On the road into Saweni Beach is **South Sea Orchids** (☎ 662 206, fax 666 283), owned by Donald and Aileen Burness, whose great-grandfather was the interpreter at the signing of the deed of Fiji's cession to Great Britain in 1874 (he is the man with the long white beard on the F$50 note). See Cession to Britain under History in the Facts about Fiji chapter. Donald and Aileen have an collection of old Fijian artefacts, landscaped gardens, a private collection of orchids and a commercial nursery.

Places to Stay & Eat *Saweni Beach Apartment Hotel* (☎ 661 777, fax 660 136), about 6km south of Lautoka, is part of the Cathay budget accommodation chain. It has camp sites for F$5.50 per person and dorm beds for F$9.90 per person (with a maximum of two people per room). It also has 12 clean and spacious one-bedroom apartments, which are self-contained and fan-cooled. Doubles cost F$41.80/46.20 for oceanview/beachfront plus F$8.80 for an extra person. The 'brown house' on the beach is a good option. The master bedroom with en suite costs F$35 while twin bedrooms are F$30 each. There are no organised activities – only come here if you want to have a peaceful time. There is a small swimming pool and a bar, but no restaurant. There is, however, a small shop and restaurant nearby, otherwise you'll have to self-cater.

Getting There & Away To get to Saweni Beach, turn off the Queens Road about 6km south of Lautoka, from where it is about 2km to the beach. Local buses leave from Lautoka bus station to Saweni Beach six times a day, with the first leaving at 6.45 am and the last at 5.15 pm. Otherwise, catch any local bus to Nadi and walk in from the turn-off. Taxis cost about F$6 to Lautoka and F$15 to the airport.

South Sea Orchids offers 1½-hour tours of its property. The tours are normally pre-booked through Fiji Tours Tourist Transport (☎ 723 311). Alternatively, you can arrange your own visit by contacting South Sea Orchids in advance. Expect to pay about F$30 for a return taxi ride from Lautoka if you want the cab to wait while you take the tour.

Vuda Point

Vuda Point peninsula juts out towards the Mamanucas between Nadi and Lautoka. The first Melanesians are believed to have arrived in Fiji at this spot. The area is mostly farmland with a couple of resorts and the Vuda Point Marina. Shell, Mobil and BP oil terminals also occupy this beautiful point.

Places to Stay Vuda Point has a couple of places to stay. About 2km along Vuda Point Rd on the left is *Anchorage Beach Resort* (☎ 662 099, fax 665 571, ✉ tanoahotels@ is.com.fj), now part of the locally owned group of Tanoa hotels. It has good views of the Vuda Point area from the hill. The beaches here are a bit better than around Nadi, but don't expect bright-white sand and crystal water. Gardenview/oceanview rooms are F$132/143 for singles or doubles. An extra adult costs F$24. It is possible to get discounts during the low season. It has a restaurant-bar with panoramic views. Breakfast and lunch cost less than F$10 (F$12.50 to F$16 for dinner).

First Landing Resort (☎ 666 171, fax 668 882, ✉ firstland@is.com.fj) is a new resort on the water's edge. It has air-con cottages with verandas for F$198 for up to four people, including breakfast. It has a lovely free-form swimming pool and pleasant beachfront restaurant.

Places to Eat For an affordable lunch try *The Hatch* coffee shop at the marina. It has sandwiches, burgers and Chinese dishes. The marina also has a good store (open 7.30 am to 7 pm daily). Next door, the *First Landing Resort* (☎ 666 171, fax 668 882) has outdoor dining decks on a sandy beach. It is a special place to dine and gaze at the Mamanucas, especially at sunset. Main meals cost F$14 to F$26 for wood-fired pizza, seafood, steak, curry and pasta dishes. Pizza is half-price on Monday nights.

Getting There & Away The Queens Road bypasses the turn-off to Vuda Point. The turn-off is about 10km south of Lautoka and about 13km north of Nadi airport, at the top of a steep hill. The marina is about 3.5km off the old Queens Road. A taxi between here and the airport costs about F$12.

Viseisei Village

The Queens Road now bypasses Viseisei, which is 11km south of Lautoka and 12km north of Nadi airport. It is not a typical Fijian village and it receives many tourists on organised tours. The villagers are relatively wealthy, as the *mataqali* (extended family or landowning group) own and lease several of the Mamanuca islands to resorts. Viseisei was the home of the late Dr Timoci Bavadra, whose government was deposed by the coup in 1987. Local buses between Nadi and Lautoka go past the village.

Garden of the Sleeping Giant

These landscaped gardens have the Sabeto mountain range (or Sleeping Giant Ridge) as a backdrop, and are a peaceful place to have a picnic or spend a couple of hours relaxing among the orchids, lily ponds and tracks up into the forested foothills. Founded by American actor Raymond Burr in 1977 to house his personal orchid collection, it is now owned by a Hawaiian corporation. Admission is a bit steep at F$9.90/24.90 for adults/families. Children five to 15 years get in for F$4.90, and it's free for those under five. The gardens are open from 9 am to 5 pm daily or Sunday by appointment (☎ 722 701).

Hindu Symbolic Rites

A Hindu temple symbolises the body, the residence of the soul. Union with God is achieved through prayer and by ridding the body of impurities (meat cannot be eaten on the day of entering the temple, and shoes must be removed).

Water and fire are used for blessings. Water carried in a pot with flowers is symbolic of the Mother, while burning camphor symbolises the light of knowledge and understanding. The trident represents fire the protector and the three flames of purity, light and knowledge.

The breaking of a coconut represents the cracking of three forms of human weakness: egotism (the hard shell), delusion (the fibre) and material attachments (the outermost covering). The white kernel and sweet water represent the pure soul within.

Fire walking is a means to become as one with the Mother. Hindus believe that the body should be enslaved to the spirit, and denied all comforts. They believe life is like walking on fire and that a disciplined approach, like the one required in the ceremony, helps them to achieve balance, self-acceptance and to see good in everything.

ROBYN JONES

Getting There & Away The gardens are about 6km north of Nadi airport. From the Queens Road, turn inland and continue on the gravel Wailoko Rd for about 2km. A taxi from Nadi will cost around F$12.

Lomolomo Guns

There is an abandoned WWII battery at the foot of the Sabeto Mountains. The battery was built to protect Nadi Bay. If you feel like a walk and a great view, take a bus along the Queens Road from Nadi heading towards Lautoka, and ask the driver to let you off at the dirt road (about 8.5km north of the airport) that leads to a school about 400m up the road. Ask the locals if it's OK to visit and for directions. The easiest track is to the left of the school. You'll have a great walk and a great view.

Queens Road & Coral Coast

The Queens Road follows the western and southern perimeter of Viti Levu, between Lautoka and Suva. It is a sealed road and a scenic drive or bus ride as it generally hugs the coast. Most of the roads that head inland off the highway are unsealed.

There are many resorts along this stretch, as well as a few budget places geared towards backpackers. Highlights are Natadola Beach, the Sigatoka Sand Dunes, the Tavuni Hill Fortification and the Sigatoka Valley.

Both Sunbeam Transport Limited (☎ 500 168) and Pacific Transport Limited (☎ 500 676, Sigatoka) have regular buses along the Queens Road (see the Getting Around chapter).

NAISALI

Naisali is a 42-hectare, privately owned island, about 12km south-west of Nadi. It is a long, flat island, just 300m off the mainland, with a dark-sand beach. *Sonaisali Island Resort (☎ 706 011, fax 706 092, ✆ info@sonaisali.com.fj)* opened in 1992 and has 32 hotel suites in a double-storey building. All rooms have sea views to the Mamanucas, a bar fridge, air-con, fan and twin queen-sized beds and cost F$297 per night. There are also 48 thatched bure, which include: oceanview bure with twin queen-sized beds, high ceilings and elevated verandahs for F$363 per night; beachfront executive bure with similar layout but with king-sized beds and private spas on decks overlooking the sea for F$407 per night; and two-bedroom beachfront family bure for F$473 per night.

Restaurants include the *Poolside Pergola, Kula Koffee Korner* and the *Sunset Terrace* for dining. A full buffet-style breakfast is included in the accommodation rates. Optional meal packages, including a two-course lunch and a three-course dinner, cost F$58/29 per adult/child, or from F$19 to F$27 for a la carte dinner courses. The resort accepts children of any age and has child-minding services for a small fee. It has a good swimming pool, a sunken bar and tennis courts. Windsurfing lessons and diving lessons in the pool are free. Other activities include catamaran sailing, canoeing, water skiing, snorkelling and diving.

Dive Sonaisali takes trips to the Mamanuca Group. Dive sites are about 20 minutes away by boat. Prices including full equipment rental are F$150 for a two-tank dive day trip and F$450 for 10 tanks over five days.

Getting There & Away

The Sonaisali Island Resort is a 25-minute drive from Nadi airport. Turn off the Queens Road at Nacobi Rd (unsealed) and drive for a couple of kilometres past a swampy area to the resort landing and taxi stand. It is only about three minutes away on a free boat shuttle from the mainland across to Naisali. Most guests are on prearranged packages.

MOMI BAY

South of Nadi the Queens Road winds through cane fields, and the first interesting detour is towards Momi Bay and along the coast on the old Queens Road. It's recommended if you are taking a leisurely drive. The turn-off is about 18km from Nadi (27km from the airport, 46.3km from Lautoka). Some local buses take this route, but if you jump off you may have to wait a while for the next one. The 29km of unsealed road takes you through beautiful farmland, cane fields and pine plantations. There are lots of small temples and mosques in the area.

The **Momi Guns** site is worth a quick visit. It is a WWII battery on a hilltop overlooking the strategic Navula Passage, about 6km from the Queens Road turn-off, coming from Nadi. The camouflaged bunkers have been restored and there is a display with historical photos. During WWII Fiji formed a strategic link between the USA and Australia, and New Zealand and Fijian soldiers were posted here. The site, open daily except Sunday, is run by the National Trust.

Places to Stay & Eat

The only accommodation in the Momi Bay area is *Seashell Surf & Dive Resort* (☎ 706 100, fax 706 094, ✆ seashell@ is.com.fj). Camping is F$12 per tent. The six five-bed dorm rooms are on top of the restaurant-bar area in a big, partitioned, shed-like space. They have fans and lockers; beds are F$11. The front rooms have sea breezes and a view. Fan-cooled lodge rooms with shared facilities cost F$45/50 for singles-doubles/triples. Fan-cooled bure with cooking facilities and fridge cost F$90 for doubles or triples, F$120 for up to six people in the family bure. Self-caterers should bring supplies from the markets in Sigatoka or Nadi. There are no cooking facilities for campers or for the dorm accommodation. Restaurant meals are about F$6.50/16.50 for lunch/dinner and there are backpacker specials and cheap snacks at the coffee shop and local shop. Meal plans are from F$25 to F$33.50.

The site is on the edge of a mangrove and, as with much of the Coral Coast, the beach is not great. Swimming, snorkelling and windsurfing are only practical at high tide. However, there's a swimming pool and volleyball, tennis and windsurfing facilities, as well as other watersports equipment for hire. Island hopping is F$60 per person. Diving with Scuba Bula is F$90 for a two-tank dive, F$400 for an open-water course. Snorkelling trips are F$15. Day trips to Castaway Island in the Mamanucas can also be arranged.

Surfing can become quite expensive, as it requires van and local boat transfers. It costs F$25 to go out to the reef-breaks around Namotu, and F$35 to get to Cloudbreak. Nearby breaks include Namotu (left-hand wave), Wilkes (right-hand wave), Desperation and Swimming Pool. Whether or not you will be able to access Cloudbreak is another matter as there are politics involved. At the time of writing, Tavarua Island Resort had priority over Cloudbreak through negotiations with the local villagers. Refer to Tavarua in the Mamanucas chapter for more information on accessing this break.

Getting There & Away
From Nadi, turn off the Queens Road at the Old Queens Road. Travel about 11km then take a turn-off to the right and continue for another 1.5km. The resort is about 30km from Nadi: Airport transfers by resort minibus are F$10 and taxis are F$33 (45 minutes). Local buses (Dominion Company) depart from Nadi bus station (four times daily, one hour). There are also daily buses from Sigatoka (20km) and taxis charge F$40.

LIKURI
This small offshore coral island, near the passage into Likuri Harbour north of Natadola Beach, has lovely white-sand beaches. It was previously known as Robinson Crusoe Island and is now mostly visited by day-trippers. A day cruise costs F$69 per person (☎ 700 026, fax 700 010). There are daily trips from Nadi and Coral Coast hotels, except Monday and Saturday, leaving at 10 am and returning at 4.30 pm. Activities on the island include windsurfing, snorkelling, volleyball and use of paddle boards. The price includes meals, drinks and pick-up from hotels.

There is also a cruise to the island combined with a trip on the Coral Coast Scenic Railway (see Yanuca & Around later in this chapter).

Getting There & Away
The local boat landing is at the first bridge on the road to Natadola Beach (Maro Rd).

It is about a 15-minute boat ride to the island. There are also various organised tours in conjunction with the Coral Coast Scenic Railway.

NATADOLA BEACH
In between Momi Bay and Sigatoka is the gorgeous white-sand Natadola Beach. It is mainland Viti Levu's best beach; most other beaches in this area and along the Coral Coast have wide, flat fringing reefs that only allow swimming at high tide. Take care when swimming here, however, as conditions vary and there can be strong currents. Sometimes there is good body surfing. If you want to snorkel, surf or windsurf take your own gear. The setting is idyllic, but watch your valuables as there have been reports of theft. The small up-market resort opposite the beach is the only development so far, however, several large resort chains have their eyes on the site, pending government infrastructure. Hopefully further development won't cut off public access to the beach.

Local villagers offer horse riding along the beach (F$5 to F$10) and sell green coconuts for drinking, shells, and seed and shell necklaces (F$2 to F$4). Some can be a bit pushy and seem to think that all travellers have spent F$260-plus per night for resort accommodation. Make sure you have loose change. Locals are not allowed to enter the resort and travellers cannot have a drink without buying lunch. Consider bringing your own picnic and drinks. There is no public telephone, although the resort should let you use its phone in an emergency.

Places to Stay & Eat
Natadola Beach Resort (☎ 721 001, fax 721 000, ✆ natadola@is.com.fj) is a cute, small-scale, luxury resort. It has eight comfortable fan-cooled rooms with fridge, tea- and coffee-making facilities and private courtyards. Three more rooms were under construction at the time of writing. It has an attractive swimming pool and landscaped garden. Prices are F$405/480 for a standard room/two-bedroom suite (up to four

people), including all meals and transfers, or F$262/337 for rooms only. The resort does not accept children under 16 years. Snorkelling gear and boogie boards are available for guest use.

The resort's *restaurant-bar*, with open-plan courtyard and Spanish-style rendered walls, is open to the public. The food is good and the menu changes daily with lunches around F$12, dinner F$20 to F$28. House guests can also have their meals by the private pool or on the beach.

Local villagers are becoming interested in a share of the tourism dollar and it may be possible to arrange *village stays* in nearby Sanasana village. Expect to pay about F$25 for accommodation and meals in a two-bed bure with toilet and bathroom. Ask for Ilami Nabiau at the police post at the Queens Road-Maro Rd turn-off or contact Save (☎ 500 800) or Baravi (☎ 508 222) in Sanasana village, or write c/o PO Box 551, Sigatoga.

Getting There & Away

Natadola Beach is fairly isolated and makes a good day escape from Nadi. The Maro Rd turn-off heads south to Natadola off the Queens Road, 36km from Nadi (45km from the airport, 66km from Lautoka) just past the police post. There is a temple with a life-sized goddess on the corner. Continue along the gravel road for 9.5km, past a school, a mosque and two bridges, and turn left at a T-junction. You will pass another mosque before reaching the beach.

While there are no direct buses from Nadi, there are regular Paradise buses from Sigatoka bus station to Vusama/Natadola (F$1.50, about one hour). There are six buses daily (fewer on Saturday, none on Sunday), the first leaving Sigatoka at about 6.30 am and the last at about 5.45 pm. The Coral Coast Scenic Railway runs tours to this beach (see Yanuca & Around later in this chapter). Keen walkers could follow the track between Yanuca and Natadola Beach. It is a pleasant 3½-hour walk. You can catch the train or bus back. It is also possible to hire bikes or take an organised bike tour from Sigatoka.

YANUCA & AROUND

Past the turn-off to Natadola, the Queens Road continues south-east, winding through hills and down to the coast at Cuvu Bay. About 50km from Nadi, on the offshore island of Yanuca (not to be confused with another Yanuca in Beqa Lagoon), is *Shangri-La's Fijian Resort* (☎ 520 155, fax 500 402, ℮ fijianresort@is.com.fj). This privately owned, 43-hectare island, known just as the Fijian Resort, is linked to the mainland by a causeway. The huge resort, which opened in the late 1960s, covers the entire island and employs over 500 staff. It has 436 air-con rooms in five different wings, all with private balconies, sea or lagoon views, 24-hour room service, tea- and coffee-making facilities and minibar. Rates for standard rooms are F$355/390 seaview/lagoonview for singles or doubles. Studios and suites are F$401.50 to F$528 and self-contained beach bungalows are F$632.50 to F$742.50. Most guests, however, receive some sort of package discount. There are convention facilities, TV and games rooms, beautiful gardens and plenty of space – although they can be a bit of a hike from some of the accommodation wings.

The Fijian Resort is very family-oriented: up to two children are allowed to share with parents for no extra charge; children under 12 can eat buffet-style meals for free; and there is a teenagers' club and 'little chiefs' club'.

There are six food outlets to choose from: Expect to spend at least F$7/10/20 for breakfast/lunch/dinner. Meals at the Golden Cowrie restaurant are between F$18 and F$39. There is a 'no cash' policy, so visitors will have to open an account at reception.

Nonmotorised sports are included in the price. Facilities include a nine-hole golf course, a gym, two swimming pools, tennis courts, croquet and lawn bowls. You can also go snorkelling, para-sailing, water skiing, fishing and sailing. Diving is with Sea Sports, which gives free lessons in the pool. A two-tank dive costs F$132, or F$487 for an open-water course.

VITI LEVU

Things to See & Do

The station for the **Coral Coast Scenic Railway** (☎ 520 434, fax 500 402) is on the Queens Road near the causeway entry to the Fijian Resort. It offers scenic rides along the coast on an old, diesel sugar train, past villages, forests and sugar plantations, to the beautiful Natadola Beach. The railway was once used for transporting cane and passengers to the Lautoka Mill. The 14km trip takes about 1¼ hours, leaving at 10 am and returning at 4 pm (F$69 including barbecue (BBQ) lunch at the Natadola Resort). Children under 12 are half-price or free if under six. It is a popular trip with families and guests of the Fijian Resort suffering hangovers or sunburn, but for those on a tight budget it is probably a waste of money. Better value is a train-bus-boat day trip for F$99, combining a one-way train ride and a trip to Likuri.

On the highway opposite the entrance to the Fijian Resort is the **Ka Levu Cultural Centre**. It has a replica of a traditional village, which will interest families. Entry is F$10. There is a *restaurant (☎ 520 729)*, previously known as Tomlu's Restaurant, which is open for lunch and dinner.

Getting There & Away

The Fijian Resort is about a 45-minute drive from Nadi and 11km west of Sigatoka. There are regular express buses, minibuses and carriers travelling along the Queens Road (see the Getting Around chapter). A taxi to Nadi airport is about F$56 while a coach is F$17. There is an Avis desk at the Fijian Resort.

SIGATOKA

pop 8000

Sigatoka (pronounced sing-a-toka) is a small town 61km south-east of Nadi and 127km west of Suva. The town is near the mouth of the Sigatoka River, Fiji's second-largest river. It is predominantly a farming community as well as a service town for tourists drawn to the Coral Coast resorts. There is a produce market in the heart of town, a few souvenir shops and a large mosque. At the time of writing the bus station was next to the market but it may be moving to a new site at the western end of the town. Sigatoka's most bizarre sight is the fantasy-style mansion on the hill behind the town. There are a few places to eat and a couple of budget places to stay, including a surf resort near the Sigatoka Sand Dunes.

Information

Gerona Medical and Surgical Clinic (☎ 520 128, 520 327 after hours) is on the Sigatoka Valley Rd. Clinic hours are from 8.30 am to 4.30 pm weekdays, to 1 pm Saturday and from 7 to 9 pm daily.

Activities

Horse Riding Ratuva's Horse Riding (☎ 500 860) has horses for hire for riding along the beach. It charges F$20 per hour and F$15 per hour for groups of five or more. Its house is on a hill about 5.5km from Sigatoka on the left towards Nadi.

Surfing Sigatoka has Fiji's only beach-break. Most other areas have fringing reefs but here the fresh water has prevented their formation. The break is over a large, submerged rock platform covered in sand. Surfing is at the point-break at the mouth of the Sigatoka River and beach-breaks pound the shore.

Organised Tours

River Cruising Bounty Cruises & Tours (☎ 500 669) has two-hour cruises (F$25) three times daily, except Sunday, to a nearby village for mat-weaving and pottery demonstrations. These boats were originally used to shuttle people across the Sigatoka River when the bridge was damaged after a cyclone. A much cheaper alternative is to visit these villages independently; just hop on a local bus. The Bounty office is opposite the Westpac Bank, on the river's edge between the two bridges.

Places to Stay

Sigatoka town is not the most interesting place to spend a night, but it can be a convenient stopover and base for exploring the local attractions. The *Sigatoka Club*

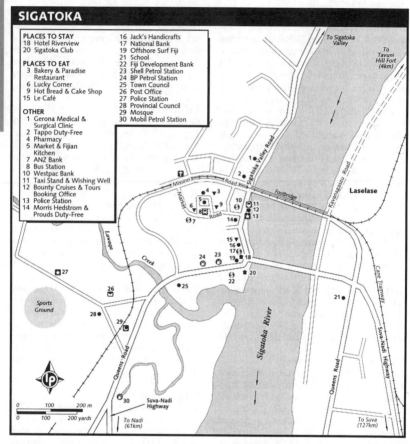

SIGATOKA

PLACES TO STAY
18 Hotel Riverview
20 Sigatoka Club

PLACES TO EAT
3 Bakery & Paradise
   Restaurant
6 Lucky Corner
9 Hot Bread & Cake Shop
15 Le Café

OTHER
1 Gerona Medical &
   Surgical Clinic
2 Tappo Duty-Free
4 Pharmacy
5 Market & Fijian
   Kitchen
7 ANZ Bank
8 Bus Station
10 Westpac Bank
11 Taxi Stand & Wishing Well
12 Bounty Cruises & Tours
   Booking Office
13 Police Station
14 Morris Hedstrom &
   Prouds Duty-Free

16 Jack's Handicrafts
17 National Bank
19 Offshore Surf Fiji
21 School
22 Fiji Development Bank
23 Shell Petrol Station
24 BP Petrol Station
25 Town Council
26 Post Office
27 Police Station
28 Provincial Council
29 Mosque
30 Mobil Petrol Station

To Sigatoka Valley

To Tavuni Hill Fort (4km)

Laselase

Sports Ground

Sigatoka River

Cape Tramway

Suva-Nadi Highway

Queens Road

To Nadi (61km)

To Suva (127km)

0   100   200 m
0   100   200 yards

Suva-Nadi Highway

(☎ 500 026) by the river is the local hotel and watering hole with pool tables and F$4 meals. Les offers spacious simple rooms for F$24/36 singles/doubles and a five-bed dorm for F$11 per bed. Also check out the **Hotel Riverview** (☎ 520 544, fax 520 016) on the opposite side of the road. It has rooms for F$35/45.

Places to Eat

For nice lunches for around F$5.50, try **Le Café** on the main street near the larger bridge. There are two **bakeries** and many cheap eateries near the market and bus sta-

tion. The **Fijian Kitchen** at the market serves simple Fijian dishes. The **Paradise Restaurant** (☎ 520 871) above a bakery near the market is open daily for lunch and dinner except Sunday. It has Chinese, Indian and Fijian meals for around F$5. Both hotels also serve meals. Self-caterers can stock up at the **market** and the Morris Hedstrom **supermarket**.

Getting There & Away

The cheapest and most fun way to travel along the Coral Coast from Suva or Lautoka is by open-air bus. Express buses running from Suva take about 2¾ hours, while the trip from Lautoka takes about 2¼ hours. Add about an hour for nonexpress buses.

Alternatively, United Touring Fiji (UTC; ☎ 722 811) has express air-con coaches going from Nadi International Airport to Korolevu. There are also carriers and Viti minibuses as well as taxis (see the Getting Around chapter).

AROUND SIGATOKA
Sigatoka Valley

The Sigatoka River's tributaries originate as far away as Tomanivi (Mt Victoria) and the Monasavu Dam. The river has long provided a line of communication between mountain peoples and coast dwellers, and the fertile river flats are productive agricultural land. Almost 200 archaeological, cultural or historically significant sites have been found in and around the valley; many are being taken over by farmland or housing.

This fertile river valley is known as Fiji's 'salad bowl'. Cereals, vegetables, fruits, peanuts and sugar cane are grown here, mostly on small-scale farms. The Sigatoka Valley Rural Development Project (SVRDP) coordinates cropping programs and provides training for farmers on up-to-date techniques and irrigation systems. Much of the produce ends up at the municipal markets, and vegetables such as eggplant, chilli, okra and root crops like *dalo* (taro), *tavioka* (cassava) and yams are exported to Canada, Australia, New Zealand and the USA. It's a great landscape to fly over, with the mountains, the patchwork valley, the muddy brown river flowing into the blue ocean, and the Coral Coast's vast fringing reef.

Two valley villages are known for their **pottery**: Lawai and Nakabuta. The latter is home to one of Fiji's best potters, Diana Tugea. Visitors are welcome at both villages. If turning up unannounced, you should ask the first person you meet to guide you. They will take you to a pottery bure with various works on display. Large, smooth cooking pots are the traditional pots from this area, but small items such as pottery pigs and bure are also sold to tourists who visit the area.

Getting There & Away Paradise Valley buses travel up the Sigatoka Valley on the western side. Lawai is about 4km north of Sigatoka. Nakabuta is twice as far (F$3 to F$5 by taxi, 50 cents by bus, or a 10-minute drive). There are regular buses to Naduri, which pass Lawai and Nakabuta (every one to two hours from about 6.30 am to 7.30 pm). On weekends services are less frequent. It is a scenic ride to Keiyasi village about 55km upriver (F$5, about four hours return). Check timetables carefully: The morning buses generally return, while the afternoon buses stay in the village overnight.

Some people may enjoy going upriver by boat. See River Cruising under Sigatoka earlier in this section. It isn't very good value, though – heading inland by local bus also offers beautiful scenery.

Sigatoka Sand Dunes

This is a large formation of windblown dunes along a windswept beach near the mouth of the Sigatoka River. The dunes are about 5km long, up to 1km wide and on average about 20m high, rising to about 60m at the western end. Do not expect golden Sahara-like dunes, as the fine sand is a grey-brown colour and largely covered with vines and shrubs. The dunes have been forming over millions of years. The alluvial sediment washed downriver and out to sea is brought ashore by waves and then blown inland by the south-east trade winds.

Human skeletal remains and pottery shards discovered here suggest that there was a village near the eastern end of the dunes in prehistoric times. The state-owned part of the area was declared a national park in 1989 in an attempt to help preserve the site.

The dunes are quite spectacular and a great place for a walk, although, it's an isolated spot. There have been frequent muggings at the eastern end near Club Masa, so don't take any money or valuables with you. Enter through the Sigatoka Sand Dunes visitor centre at the western end of the dunes, 4.5km west of Sigatoka on the Queens Road. From here there are trails to the dunes; avoid eroding the fragile dunes. Allow about one

VITI LEVU

AROUND SIGATOKA & KOROTOGO

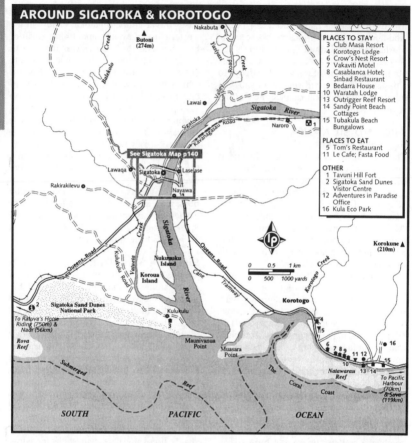

PLACES TO STAY
3 Club Masa Resort
4 Korotogo Lodge
6 Crow's Nest Resort
7 Vakaviti Motel
8 Casablanca Hotel;
  Sinbad Restaurant
9 Bedarra House
10 Waratah Lodge
13 Outrigger Reef Resort
14 Sandy Point Beach
  Cottages
15 Tubakula Beach
  Bungalows

PLACES TO EAT
5 Tom's Restaurant
11 Le Cafe; Fasta Food

OTHER
1 Tavuni Hill Fort
2 Sigatoka Sand Dunes
  Visitor Centre
12 Adventures in Paradise
  Office
16 Kula Eco Park

hour each way to walk to the beach. The park entry fee is F$5. Tui, the manager, may be able to arrange village stays.

Places to Stay *Club Masa Resort (☎ 925 717, postal address: PO Box 689, Sigatoka)* is a surfie hangout near the beach at the edge of the Sigatoka Sand Dunes near Kulukulu village. The place has seen better days and at the time of writing was operating haphazardly. There have been reports of knifepoint robberies at the dunes nearby. Nevertheless, camping is F$15 per person, a dorm bed F$22 and singles/doubles in a

cabin F$25/30. Prices include breakfast and dinner, and lunch can be ordered. There is a kitchen-bar, sitting room and dining on the verandah, but there was no power at the time of writing. It has ocean and river access for water sports but you need to bring your own gear or hire it from Nadi. See the Activities entry under Sigatoka earlier in this chapter for information on surfing.

Getting There & Away There are regular buses along the Queens Road.

Club Masa is south-west of Sigatoka near the mouth of the river and the dunes.

Turn off the Queens Road at Kulukulu Rd, about 2km south-west of Sigatoka. Continue a farther 2km along the dusty road. Turn left at the T-junction facing the dunes at the end of Kulukulu Rd and continue for about 1km. Club Masa is about a 200m walk across the paddock from the village towards the beach. There are Sunbeam buses that depart from Sigatoka bus station for Kulukulu village six times daily, less often on Sunday. If you choose to walk from Sigatoka, take drinks, as it's a long way in the heat. A taxi will cost about F$4 from Sigatoka. It's a 50-minute drive from Nadi airport (F$60 by taxi).

Tavuni Hill Fort

The Tavuni Hill Fort is one of the most interesting sights in the area. Defensive sites such as this were used in times of war. While there are many like it scattered all over Fiji, this is the most accessible for visitors. The site has been restored and has an information centre. It was set up in a combined effort between the Ministry of Tourism and the people of Naroro, and received funding from the European Union (EU). It now provides income to the local villagers whose ancestors lived in the fort.

The defensive fort was established by a clan of Tongans led by Chief Maile Latemai. The mid- to late-18th century was an era of political and social upheaval in Tonga and the chief left his country to escape a family dispute. He and his entourage of servants sailed all the way in a double-hulled canoe and arrived in the Sigatoka area in about 1788. They originally set up in Korotogo but were kept on the move by constant tribal warfare. Eventually the newcomers were accepted by the local tribes and the chief was given some land and a local wife.

The steep limestone ridge, about 90m high at the edge of a bend in the Sigatoka River, was an obvious strategic location for a fortification. From this position the surrounding area could easily be surveyed, both upstream and downstream. Substantial earthworks were carried out to form *yavu* (bases for houses) and terraces for barricade fencing. There are also a number of grave sites, a *rara* (ceremonial ground), a *vatu ni bokola* (head-chopping stone), and some beautiful curtain figs and an *ivi* (Polynesian chestnut tree) on the site.

Admission with guided tour is F$3/6/15 per child/adult/family. The guide will probably joke about his cannibal past and pinch you to see how tasty you might be! The reception bure has display material and toilets, and sells souvenirs, posters and drinks. It is open 8 am to 5 pm daily, except Sunday.

The Kai Colo Uprising

The last significant tribal conflict in Fiji was the Kai Colo Uprising of 1875–6. The Kai Colo (mountain people of inland Viti Levu) disagreed with the cession of Fiji to Great Britain in 1874 and did not appreciate the imposition of the new politics and religion by the colonial regime.

The measles epidemic of 1875 destroyed about one-third of Fiji's population, totally wiping out some villages. The Kai Colo interpreted this both as a deliberate effort by the European invaders to destroy them and as a punishment from their gods for discarding the traditional ways. Any faith in the new church dissolved and they returned to the old religion and tribal warfare, descending into the Sigatoka Valley and attacking and burning villages of their traditional enemies.

This was seen by the colonial government as a direct threat to the viability of their fledgling administration. To quash this 'rebellion' and set an example to others, Sir Arthur Gordon formed a constabulary of over 1000 Fijian men under the Nadroga Chief Ratu Luki. This force ascended the valley, destroying hill forts and hanging, imprisoning or dispersing the chiefs involved. Sir Gordon's strategy was to pit Fijian against Fijian, on the one hand reinforcing the link with the new laws and, on the other, distancing the colonial government from the bloodshed.

Getting There & Away Tavuni is about 4km north of Sigatoka on the eastern side of the river, above Naroro village. There are regular local buses that pass Tavuni Hill (about 50 cents). They leave Sigatoka bus station along Kavanagasau Rd heading for Mavua (seven times on weekdays between about 7.45 am and 5.30 pm). A taxi to the fort is about F$8 return.

KOROTOGO & AROUND

Past Sigatoka and across the river, the Queens Road heads back towards the shore again at Korotogo. Korotogo is about 8km east of Sigatoka. At the time of writing, the Outrigger Reef Resort was undergoing a complete redevelopment and the Queens Road was being diverted from the foreshore to around the back of the town. The area has a range of accommodation on or across the road from the beach, a few places to eat, a souvenir shop and a travel agent. Most parts of the beach are suitable for swimming and snorkelling at high tide only. Sovi Bay, east of Korotogo, is OK for swimming, however, be careful of the channel currents.

The section of the Queens Road between Korotogo and Korolevu is one of the most beautiful. The road winds along the shore, with scenic views of bays, beaches, coral reefs and mountains. Travelling at sunset or sunrise can be quite spectacular.

Kula Eco Park

This wildlife park (☎ 500 505, fax 520 202, ✉ mitman@is.com), previously Kula Bird Park, is north-east of Outrigger Reef Resort. It has recently been redeveloped into a wildlife sanctuary and educational centre for children. It has a captive-breeding program for the endangered Fiji peregrine falcon, and Fiji's crested and banded iguanas. There are also bushwalking paths through forests. It is open from 10 am to 4.30 pm daily and admission is F$11/5.50 for adults/children.

Diving

Sea Sports (☎ 500 225) takes dive trips to some of the Coral Coast reefs and passages. A two-tank dive costs F$132 and an open-water course is F$487.

Organised Tours

Adventures in Paradise (☎ 520 833, fax 520 848, ✉ wfall@is.com.fj) offers day trips (F$99) to the Naihehe cave (see the Viti Levu Highlands section later in this chapter), and a half-day tour (F$79) to Biausevu and the Savu Na Mate Laya waterfall near Korolevu. Tours include a village visit, kava ceremony, lunch and transport from Coral Coast and Nadi hotels. Its office is in a small group of shops just west of Outrigger Reef Resort.

Mountain bikes can be hired from the Adventures in Paradise office for F$13/25 for a half/full day. Independent Tours (☎/fax 520 678) has guided bike tours for two to six people. A day tour of the Sigatoka area is F$79. Half-day tours to the Nausori Highlands are F$49. A three-day tour of the Sigatoka Valley and Nausori Highlands, with village stays, is F$299. Book in advance.

Places to Stay – Budget

The hillside *Vakaviti Motel* (☎/fax 520 424, ✉ *bulavakaviti@is.com.fj*) is about 500m west of Outrigger Reef Resort, just across the road from the beach. It has a block of four rooms opening onto a swimming pool and overlooking the ocean – F$55 for up to three people. One of the rooms is a six-bunk dorm (F$12 per person). These rooms have ceiling fans, cooking facilities and private bathrooms. There is also dorm accommodation in the spacious surf shack. The shack has two- and four-bed rooms, a sitting area and a kitchen (F$15 per person). There is another dorm building for up to six people at the bottom end of the garden, also for F$15 per person.

There are discounts for YHA members and long stays. The friendly owner, AJ, an ex-Rugby Union player who was the first Fijian to play for the New Zealand All Blacks team, will help you organise activities or tours around the area.

Crow's Nest Resort has a nice little elevated six-bed dorm (no cooking facilities) on top of its restaurant and overlooking the pool for F$25 per bed (bathroom downstairs). In the low season you'll pay F$15

Ratu Sukuna, Suva

Thurston Gardens, Suva

City Square, Suva

Sri Siva Subramaniya Swami Temple, Nadi

Canoeing, Castaway Island in the Mamanucas

Biausevu waterfall, Korolevu, Coral Coast

Sigatoka Valley, Viti Levu

Sunset near Momi Bay, Viti Levu

and may find you have it to yourself! See Places to Stay – Mid-Range later for more details.

The Mediterranean-style **Casablanca Hotel** *(☎ 520 600, fax 520 616)* next door to Vakaviti looks a bit incongruous for the South Pacific, but the price is fair and the staff are friendly and helpful. It is managed by Mostafa, an Egyptian-Australian, and his Fijian wife. The eight clean, spacious rooms with bathroom, cooking facilities and fridge cost F$45/55 for singles/doubles, F$8 for an extra person. Some rooms interconnect and the largest room with its own balcony is F$60 for singles or doubles. All rooms have ocean views and there is a pleasant garden and saltwater swimming pool. See Places to Eat later in this section for information on its Sinbad restaurant.

Another good budget place is **Tubakula Beach Bungalows** *(☎ 500 097, fax 500 201, ⓔ tubakula@fiji4less.com)* on the beachfront east of Outrigger Reef Resort. It is run by the same people who own the Cathay Hotel in Lautoka, Saweni Beach Apartment Hotel near Lautoka, South Seas Resort in Suva and Travel Inn, also in Suva. It has 27 A-framed, fan-cooled, self-contained bungalows. Prices vary according to position: from F$50 to F68 for up to three, plus F$10.50 per extra person. Dorm accommodation costs F$13.50 per night (three to four beds) in eight small rooms with communal cooking facilities. It also has good-value renovated 'superior' bungalows (F$70/86 for poolside/beachfront bungalows for up to three people). There are spacious grounds, a swimming pool and a minimarket.

Waratah Lodge *(☎ 500 278)* between Bedarra House and Le Café is less appealing. It has three A-framed cottages and two three-bed flats in a garden with a swimming pool. The cottages have fridges and cooking facilities and cost F$35/44 for singles/doubles, and F$10/3 for each extra adult/child, to a maximum of six or nine. The cottages are in poor condition but it could be a way for a group to stay cheaply while exploring the surrounding area.

If you have nowhere else to go, consider **Korotogo Lodge** *(☎ 500 733)*. It is 5km east of the Sigatoka bridge on the inland side of the road, next door to Tom's Restaurant. The place is run-down and the rooms are dingy. A bed in the six-bed dorm costs F$10 per person. There are also four double units. You can camp for F$5.50.

Places to Stay – Mid-Range

Crow's Nest Resort *(☎ 500 513, fax 520 354, ⓔ crowsnest@is.com.fj)* is 7km east of Sigatoka town in Korotogo. It is on a hillside site across the road from the beach. The 17 self-contained, split-level units have balconies and sea views. Each has a double bed and two single beds, ceiling fans, aircon, cooking facilities and refrigerator. Rates are F$169 for up to four people; an extra person is F$20. The resort has a swimming pool and a sun-deck adjacent the restaurant (see Places to Eat later). It also has dorm accommodation (see Places to Stay – Budget earlier).

Farther east of the Crow's Nest Resort, and past the Casablanca Hotel, is the pleasant **Bedarra House** *(☎ 500 476, fax 520 116, ⓔ bedarra@is.com.fj)*. The main building, more like a mansion than a hotel, has only four rooms (two family rooms and two double rooms), but a new wing was being built at the time of writing. The family rooms are spacious and can fit four. The hotel has a swimming pool, nice gardens and one of the best restaurant-bars in the area. Daily tariffs, including breakfast, are F$132 for up to four people.

Sandy Point Beach Cottages *(☎ 500 125, fax 520 147)* is a family-oriented resort with five self-contained cottages in spacious grounds on a nice stretch of beach just east of the Outrigger Reef Resort site. Rooms are F$65/80 for singles/doubles-triples and F$130 for a family cottage, which sleeps five people. There is a 10% discount if you stay longer than 28 days and you should book ahead for the busy months of June to September. There is a freshwater swimming pool but no restaurant. Resort owner Bob Kennedy uses his parabolic bowl (satellite dish) to receive the latest weather maps and keep an eye on cyclones.

Places to Stay – Top End

At the time of writing the Reef Resort had been largely demolished to make way for the enormous new *Outrigger Reef Resort*. It is to have 255 rooms and bure.

Places to Eat

Bedarra House Restaurant (☎ 500 476) is open for visitors and has excellent food and a friendly bar; mains are F$13 to F$19. The *restaurant* at the Crow's Nest Resort in Korotogo is decked out with Paddy Doyle's nautical memorabilia. It has European and local dishes from F$6 to F$16.

The Swiss chef Jean Pierre at *Le Café (☎ 520 877)* in Korotogo offers tasty pizzas and European-style food for around F$7. It's open 4 pm to 10 pm daily. The small group of shops next door to Le Café includes a general store *Fasta Food*, an inexpensive eat-in or takeaway. It has pizzas and simple meals. Mostafa at the *Sinbad Restaurant* at the front of the Casablanca Hotel has Chinese, curries, pizza and European dishes for F$4 to F$10. *Tom's Restaurant (☎ 520 238),* about 5km east of Sigatoka, has seafood and good Chinese meals from F$4 to F$12. It is open from noon to 3 pm and 6 to 10 pm weekdays, and also on Sunday night, and provides free transport for customers within the Korotogo area after 9 pm.

Once open, the *Outrigger Reef Resort* will provide a few more options.

Getting There & Away

There are regular express and local buses along the Queens Road. A taxi from Korotogo to Sigatoka is about F$4, around F$30 to Nadi. Sunset Express has air-con buses with TV from Nadi to Korotogo (about F$5, four daily).

KOROLEVU & AROUND

The village of Korolevu is 31km east of Sigatoka (24km from Korotogo) and 71km west of Pacific Harbour. There are many resorts spread along this stretch of the coast, from backpacker to top-end places.

There is a souvenir shop east of Korolevu: Baravi Handicrafts (☎/fax 520 364) sells local crafts, clothes and jewellery and is open daily.

East of Korolevu, the Queens Road turns away from the shore and climbs over the southern end of Viti Levu's dividing

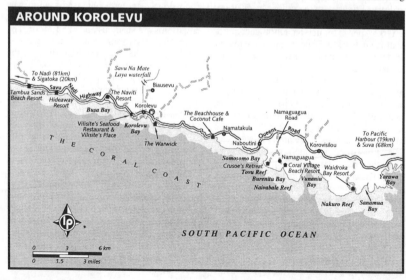

AROUND KOROLEVU

To Nadi (81km) & Sigatoka (20km)

Savu Na Mate Laya waterfall

Biausevu

Tambua Sands Beach Resort
Savu
Nadi Highway
Hideaway Resort
The Naviti Resort
Korolevu
Busa Bay

Vilisite's Seafood Restaurant & Vilisite's Place
Korolevu Bay

The Warwick

The Beachhouse & Coconut Cafe
Namatakula
Naboutini

Namaguagua Road

Queens Road

Korovisilou

To Pacific Harbour (19km) & Suva (68km)

THE CORAL COAST

Somosomo Bay
Crusoe's Retreat
Tovu Reef
Burenitu Bay
Naivabale Reef

Namaguagua
Coral Village Beach Resort
Vunaniu Bay

Waidroka Bay Resort

Yarawa Bay

Nakuro Reef
Sanamua Bay

SOUTH PACIFIC OCEAN

0   3   6 km
0   1.5   3 miles

mountain range. To the east of this range the road improves and the area is scenically different, with more rainforest. From here the road winds its way past wider bays.

Activities

Adventures in Paradise (see Organised Tours under Korotogo & Around earlier in this chapter) has trips to the village of Biausevu, inland from Korolevu, and a local waterfall where you can **swim**. The turn-off to Biausevu is about a 15-minute drive east of Hideaway Resort. The village is 2.5km inland, and the waterfall is an easy 15- to 30-minute walk from the village.

The Pro Dive (☎ 530 199, fax 530 300, ✉ prodivefiji@is.com.fj) operation has dive trips for most hotels and resorts along the Coral Coast. Rates are F$135 for a two-tank dive or F$480 for an open-water course. Waidroka Bay Resort has its own dive setup (see Places to Stay later in this section).

Surfing is possible at Hideaway Resort and offshore from Waidroka Bay Resort.

Places to Stay – Budget

The Beachhouse (☎ 530 500, fax 450 200, ✉ beachouse@is.com.fj) is 7km east of Korolevu and 89km from Suva, just off a bend in the Queens Road. It is popular with budget travellers for its friendly atmosphere and nice beach setting. It has a couple of double-storey timber buildings with double rooms upstairs, and dorm rooms downstairs (maximum of five in each). Bathrooms and toilets are in an adjacent building. Prices are F$16.50 per bed in the dorm, F$38.50 per double room and F$8.80 per person for camping. Meals are at Coconut Cafe in the restored cottage on the site (see Places to Eat later). There is also a simple communal kitchen at the back.

Use of canoes is free, there is snorkelling equipment for hire, and a trip to Suva is F$12 per person. Take care while swimming, currents can be dangerous and there have been drowning here. There are plenty of buses shuttling along the Queens Road (to Suva or Nadi costs approximately F$5) and drivers will pick up and drop off at the gate from both directions.

Waidroka Bay Resort (☎ 304 605, fax 304 383, ✉ waidrokaresort@is.com.fj) is on a beautifully secluded section of the coast, 69km west of Suva and 4km off the Queens Road through steep hills and forest. Waidroka is the Fijian word for fresh water, referring to the spring creek that flows through the forest to the bay. Run by an American couple and their son, the resort caters mainly for adventurous divers and surfers. The lodge is very simple (maximum of three people in a room with shared facilities) for F$54 per person per night. The big, eight-bed dorm bure is F$18 per night. The four oceanfront bure are much more comfortable, with ceiling fans, tea- and coffee-making facilities and verandahs facing to the bay. Rates are F$99/134 for a double/triple per night. The restaurant is open from 8 am to 8 pm. Meal packages are F$30 per day, otherwise lunch snacks are under F$10 and dinner is from F$8.50 to F$20. It is a remote place and there are no self-catering facilities.

Diving in the bay and off the outer reef is F$95 for a two-tank dive, plus F$15 for equipment rental. Snorkel trips are F$10 per person but you can also snorkel along the shore. If conditions are right, it is possible to surf a couple of breaks a half-hour paddle from the beach (F$15 per person for a boat). Alternatively, it is a half-hour boat trip to surf Frigate Passage (F$40 per person including lunch for a day trip). The resort can hire out surfboards (F$20 per day), but ideally bring your own. Other activities include fishing and island trips, paddle boating, kayaking, trekking, village visits and trips to Pacific Harbour.

The road into the resort is a bit rough and very steep in parts but you shouldn't need a 4WD. Transfers from Nadi airport or from the Queens Road can be organised if you call ahead.

Vilisite's Place (☎ 530 054), on the Queens Road between the Naviti and Warwick resorts, has a building next to its restaurant with three fan-cooled rooms. Rooms with an en suite and fridge are F$44/55 for singles-doubles/triples. The rooms are OK but they have a small window facing the back of the building and are certainly not designed to make the most of the sea views.

Coral Village Beach Resort (☎ 500 807, fax 308 383) is in a coastal valley next to Namaquaqua village and near Crusoe's Retreat. The turn-off is 50km from Sigatoka and 77km from Suva. Maggie and Tony run the small low-key resort. It's an isolated spot with a good beach lagoon and offshore reef for swimming and snorkelling. It has double or twin fan-cooled standard/deluxe bure for F$55/59 per person, five-person family bure for F$55 per person and eight-bed dorm for F$36 per bed (no cooking facilities). Rates include two meals per day (breakfast and dinner) at the restaurant-bar.

Activities include volleyball, nature walks, fishing, and snorkelling trips At the time of writing, a diving operation was being set up by an Australian couple. There is a local dance, as well as kava drinking, on Tuesday night for F$7.50 per person. The road into the resort is about 5km off the Queens Road, so call ahead to be picked up at the turn-off. There are regular buses to/from Nadi and Suva.

Places to Stay – Mid-Range

Waidroka Bay Resort has comfortable, fan-cooled, oceanfront bure for F$99/134 for doubles/triples (see Places to Stay – Budget earlier in this section).

Tambua Sands Beach Resort (☎ 500 399, fax 520 265) is approximately halfway between Nadi and Suva, west of Hideaway Resort. The resort has 25 bure along a reasonably good beach costing F$115 for doubles, and six garden bure for F$88 (each extra adult costs F$15). Bure are very simple and are fan-cooled with private bathrooms and tea- and coffee-making facilities. Cooking facilities, however, are not available. Meals at the resort's restaurant cost around F$8/9/21 for breakfast/lunch/dinner. The resort also has a small swimming pool and nice setting, but the services and facilities are average. Most activities, including village tours, horse riding, snorkel hire and deep-sea fishing, will cost you extra.

Places to Stay – Top End

Hideaway Resort (☎ 500 177, fax 520 025, ✉ hideaway@is.com.fj) is a popular resort on a good stretch of beach in the Korolevu area. The accommodation is smart and in a well-maintained garden. Rates are F$215/190 for fan-cooled beachfront/oceanview bure for up to three people. Beachfront bure with air-con cost F$225. The frangipani bure at the back are new, with cute outside bath/shower (F$200 for up to three people). The two-bedroom bure (maximum six people) for F$355 are fan-cooled and well ventilated. The new, deluxe, air-con villas on the beachfront are spacious, with king-sized beds and fresh-air bathroom for F$265. Rooms have tea- and coffee-making facilities and fridges, and all rates include a cooked breakfast. Main meals in the open-plan restaurant-bar are between F$10 and F$20, and there is a five-day meal plan for F$120.

The resort has a good atmosphere, with lots of amenities and entertainment. It has boutiques, a Thrifty car-rental desk and a foreign-currency exchange. Child-minding and baby-sitting can be arranged. It has lovo nights on Sunday, a nightly house band, weekly fire walking, mekes twice-weekly and a kava ceremony weekly. Swimming here is good at high tide, but the channel currents can be dangerous under certain conditions (the channel area is marked by buoys). The resort has a nice swimming pool and nonmotorised activities, such as shore snorkelling, minigolf, tennis, volleyball, archery and using the gym, are included in the tariff. Diving is with Pro Dive (see Activities under Korolevu & Around earlier in this section). Windsurfing, deep-sea fishing, massage and night tennis are also available. There is a right-hand break about 100m from the shore – one of the few sites in Fiji where you don't need a boat to go surfing. It is possible to surf all year round but your chances of good surf are better between May and September.

Korolevu has two other large resorts, both members of the Warwick International Hotel chain and within a few kilometres of each other. Guests can use either resort's

Fire Walking

Fijian *Vilavilairevo* (literally 'jumping into the oven') is practised on the island of Beqa, off southern Viti Levu. The ability to walk barefoot on white-hot stones without being burned was, according to local legend, granted to a local chief by the leader of the *veli,* a group of little gods. Now the direct descendants of the chief *(Tui Qalita)* serve as the *bete* (priests) who instruct in the ritual of fire walking. The spirits of the little gods are summoned to watch the performance held in their honour.

Preparations for fire walking used to occupy a whole village for nearly a month. Firewood and appropriate stones had to be selected, costumes made and various ceremonies performed. Fire walkers had to abstain from sex and refrain from eating any coconut for up to a month before the ritual. None of the fire walkers' wives could be pregnant, or it was believed the whole group would receive burns. Pregnant women were also barred from the vicinity of the pit.

Traditionally, fire walking was only performed on special occasions in the village of Navakaisese. Nowadays it is performed for commercial purposes and has little religious meaning. Other villages on Beqa, as well as villages from neighbouring Yanuca, use fire walking as a source of income. Time and cost considerations in modern resort performances has led to a reduction in the size of the original fire pits, which took longer to prepare and required a tremendous amount of firewood. Costumes can now be reused and *tabu* (taboo) periods have been reduced to a few days. There are regular fire-walking performances at the Pacific Harbour Cultural Centre, at resort hotels such as the Centra and the Sheraton, and at Suva's annual Hibiscus Festival.

Hindu Hindu fire walking is part of an annual religious festival coinciding with a full moon in July or August and lasting 10 days. It takes place at many temples in Fiji, including the Mariamma Temple in Suva.

Preparations for the ceremony are overseen by a priest and take three to 10 days, with the fire walking the climax of the ritual. During this period participants isolate themselves, abstain from sex and eating meat, and meditate to worship the goddess Maha Devi

They rise early, pray until late at night, survive on little food or sleep and dress in red and yellow, which symbolises the cleansing of physical and spiritual impurity. Yellow turmeric is smeared on the face as a symbol of prosperity and power over diseases.

On the final day the participants at the Mariamma Temple bathe in the sea and rites are performed by the priests who pierce the tongues, cheeks and bodies of the fire walkers with three-pronged skewers. The fire walkers then dance in an ecstatic trance for about 2km back to the temple for the fire walking.

Devotees' bodies are whipped before and during the ceremony. The Tamil word for fire pit, *poo kuzhi,* is the same as for flower pit. If fire walkers are focused on the divine Mother they should not feel pain.

A decorated statue of the goddess is placed facing the pit for her to watch and bless the ceremony. It only takes about five seconds to walk along the pit, which is filled with charred wood raked over glowing coals, and the walk is repeated about five times. The ceremony is accompanied by sacred chanting and drumming.

Hindu fire walking is a religious sacrament performed mostly by descendants of southern Indians. It is a means by which a devotee aspires to become one with the Mother. Their body should be enslaved to the spirit and denied all comforts. They believe life is like walking on fire; a disciplined approach, like the one required in the ceremony, helps them to achieve a balanced life, self-acceptance and to see good in everything.

facilities. *The Naviti Resort (☎ 530 444, fax 530 099, ✆ naviti@is.com.fj)* is popular with families and has good facilities for children. It is on an interesting site with a protected beach, a hilly backdrop and a small, private island. The 140 air-con rooms, with tea- and coffee-making facilities and minibar, are F$275/350/650 for mountainview/oceanview/suites. Rates are for doubles and up to two children. To include all meals, add about F$80/55 per adult/child, otherwise the resort's restaurants offer main meals from F$15 to F$24.

The resort has five tennis courts, a nine-hole golf course, a good swimming pool, a games room, a couple of shops and a currency exchange. It has an extensive list of activities and nonmotorised sports such as badminton, catamaran sailing, windsurfing, kayaking and snorkelling, which are included in the price. Baby-sitting is available 24 hours for F$1.50 per hour and there is a baby pool, children's menu, fun park and playground. There is reasonably good access for disabled people and prams.

There is a free shuttle bus from The Naviti Resort (five minutes) to *The Warwick (☎ 530 555, fax 530 010, ✆ warwick@is.com.fj)*. With 250 rooms it is one of the largest resorts in Fiji. It has a spacious lobby, shops, tour desk, laundrette, gym and convention facilities and all rooms have TV and air-con. Mountainview rooms cost F$260 for up to two adults and two children, F$15 for an extra adult. Oceanview rooms are F$30 extra. The 'Warwick Club' has rooms on the third level for F$450 and suites for F$600, including breakfast, afternoon tea and cocktails in the club lounge, slippers and gowns.

It has four restaurants (see Places to Eat later). Entertainment includes a weekly meke and fire walking. The resort has shops, a tour desk, two swimming pools, tennis and squash courts, minigolf and a kids' club. Activities include golf, tennis, squash, horse riding, windsurfing and fishing. Diving is with Pro Dive.

The two resorts are about 90km from Nadi airport. The Naviti is a few kilometres west of Korolevu, while the Warwick is about 2km east of Korolevu. Taxis to the airport cost about F$65 for the 1½-hour ride, F$30 for the 20-minute drive to Sigatoka (28km).

Crusoe's Retreat (☎ 500 185, fax 520 666), previously gay-friendly Man Friday Resort, has been under new management since 1998. Gone is the lively entertainment, now it's much more low-key. It has a beautiful, hilly beachfront setting, well off the beaten track. There are 26 spacious, fan-cooled bure with mosquito nets, tea- and coffee-making facilities, fridge, queen-sized beds and double showers. Rates are F$200/225 for seaview/seaside singles or doubles. Some of the hillside units have lots of steps.

Dinner is served buffet and a la carte, with different theme nights. Visitors are welcome at the restaurant-bar and can use the resort facilities for a charge. There is a tennis court and a foot-shaped saltwater swimming pool. Use of the glass-bottomed boat and snorkelling equipment is free. Diving can be arranged with Pro Dive. Crusoe's Retreat is 90km from Nadi, 80km from Suva and 5km from the Queens Road.

Places to Eat

Coconut Cafe at the Beachhouse colonial cottage, near Korolevu, is a nice place for a break if you are travelling along the Coral Coast. It has coffee and fresh-fruit smoothies. Breakfast is F$3 to F$5.50, a light lunch is F$4 to F$7, and dinner is around F$7 (order before 4 pm). It's a popular spot with backpackers (see Places to Stay earlier for details of how to get there).

Vilisite's Restaurant (☎ 530 054), between the Naviti and Warwick hotels, has a verandah overlooking the water. It has a la carte and set-menu dishes for lunch and dinner. Octopus, fish fillets and fruits are F$19.50, while a meal of 16 king prawns, fried rice and a fruit platter is F$32.

The larger resorts also have restaurants where visitors are welcome. At The Warwick resort, *Papagallo Restaurant* serves good pizza and pasta dishes for F$10 to F$20 and main meals for F$16.50 to F$28. It also has an interesting seafood restaurant (dinner only), *Wicked Walu,* which is on a tiny island linked to the resort by a causeway. Meals here cost F$20 to F$34.

PACIFIC HARBOUR

The scenery along the Queens Road begins to change as you pass Korolevu and head towards Suva. The vegetation becomes greener and denser as you approach the wetter eastern side of Viti Levu. In the Deuba and Pacific Harbour area, the Queens Road hugs the coast, with the offshore island of Beqa in sight. There are roadside stalls selling fruit and vegetables.

Pacific Harbour is 78km east of Sigatoka (139km from Nadi) and 49km west of Suva. It is an unusual town for Fiji, planned as an upmarket housing and tourism development with meandering drives, canals and a golf course. It rains a lot here and many will find the town itself fairly boring. However, the Beqa Lagoon offshore has world-class diving and a surf-break, and the beach at Deuba, about 1km west of Centra Resort, is the closest reasonable beach to Suva. Just 45 minutes by car from Suva, Pacific Harbour is a convenient weekend beach escape from the capital, and some residents commute daily to work in Suva. Pacific Harbour has two large hotels, villa units and apartments for rent and a couple of budget places to stay. It also has a few restaurants and a touristy cultural centre and marketplace.

Things to See

The **Fijian Cultural Centre & Marketplace** (☎ 450 177, fax 450 083) is about 1km east of Centra Resort. The place has seen better days, as now it just has a few gift shops and a restaurant. It is geared towards tourists and, specifically, tour groups by the busload. The cultural centre (closed for renovation at the time of writing) is OK for a quick caricature of Fijian history. Children may enjoy taking the **Lake Tour** in a *drua* (double-hulled canoe) around the small islands that have an artificial village with a 'warrior' as skipper and guide. There is a temple, chief's bure, cooking area with utensils and a weaving hut. Fijian actors dressed in traditional costumes carry out a mock battle. The boat stops along the way to show traditional techniques for canoe making, weaving, *tapa* (also known as *masi*, or bark cloth) and pottery.

Activities

Centra Resort allows visitors to join its organised tours and use the resort's facilities. Dinghy sailing, windsurfing, or coral viewing in a glass-bottomed boat costs F$15 and a one-hour horse ride is F$9/15 per adult/child. Cruises to offshore Yanuca are F$59 per person.

Diving Aqua-Trek (☎ 702 413, fax 702 412) at Centra Resort has the best diving operation in the area. Rates are F$165 for a two-tank dive, F$600 for an open-water course. Dive Connections (☎ 450 541, fax 450 539, @ diveconn@is.com.fj) is opposite the Centra next to the canal at 16 River Dr. It takes dive trips on either the 12m *Scuba Queen* or 7m aluminium *Dive Master*. A two-tank dive, including all equipment and picnic lunch, costs F$130, F$100 for just tanks and weights. An open-water course is F$395. For snorkellers, trips are F$45 including lunch. Some readers, however, have expressed dissatisfaction with the standards of this dive operation. It has a comfortable, self-contained one-bedroom unit to accommodate its divers.

The 33m live-aboard yacht *Nai'a* (☎ 450 382, fax 450 566, @ naia@is.com.fj) is based at Pacific Harbour and has the reputation of being the best in Fiji. It has eight aircon rooms and takes up to 18 passengers.

Fishing Dive Connections also charters its dive boats for fishing trips for F$320/550 for a half/full day, including lunch and all fishing gear. Baywater Charters (☎ 450 235, fax 450 606) also has charter boats for fishing as well as for picnic and snorkelling trips to Yanuca island. Charters organised through the Centra are F$400/650 for half/full-day game-fishing tours.

Surfing There is first-class surfing at Frigate Passage and surf camps on Yanuca (see Yanuca later in this chapter).

Golf The Pacific Harbour Golf & Country Club (☎ 450 048) has an 18-hole, par-72 championship course, considered one of the best in Fiji. Designed around lakes and canals, it has a clubhouse and is about 2km off the Queens Road. Green fees are F$19/25 for nine/18 holes. Club and cart hire is extra and golf lessons are available.

Organised Tours

Tour operation Rivers Fiji (☎ 450 147, fax 450 148, ☻ riversfiji@is.com.fj), based at Pacific Harbour, and Discover Fiji Tours (☎ 450 180, fax 450 549), based at Navua, both have trips to the Namosi Highlands north of Pacific Harbour. See the Viti Levu Highlands section later in this chapter.

Wilderness Ethnic Adventure Fiji (☎ 387 594, fax 300 584) offers tours to the Navua River, picking up passengers from Pacific Harbour as well as from Suva hotels (see under Organised Tours in the Suva section later in this chapter).

Places to Stay – Budget

Club Coral Coast (☎ 450 421, fax 450 900) has good family rooms with a double bed and a mezzanine level with twin single beds for F$60/70 for singles/doubles, F$10 per extra person. It also has tight bunk rooms with shared facilities for F$20/30. It has a lovely swimming pool and a tennis court. Coming from the west, turn left just before the Japanese restaurant, cross the canal and turn left again at Belo Circle.

Accommodation at the *flat* next to the Dive Connections office in Pacific Harbour is excellent value: F$30/40/55 for singles/doubles/triples. It has hot showers and a good kitchen. Contact Dive Connections for bookings (☎ 450 541, fax 450 539, ☻ diveconn@is.com.fj).

Deuba, on the Queens Road just a kilometre west of the Centra and a few minutes' walk from the local beach, also has a couple of budget places to stay.

Coral Coast Christian Centre (☎/fax 450 178) is run by two couples, Joe and Heather, and Paul and Jo-Anne. It has cheap, clean accommodation with good communal facilities. Camp sites cost F$5.50. Dorm cabins (maximum of five people in each) with fan, shared bathroom and cooking facilities are F$13/22 for singles/doubles, F$9/5 for each extra adult/

child. The centre also has six self-contained units, each with private bathroom, hot water, refrigerator and cooking facilities, for F$27.59/44 singles/doubles, F$16.50/6.60 per extra adult/child. Discounts are given for stays of over one week. Alcohol and kava are not permitted here. Bring insect repellent.

Deuba Inn (☎ 450 544, fax 450 818), next door to Club Coral Coast, used to be an old homestead and pineapple-canning factory. It now has budget accommodation with a garden and restaurant. It has beds in awful prefab boxes with shared bathroom for F$16.50/26.40 for singles/doubles. The dorm can fit five people for F$7 per person. There are also four self-contained units of varying sizes with cooking facilities for F$50 to F$60 for three people and F$5 per extra person (maximum five at a squeeze). See Places to Eat later for information on the inn's restaurant.

Places to Stay – Mid-Range

Pacific Harbour Villas (☎/fax 450 959) can be a good option for families or groups. The villas are spacious houses on the quiet backstreets around the golf course. They have twin or double bedrooms, open-plan lounge, dining and kitchen areas, and gardens, some with swimming pools. They are mostly owned by people who live abroad and are normally rented for long periods. The villas won't provide the ultimate Fijian experience but might be convenient to use as a base to go diving or visit the surrounding area. Prices for villas are F$95 per night for standard two-bedroom units for a minimum stay of three days. Long-term discounts are available. Ideally, if you stay at one of the rear units you should have your own transport.

Fiji Palms Beach Club (☎ 450 050, fax 450 025) is next door to the Centra Resort and has spacious, self-contained apartments with two bedrooms, air-con and fans (sleeping up to six people). Prices are F$150 for one night or F$900 per week. It has a bar and nice swimming pool, spa pool, BBQ and shop; guests can use the facilities of the Centra.

Korean Village (☎ 450 100, fax 450 270) was in receivership at the time of writing. It is a large building with 22 rooms and is painted pink everywhere, but this will no doubt change with the new ownership. It has standard and deluxe rooms, huge suites, one penthouse, a restaurant and a swimming pool. To get there, turn down Great Harbour Drive just west of the Fijian Cultural Centre & Marketplace. It is near the golf course, on Fairway Place, just north of the canal.

Places to Stay – Top End

The *Centra Resort* (☎ 450 022, fax 450 262, ❷ centrapacharb@is.com.fj), previously the Pacific Harbour Hotel, was built in the early 1970s. Air-con rooms with fridge, tea- and coffee-making facilities and TV cost F$143 for singles or doubles, F$25 for an extra adult, or up to two children under 16 years old can share with parents free of charge. A suite is F$275. The restaurant has an all-day menu (see Places to Eat later in this section). Canoeing and daytime tennis are included in the room rate but most other activities and organised tours cost extra. The resort has spacious grounds, a swimming pool, tennis, windsurfing, snorkelling, diving, horse riding, tennis, a kids' club and an OK dark-sand beach for swimming. There is a money exchange and shop. There are fire-walking performances on Friday night. Diving is with Aqua-Trek (see Activities earlier).

Places to Eat

If you are after good, cheap and simple food, try *Kumaran's Restaurant and Milk Bar* (☎ 450 294), across the Queens Road from the Centra entrance. It has Indian, Chinese and European food to eat-in or take away: F$5 to F$10 for mains. There is also a couple of cheap *takeaways* in the Fijian Cultural Centre & Marketplace. *Oasis Restaurant* (☎ 450 617) is open for lunch and dinner, with burgers and sandwiches from F$4.50 to F$7 and mains for F$15 and above. *Nautilis Restaurant* at Centra Resort welcomes visitors. It has an all-day menu, with meals from F$12.50 to F$22.50.

Sakura House (☎ 450 300), opposite the Centra, has Japanese dishes (F$20 to F$30) and European-style steak dishes (F$10 to F$15). It is open daily for dinner. *Loraini's Restaurant* at Deuba Inn specialises in seafood dishes. Happy hour is from 6 to 7 pm at the Planters Bar.

Getting There & Away

Pacific Harbour is 139km from Nadi and 49km west of Suva. It is about an hour's express bus ride from Suva and around three hours from Nadi. There are frequent Pacific Transport and Sunbeam Transport Lautoka-Suva buses travelling the Queens Road as well as Viti minibuses and carriers. The first bus from Pacific Harbour to Lautoka leaves at about 7.50 am and the last at around 7 pm. The first bus to Suva leaves at 8.45 am and the last is at 9.40 pm.

NAVUA

This agricultural region is 39km west of Suva and 143km from Nadi. Early in the 20th century sugar cane was planted and a sugar mill built, but this activity ceased as the drier western region proved more productive. The delta region then turned to dairy farming, cattle grazing, rice growing and other crop growing. The small town of Navua, on the banks of the wide Navua River, is about a 20-minute drive from Suva. It serves the local farming community and has a produce market. Many of the old buildings in the town date from the beginning of the 20th century.

Upriver there are beautiful gorges, waterfalls, forests and spectacular mountains. The best way to explore this relatively inaccessible area is by river.

Organised Tours

Discover Fiji Tours (☎ 450 180, fax 450 549) has several tours to the Navua River area. The 'Magic Waterfall' trip costs F$80 per person and includes lunch and *bilibili* (bamboo rafting) down the Navua River to Nakavu village. You can be picked up and dropped off at Pacific Harbour and Suva hotels. A five-hour trip with a cruise up the Navua River in a 25-horsepower punt

(1½ hours upriver, one hour downriver) to Namuamua village for lunch costs F$55. It also offers one- to four-day guided treks across Namosi Highlands, with camping overnight in villages, and a three-day, two-night camp on the banks of the Navua River.

There are also market boats and local buses to/from Namuamua and Nukusere villages about 20km upriver. The trip can take up to two hours, depending on the river's water level.

Bure Kalou

In the days of the old religion, every village had a temple, or *bure kalou*. These had a high-pitched roof and usually stood on terraced foundations. The *bete*, or priest, who was an intermediary between the villagers and the spirits, lived in the temple and performed various rituals, including feasting on slain enemies and burying important people. A strip of white *masi* (bark cloth), usually hung from the ceiling, served as a connection to the spirits. These bure were also used as meeting houses for men. The construction of such a temple required that a strong man be buried alive in each of the corner post holes.

ROBYN JONES

Getting There & Away

The regular express buses along the Queens Road stop at Navua. They take about 50 minutes from Suva and about 3¼ hours from Nadi.

ORCHID ISLAND CULTURAL CENTRE

The **Orchid Island Cultural Centre** (☎ 361 128, fax 361 064) is 7km west of Suva and 42km from Pacific Harbour. The place has gone downhill, however, it still has an interesting replica of the *bure kalou* (a large ancient temple), a tour through the chief's house, demonstrations of masi making, basket weaving and pottery. The centre also has the remains of a small zoo with a banded iguana, snakes and Fijian flora. Admission at F$10 per person (free for children under 15 years) is a bit steep for what's offered. The centre is open from 9 am to 4 pm weekdays and from 8 am to 1 pm Saturday. You can get to the centre on Queens Road non-express buses.

ISLANDS OFF SOUTHERN VITI LEVU

The 360-sq-km **Beqa Lagoon** lies south of Pacific Harbour. It has 64km of barrier reef and encloses two islands: Beqa and Yanuca. The lagoon is famous for its dive sites, which include: Side Streets, with soft corals, coral heads and gorgonian fans; Frigate Pass, a 48m wall dive with large pelagic fish including white-tip reef sharks; and Caesar's Rocks, with coral heads and swim-throughs. Surfing is first-class at **Frigate Passage**, south-west of Yanuca. It has left-hand waves, which can get really big. The break has three sections, which join up under the right conditions: the outside take-off; a long, walled speed section with a possibility of stand-up tubes; and an inside section breaking over the shallower section of reef and finishing in deep water.

Beqa

Beqa is a volcanic island about 7.5km south of Viti Levu's Navua delta, and is visible from the Queens Road near Pacific Harbour and even from Suva. It is 35 minutes by boat from Pacific Harbour. The volcanic island is about 7km in diameter with an area of 36 sq km and a deeply indented coastline. The rugged interior is dominated by ridges averaging heights of 250m and sloping steeply down to the coast. The surrounding coral reef is famous for its dive sites. Beqa has one upmarket resort and eight villages. The villagers of Rukua, Naceva and Dakuibeqa are known for the tradition of fire walking.

Marlin Bay Resort (☎ *304 042, fax 304 028,* ✉ *george@is.com.fj*) has 12 luxury bure on a nice coconut-tree-fringed beach on the western side of the island. There is a large restaurant-lounge bure and a pool. The resort caters mostly for divers on pre-booked packages. Rates are quoted in US dollars and work out to about F$370 per bure for a minimum of three nights (half-price for children under 10 years). Meal plans are F$110 per person per day. Rates include snorkelling, kayaking, a two-tank dive-boat trip, unlimited shore diving, hiking to waterfalls and village visits. Game fishing can be arranged for an additional price. Two-tank dive trips cost F$160; instruction can also be arranged. Boat transfers are F$100 per person return.

Lalati Resort (☎ *472 033, fax 472 034,* ✉ *lalati@is.com.fj*) opened in Beqa late in 1999. It has five two-bedroom bure with verandahs that overlook a sandy beach at the mouth of Malumu bay on the eastern end of Beqa island. It claims to be an 'upscale but casual ecologically friendly resort' and specialises in diving around Beqa Lagoon and surfing at Frigate Passage. Rates, including three gourmet meals per day (alcohol costs extra), diving, surfing, and the use of kayaks and windsurfers, are F$540 per person per night. Transfers from Pacific Harbour by one of Lalati's 10m catamarans take about 25 minutes and are included in the price.

Mikaele Funati (☎ 387 591, fax 300 945) organises *village stays* in Beqa, including boat trips from Navua, three days' accommodation, meals and two day excursions to the reef and beaches for F$130 per person. Call in advance for bookings. Trips normally leave Tuesday and Friday.

Yanuca

Not to be confused with Yanuca (Shangri-La's Fijian Resort) near Sigatoka, or Yanuca near Ovalau, this small island with beautiful beaches is within the Beqa Lagoon, 9km west of Beqa. **Frigates Passage** surf-break is nearby. The island is visited mainly by day-trippers, divers and surfers. It has one small village and two surf camps.

Penaia at *Frigate Surfriders* (☎/*fax 450 801*) has a camp on a small white-sand beach. He charges F$75 per person per night in the beach-hut dorm or for camping (own tent). Nonsurfers pay F$35. Prices include three meals and daily surf trips. Boat transfers are F$40 return. Other activities, including snorkelling, diving, canoeing and trekking, can be arranged.

Batiluva (☎ *450 202, fax 450 067*) also has a surf camp at Yanuca offering accommodation and surf trips for similar prices to Frigate Surfriders.

Vatulele

The island of Vatulele is 32km south of Korolevu, off Viti Levu's southern coast and west of Beqa Lagoon. It is 13km long with a total area of about 31 sq km. It is mostly flat, the highest point being just 33m above sea level, with scrub and palm vegetation. The western coast is a long escarpment broken by vertical cliffs formed by fracturing and uplifts. A barrier reef up to 3km offshore forms a lagoon on the northern and eastern ends. There are two navigable passages at the northern end of the barrier reef.

Vatulele has four villages with total of 950 people, and one exclusive resort on land leased from the *mataqali* (landowning groups). The villagers live mostly off subsistence farming and fishing and are one of Fiji's two main producers of masi. Vatulele is also known for its **archaeological sites**, including ancient rock paintings of faces and stencilled hands, and for its geological formations, including limestone caves and pools inhabited by sacred red prawns.

Places to Stay & Eat The exclusive *Vatulele Island Resort* (☎ *720 300, fax 720 062,* ✉ *vatulele@is.com.fj*) is definitely one of

Sacred Red Prawns

Near the north end of Vatulele the limestone is honeycombed with caves and pools, which, despite being inland from the shore, are affected by tidal movements. These pools are the habitat of the famous red prawns, or *ura buta*, meaning 'cooked prawns'. The islanders have great respect for red prawns and won't eat or harm them. They believe that anyone who takes the prawns will be shipwrecked when they sail away from the island. The prawns are known to respond when called by traditional magic chants and there is a local legend to explain their origin:

There was once a beautiful but cold-hearted young woman called Yalewa, who treated her many suitors with disdain, preferring to play with her friends instead. She told her chiefly father that she would only accept a man who was brave and creative and who had godly powers – she would never marry anyone who came to the island by mere canoe. One day an ingenious and hopeful young chief arrived from across the sea on a string of stepping stones, bringing with him a basket of cooked prawns as a present. Yalewa was not impressed. She angrily and ungraciously struck him with the basket, scattering its contents. The prawns came alive and can be found in the pools of Vatulele to this day. The frightened suitor fled home across the stepping stones and never returned.

Fiji's best top-end resorts, with a price to match. It is the only place to stay on the island. The location is idyllic and the architecture stunning – a mix of thick, Santa Fe-style, rendered walls with the lofty thatched roofs of traditional Fijian bure. It was developed by Australian TV producer Henry Crawford and Fijian Martin Livingston and opened in 1990. Martin manages the resort and ensures there is never a dull moment. The 16 open-plan, split-level bure are well spaced for privacy, each with an outdoor terrace and its own stretch of white-sand beach and turquoise lagoon. Every element is thoughtfully designed, right down to the shower outlet. There are no excuses if you can't relax here! The materials, including huge, sculptural, strangled fig trunks, were imported from the main island, and the site was selectively cleared by 100 men with cane knives to minimise impact. In keeping with this philosophy, motorised sports are not available.

The minimum stay is four nights, at a nightly price of F$968/1936 for singles/doubles. Children are only accepted during family weeks (early July. and late September); the charge is F$132 each for a maximum of two children. Gourmet meals, beverages and alcohol are included in the rate and can be served anywhere you wish, although everyone usually dines at the same table in the main bure.

Activities such as snorkelling, windsurfing, tennis and hiking are included in the rate. Diving is F$198 for a two-tank trip, F$1108 for an open-water course. Dive packages and game fishing are also available.

Getting There & Away Unless you are a resort guest you are unlikely to be able to visit this beautiful island. The island has an airstrip and return transfers are by resort charter plane to Nadi (F$616 per adult, 25 minutes).

Suva

pop 167,975

While Nadi is the country's tourism centre, Suva (pronounced soo-va) is the political and administrative capital, the major port and Fiji's educational, commercial and industrial centre. It is the largest South Pacific city and an important regional centre, with the University of the South Pacific (USP), the Forum Secretariat and many embassies.

Suva and its surrounding urban area have about half of Fiji's total urban population. It is a multiracial and multicultural centre with a cosmopolitan feel. A large number of public servants, expats and students from throughout the Pacific region live here. Urbanisation, poverty and crime are becoming increasingly problematic and about 60% of Suva's inhabitants are squatters living in settlements on land that has no formal title.

The city is mostly low-rise with some high-rise blocks. There are gardens, churches, mosques, temples and some interesting remnants of the colonial past. Suva's topography is beautiful, with scenic views to the mountains across the bay. The climate here is notoriously hot, wet and humid, although the tropical rain (about 3000mm per year) often comes as refreshing change at the end of the afternoon.

History

The Fijians who originally lived on the Suva peninsula were traditional rivals of the Rewans of the Rewa Delta to the east. Chief Cakobau of Bau was also an enemy of the Rewans, and in the 1850s, with help from King George of Tonga, he defeated them in the battle of the Kaba Peninsula.

Until the 1870s there were few Europeans in the area. The majority of Suva's settlers and fortune hunters came from Melbourne, Australia, where there was an economic downturn after the gold rushes. In 1868 the newly formed Polynesia Company

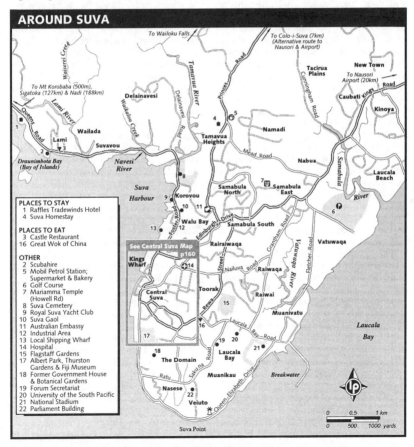

AROUND SUVA

To Wailoku Falls
To Colo-i-Suva (7km)
(Alternative route to
Nausori & Airport)

Waiserei Creek
Tamavua River
Princes Road
Tacirua Plains
To Nausori Airport (20km)
New Town
Cunningham Road
Caubati
Kings Road

To Mt Korobaba (500m),
Sigatoka (127km) & Nadi (188km)
Lami River
Queens Road
Delainavesi
Wailoku Creek
Waikalou Creek
Delainavesi Road
Foster Road
Kinoya

Wailada
Lami
Suvavou
1
2
3
Tamavua Heights
4
5
Namadi
Mead Road
Nabua
Samabula

Drauminbota Bay
(Bay of Islands)
Navesi River
Suva Harbour
8
Korovou
9
Samabula North
7
Samabula East
Laucala Beach

PLACES TO STAY
1 Raffles Tradewinds Hotel
4 Suva Homestay

10 11
Walu Bay
Edinburgh Drive
Samabula South
River

PLACES TO EAT
3 Castle Restaurant
16 Great Wok of China

13 12
Rairaiwaqa
Grantham Road
Vatuwaqa
Vatuwaqa

OTHER
2 Scubahire
5 Mobil Petrol Station;
   Supermarket & Bakery
6 Golf Course
7 Mariamma Temple
   (Howell Rd)
8 Suva Cemetery
9 Royal Suva Yacht Club
10 Suva Gaol
11 Australian Embassy
12 Industrial Area
13 Local Shipping Wharf
14 Hospital
15 Flagstaff Gardens
17 Albert Park, Thurston
   Gardens & Fiji Museum
18 Former Government House
   & Botanical Gardens
19 Forum Secretariat
20 University of the South Pacific
21 National Stadium
22 Parliament Building

See Central Suva Map p160
Kings Wharf
14
Nailuva Road
Raiwaqa
Fletcher Road
Central Suva
Toorak
Raiwai
Muanivatu

15
Rewa Street
Laucala Bay Road
16
17
18
19 20
21
The Domain
Laucala Bay
Laucala Bay
Ratu Sakuna Road
Muanikau
Breakwater
22
Nasese
Veiuto
Queen Elizabeth Drive
Suva Point

0   0.5   1 km
0   500   1000 yards

had agreed to clear Cakobau's inflated debts (owed to American settlers) in return for land, including over 9000 hectares in the Suva area, and the right to trade in Fiji. While not his land to sell, the powerful Chief Cakobau had the Fijian village relocated from the present site of Government House. Cakobau, claiming to be *Tui Viti,* or King of Fiji, had already attempted to cede Fiji to Britain for payment of these debts in 1862.

In 1870 a group of forty Australians from Melbourne arrived in what is now downtown Suva. The dense reeds were cleared for farming and they tried growing cotton and then sugar cane. Their attempts at farming on the thin topsoil and soapstone base of the Suva peninsula failed and most of the settlers' efforts ended in bankruptcy. Two Melbourne merchants, WK Thomson and S Renwick, turned this financial ruin to their advantage by encouraging the government to relocate the capital from Levuka to Suva so as to increase land values. Levuka had insufficient room for expansion, being squeezed between the beachfront and tall hills immediately behind, and the government was looking for a fresh start for white settlement. Galoa, in Kadavu, and Nadi were also considered as sites for the new capital, but the merchants gave incentives in the form of land grants. Colonel WT Smyth, who recommended the move, had not visited Suva during the hottest and rainiest season, and opinion has it that he might have decided otherwise if he had.

The government officially moved to Suva from Levuka in 1882. In the 1880s Suva was a township of about a dozen buildings. Later, sections of the seashore were reclaimed and trading houses constructed, and by the 1920s it was a flourishing colonial centre with many prominent public and private buildings. Large-scale land reclamation was carried out in the 1950s for the Walu Bay industrial zone.

The contorted layout of downtown Suva is blamed on Colonel FE Pratt, who was the surveyor general of the Royal Engineers in 1875. Although many were not happy with the layout, the original plans were not modified due to a lack of funds, and in some areas the town grew haphazardly anyway. The area south of the Nubukalou Creek was developed first and the mud and soapstone roads were often impassable. Later the town extended east to the domain and north-east to Toorak. This residential suburb on the hill overlooking the bay was once one of the premium areas, and though it has now fallen from grandeur it is thought to have been named after Melbourne's exclusive suburb of Toorak.

Orientation

Suva is on a peninsula about 3km wide by 5km long, with Laucala Bay to the east and Suva Harbour to the west. Most of the peninsula is hilly apart from the relatively flat area downtown near the wharf and market. There are three major roads in and out of the city: the Queens Road via Lami to the west; Princes Rd along the Tamavua ridge to the north; and the Kings Road to the north-east towards Nausori. Drivers may find central Suva's meandering one-way streets, angled intersections and contorted loops a bit challenging at first.

The Queens Road from Nadi skirts Suva Harbour and enters downtown Suva from the north. If you're driving, pass the prison and industrial area and cross the bridge over the Walu Bay inlet. At the roundabout, Edinburgh Dr heads uphill to the left to Samabula, and from there you can follow the Kings Road through to Nausori International Airport. Princes Rd heads north from Samabula through Tamavua Heights and is a scenic route to Nausori. Alternatively, at the roundabout at Walu Bay, follow Rodwell Rd past the bus station and market, and across Nubukalou Creek to central Suva.

The suburb of Toorak is on the hill overlooking the market. This area has some no-through streets. Waimanu Rd, an extension of Victoria Parade and Renwick Rd, takes you up past Suva Hospital to Samabula.

Suva's GPO and main business strip is along Victoria Parade, which runs parallel to the waterfront. If you keep heading south you will pass the Government Buildings, Albert Park and Thurston Gardens, where Victoria Parade becomes Queen Elizabeth

Dr. This then passes Government House and Suva Point, and finishes near the USP and the National Stadium, on the eastern side of the peninsula on Laucala Bay. From Laucala Bay you can either head north to meet the Kings Road, or head west back to central Suva via Laucala Bay Road.

Maps The best source of maps is the Department of Lands & Surveys, Room 10, Records & Reprographic Subsection, Government Buildings, Suva. Here you can buy *Suva, Lami & Environs* and maps of other parts of Fiji. Opening hours are 9 am to 3.30 pm (to 3 pm Friday), but it's closed from 1 to 2 pm for lunch. The Post Shop at the GPO and some bookshops and newsagencies also stock this map. The FVB also has brochures and maps.

Information
Tourist Offices The main source of good tourist information is the Fiji Visitors Bureau (FVB; ☎ 302 433, fax 300 970, @ infodesk@fijifvb.gov.fj, PO Box 92), which has its head office in Suva on the corner of Thomson and Scott Sts. Check out its Web site at www.bulafiji.com. The staff are helpful and friendly. Like the Nadi International Airport office, it has an extensive stock of brochures for you to browse through and get lost in. It is open from 8 am to 4.30 pm Monday to Thursday (to 4 pm Friday and to noon Saturday). It is closed Sunday and on public holidays. It also has a 24-hour, toll-free visitors' helpline (☎ 0800 721 721) to handle complaints and emergencies.

The Tourism Council of the South Pacific (☎ 304 177, fax 301 995, @ spice@is.com.fj) has an office on the corner of Loftus St and Victoria Parade (on the 3rd floor, above Dolphin Plaza). For more information see Tourist Offices in the Facts for the Visitor chapter.

In addition to those publications already mentioned in the Tourist Offices section of the Facts for the Visitor chapter, the following may also be useful:

Spotlight on Suva This is a local advertising newspaper (free) that also has information on restaurants, shops, tours and activities.

Suva: A History and Guide by Albert J Schutz is published by Pacific Publications, Sydney, 1978.

Money Westpac Bank (☎ 300 666, fax 300 275), at 1 Thomson St, and the ANZ bank (☎ 301 755, fax 300 267), at 25 Victoria Parade, are the best places to change money in Suva. The Suva branches of the ANZ and Bank of Hawaii have ATMs. Bank hours are 9.30 am to 3 pm Monday to Thursday (to 4 pm Friday). Thomas Cook (☎ 301 603), at 21 Thomson St, also changes travellers cheques and foreign currency and is open from 8.30 am to 5 pm weekdays, (to noon Saturdays). Some hotels, including the budget South Seas Private Hotel and Travel Inn, will also change travellers cheques for guests at the going bank rate. The Centra will exchange foreign currency on Sunday, but at lower rates than banks.

Post & Communications There are many cardphones around the city, including in the arcade next to the GPO. Fintel, or Fiji International Telecommunications (☎ 312 933, fax 301 025), 158 Victoria Parade, provides international phone calls, faxes and telegrams. It also provides line to connect your own notebook computer to the Net. It is open 8 am to 8 pm Monday to Saturday.

Email & Internet Access The Republic of Cappuccino (☎ 300 333), in Dolphin Plaza on Victoria Parade, has email and Internet services. It is open 7 am to 11 pm daily (from 10 am Sunday). For Internet access, but no coffee, visit the Alpha Computer Centre (☎ 300 211, fax 302 089, @ alphacomputer@is.com.fj) on Victoria Parade. Alpha is also one of several shops that sells PCs in Suva. If staff there can't repair your PC they should be able to put you in touch with people who can.

Travel Agencies Travel agencies in Suva include:

Air Fiji (☎ 314 666, fax 300 771) 185 Victoria Parade
Air New Zealand (☎ 313 100, fax 302 294) Queensland Insurance Building, Victoria Parade

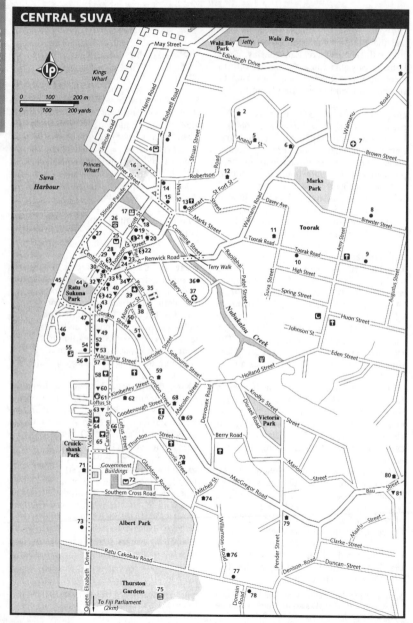

CENTRAL SUVA

CENTRAL SUVA

PLACES TO STAY
1   Outrigger Hotel;
    Papa La Pizza
2   Tropic Towers Apartment
    Hotel
5   Colonial Lodge
6   Annandale Apartments
11 Uptown Motel
12 Capricorn Apartment Hotel
38 Town House Hotel;
    Roof Top Bar
50 Sunset Apartment Hotel
59 Southern Cross Hotel
62 Coconut Inn
68 Elixir Motel Apartments
69 Berjaya Hotel; Kampong Ku
70 Travel Inn
71 Centra
74 Suva Motor Inn
76 South Seas Private Hotel
79 Suva Peninsula International
    Hotel
80 Suva Apartments

PLACES TO EAT
18 Crown of India;
    Pizza King; The Wishbone
    & The Wedge
23 Chef's Restaurant
    & Ice Cream Parlour
28 Govinda Vegetarian
    Restaurant
30 Cardo's Chargill
32 McDonald's
34 Lantern Palace;
    Hare Krishna Restaurant
40 Palm Court Bistro;
    Sunflower Airlines
45 Tiko's Floating Restaurant;
    Tingles

48 JJ's Bar & Grill
49 New Peking
53 Bad Dog Cafe; Lucky Eddies;
    Pizza Hut; O'Reilly's
60 Daikoku Restaurant;
    Traps Bar
63 Dolphin Plaza Food Court;
    Republic of Cappuccino;
    Tourism Council of the
    South Pacific
66 Old Mill Cottage
81 Noble House; Aberdeen Grill;
    Taipan Restaurant;
    Scandals Disco

OTHER
3   Supermarket
4   Bus Station; Taxi Stand
7   Hospital
8   Fiji Recompression Chamber
    Facility
9   Indian Cultural Centre
10 Laundry
13 Beachcomber Cruises;
    Patterson Brothers Shipping
14 Morris Hedstrom
    Supermarket
15 South Pacific Recordings
16 Suva Municipal Market
17 Village 6 Cinema Complex
19 Consort; Shipping Line
20 Desai Bookshop; Bakery
21 Fiji Visitors Bureau (FVB)
22 Money Exchange;
    Garrick Hotel Building
24 Jack's Handicrafts;
    Thomas Cook;
    Prouds Duty-Free
25 GPO; Fiji Philatelic Bureau;
    AJ Swann Drug Store Ltd

26 Telephone Exchange
27 Curio & Handicraft Centre
29 Westpac Bank
31 Air Pacific; Qantas
33 ANZ Bank
35 Roman Catholic Cathedral
36 Suva Bookshop
37 Boulevard Medical Centre;
    Central Pharmacy;
    Downtown Boulevard
    Shopping Centre Food Court
39 Police Station
41 Air New Zealand
42 Bank of Hawaii
43 National Bank
44 Public Toilets
46 Town Hall & Suva City
    Council
47 Fiji International
    Telecommunications (Fintel)
51 Emosi's Shipping
52 Air Fiji
54 Old Town Hall; Ashiyana;
    Ming Palace; Jackson
    Takeaway; Greenpeace
55 Suva Olympic Pool
56 Suva City Library
57 Government Crafts Centre
    & Ratu Sakuna House
58 Birdland R&B Club
61 Shell Petrol Station
64 Golden Dragon Nightclub
65 The Barn
67 St Andrew's Church
72 Post Office
73 Grand Pacific Hotel Building
75 Fiji Museum; Botanic
    Gardens Clock Tower
77 Alliance Française
78 Spachee

Air Pacific (☎ 304 388, fax 302 860) CML Building, Victoria Parade

Hunts Travel (☎ 315 288, fax 302 212) 1st floor, Dominion House arcade. Hunts is a general agent for international air tickets.

Qantas Airways (☎ 311 833, fax 304 795) CML Building, Victoria Parade

Sunflower Airlines (☎ 315 755, fax 305 027) 1st floor, Queensland Insurance Building, Victoria Parade

See the Getting There & Away entry later in this section for contact details of inter-island-ferry agencies.

Bookshops The University of the South Pacific has two good bookshops: the USP Book Centre at the Services Centre, which stocks textbooks as well as books about the South Pacific, and the Institute of Pacific Studies (☎ 313 900, 212 018, fax 301 594), a publisher with an interesting catalogue, including over 250 titles by local authors. Its small bookshop, also at the USP, accepts cash and mail orders. The Fiji Museum has a few interesting books for sale, as does Desai Bookshop at the Dominion House arcade, near the FVB.

Libraries The Fiji Museum (☎ 315 944, fax 305 143, @ fijimuseum@is.com.fj) has a good reference library. You need to pay a small fee/donation and call in advance to request a visit. The Suva City Library, on Victoria Parade next to the old town hall, has a small library on the ground floor.

The best Pacific collection is at the university library, a large resource centre for the whole of the South Pacific region. Visitors can pay a F$50 deposit to borrow books from the general library. Books from the Pacific collection, however, cannot be borrowed and visitors can only use this part of the library for one day. Opening hours are 8 am to 10 pm Monday to Thursday (to 6 pm Friday), from 9 am to 6 pm Saturday, and from 1.30 to 6 pm Sunday. Reduced hours apply during vacation breaks.

Spachee, the South Pacific Action Committee for Human Ecology & Environment (☎ 312 371, fax 303 053), at the corner of Ratu Cakobau and Domain Rds, has a small reference library. The organisation aims to create awareness of issues that affect environment, sustainability and growth in the South Pacific region.

Greenpeace (☎ 312 861, fax 782), on the first floor above old town hall building on Victoria Parade, also has a reference library.

Cultural Centres The Fiji Museum promotes indigenous Fijian culture (see Fiji Museum later in this section). Other cultural centres include:

Alliance Française (☎ 313 802, fax 313 803) 77 Cakobau Rd, Suva
Indian Cultural Centre (☎ 300 050) 271 Toorak Rd, Suva. This centre promotes Indian culture, with lectures and theatre, and language, music and dance classes.

Laundry Most resorts and hotels will do your laundry for about F$5 a load. Same-day laundry and dry-cleaning services are also available in Suva.

Medical Services Boulevard Medical Centre has a good reputation and is conveniently located in downtown Suva with a pharmacy nearby. Visits to the GP are usually F$10 to F$20, although if you have an International Student Card you should be able to attend the university medical clinic for free.

AJ Swann Drug Store Ltd (☎ 302 743) in the arcade next to the GPO, Thomson St. Opening hours are 8 am to 6 pm weekdays, 8 am to 1.30 pm Saturdays and 9 am to noon Sundays and public holidays.
Boulevard Medical Centre (☎ 313 355, fax 302 423) 33 Ellery St. Opening hours are from 8.30 am to 5 pm weekdays and 8.30 am to 11.30 am Saturdays.
Central Pharmacy (☎ 303 770) Shop 13, Downtown Boulevard Shopping Centre. Opening hours are 8 am to 5.30 pm weekdays and 8 am to 1 pm Saturdays.
Colonial War Memorial Hospital (☎ 313 444) Waimanu Rd
Fiji Recompression Chamber Facility (☎ 850 630, fax 850 344) cnr Amy & Brewster Sts.
Flagstaff Pharmacy (☎ 304 001) 7 Rewa St, Flagstaff. The pharmacy is a 10-minute drive from downtown Suva towards the USP. It's open Monday to Saturday from 9 am to 8 pm, and on Sundays and public holidays from 5 pm to 8 pm, but ring to confirm opening hours.
Samabula Drug Store (☎ 385 900) 77 Ratu Mara Rd, Samabula. Opening hours are 8.30 am to 8 pm Monday to Saturday, 5 pm to 8 pm Sundays and 9 am to 7 pm on public holidays.

Emergency Some useful emergency numbers are:

Emergency	☎ 000
FVB Emergency Hotline	☎ 0800 721 721
Police	☎ 311 222
Tourist Police	☎ 302 433 + 215
Ambulance	☎ 301 439
Fiji Recompression Chamber	
Facility, emergency	☎ 362 172

Walking Tour

Most of the colonial buildings and places of interest are concentrated in central Suva, and it is easy to get around on foot. Allow a few hours for this tour, to take breaks along the way and avoid the midday heat. Most places are closed on Sundays, and Saturday mornings are the busiest, especially around the market.

Using the Central Suva map as a guide, begin at the **FVB** building (1912). Opposite is the **Garrick Hotel** (1914), now the Sichuan Pavilion Restaurant. Pause at the tiny park in front of Proud's Duty-Free shop. The historical marker here commemorates the arrival of the first missionaries in 1835, the annexation of Fiji by Britain in 1874, public land sales in 1880 and the proclamation of Suva as the capital of Fiji in 1882. Head down **Victoria Parade**, Suva's main street, which is lined with shops, banks, airline offices, nightclubs and many colonial buildings. Cross Ratu Sukuna Park to the waterfront for a view across Suva Harbour to the mountain ranges and the distinctive **Joske's Thumb**. Head north to the **Curio & Handicraft Centre** for a browse through the souvenir stalls (8 am to 5 pm from Monday to Saturday).

Then walk along the foreshore to the **Suva Municipal Market**. This bustling produce market is a must-see. It is a good place to buy kava for village visits (the unpounded roots are better) and to sample local foods. Vendors sell exotic fruit and vegetables, *nama* (seaweed), fish, crabs, spices, brightly coloured Indian sweets and savouries, and fruit drinks from glass tanks. The top floor has mostly tobacco and kava. You will probably be offered to try a bowl. The multiracial and multicultural mix of people and produce is interesting.

Head south-east to busy Cumming St, which in the 1920s was known for its *yaqona* saloons and 'dens of iniquity'. At the end of Cumming St turn right into Renwick Rd and left at Pratt St. On the left is the **Roman Catholic Cathedral** (1902), one of Suva's most prominent landmarks. Head right at Murray St, right again at Gordon St, and then left back on to Victoria Parade. Continue along past the **Fintel building** (1926) and the **old town hall** (1904). The old town hall building now houses several restaurants but was once used for dances, bazaars and performances. The **Suva Olympic Pool** is set back between this building and the **Suva City Library** (1909).

Turn left at Macarthur St (consider a stop at the Bad Dog) and have a browse in the **Government Crafts Centre**. Turn right along Carnavon St, where you can stop for coffee at the Republic of Cappuccino, or for food at the Old Mill Cottage. Opposite the Old Mill Cottage is a **rusting cog wheel** uncovered during excavations for the Native Lands Trust Board (NLTB) building. It is thought to be a remainder of the sugar mill previously on this site. Built in 1873 and owned by Brewer & Joske, it was Fiji's first mill. Growing sugar cane in this wet area, however, proved unsuccessful.

The impressive **Government Buildings** (1939 and 1967) at the end of Carnarvon St required heavy foundations as they were

Ratu Sukuna & the Native Lands Trust Board

By 1905, 17% of Fijian land had been sold to non-Fijian landowners, when the colonial government imposed a decree to prevent the sale of any more native land. Ratu Sukuna, who was the first Fijian to be educated overseas and the first to receive a university degree (in law, from the University of Oxford), spent years studying the boundaries of land owned by the many *mataqali* and *yavusa* (Fijian landowning groups). He negotiated with every mataqali in Fiji and the Great Council of Chiefs to resolve land disputes.

One of his most significant contributions to Fiji was the setting up of the Native Lands Trust Board (NLTB) in 1940. The NLTB endeavoured to prevent Fijians from entering long leases for quick profits at the expense of the needs of future generations, as well as to make surplus land available for lease.

The plaque on Sukuna's statue outside the Government Buildings reads: 'Ratu Sir Lala Sukuna, Tui Lau, Statesman Soldier, Paramount Chief and Leader of Men, 1888–1958'. The anniversary of his death is commemorated with a national holiday.

built on reclaimed land over a creek bed. The Department of Lands & Survey is of interest, as it was the scene of the 1987 coup. Parliament has now moved to new premises, but government departments and the courts remain. The statues of two influential Fijians (Ratu Cakobau and Ratu Sukuna) are in the front gardens on Victoria Parade.

Farther along Victoria Parade is **Albert Park**, which was named after Queen Victoria's husband. The Polynesia Company gave this land to the government as an incentive for moving the capital to Suva. It has a cricket ground, tennis courts and the **Kingsford Smith Pavilion**, named after the famous aviator who landed here. On the foreshore opposite the park is the **Grand Pacific Hotel** building (1914), built by the Union Steamship Company. It is a fantastic site looking across the bay to the mountains. Its ship-style architecture is reminiscent of the 1st-class ship accommodation of the era, with rooms opening onto a deck-like verandah and with an internal balcony over an entertainment area. Elegant in its heyday, the building awaits its long-promised renovations and sits boarded-up and neglected. It is owned by the people of Nauru.

At this point Victoria Parade becomes Queen Elizabeth Dr. Continue along the waterfront to the **former government house** (1928). Now that Fiji is a republic, the house has become the president's residence. The precinct is not open to the public and the entrance is guarded by a soldier in a red shirt and white handkerchief sulu. In 1921 the original government house (1882) on this site, built for Governor Des Voeux, was struck by lightning and burnt down.

Return north to **Thurston Gardens** (1913), near Albert Park. The gates are open from 6 am to 6.30 pm daily. These botanical gardens are named after Sir John Bates Thurston, an amateur botanist who introduced many ornamental plant species to Fiji. The **Botanic Gardens Clock Tower**, near the entrance to the Fiji Museum, was built in 1918. Finish the walking tour at the Fiji Museum, or if you still have the time and energy, visit the parliament buildings (it's probably worth taking a taxi).

Fiji Museum

The Fiji Museum (☎ 315 944, fax 305 143, ✉ fijimuseum@is.com.fj), in the grounds of Thurston Gardens, is definitely worth a visit. It has a fascinating collection of artefacts, including *drua*, weapons, ceremonial *tabua*, kava bowls, necklaces, breastplates, tools and cooking utensils, and Reverend Baker's old boot, which was reportedly cooked along with his body parts. There is a room upstairs with beautiful examples of masi bark cloth. Exhibits cover aspects of Fiji's history, such as the Tongan influence, early traders and settlers, blackbirding and Indian indenture.

The museum also undertakes archaeological research, collects and preserves oral traditions and publishes such works as *Domodomo*, a quarterly journal on history, language, culture, art and natural history. It also organises exhibitions and craft demonstrations. Fiji's best-known potters, Taraivini Wati and Diana Tugea, give joint

---

Kingsford Smith

Charles Kingsford Smith was the first aviator to cross the Pacific, flying in his Fokker trimotor, *The Southern Cross,* from California to Australia. The longest leg of the flight was the 34-hour trip from Hawaii to Fiji. Suva's Albert Park, with its hill at one end and the Grand Pacific Hotel at the other, was made into a makeshift landing strip for his arrival. Trees were still being cleared after he had already left Hawaii. Kingsford Smith and his crew arrived on 6 June 1928, and were welcomed by a crowd of thousands, including colonial dignitaries who had gathered at the Grand Pacific Hotel to witness and celebrate this major event. The pilot had to spin the plane around at the end of the park to avoid crashing. Because the park was too short to take-off with a heavy load of fuel, they had to unload, fly to Nasilai Beach and reload for take off to Brisbane and Sydney. Kingsford Smith and his crew were presented with a ceremonial *tabua* (whale's tooth) as a token of great respect.

VITI LEVU

Drua

A *drua* (double-hulled canoe) named *Ra Marama* was given to King George of Tonga by Ratu Cakobau for help in his war against the people of Rewa. Built in the early 1850s, it was over 30m long, with an 18m-high mast, 90 sq m of deck space and could carry more than 150 people. It could sail faster than the European sailing ships of the era. Some drua could carry up to 300 people and building could take as long as seven years.

Work began with the felling of two large trees, which were spliced together to form the keel. The hulls were made from split logs, and mulberry bark was used as a caulking material. Construction involved ceremonial human sacrifices, and the completed vessel was launched over the bodies of slaves, which were used as rollers under the hulls.

demonstrations at the museum on the first Thursday of each month, and Wati can also be seen each Thursday and Friday.

Lack of space and funding are perennial problems. A design competition for new premises has been held, and the museum must raise through donations F$10 to F$15 million. Admission is F$3.30 (children free). Opening hours are 9.30 am to 4 pm weekdays, 1 to 4 pm weekends. The Friends of the Fiji Museum Society publishes a quarterly newsletter called *Time Connections*. Annual subscriptions cost F$15/30 for students/individuals living abroad. For more information call ☎ 315 944, fax 305 143, or write to PO Box 2023, Government Buildings, Suva. Volunteers are needed in the Collections, Archaeology and Education departments to organise archives and artefacts, and to organise children's projects and archaeology field programs.

Parliament of Fiji

The parliament complex (☎ 305 811) opened in June 1992. It consists of the *vale ni bose lawa* (parliament house) and separate buildings for committee facilities and parliament, government and opposition offices. Both the House of Representatives and the Senate meet in the same chamber at different times.

The parliament is of architectural interest. Designed by Viti Architects, the concept was to integrate traditional Fijian building forms and crafts with a contemporary feel and modern technology, addressing shade, natural light and ventilation. It also reinforces the direction of the postcoup government towards maintaining traditional indigenous-Fijian values. The building, with its stone base and dominant roof form, is based on form of the traditional *vale* (family house). The site and landscaping form a symbolic link between the land and the sea. The complex is planned around courtyards and uses landscaping and covered walkways to link the various buildings. Internally, Fijian elements include masi banners, *lalawa-magimagi* (weaving of the ceiling structure and round concrete columns), extensive use of timber, and crafted furniture.

The buildings are visible from Queen Elizabeth Dr but the visitors' entry is off Battery Rd, with ceremonial access from Ratu Sukuna Rd. The complex is 5km from the city centre and the easiest way to get there is by taxi, otherwise take a bus along Queen Elizabeth Dr and walk along Ratu Sukuna Rd for about 1km. Visiting hours are 8 am to 1 pm and 2 to 4.30 pm weekdays. Entry is free.

University of the South Pacific

The Laucala campus (☎ 313 900, fax 301 305) is the main campus of the regional university for 1.5 million people of 12 South Pacific countries. It has 11,000 students, including part-timers and distance learners. See its Web site at www.usp.ac.fj. It has Schools of Humanities, Agriculture, Law, Pure & Applied Sciences and Social & Economic Development. There are also seven institutes: Applied Sciences; Education; Marine Resources; Management & Development; Justice & Applied Legal Studies; Pacific Studies and Research, Extension & Training in Agriculture. The Law School and Pacific Languages Unit are in Vanuatu, while the Agriculture School is at the Western Samoa campus.

The Reverend Baker

The Wesleyan Methodist missionary, Thomas Baker, was killed on 21 July 1867 by the Vatusila people at Nabutautau village, in the isolated headwaters of Sigatoka River in the Nausori Highlands. A few years earlier he had been given the task of converting the people of the interior of Viti Levu to Christianity. Out of impatience, martyrdom, foolhardiness or the urge for success, he ignored advice to keep to areas under the influence of already converted groups. Many felt it was almost inevitable that he would offend the highlanders in some way.

One theory maintains that the Reverend's death was political. The highlanders associated conversion to Christianity with subservience to the chiefdom of Bau and were opposed to any kind of extended authority.

Another version is that the local chief borrowed Baker's comb while the missionary was out. Insensitive or forgetful of the fact that the chief's head was considered sacred, Baker snatched the comb from the chief's hair. Villagers were furious at the missionary for committing this sacrilege and killed and ate him in disgust. His flesh was shared among neighbouring villages. One local laughingly recounts the story of his ancestors: 'We ate everything, even tried to eat his shoes'. Baker's shoe is exhibited in the Fiji Museum. Twenty years after Baker's death, a mission teacher, guided by a repentant eater, recovered the Reverend's humerus from within the overgrown fork of a large shaddock tree. The bone had been placed there as a trophy.

USP is a fee-paying institution and most students rely on scholarships. Competition to obtain scholarships is fierce, and the government's policy of 'positive discrimination' is controversial. Scholarships are awarded by the Government Public Service: 50% are allocated to indigenous Fijians, while Indian, Chinese, European and other races compete for the remaining 50%. The Native Lands Trust Board also has scholarships specifically for indigenous Fijians.

The campus, on the site of a former New Zealand seaplane base, is a pleasant place to visit. Many of the buildings have been financed by the Australian or New Zealand governments. The main entrance is off Laucala Bay Rd and is a 10 to 15-minute drive from downtown Suva. Inside the entrance, on the right, is a small botanical garden, with Pacific plants, which is open from 8 am to 4 pm weekdays. There are frequent buses to the USP: the Vatuwaqa bus departs opposite the Dominion arcade in Thomson St, near the FVB. The taxi fare from the city is about F$2.

Colo-i-Suva Forest Park

The Colo-i-Suva Forest Park (pronounced tholo-ee-soo-va) is comprised of about 245 hectares of forest in the hills north of Suva. Great for escaping the capital on a hot day, it has three natural swimming pools (with rope swings), about 6.5km of walking track and a 500m-long nature trail. The park has toilets, shelters, BBQ pits and picnic tables.

The Waisila Creek flows down to Waimanu River and is the water catchment for the Nausori/Nasinu areas. The forest here was logged in the late 1940s and early 1950s, and while the surrounding area has been extensively cleared, the park area was replanted with introduced mahogany. It is now managed by the Department of Forestry. The Visitor Information Centre at the park's Forest Station (☎ 320 211) is on the left on the top of the hill (entry F$5 per person).

You have to travel about 2km along the gravel Kalabu Rd from the forest station to reach the Upper Pools car park, and then walk about 250m to the pools. If on foot, hike in along the Falls Trail (from Princes Rd to the Waisila Falls it's about 800m, and then it's a farther 570m to the Upper Pools). There is a security booth at the car park, attended from 9 am to 4 pm daily, but watch your belongings anyway. Leave anything valuable at the Visitor Information Centre, not in your car. Camping is no longer allowed because there have been robberies in the past.

The park is popular with bird-watchers. There are about 14 bird species, among which you may see or hear barking pigeons, sulphur-breasted musk parrots, Fiji warblers and golden doves.

Take high-speed film as the forest is quite dense, and wear hiking boots because it can be slippery in the wet.

Getting There & Away The park is about 11km north of Suva. The Sawani bus leaves Suva bus station every half-hour (20 minutes, F$0.65). The forest station is on the left on top of the hill. If driving, take Princes Rd out of Suva, past Tamavua and Tacirua villages.

Activities

Not much happens in Suva on Sunday so try to organise activities in advance or attend a Fijian church service to hear some great singing.

Bushwalking Colo-i-Suva Forest Park is an easy place for bushwalking close to Suva (see earlier in this section for details). You can also hike to Mt Korobaba, about a one-to two-hour walk from the cement factory near Lami. Joske's Thumb is an enticing spectacle from Suva. A climb to this peak was featured in the film *Journey to the Dawning of the Day*.

Keen walkers should contact the Rucksack Club. The president and membership changes regularly, as most of the 80 to 100 members are expats on contract in Fiji. Ask the FVB for the latest contact number. The club is dedicated to appreciating Fiji's natural beauty and culture through outdoor-walking adventures. It has fortnightly meetings, with guest speakers and performers, at St Andrew's Church (a small, simple weatherboard structure that dates back to 1895) on the corner of Gordon and Goodenough Sts.

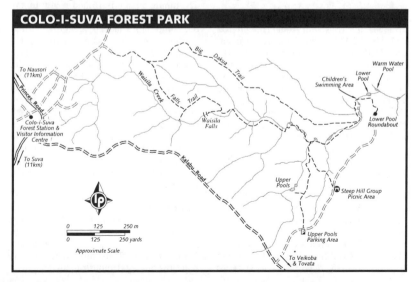

COLO-I-SUVA FOREST PARK

Weekly activities include bushwalks and trips inland or to other islands. For further information, write to PO Box 2394, Government Buildings, Suva.

Swimming The Suva Olympic Swimming Pool, 224 Victoria Parade next to the Suva City Library, is a welcome retreat on a hot day. It's cheap, is seldom crowded and is reasonably clean (open from 10 am to 6 pm weekdays from April to September, and from 6 am to 7 pm weekdays and 8 am to 6 pm Saturdays from October to March). Admission is F$1.10 for adults. Change cubicles are available for a small charge. Keen lap swimmers could also try the university's 25m pool (F$2 admission, open from 7 am to 6 pm daily).

The nearest decent beach is at Deuba, Pacific Harbour. It is a 50-minute drive from Suva, although by local bus it can take much longer. Alternatively, there are the freshwater pools at Colo-i-Suva Forest Park. There are also freshwater pools at Wailoku Falls. Take a Wailoku bus from the Suva bus station, get off at the end of the line, walk down the gravel road to the creek and then walk upstream for about five minutes.

Diving The Centra hotel in Suva also arranges dive trips with Aqua-Trek (☎ 702 413, fax 702 412) at the Centra resort in Pacific Harbour. Scuba Hire (☎ 361 088, fax 361 047), 75 Marine Drive, Lami, has dive trips to Beqa Lagoon and runs diving courses. The *Nai'a,* a 33m live-aboard yacht (☎ 361 382, fax 362 511), is based at Pacific Harbour. It has a 12-person crew, a photo-processing room with E6 processing, and takes up to 18 passengers.

Surfing There is a surf-break near Suva lighthouse, but you need a boat to get there. Trips with Matthew Light (☎ 998 830) cost F$20. Ed Lovell from the Fiji Surf Association (☎ 361 358) may be able to give some advice on local conditions.

Sailing Visiting yachties can get membership at the Royal Suva Yacht Club (☎ 312 921, fax 304 433, @ rsyc@is.com.fj). Fees

for the marina are F$15/30 for one person/two or more people per week at an offshore mooring. The club has bathrooms with hot water and a laundromat (F$3.50 per load wash and dry), which are open 24 hours a day. Even without a yacht, overseas visitors are welcome and can be signed in for weekend social activities. The clubhouse has great views of the Bay of Islands and the mountains, including Joske's Thumb, and is a pleasant place to spend a few hours. The cafe is reasonably priced and has the best homemade pies in Suva (F$5). It's often possible to take a trip across the bay or out to the offshore island of Nukulau on weekends with one of the practising crews. The office is open from 8 am to 5 pm weekdays and 8 am to noon Saturdays. On Tuesday evenings there is a BBQ with half-price beer from 6 to 7.30 pm.

Organised Tours

Wilderness Ethnic Adventure Fiji (☎ 387 594, fax 300 584) offers several tours, which pick up from Suva hotels. An all-day trip with canoeing/rafting on the beautiful Navua River includes a BBQ lunch and costs F$69 per person. Expect to get wet. The minimum age is 15 and if you're any older than 45 you have to sign a liability disclaimer! Life jackets are provided but you must be able to swim. A trip up the Navua River by motorboat with a village visit costs F$59. A half/full-day Rewa Delta and Nasilai village tour is F$39/54 per person. The tour includes a visit to a Hindu temple and the St Joseph Catholic Church (1901), as well as entertainment and demonstrations of pottery or mat weaving.

Discover Fiji Tours (☎ 450 180, fax 450 549), based in Navua, also offers trips to a waterfall up the Navua River (see under Navua in the Queens Road section earlier in this chapter).

Special Events

Check with the FVB to see if there are any special events coinciding with your stay. In August, Suva has a week-long **Hibiscus Festival** that has floats, processions and Fijian fire-walking demonstrations.

There are several Hindu religious festivals observed in Suva and around the country. Fire walking and body piercing is held at the Mariamma Temple, Howell Rd, Samabula, also in August.

In March or April each year, there is a party on the shores of Laucala Bay to celebrate the birth of Lord Rama, with offerings, flowers and swimming in the bay.

Places to Stay

The capital has a variety of places to stay. There are some good budget options, as well as many mid-range hotel rooms and long-term apartments, and a few top-end hotels. The closest island resort is Toberua to the east. See Nausori & the Rewa Delta in the Kings Road section later in this chapter for more information.

Places to Stay – Budget

Hostels The Cathay chain runs two budget accommodations in Suva (South Seas Private Hotel and Travel Inn), both with clean and spartan rooms. They are affiliated with the HI New Zealand and Backpacker Resorts International. At both Cathay hotels travellers cheques are accepted, but not credit cards. Small discounts are available for long stays and for those with Nomads Dreamtime cards, YHA or VIP cards.

South Seas Private Hotel (☎ 312 296, fax 340 236, ◙ southseas@fiji4less.com, 6 Williamson Rd) is a classic, old, double-storey weatherboard building near the Thurston Gardens and is a good option for the budget traveller. It offers a variety of rooms, so take a look at few before choosing. Dorms (maximum of five people) cost F$9.50 per person, single rooms are F$16, double or twin rooms are F$24 (the double room at the back next to laundry is well ventilated and has windows facing the green backyard), and triple family rooms are F$32. All rooms have shared facilities. Rooms with en suite are F$36 for single or double occupancy. All rooms have fans and the bathrooms are clean and have solar hot water. Downstairs there is a communal lounge, kitchen and dining and there's a book exchange. You can keep gear in a storage room, and staff are generally friendly. As with many budget places you may find the occasional cockroach.

Cathay also runs *Travel Inn (☎ 304 254, fax 340 236, ◙ travelinn@fiji4less.com, 19 Gorrie St)*. It is in a convenient location in a quiet street near the Government Buildings, within an easy walk to the city centre. The old building, a bit reminiscent of a prison with rooms in a U-shape around a central stairway, has singles, doubles or twin fan-cooled rooms. Its rooms are paired to share a bathroom and a small area with a table, sink, refrigerator and a common door to the outside. Singles/doubles cost F$18.50/27 and self-contained apartments are F$44/55 for three/four people. There is a small but reasonably good communal kitchen and dining area, which is open from 7 am to 7.30 pm.

Sunset Apartment Motel (☎ 301 799, fax 303 446), on the corner of Gordon and Murray Sts near the city centre, has a clean 12-bed dormitory. It has one bathroom, two toilets, a refrigerator, lockers and a small sitting area, but no cooking facilities, for F$8.70 per person.

Coconut Inn (☎ 305 881, 8 Kimberley St) is a small, rock-bottom hotel that has cramped and stuffy four to six-bed dorms for F$10 per person. It has a small sitting area at reception, a kitchen where you can cook, but poor atmosphere.

On the university campus there is good accommodation at *USP Lodges (☎ 212 614, fax 314 827, ◙ ganesan-r@usp.ac.fj)*. It offers self-contained units with cooking facilities for F$45/55 a single/double, and rooms with shared facilities in two double buildings on the upper and lower campus for F$35/40. Advanced booking are required.

B&Bs *Colonial Lodge (☎/fax 300 655, 19 Anand St)* is an excellent small-scale place to stay. The restored colonial home has private rooms, and verandah upstairs with bay views. Beds in the dorm downstairs cost F$14.50, while a twin-bed, shared-facilities room is F$25/40 for singles/doubles and an en suite room F$35/60. Rates include a cooked breakfast. The food is good and the three-course dinners are good value.

Hotels & Motels *Tropic Towers Apartment Hotel* (☎ *304 470, fax 304 169, 86 Robertson Rd*) is a short walk up the hill from the bus station and the Suva Municipal Market. The budget rooms in this old building cost F$33/44 with fan/air-con for singles or doubles with shared bathroom and kitchen (the upstairs rooms are better). There is a sitting room with TV and guests can use the hotel's pool facilities and have a load of washing done for F$3. It also has mid-range rooms (see Places to Stay – Mid-Range, later in this section).

Uptown Motel (☎ *306 044, fax 306 094, 55 Toorak Rd*), above a furniture shop, looks dodgy from the outside but is surprisingly clean inside and has friendly staff. It has 13 rooms, which are OK-value. The dorm (maximum of six people) is F$10 per person. Large double rooms with private bathroom, fridge and phone are F$33/35 for fan/air-con for singles or doubles.

Outrigger Hotel (☎ *314 944, fax 302 944, 349 Waimanu Rd near the hospital*) appears to be improving its previously run-down facilities and poor services. It now has reasonably clean 10-bed dorm accommodation with air-con, fans and private bathroom (which they call intercom rooms) for F$20 per bed, and air-con private rooms for F$49 for singles or doubles. Some rooms have a good view of Suva Harbour and the mountains. It also has a bar and pizzeria on the roof-garden, which has great views (see Pizzerias under Places to Eat later in this section).

There are also several places reputed to be frequented by prostitutes and their clients, which you may prefer to avoid, including: *Saf's Apartment Hotel* and *Motel Capital* on Robertson Rd; *Oceanview Private Hotel* and *New Haven Motel* on Waimanu Rd and *Amy Apartment Hotel* on Amy St.

Places to Stay – Mid-Range

B&Bs *Suva Homestay* (☎ *370 395, fax 370 947,* ✆ *homestaysuva@is.com.fj, Princes Rd, Tamavua*) is a great place to rest travel-weary bones. This renovated colonial house is in large grounds on the Tamavua ridge, with spectacular views over Suva Harbour.

It is a F$3 taxi fare from downtown. Accommodation here is comfortable and homey, with special attention given to details. All five rooms have air-con, fans and en suites. The downstairs 'blue-and-white room' has a deep bath, while the two large rooms upstairs both have fantastic bay views. Rates for B&B are F$115 per night in the downstairs rooms and F$130/140 for singles/doubles upstairs. An excellent breakfast is served on the terrace overlooking the pool and bay. This place is impeccably clean, has a dog, a cat and a laundry service, and home-cooked dinners can be provided for F$25 per person. Book in advance (no young children).

Hotels The 110-room *Raffles Tradewinds Hotel* (☎ *362 450, fax 361 464*), Queens Road, Lami, is about 10 minutes' drive north-west of Suva. It used to be a top-end hotel but now is a bit run-down. Nevertheless, it is right on the water's edge, with great views over the Bay of Islands. Rooms here cost F$102/116 for singles/doubles, but look out for special discounts. Up to two children sharing with parents are free. Suites are more spacious and cost F$154. Hotel amenities include a floating restaurant, swimming pool and bar.

Suva Peninsula International Hotel (☎ *313 711, fax 300 804*), on the corner of Macgregor Rd and Pender St, has undergone refurbishing in most of its 40 units and is popular with Fijian businessmen. Standard rooms are fairly small but clean with air-con, phone, and tea- and coffee-making facilities. Rooms cost F$70/90 for singles/doubles. The more spacious deluxe versions with similar facilities and bigger bathrooms are better value for F$90/110.

The Korean-owned *Southern Cross Hotel* (☎ *314 233, fax 302 901, 63 Gordon St*) has 34 rooms with air-con, minibar and TV for F$88 for singles or doubles. There is a nightclub downstairs (some rooms can therefore be noisy) and a pool at the back. See Places to Eat later in this section for information on the Korean restaurant on the top floor, Seoul House, and Entertainment, also later in this chapter, for information on the disco.

Apartments Suva has a number of mid-range apartments with self-catering facilities, ranging from small blocks to hotel-style amenities such as *Suva Motor Inn (☎ 313 973, fax 300 381)*, corner of Mitchell and Gorrie Sts. It is conveniently located near the Government Buildings and parks. The building is designed around a central courtyard with a swimming pool and waterslide. Some rooms can be noisy. It has 36 air-con studio units with TV and kitchenette for F$100 a single or double, F$20 per extra person. Some have a balcony facing the bay. There are also eight good two-bedroom apartments with kitchenette and dining area for F$170 a single or double, F$10 for each extra person, up to a maximum of six people.

Tropic Towers Apartment Hotel (☎ 304 470, fax 304 169, 86 Robertson Rd) is a four-storey apartment block (no lift) on the hill up from the bus station and the Suva Municipal Market. It offers nondescript but clean and comfortable apartments with air-con, phone, TV and cooking facilities for F$77/88/99 for singles/doubles/triples. It has a swimming pool, bar, a small shop and a secure parking area.

The *Capricorn Apartment Hotel (☎ 303 732, fax 303 069, 7–11 Fort St)* is a four-storey building arranged around a swimming pool and garden area. It has 25 studio rooms and nine deluxe apartments, all with private facilities including a kitchenette, refrigerator, TV and air-con, and some have balconies overlooking Suva Harbour. Standard rooms here are getting a bit old and cost F$93.50/104.50 upstairs/downstairs for singles or doubles. It is better value to pay F$115.50/126.50 for the deluxe one/two-bedroom accommodation (maximum of five people).

Town House Hotel (☎ 300 055, fax 303 446, 3 Foster St) is a five-storey building with very simple, if slightly shabby, self-contained units with air-con, TV, cooking facilities and refrigerator. A bedsit room is F$46/58 for singles/doubles, while one-bedroom apartments cost F$58/68, F$12 per extra adult and F$7.70 per extra child. You can get to the rooftop bar via a rickety external lift for views of the cathedral, city

and bay. Nearby, and run by the same owners, is *Sarita Flats (☎ 300 055, fax 303 466, 39 Gordon St)*. It offers cramped bedsit room apartments for F$55 doubles or two-bedroom apartments for F$80 doubles plus F$12 for each extra adult (up to six). The apartments are spartan but clean with air-con, TV and kitchen.

Sunset Apartment Motel (☎ 301 799, fax 303 446), on the corner of Gordon and Murray Sts, is very close to the city centre. The four-storey building (no lifts) has 15 self-contained basic apartments, nine of which are two-bedroom units. Units with air-con, TV, phone, kitchen, sitting area and verandah cost F$66/77/88 for doubles/triples/quads. Double rooms downstairs without cooking facilities are not good value for F$41.60/46 for singles/doubles.

Opposite Berjaya Hotel, on the corner of Malcolm and Gordon Sts, is *Elixir Motel Apartments (☎ 303 288, fax 303 383)*, which can be busy and noisy at times. The entrance has a security door and camera. The 15 two-bedroom apartments (maximum of three people) with cooking facilities are OK-value for F$55/66 with/without air-con. There is a 10% discount for stays of more than one week.

Other self-contained apartments include the new annex of *Suva Apartments (☎ 304 280, 17 Bau St)* about 1.5km from the city centre opposite Noble House. It has good-value, self-contained, air-con apartments for F$50/65 for singles/doubles.

Annandale Apartments (☎ 311 054, fax 302 171, 265 Waimanu Rd) has shabby but spacious two-bedroom apartments, with ceiling fan, large kitchen and big fridge, and balconies (some with harbour view) for F$45 for singles or doubles and F$60 for up to four people.

Places to Stay – Top End

Centra (☎ 301 600, fax 300 251), previously known as Suva Travelodge, is on Victoria Parade, on the waterfront opposite the Government Buildings. It is popular with business travellers for its proximity to Suva's CBD. There are 130 standard rooms with tea- and coffee-making facilities, phone, TV and air-con for F$154/170.50 for singles/doubles. Renovated deluxe versions are F$225 for singles or doubles and a suite is F$406 for singles or doubles. It has a swimming pool, restaurant and entertainment area with a nightly house band.

Also near central Suva, the Best Western chain of hotels operates *Berjaya Hotel* (☎ 312 300, fax 301 300) on the corner of Malcolm and Gordon Sts. The nine-storey building, previously the Suva Courtesy Inn, has 48 air-con, motel-type rooms and suites. Rooms are all of similar layout, with one double bed, a couch, tiled floor, TV, mini-bar, and tea- and coffee-making facilities. Rooms on the lower floors cost F$134 for singles or doubles, while upper-floor rooms with views of the mountains and harbour are F$146. Amenities include a swimming pool, coffee shop and a reasonable-quality Chinese-Malaysian restaurant.

Those after a more homey environment should consider *Suva Homestay* (see Places to Stay – Mid-Range earlier in this section). The closest island resort is *Toberua Island Resort* (see Toberua in the Kings Road section later in this chapter).

Places to Eat

Restaurants Suva doesn't have as much variety as Nadi, but does have some good restaurants. *Old Mill Cottage* (☎ 312 134, 49 Carnavon St), just around the corner from the Dolphin Plaza Food Court, is probably the best bet for lunch or a fruit-salad. This old weatherboard home with a verandah has been converted into a cute cafe, which is popular with government workers on their lunch break. The Fijian, Indian and Chinese food here is well prepared and very good value for around F$5.50 a dish. Try the *palusami* (corned beef wrapped in taro leaves and then cooked in coconut milk), a traditional Fijian dish. It's open 7 am to 6 pm weekdays, to 5 pm Saturdays.

JJ's Bar & Grill (☎ 305 005, 9–10 Gordon St) is a trendy place for lunch or dinner. It has a choice of indoor air-con or outdoor courtyard dining. It has excellent international-style food, with dishes from F$6 to F$19. Another good place is *Cardo's*

Chargrill (☎ 314 330), an air-con restaurant and bar in Regal Lane. It specialises in beef steak, but also has chargrilled chicken and seafood. The steaks are not cheap (starting at F$18.50) but are great by Fijian standards. Styles include Japanese and Cajun. Cardo's current owner claims to be descended from an Argentinian on board a boat that was pirated while passing through Fiji's Koro Sea in the 19th century.

Tiko's Floating Restaurant (☎ 313 626), a converted Blue Lagoon Cruiser, is anchored at the sea wall near Ratu Sukuna Park. Seafood is its speciality, with dishes from F$7 to F$30. It's open for lunch on weekdays and dinner daily except Sunday. There is a disco below deck. When there is a bit of a swell the rocking and the fresh sea breeze can be pleasant even if the food isn't the best value.

Noble House (☎ 304 322, fax 300 504, 16 Bau St), towards Flagstaff, is comprised of two fine-dining restaurants run by the amiable Jackson Yee. This grandiose building was built to replace the original house, which burnt down in 1981. The *Aberdeen Grill* serves steak and seafood dishes for around F$15 to F$20. It is open noon to 2.30 pm and 6.30 to 10.30 pm weekdays, and on Saturday evenings. In a large ballroom setting, the *Taipan Restaurant* offers mostly Cantonese dishes for F$5 to F$30. The Taipan has fine food but is not up to the standard of the Great Wok (see the following Chinese food entry). There is also a disco (called Scandals) on the premises: see Entertainment later in this section.

Other restaurants include the *Centra*, where smorgasbord lunch is F$12.

Indian Try *Hare Krishna* (☎ 314 154), on the corner of Pratt and Joske Sts, for good cheap vegetarian meals. The downstairs cafe (open 9 am to 7.30 pm weekdays, to 3.30 pm Saturdays) has good-quality ice cream and gaudy-coloured sweets. The air-con restaurant upstairs is open for lunch and early dinner to 7.30 pm weekdays. *Govinda Vegetarian Restaurant,* next the Westpac on Victoria Parade, also has inexpensive vegetarian meals. *Crown of India* (☎ 300 679), upstairs in a building opposite the Village cinema, has very good food and friendly staff. Curries are from F$5 to F$7.50, tandoori F$9 to F$15.50. *Ashiyana (☎ 313 000)*, in the old town hall, has good Indian dishes for F$8. It is open daily for lunch and dinner.

Chinese Suva has many Chinese restaurants. Perhaps the best is **Great Wok of China** *(☎ 301 285)*, on the corner of Bau St and Laucala Bay Rd, Flagstaff. The food is excellent, with dishes costing an average of F$12. It specialises in Sichuan cuisine. Try the bêche-de-mer if you are game (yuk!). It is open noon to 2 pm and 6.15 to 10.45 pm weekdays, and on Saturday nights.

Lantern Palace (☎ 314 633, 10 Pratt St) downtown has friendly staff, and dishes are reliable and good-value for around F$8. As well as Chinese food, it serves sizzling Mongolian dishes, steaks, salads and fish and chips. It is open 11.30 am to 2.30 pm daily except Sundays, and from 5 to 10 pm daily.

Ming Palace (☎ 315 111) is inside the grandiose old town hall building. It can cater for up to 250 people, however, the food is bland and there are usually only a few people dining. Chinese and European dishes cost from F$8 to F$10. It is open 11.30 am to 2.30 pm and 6 to 10 pm weekdays and Sunday evenings. *New Peking (☎ 312 939, 195 Victoria Parade)* is a stuffy place just opposite the Suva City Council building. Nevertheless, it has cheap Chinese and European dishes (from F$5 to F$9).

Malaysian Berjaya Hotel has a reasonable Chinese-Malaysian restaurant called *Kampong Ku*. Mains are from F$8 to F$15 and the steamboat (where you cook the ingredients yourself in a boiled broth, at your table) is F$18.50. Thursday is buffet night (F$15.50).

Korean *Seoul House,* at Southern Cross Hotel, caters mostly for groups of Korean tourists. Main dishes from are F$8 to F$16. Sashimi is served on Wednesday and Sunday nights (F$13 to F$17 for a large platter).

Japanese *Daikoku Restaurant (☎ 308 968)* on Victoria Parade has quality Japanese food and steep prices. Main a la carte meals range from F$18 to F$29, teppanyaki costs F$22 to F$48, and sushi is F$7.

Pizzerias *Pizza Hut (☎ 311 825)*, on Victoria Parade near the Bad Dog Cafe, serves OK, inexpensive pizzas. *Pizza King (☎ 315 762)* at the Harbour Centre has F$6 pizzas but they are not as good as Pizza Hut's. It is open from 11 am to 2 pm and 7 to 10 pm daily. *Papa La Pizza (☎ 349 351)*, at Outrigger Hotel, also serves reasonable pizzas (F$13 to F$20 for a large size). It is a bit run-down but the roof-garden bar has great views. Take a taxi from downtown (F$1.50) or the frequent hospital bus from the station (F$0.30), or walk up Waimanu Rd (about 30 minutes).

Cafes *Republic of Cappuccino (☎ 300 333)*, on Victoria Parade at Dolphin Plaza, has snacks, fresh juices, good coffee and Internet services. It's open 7 am to 11 pm Monday to Saturday, and from 10 am to 7 pm Sunday.

Bad Dog Cafe (☎ 304 662, on the corner of Macarthur St and Victoria Parade, has tasty food and huge coffees and is open from 11 am to 11 pm Monday to Wednesday, to 1 am Thursday to Saturday. It has an extensive list of foreign beers as well as wines available by the glass. It is a good place to escape the midday heat and receive a blast of air-con or to watch nightclubbers go by on Friday and Saturday nights.

Palm Court Bistro (☎ 304 662, shop 17, Queensland Insurance Building) off Victoria Parade is recommended for quick lunches and good cakes. Sandwiches and salads are from F$2 to F$4, burgers are F$3.50 and pizzas, quiches and pastries are under F$3. It is open from 7 am to 5.30 pm weekdays, from 7 am to 2.30 pm Saturdays. *Old Mill Cottage* (see Restaurants earlier in this section) is also recommended for coffee and cakes.

Berjaya Hotel's coffee shop has light meals from F$5 to F$15.

Fiji Museum Cafe overlooks Thurston Gardens. It serves vegetarian *thali* (curries and roti) for under F$5 (open 7.30 am to 4.30 pm weekdays, from midday at weekends).

The university has a couple of cheap places to eat. Food at the USP *canteen* (F$5 for visitors) is predictably ordinary. *Mango Tree Kona* is a better option and the verandah is a good spot to sit and watch students go by.

Fast Food Suva has two *food courts*: one at Downtown Boulevard Shopping Centre on Ellery St, the other at Dolphin Plaza on the corner of Loftus St and Victoria Parade. Both have a good variety of takeaway-food outlets, including pizza, pasta, Chinese, curries and Fijian dishes for around F$5. Dolphin Plaza is popular with locals for Sunday lunches. *Jackson Takeaway* in the old town hall has good-value Chinese food for under F$3.50. If you have a hankering for a burger, there is *McDonald's* on Victoria Parade.

Self-Catering *Suva Municipal Market* is the best place for fish, fruit and vegetables. There are a couple of supermarkets downtown on Rodwell Rd facing the market and bus station. There are *bakeries* downtown, including a hot-bread kitchen in the Harbour Centre arcade, down Thomson St from the FVB office.

Entertainment

Suva, with its cosmopolitan population and high number of university students, has the most diverse nightlife in Fiji. On Friday and Saturday nights, Victoria Parade swarms with nightclubbers and barhoppers. Watch out for pickpockets in the crowded discos, though. Most of the nightclubs and pubs have a happy hour with cheaper drinks.

Check out the *Fiji Times* entertainment section for upcoming events and what's on at nightclubs.

Cinemas The Village 6 *cinema complex* (☎ 311 109) is on Scott St, near Nubukalou Creek. Tickets cost from F$3 to F$4. See the cinema section of the *Fiji Times* for what's screening.

Discos *Lucky Eddies* (☎ 312 884), on Victoria Parade opposite the old town hall, is the most lively yet relaxed of the main nightclubs. It is open 8 pm to 1 am nightly. Entry is F$4, Sunday to Wednesday is free.

If you'd prefer something quieter and smaller in scale, try *Tingles* (☎ 313 626), below deck on Tiko's Floating Restaurant moored off Ratu Sukuna Park. It plays disco and reggae music and is open to 1 am Friday and Saturday nights (free entry).

Other discos include *Scandals*, at Noble House on Friday and Saturday nights (frequented mainly by under-25 year olds), and the rough and rowdy *Chequers*, at Waimanu Rd between Cunningham and Marks Sts, which has a house band nightly except Sunday. Southern Cross Hotel has a *disco* and live house band, playing Fiji rock'n'roll to a mostly local audience. Its long happy hour is from 4 to 7 pm. Admission is F$2, and it is open till 1 am Monday to Saturday.

Jazz *Birdland R&B Club* (☎ 303 833, 6 Carnavon St) is an underground venue offering live jazz and rhythm and blues on Thursday and Saturday nights. Admission is free and happy hours are from 6 to 9 pm. The *Centra* has a house band that play nightly.

Pubs & Bars *O'Reilly's* (☎ 312 968) is a very popular Irish bar on the busy corner of Macarthur St and Victoria Parade. It is great for an evening beer, with a friendly atmosphere, a mixed crowd, pool tables and music. Evidently, the back right-hand side of the bar is the place to be if you are gay. Farther down Victoria Parade, before the Shell petrol station, *Traps Bar* (☎ 312 922) has happy hour (half-price drinks) from 5 to 8 pm. The Fiji Writers' Association's Niu Wave Writers have monthly performances here with music and comedy. The bar has lots of small rooms with Spanish-style white rendered walls and dark timber, and it also plays videos.

Roof Top Bar, at the Town House Hotel, while a bit basic, has nice views of the cathedral, city and bay, and may be an option for escaping the busy city streets for a beer.

Most bars open from 5 or 6 pm until 1 am on weekdays, to midnight on Saturdays, and many now open on Sundays.

Country Music *The Barn (☎ 307 845),* on Carnavon St, is a popular venue with older crowds. It has bands with mainly country music, barn dances and a bar. Entry is F$5. The bouncers wear cowboy hats and make you tuck in your shirt to enter. It is open from 5.30 pm to 1 am Monday to Saturday, with happy hour from 5.30 to 9.30 pm.

Spectator Sports
Fijians are fanatical about their rugby, and even if you aren't that keen on the game it's worth going to a match to watch the crowd. Ask at the FVB if there will be a match during your stay.

Shopping
There are lots of souvenir shops along Victoria Parade. The Government Crafts Centre (☎ 211 222, fax 302 617), on Macarthur St, assists rural artisans and has quality items, but is generally more expensive than elsewhere. It's a good idea to look around and compare quality and price. Opening hours are from 8 am to 4.30 pm Monday to Thursday (to 4 pm Friday) and from 8 am to 12.30 pm Saturday. The Centra often has exhibitions of work by local artists. The Suva Curio & Handicraft Centre, on Stinson Parade, is interesting for a stroll. Be prepared to bargain! Some of the artefacts are not even genuinely Fijian and if there is a cruise ship in port, prices will skyrocket. Watch out for annoying sword sellers who will pretend to be your friend and then demand that you buy a souvenir with your name on it – just walk away, you are under no obligation to buy.

Try South Pacific Recordings (☎ 313 405, fax 304 883), in Usher St near Suva Municipal Market, for tapes or CDs of local musicians. The Fiji Museum Shop has good postcards, posters and books. The Fiji Philatelic Bureau (☎ 312 928, fax 306 088) at the GPO building, PO Box 100, Suva, has stamps and first covers from Fiji and other Pacific Islands.

Getting There & Away
Suva is well connected to the rest of the country by air and inter-island ferry, and to western Viti Levu by buses and carriers. Most international flights, however, arrive at Nadi International Airport.

Air Nausori airport is 23km north-east of central Suva. See the Getting Around chapter for air routes and prices, and Travel Agencies earlier in this section for contact details.

Bus & Carrier There are frequent express buses operating along the Queens Road and Kings Road. Pacific and Sunbeam express buses leave from Suva's Rodwell Rd bus station. If you can cope with busy bus stations and sometimes crowded buses, they are more fun and better value than the 20-seater tourist buses, which stop at all hotels along the Coral Coast.

Small trucks or carriers, with tarpaulin-covered frames on the back, also take passengers.

Fiji Holiday Connections (☎ 720 977) Nadi. This company operates a minibus shuttle between Nadi and Suva along the Queens Road that will pick up and drop off at hotels along the Coral Coast.

Pacific Transport Limited (☎ 304 366). Pacific has regular buses (open-air type) from Lautoka to Suva via the Coral Coast, on the Queens Road.

Sunbeam Transport Limited (☎ 382 122). Sunbeam has a Kings Road as well as a Queens Road service to Lautoka.

UTC (United Touring Fiji; ☎ 312 287). UTC offers an express air-con coach service from Suva to Nadi along the Queens Road, stopping at the larger hotels along the way.

Boat From Suva there are regular ferry services to Vanua Levu and Taveuni (Patterson Brothers, Beachcomber Cruises and Consort Shipping) and to Ovalau (Patterson Brothers and Emosi's Shipping). See the Getting Around chapter for details. There are also irregular boats that take passengers from Suva to Kadavu, Lau and Rotuma (see these chapters).

Beachcomber Cruises (☎ 880 216, fax 880 202) Suite 8, Epworth Arcade, Nina St, Suva

Consort Shipping Line (☎ 302 877, 313 344, fax 303 389) Dominion House Arcade, Thomson St, behind the FVB. The office is open from 8 am to 4 pm Monday to Friday (closed noon to 1 pm for lunch), and from 9 am to noon Saturdays.

Emosi's Shipping (☎ 313 366) 35 Gordon St, Suva. Emosi has a daily Viti Levu-Ovalau service by minibus from Suva to Bau Landing then a small boat via Leleuvia.

Patterson Brothers Shipping (☎ 315 644, fax 301 652) Suite 1 & 2, Epworth Arcade, Nina St, Suva

Getting Around

It is easy to get around central Suva on foot. Local buses are cheap and plentiful. The busy local bus station is next to the market; just ask bus drivers or locals about timetables. There are relatively few buses in the evening and there is reduced service on Sundays.

Taxis are cheap for short trips, and in Suva they actually use the meter! Suva's one-way looping streets may make you think the taxi driver is taking you in the wrong direction. Drivers along Victoria Parade may get caught on a long run around the market and wharf area. See the Getting Around chapter for car rental companies, and Nausori in the Kings Road section later in this chapter, for how to get to/from Nausori airport (about 23km from Suva).

Kings Road

The Kings Road links Suva to Lautoka around eastern and northern Viti Levu. It is 265km from Suva to Lautoka on the Kings Road, compared to 221km along the Queens Road. This route is just as beautiful as the Queens Road, and is perhaps more interesting for the variety of landscapes and towns and villages it passes through. It is recommended for travel either by bus or car.

There are relatively few places to stay along this route. Korovou, Rakiraki, Tavua and Ba each have a simple hotel. There is also an upmarket resort near Rakiraki and several other offshore resorts on Nananu-i-Ra.

NAUSORI & THE REWA DELTA
pop 22,000

The township of Nausori is on the eastern bank of the Rewa River, 19km north-east of downtown Suva. It has the country's second-largest airport and is an important agricultural, market, transport and service centre.

The town developed around the CSR sugar mill, which operated here between 1882 and 1959. Growing sugar, however, was more successful on the drier western side of Viti Levu, and the sugar mill was taken over by the Rewa Rice Mill, which still operates today. Irrigation developments of the 1970s turned the Rewa Delta, like the Navua Delta and the Bua River flats in south-western Vanua Levu, into a major rice-producing area. Other industries include light manufacturing, stock food production and timber milling. Nausori is also the headquarters for district offices of the Central Division. Most of the population are farm labourers and industry workers.

The town itself isn't very interesting for travellers. There are a couple of banks and some inexpensive eateries near the market and bus stations. If you are desperate, *Kings Hotel* (☎ 478 833), in the main street near the silos, has a couple of very ordinary rooms (with bathrooms) around the back of the pub/nightclub for F$16.50/21.45 for singles/doubles. They are reputed to be rented by the hour by prostitutes and their clients.

There are three important boat landings near Nausori: Bau Landing, Wainibokasi Landing and Nakelo Landing (see the Bau, Nasilai Village and Toberua entries respectively, later in this section). There are regular buses to all three landings from Nausori. From Nakelo Landing there are local village boats, which you may be able to join or hire to explore the area. Chat with locals and you may be invited to visit their villages.

Nausori International Airport

The airport is about 3km south-east of Nausori, 22km from Suva. Air Fiji and Sunflower Airlines are Fiji's domestic carriers. See the Getting Around chapter for details. Air Fiji, Air Pacific and Royal Tongan Air-

Natadola Beach, Viti Levu

Queen's Wharf, Lautoka on Viti Levu

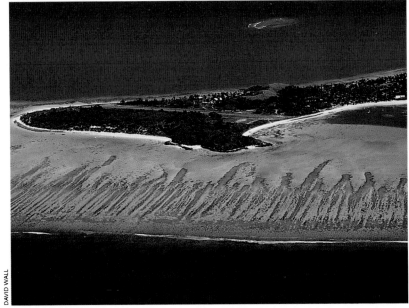

Mana island, Mamanuca Group

The Mamanucas: Who said 'blue and green should never be seen'?

Ring-Ditch Fortifications

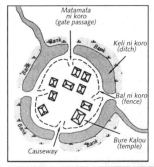

Matamata
ni koro
(gate passage)

Bank

Keli ni koro
(ditch)

Bank

Bal ni koro
(fence)

Bank

Bure Kalou
(temple)

Causeway

Defensive fortifications in lowland areas took the form of ring-ditches *(korowaiwai)*. There are many of these eroded circular mounds remaining in the Rewa Delta and you may be able to spot some if you fly over the area. In times of war they were a necessity for the survival of a village, forming protection against surprise attack. The habitation area was encircled by a war ditch, usually about 10m wide with steep battered sides and a palisade, or strong fence, on top of the inner bank. Entry was through narrow causeways or drawbridges and gates. The ditch sometimes had danger-ous bamboo spikes hidden in the muddy water. Important villages could be surrounded by up to four concentric ditches with offset causeways to divide and expose at-tackers. Fences were made of coconut posts and bamboo or bundles of reeds. According to AJ Webb, writing in 1885, 'Before the introduction of firearms, these places were simply impregnable to assault, and could only be taken through treachery or by starving the beleaguered.'

lines have international flights through here, but otherwise it is mostly used for do-mestic purposes. The airport premises are small and low-key, with a newspaper stand (with a few magazines and books) and a snack counter. An ANZ bank opens for in-ternational flights only.

Getting There & Away There are no di-rect local buses to/from Suva and the air-port, but Nausori Taxi & Bus Service (☎ 312 185, 304 178) has regular buses to/from the Centra hotel in Suva (F$2.10). Otherwise, a taxi from the airport to/from Suva costs about F$17. Alternatively, cover the 3km to Nausori's bus stations by taxi (about F$2.50), and catch one of the fre-quent local buses to Suva bus station for about F$1. Allow plenty of time, as some buses crawl while others speed.

Nasilai Village & Naililili Catholic Mission

Nasilai village is home to the well-known potter Taraivini Wati (see Arts in the Facts about Fiji chapter). Pottery is a major source of income for the village, and when large orders are placed from hotels and em-bassies, everyone participates in the process, helping to collect and prepare the

clay and make the pots. When a baby girl is born in the village, a lump of clay is placed on her forehead. They believe that she will then automatically know how to carry on the pottery-making tradition.

The Naililili Catholic Mission was built at the turn of the century by Catholic mis-sionaries from France. The stained-glass windows incorporate writing in Fijian and were imported from Europe. The delta area on which the mission is built is a flood plain and so the priests no longer live here.

Getting There & Away Wilderness Eth-nic Adventure Fiji (☎ 387 594, fax 300 584) runs tours of the Rewa Delta and Nasilai village, departing from Suva hotels. There are also regular buses to Wainibokasi Land-ing from the Nausori bus station. If driving from Nausori, head south-east for about 6km on the road that runs parallel to the Rewa River. Pass the airport entrance and turn right at the T-junction. The landing is a farther 1km before the bridge across the Wainibokasi River. There you can catch a boat to the Naililili Catholic Mission, which is almost opposite the landing, or take a short trip downriver to Nasilai village. Ask a local for permission to visit the village and take along some kava.

VITI LEVU

Bau

If you fly over Bau today it is bizarre to think that in the 19th century such a tiny speck of an island was the power base of Cakobau and his father Tanoa (see History in the Facts about Fiji chapter). In the 1780s there were 30 bure kalou on the small chiefly island, including the famous Na Vata ni Tawake, which stood on a huge yavu faced with large panels of flat rock.

Also of interest are its **chiefly cemetery**, **old church** and a **sacrificial killing stone** on which enemies were slaughtered prior to being cooked and consumed.

To visit the island you must be invited by someone who lives there or have permission from the Ministry of Fijian Affairs. Dress conservatively, take a large *waka* (bunch of kava roots) for presentation to the *turaga-ni-koro* (chief), take off your hat and don't walk around unescorted (see the Dos & Don'ts section in the Facts for the Visitor chapter).

Getting There & Away There are regular buses from Nausori bus station to Bau Landing, which is north-east of Nausori airport. If you are driving from Nausori, turn left before the airport and after about 4km turn left at the intersection and follow the road to its end. Local boats cross to Bau, which is just offshore from the mainland. Boats also leave from Bau Landing for Viwa.

Toberua

Toberua is a small island just off Kaba Point, the easternmost point of Viti Levu, about 30km from Suva. *Toberua Island Resort (☎ 302 356, 472 777, fax 302 215, ✉ toberua@is.com.fj)* was originally built in 1968 as an American millionaire's hideaway and was one of the earliest luxury resorts established in Fiji. Despite its proximity to Suva, Toberua has its own weather patterns, receiving about a third of Suva's annual rainfall. Its 14 fan-cooled bure have polished hardwood interiors, a king-size and a single bed, tea- and coffee-making facilities, a fridge and indoor/outdoor bathrooms. Rates are F$390/455/498 for singles/doubles/triples. Up to two children under 16 years can share with parents free of charge (babysitting can be provided). Meal plans for adults are F$81/98 for two/three meals per day and F$10 to F$45 for children depending on age. The resort also organises day trips to the island from Suva for F$120 per person, including lunch and use of a bure.

The island's total area is just under two hectares at high tide, but when the tide is out it extends to 12 hectares and the exposed beach is used for golf. Other activities included in the price are snorkelling, windsurfing, catamaran sailing, paddle boating and tours to the nearby island bird sanctuary and mangroves. Diving, including equipment, is F$70 per dive, F$550 for an open-water course.

Getting There & Away Toberua Island Resort organises transfers for guests. The trip involves a taxi from Nausori airport/Suva to Nakelo Landing (F$14/28) followed by a boat (F$17.50/35 per child/adult, 40 minutes).

There are also regular local buses from Nausori bus station to Nakelo Landing, which is on the banks of the Wainibokasi River, south-east of the airport. If driving from Nausori, turn left before the airport and then take the first right. Follow the road for about 5km and turn right before Namuka.

Getting There & Away

The Kings Road from Suva to Nausori is the country's busiest and most congested stretch of highway. The Nausori bus station is in the main street. Sunbeam Transport (☎ 479 353) has regular buses to Lautoka via the Kings Road and there are four express services on weekdays (the first at 7.15 am and the last at 6.45 pm; ring to confirm weekend timetables).

KOROVOU & AROUND

The Kings Road between Suva and Rakiraki is mostly sealed, except for the 56km section between Korovou and Dama. Korovou (one of many towns known literally as 'new village') is not much more than a transport intersection, about 50km north of Suva and 31km from Nausori airport. There are a few shops near the bus stop, where you can buy a snack, and there's a post office across the river near the roundabout. At the roundabout, the Kings Road continues to the north-west and into the hills. Another unsealed road follows the coast to Natovi Landing (a 20-minute drive), from where there are bus/ferry services to Labasa (Vanua Levu) and Levuka (Ovalau). See the Getting Around chapter for details. It is possible to meet the Kings Road again farther on, but only if you have a 4WD, as the road deteriorates as you approach Mt Tova.

Korovou itself isn't very interesting, however, *Tailevu Hotel* (*☎ 430 028, fax 430 244*) has a variety of budget accommodation. It's on the hill overlooking the roundabout. Dorm accommodation is F$8. Rooms with en suite are F$25/35 for singles/doubles. There is a family room that sleeps five people for F$50, as well as self-contained cottages (maximum four people) for the same price. You can also camp; sites are F$8 per night. Meals in the restaurant are from F$4 to F$7.50 for a main or up to F$10.50 for seafood; half a cray goes for F$15.50. It becomes a nightclub on Thursday, Friday and Saturday nights.

Tailevu Hotel can arrange trips and activities, including a visit to **Wailotua Snake God Cave** about 23km west of Korovou on the Kings Road. Alternatively, inquire about the cave at Wailotua village and for a small fee the hotel will arrange a guide. The cave is about 1½ to two hours' walk from the village.

It is an interesting trip along the Kings Road from Korovou to Rakiraki. The road passes through dairy-farming country and then winds through hills and along the Wainibuka River, and past many small villages where you'll receive a friendly wave. The unsealed section is usually passable although somehow *we* managed to get bogged! It's a slow trip – watch out for mad drivers and the odd timber truck, which hurtle along the gravel, and expect delays at milking time when cows plod along the road. The ones we saw all seemed to have

sore feet! You may see the occasional bilibili on the river. About 14km from Korovou the Kings Road crosses the beautiful **Uru's Waterfall**.

Natovi Landing

There is a general store at Natovi Landing but not much else. Patterson Brothers has a bus/ferry service (daily except Sunday) between Suva-Natovi and Nabouwalu, Vanua Levu. It also has a Suva-Natovi-Ovalau bus/ferry service (daily except Sunday) to Buresala Landing, with a bus connection to Levuka. Ferries also depart for Nabouwalu, Vanua Levu from Ellington Wharf near Rakiraki. See the Getting Around chapter for more information and bus connections.

Getting There & Away

Sunbeam Transport has regular buses between Korovou and Suva on weekdays between 10.55 am and 9.20 pm, and to Lautoka between 8 am and 6.30 pm.

RAKIRAKI & AROUND

Rakiraki is the northernmost town in Viti Levu, 157km north-west of Suva and 141km north-east of Nadi. Inland from Rakiraki, about 2km off the Kings Road past the sugar mill, is the township of **Vaileka**, where you will find a bus station, taxi stands, banks, market, supermarket and a few cafes.

It's a great trip, with stunning scenery from Korovou across the mountains, down past Viti Levu Bay and through to Ra province and Rakiraki. The road winds through hills and along the Wainibuka River past many small villages. The climate on the northern side of the mountains is similar to that of western Viti Levu, and it is sugar-cane-growing country. According to local legend, the imposing mountains of the **Nakauvadra Range** are the home of the great snake-god Degei, creator of all the islands. The opening and closing of his eyes is the cause of night and day, and thunder is said to be Degei turning in his sleep.

The turn-off to **Ellington Wharf** is about 5km east of Rakiraki off the Kings Road (at the 112.4km post from Lautoka), and it is

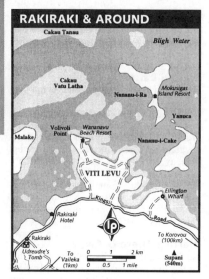

RAKIRAKI & AROUND

then a farther 1.5km to the wharf. From there you can cross to the island of Nananu-i-Ra (see Nananu-i-Ra later in this section for more information). Ferries also leave here for Nabouwalu, Vanua Levu.

Heading west out of Rakiraki towards Nadi, look out for **Udreudre's Tomb**, the resting place of Fiji's most notorious cannibal. It is by the roadside on the left, about 100m west of the Vaileka turn-off.

About 10km west of Rakiraki near Vitawa is a large outcrop known as **Navatu Rock**. There was once a fortified village on top of the rock and it was believed that from here spirits would depart for the afterlife.

Naiserelagi Catholic Mission
About 25km east of Rakiraki, overlooking Viti Levu Bay, is an old mission (1917), which is famous for its mural depicting a black Christ. It is the work of French artist Jean Charlot, who painted it in 1962. The three panels incorporate biblical scenes with Christ on the cross in a masi sulu. Fijians are depicted offering mats and tabua, and Indians offering flowers and oxen. There is a tanoa at Christ's feet. Visitors are welcome and a small donation is appreciated.

From Vaileka, take the Flying Prince local bus for F$1.20, ideally before 9 am when buses are more regular. Otherwise it will cost F$30 by taxi. Naiserelagi is just south of Nanukuloa village, on the right past the school. The mission is on the hill, about 500m up a winding track. Alternatively, Rakiraki Hotel can arrange half-day tours, departing at about 8 am.

Organised Tours
A local guide takes waterfall trips to Nayaulevu village (up to four people, F$30 each, including lunch). Book at Rakiraki Hotel.

Places to Stay
There are two places to stay on the mainland in the Rakiraki area. *Rakiraki Hotel* (☎ 694 101, fax 694 545), on the Kings Road 1.8km east of the Vaileka turn-off, offers reasonably good-value rooms with fans for F$35/40 for singles/doubles, and air-con rooms for F$88/99. The rooms are musty but otherwise pretty standard and the hotel has a pool, half-size tennis court, lawn bowling and nine-hole golf course nearby. You can get about a 30% discount for air-con rooms between November and early

---

Ratu Udreudre

In 1849, some time after Ratu Udreudre's death, Reverend Richard Lyth asked Udreudre's son about the significance of a long line of stones. Each stone, he was told, represented one of the chief's victims, and amounted to a personal tally of at least 872 corpses. Reverend Lyth said:

Ravatu assured me that his father eat all this number of human beings – he was wont to add a stone to the row for each one he received – they were victims killed in war he eat them all himself – he gave to none, however, much he had on hand – it was cooked and recooked (by which it was preserved) until it was all consumed – he would keep it in a box so that he might lose none…he eat but little else very little vegetable – and being an enormous eater he was able to get through a great deal.

April. The restaurant-bar is open to visitors (see the following Places to Eat entry).

Those wanting a mid-range resort should try *Wananavu Beach Resort* (☎ 694 433, fax 694 499, ✉ wananavuresort@is.com.fj), at the northernmost point of Viti Levu, east of Rakiraki. The resort opened in mid-1994 and is run by a New Zealand family. From its hillside position there are beautiful views of Nananu-i-Ra island and Viti Levu's coastline. Each of the 15 comfortable deluxe bure have cross ventilation, ceiling fan, refrigerator, tea- and coffee-making facilities and balcony, and at a pinch can accommodate up to four people. Rates for doubles, including airport transfers, are F$165/200/220 for gardenview/oceanview/beachfront bure, F$20 for an extra person. There are also two self-contained two-bed villas for F$300. Ask about walk-in deals. See the following Places to Eat section for details about its restaurant.

There is a beach nearby, a marina, nice swimming pool, tennis and volleyball courts, diving and snorkelling. Diving is available with Ra Divers, based at the resort.

Coming from Lautoka, continue northeast along the Kings Road for about 3.5km past the Vaileka turn-off. Follow the unsealed (sometimes muddy) road to the north for about 3km to the resort. Airport transfers from Nadi are F$85 by taxi.

Places to Eat

The restaurant-bar at *Rakiraki Hotel* is open to visitors. Mains cost from F$11 to F$15, including curries, roasts, fried fish, grilled steak and vegetables. Visitors are also welcome at *Wananavu Beach Resort's* restaurant-bar. It's a great spot and the food is very good (similar dishes to those at Rakiraki Hotel). International and Fijian dishes are F$18.50 to F$24 for a main.

Vaileka has a few cheap *cafes* near the bus station, and a *cake shop* at the Community Centre building. Ellington Wharf has a small *kiosk* that only sells cola and a few tins and snacks.

Make sure you don't drink the tap water in Rakiraki: It has been deemed unsafe for human consumption.

Getting There & Away

Sunbeam has regular express buses along the Kings Road from Suva and Nadi, which stop at Vaileka and the turn-off to Ellington Wharf. A taxi from Vaileka to Ellington Wharf is around F$8.

Nananu-i-Ra is a 15-minute boat ride from Ellington Wharf. All the resorts on Nananu-i-Ra have their own boat transfers. Arrange your pick-up in advance (there is no phone at Ellington Wharf). Boat transfers for the budget resorts are around F$18 return.

Kon Tiki Lodge has a minibus service from Nadi for their guests, F$17 one way. Alternatively, PVV Tours (☎ 700 600, fax 701 541) has daily Nadi-Ellington Wharf minibus transfers (F$22 one way, 2½ hours) and a boat to Nananu-i-Ra (F$8.25 one way per person). The PVV bus is more expensive than the ordinary bus, however, it does pick up from hotels and stop along the way for supplies. Sharing a taxi is another option (about F$65 to Nadi).

From Ellington Wharf there is a Patterson Brothers' ferry three times a week to Nabouwalu, south-west Vanua Levu (see the Getting Around chapter).

NANANU-I-RA

Nananu-i-Ra is a 350-hectare island, roughly triangular in shape with steep hills, many scalloped bays, white-sand beaches and mangroves. It's about 3km north of Ellington Wharf. **Bligh Water** is to the north and the surrounding reefs are good for diving. Nananu-i-Ra is popular with travellers for its relative ease of access, good beaches, dry climate and good snorkelling. It is a quick and inexpensive option for getting away from the Nadi area. The island has some private homes and a few places to stay. Most of the residents are of European descent, so don't come here expecting to have much contact with indigenous Fijian culture.

The island has no roads and much of the land is privately owned, so stick to the beach.

While snorkelling, expect to see coral, abundant fish, and, on the north side of the island, many sea snakes.

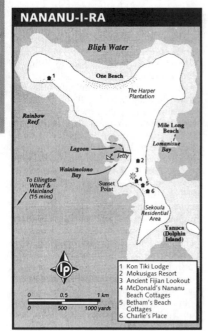

NANANU-I-RA

Bligh Water

One Beach

The Harper Plantation

Rainbow Reef

Mile Long Beach

Lomanisue Bay

Lagoon Jetty

Wainimolono Bay

To Ellington Wharf & Mainland (15 mins)

Sunset Point

Sekoula Residential Area

Yanuca (Dolphin Island)

0   0.5   1 km
0   500   1000 yards

1 Kon Tiki Lodge
2 Mokusigas Resort
3 Ancient Fijian Lookout
4 McDonald's Nananu Beach Cottages
5 Betham's Beach Cottages
6 Charlie's Place

Diving

Ra Divers (☎ 694 511), based at Wananavu Beach Resort on the mainland, will pick up from each of the budget resorts on Nananu-i-Ra. It charges F$120 for a two-tank dive, plus F$20 equipment rental, and F$450 for an open-water course. It will also take snorkellers for F$7.50 if there is space on the boat. Ra Divers also has fishing trips, including day trips to Turtle Bay (a turtle-breeding ground in October/November).

Action Diving (☎ 694 454, fax 694 829) based at Mokusigas Resort, has diving and fishing for resort guests and will allow others to join if space allows. It has lessons in German and English. Diving is F$130 for a two-tank dive, F$450 for an open-water course. Snorkelling/fishing is F$25/30 per person.

Places to Stay – Budget

There are four inexpensive places to stay on the island and one upmarket resort.

Take cash, as none of the budget places accept credit cards. Most places, with the exception of Kon Tiki Lodge, provide some food, but it is a good idea to pick up some supplementary supplies (especially fruit and vegetables). Rob's shop at Betham's Beach resort sells bread, milk, frozen meat and some alcohol, and McDonald's Nananu Beach Cottages has an outdoor cafe. All the budget places provide linen and cutlery. Both Betham's and McDonald's have snorkelling gear for F$10 per day and kayaks and rowboat for F$5 per hour. It's a good idea to book accommodation in advance, especially if you want a cottage, as the island can get crowded. Water supply is sometimes a problem. Outsiders may be allowed to use Mokusigas Resort's bar and restaurant if it is not busy, but it is essential to book first.

Three of the budget places are close together on the same beach, so if you are not happy you have the potential to swap. Prices are competitive. *Charlie's Place* (☎ 694 676), run by Charlie and Louise, is popular and good value-for-money. The eight-bed dorm here is F$16.50 per person. There are also two self-contained cottages with well-equipped kitchens and laundry for F$60 a double (plus F$8 per person up to a maximum of seven). One is more spacious, good for families, with views both ways from the hill, but is closer to the generator. A two-course dinner is F$10. Charlie and Louise give guests mangoes when they are in season.

McDonald's Nananu Beach Cottages (☎ 694 633), previously known as Nananu Beach Cottages, has dorm accommodation with fan (maximum of six people) for F$16.50, and twin rooms with shared bathrooms for F$44 for singles or doubles. Self-contained cottages sleep up to five and are F$60.50 for doubles, F$9 per extra person. Meal packages (three meals) are F$24.50. It has an outdoor cafe, which serves toasted sandwiches for F$3.50 and pizzas from F$12 to F$15 (enough for two). Day trips for snorkelling are F$10 with lunch.

Betham's Beach Cottages (☎/fax 694 132), between Charlie's and McDonald's, has two dorms with cooking facilities, fridge and freezer but no fan, sleeping six to 10 people, for F$16.50 per person. The four self-contained beachfront cottages are F$66 each, F$10 per extra person. It has a small shop that sells a few food items, including bread, milk and frozen meat at reasonable prices.

Kon Tiki Lodge (☎ 694 290, 722 836 Nadi) is near the north-west point of the island on a lovely beach with good snorkelling. It is about 1½ hours' walk from the other budget places. Accommodation is for self-caterers only. There is a small shop with a few basics but we recommend you bring your own food. Camping is F$10 per tent. The dorm (up to 10 beds per room) has its own kitchen and costs F$16.50 per bed. Beachfront bungalows have two bedrooms and shared kitchen and bathroom for F$38.50 a double. Traditional bure with mosquito nets and shared facilities are F$33 a double. It is a good place to sit up at night exchanging stories with fellow travellers and drinking kava. Activities include volleyball, fishing, snorkelling (F$4 equipment hire) and diving with Ra Divers.

Places to Stay – Top End

The more upmarket *Mokusigas Resort (☎ 694 444, fax 694 404)* is on a narrow, steep ridge with beautiful views to the water on both sides. The name translates loosely as 'killing time'. If you don't like steep paths you'd better avoid this resort. It has 20 suites, each with ceiling fans and balcony, which are from F$260 to F$350, depending on the view, furnishing and extras such as ground coffee, for a maximum of three people. Rates include breakfast and transfers. Main meals in Bligh's Restaurant are in the F$18 to F$19 range. Activities include snorkelling, windsurfing, canoeing, fishing, tennis and working out in the gym. Action Diving has its dive shop here (see the earlier Diving entry in this section).

Getting There & Away

For getting to/from Ellington Wharf and the island, see Getting There & Away in the earlier Rakiraki & Around section.

TAVUA & AROUND

Midway between Rakiraki and Tavua is **Yaqara**, the largest cattle station in Fiji (7000 hectares). The land extends from the Kings Road all the way up to the mountain ridge. Run by the government for commercial and research purposes, it has orchards and over 4000 head of cattle.

Tavua is a small, quiet agricultural town 67km from Lautoka and 100km from Nadi. It has a market, so if heading inland do your shopping here. Buses leave here at 3 pm daily for the hill town of Nadarivatu, although at the time of writing this service had been suspended due to poor road conditions. Farther along this inland route is Monasavu Dam and the road eventually ends up in Suva. Don't attempt this trip unless you have a 4WD (see the Viti Levu Highlands section later in this chapter).

From Tavua, the road past the hospital leads inland for about 9km to **Vatukoula**. It's a gold-mining town of about 5000 residents.

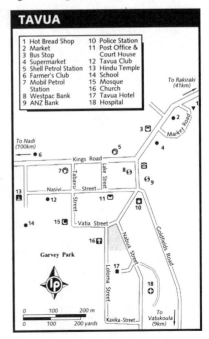

TAVUA

1 Hot Bread Shop	10 Police Station
2 Market	11 Post Office &
3 Bus Stop	Court House
4 Supermarket	12 Tavua Club
5 Shell Petrol Station	13 Hindu Temple
6 Farmer's Club	14 School
7 Mobil Petrol	15 Mosque
Station	16 Church
8 Westpac Bank	17 Tavua Hotel
9 ANZ Bank	18 Hospital

To Rakiraki (41km)

To Nadi (100km)

Kings Road

Market Road

Tabavu Street

Lake Street

Nasivi Street

Vatia Street

Nabua Street

Loloma Street

Garvey Park

Goldfields Road

To Vatukoula (9km)

Kavika Street

0   100   200 m
0   100   200 yards

The Emperor Gold Mining Company began mining here in the 1930s. The ore is mined from a narrow vein on the edge of an extinct volcano. Most mining is underground, but there are also open cuts. Gold is Fiji's third-largest earner of foreign exchange and the company employs about 1500 people. The early 1990s saw bitter strikes by workers over wages and conditions. If you have time to kill, it may be worth taking a ride to see the difference between the housing for workers and their bosses. There are regular buses to Vatukoula from Tavua.

From Vatukoula, drivers may take the scenic back road to Ba, which passes cane farms and Indian settlements. Rosie Tours has excursions that include Vatukoula on their itineraries, and the Tavua Hotel can also organise trips.

Places to Stay & Eat

The only place to stay in the area is the budget *Tavua Hotel* (☎ 680 522, fax 680 390). It is a classic old hotel with colonial character and rather sleepy service. It has 11 basic rooms with en suites, and is OK-value for F$33/44 for singles/doubles. There is also a musty six-bed dorm for F$11 per person, a three-bed room for F$55 and one air-con room for F$66. Some rooms have a fridge. There is a spacious semicircular lounge upstairs and a bar and large dining room downstairs. Meals are unexciting and range from F$8 to F$12. The swimming pool was not particularly clean on our visit. This place is an option for spending a night before heading inland to Nadarivatu on Tomanivi (Mt Victoria). See the Viti Levu Highlands section later in this chapter for more information.

BA

pop 12,500

Ba is an agricultural town 38km north-east of Lautoka and 71km from Nadi. The Ba district is the largest in Fiji, with a predominantly

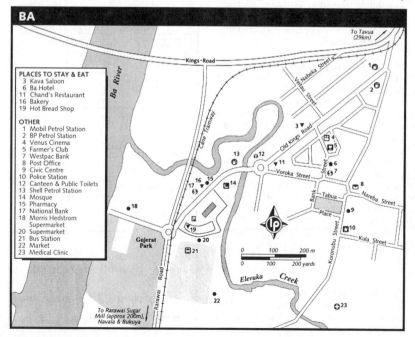

BA

PLACES TO STAY & EAT
3 Kava Saloon
6 Ba Hotel
11 Chand's Restaurant
16 Bakery
19 Hot Bread Shop

OTHER
1 Mobil Petrol Station
2 BP Petrol Station
4 Venus Cinema
5 Farmer's Club
7 Westpac Bank
8 Post Office
9 Civic Centre
10 Police Station
12 Canteen & Public Toilets
13 Shell Petrol Station
14 Mosque
15 Pharmacy
17 National Bank
18 Morris Hedstrom
   Supermarket
20 Supermarket
21 Bus Station
22 Market
23 Medical Clinic

To Tavua (29km)

Kings-Road

Ba River

Cane Tramway

Vesa Nabeka Street

Veitari Street

Old Kings Road

Voroka Street

Nareba Street

Bank

Tabua Place

Koronubu Street

Kula Street

Gujerat Park

Elevuka Creek

Rarawai Road

To Rarawai Sugar Mill (approx 200m),
Navala & Bukuya

0   100   200 m
0   100   200 yards

Fiji-Indian population. It's an expanding commercial centre, dependent on cane growing and the Rarawai Sugar Mill. There's also a sawmill that harvests pine and local hardwood. Other industries include production of clothing, building materials, steel, confectionery, poultry and chalk.

The Kings Road now bypasses the town, and the new bridge over the Ba River was financed by the EU. The original bridge was wiped out by Cyclone Kina in 1993. There is a large mosque downtown, near the Elevuka Creek.

Soccer is popular in the region and the local team often wins national tournaments. Ba has Fiji's best racecourse, and the town's horse-racing and bougainvillea festivals are in September.

Places to Stay & Eat

There is not much reason for the average traveller to stay here, however, the *Ba Hotel (☎ 674 000)* on Bank St has gaudy but clean rooms. It is the only place to stay in town and caters mainly for local business people. It has 11 air-con rooms with en suite, tea- and coffee-making facilities, fridge and phone for F$44/55 for singles/doubles. There are also two fan-cooled rooms (F$30 for singles) and a suite for F$66. Main meals at the hotel restaurant-bar are around F$8 and there is an OK swimming pool. *Farmer's Club* next door is a good place for a drink. There are lots of very cheap but fairly grotty places to eat along Ba's main street. *Chand's Restaurant (☎ 670 822),* just east of the river on the main street, has meals for F$4 to F$9. It's open daily except Sunday night. *Kava Saloon* is a Fiji-Indian haunt with cheap fast food and a pool table.

Viti Levu Highlands

The interior of Viti Levu is one of the best places to experience traditional Fijian culture. There are small, largely self-sufficient villages and settlements scattered through the hills. Koroyanitu National Heritage Park and the Nausori Highlands have some

fantastic landscapes and are good for trekking. Remember to take a jumper with you, as the temperatures are cooler in these mountainous inland areas.

KOROYANITU NATIONAL HERITAGE PARK

If you are a keen walker or nature lover, the Koroyanitu National Heritage Park, in the mountains about 10km south-east of Lautoka, is definitely worth a visit. Contact the Abaca Visitor Centre (☎ 666 644, after the beep dial 1234) for more information. The park is being developed by the Native Lands Trust Board (NLTB) and South Pacific Regional Environment Programme (SPREP) to provide income for the locals through ecotourism.

Abaca (pronounced am-b**arth**-a) village is at the base of **Mt Koroyanitu** (Mt Evans). The area has beautiful nature walks, native rainforests, waterfalls, archaeological sites and swimming. *Nase Lodge* is about 400m from the village and has bunk beds, a living area, cooking facilities, a cold-water shower and toilet. Dorm beds cost F$15 and camp sites cost F$10 per person. Village stays are F$30 per night, including all meals, for a minimum stay of three nights. Meals at the village will cost you F$5/7/10 for breakfast/lunch/dinner, but you should also take some groceries as there is only a small village shop. There are BBQ facilities and a lovo and entertainment on Thursday night (F$20 per person).

Admission to the park is F$5, plus F$5 to F$10 for guided hikes, which include a full-day hike to Mt Koroyanitu and the remains of a fortified village. There is also a two-hour hike to the terraced gardens at Tunutunu and to the Navuratu village site. Those who make the one-hour climb to the summit of **Castle Rock** will be rewarded with panoramic views of the Mamanucas and Yasawas. If you are a keen walker, there is a two-day hike through highland villages, including a climb over Fiji's sleeping giant (Mt Batilamu), which also provides gorgeous views of Nadi Bay. The hike includes an overnight stay in Fiji's highest bure near the top of Mt Batilamu.

VITI LEVU

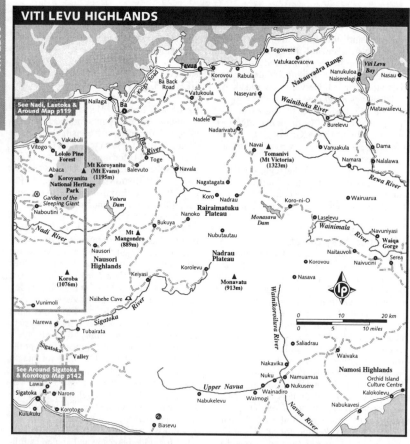

VITI LEVU HIGHLANDS

Getting There & Away

A carrier departs from Lautoka (daily except Sunday) from the Cathay Hotel at 9 am, returning at 4 pm. It costs F$8 per person each way. Alternatively, you could hire a carrier on Yasawa St next to the Lautoka bus station. If driving from Nadi, turn right off the Queens Road at Tavakubu Rd, past the first roundabout after entering Lautoka. Continue for about 6.5km past the police post and the cemetery, then turn right into the signposted Abaca Rd. It is a farther 10km of gravel road up to the village, suitable for 4WD only.

NAUSORI HIGHLANDS

The Nausori Highlands have some fantastic landscapes and remote villages, which retain many interesting traditional beliefs and culture. Sunday is a day of rest, church and spending time with the family, so visits on that day are not recommended, as they may be disruptive and unappreciated by the chief.

Navala
pop 800

Navala is Fiji's most picturesque village, set in a superb landscape on a sloping site on the banks of the Ba River. While most

Fijian villagers now prefer concrete-block and corrugated-iron constructions, all of the houses in Navala are traditional bure; only the school and radio shed (housing the village's emergency radio telephone) are concrete blocks and these are out of sight. Obviously the chief enforces strict town-planning rules! Navala is a relatively large village and the houses are laid out in avenues with a central promenade down to the river. The buildings are rectangular in plan and of timber-pole structure, with sloping stone plinths, woven panel walls and hipped thatched roofs. Kitchens are in separate bure.

It is a photographer's paradise but you need to get permission to take shots, even from across the bridge. The turaga-ni-koro, Karoalo Vaisewa, allows tourists to visit and take photos but they must present a *sevusevu* (a gift such as yaqona) and donation of F$15. If you arrive independently, ask the first person you meet to escort you to the chief.

Places to Stay & Eat *Bulou's Lodge & Backpacker Hostel (☎ 666 644-2116)* near Navala village is run by a retired Fijian couple, Seresio and Bulou N Talili, and their son Tui. The traditional bure sleeps about six people or you can stay in their house and be part of the family; they have a cold-water, improvised shower and no electricity. All meals and kava are included in the F$35 nightly fee and if you are staying three nights a lovo is included. Activities include horse riding (F$10 for a couple of hours) and trips up to the Talili's farm (a two-hour walk uphill), from where you can see the sea in the distance. There are also bilibili trips in the dry season. Take some food as a present for the hostel owners and leave a donation for the village community centre project. Coming from Ba, the lodge is 1km past Navala and on the right about 50m before a river crossing.

Getting There & Away There are local buses from Ba to Navala (1½ hours) daily, except Sunday. One leaves Ba at midday, returning from Navala about 1.30 pm. Only

the late afternoon bus goes as far as Bulou's; ring in advance and the hostel will pick you up from Navala. Carriers cost about F$18. The rough, gravel road has a few patches of bitumen on the really steep bits. While only about 26km away, Navala is about an hour's drive from Ba, past the Rarawai Sugar Mill, through beautiful rugged scenery. The Ba River floods occasionally and the concrete bridge just before the village becomes impassable. Some organised tours from Nadi also visit Navala.

Bukuya
pop 700
The village of Bukuya is at the intersection of the roads from Sigatoka, Nadi and Ba. The drive from Sigatoka up the Sigatoka Valley is about 1½ hours, as is the journey from Ba via Navala. From Nadi along the Nausori Highlands Rd it takes about 1½ to two hours. The chief here is an ex-boxing champion.

Places to Stay & Eat About the only traditional bure in Bukuya are at *Peni's* (☎/fax 700 801, Nadi). Peni's has nine thatched bure and large dining bure, built for travellers. It is situated on a hill on the edge of the village. Rates seem to be pretty arbitrary, depending on how much they think you can spend! The longer the stay the cheaper the rate. Expect to pay about F$150/200 for singles/doubles for three days and two nights, including meals and return transport from Nadi (minimum five people). Bure are small and very simple, with lino over compacted earth floors, and various living things making their homes in the roof. There are shared flush toilets and cold showers. Camp sites are F$22 per person per night, including meals, plus F$40 for return transport from Nadi.

The food is good, with plenty of home-grown fruit and vegetables. Meals include *palusami* (corned beef, onion and *lolo*, or coconut cream, wrapped in dalo leaves and baked in a lovo), dalo leaves, roots, pineapple, pawpaw, potatoes, and noodles mixed with green beans and canned meat. Peni's also has lovo nights. Villagers are more or less self-sufficient in food, except for salt and meat. The small *shop* opposite Peni's sells confectionery, soap, dried biscuits, tinned fish and cigarettes. Another *shop* in the village has refrigerated meats.

Activities may include waterfall tours, horse riding (F$15 per day), pig hunting (F$20 per person), trekking and visits to the chief's bure, the local school and Sunday church (Methodist). However, you are unlikely to be offered more than one activity per day and some activities are not feasible in wet conditions, or if the hostel's carrier is otherwise engaged. We have received a few letters from disappointed travellers. Try not to pay for everything upfront. Do not expect anything to be strictly organised, as 'Fiji time' definitely operates here. If activities are not happening, you may have to be prepared to just appreciate the good food and get into the slow-paced Fijian village lifestyle.

We spent two weeks at Peni's place in Bukuya. Accommodation is basic and activities sometimes haphazard, but after all, this is Fiji time. We loved it, and if you go there expecting a taste of village life and are prepared to take things as they come, you'll have a better time than at any of the beach resorts! If you're travelling with kids it's nothing short of perfect – the villagers love children.

Adrienne Robinson

Getting There & Away All roads to Bukuya are rough and unsealed, and are best suited to a 4WD. Peni's son George hurtles up and down the hills in his carrier with his load of travellers bouncing in the back. Don't expect comfort – it's a bone-crunching ride and if you are lucky there may be a few bits of sponge to sit on.

There are several operators that take day trips into the highlands (see Activities in the Nadi, Lautoka & Around section earlier in this chapter).

SIGATOKA VALLEY
The **Naihehe cave**, about an hour's drive upriver from Sigatoka, was once used as a fortress by hill tribes and has the remains of a ritual platform and cannibal oven. Adventures in Paradise (☎ 520 833, fax 520 848, ✉ wfall@is.com.fj) offers an interest-ing guided tour to this historic spot. Independent Tours (☎/fax 520 678) offers guided bike trips of the valley (see Korotogo in the Queens Road & Coral Coast section earlier in this chapter).

NAMOSI HIGHLANDS
The Namosi Highlands north of Pacific Harbour have some spectacular mountain scenery, with rainforests, deep river canyons, waterfalls, birdlife and isolated villages.

Tour company Rivers Fiji (☎ 450 147, fax 450 148, ✉ riversfiji@is.com.fj), based in Pacific Harbour, has trips to the Wainikoroiluva (Luva Gorge) and Upper Navua Rivers. A day trip to the Upper Navua River costs F$180, with food and equipment included. It involves a one-hour road trip to Nabukelevu village, followed by seven hours by boat (raft and punt) to Wainadiro or Waimogi. A day trip to Luva Gorge costs F$160 from Suva or the Coral Coast, F$175 from Nadi. This involves a two-hour road trip to Nakavika village, followed by four hours' inflatable kayaking to Namuamua and 1½ hours by motorised longboat to Nakavu or Navua. Food, drinks and equipment are included.

Discover Fiji Tours (☎ 450 180, fax 450 549), based at Navua, has two-day guided treks across Namosi Province, camping overnight in villages, as well as trips with village visits and bilibili expeditions on the Navua River (see Navua in the Queens Road & Coral Coast section earlier in this chapter).

NADARIVATU, NAVAI & KORO-NI-O
About 3km east of Tavua, a gravel road heads inland off the Kings Road to the forestry settlement of Nadarivatu and across the highlands to Suva. The road winds up gently at first, then climbs sharply to Fiji's highest mountain range. It becomes more and more spectacular, with vistas of the coast and offshore islands.

Nadarivatu, 30km south-east of Tavua, is in one of the most beautiful highland areas of Fiji. A large part of this area is covered with pine plantations, which are harvested and replanted. The cool, fresh mountain air

Cannibalism

Archaeological evidence from food-waste middens shows that cannibalism was practised in Viti from 2500 years ago until the mid- to late-19th century, by which time it had become an ordinary, ritualised part of life. In a society founded on ancestor worship and belief in the afterlife, cannibalising an enemy was considered the ultimate revenge. A disrespectful death was a lasting insult to the enemy's family.

Bodies were either consumed on the battlefield or brought back to the village spirithouse, offered to the local war god, then butchered, baked and eaten on the god's behalf. The triumph was celebrated with music and dance. Men performed the *cibi*, or death dance, and women the *dele* or *wate*, an obscene dance in which they sexually humiliated corpses and captives. Torture included being thrown alive into ovens, being bled or dismembered, being forced to watch their own body parts being consumed or being forced to eat some of themselves!

Women and children joined in the eating, but were banned from the formal sacrificial rites and feasting in the spirithouse and men's house, known at that time as *bure*. Raw and cooked human flesh was handled like any other meat and eaten with the fingers. Priests and chiefs, as living representatives of the gods, could not touch any kind of food as their hands and lips were considered *tabu* (sacred). They were normally fed by a female attendant who carefully avoided touching the lips, but for cannibalistic feasts the men fed themselves with special long-pronged wooden forks. Considered sacred relics, these forks were kept in the spirithouse and were not to be touched by women or children.

Mementos were kept of the kill to prolong the victor's sense of vengeance. Necklaces, hairpins or ear-lobe ornaments were made from human bones, and the skull of a hated enemy was sometimes made into a *tanoa*, or kava drinking bowl. Meat was smoked and preserved for snacks, and war clubs were inlaid with teeth or marked with tally notches. To record a triumph in war, the highlanders of Viti Levu placed the bones of victims in branches of trees outside their spirithouses and men's houses, as trophies. The coastal dwellers had a practical use for the bones: leg bones were used to make sail needles and thatching knives. Sexual organs and foetuses were suspended in trees. Rows of stones were also used to tally the number of bodies eaten by the chief.

Early European visitors and settlers were understandably obsessed with cannibalism, recording gruesome but nevertheless fascinating stories. At this time Fiji was in a state of upheaval, and warring was intense. Traders and beachcombers had a significant and disruptive influence on the population, introducing arms and altering the balance of power.

---

will make you pull out that forgotten jumper or jacket. Almost opposite the now dilapidated and unused Forestry Rest House is a fragment of the legendary **stone bowl** after which the town was named. Locals believe there was once a spring originating from the bowl which became the source of the mighty Sigatoka River. From Nadarivatu there is a walking trail up to the old fire tower on Mt Lomalagi (meaning 'sky' or 'heaven' in Fijian). The hike is about 1½ hours each way and the view from the top is great on a clear day.

It is possible to *camp* at Nadarivatu, but first seek permission from the Forestry Office (☎ 689 001). The office can also arrange a *homestay* with one of the forest worker's families or in the forest workers' dorm. Bring provisions and give either some money, groceries or clothing to cover your costs.

Nadarivatu was once a summer-holiday destination for Vatukoula mine bosses. The gold-mine *rest house* is spacious and has an open fire. It is for the use of mine workers but, on the off-chance that it is available, seek permission to stay there from the manager at Vatukoula's Emperor Gold Mining Company (☎ 680 630, ext 400). You may have to pay in advance at Vatukoula. Buli Tamani and family (☎ 689 005) are the caretakers.

Navai is about 8km south of Nadarivatu at the foot of Fiji's highest peak, **Tomanivi** (Adam and Eve's place; 1323m), also known as Mt Victoria. The Wainibuka and Waini-mala Rivers (eventually merging to form the Rewa) originate in this area, as does the Sigatoka River. Fiji's staple root crop, tavioka, grows poorly here (locals believe this to be Adam's punishment), but many other vegetables thrive at this altitude. Villagers only grow food for their own use nowadays, after a farm scheme proved uneconomical.

A hiking trail to Tomanivi begins at Navai village. Guides can be hired for F$10. Allow at least three hours for the climb up and two hours down. The last half of the climb is practically rock climbing and can be extremely slippery after rain.

Past Navai the road deteriorates, and is recommended for 4WD vehicles only. **Monasavu Dam** and Koro-ni-O (village of the clouds) are about 25km to the southeast. The Wailoa/Monasavu Hydroelectric Scheme provides about 93% of Viti Levu's power needs (about 89% of Fiji's needs), with a generating capacity of 80MW. It was completed in 1983 at a cost of F$233 million and has greatly reduced Fiji's reliance on diesel imports. The road improves again at Serea and continues through to Suva.

Getting There & Away

Local buses depart from Tavua (opposite the market) at 3 pm daily (except Sunday) up to Nadrau, a village near the Monasavu Dam. The bus returns to Tavua the following day about 7 am. The service, however, had been suspended at the time of writing due to poor road conditions. It's a winding trip up into the mountains (about 1½ hours). If driving, it's advisable to take a 4WD. The inland road that cuts across from Vatukoula is barely passable; avoid it unless you have a 4WD or are hitching with a carrier.

Mamanuca Group

The Mamanuca Group comprises about 20 small, varied islands. The group is just off the western coast of Viti Levu in a lagoon formed between the Great Sea Reef and the mainland. Due to their proximity to Nadi and Lautoka, the islands here are popular for day trips, and most of Fiji's tourists visit or stay at one of the Mamanuca resorts.

Like the Yasawa Group to the north, the Mamanucas are very scenic, with beautiful white-sand and reef-fringed beaches. Most of the habitable islands support a tourist resort and/or a Fijian village community. Only a few of the smaller islands, such as Monu and Monuriki, retain significant areas of forest with native birds and reptiles. Most of the islands have grassland and some have dry forest areas. Coconut palms are found on the small sandy islands. Fire and goats and other introduced animals have degraded the original vegetation.

The Mamanuca islands are usually sunnier and drier than Viti Levu. You often see heavy rain clouds hanging over Nadi and Lautoka while these offshore islands remain unaffected. The resorts usually bring in their water from the mainland by barge, and rely on generator power. The majority of resorts are on land leased from nearby villages.

Activities

Most resorts have their own activities, including snorkelling, windsurfing, fishing and other water sports.

Diving Mamanuca dive sites have an abundance of fish and corals. Gotham City is three pinnacles in a passage in the Malolo Barrier Reef, and has soft coral and is named after the batfish. You are likely to see big fish at The W dive site, which is outside the reef on the edge of an abyss.

Inside the Malolo Barrier Reef is the famous Supermarket, at a depth of 5m to 30m, where several currents converge. Here brave

HIGHLIGHTS

- Snorkel or dive in azure waters amid beautiful coral reefs.
- Visit Beachcomber Island to party and parasail over the beautiful coral islet.
- Surf the fantastic breaks of the southern Mamanucas.
- Sail or cruise around the island group.
- Fly in a small plane over tiny islets with reef-fringed white-sand beaches.

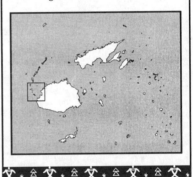

divers feed grey, white and black-tip reef sharks and the occasional bronze whaler.

North Reef, also known as the Circus, has lots of clown fish, schools of pelagics, plate corals, nudibranches, feather stars and a series of pinnacles. Other sites include the Fish Store, Driwas Dream, Yadua Island, Barrel Head, Camel Humps, a cruise-ship wreck and the remains of a WWII B26 bomber. See Activities in the Facts for the Visitor chapter for more information.

Many resorts have their own dive operations. Subsurface has dive shops on Beachcomber Island (Tai) and Malololailai (Plantation Island) and is a well-respected operation. The Fiji Recompression Chamber Facility in Suva is 45 minutes away from the Mamanucas by helicopter.

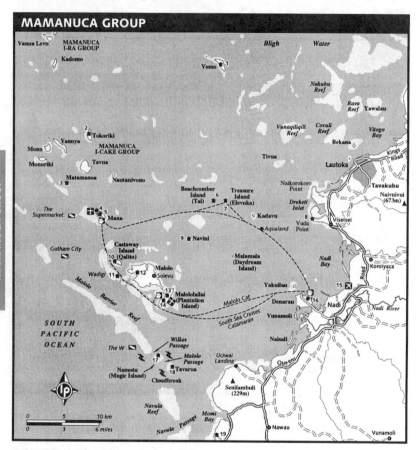

MAMANUCA GROUP

MAMANUCA GROUP

Surfing There are excellent surf-breaks at Malolo and Wilkes passages. Surfers will have to weigh up the cost and convenience of staying at resorts close to the breaks against staying at cheaper resorts on the mainland, but with extra transport costs for each surf trip. Seashell Surf & Dive Resort, near Momi Bay on Viti Levu, arranges trips to some of the Mamanuca breaks.

Organised Tours

Captain Cook Cruises This company (☎ 701 823, fax 702 045, ✉ captcookcrus@is.com.fj) offers a day cruise to Tivua, a tiny coral island, on board the *Ra Marama*, a 33m sailing ship. It departs Denarau Marina at 10 am and returns at 5 pm (F$79/39.50 per adult/child). The cost includes transfers from Nadi hotels, guided snorkelling, coral viewing in glass-bottom boats, paddle boats and a barbecue (BBQ) lunch. The starlight dinner cruise aboard MV *Lady Geraldine* (F$83/41.50 per adult/child, three hours) includes a three-course meal (wine and spirits extra); it departs Denarau Marina daily at 5.30 pm. It also has a three-day, two-night cruise/camping trip to the Mamanucas and the southern Yasawas (see Organised Tours in the Yasawa Group chapter for more information).

MAMANUCA GROUP

1 Vomo Island Resort
2 Tokoriki Island Resort
3 Matamanoa Island Resort
4 Mana Island Resort
5 Ratu Kini's Boko's Village Resort;
   Mereani Vata Backpacker's Inn
6 Beachcomber Island Resort
7 Treasure Island Resort
8 Vuda Point Marina
9 Navini Island Resort
10 Castaway Island Resort

11 Wadigi Island Lodge
12 Malolo Island Resort
13 Musket Cove Resort;
    Musket Cove Marina; The Trader
14 Plantation Island Resort;
    Ananda's Restaurant
15 Nadi International Airport
16 Denarau Marina
17 Namotu Island Resort
18 Tavarua Island Resort
19 Seashell Cove Resort

South Sea Cruises Apart from the Island Express *(Tiger IV)* catamaran transfers (see Getting Around later in this section), South Sea Cruises (☎ 750 500, fax 750 501, ✆ southsea@is.com.fj) has water taxis from Denarau, as well as combination and full-day cruises on board the *Seaspray* to Castaway Island (Qalito; F$95 including lunch, nonmotorised water sports and use of the resort facilities).

A half-day/full-day cruise to Aqualand, a small, sandy island south-east of Treasure Island, is F$59/79, including pick-up from Nadi hotels, and lunch. Water sports there include snorkelling, water-skiing, windsurfing, parasailing, banana rides, and use of coral viewing boards and water scooters. Nonmotorised water sports are free and there is an F$80 pass for the motorised activities.

Oceanic Schooner Company This company (☎ 722 455, fax 720 134) offers a five-island Champagne day cruise aboard the 30m schooner *Whale's Tale,* including Champagne, continental breakfast, buffet lunch, an open bar and snorkelling gear. What else could you possibly need? Well, F$160.

Fun Cruises Fiji This company (☎ 702 443) offers day trips to uninhabited Malamala (Daydream Island; F$69 on weekdays). Children under 16 years pay half-price (under 12s are free). Included are a BBQ lunch and drinks, including wine and beer, snorkelling, and coral viewing. The cruise to the island takes one hour.

Blue Lagoon Cruises This company (☎ 661 662, fax 664 098, ✆ blc@is.com.fj) has combined Mamanuca and Yasawa islands cruises from Lautoka using three different luxury boats. For more information, see Organised Tours in the Yasawa Group chapter.

Accommodation
There are only a few budget places to stay in the Mamanucas: the backpacker hostels on Mana and dormitory accommodation at Beachcomber Island Resort. Unless your time is very limited, the Yasawas, Nananu-i-Ra and Taveuni have better options for budget travellers.

Most of the resorts cater for those willing to pay mid-range to top-end prices, and usually guests are package-deal customers who have pre-arranged their trip from overseas. Some resorts have excellent facilities and services for families, while others don't accept young children. The resorts on Tavarua and Namotu, near the surf-breaks in the southern Mamanucas, cater mostly for surfers.

Getting There & Away
See the individual island sections later in this chapter for specific getting there and away information.

Getting Around
It is relatively difficult and costly to explore the Mamanucas, unless of course you have your own yacht. Yachts can be hired at Musket Cove Marina on Malololailai. Most resorts have island-hopping trips for

their guests but, as they prefer not to promote their competition, they stop only briefly.

Tiger IV (also known as the Island Express) of South Sea Cruises (☎ 750 500, fax 750 501, @ southsea@is.com.fj) is a 27m fast catamaran that shuttles from Denarau Marina to some of the Mamanuca islands: Castaway Island, Malolo, Mana (F$41 one way), Treasure Island (F$35) and islands between the above resorts (F$25). Matamanoa and Tokoriki are linked by small launch to Mana (F$66). Coaches pick up and deliver guests to Denarau Marina from hotels and resorts in Nadi (free) and on the Coral Coast (F$15). South Sea Cruises also offers day trips from Denarau Marina to Mana (F$85) and Castaway Island (F$95), including lunch, nonmotorised sports and use of resort facilities. Children five to 15 years pay half-price, those under five are free. South Sea Cruises also has a water-taxi service, which is expensive unless you are in a large group.

Malolo Cat (☎ 702 774), a fast and comfortable 17m catamaran, shuttles between Malololailai (Musket Cove and Plantation Island Resorts) and Denarau Marina three times daily (F$75/37.50 for an adult/child return, 50 minutes one way).

The price of a light-plane ticket is comparable with catamaran prices, and the trip by air is much quicker and more scenic. Sunflower Airlines and Air Fiji have several flights daily from Nadi to Mana (from F$47 one way) and Malololailai (from F$37). Turtle Airways offers more-expensive seaplane flights to the Mamanuca resorts, as does Island Hoppers (by helicopter). For more information, see Charter Services & Joyflights in the Getting Around chapter. Note that weight limits apply to all flights.

Local boats are used to transport backpackers between Mana and Malolo.

Dangers & Annoyances Travelling by small boat in rough weather can be a problem. This mostly applies to backpackers travelling from Nadi to Mana; you and your gear are likely to get wet. If the weather conditions look suspect, the boat is overcrowded or there are no life jackets on board, consider alternative means of transport.

BEACHCOMBER ISLAND

Beachcomber Island, also known as Tai island, is about 20km offshore from Nadi airport. The island measures only two hectares at low tide, but has a great garden and is circled by a beautiful beach. *Beachcomber Island Resort* (☎ 661 500, fax 664 496, @ beachcomber@is.com.fj) has been operating for more than 28 years. It takes only 10 minutes to walk around the island, which is completely covered by the resort. It caters for up to 200 guests, plus day-trippers. While it is not a secluded oasis, it has the reputation of having the best party atmosphere in the Mamanucas, and attracts a young singles crowd. Entertainment includes live music and grooving on the sand dance floor.

Bunk beds in the 84-bed *bure* (thatched dwellings) cost F$69. Lockers are provided. Alternatively, fan-cooled single/double rooms with fridge are good value at F$165/220. There are also 20 nice beachfront bure for F$250/300. Each has an en suite, fan, fridge and tea- and coffee-making facilities. Children under six are free. All prices include good buffet-style meals.

Most activities cost extra, but snorkelling equipment is free for house guests; day visitors pay F$5 for all-day hire plus a F$40 refundable deposit. Also on offer are water-skiing (F$30 per hour), parasailing (F$50), catamaran sailing (F$25 per hour), windsurfing (F$10 per hour), jet-skiing (F$80 per half-hour), canoeing (F$14 per day) and fishing trips (F$200 for a maximum of four people for two to three hours). Subsurface (☎ 666 738, fax 669 955, @ subsurface@is.com.fj) is an excellent diving operation based on the island. It has Japanese- and English-speaking dive instructors. Mixed-gas diving (nitrox) is also available. A two-tank dive is F$140, open-water courses are F$495. Speciality courses are also available. Diving is half-price during February and March for those staying at least five nights.

Getting There & Away

Transfer is by the resort's fast catamaran *Drodrolagi* and includes courtesy bus pick-ups from the airport, and Nadi and Lautoka hotels. Day-trippers can go by the fast catamaran (25 minutes from Denarau Marina) or aboard the 39m schooner *Tui Tai* (70-minute cruise departing from Lautoka Queen's Wharf), which has bar facilities on board. Return day trips (F$60/30 per adult/child) by either boat include buffet lunch. Beachcomber also offers speedboat transfers for late flight arrivals, with a F$20 surcharge.

TREASURE ISLAND

Treasure Island, also known as Elevuka, is a short distance from Beachcomber Island. The six-hectare coral island is covered by *Treasure Island Resort (☎ 666 999, fax 666 955, ✉ treasureisland@is.com.fj)*, which caters mostly for families. Accommodation in one of 67 comfortable beachfront bure costs F$395. Each has air-con, fan, fridge, and tea- and coffee-making facilities, and can take up to three adults, or two adults and two children under 16 years. Optional meal packages cost F$55/62 for two/three meals daily; otherwise expect to spend F$13/17/36 per person for breakfast/lunch/dinner.

There is nightly entertainment in the large, open dining room/bar, a games room and a freshwater pool. The resort caters well for kids, with a children's pool, playground and baby-sitting provided. Activities included in the price are windsurfing, canoeing, snorkelling, volleyball, golf, use of catamarans, paddle boats and sail boats, coral viewing and fishing. Diving trips cost F$130 for two tanks or F$520 for open-water certification.

Getting There & Away

Treasure Island Resort is serviced by South Sea Cruises Island Express catamaran. See Getting Around earlier in this chapter for more information.

NAVINI

Navini, a tiny island centrally located in the Mamanuca Group, is surrounded by a white-sand beach and offshore reef. *Navini Island Resort (☎ 662 188, fax 665 566, ✉ naviniisland@is.com.fj)* caters for a maximum of 22 guests. It is a good place

for families or couples who want a friendly intimate atmosphere away from crowds of tourists. The 30 staff outnumber the guests – one of the reasons why there are lots of return customers. The resort shop has souvenirs, toiletries, books and book lending.

The nine bure are all within 10m of the beach. The two one-bedroom bure (maximum three people) cost F$360. The two more spacious 'premier' bure with queen-size beds and verandah on two sides cost F$390. The three duplex bure have sitting rooms (maximum five people) and are F$420. The deluxe honeymoon bure, which has two rooms, a verandah and a private courtyard with spa, costs F$495. A 10% discount applies for stays of over one week. All guests usually eat at the same table or you can choose a private candlelight dinner if you wish. A meal plan is F$68 per adult, F$37 for children five to 12 years old or F$22 if under five. The food is good, especially the fresh fish.

Snorkelling is excellent just off the beach along the edge of the surrounding reef. Kayaking, windsurfing, volleyball, use of coral viewing boards, and morning trips, including fishing and visiting other resorts or villages, are included in the price. Diving can be arranged with Subsurface at Beachcomber Island. Guests staying on other islands cannot visit Navini.

Getting There & Away

Most guests are picked up from Nadi or Lautoka hotels, taken by car to Vuda Point Marina and then spend 30 minutes in a speedboat. Return transfers cost F$135/68 for an adult/child aged five to 12; children under five are free.

MALOLOLAILAI

Malololailai, also known as Plantation Island, is approximately 20km west of Denarau Island. This 240-hectare island is the second-largest of the Mamanuca Group. Apart from two resorts, there is a time-share resort, a marina, a Subsurface dive shop, two grocery stores, a restaurant near the airstrip, and a gift shop on the hill above Musket Cove.

Musket Cove Marina

In September each year, the Musket Cove Yacht Club (☎ 662 215, fax 662 633) hosts Fiji Regatta Week and the Musket Cove to Port Vila yacht race. Yachts can anchor at the marina (year round) from F$36 a week, and stock up on fuel, water and provisions at the general store. The marina also offers a choice of charter yachts ranging in size from 6m to 32m; charter rates vary depending on duration and extent of services required.

Diving

Subsurface at Musket Cove (☎ 622 215, fax 662 633, ☻ subsurface@is.com.fj) is a well-equipped dive shop, with fast dive boats and quick access to great dive sites at the Malolo Barrier Reef. A two-tank dive costs F$140, a six-tank package F$320 and an open-water course is F$495. Plantation Island Resort has its own diving concern, Plantation Divers. It offers two-tank dives (F$120) and six-tank packages (F$320).

Surfing

There is no official transport to Namotu Lefts and Wilkes Passage surf-breaks, but 'Big Johnnie' from the local village can get you there. His boat, however, does not have life jackets, radio, flares or insurance. He can be contacted at Plantation Island Resort's boatshed, and if one/two-three/four-five people go, rates are F$40/30/25 per person. *Emotional Rescue* (☎/fax 666 710, ☻ sailfiji@is.com.fj), a fast, 17m yacht available for charter for F$1000 per day for a maximum of eight people, also offers access to the main surf-breaks.

Places to Stay & Eat

Plantation Island Resort (☎ 669 333, fax 669 423, ☻ plantation@is.com.fj), established in the late 1970s, was one of Fiji's first resorts. It has a good white-sand beach. However, if you are after a quiet, secluded holiday this is not the place for you.

The resort caters well for families who are on tight budgets, and the atmosphere is often fun and lively, especially for children. The 23 two-bedroom bure are popular and often booked out. They cost F$385/470 for beachfront/garden bure (singles or doubles or F$490/570 for six adults). The 66 one-room studio bure set in the garden are F$280 (doubles). Air-con hotel rooms, catering for up to two adults and two children under 16, cost F$190. Expect to get at least 25% discount off these rates in package specials or walk-in rates.

Buffet breakfast is included in the price. Expect to spend around F$10 to F$20 per person for lunch, F$17 to F$24 for dinner mains or F$22 to F$25 for set-menu nights. There are no cooking facilities.

The resort has a creche and baby-sitting service, two swimming pools and a games room. Activities included are snorkelling, volleyball, putt putt golf, canoeing and windsurfing. It also has a nine-hole golf course, a tennis court and lawn-bowls rink. Diving, water-skiing, paragliding, game fishing, island hopping and jet-skiing cost extra.

Musket Cove Resort (☎ 662 215, fax 662 633, ☻ musketcovefiji@is.com.fj) is adjacent to Musket Cove Yacht Club and marina. It is set in spacious gardens with a poolside restaurant, beachfront walking trail and a cute island bar linked by the marina. The beach here is tidal and not as nice as at the Plantation Island Resort; however, guests from the two resorts are welcome to use both beaches and facilities. It caters well for families as well as for those after a quiet holiday. The owners are Dick and Carol Smith, who established both Castaway and Plantation Island Resorts.

Beachfront/lagoon bure sleep three people and cost F$260/372. Self-contained seaview bure sleep four and cost F$340. The double-storey villas, which have a spa, two bathrooms, cooking facilities, and sleep up to six people, cost F$480. Prices quoted are for double occupancy: Each additional adult is charged F$15. All units have ceiling fans. The resort also has good air-con rooms on the first floor of the administration building for F$220. There is a 20% discount for all types of accommodation during the low season, from mid-January to the end of May and from November to 20 December. Dinner mains at Dick's Place, the resort's bistro and bar, cost from F$18 to F$27, but there is a three-course set menu for F$21.50 and meal plan for F$55. Dick's Place serves international cuisine with some Indian and Fijian dishes, weekly BBQs and pig-on-the-spit.

Activities such as windsurfing, canoeing, hand-line fishing and snorkelling are included. Game fishing, diving and use of catamarans cost extra.

Lagoon Resort Time Share (☎ 662 215/ 09-357 0503 New Zealand, fax 358 4269 New Zealand) has five two-bedroom and 15 one-bedroom bure. The units are spacious, clean and have kitchen facilities. Although it is a time-share resort, you may be able to arrange to stay here if you ring the New Zealand number. Guests can also use the Musket Cove Resort's facilities.

There is a well-stocked supermarket, *The Trader*, near Musket Cove Marina and a small general store and a restaurant between the airstrip and Plantation Island Resort. *Ananda's Restaurant*, next to the general store, has mains for around F$17 and kids' meals for F$8. It makes a change from the resort restaurants, the food is good, and there is sometimes live music.

Getting There & Away

Plantation Island and Musket Cove Resorts are serviced three times daily by the catamaran *Malolo Cat*. Return fares from Denarau Marina near Nadi cost F$75/37.50 per adult/child and take 50 minutes one way. Malololailai has a landing strip with shuttle services from Nadi by both Sunflower Airlines (F$44 one way) and Air Fiji (F$37). The flight takes about 10 minutes and gives a superb aerial view of the island.

TAVARUA

This 12-hectare coral island is at the southern edge of the Malolo Barrier Reef, which encloses the southern Mamanucas. It is surrounded by beautiful white-sand beaches and has great surf nearby at Cloudbreak and Restaurants. Waves are for experienced surfers only, as they're overhead to well overhead on good days. Cloudbreak, about 2.5km offshore, has waves averaging 2m to 3m. The resort boat will drop off surfers at

Restaurants, about 400m paddling distance from the resort, where waves average 2m.

Tavarua Island Resort (☎ 723 513, fax 706 395, ✆ tavarua@is.com.fj) is run by Americans and most of the guests are American surfers. The resort, which runs on solar and generator power, has 12 simple bure elevated and spaced along the beach, one toilet block, and a restaurant-bar overlooking the Restaurants surf-break. Behind each bure is a screened open-air solar shower. The toilet block is a bit of a walk from some of the bure.

The daily rate is about F$288/412 for singles/twins, which includes all meals, transfers from Uciwai Landing and boat trips to the surf-break. Drinks are extra. There are also two new family bure. These have en suites with hot and cold water.

Serious surfers are advised to bring three boards, as boards can easily be snapped by the powerful waves. A boat with a radio stays with surfers out at Cloudbreak and, if necessary, any accident victims can be transferred quickly to the mainland by helicopter. Game fishing, windsurfing and diving can also be arranged. Depending on the group of guests, nonsurfers may feel a bit left out.

The minimum stay is one week and bookings need to be made well in advance, although in the low season (December to February) they may accept 'walk-ins'. Book with Tavarua Island Tours, California, USA (☎ 805-686 4551, fax 683 6696).

Getting There & Away

The resort organises pick-ups from the Nadi area. Guests are driven to Uciwai Landing and there's a half-hour boat ride to the island.

NAMOTU

Namotu, a cute 1.5-hectare island next to Tavarua, is not much more than a sand bar. *Namotu Island Resort (☎ 706 439, fax 706 039, ✆ namotu@is.com.fj)* is an intimate resort catering for a maximum of 24 people. While ideally suited to surfers and windsurfers, it is also popular with divers, fishermen and honeymooners. The hexagonal restaurant-bar is surrounded by a

MAMANUCA GROUP

verandah with great views of the ocean and swimming pool. Accommodation prices include three meals a day (varied cuisine) and unlimited surfing. Drinks are extra. The two larger beach bungalows cost F$968 for up to four people and sleep two extras for F$242 each. Double beach bungalows cost F$628 and shared rooms are F$242 per person. Children under 12 years are not accepted at the resort.

Surf-breaks include Swimming Pool, which is good for beginners, Wilkes Passage and Namotu Lefts. Use of kayaks and snorkelling gear is included in the price. Surfboards can be hired from Nadi surf shops. Windsurfers have to bring their own equipment. Diving can be arranged with resorts on Malololailai island.

Check in and check out is on a Saturday to Saturday basis only. Generally, guests book and pay in advance, but Namotu does occasionally take 'walk-ins'.

Getting There & Away
The resort will arrange for a driver to pick up its guests from Nadi airport or from Nadi hotels.

MALOLO
Malolo is the largest of the Mamanucas and has two villages, a resort and a time-share facility (called *Lako Mai*). It has a variety of vegetation, including mangroves and coastal forest. The island's highest point is Uluisolo (218m), which was used by locals as a hill fortification and by the US forces in 1942 as an observation point. There are panoramic views of the Mamanuca islands and the southern Yasawas.

Malolo Island Resort (☎ 669 197, fax 669 197, @ malolo@is.com.fj) opened in 1999 on the former Club Naitasi site. The old resort has been thoroughly renovated. All rooms have air-con, fridge, fans and verandahs. Oceanview/beachfront bure cost F$300/375 for two adults and two children, or F$475 for deluxe versions. The resort has two bars and restaurants, including the Tree Tops Restaurant offering gourmet dinners overlooking the resort. Optional seven-night meal packages are F$300. This daily rate includes all nonmotorised water activities, a kids' club, and nature and cultural walks around the island.

Getting There & Away
Malolo Island Resort is serviced by South Sea Cruises' Island Express catamaran (see Getting Around earlier in this chapter).

WAIDIGI
This small island of about 1.2 hectares is just west of Malolo island. *Wadigi Island Lodge* (☎/fax 720 901, @ waidigiisland@is.com.fj), run by Ross and Jenny Allen, comprises three bedrooms, lounge, dining decks and gorgeous views. It caters for a maximum of six people (no children under 12). All meals are included as is the use of snorkelling gear, kayaks, windsurfers and a 4m aluminium boat. Transfers are via Malololailai.

CASTAWAY ISLAND
Reef-fringed Castaway Island, also known as Qalito, is 27km west of Denarau. *Castaway Island Resort* (☎ 661 233, fax 665 753, @ castaway@is.com.fj) covers about one-eighth of the 70-hectare island; the remainder has tropical vegetation. The 65

Americans on Malolo

A US expedition led by Commandant Charles Wilkes visited Fiji in 1840 as part of its exploratory journey of the Pacific. The team, including scientists, artists and a language expert, produced the first reasonably complete chart of the Fiji islands. They ran into strife in the Mamanucas, however, when a disagreement with the people of Malolo got out of hand. Wilkes and his sailors tried to take a local person as hostage and the Fijians retaliated by killing some of the Americans, including Wilkes' nephew. In response, the Americans set alight two villages and killed more than 50 people.

American troops again 'invaded' Malolo in 1942, while training for combat against the Japanese. They set up an observation and signals station on Uluisolo.

simple fan-cooled bure are quite spacious, sleeping four adults or a family of five, and have fridges and interesting *masi* (bark cloth)-lined ceilings. Prices are $445/475/515 for garden/oceanview/beachfront bure. There is a nice swimming pool/bar and a great dining terrace perched on the point overlooking the water. The all-day casual dining menu has meals for F$10 to F$14; the a la carte dinner is F$14 to F$22; or pay F$50 per day for unrestricted selection from lunch and dinner a la carte menus.

The resort has a clinic with a nurse, creche and kids' club, which is free during the day for those over three years old. Otherwise, baby-sitting is F$3.50 per hour. Catamaran sailing, snorkelling, surf-ski paddling, windsurfing, volleyball and tennis are included. Other activities such as diving, jet-skiing, parasailing, water-skiing, fishing and island hopping cost extra.

Castaway Dive Centre is reliable and charges F$140 for a two-tank dive and F$360 for a six-tank package. There is a small discount if you have your own equipment. Open-water courses are F$495 per person in a group or F$600 for individual lessons. Underwater photography courses are also offered.

Getting There & Away
Castaway Island Resort is serviced by South Sea Cruises' Island Express catamaran transfer. The island can also be visited as a day trip (see South Sea Cruises earlier in this chapter under Organised Tours).

MANA
The beautiful island of Mana is about 30km west of Denarau. With its grassy hills, lovely beaches and wide coral reef, it is spectacular to fly over. Accommodation includes a large luxury resort and two backpacker hostels. The upmarket Mana Island Resort stretches between the north and south beaches over 80 hectares of leased land. The resort holds weddings at Sunset Beach at the far western end of the island. Snorkelling here is quite good with lots of tiny colourful fish. Also check out the south beach pier, where the fish go into a frenzy

under the lights at night. Hike up to the tallest hill for a lovely view.

Places to Stay – Budget
There are two backpacker hostels on the south-eastern edge of Mana Island Resort near the south beach. The resort has erected a huge fence to make it clear that its facilities, such as beach shelters and deck chairs, are for its own guests only.

While the hostels appear to be part of the same complex, they are run by brothers who are very competitive. Politics aside, the staff of both are usually friendly and the party atmosphere can be fun, but it's not a quiet escape. There have been mixed reports about both hostels; avoid paying too much upfront so that you have an option to change if you are not happy. Only cash is accepted and beware of theft on the beaches and in the dorms. It's best to bring your own soap, towel, snacks, torch, kava and mosquito repellent. There is nowhere to buy ingredients for cooking and backpackers are not allowed to use Mana Island Resort's restaurants. Activities include bushwalking, swimming, snorkelling, kava parties and volleyball.

Ratu Kini Boko's Village Resort (☎ 669 143, 721 959 Nadi, fax 720 552) has five dorms of various sizes and types, from a concrete house to traditional bure. The largest takes a maximum of 16 people. Prices including meals are F$35 for a dorm bed and F$22.50 per person for camping. Food is usually OK and is served buffet-style. Activities include a BBQ on a 'honeymoon island' and snorkelling trips for F$5 per person for the boat plus F$5 to hire gear.

Mereani Vata Backpacker's Inn (☎ 663 099, 703 466 Nadi) has up to 24 people squeezed into one dorm for F$30 per person, including three meals. There are also four double rooms for F$35 per person, including meals. It seems that food quality and quantity here can vary. Activities available include reef-fishing trips for F$5, four-island sightseeing for F$20, snorkelling (including equipment) for F$6 per day and a weekly kava ceremony.

Places to Stay – Top End

Japanese-owned *Mana Island Resort* (☎ 661 210, fax 662 713, ✉ mana@is.com.fj) was established in the early 1970s when the original Australian owner built 60 of the garden bure. Presently, with its 128 bure and 32 hotel rooms, it is one of the largest island resorts in Fiji. Garden bure cost F$280/500 a double/duplex (up to six people), and spacious, deluxe, oceanview, aircon bure cost F$430/720. Up to two children under 16 years are free. Deluxe oceanview bure cost F$430/720. The deluxe bure are spacious, elevated, have a porch, fan, air-con, fridge and solar power. Deluxe air-con hotel rooms on the northern beachfront cost F$430 a double. Resort facilities include a circular pool, two tennis courts, volleyball, games room, kids' club, library and play centre for children. The price includes all nonmotorised water sports. South Sea Cruises offers trips on a semisubmersible reef viewer.

The resort has three good restaurants. The south beach restaurant is the most pleasant as it is right on the beach. Mains cost F$15 to F$26.50. Meal plans are available and children's meals are about half-price. There is a weekly *lovo* (traditional Fijian banquet) and a *meke* (dance performance) three times a week.

There are good dive sites at the main reef off Mana. Aqua-Trek (☎ 702 413, fax 702 412) caters mostly for resort divers. A one-tank boat dive costs F$80, including equipment, a six-tank package costs F$390 and open-water courses cost F$520.

Getting There & Away

The backpacker resorts charge F$30 per person one way for boat transfers. Boats depart from Wailoaloa Beach (taking 45 minutes to 1½ hours, depending on weather conditions and the tide). The small boats to the island can be a problem in rough weather. Ideally, get informed about weather conditions, and avoid overcrowded boats with no life jackets or radio on board. Flying is the quickest and most scenic way to get to Mana, but it may not be an option for backpacker resort guests, as the airstrip

is part of Mana Island Resort (for the use of its guests only).

Sunflower Airlines and Air Fiji have a 15-minute shuttle from Nadi airport to the Mana airstrip several times daily (F$56 with Sunflower Airlines, one way, or F$47 with Air Fiji). The island is also serviced by South Sea Cruises' Island Express catamaran (see Getting Around earlier in this chapter).

MATAMANOA

Matamanoa is a small, high island north of Mana. *Matamanoa Island Resort* (☎ 660 511, fax 661 069, ✉ matamanoa@is.com.fj) is on a high point overlooking a beautiful beach. There are concrete paths through the garden to the 20 bure. The layout is fairly tight but buildings are staggered to increase privacy. Each bure has a verandah and views to the beach (half facing sunrise, half sunset), ceilings decorated with *tapa* (*masi*, or bark cloth), and tea- and coffee-making facilities. Prices are F$400 for doubles and F$52 for each extra adult (maximum of four people). There are also 11 air-con units with beach or garden views for F$180 a double. Matamanoa does not cater for children under 12 and is best suited to couples who want a relaxing holiday. The minimum stay is three days. Rates include breakfast (meal plans cost F$56/28 per adult/child).

The resort has a swimming pool and tennis courts, which are shaded during the day and lit at night. Nonmotorised water sports are included in the price. Other activities offered include a 'honeymoon island' picnic, island hopping and trips to the nearby village of Tavua (on Tavua island), which is famous for its pottery. Diving is with Aqua-Trek, based on Mana. Two-tank dives cost F$165, including equipment, while open-water certification costs F$600.

Getting There & Away

Matamanoa Island Resort is serviced by South Sea Cruises' Island Express catamaran to Mana and then by shuttle boat to Matamanoa. Alternatively, Sunflower Airlines and Air Fiji fly to Mana; from there take a shuttle boat (see Getting Around earlier in this chapter). The island also has a helipad. See Charter Services & Joyflights in the Getting Around chapter for information on Island Hoppers (F$184 each way).

TOKORIKI

The small, hilly island of Tokoriki has a beautiful, long white-sand beach facing west. Its position near the northern end of the Mamanucas gives it a special feeling of remoteness. You can visit for the day, or stay at the resort.

Tokoriki Island Resort (☎ 661 999, fax 665 295, ✉ tokoriki@is.com.fj) caters largely for families and couples, much of it repeat business. It has 27 beachfront bure with fans and fridges, while deluxe bure also have air-con and private open-air showers. Rates are F$430/490 for regular/deluxe for up to four people, breakfast included. If you stay seven nights, you pay for six.

The resort has a pleasant dining terrace where lunch is served from F$11 to F$13 and dinner from F$20 to F$28. There is a smorgasbord three nights a week, a lovo and a meke once a week, and a children's menu. Activities include tennis, canoeing, sailing, reef fishing, diving, snorkelling, a visit to Yanuya village (on Yanuya island) and island hopping (four people for F$50 each). Nonmotorised water sports are included in the rate. Diving is with Dive Tropex. Two-tank diving trips cost F$130 and open-water courses are F$520.

On top of the hill is a cross in memory of the initial owner and developer, Australian Gordon Morris, who died in an accident while building the resort.

Getting There & Away

Tokoriki Island Resort is serviced by South Sea Cruises' Island Express catamaran to Mana and then by shuttle boat to Tokoriki. Sunflower Airlines and Air Fiji fly to Mana, from where you can take a shuttle boat to Tokoriki (see Getting Around earlier in this chapter).

VOMO

This wedge-shaped 90-hectare island rises to a magnificent high ridge and has lovely beaches, good snorkelling and diving.

Upmarket *Vomo Island Resort* (☎ 666 122, fax 668 500, ✉ vomo@is.com.fj), formerly Sheraton Vomo Island, has 28 very comfortable air-con villas, each with a spacious bathroom and spa, a mosquito-proof deck and a separate lounge. Peak-season rates are F$847/F$350 per double/child, or F$3190 for a deluxe versions for up to four people. Rates include all meals, a laundry service and nonmotorised activities. There is a minimum stay of three nights.

Facilities include a pool, a golf course and three venues for dining. One couple at a time can picnic just offshore on the beautiful 'honeymoon island' Vomolailai. Activities include day trips to other islands, hiking, sailing, windsurfing, snorkelling and diving.

Getting There & Away

Guests have the choice of arriving at the island by helicopter (F$370 return, 15 minutes from Nadi airport or Denarau), seaplane (F$220 return, 20 minutes from Wailoaloa Beach) or launch (F$440, one hour from Denarau).

MAMANUCA GROUP

Yasawa Group

The Yasawa Group is a chain of 20 ancient volcanic islands that extends in an almost straight line for 90km within the Great Sea Reef. The southern islands begin 40km north-west of Viti Levu. Of these 20 islands, four are large and elevated, with summits up to nearly 600m above sea level. The land is mostly hilly and the climate is relatively dry. The climate and the group's white-sand beaches, spectacular crystal-clear lagoons and rugged volcanic landscapes make it one of Fiji's main tourist destinations. Most people visit the islands on cruises as there are not many places to stay.

After the famous mutiny on the *Bounty* in 1789, Captain William Bligh passed through the island group on his way to Timor. His longboat was chased by Fijian canoes.

The people of the Yasawas have their own dialect, known as Vuda. The traveller may notice that *cola* (pronounced thola) is sometimes used instead of *bula* (cheers), or *vina du riki* instead of *vinaka vakalevu* (thank you very much).

The Yasawas has a sparse population of 5000 people. There are no banks, postal services or medical services. The upmarket resorts have phones and some of the smaller resorts have radio phones for emergencies.

Hurricane Gavin in early 1997 devastated much of the Yasawas and was followed by the biggest drought for 100 years.

Activities

Hiking Bring hiking boots, as the high islands such as Wayasewa and Waya are great for trekking.

Diving The Yasawas have lots of spectacular reefs with brilliant corals, walls, underwater caves and many unexplored areas. Westside WaterSports has a dive shop on Tavewa that caters for the backpacker resorts as well as Blue Lagoon Cruises passengers. There is also a local diving

HIGHLIGHTS

- Cruise, kayak or take a sailing safari through the beautiful waters and high islands.
- Snorkel or dive the reefs to see the hard coral and abundant fish life.
- Hike on the high islands of Waya and Wayasewa.
- Visit a village for a *kava* ceremony and *meke* performance.

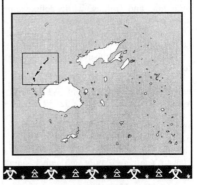

operation based at Wayalailai Resort on Wayasewa. The upmarket resorts of Yasawa Island Lodge and Turtle Island (Nanuya Levu) provide diving for their guests, as do Captain Cook Cruises and Blue Lagoon Cruises.

Kayaking Southern Sea Ventures (☎ 02-9460 3375, fax 02-9460 3376 in Australia, ✉ cventure@tpg.com.au) runs 11-day kayaking trips around the Yasawas. The trips are run between July and October and cost F$2590 per person. This price includes all meals, two-person fibreglass kayaks and camping and safety equipment. It takes a maximum of 10 people per group. Expect to paddle for three to four hours daily. Other activities include swimming, snorkelling and village visits.

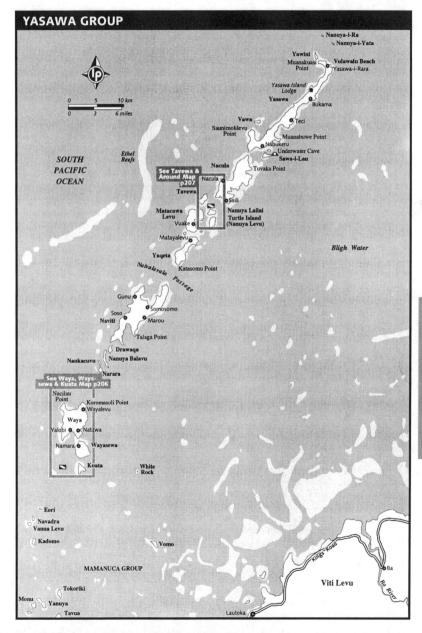

YASAWA GROUP

Nanuya-I-Ra
Nanuya-i-Yata

Yawini
Muanakuasi
Point
Vulawalu Beach
Yasawa-i-Rara

Yasawa Island
Lodge
Yasawa
Bukama

Vawa
Teci
Saunimolilevu
Point
Muanabuwe Point

Nabukeru
Underwater Cave
Sawa-i-Lau
Nacula
Tuvaka Point
See Tavewa &
Around Map
p207
Nacula
Tavewa
Sisili

Matacawa
Levu
Nanuya Lailai
Turtle Island
(Nanuya Levu)
Vuake

Matayalevu
Yaqeta
Bligh Water
Katasomu Point
Naivalavala Passage

SOUTH
PACIFIC
OCEAN

Ethel
Reefs

0   5   10 km
0   3   6 miles

Gunu
Somosomo
Soso
Naviti
Marou
Talaga Point

Drawaqa
Naukacuvu
Nanuya Balavu
Narara

See Waya, Waya-
sewa & Kuata Map p206
Nacilau
Point
Koromasoli Point
Wayalevu
Waya
Yalobi
Natawa
Namara
Wayasewa
Kuata
White
Rock

Eori
Navadra
Vanua Levu
Kadomo
Vomo

MAMANUCA GROUP
Kings Road
Ba
Ba River

Tokoriki
Viti Levu
Monu
Yanuya
Tavua
Lautoka

YASAWA GROUP

Coral's True Colour

Coral is usually stationary and looks decidedly flowery, but it's an animal, and a hungry carnivorous animal at that. Although a 3rd century AD Greek philosopher surmised that coral was really an animal, it was still generally considered to be a plant until only 250 years ago.

Corals are coelenterates, a class of animals that includes sea anemones and jellyfish. The true reef-building corals or Scleractinia are distinguished by their lime skeletons. It is this relatively indestructible skeleton that forms the reef, as new coral continually builds on old, dead coral and the reef gradually builds up.

Coral takes a vast number of forms but all are distinguished by polyps, the tiny tube-like fleshy cylinders that look very like their close relation, the anemone. The top of the cylinder is open and ringed by waving tentacles, which sting and draw any passing prey into the polyp's stomach (the open space within the cylinder).

Each polyp is an individual creature, but each can reproduce by splitting to form a coral colony of separate but closely related polyps. Although each polyp catches and digests its own food, the nutrition passes between the polyps to the whole colony. Most coral polyps only feed at night: During the daytime they withdraw into their hard limestone skeleton, so it is only at night that a coral reef can be seen in its full colourful glory.

Hard corals may take many forms. One of the most common and easiest to recognise is the staghorn coral, which grows by budding off new branches from the tips. Brain corals are huge and round with a surface looking very much like a human brain. They grow by adding new base levels of skeletal matter and expanding outwards. Flat or sheet corals, like plate coral, expand at their outer edges. Many corals can take different shapes depending on their environment. Staghorn coral can branch out in all directions in deeper water or form flat tables when they grow in shallow water.

Like their reef-building relatives, soft coral is made up of individual polyps, but does not form a hard limestone skeleton. Without the skeleton that protects hard coral, it would seem likely that soft coral would fall prey to fish, but it seems to remain relatively immune either due to toxic substances in its tissues or to the presence of sharp limestone needles, which protect the polyps. Soft corals can move around and will sometimes engulf and kill hard coral.

Corals catch their prey by means of stinging nematocysts (a specialised type of cell). Some corals can give humans a painful sting. The fern-like stinging hydroid is one that should be given a wide berth.

Organised Tours

Cruises are a great way to see the Yasawas, either by cruise ship or sailing ship. In one trip you can see beautiful white-sand beaches, experience excellent snorkelling or diving, visit villages and have good food and comfortable accommodation. Seasonal kayaking trips are also available. Operators include Captain Cook Cruises and Blue Lagoon Cruises.

Captain Cook Cruises (☎ 701 823, fax 702 045, @ captcookcrus@is.com.fj), 15 Narewa Rd, Nadi, offers a three-night Mamanuca and southern Yasawa cruise, a four-night Yasawa cruise and a seven-night combination cruise on board the MV *Reef Escape*. The 68m cruise boat has a swimming pool, bars, lounges and air-con accommodation on three decks, including cabins with bunk beds, staterooms and deluxe staterooms. Prices per person, twin share, including all meals and activities (except diving), are F$1080/1285 (three-night cruise) or F$2268/ 2699 (seven-night cruise) for cabin/ stateroom. Children under two years are free; those up to 15 years pay F$100 per night. Cruises depart from Denarau Marina on Denarau Island, west of Nadi.

Captain Cook Cruises also offers interesting tall-ship Sailing Safaris on board the SV *Spirit of the Pacific*. It has three- or four-day cruises to the southern Yasawas, including swimming and snorkelling trips, fishing tours, island treks, village visits, campfire barbecues (BBQs) and *lovo* (food cooked in a pit oven) feasts. Prices per person, twin share, are F$495/599 for three/four days. Accommodation is in simple *bure* (thatched dwellings) ashore, or aboard in fold-up canvas beds below the deck cabins.

Blue Lagoon Cruises (☎ 661 662, fax 664 098, @ blc@is.com.fj), 183 Vitogo Parade, Lautoka, offers three-, four- or seven-day Club Cruises to the Yasawas aboard the motor yachts MV *Yasawa Princess* (54m, 33 cabins), the MV *Nanuya Princess* (49m, 25 cabins) and the MV *Lycianda* (39m, 21 cabins). Gold Club Cruises are aboard the luxury MV *Mystique Princess* (56m, 36 staterooms). Club cruises cost from F$775/1122/3080 for two/three/six nights in twin-share cabins. Seven-day Gold Club Cruise prices start at F$3332 for twin deluxe staterooms. Children under two pay 11% and those under 16 years sharing with an adult are charged from F$220 to F$1100, depending on the type of cruise. All accommodation has air-con and en suites, and the boats have saloon and sundeck areas. Transfers, cruise activities and food are included but drinks, snorkelling, diving and equipment hire is extra. Cruises depart from Lautoka's Queens Wharf on Viti Levu. Diving is with Westside WaterSports (see Diving under Tavewa later in this chapter).

Accommodation
Camping is available at Wayalailai Resort (Wayasewa) and at Coral View and David's Place on Tavewa. In addition, other budget places are Octopus Resort on Waya and Otto & Fanny Doughty's on Tavewa. Most places have a minimum stay and ask for payment upfront. It is difficult to swap between islands as transport is limited. Self-catering is possible at Otto & Fanny's. On Waya and Wayasewa you will probably have more contact with village culture than on Tavewa. The Yasawas also has two luxury resorts: Turtle Island and Yasawa Island Lodge. Alternatively, you could try a floating resort (see the previous Organised Tours entry).

Getting There & Away
The upmarket resorts have charter plane services for guests, while most visitors to the budget resorts travel by small boat. There are regular cruises and seasonal kayak trips. Unfortunately there is no really cheap and easy way to hop from island to island in the Yasawas unless you have your own yacht or sea kayak!

Dangers & Annoyances Visitors to the budget resorts travel by small boat. The trip is quite long, across an exposed stretch of water, and weather conditions can quickly change. In the past passengers have been stranded for hours due to engine failure and in 1999 an overcrowded boat sank! Fortunately no one died but, as one traveller has told us, it's worth checking if boats have sufficient life jackets and a marine radio. The traveller, who was on the sinking boat, says it pays to plan ahead and check with your resort about whether its boats are licensed by the Fijian government.

Depending on the weather and your state of mind, the trip can be a fun adventure or uncomfortable, vomit-inducing and frightening! Exposure to rain or too much sun may also be a problem if the boat doesn't have a roof.

KUATA
Kuata is a small island about 1.5km south of Wayasewa. It has caves, volcanic rock formations, coral cliffs on the southern end, and great snorkelling just offshore. It is a short boat ride from Wayasewa (see the following entry).

WAYASEWA
Also known as Wayalailai (little Waya), Wayasewa is in the southern Yasawas, about 40km north-west of Lautoka. It has good beaches and coral reefs. The Fijian Government declared Namara village unsafe and had it moved to its present location in 1975 after a rockslide from the cliff damaged some of the buildings. The new **Namara** (Naboro) village also has a spectacular setting. The high grassy hills to the south form a theatrical backdrop for

meke (dance performances that enact stories and legends) in the late afternoon light. Villagers welcome tourist groups and present meke and host *kava* ceremonies (see Dos and Don'ts in the Facts about Fiji chapter for information on *yaqona* drinking). Many of the photos in Glen Craig's photography book *Children of the Sun* were taken on Wayasewa and Waya.

Wayalailai Resort (☎ *669 715*) is owned and operated by the villagers of Wayasewa and is the closest Yasawa resort to the mainland. It is at the base of a spectacular cliff where the old Namara village used to be.

WAYA, WAYASEWA & KUATA

0   2.5   5 km
0   1.5   3 miles

Nacilau Point
Nova Bay
Nalauwaki Bay
Koromasoli Point
Vatukavika Point
Bekua Point
Rurugu Bay
Wayalevu
Likuliku Bay
Nalauwaki
Octopus Resort
(567m) ▲
Varaguru Reef
Naiyala Reef
Waya
(429m) ▲
Liku Bay
Captain Cook Cruises' Bure
Motukuro Point
Bavu Reef
Lovoni Camping
Bligh Water
Adi's Place
Natawa
Batinareba (510m) ▲
Yalobi
Vunadilo Point
Yalobi Bay
Nativaga Point
Bonini Point
Loto Point
Namara Village (Naboro)
Tubucikawa Reef
Wayasewa
Yegusu Reef
Ilo Reef
(349m) ▲
Naqalia Point
Old Namara Village
Wayalailai Resort
SOUTH PACIFIC OCEAN
Likunivisawa Point
(171m) ▲
Yakawe Reef
Kuata
Nacilau Point
Lotoikuata Point

The five simple beachfront bure have en suites and offer the best accommodation at F$100 per couple. Beds in a 19-bed bure or a smaller eight-bed dorm cost F$35. Accommodation in the old schoolhouse, which is partitioned into 13 basic single rooms, costs F$40. Camp sites cost F$25 per person. The minimum stay is three days. All rates include three meals a day. Mosquito nets are provided. There are shared cold-water showers and flush toilets; however, water supply can be restricted. Drinks and snacks can be bought at reasonable prices, and the restaurant-bar has a lovely raised deck overlooking the beach. There is generator power and a radio telephone for emergencies.

Wayalailai has a good beach. Snorkelling off the beach is OK, but the best place is off Kuata, a short boat ride away (F$3 per person). However, gear (F$3 hire per day) is limited. Two-tank diving trips cost F$100. Guided hikes around the island cost F$3 per person. The hikes to the top of the cliff passes through high grass, trees and sharp rocks. From the hilltop you have excellent views of the whole Yasawa Group. Other activities include fishing (F$7), volleyball, village visits (F$10) and the inescapable kava ceremony. There are no boat trips or guided treks on Sunday, to respect the Fijian day of rest, however, you can attend the local church.

Getting There & Away
Transport to the island is by small boat (F$70 return, about 1½ to two hours, 40km). Guests can be picked up and dropped off at Lautoka and Nadi hotels.

WAYA
Waya has rugged hills and beautiful beaches and lagoons. There are four villages, a nursing station and a boarding school on the island. It is easy to walk around Waya and hike to the top of Yalobi Hills, from where you can see the entire Yasawa islands chain.

Places to Stay & Eat
Octopus Resort (☎ *666 337, fax 666 210*) is a good alternative to the busier budget

places in the Yasawas. It has a lovely beach, a good reef for snorkelling, and a secluded atmosphere. It has three simple bure with en suites and mosquito nets. Accommodation costs F$99 for singles or doubles, while sharing a bure with a maximum of four people is F$35/10 per adult/child. Camping is F$25 per person. Rates include breakfast and dinner (lunch costs F$4). You can buy alcohol (F$3.20 a stubbie). There is solar electricity for lighting, and facilities are simple but comfortable. New owners took over in early 1999 with plans to build a few more bure.

Activities with Octopus Resort include village visits, island hopping, picnics or fishing trips (F$15 per person), a hiking tour (F$10) and volleyball. Diving can be arranged through Wayalailai Resort. The use of snorkelling gear and, if you are game, the corrugated-iron kayak, is included in the accommodation price.

There are a couple of other budget places on Waya. However, these places were unlicensed at the time of writing and the Fiji Visitors Bureau (FVB) has had complaints from travellers: Check with the FVB prior to going. *Adi's Place* (☎ *660 566 at the Cathay Hotel, Lautoka*) at Yalobi is on a nice white-sand beach in a protected bay. The owner, Adi Sayaba, offers very simple accommodation for F$35 per person in a 12-bed dorm, or F$40 per person in a double room. Camping is F$20 per tent. Three meals are included. The other budget place is *Lovoni Camping*, north of Natawa, village, run by Adi's cousin Semi. You can camp here for F$25 per person, including meals. It takes about half an hour to walk here from Adi's.

Getting There & Away
The Octopus Resort picks up its guests from Vuda Marina on Viti Levu (F$80 return, two hours). A taxi between the marina and the airport costs around F$18. There are also local buses. Transfers to Adi's Place cost F$35/70 per person one-way/return, including pick-up from Nadi/Lautoka hotels. Check with the FVB to see if transfer boats are licensed.

TAVEWA
Tavewa is a small, low island (measuring about 1km wide and 3km long) around the middle of the Yasawa Group, with nice beaches and good swimming and snorkelling. The island is comprised of freehold land and there is no village or chief – there are just three budget resorts and a dive operation. The best beach is at the lovely Savutu Point at the southern end of the island. Be warned – it can sometimes get overcrowded at Tavewa's backpacker resorts.

Diving
Tavewa's Westside WaterSports (☎ 661 462, @ westside@is.com.fj) caters for the budget resorts and for Blue Lagoon Cruises passengers (a two-tank dive costs F$110, while an open-water course is F$390). The dive shop is on the beach in front of Otto & Fanny Doughty's (see the following Places to Stay & Eat entry).

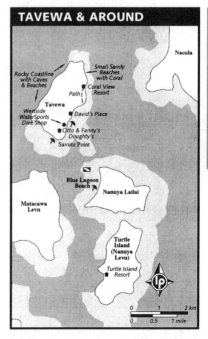

TAVEWA & AROUND

Nacula

Rocky Coastline with Caves & Beaches

Small Sandy Beaches with Coral

Coral View Resort

Path

Tavewa

Westside WaterSports Dive Shop

David's Place

Otto & Fanny's Doughty's

Savutu Point

Blue Lagoon Beach

Nanuya Lailai

Matacawa Levu

Turtle Island (Nanuya Levu)

Turtle Island Resort

0   1   2 km
0   0.5   1 mile

YASAWA GROUP

Places to Stay & Eat

Otto & Fanny Doughty's (☎/fax 661 462), just inland from Savutu Point, has a variety of accommodation among the coconut palms. The large six-bed dorm bure is good and costs F$60 per person, including meals. The two other self-contained bure can fit three to four people. The one near the beach is the most secluded. There are also two good, new units without cooking facilities. The one nearest the beach catches the sea breeze and has a veranda. Prices are F$80 per unit, plus F$25 per person for three meals. All units have a kitchen, dining table and lounge chairs. Book through Westside WaterSports.

There is no shop on the island, so bring your own food and drinks. The generator provides electricity from 6 to 10 pm. While the beautiful beach at Savutu Point is seemingly remote, avoid the temptation to skinny-dip as Fanny does not appreciate the local kids being corrupted! Fanny's afternoon tea, from 3 to about 4.30 pm, is very popular. Three pieces of cake (chocolate or banana) with coffee, tea or juice costs just F$2, and ice cream is F$1 per scoop. She will also provide lunch and dinner if you give advance warning.

The two other budget resorts on Tavewa are fairly similar to each other in feel and quality. Both have spacious grounds adjacent to the beach. Ideally, pay for your one-way transfer only, so if unhappy you can check out the competition. Both are popular with backpackers and have volleyball, nightly music and kava sessions, fishing, beach trips to nearby islands, village visits and trips to Sawa-i-Lau caves (about F$20 per person, depending on numbers). Canoes and snorkelling and fishing gear can be hired at the dive shop.

Coral View Resort (☎ 662 648 island, 724 199 Nadi), run by Don and Alumita Bruce, has a good atmosphere. Its spacious flat grounds overlooking the water are good for campers. It charges F$29 per person for camping (own tent), F$35 for dorm beds, F$77 for standard double bure and F$88 for superior double bure, which have extra furniture but are set back from the beach.

All prices include three basic meals. The dorm bure have concrete floors, mosquito nets and three to eight beds. When busy, the rooms in the building at the back near the generator are used as dorms, but it is noisy and stuffy there. There is a shared facilities block with flush toilets, and a kitchen and dining hut near the beach.

There is very good coral about 30m from the beach and lovely Savutu Point is a 20-minute walk along the beach. There are trips to Malakati village on Nacula Island, and to Blue Lagoon Beach on Nanuya Lailai, about 10 minutes away.

David's Place (☎ 663 939, ☎/fax 721 820 Nadi airport), run by David Doughty, also has a friendly atmosphere. Camping costs F$27 per person, dorm beds (up to 10 people) F$35 and accommodation in traditional-style double bure F$77. The bure have mosquito nets and concrete floors and are occasionally visited by crabs and mice. If it's filled to capacity you will probably have to queue for the showers and toilets. There is no shop and no cooking; prices include three simple meals a day with lovo and BBQ nights. There is usually plenty of food provided. Guests gather in the dining room for music and dancing every night, along with a grog session. It has introduced afternoon tea (F$1.50) to compete with Fanny.

Free activities include snorkelling at nearby islands, volleyball, hiking and fishing. Trips to Sawa-i-Lau caves and a Naisisili village visit cost F$20 per person for a group of eight. A trip to Nanuya Lailai (minimum of six) costs F$5 per person.

Getting There & Away

Boat transfers (three hours minimum) from Viti Levu to the island of Tavewa cost F$50/100 one way/return. Resorts charge other resort guests more for transfers. The return trip to Coral View Resort costs F$80, departing from the Cathay Hotel, Lautoka, at 8 am on Tuesday and Saturday, and 2 pm on Wednesday, and returning from the island on Monday, Wednesday and Friday mornings.

The boat from David's Place (for 12 to 15 passengers) leaves Lautoka for the island on

Malololailai island, Mamanuca Group

Sports day on Wayasewa in the Yasawas

The Yasawas' Turtle Island (Nanuya Levu), where some of the movie *The Blue Lagoon* was filmed

Paint the town red at Levuka on Ovalau

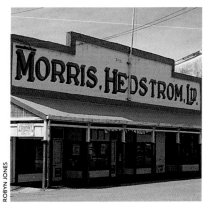
Stock up in Levuka, Ovalau

Bishop tomb, Ovalau

Wairiki Catholic Mission, Taveuni

Tuesday, Thursday and Saturday at about 9.30 am and returns on Monday, Wednesday and Friday from around 8 am. Otto and Fanny's guests transfer with Coral View (for F$5 extra) or, for groups of five or more, with Westside WaterSports.

SAWA-I-LAU
Sawa-i-Lau is the odd limestone island amid high volcanic islands. As limestone forms under water, it is thought to have formed a few hundred metres below the surface and then uplifted over time. It has a great dome-shaped cave, which extends about 15m above the water surface. You can swim in the pool, which is well lit by daylight. With a guide and a torch you can swim through an underwater passage into other caves leading off it. The limestone walls have carvings, paintings and inscriptions of unknown meaning. Similar inscriptions also occur on Vanua Levu in the hills near Vuinadi village, Natewa Bay and near Dakuniba village on the Cakaudrove Peninsula.

Getting There & Away
Many of the Yasawa backpacker resorts offer trips to the caves and the cruise ships call here.

TURTLE ISLAND
Turtle Island (Nanuya Levu) is a 200-hectare, privately owned island about 2.5km long and about 900m wide. It has protected sandy beaches, rugged volcanic cliffs and surf. The 1980 film *The Blue Lagoon*, starring Brooke Shields, was partly filmed on Turtle Island, as was the original 1949 version starring Jean Simmons.

Exclusive *Turtle Island Resort* (☎ 722 921/663 889, fax 720 007, @ turtle@is .com.fj) is owned by American Richard Evanson, who after making his fortune in cable television bought the island in 1972 as his own personal hideaway. There are 14 bure, each with two rooms, spaced along the western beach. Prices are F$1668/2000

for deluxe/grand bure per night for doubles, inclusive of all food, drinks and activities. Children are allowed only at specific times during July and Christmas holidays. Guests can partake in deep-sea fishing, sailing, windsurfing, canoeing, snorkelling, diving, horse riding and village trips. The island has 14 private beaches for use by guests. There is a six-night minimum stay.

Getting There & Away
Guests are transferred to Turtle Island Resort by Turtle Airways seaplane charter, a 30-minute flight from Nadi.

YASAWA
Yasawa, the northernmost island of the group, has six small villages and an upmarket resort. *Yasawa Island Lodge* (☎ 722 266, fax 724 456, @ yasawaisland@is.com .fj) is a luxury resort on a gorgeous beach. The 16 bure are spacious with separate living and bedroom areas, sundecks, king-size beds, double showers, separate dressing rooms, ceiling fans and air-con. Rates start at F$980 a double per day, including all a la carte meals (drinks extra) and activities (except for diving, game fishing and massage). The bar/dining area is in a large octagonal bure, which opens onto verandas. Lobster omelettes are offered for breakfast. The resort has its own dive shop and other pastimes include 4WD safaris, picnics on deserted beaches, snorkelling, tennis, bushwalking and use of dinghies and sailboards. There is no minimum stay and children over 12 years are accepted for an extra F$165 per day. The resort has its own diving operation, which charges F$130 for two-tank dive trips. It also offers open-water dive certification for F$925, but advance notice is required.

Getting There & Away
Transfers to the resort's airstrip are by Sunflower Airlines charter from Nadi (30 minutes, F$200 per person each way).

Lomaiviti Group

The Lomaiviti Group, also known as the Central Group, lies off the east coast of Viti Levu. It has seven principal islands and many smaller ones. Ovalau is one of the largest and closest to Viti Levu. Levuka, Ovalau's main town, was Fiji's earliest European settlement and the country's first capital. To the south of Ovalau are the islands of Moturiki, Caqelai and Leleuvia. The tiny coral islands of Leleuvia and Caqelai both have budget accommodation, good snorkelling and lovely beaches. Hawksbill turtles lay their eggs on these beaches.

Gau is the southernmost and the largest island of the group. Wedge-shaped Koro rises abruptly from deep water. Ferries stop here between Viti Levu, Vanua Levu and Taveuni. Both Koro and Gau have airstrips. Lying to the east are Nairai and Batiki, both lower than their neighbouring islands and surrounded by large coral reefs. Makogai, north-east of Levuka, was formerly a leper colony for the south-west Pacific, but is now home to a Department of Agriculture research station. Wakaya, also north-east of Levuka, used to be a private plantation. It now has an exclusive resort and property development.

The climate of these islands is sunnier and drier than that of the east coast of Viti Levu.

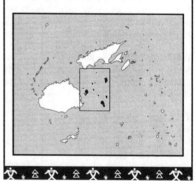

Ovalau

Ovalau's rugged volcanic landscape with its sharp peaks and central crater is beautiful, and the historic town of Levuka is definitely worth a visit. You can hike to the extinct caldera that is the site of Lovoni village. This large crater has vents on its northern and eastern sides, and is broken to the south-west by a river valley. The Bureta airstrip and Buresala ferry landing are on the western side of the island, while Levuka is on the eastern coast. A gravel road winds around the perimeter of Ovalau and is quite steep in the northern section. Another road follows the Bureta River inland to Lovoni village.

There's plenty of budget accommodation in Levuka, and camping at Rukuruku and Ovalau holiday resorts. For most people a couple of days is plenty of time to explore Levuka, but you should add another day for a hiking trip to the village of Lovoni in the centre of the island. If you want to visit beautiful white-sand beaches, consider spending time on the offshore coral islands of Leleuvia and Caqelai.

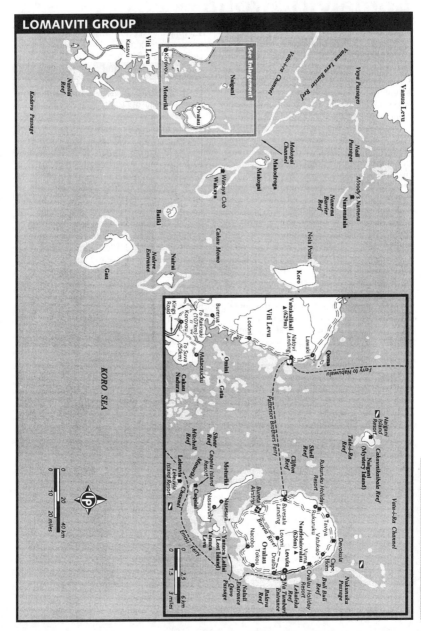

LOMAIVITI GROUP

Viti Levu

Kasavu

Korovou

Nasilai
Reef

Kadavu Passage

Naigani

See Enlargement

Moturiki

Ovalau

Vanua Levu

Vanua Levu Barrier Reef

Vanua-i-Ra Channel

Vatu-i-Ra Channel

Vuya Passages

Nadi
Passages

Moody's Namena

Makogai
Channel

Makodroga

Makogai

Wakaya Club

Wakaya

Batiki

Cakau Momo

Namena
Barrier
Reef

Namenalala

Nola Point

Koro

Nairai

Nateve
Entrance

Gau

KORO SEA

Kings
Road

To Rakiraki
(107km)

Korovou

To Suva
(50km)

Bureua

Natovi
Landing

Lodoni

Lawaki

Qoma

Vatukalikali
▲ (62m)

Viti Levu

Matavulu

Omini

Gata

Cakau
Ndaura

Patteson Brothers Ferry

Ferry to Nabuwalu

Mitchell
Reef

Monuriki

Silver
Reef

Caqelai Island
Resort

Caqelai

Nasauvuki

Naisasara

Nasesara
Yanuca
Levu

Leleuvia
Island Resort

Leleuvia
Channel

Enoši Ferry

Yanuca Lalilai
(Lost Island)

Moturiki

Yanuca
Lailai
Passage

Naigani
Island
Resort

Naigani
(Mystery Island)

Cakaunikebula Reef

Tai-i-Ra
Reef

Shell
Reef

Rukuruku Holiday
Resort

Clifton
Reef

Rukuruku

Vuma

Vatukalo

Nandelalaovalau

Nabouono
Drakai

Buresala
Landing

Levuka

Levoni

Buretai
Airstrip

Burela River

Nacobo

Tokou

Nandelaloavalau ▲ (626m)

Ovalau

Tavuya

Devotula

Cape
Horn

Bali Buli
Reef

Ovalau Holiday
Resort

Lekaleka
Reef

Na Tumboru

Badovu
Reef

Nahili
Entrance

Qovu
Entrance

Nukunuku
Passage

Vatu-i-Ra Channel

0   1.5   2.5   6.4 km

0   3 miles

0   10   20   40 km

0   20 miles

LOMAIVITI GROUP

LEVUKA
pop 3000

Levuka is the administrative, educational and agricultural centre for the Lomaiviti Group and Eastern Division, and one of Fiji's official entry ports. Its harbour is protected by the Lekaleka Reef.

As early as 1806 sandalwood traders stopped at Levuka for supplies of food and water. Traders began settling here in the 1830s and many married Fijian women. With the protection of the chief of Levuka they built schooners and traded throughout Fiji for bêche-de-mer, turtle shell and coconut oil. The settlement was occasionally raided by Lovoni villagers, from the centre of Ovalau. By the 1850s Levuka had become increasingly rowdy, with a reputation for wild drunkenness and violence.

The town's heyday was in the mid to late 19th century. In the 1870s a flood of planters and other settlers came to Fiji, and the booming town had a population of about 3000 Europeans. It seems incredible now that quaint little Levuka once had 52 hotels on Beach St and was the wild, lawless centre of the blackbirding trade and a popular port for sailors, whalers and traders. In 1888 and 1905, the buildings at the north end of the town were swept away by hurricanes.

Until 1825 the coastal villagers were allied with the chiefs of Verata (a village on Viti Levu's Rewa Delta), after which they changed allegiance to the chief of Bau (Bau is an island off the south-east coast of Viti Levu). Bau's powerful Ratu Seru Cakobau attempted unsuccessfully to form a national government here in 1871, and in 1874 ceded Fiji to Great Britain. Fiji thus became a British colony and Levuka was proclaimed its capital. For more information see the History section in the Facts about Fiji chapter.

Levuka was unable to develop as a capital due to the constraints of terrain, and the government was officially moved to Suva in 1882. By the end of the 19th century trade also began shifting to Suva, and with copra markets plummeting in the 1930s the town declined further. These days the island's main employer, the Pacific Fishing Company (Pafco), is located in Levuka. The rest of the town seems to have been frozen in time – slow-paced and picturesque, it looks like a Wild West tumbleweed town transposed to the Pacific. Many surprisingly intact, colourful old buildings date back to Levuka's boom period and tourism is becoming increasingly important. The Department of Town & Country Planning declared Levuka a historic town in 1989, and it has recently been nominated for Unesco World Heritage listing. If the town is listed, the local economy stands to benefit.

The population is mainly of mixed Fijian and European descent. Many descendants of traders live in the town – including those of American David Whippy, a beachcomber who was later appointed US vice-consul by Commodore Wilkes.

Tabua

Tabua (carefully polished and shaped whales' teeth) were believed to be shrines for the ancestor spirits. Tabua were, and still are, highly valued items and essential to diplomacy. Used as a powerful *sevusevu* – a gift presented as a token of esteem or atonement – the acceptance of tabua binds a chief morally and spiritually to the gift-giver and the desired outcome of that person.

Traditionally, a man's body was accompanied to the grave by a tabua – along with a war club or a musket and his strangled wives – to help defend his spirit on its hazardous journey to the afterworld. Without the company of a tabua his spirit would be left in 'lonely limbo'.

Originally tabua were rare, obtained only from washed-up sperm whales or through trade with Tonga. However, European traders introduced thousands of whale teeth and replicas of teeth in whalebone, elephant tusk and walrus tusk. These negotiation tools became concentrated in the hands of a few increasingly powerful chiefdoms, consequently increasing their power.

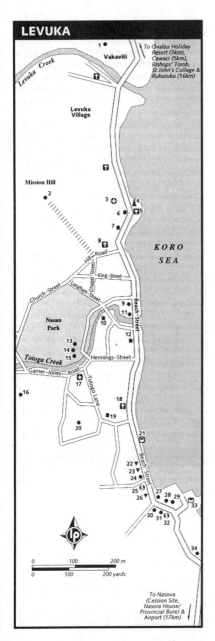

Orientation & Information

Levuka is squeezed between the steep mountains and the water's edge. The Beach St oceanfront promenade is lined with historic shopfronts. This main street continues as a ring road around the island's perimeter. The Pafco tuna cannery is at the southern end. Its modern building contrasts starkly with the rest of the town.

Ovalau Tours & Transport Limited (OT&T, ☎ 440 611), on Beach St, is a useful source of information. You may also want to try the community centre, in the Morris Hedstrom building, and the Whale's Tale restaurant.

Westpac and the National Bank of Fiji, both at the southern end of Beach St, will change travellers cheques and are open from 9.30 am to 3 pm weekdays. The post office is open from 8 am to 1 pm and 2 to 4 pm weekdays, and from 8 to 10.30 am Saturdays. It is near Queens Wharf at the southern end of Beach St. There is a cardphone outside.

Air Fiji Travel Centre (☎ 440 139, fax 440 252) is opposite the community centre. Patterson Brothers Shipping (☎ 440 125) is near the market on Beach St. Also check OT&T under Organised Tours later in this chapter.

In an emergency, dial ☎ 000 for the ambulance or police. Otherwise, you'll find the Levuka Hospital (☎ 440 152) is at the northern end of Beach St, below Mission Hill, and the police station (☎ 440 222) is in Totogo Lane.

Walking Tour

A good place to start is Nasova, about 10 minutes' walk south of the Pafco cannery, where the Deed of Cession was signed in 1874. **Cession Site** has a memorial commemorating the event and is surrounded by a picket fence. Prince Charles once stayed in the **Provincial Bure** (1970), and **Nasova House** (1869) is thought to be part of the original colonial governors' complex. The weatherboard structure, with its top-hinged windows propped open, is typical of the domestic colonial architecture.

The tuna cannery (Pafco), at the southern end of Levuka, employs about 1000 people, roughly 30% of Ovalau's working population. Canned fish exports are Fiji's largest earner after sugar, tourism and gold. The factory was established in 1964, as a joint venture between two Japanese companies and the Fijian government, to boost the town's dying economy. However, Levuka's economy has always been insecure and rumours circulate about the plant being moved to Suva.

Originally it was a transit depot for Taiwanese, Japanese and Korean long-line fishing vessels operating around the western Pacific. In 1987 the Fijian government bought out its partners, and 2% of Pafco is now owned by Ovalau citizens. Pacific Packaging Limited, a joint-venture canmaking plant, was built in 1989, and in 1992 there were further expansions with a wharf development, offices and freezer storage. The F$17 million extension was built with Australian support. The facility processes about 15,000 metric tonnes of tuna (skipjack, yellow fin and albacore) per year from waters around Fiji and other Pacific nations, including the Solomon Islands and Kiribati. It is packed under about 30 different brand-names.

Walk north along **Beach St** where Levuka's shop facades are typified by parapet walls, and verandahs link to form walkways. The streetscape dates from the late 19th and early 20th centuries. Most of the buildings are of simple timber construction. The facade of the former **Morris Hedstrom** trading store (1868), featuring massive graphics, has been retained, but it now houses the Levuka Community Centre, library, museum, and YWCA. The **museum** and **library** (together in one building) has a collection of old artefacts, clubs and adornments as well as traders' and settlers' carpentry tools, demijohns, bottles, guns, photos, a sitar and a WWI gas mask. The opening hours are from 9 am to 5 pm on weekdays and from 9 am to noon Saturdays. Entry is F$2.

Many of Levuka's original religious and community buildings are still intact. Visit the **Sacred Heart Church** (1858) on the main street, then explore the backstreets. The **Marist Convent School** (1891) was established by the Marists (Congregation of Mary) who arrived from France and Australia, and is now a primary school for students from all over Fiji. The symmetrical form of the coral-stone and timber building is impressive against the mountain backdrop.

The little weatherboard **police station** on Totogo Lane dates from 1920, and across the creek in Nasau Park you'll find Fiji's first private club – the colonial-style timber **Ovalau Club** (1904). Ask the bartender to show you a letter written by Count Felix von Luckner during WWI, on Katafaga in northern Lau. Before von Luckner's eventual capture on nearby Wakaya, German ships cruised these waters, sinking Allied vessels. During the war most of the local German traders were forced to give up their businesses. Next door to the Ovalau Club is the **town hall** (1898), also known as Queen Victoria Memorial Hall, built in typical British colonial style. Here too, is the **Masonic Lodge** (1924), a classic revival-style building. It was the South Pacific's first masonic lodge.

Return across the creek, following Garner Jones Rd and the Totoga Creek west to the **Levuka Public School** (1881). The building has been stripped of its ornate trimmings. It was Fiji's first formal school, with a European-style education, and many of Fiji's prominent citizens were educated here. If you continue up the steps behind the school you will come to a popular resting spot where you can pause and chat to passers-by. Walk back down to Garner Jones Rd and turn left into Church St and past Nasau Park. There are many old colonial homes on the hillsides. If you are reasonably fit, the **199 Steps of Mission Hill** are worth climbing for the fantastic view.

The simple coral and stone Gothic-style **Navoka Methodist Church** (1860s) near the foot of the steps is one of the oldest churches in Fiji. Head south along Chapel St then east along Langham St and across the creek. **The Royal Hotel** (1860s) is the lone survivor of the once-numerous pubs of the era, and its timber-framed structure was rebuilt in 1903. Originally it had an open verandah with lace balustrading, but this was built in to increase the size of the rooms.

Back on Beach St continue north to **Niukaube Hill**, on a point near the water. This was once the site of Ratu Cakobau's supreme court and parliament house. It now has a memorial to locals who fought and died in WWI and WWII.

Levuka village is a 200m farther north. With the chief's permission you can climb the prominent **Gun Rock**. In 1849 Commodore Wilkes, of the US Exploring Expedition, pounded this peak with cannon fire in an attempt to impress the Tui Levuka. From here you have a great view of Levuka township.

Walk or take a taxi the 5km to Cawaci, where you will find **Bishops' Tomb** (1922) on a point overlooking the sea. Fiji's first and second Roman Catholic bishops are entombed here. The tomb has Gothic and Italianate influences. From here you can see **St John's College** (1894), where the sons of Fijian chiefs were educated in English. This interesting Gothic-revival-style building is constructed of limestone and coral.

Activities

Cycling Cycling is a good way to explore Levuka. The road to the south is fairly flat, and the north is OK until about Vatukalo, after which it gets very hilly. Mountain bikes are available for hire for F$10/15 per half/full day. Inquire at OT&T (☎ 440 611).

Diving & Snorkelling Diving can be quite good, and there are some unexplored sites in the area. You may see pilot whales, hammerheads and manta rays. Nobby, at Ovalau Watersports (☎ 440 611, fax 440 405), behind the OT&T office, has good gear and instructs in English and German. A two-tank dive costs F$120 and it is $F460 for the open-water course. Reef snorkelling trips are F$30. There is also a dive operation on Leleuvia (see the Leleuvia section later in this chapter).

Organised Tours

One of Ovalau's highlights is the hike to Lovoni village, uphill through rainforest and into the crater of the extinct volcano at the island's centre. Present a *sevusevu* (a gift such as *yaqona*, or kava), at the village, have a Fijian lunch and swim in river pools. Epi's tours are popular and recommended; Epi will explain local customs, the history of Lovoni people, and their traditional and medicinal uses of plants. Tours leave from Levuka Monday to Saturday and cost F$20, including lunch and return transport. Contact Epi at the Whale's Tale (☎ 440 235) or at The Royal Hotel (☎ 440 024).

Ovalau Tours & Transport Limited (☎ 440 611, fax 440 405, ✉ otttours@is.com.fj), on Beach St, offers guided walking tours, day trips and overnight packages. Some of the money raised from its tours helps fund restoration of historic homes. The 'tea and *talanoa*' ('have a chat') tours take you inside the homes of local residents, such as Rosie Morris, Bubu Kara and Aunty Ella Bryson. It's a great way to get a local perspective on life in Levuka. It costs F$17.50 per person from Levuka or F$94 for a full-day trip, including return transfers from Bureta airstrip, breakfast, lunch and an extended tour of the town.

Devokula is a cute, mock-traditional village built and run by the nearby Bolakula village youth club. Here you can participate in presenting a sevusevu, watch handicraft demonstrations and try the local food. Devokula village tours cost F$25 per person, including lunch. The Levuka and Devokula village full-day excursion costs F$94 per person, including airport transfers, breakfast and lunch. Overnight stays at Devokula village cost F$77.50 per person twin share (children under 12 years cost F$27.50 and children under 2 years are free) or F$55 per person in the dorm. Rates include all meals, guided walks and cultural performances. Accommodation at Devokula is pretty basic, with sleeping mats in traditional *bure* (thatched dwellings). Stays at Devokula can be arranged through OT&T Tours in Ovalau or with Jeremaia Tukutuku (☎ 440013, fax 440 405).

Places to Stay

Fiji's oldest hotel, *The Royal Hotel* (☎ 440 024, fax 440 174), next to Totoga Creek, is one of the town's best options. The old weatherboard building oozes colonial atmosphere, even if it is getting a bit worn at the edges, and has been run by the Ashley family for generations. There is a licensed bar (for houseguests only), billiard room, dining room with garden views, guest lounge and a video room.

The hotel has 15 fan-cooled rooms upstairs, each with a small en suite. They are reasonably comfortable and cost F$17.60/27.50/33 for singles/doubles/triples. The dorm accommodation is good, in a large four-bedroom building at the back of the garden. It has a kitchen and sleeps 14 people for F$10 per person. There are also three weatherboard cottages of two, three and five rooms, each with en suites, air-con and shared kitchen. If you'd prefer something new, the air-con one-bedroom cottages are very good and cost F$77 for a maximum of three people.

Mavida Guest House (☎ 440 477, PO Box 4 Levuka), at the northern end of Beach St near Niukaube Hill, is another good budget option. Parts of the guesthouse date from the late 1860s. It is a pleasant place with lots of sitting areas, and is actually two buildings joined by a covered space for parties and kava drinking. There is a dorm sleeping four people for F$8 per person; fan-cooled rooms with shared bathrooms and hot water are F$12/24 for singles/doubles; and better rooms in the old house are F$15/30. All prices include breakfast, and lunch and dinner can be ordered for F$6 per meal.

Inquire about *Sailor's Home* at OT&T. It is a large colonial weatherboard house on the hill opposite the Niukaube Hill War Memorial, about 50m north of Mavida Guest House. It has two bedrooms, a kitchen, dining room and two sunrooms with views. It sleeps up to seven and costs F$99.

Emosi and Mary of Leleuvia Island Resort have two accommodation places in Levuka. *Old Capital Inn I* (☎ 440 057) on Togotogo Lane is a double-storey building at the back of Sacred Heart Church. It has a sitting room, and upstairs are fan-cooled rooms with shared facilities for F$13/26 for singles/doubles. The dorm (maximum of four people) costs F$9, with a breakfast of toast, eggs and fruit included. There is also a restaurant downstairs (see Places to Eat). *Old Capital Inn II* (☎ 440 013) charges F$12/24 for singles/doubles for fan-cooled rooms, with breakfast served at Old Capital Inn I. Dorm accommodation (maximum of four people) costs F$9, including breakfast. It also has two self-contained cottages, one costing F$18/25, while the other, which sleeps three, is F$16/25/30 a single/double/triple. The rooms have mosquito nets and fans.

Ovalau Holiday Resort (☎ 440 329, PO Box 113, Levuka) is an option if you want an extra-quiet budget place. It's about 3km north of Levuka, facing a small bay at Lawaki past Vuma village, and is run by the Praan family, who also own Cafe Levuka. You can camp here for F$10 per person, or a bed in the 17-bed dorm is F$16.50, including breakfast. It has six fan-cooled bedrooms, two toilets, a shower, central kitchen and a small sitting area. There are no mosquito nets, but coils are provided. There are also five self-contained weatherboard units with verandahs. Each has two bedrooms and a sitting area and can accommodate up to six people. Singles/doubles/triples cost F$75/99/121 and children under 12 are free. Meals at the restaurant-bar are F$4.50 to F$12.50 for lunch or dinner. The sandy beach is not great but the snorkelling is OK and equipment use is free. Kayaks can be hired for F$5 per hour and there's also a small swimming pool. It is about a 50-minute walk from Levuka, around F$5 by taxi, but transport is also provided free by the resort.

There is also accommodation at the *Devokula Village* bure. See Organised Tours earlier in this chapter.

Places to Eat

Restaurants *Whale's Tale (☎ 440 235)*, a small restaurant run by Australians Liza and Julia Ditrich, has the best food in town. The cooking is home-style and the ingredients are always fresh. The fruit smoothies, vegetable stir-fry and banana crepes with chocolate sauce are all recommended! A three-course special costs F$12.

Kim's (☎ 440 235) is another good and inexpensive option. It serves huge bowls of soups for F$2 to F$4 and large main dishes of chicken, beef or fish for F$5 to F$9. The Sunday evening buffet is recommended at F$9.90, including dessert. Get there early or book to get a table on the balcony overlooking the water.

The restaurant at *Old Capital Inn I* on Totogo Lane serves breakfast, lunch and dinner. Mains are under F$5, with dessert thrown in for free. It also has a Sunday evening buffet for F$7. *Cafe Levuka*, opposite the Morris Hedstrom building, also has OK food.

Self-Catering There is a *produce market* on the north side of Totoga Creek, a *supermarket* near the community centre and a few *general stores* along the main street.

Entertainment

Levuka's wild days are long gone and the sleepy town doesn't offer much night-time entertainment. For a drink, try *Ovalau Club* or *Levuka Club*. The bar and video nights (very popular with TV-starved travellers) at *The Royal Hotel* are for guests only.

Getting There & Away

Air Air Fiji has twice-daily Levuka-Suva flights from Nausori airport to Bureta airstrip (12 minutes) on Ovalau for F$35/70 one way/return or F$50 if you choose an excursion fare.

The Bureta airstrip is on the south-western side of Ovalau, about one hour's drive to/from Levuka (costing F$3 by minibus or F$17 by taxi). Minibuses and taxis to the airport depart from outside the Air Fiji Travel Centre in Beach St, opposite the community centre.

Boat Patterson Brothers Shipping (☎ 440 125), near the market on Beach St, has a bus and ferry service from Suva to Levuka via Natovi. In all the trip takes about 5 hours, including waiting around at Natovi. From Natovi there are ferry services to Nabouwalu and Savusavu on Vanua Levu as well as to Taveuni (see the Getting Around chapter).

Emosi's Shipping (☎ 440 057 at Old Capital Inn I) has small boat services from Suva to Levuka via Leleuvia (see the Getting Around chapter).

Getting Around

Levuka is relatively easy to get around on foot. There is a taxi stand opposite the Whale's Tale restaurant in Beach St. Carriers (small trucks with a tarpaulin-covered frame on the back) can also be hired from here. Minibuses or taxis heading to the airport depart from outside Air Fiji Travel Centre in Beach St. Regular village trucks also depart for Lovoni and Rukuruku. Mountain bikes can be hired through OT&T (see the Activities section earlier).

LOVONI

Lovoni village is nestled within a spectacular extinct volcano crater, in the centre of Ovalau. The village has no accommodation for travellers at present but there are guided walks to visit the village from Levuka. (The hike can be steep and muddy so good boots are absolutely essential.) Of interest is the **chief's burial site** opposite the church, and **Korolevu hill fortification**, high on the crater rim, where villagers took refuge in times of war.

LOMAIVITI GROUP

The Enslavement of the People of Lovoni

In 1870-71 Ratu Cakobau's warriors fought a war against the Lovoni highlanders, who had been raiding the settlement of Levuka and were a threat to Cakobau's authority. Repeated attempts to penetrate the enemy fort were defeated, so Cakobau sent a Methodist missionary to subdue the people. At the time, Lovoni had a dwarf priest who had the ability to foresee the future. The priest was the first to notice the approaching missionary and, seeing a kind of brightness emanating from him, believed the missionary's powers had been stripped from him. The missionary held up the Bible, from which he read in Bauan. He referred to the people of Lovoni as the lost sheep of Fiji and invited them to a reconciliation feast on 29 June 1871, organised by Cakobau. The warriors came down to Levuka, and in good faith put aside their weapons. However, as they started their meal, Cakobau's warriors caught them off guard, quickly surrounding and capturing them.

Ratu Cakobau sold the prisoners as slaves, his takings helping him form government. Families were separated and Lovoni villagers were dispersed as far Kavala (in the Kadavu Group), Yavusania (near Nadi on Viti Levu), Lovoni-Ono (in the Lau Group) and Wailevu (on Vanua Levu). The dwarf priest and two Lovoni warriors were sold to an American circus.

The villagers of Lovoni are extremely proud people. They believe that since Cakobau was only able to defeat them by using trickery, not by war, they are the strongest tribe in Fiji (see 'The Enslavement of the People of Lovoni' boxed text for more information). Men from Lovoni display their superiority by wearing hats in other villages, even in the chiefly village of Bau. This is normally seen to be extremely disrespectful.

On 7 July each year the enslavement of the Lovoni people is commemorated. People of all religions gather in the same church and the history is read out. There is a plaque at the church with a translation that reads:

This is a memorial stone commemorating the hundred years since Reverend Frederick Langham DDE walked up to Korolevu (old hill fort), Lovoni, Ovalau and ended the war of 1871. He took the people down to Levuka and they were captured and sold on 7.7.1871. We should fear and worship God because our grandfathers never surrendered to any tribe, they only surrendered to God's word. We should worship him because there is no other god in this world that is greater than him.

Getting There & Away

You can hike in from Levuka with a local guide (see Organised Tours earlier in this chapter for more information). There is also a Levuka-Lovoni truck leaving Levuka at 7 and 11 am daily, except Sunday, and returning at about 3 pm.

RUKURUKU

The village of Rukuruku, about 17km from Levuka, on north-western Ovalau, has a **black-sand beach** and a view of Naigani island. There is a small **waterfall** about 20 minutes' walk up the valley from Rukuruku Holiday Resort. Naigani Island Resort will pick up guests from **Taviya** village, about 1km north-east of Rukuruku.

Places to Stay & Eat

If you're after solitude, consider *Rukuruku Holiday Resort (☎ 440 611 via OT&T, Levuka, fax 440 405)*. At the time of writing, it was about to be reopened after renovations. It has a camp site with toilets, showers and cooking facilities for F$6 per person. The dorm accommodation has an en suite bathroom and costs F$10 per person, including breakfast. The bungalow sleeps seven and is F$15 per person, including breakfast. A portable gas stove is available for guest use. A 'deluxe' bure, for a maximum of four people, is F$65 per night. Snorkelling here involves a 15-minute boat ride from Rukuruku.

There is a dining room for meals at the resort, and the shop in Rukuruku sells canned food but not much else.

Getting There & Away

The Rukuruku carrier (a large, red-framed truck with a white-and-green canopy) has a daily trip (except Sunday) between Beach St, Levuka, and Rukuruku (F$1.50, one hour). Hiring a van, which will carry up to 12 people in one trip and will pick up and return at your leisure, will cost F$25 each way. A taxi is about F$20 each way. Rukuruku Holiday Resort will pick up travellers from Buresala Landing by boat at a cost of F$10 (a 20-minute journey) or from Naigani for F$50.

Other Lomaiviti Islands

YANUCA LAILAI

Yanuca Lailai (Lost Island) is an uninhabited island close to Levuka and adjacent to Moturiki. It has a hill with a short, **golden-sand beach** (about 200m long), and the rest of the island is rocky. It is too shallow to swim at low tide – but bring your own gear for snorkelling.

The island has rudimentary accommodation, but when we visited no-one was there and it seems to be an irregular operation. (Apparently, people sometimes get stranded on Yanuca Lailai.) There are four very simple shed-like bure for F$22 per person. The facilities include one flush toilet, one pit toilet, one shower (pump type out in the open), one covered sitting area and a tiny kitchen. You can camp here for F$10 per person. A day trip with lunch costs F$10, three meals cost F$14 and fishing trips are F$5. Arrange trips with Levi in Levuka, if you can track him down – try at the community centre.

MOTURIKI

The island of Moturiki is south-west of Ovalau. It has a hilly topography and is home to 10 villages, but it has no place for travellers to stay. Both Leleuvia and Caqelai resorts will take guests staying on those islands to Niubasaga on Moturiki for Sunday church services.

CAQELAI

Just south of Moturiki lies Caqelai – a gorgeous coral island. It is only a 15-minute walk around the island's beautiful **white-sand beaches**, which are fringed with palms and other large trees. If you're lucky you may see **dolphins** and **baby turtles**.

The island is owned by the Methodist Church of Moturiki, which runs the small, budget *Caqelai Resort*. Those who are after a secluded spot and don't mind roughing it will love it here. The facilities are very basic, with shared bucket showers and bucket-flush toilets.

There are various small Fijian-style bure with pandanus-leaf lining and sand or concrete floors. Most have a small verandah and those along the beachfront catch the sea breeze. One bure has rough-hewn, coconut-board walls and a raised floor. Dorm accommodation, for up to 12 people, is in a spartan weatherboard building with foam mattresses, and unlike the bure the dorm has power. Dorm beds cost F$25/11 per person with/without meals, camping is F$20/6 and bure are F$28/14. Mosquito nets are provided. The food is good here but, alternatively, guests can use the kitchen for F$3 per day. There is an open shelter on the beach with a long table. There is a small shop but it's best to BYO alcohol, drinks and snacks.

There is good snorkelling off the beach; the resort has some gear but ideally you'll bring your own. At low tide it is possible to walk out to Snake Island (named after the many black-and-white banded sea snakes found here), where it's also good for snorkelling. Diving can be arranged with Leleuvia's dive shop (see the following Leleuvia section). Guests are taken on village trips to Niubasaga on Moturiki for the Sunday church service. Other activities include rugby and volleyball as well as singing, dancing and kava drinking beside a bonfire on the beach.

Getting There & Away

Contact the Royal Hotel (☎ 440 024) in Levuka to arrange transport from Levuka by small boat (F$10 per person, 30 minutes). There's a shopping run to Levuka each morning costing F$2.50 one way. Return transport to/from Verata or Bau Landing, Viti Levu, costs F$20. Emosi's Shipping's Leleuvia service will also drop off passengers on Caqelai for an extra F$10 (see Getting There & Away in the following Leleuvia section).

LELEUVIA

Leleuvia is a 7-hectare coral island with golden-sand beaches. At low tide a vast area of sand and rock is exposed. You can easily walk around the island and explore the rockpools, where you'll find lots of sea slugs and tiny octopuses. At low tide it's not so far to walk out to swim on the western side. There is a view of the local 'honeymoon island'; a private island for romantic picnics.

Leleuvia Island Resort (☎ 301 584, 313 366 Suva office) has an assortment of bungalows spread over the island. There are coconut-log cabins with tapa cloth lining, thatched-roof bure with woven walls, and very basic weatherboard units with concrete floors and private bathrooms. Beachfront bungalows with private bathrooms cost F$33/55 for singles/doubles, while bure with shared facilities are F$15/30. Some bure and bungalows have cooking facilities, otherwise a basic meal package costs F$13. Accommodation in eight-bed dorms cost F$12 and camping is F$8 per person. The shared facilities include four showers (pumped rainwater) and four flush toilets. There is a small shop and a communal cooking area.

Here you can play volleyball, have a massage, socialise with fellow backpackers and laze on the beach. The resort's Nautilus Dive Fiji is reasonably organised and offers two-tank dives for F$95 and open-water courses for F$390. Dive sites include Snake Island, Challis Reef, Coral Garden, Smiley's and Shark Reef. The boat trip to snorkel at Shark Reef or Snake Island is F$15 per person and includes gear.

Getting There & Away

Emosi's Shipping (☎ 313 366) has an office at 35 Gordon St, Suva (see the Getting Around chapter). The bus leaves Suva for Bau Landing at noon daily, except Sunday, stopping for supplies at Nausori on the way.

Transfers to the island from Bau Landing take about one hour on a 12-person boat. Leleuvia-Suva costs F$20/40 one way/return and the Suva-Leleuvia-Levuka trip (three times a week) is F$25/50. The boat passes near Bau, a tiny island of great historical importance. Conditions can get very choppy and passengers and their gear can arrive drenched. Don't go if there aren't enough life jackets or if the boat is overcrowded. To get to Leleuvia from Levuka, ask at OT&T (see Organised Tours earlier in this chapter). The boat leaves Levuka at about 9 am.

WAKAYA

Wakaya is an 880-hectare island that is privately owned by David and Jill Gilmour. It is about 20km east of Ovalau and is visible from Levuka. It has forests, cliffs, beautiful white-sand beaches, and archaeological sites, including a **stone fish trap**. Feral horses, pigs and deer freely roam the island. There are roads, millionaires' houses and a marina.

On 80 hectares at the north-west end of the island is *Wakaya Club (☎ 448 128, or ☎ 1800 124 205 in Australia, ☎ 0800 968 986 in the UK, ☎ 1800 828'3454 in North America, fax 448 406, ✉ wakaya@is.com.fj)*. This is one of Fiji's most exclusive resorts, ranking with Vatulele Island Resort, Turtle Island Resort and Yasawa Island Lodge. It caters for a maximum of nine couples, and no children under 16 years are allowed. Each of the eight air-con units has a living room, a separate bedroom, a four-poster king-size bed, bar, VCR/DVD set, CD player, shower and separate bath. Rates for gardenview/oceanview units are F$2580/2800 a night per couple, with a five-night minimum stay.

The club's Governor's Bure has all the standard-unit features plus extra space, a wide verandah, a hammock and private beach and costs F$3565 a night per couple. Also on offer is the Vale 'O' ('House in the Clouds'), the hilltop three-bedroom home of the Gilmours. Among other features are a swimming pool, a lighted tennis court and a *boules* court. Accommodation at the Vale 'O' is F$7700/9900/12,100 for one/two/three couples per night! The resort has a golf course, tennis, croquet and masseurs. The rates include all meals, drinks and the use of sporting facilities and equipment – the prices exclude deep-sea fishing, diving courses and boat charters. The daily rate includes two one-tank dives a day from the glass-bottomed boat. An open-water course (four days) costs F$1980/3080 for singles/couples and Discover Scuba Diving charges F$300 per person for three hours. There are dive sites only five minutes by boat from the club.

Getting There & Away

Resort guests are transferred by Air Wakaya in the island's own twin-engine 1992 Britten Norman Islander plane. The flight from Nadi International Airport takes 45 minutes and costs F$1560 per couple from Nadi, or F$780 per couple from Suva. The island is a 20-minute speedboat ride from Levuka.

NAIGANI

Naigani, also known as Mystery Island, is a mountainous island about 10km offshore from Ovalau. With an area of 220 hectares, the island has white-sand beaches, lagoons, a fringing coral reef, the remains of a **precolonial hillside fortification** and 'cannibal caves'. According to locals, 1800 villagers were slaughtered here by marauding tribes. Out of respect, no-one now visits the place.

Naigani Island Resort (☎ 300 925, 312 069, fax 300 539, ✉ *naigani@is.com.fj),* on the grounds of an old copra plantation, caters to couples, families and small groups. The 17 spacious garden and beachfront villas are excellent value. Two-bedroom, fan-cooled villas cost F$218 (up to six people), while studios are F$165. Ask about reduced walk-in rates. The bar and restaurant is in the restored plantation homestead, and daily meal packages are F$40/55 for two/three meals.

The resort has child-care and kids' campouts. There's a golf course, a pool with swim-up bar and a water slide. Snorkelling is excellent immediately offshore and there are good dive sites nearby. It has its own diving operation. Other activities include nature-trail walks, kayaking, windsurfing, fishing and day excursions to Levuka. The resort has an office in Suva, upstairs at 22 Cumming St *(☎ 312 069, fax 302 058).*

Getting There & Away

Return transfers to/from Suva, via Natovi Landing, are F$60/30 per adult/child. It is about a 1½-hour drive from Suva to Natovi, then a 30-minute boat ride. Return launch transfers to/from Taviya village, near Rukuruku on Ovalau, are F$45.

NAMENALALA

The 44-hectare volcanic island of Namenalala is on the Namena Barrier Reef, 25km off the south-eastern coast of Vanua Levu and about 40km from Savusavu. Namenalala has lovely **beaches** and the island is a natural sailors' refuge. There is an old **ring fortification** on the island but no longer any villages – just one upmarket resort.

Moody's Namena (☎ 813 764, fax 812 366, ✉ *moodysnamena@is.com.fj)* accommodates up to 12 guests in six hexagonal timber and bamboo bure with verandahs, on a forested ridge. Accommodation, including meals, is F$378 per person with a minimum stay of five nights. Children under 16 years cannot stay here. Wine is complimentary with dinner and heart of palm is a speciality.

Divers must be certified to dive here, and provide a certification card as proof. Diving on the barrier reef is excellent and costs F$82 per tank. Weights, weight belt, tank, air, boats and dive guide are provided; if you haven't brought all your gear you'll have to rent it from Savusavu or Nadi. All other activities – windsurfing, fishing, snorkelling, barrier reef excursions (for snorkelling and diving), beach BBQs, beach volleyball, use of canoes and paddle boards – are included in the rate. The island has a nature reserve for bird-watching and trekking, and a giant clam farm. It is home to seabirds, and red-footed boobies and hawksbill and green turtles lay their eggs on the beaches between November and March. The resort closes between March and April.

Getting There & Away

Guests arrive by charter yacht from Savusavu (F$185 per person each way) or by charter seaplane from Nadi (F$264 per person, one hour, minimum of two people). The resort arranges share fares.

Vanua Levu

With an area of 5538 sq km Vanua Levu (Big Land) is Fiji's second-largest island. It is just over half the size of Viti Levu. It is also the archipelago's second most populated island, with 18% of the country's total population. The main industries here are sugar and copra (dried coconut), and until recently, gold was being mined at Mt Kasi in the island's south-west. The Fijian administration divides the island into the provinces of Cakaudrove (the south-east), Bua (the south-west) and Macuata (the north-west). Vanua Levu, together with Kioa, Rabi, a number of smaller offshore islands, Taveuni, Qamea, Laucala, Matagi and the Ringgold Isles, is known as Fiji's North.

Vanua Levu has an irregular and deeply indented coast. A large peninsula to the north-east forms the huge Natewa Bay and there is another large bay, Savusavu Bay, on the southern side of the island. As on Viti Levu, a mountain range runs along much of Vanua Levu's length dividing the island into a wetter eastern side and a drier western side.

The south-east coast has a predominantly indigenous Fijian population. The landscape here is scenic with many bays, rainforests and coconut plantations. Savusavu is the main tourist destination.

The central north has a higher population of Fijians of Indian decent, concentrated around Labasa, Vanua Levu's largest town and administrative and business centre. As well as native forest, there are lots of sugarcane plantations and commercial pine plantations. Much of the western coast is remote and accessible only by boat.

Vanua Levu is relatively undeveloped, and except for around Savusavu, infrastructure and services for travellers are limited. Due to its proximity to Viti Levu and easy access via frequent ferry and flight services, Vanua Levu is attracting an increasing number of visitors. As in Viti Levu's interior, the traveller is more likely to gain an insight into the traditional Fijian way of

HIGHLIGHTS

- Snorkel or dive the Rainbow Reef.
- Kayak around Savusavu Bay.
- Drive the Hibiscus Hwy, passing forests, plantations and rural villages.
- Take in the island's rugged landscape and beautiful bays.

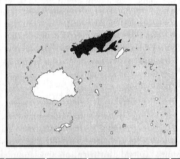

life. The island is volcanic in origin and has few sandy beaches. The reefs, however, offer some excellent snorkelling, diving, kayaking and bird-watching. The indented coastline with many bays is also great for kayaking and the rainforest is good for bird-watching. The wild and rugged interior has potential for hiking, but there is little in the way of organised treks. Villagers are less familiar with tourists than on Viti Levu and you cannot wander through the countryside without permission from the landowners. There are interesting archaeological sites at Nukubolu near Savusavu and at Wasavula near Labasa.

Activities

Hiking Contact Tui at Lomalagi Resort east of Savusavu. He can organise walking tours of the Tunuloa Peninsula and camping at a village on the island of Yanuca, north-east of Taveuni.

Diving Vanua Levu's diving operations are concentrated in the Savusavu area. The famous Rainbow Reef, off south-eastern Vanua Levu, is generally accessed from Taveuni but can also be accessed from Buca Bay. The Great Sea Reef, the long barrier reef running along the island's northern coast, is largely unexplored. The upmarket Nukubati Island Resort organises dives here. *Fiji Aggressor*, a diving boat, berths at Savusavu.

Kayaking Savusavu company Eco Divers-Tours takes organised tours of Savusavu Bay and has kayaks for hire all year.

Getting There & Away

There are frequent ferry and flight services from Viti Levu to Vanua Levu. Both Savusavu and Labasa have airports (see the Air Fares Chart in the Getting Around chapter for more information).

Patterson Brothers Shipping, Beachcomber Cruises and Consort Shipping operate passenger ferry services between Viti Levu, Vanua Levu and Taveuni. Prices are competitive. All three have services between Suva and Savusavu. Patterson Brothers also has services between Nabouwalu, in southwestern Vanua Levu, and Natovi Landing and Ellington Wharf on Viti Levu (see Nabouwalu later in this chapter and Ferry in the Getting Around chapter for details).

The roll-on roll-off ferries will take cars or bicycles, but since both can be hired in Savusavu it is probably not worth the expense. Besides, rental companies normally won't allow their vehicles to be taken on the ferries.

Getting Around

There are unsealed roads around most of the island's perimeter. The road from Labasa to Savusavu over the central mountain range is sealed but not well maintained. The island's main routes are well serviced by buses, but it is also fun to explore by 4WD. Budget Rent a Car (Labasa and Savusavu) and Avis Rent A Car (Savusavu) have 4WD vehicles for hire. Avoid driving at night as there are lots of wandering animals and pedestrians and service stations are scarce. Another long unsealed road links Labasa to Savusavu across the north and along the coast of Natewa Bay. It passes small villages but don't expect to be able to buy lunch or petrol.

SAVUSAVU & AROUND
pop 2000

Sleepy Savusavu is Vanua Levu's second-largest town. It is on the peninsula dividing Savusavu Bay from the Koro Sea. The main street, which runs parallel to the water's edge, has a market, a few shops and a yacht club. The view of the islet of Nawi, about 250m offshore, and beyond to the western

---

Bêche-de-Mer

European traders flocked to Fiji in the early 19th century to procure the lucrative *bêche-de-mer* (sea cucumber). It fetched huge profits in Asia, where it is considered a delicacy and aphrodisiac.

You are likely to see some of these ugly slug-like creatures while snorkelling or diving. They feed on organic matter in the sand and serve an important role as cleaners in the lagoon ecosystem. There are various types: some are smooth and sticky, some prickly, some black and some multicoloured. After being cut open and cleaned, they are boiled to remove the salt, then sun-dried or smoked. Many find the taste revolting, but it is highly nutritious, with 50% to 60% protein.

Bêche-de-mer is still a lucrative commodity, both for local use and for export, and unscrupulous traders are delivering dive equipment to remote areas and promising high rewards. Villagers of the Bua region are renowned for harvesting the creature. Usually untrained and unaware of the risks, they are encouraged by the traders to dive in deep waters, risking their health and lives by using faulty or dirty air-compression equipment. Many end up with the bends and a stint in the Fiji Recompression Chamber, and several have died.

VANUA LEVU

VANUA LEVU & TAVEUNI

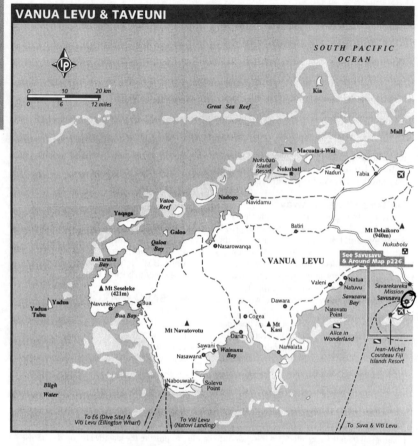

mountain range across the bay, is picturesque and sunsets can be spectacular. Savusavu Bay was once a caldera and the area still has lots of geothermal activity, with **hot springs** near the wharf and vents of steam along the water's edge. Locals sometimes use the springs behind the playing field for cooking.

Copra production was the area's main business during the second half of the 19th century, but profitability began declining early this century. Until the mid-1980s, most copra was sent to Suva for processing. Despite the building of a copra-processing facility in Savusavu, considerably reducing freight costs, farmers are still struggling to remain viable.

Tourism is expanding and the town is now well serviced by airlines and ferries. Its slogan is 'the hidden paradise'. The port is a natural cyclone shelter and a popular stop for cruising yachties who can carry out immigration formalities here.

There is an **archaeological site**, known as Nukubolu, in the mountains north of Savusavu near Biaugunu. The Nukubolu people lived here prior to the cession of Fiji to Britain until a disagreement between

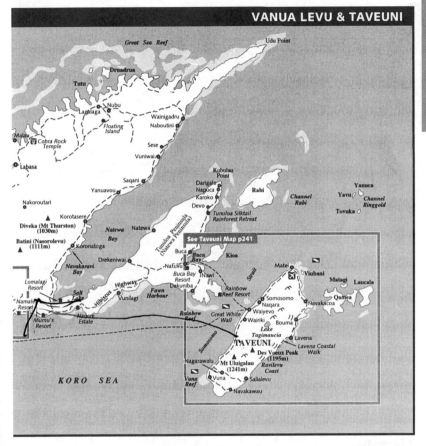

VANUA LEVU & TAVEUNI

their chief Tui Koroalau and Tui Cakau (chief of Cakaudrove). Tui Cakau had sent *tabua* (the teeth of sperm whales, which have a special ceremonial value for Fijians) along with a request for pigs to the Tui Koroalau. However, Tui Koroalau refused the request and sent back the tabua. This was considered a grave insult and war broke out. The Nukubolu people retreated inland but could not escape defeat by the forces of Cakaudrove.

The remains of the extensive village are on the banks of a creek, near some hot springs in a fertile volcanic crater. There are well-preserved stone building foundations, terraces and carefully constructed thermal pools. Locals dry *kava* (the Polynesian pepper shrub) on corrugated-iron sheets laid over the pools, and bathe in the hot springs when sick.

If you have your own 4WD, you can visit **Biaugunu** village. Be sure to take a *sevu-sevu* (a gift, such as *yaqona,* or kava) for the chief (Seru). The turn-off is about 20km north-west of Savusavu. Continue about 8km inland and over a couple of river crossings. The Nukubolu site is earmarked to become a future national park (called Waisali

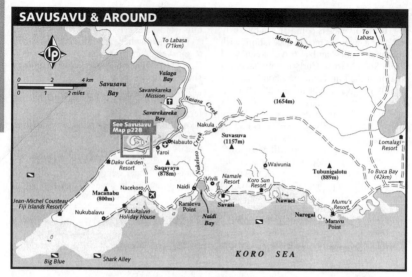

SAVUSAVU & AROUND

Rainforest Reserve) and an ecotourism project, with Eco Divers-Tours as park managers. It is about 30 minutes' walk from the village, along a muddy track through large stands of bamboo and across a shallow river. At the time of writing, however, villagers had not reached a consensus on whether to allow tourism, and unless the site has been cleared, visiting is pointless. There is reportedly also a fortification in the surrounding mountains. You should be able to arrange a guided walk for a small fee.

Information

ANZ bank and Westpac have branches in the main street, opposite the bus station. Both change cash and travellers cheques. The post office is at the eastern end of town near Buca Bay Rd. There are cardphones inside the post office and also at Copra Shed Marina (☎ 850 457, fax 850 989, ✉ coprashed@is .com.fj). Once a dilapidated old copra shed, the building has been renovated and turned into the service hub of the town. Here you can find Eco Divers-Tours (☎ 850 122), Beachcomber Cruises (☎ 850 266, fax 850 499), Sunflower Airlines (☎ 850 141), Air Fiji (☎ 850 173, fax 850 702), Savusavu

Yacht Club, a bar, toilets, hot showers, two accommodation units, a boutique, a bookshop and a pizza restaurant on the water's edge. The marina has a same-day laundry service, provided you put your washing in early in the morning (F$7 a bag).

Moorings at the yacht club cost F$5 per day or F$150 per month. Savusavu is an official point of entry for yachts, with customs, immigration, health and quarantine services.

Call ☎ 850 444 for the hospital or an ambulance, or ☎ 850 222 for the police.

Activities

The main attraction for most travellers to Savusavu is its reefs. There are good **dive sites** at the entrance to Savusavu Bay, the protected inner Savusavu Bay and along the coast towards Taveuni. Eco Divers-Tours, in conjunction with Jean-Michel Cousteau Fiji dive operation, has buoyed dive sites including Big Blue, Shark Alley, The Grotto and Alice in Wonderland. Jean-Michel Cousteau Fiji offers snorkelling, diving and dive courses for its guests (see under Places to Stay – Top End later in this chapter).

Eco Divers-Tours (☎ 850 122, fax 850 344, ✆ ecodivers@is.com.fij), run by Curly and Liz Caswell, has a dive shop with equipment sales and a travel agency at Copra Shed Marina. Curly is national coordinator of the Fiji Recompression Chamber Facility in Suva and the president of the Fiji Dive Operators Association (FDOA). A two-tank dive trip costs F$143, including equipment, and a 10-tank special is F$525, an open-water course costs F$450 (with manuals). Two-hour snorkelling trips are F$18 each for a group of three or four and F$25 each for two people. Weekly accommodation/dive packages are available. Combination dive/snorkelling groups can be accommodated. Eco Divers-Tours has good boats and offers two-tank morning dives and one- or two-tank afternoon dives as well as dusk and night dives. It's best to book ahead.

Fiji Aggressor (☎ 504-385 2628, fax 384 0817 USA, or vessel cellular ☎ 998 820, ✆ divboat@compuserve.com) is the new live-aboard diving operation based in Savusavu. It is part of the worldwide Aggressor fleet of luxury live-aboard boats. *Fiji Aggressor* is a 32m-long boat with eight cabins to accommodate a maximum of 16 guests. It has sundecks, air-con saloons and staterooms, a wheelchair lift, disabled access, quality diving gear and photo equipment. Cruises cost F$8600 per person, twin share and normally leave on Saturday returning the following Saturday. It includes 5½ days of diving.

Eco Divers-Tours (☎ 850 122, fax 850 344, ✆ ecodivers@is.com.fij) also organises **village visits**, trips to **copra plantations** and a mill (F$20), and **rainforest** or **waterfall walks** (F$30). It hires out ocean kayaks (F$35 per day) and mountain bikes (F$20 per day). Eco Divers-Tours also offers interesting **kayak expeditions** along the coast of Savusavu Bay, staying overnight in Fijian villages. A six-day kayaking expedition will cost you F$699 per person in a group of six.

Yachting is popular in Savusavu. Savusavu Yacht Club, next to Eco Divers-Tours, has sailboats for hire. You can also

go **water-skiing** (F$25 for 15 minutes) or hire windsurfers (F$10 per hour).

There is nowhere around Savusavu town to snorkel, apart from snorkelling trips with Eco Divers-Tours. If you have your own **snorkelling** gear, you could try an exploratory snorkel, and if you are confident, try along the coast near Mumu Resort. Alternatively, take the Labasa bus, which takes the route along Natewa Bay, and get off about 40km from Savusavu, where the reef is close to the beach around Navakaravi Bay (before Koronatoga). There are some white-sand beaches along this coast but it is largely rock, mangrove or coral. The return bus from Labasa to Savusavu passes about 3 pm. Don't miss it – there is nowhere to stay in the area!

Places to Stay – Budget

The four-bed fan-cooled dorm rooms on the lower level of *Hot Springs Hotel* (☎ 850 195, fax 850 430, ✆ hotspring@is.com.fj), which is on the hill overlooking the lovely bay, are good value for F$15 per person.

Hidden Paradise Guest House (☎ 850 106) is popular with locals and budget travellers who want somewhere quiet to stay. It is west of the copra shed next door to the Shell petrol station. Six clean rooms are in a building at the back of a general store and restaurant. Security is obviously a priority judging by the bars on the windows and doors. There are shared toilets, cold showers, cooking facilities, and a covered clothes drying area. Prices are F$15/30/45 for singles/doubles/triples, including breakfast of sweet porridge, fruit, eggs, toast, chips and sausage. Locals play soccer in the afternoons at the sportsground at the back.

Savusavu Bay Accommodation (☎ 850 100), upstairs in a double-storey building on the main street, also calls itself 'hidden paradise' but has little atmosphere. Fan-cooled rooms, each with a small en suite and porch, cost F$15/19, or F$38.50 for air-con. An air-con room with four beds costs F$55.

David's Holiday House (☎ 850 149), back from the waterfront, is near the hot springs behind the sportsground. The place is simple but the atmosphere is friendly.

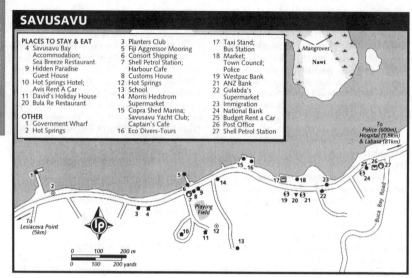

SAVUSAVU

PLACES TO STAY & EAT
4 Savusavu Bay
   Accommodation;
   Sea Breeze Restaurant
9 Hidden Paradise
   Guest House
10 Hot Springs Hotel;
   Avis Rent A Car
11 David's Holiday House
20 Bula Re Restaurant

OTHER
1 Government Wharf
2 Hot Springs

3 Planters Club
5 Fiji Aggressor Mooring
6 Consort Shipping
7 Shell Petrol Station;
   Harbour Cafe
8 Customs House
12 Hot Springs
13 School
14 Morris Hedstrom
   Supermarket
15 Copra Shed Marina;
   Savusavu Yacht Club;
   Captain's Cafe
16 Eco Divers-Tours

17 Taxi Stand;
   Bus Station
18 Market;
   Town Council;
   Police
19 Westpac Bank
21 ANZ Bank
22 Gulabda's
   Supermarket
23 Immigration
24 National Bank
25 Budget Rent a Car
26 Post Office
27 Shell Petrol Station

Mangroves
Nawi

To
Police (600m),
Hospital (1.5km)
& Labasa (81km)

Buca Bay Road

To
Lesiaceva Point
(5km)

Playing
Field

0   100   200 m
0   100   200 yards

It has a good freestanding dorm (no fan) that sleeps seven for F$10 per person. Camp sites in a cute garden cost F$6. The house has various fan-cooled rooms and a kitchen where you can do your own cooking, a dining area and shared bathroom. Rooms cost F$14/20 including breakfast of toast, eggs, fruit and cocoa. The family room sleeps four for F$30. If you stay more than seven days, a 10% discount applies and laundry is free. Horse riding is free for guests.

There is good accommodation at the *Copra Shed Marina* (☎ 850 457, fax 850 989, @ coprashed@is.com.fj), but it is often booked out on long-term leases or rented by yachties. Studio one is a spacious one-room apartment on the first floor, which used to be the bar. A night here costs F$55. Studio two has two bedrooms and costs F$75. Both units have kitchenette and mosquito nets, but the studio one bathroom is downstairs.

If you want something secluded and self-contained, try *Vatukaluvi Holiday House* (☎ 850 143, 850 561, postal address: PO Box 3, Savusavu). It is a 15-minute drive from the town on a rocky point. It overlooks the Koro Sea and a couple of cute islands with lone coconut trees. You can snorkel and there are hot springs nearby. The house has a mezzanine and a deck and sleeps up to six people. It is ideal for a couple or a family interested in self-catering, and costs F$55 per night. A taxi to Savusavu costs F$5. The owner is Geoff Taylor, a geologist who has an office at the Marina. Bookings are recommended.

Mumu's Resort (☎ 850 416, fax 850 402) is about 17km east of Savusavu on a ruggedly beautiful site, but the place is a bit run-down and water supply and power can be erratic. The owner, Philipina Rosie Edris, has lots of guard dogs, but beware of leaving valuables in the bure near the road. The various shacks and bure on site are products of her late husband Gordon's creative imagination. Concrete paths wind between the trees, which cling to the volcanic rock.

The camp site is on top of the hill, under the pine, pandanus and coconut trees. Camping costs F$4.50/8. The six-bed dorm or 'lagoon house' costs F$14 per person. It has cooking facilities, a shower and a toilet. The noisy generator may still be a problem.

The 'dream house' is fantastic, especially on a stormy night. It is perched on a rocky, exposed cliff and has access through a crevice to a rocky beach. The spacious front bedroom has a double and single bed; an adjoining room has two single beds; and behind is a simple kitchen and bathroom with cold water. It costs F$70 per night. The 'tank house' is a simple concrete block structure and costs F$40 for singles and doubles. A Fijian bure is F$50 for a double and the pool house is F$120 for five people. Mosquito nets are provided.

The main house has a comfortable meals/ sitting area and pet parrots. Food is simple and costs F$8/7/15 for breakfast /lunch/dinner. You can use the cooking facilities; it costs F$1 for the gas.

There is a sitting area and natural rock pool on the point, where you can dip with the colourful fish. While there is no sandy beach, snorkelling is good. At low tide you can walk out to the' lagoon between the nearby islands. It has beautiful soft coral and lots of fish. There is another channel to the east of the resort where it is possible to swim through caves and see large parrot fish. Take care with the currents. Local buses (F$1 to Savusavu) pass five times a day (once only on Sunday) and a taxi to/from Savusavu is F$12.

Places to Stay – Mid-Range

The four-level *Hot Springs Hotel* (☎ 850 195, fax 850 430, ☻ hotspring@is.com.fj) is Savusavu's most prominent landmark. It was built as part of the Travelodge chain and rooms are of typical hotel layout with en suites, a double and a single beds, phone, fridge, tea- and coffee-making facilities, and a verandah. Garden or oceanview fan-cooled rooms cost F$80 for singles or doubles (F$125 for air-con). An extra person in any of the rooms costs F$22. It has a deck area with a freshwater swimming pool and great views.

About 15 minutes' walk south-west of Savusavu is *Daku Garden Resort* (☎ 850 046, fax 850 334, ☻ daku@is.com.fj). This small, quiet resort, run by Lily and Rex for the Anglican Diocese of Polynesia, can

cater for groups of up to 20 people. It has lovely views to the bay.

It has six simple fan-cooled bure with fridge, tea- and coffee-making facilities and bathrooms with hot water for F$66/100/140. The four fan-cooled villa units are clean, spacious and equipped with cooking facilities. They are ideal for families and can sleep up to five people. The self-catering villa units cost F$110 for doubles plus F$22 for each extra person. Children under 12 pay half-price. The unit on the hill has the best sea view. Meals here are huge, plenty for two to share, and cost F$8.50/12.50/20 for breakfast/lunch/dinner. Meal plans are available for F$38.50 per person. Package rates are also available and credit cards are accepted.

The resort has a pool. Activities such as volleyball; *meke* (dance performances that enact stories and legends); visits from guest speakers; trips to villages, schools and plantations; snorkelling trips and island picnics can be organised for groups. Diving can be arranged with Eco Divers-Tours. Free transport is provided for guests to/from the airport. A taxi to/from Savusavu costs F$1.50.

Naqere Estate (☎ 880 022, ☻ denise@ is.com.fj) is a nice beachfront B&B on a 4.5-hectare copra plantation, about 25km from Savusavu along Buca Bay Rd. Accommodation in double bedrooms with bamboo king-size beds costs F$200 per day per person plus F$100 per additional person (maximum of four, no children). The rooms have a shared bathroom and the price includes three home-cooked meals per day. Activities include snorkelling and kayaking.

At the time of writing, *Koro Sun Resort* (☎/fax 850 262, ☻ info@korosunresort.com) was preparing to open. It intends to offer accommodation in 15 luxury bure with king-size beds for F$330/385, or in honeymoon bure for F$225. Activities include diving (three-day packages for F$530) and snorkelling trips, windsurfing, canoeing, hiking and village visits. The resort is on a nice sloping site with large trees, about 13km east of Savusavu. A taxi to/from Savusavu costs about F$10.

Places to Stay – Top End

Jean-Michel Cousteau Fiji Islands Resort (☎ 850 188, fax 850 340, ❷ fiji4fun@is.com.fj) is about 5km south-west of Savusavu at Lesiaceva Point, where Savusavu Bay joins the Koro Sea. It offers 25 comfortable, fan-cooled bure with king-size beds, large deck, hammock and private screened garden. Doubles cost from F$890 in gardenview bure to F$1375 for the new oceanfront split-level bure, which are about 50% more spacious. A third person aged 11 to 16 will pay F$140 or, if over 17 years, F$190. Gourmet meals are included in the price and served at an open-air restaurant or on the pier.

The resort has a swimming pool, gym, tennis courts, an interesting gift shop, a darkroom and a conference room with a video library. Activities include village visits, underwater-photography lessons, birdwatching, snorkelling, kayaking, volleyball, tennis, yoga, massage, rainforest hikes and lessons on local customs and herbal medicine. The kids' program has fun activities and theme days and costs an extra F$80/160 for one/two or more children. Jean-Michel Cousteau Fiji dive rates are F$185 for a two-tank dive plus F$60 for equipment rental. An open-water course costs F$720. The company has a great video setup where nondivers can watch and talk to the people who are diving.

Namale Resort (☎ 850 435, fax 850 400, ❷ namale@is.com.fj) is an exclusive resort built in a multilevel landscaped garden on the Hibiscus Hwy 9km east of Savusavu. The resort caters for up to 20 guests; it is lovely, but also horribly expensive. Rates are F$1260/1480 a single/double for garden bure and F$1700 for the oceanview honeymoon bure with garden bathtubs. Prices include all meals, drinks (alcoholic and nonalcoholic), transfers from Savusavu airport and all activities apart from diving. Children over 12 are accepted, but are required to stay in and pay for their own bure! The garden bure are very private, have outdoor decks and are a short walk from the beach. The resort has an impressive entertainment/restaurant bure, but it is for the exclusive use of guests. Diving rates are F$370 for a two-tank dive, and F$1650 for a five-day package. Activities include tennis, horse riding, village trips and waterfall and blowhole visits.

About 24km offshore, south-west of Savusavu, is Moody's Namena, on the island of Namenalala (see the Lomaiviti Group chapter for more information).

A new upmarket place to stay is *Lomalagi Resort (☎ 816 098, fax 816 099, ❷ lomalagi@is.com.fj)*, which opened in 1998. It is about 24km east of Savusavu, hidden high on a hill overlooking the huge and beautiful Natewa Bay. It has 12 villas spread over the 10 hectares of former coconut plantation and is connected by long wooden walkways and a pool. The villas are simple, spacious and comfortable with queen-size bed, fan, bath, kitchen and a large deck with spectacular views of the bay. The resort provides snorkelling gear, sea kayaks and mountain bikes. Village visits, fishing and reef snorkelling trips, horse riding and diving can be arranged. It has a restaurant near the S-shaped salt-water swimming pool and ,a pool table in the games pavilion. Prices are F$800 per couple per night (three-night minimum, no children allowed) plus an optional meal plan for F$220 per couple. The resort is about 5km uphill from the Buca Bay Rd turn-off (take the road north at marker 30.3).

Places to Eat

Your options are pretty limited in Savusavu. One of the most reliable places to eat is *Captain's Cafe (☎ 850 511)* at Copra Shed Marina near the bus station. It has snacks and good pizza (F$8 to F$16 for a medium size), and it has a great spot on the outdoor deck, with beautiful views of Viwa and the volcanic mountains across the bay. *Sea Breeze Restaurant*, at the western end of the town below Savusavu Bay Accommodation, has good large serves of curry and Chinese for under F$5. The best value curries are at the *Harbour Cafe*, two doors west of Customs House. *Bula Re Restaurant* in the middle of the town has OK Chinese for F$5 to F$8, and some Fijian dishes for F$6 to F$9. The restaurant at the front of *Hidden Paradise Guest House* serves Indian curries, rice, roti (flat Indian bread) and *tavioka* (cassava) for under F$5. Also try the restaurant at *Hot Springs Hotel* for medium-priced meals with views.

Savusavu has a couple of supermarkets, a few general stores and a *market* with an OK range of fruit and vegetables.

Entertainment

Savusavu Yacht Club has a small bar on the water's edge at Copra Shed Marina. If you befriend one of the yachties they'll sign you in. *Hot Springs Hotel* has happy hour from 5 to 7 pm and occasional dances. The 43-year-old *Planters Club*, near Savusavu Bay Accommodation, is frequented by the local copra farmers but visitors are welcome and will be signed in. The club's old colonial weatherboard building has a verandah with a view to the water. There are pool and table-tennis tables. Bill and Mary McLaren have been running the club for about 25 years. Though copra farming is on the wane, they still organise dances once every three to four months, where the oldies turn up in black tie, white jackets and evening frocks.

You might like to watch locals play rugby and soccer on the playing field behind the Shell petrol station.

Getting There & Away

Air Savusavu airstrip is 3km south of the town. The trip from Nadi takes about an hour, and from Suva 45 minutes. The flight over the reefs and down to Savusavu through the coconut plantations is superb. The airport has toilets, and locals sell roti, cake and fresh lemon juice at arrival and departure times. Sunflower Airlines has flights Savusavu-Nadi and Savusavu-Taveuni twice daily. Air Fiji has direct flights to Nadi and Suva twice daily, and to Taveuni once daily (see the Air Fares Chart in the Getting Around chapter for prices). Contact details for the airlines are:

Air Fiji (☎ 850 173) Savusavu and airport
Sunflower Airlines (☎ 850 141) Savusavu;
  (☎ 850 214) airport

Bus Buses travelling the sealed highway from Savusavu over the mountains to Labasa (about F$5, three hours, four times daily) depart from 7.15 am to 3.30 pm Monday to Saturday and from 9.30 am to 3.30 pm on Sunday. The long route from Savusavu to Labasa around the north along Natewa Bay is quite scenic (taking nine hours and departing at 9 am). At 1 pm a bus goes as far as Wainigadru and, at 4.30 pm, to Yanuavou.

Buses from Savusavu to Napuca (F$4.70, 3½ hours), at the tip of the Tunuloa Peninsula, depart at 10.30 am and 2.30 pm daily. The afternoon bus stays there overnight and returns at 7 am. A 4 pm bus goes to Drekeniwai and on to Buca Bay (F$3.20), where it stays overnight.

Buses also travel along the south-east coast towards Mt Kasi. The 11 am bus goes as far as Valeni and the 2 pm bus travels to Mt Kasi gold mine (taking about two hours).

For confirmation of bus timetables, ring Vishnu Holdings (☎ 850 276).

Boat For Suva-Savusavu, Savusavu-Taveuni and Savusavu–Buca Bay–Taveuni ferry services, see Ferry in the Getting Around chapter.

Getting Around

The Savusavu bus station and taxi stand are downtown, near the market. There's no shortage of taxis. They can be hailed on the street or booked – try Hot Spring Taxis (☎ 850 226). Rates are about F$15 per hour. Local buses do pass the airport every so often, however, a taxi to/from Savusavu costs only F$2. There are buses from Savusavu to Lesiaceva Point (Jean-Michel Cousteau Fiji Islands Resort, F$0.50, 15 minutes). The bus leaves Savusavu between 6 am and 5 pm five times daily, except on Sunday.

Avis Rent A Car (☎ 850 911), at Hot Springs Hotel, and Budget Rent a Car (☎ 850 700), near the post office, have 4WDs; it's a great way to explore the area if you can afford it. Eco Divers-Tours has mountain bikes for hire.

TUNULOA PENINSULA

Tunuloa Peninsula, also known as Natewa or Cakaudrove Peninsula, makes up the southeastern section of Vanua Levu. It is a good area for bird-watching, hiking or for exploring by bus or 4WD. The gravel Hibiscus Hwy is scenic, running from Savusavu to the road's end at Darigala, passing copra plantations, old homesteads, villages and forests. About 20km east of Savusavu there is a turnoff to the north. This road follows the western side of Natewa Bay, an alternative 4WD route to Labasa. About 35km from this intersection further along the Hibiscus Hwy is the turn-off into the village of **Drekeniwai**, where former prime minister Sitiveni Rabuka was born.

Another road turns off to Buca Bay, which is about 65km from Savusavu (1½ hours by bus). Most travellers pass through **Buca Bay** on the way to/from Taveuni. Ferries leave from Natuvu, Buca Bay, and cross the Somosomo Strait to Taveuni. The beach here is black sand. There is excellent budget accommodation near the wharf. The ferry passes the island of **Kioa**, which is inhabited by Polynesians from Vaitupu atoll in Tuvalu (formerly Ellice Islands). Their home island suffered from poor soils and overcrowding and after WWII the community decided to purchase another more fertile island and relocate some families to reduce the pressure. The island was purchased in 1946 with money they had earned working for the Americans, who had occupied their islands during WWII. About 600 people now live here in one village.

South of Buca Bay, at the south-eastern end of Vanua Levu, is the village of Dakuniba, where **petroglyphs** on boulders can be found in a creek bed nearby. Similar alphabetic rock inscriptions are also found in the Sawa-i-Lau caves in the Yasawas. The inscriptions are thought to be of ceremonial or mystical significance, but no-one knows who carved them, and their meaning is a mystery. Dakuniba means 'behind the fence', and there is a theory that the rocks may have been part of a single structure. The famous **Rainbow Reef** is offshore from Dakuniba. Diving can be arranged with Buca Bay Resort. Dive boats from the Taveuni resorts travel across the Somosomo Strait to the reef.

The scenic road up to Napuca and **Darigala** follows the eastern coast and passes copra plantations, old homesteads, villages and forest areas. The island of **Rabi**, east of the northern tip of the Tunuloa peninsula, is populated by Micronesians originally from Banaba (Ocean Island), in Kiribati. At the turn of the century the naive islanders sold the phosphate mining rights of Banaba in return for an annual payment, and their tiny island was eventually ruined. During WWII the Japanese invaded their island and many people perished. Rabi was purchased for them by a British mining company and after the war the 2000 Banaban survivors were settled there.

Places to Stay & Eat

The phone lines can be unreliable at this end of the island – persevere, though, as the resorts are worthwhile.

The pleasant **Buca Bay Resort** (℡/fax 880 370, ✆ bucabayresort@mail.is.com.fj) is within view of the ferry landing. It has a rustic bure, a swimming pool, good snorkelling nearby and diving on the Rainbow Reef. The 14-bed dorm is linked to a kitchen/bar and costs F$33 per person. The cute waterfront bure costs F$88 a double, and the family bure is F$120 a double, plus F$10 per person up to a maximum of six. There is an external bathroom bure. A room in the main house with a share bathroom is F$88 a double. The house has a communal sitting area and porch with a view to the water. Meal packages cost F$55. Dive rates with Buca Bay Divers are F$120 for a two-tank dive, including equipment, while snorkelling trips cost F$40.

South-east of Buca Bay on the eastern end of Vanua Levu and across Somosomo Strait from Taveuni is **Rainbow Reef Resort** (℡ 880 900, fax 880 901, ✆ rainbowreefrs@ is.com.fj). It is the closest resort to the famous Rainbow Reef. This small-scale, family friendly resort is on a lovely white-sand beach and has comfortable beachfront cottages among nice gardens, each with verandah, king-size bed and open-air shower. Honeymoon cottages cost F$350/ 390 a double without/with spa, and the beachfront family suite with bedroom, sitting area and children's loft is F$420. Rates include all meals and there is a three-night minimum stay. Activities include hiking, kayaking and snorkelling. Diving and tours to Taveuni cost extra. Transfers are F$100 return, by boat from Taveuni.

Tunuloa Silktail Rainforest Retreat (☎ *013 – ask the operator to connect you to radio* ☎ *759RP6,* ☎ *09 232 0188 New Zealand, fax 232 0190 New Zealand)* has been set up by a group of New Zealand bird-watchers, including Stuart Chambers, author of *Birds of New Zealand Locality Guide,* 1987. The two cottages have verandahs and are on a hill in a rainforest setting near Devo beach and the Meru and Natovotovo Rivers. The self-contained cottages have a gas stove and fridge and cost F$60 for two people, F$10 for an extra person, or F$350 weekly. The lodge sells basic ingredients for cooking, but is best if you bring your own food. Otherwise, cooked meals cost F$6/7/17 for breakfast/lunch/ dinner and are served at the communal verandah and restaurant.

The area is the habitat of the silktail, a rare bird found only on this peninsula and on Taveuni. The silktail is on the world's endangered-species list, and logging has threatened the local population. The bird is about 8cm high and is black with a white patch on its tail. Apart from bird-watching, activities include bushwalking, snorkelling, swimming and trips to the island of Rabi, east of Kubulau Point.

Getting There & Away
The ferry landing is near Buca Bay Resort. For Savusavu–Buca Bay–Taveuni services see Ferry in the Getting Around chapter.

The bus from Savusavu to Napuca (F$5, 3½ hours) departs Savusavu at 10.30 am and 2.30 pm. The afternoon bus stays in Napuca overnight and returns at 7 am. The bus passes the Tunuloa Silktail Rainforest Retreat twice daily heading for Napuca and twice on the way back to Savusavu.

There is an afternoon (4 pm) bus from Savusavu to Drekeniwai and on to Buca Bay where it stays overnight.

Timetables are liable to change so confirm in advance.

LABASA & AROUND
pop 24,095

Labasa, the largest town on Vanua Levu, is on the north-western side of Vanua Levu's mountain range, about 5km inland on the banks of the meandering Labasa River. A big centre for CSR and the sugar industry in colonial days, the district is still mainly a cane-growing area. The Labasa sugar mill was opened in 1894 and the company established cane plantations in the fertile river valleys and on reclaimed mangrove swamps. Raw sugar, molasses and timber are exported from the port at Malau, north of the town. There are some lovely big colonial residences scattered around the district. Labasa has a predominantly Fiji-Indian population, mostly descendants of indentured labourers brought to work on the plantations.

While Labasa is a bustling trade, service and administrative centre for western Vanua Levu, most travellers will find the town pretty dull. There are, however, a few interesting things to see.

Information
Most shops and services can be found on Nasekula Rd (the main street), including the National, ANZ and Westpac banks, and the post office, which has cardphones. The booking office for Sunflower Airlines (☎ 811 454) is on the corner of Nasekula Rd and Damanu St, and Air Fiji (☎ 811 188), Beachcomber Cruises (☎ 817 788) and Patterson Brothers Shipping (☎ 812 444, fax 813 460) are all found close by, also on Nasekula Rd.

The public library at the Civic Centre has a small collection of books. It is open 9 am to 1 pm and 2 to 5 pm weekdays, and 9 am to noon Saturday.

East of the river is the hospital and the provincial council's multistorey office building. Note the stone monolith in front of the building. In the old Fijian religion,

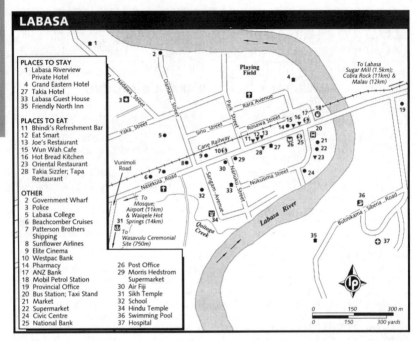

LABASA

PLACES TO STAY
1 Labasa Riverview
   Private Hotel
4 Grand Eastern Hotel
27 Takia Hotel
33 Labasa Guest House
35 Friendly North Inn

PLACES TO EAT
11 Bhindi's Refreshment Bar
12 Eat Smart
13 Joe's Restaurant
15 Wun Wah Cafe
16 Hot Bread Kitchen
23 Oriental Restaurant
28 Takia Sizzler; Tapa
   Restaurant

OTHER
2 Government Wharf
3 Police
5 Labasa College
6 Beachcomber Cruises
7 Patterson Brothers
   Shipping
8 Sunflower Airlines
9 Elite Cinema
10 Westpac Bank
14 Pharmacy
17 ANZ Bank
18 Mobil Petrol Station
19 Provincial Office
20 Bus Station; Taxi Stand
21 Market
22 Supermarket
24 Civic Centre
25 National Bank

26 Post Office
29 Morris Hedstrom
   Supermarket
30 Air Fiji
31 Sikh Temple
32 School
34 Hindu Temple
36 Swimming Pool
37 Hospital

such stones were worshipped, as it was believed that they embodied the spirit of ancestor gods.

The police (☎ 811 222) is in Nadawa St. The hospital (☎ 811 444), in Butinikama-Siberia Rd, has the same number as the ambulance.

Things to See & Do

Just a couple of kilometres south of town on Vunimoli Rd is the **Wasavula Ceremonial Site** (see the boxed text later in this chapter). It consists of two parallel linear platforms, each about 2m wide and 75m long, and spaced about 4m apart. The ceremonial platforms are lined with low stone walls, and transverse walls divide the site into segments. There are several tall stone monoliths and a *vatu ni bokola* (head-chopping stone). The site is behind some village houses, so make sure you ask permission to have a look. You can get to Wasavula by bus or taxi.

Labasa Sugar Mill (☎ 811 511) is about 1½km east of town. The crushing season is from June to December. **Waiqele hot springs** is 3km beyond the airport. Take the Waiqele bus (F$0.75).

Past the sugar mill and the Oawa River, the main road turns left. After about 5km there is a turn-off to the left to Malau wharf. Another 4.5km (about 11km north of Labasa) on the right side of the road is a Hindu temple built around the **Cobra Rock**.

The rock is about 3m high and its curved form resembles a poised cobra. Devotees bring offerings to the temple. They swear that the rock grows in size and that the roof has had to be raised several times over the years. Before entering you must remove your shoes and you should not have eaten meat that day. Several buses pass the temple, including those to Natewa Bay. A taxi costs around F$10.

Farther up the road on the left is a bus stand and a road that leads to the best **beach** in the area. It's about 3km off the main road, so it's difficult to get there unless you walk, have a car or are prepared to pay for a taxi. The road passes strange rock formations and runs through land that used to be a tidal swamp, but now has rice and cane plantations. The beach is on private land and at the farm you'll have to pay F$5 per car to visit. Continue down through the coconut trees to the beach, which is about 300m long, has a couple of huts, a toilet and a view to the port. It is popular with locals and can get crowded on holidays. It's a bit rocky and you can swim only at high tide.

About 50km north-east of Labasa is **Floating Island**, in a small lake among the cane plantations. Pandanus palms grow on a small grassy platform that moves about. Locals say that no-one has ever reached the bottom of the lake.

You can get there by the morning Lagalaga Bisongo bus, but check return timetables to make sure you don't get stranded in the middle of nowhere. Ask the driver where to get off. Take the track about 1km off the main road, and ask to see the island at the farmhouse on the right. A return trip by taxi will cost about F$45, which may be an option for a group.

Places to Stay
Labasa Guest House (☎ 812 155) in Nanuku St is conveniently located but has little atmosphere. However, it does have shared kitchen facilities. Singles/doubles cost F$16.50/22. *Labasa Riverview Private Hotel* (☎ 811 367, fax 814 337) is a good budget option. It is in the suburb of Namara, about a five-minute walk from town past the police station along Nadawa St. The double-storey building has 10 fan-cooled rooms and a bar with snooker tables facing the river. Rooms with fan and en suite cost F$30/40 or F$45/55 with air-con. Beds in the five-bed dorm upstairs, with verandah and river view, are good value for F$11. The friendly owner, Pradeep, is good for a chat and you can make tea or coffee in his office.

The best mid-range option is the upgraded *Grand Eastern Hotel* (☎ 811 022, fax 814 011, ✉ grest@is.com), between the river and Mobil's storage tanks. It has a pleasant courtyard with free-form swimming pool. Standard air-con rooms cost F$95, while spacious deluxe rooms with small porch facing the river are better value at F$115.

Friendly North Inn (☎ 811 555, fax 813 900) is opposite the hospital, east of the river. The 10 rooms are relatively new and are good value. Fan-cooled rooms cost F$30/40, or F$40/50 with air-con. All rooms have a TV and fridge. An self-contained apartment with lounge and kitchen costs F$50/55 with fan/air-con. There is also a restaurant-bar where meals are available if you order in advance. It is within walking distance from the town centre (a taxi ride costs about F$1).

Wasavula Ceremonial Site

Little is known about the origin of the Wasavula platforms, but they are thought to be related to similar sites of the *naga* cult found in Viti Levu's Sigatoka Valley. Those who betrayed ceremonial secrets would face insanity and death, so what is known about such sites is mostly based on hearsay and vague memories.

Such sites were connected with spirit/ancestor worship. They were both a venue for communicating with the founder gods and a spiritual link between the people and the earth, time, crops and fertility. The sites were thought to have been used for performing ceremonies such as the installation of chiefs and priests, male initiation rites such as circumcision, or to tell the gods that the *bokola* (dead body of an enemy) had been prepared.

Stone monoliths were seen as actual gods or the shrines of the gods. They were also used for refuge. Someone who had committed a crime could run to the village refuge stone. If they made it to the rock before being caught, their life would be spared.

The three-storey 38-room *Takia Hotel* (☎ 811 655, fax 813 527) is on the main street close to the bus station. It's a bit claustrophobic, with stuffy air-con and clashing '70s pub-style carpet. Fan-cooled rooms are F$35/45 for singles/doubles. Air-con rooms with clinical vinyl are F$55/65, or F$60/70 with gaudy carpet. Second-floor air-con suites cost F$70/80. All rooms have their own en suite, tea- and coffee-making facilities and fridge. Credit cards are accepted but you will be charged about 5% to 10% extra. Children under 12 are free; extra adults cost F$10.

Places to Eat

There is a *Hot Bread Kitchen* and *supermarket* near the bus station. There are lots of cheap eateries along Labasa's main street. *Bhindi's Refreshment Bar* is clean and has good home-made snacks including samosas and cakes. Mutton and vegetable pies cost F$1.50. Bhindi's is closed Sunday. *Takia Sizzler*, the Takia Hotel's fast-food outlet, plays Indian music and serves Chinese and Indian meals such as chop suey or curries with rice, roti, cassava, *dalo* (taro) and chips for under F$5. *Wun Wah Cafe* has just OK Chinese fare for under F$5. *Eat Smart* (☎ 816 611) has medium pizzas for F$10 and will deliver.

Probably the best restaurant in town is *Joe's Restaurant* (☎ 811 766), which has good-value Chinese-style food. The air-con *Oriental Restaurant* (☎ 817 321), on Nukusima St near the bus station and market, has Chinese, Fijian and European meals from F$5 to F$10. The *restaurant* at the Grand Eastern Hotel offers lunch from F$6 and dinner from F$11.50 to F$15.50. It has historical photos and a pleasant courtyard to relax in. *Tapa Restaurant* at Takia Hotel has reasonable meals, including grills and fish, from F$12.50 to F$25.

Entertainment

Apart from *Elite Cinema* (☎ 811 260) on Nasekula Rd, Labasa has very little nightlife (head for Suva on Viti Levu, if you need more action). Both Grand Eastern Hotel and Takia Hotel have *bars*.

Getting There & Away

Air Sunflower Airlines (☎ 812 121 airport) has four Nadi-Labasa flights daily and two Suva-Labasa flights daily. Air Fiji (☎ 811 679 airport) has six Suva-Labasa flights daily and twice-daily Nadi-Labasa flights. See the Air Fares Chart in the Getting Around chapter for prices.

Bus There are regular buses between Labasa and Savusavu. Waiqele company buses (☎ 817 680, $3.60, four times daily, twice on Sunday) depart Labasa between 7.30 am and 4 pm. There are also buses that take the long route (about nine hours) to Savusavu around the north and down along Natewa Bay. Lagalaga Buses (☎ 811 062) has trips on this route (F$9) departing at 9 am. There are also regular buses between Labasa and Nabouwalu (see Nabouwalu later in this chapter).

Getting Around

Taxis are plentiful and the main stand is near the bus station. There are several local bus companies. If you have time to kill, consider taking a bus ride around the district. There are no written timetables, so go to the bus station and ask around. You can hire 4WD vehicles from Budget Rent a Car (☎ 811 999) and Avis Rent A Car (☎ 811 688).

The airport is about 11km south-west of Labasa. It has a kiosk and a cardphone. The turn-off is about 4.25km west of Labasa, just past the Wailevu River. During the day there are regular Waiqele buses from Labasa to the airport for F$0.55. A taxi from Labasa costs F$6.

NUKUBATI

This privately owned island is just off the northern coast of Vanua Levu, about 40km west of Labasa. It is actually two small islands linked by mangroves. It takes about 30 minutes to walk around the island at low tide and 15 minutes to walk to its highest point. Once occupied by Fijian villagers, in the 19th century it was given by a local chief to a German gunsmith who settled here with his Fijian wife. In colonial days it operated as a coconut plantation.

Secluded ***Nukubati Island Resort*** (☎ *813 901, fax 813 914*) feels like it's in the middle of nowhere, certainly far from the usual tourist destinations. It has four bungalows and three honeymoon bure for a maximum of 14 guests. The spacious fan-cooled suites have separate bedroom, bathroom and sitting areas, a verandah facing a white-sand beach and a private courtyard off the bedroom. Prices, including gourmet meals, nonalcoholic drinks and transfers are F$880/990 for double bungalows/honeymoon bure. Only adult couples are accepted, except for whole island booking at F$6835 per night. The resort recommends a minimum stay of five nights.

The dining, bar and lounge pavilion has great views and plenty of room to find your own corner and read a book from the library. The restaurant has an extensive wine list and the menu specialises in seafood, fresh fruits and Fijian-style cooking including *lovo* (feast cooked in a pit oven) and curries. Wind generators and solar panels provide the electricity, and water is obtained by a desalination plant as well as from filtered rain water.

Activities include tennis, sailing, windsurfing, snorkelling and fishing. Diving on the Great Sea Reef is very good and costs F$185 for a two-tank dive. The dive shop caters for experienced divers only. Alternatively, you can just laze about and have a traditional Fijian massage. Game fishing and 4WD trips around Vanua Levu are extra.

Getting There & Away

Resort guests are transferred from Labasa to the island by a one-hour boat ride along Vanua Levu's northern coast. Alternatively, take a taxi along the coast past Naduri to the jetty, followed by a short boat ride.

NABOUWALU & AROUND

Nabouwalu is a small settlement on the south-western point of Vanua Levu. It has administrative offices, a post office, a small market and a store. Apart from the ferry landing, there's not much reason to visit this area.

Early in the 19th century, European traders flocked to the **Bua Bay** area northwest of Nabouwalu to exploit *yasi dina* (sandalwood), which grew in the rugged hills. Offshore to the north-west, the island of Yadua Tabu is home to the last sizeable population of rare and spectacular crested iguana. It became Fiji's first wildlife reserve in 1980.

Precious Cargo

In 1800 the American schooner *Argo* was on its way to the English penal colony on Norfolk Island, 100km north of Auckland, when it was shipwrecked near Oneata, east of Lakeba in the Lau Group. Many of the sailors were killed and eaten by the locals, but Oliver Slater survived by befriending powerful chiefs and helping in their wars with his knowledge of muskets and gunpowder.

The sailors brought with them a disease, thought to be Asian cholera, and a plague broke out in the Fijian islands. Known as *na lila balavu* (wasting sickness), it took a terrible toll and destroyed whole communities. Sick people were walled up in caves, strangled, or even buried alive in an attempt to avoid the spread of the disease.

Slater left Oneata with some Fijians. He lived a while in a village on Bua Bay in Vanua Levu, until he was picked up by a passing Spanish vessel. He broke the news of the precious sandalwood to be found in the nearby hills and later returned to Fiji to facilitate trade. Ships flocked to the area, which became known as Sandalwood Bay. Cargoes of the fragrant timber fetched high prices in Asia. It was traded for trinkets, muskets, alcohol and assistance in local wars. As a result the chiefs of Bua gained relative prosperity and prestige.

The sandalwood trade was short-lived as supply was soon exhausted. Slater's luck eventually ran out – the influential beachcomber was killed on Moturiki in the Lomaiviti Group.

VANUA LEVU

Places to Stay & Eat

If you do wish to stay overnight in Nabouwalu, there is a *government guesthouse* (☎ *836 027, district officer, Bua)*, which is generally used by government workers but may have vacancies. Prices are F$10 per person and there are cooking facilities. The local store has food but it is best to bring your own. There is also a *YWCA* with beds for F$15.

Getting There & Away

Patterson Brothers Shipping has a ferry service linking Nabouwalu and Ellington Wharf near Nananu-i-Ra, on northern Viti Levu, with bus connections to/from Lautoka and Labasa. It is mostly used for transporting pine trucks across the 60km of Bligh Water. The trip (F$43) involves taking a bus (3½ hours) from Lautoka, the *Ashika* ferry (3¾ hours) and another bus to Labasa (four hours). The ferry leaves Ellington Wharf early in the morning and you may be able to arrange to spend the night before on the boat. It also has a daily (except Sunday) ferry service between Natovi Landing, eastern Viti Levu, and Nabouwalu, with bus connections to/from Suva and Labasa. The trip (F$43) involves taking a bus (1½ hours) from Suva, ferry (4½ hours) and another bus to Labasa (four hours).

Buses regularly travel along the long dusty road to Labasa (F$6.50, five hours, 136km, three times daily) through Bua and Macuata provinces. Express buses take about four hours. There are no direct buses from Nabouwalu to Savusavu, but you can travel through to Labasa and catch a bus from there to Savusavu. If you are not interested in visiting Labasa, ask the driver to drop you off at the junction with the road to Savusavu. You may have to wait at the intersection for about an hour for a connecting bus to Savusavu.

The road from Nabouwalu around the southern coast to Savusavu (127km) is only passable by 4WD or carrier.

Taveuni

Taveuni is quite sparsely populated: Its 12,000 people are indigenous Fijians, people of mixed descent and foreigners. Taveuni, along with Eastern Vanua Levu and the islands of Qamea, Matagi and Laucala, form the Vanua (region) of Cakaudrove. Somosomo is the largest village and is the power base of the region's chiefly Fijian administration. The island's main source of income is agriculture, mostly copra (dried coconut) and to a lesser extent *dalo* (taro) and *kava* crops, but it is increasingly relying on tourism.

Taveuni's stunning natural beauty, both under and above water, is popular with divers, bushwalkers and nature lovers. Fortunately it is not overrun with resorts (as yet anyway) and the island is relatively compact, easily accessible, and good for outdoor activities.

History

There are a few sites of archaeological interest on Taveuni, including the remains of the old Vuna village hill fortification in the south near Vuna Point. According to local lore, the Paramount Chief Tui Vuna, who was originally from Moturiki near Ovalau, presided here. His vast army was long undefeated, partly due to the strategic location of the fort. His opponent, the Tui Cakau of Somosomo, eventually overcame him by bribing the Tui Vuna's relatives to abduct his son.

Before Europeans arrived on Taveuni, the Fijian villagers had long been trading, and occasionally warring, with the seafaring Tongans. In the mid-19th century the Tongan warlord Ma'afu, already powerful in the Lau group and attempting to extend his influence, was defeated in a battle at Somosomo, in the island's north-east.

The first European traders and settlers arrived in southern Taveuni in the early 19th century. Land was bartered or purchased from the Tui Vuna and the traders and settlers established plantations and home-

HIGHLIGHTS

- Snorkel or dive on the famous coral reefs of the Somosomo Strait and the Rainbow Reef.
- Go bushwalking and bird-watching in the rugged forested mountain landscape.
- Walk the beautiful Lavena coastal track with a rewarding swim in a waterfall pool.
- Take a guided day hike along the Vidawa Forest Walk to fortified village sites, through verdant vegetation and past waterfalls.
- Visit the stunning islands of Matagi, Qamea and Laucala.

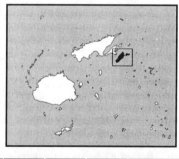

steads. Taveuni developed good shipping services and roads for the time. Taveuni's deep fertile soil grew high-quality cotton, but when cotton prices collapsed, sugar cane was planted. Sugar cane, however, failed in Taveuni's wet climate. The ruins of the 100-year-old Billyard sugar mill still stand in Salialevu, southern Taveuni. Cattle and sheep grazing had some success, as did the planting of coffee and tropical fruits, before copra plantations took over. Some descendants of the original settlers still own land in the area.

Geography

Taveuni, 42km in length and about 10km wide, is the third-largest of Fiji's islands. It is about 140km north-east of Viti Levu and just 9km from the south-eastern end of Vanua Levu across the Somosomo Strait. The 1000m-high central ridge includes two of the highest peaks in Fiji: Des Voeux Peak, at 1195m, and Mt Uluigalau, which at 1241m is the second-highest summit in Fiji. The ridge lies perpendicular to the south-easterly prevailing winds, hence the high rainfall, especially on the south-eastern side. The summit is often hidden behind clouds. The abundant rainfall and volcanic soil covered with lush vegetation makes Taveuni one of Fiji's most fertile areas.

Taveuni is a typical example of a volcanic island. Its high volcanic ridge was formed by a series of volcanoes and its rich soils are derived from basaltic lava. In the south-east there are a number of lava flows reaching the coast. Most of the coastline is rugged and there are some black-sand beaches such as Navakacoa. The beaches at Lavena and Matei have some white sand and are good for swimming and snorkelling. The smaller offshore islands of Qamea, Matagi and Laucala have stunning beaches.

Off Matei's Naselesele Point, the island's northernmost point, is a group of picturesque rocky islets. From here to Thurston Point, 12km to the south-east, the land slopes gently. The water is shallow with reefs down to the village at Lavena Point. Hereon to Salialevu the terrain is rugged, with a straight stretch of cliffs, open ocean and no roads. About halfway along, the 20m-high Savulevu Yavonu Waterfall flows directly into the sea. Salialevu has a small fringing reef and a channel, and the southern coast is eroded by the sea, forming caves and blowholes. At the southern cape, the land turns flatter again with a wide bay ending at Vuna Point, where there are again villages. There is deep water close to shore along the southern and western coasts up to Wairiki. The only reef in this section is at Vuna Point, where the reef forms an inverted U-shape extending to about 3km offshore. North of Wairiki, the Somosomo Strait currents flow over a submerged platform with abundant coral.

Climate

Expect lots of rain here; it's a rainforest area. The island is especially hot and humid in January and February and the water clarity is reduced due to plankton blooms and northerly winds from the equator (see Climate in the Facts about Fiji chapter for more information on Fiji's climate). Cyclone Gavin hit Taveuni in 1997 and washed sand from Prince Charles Beach in Matei.

Flora & Fauna

Taveuni is known as the 'Garden Island of Fiji' for its dense and verdant rainforest and exotic flora and fauna above and below the sea. Its rugged geography has hindered farming, leaving forests and wildlife relatively intact. Flora includes ferns, orchids,

Tui Cakau

Ratu Glanville Wellington Lalabalavu was Tui Cakau (paramount chief of Somosomo and of the whole Cakaudrove region) from 1996 to 1999. The former soldier, politician and administrator replaced the late Ratu Sir Penaia Ganilau. At his installation ceremony he was dressed in *masi* (bark cloth) and a sash adorned with the sacred tagimaucia flower. Youths had made the difficult climb to Lake Tagimaucia to find the rare flower. Ratu Glanville received *yaqona* (drink made from kava) from the traditional king-maker as a symbol of acceptance of the title. He was given authority and power over the land and fishing grounds of the entire province, its people and all living things, and the right to make decisions on land ownership and usage. After the ceremony, he had to remain at his home for four nights before bathing in the sea and removing the symbolic masi ceremonial attire. Ratu Glanville Lalabalavu died in November 1999, throwing the entire Cakaudrove province into deep mourning.

Temple doors, Orchid Island Cultural Centre

Ganesh – Hindu lord of beginnings, Vanua Levu

Marist Convent School, Levuka

Village church, Kadavu island

Naiserelagi Mission

Bilibili (bamboo rafting)

Korean Wharf, near Waiyevo on Taveuni

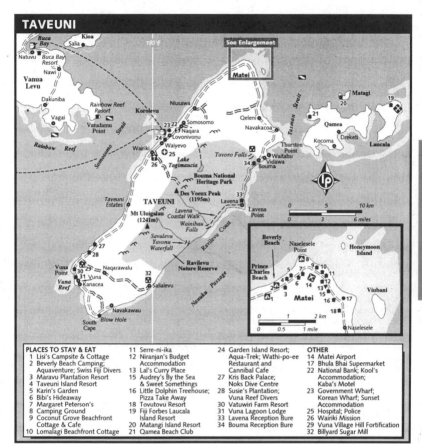

TAVEUNI

PLACES TO STAY & EAT
1 Lisi's Campsite & Cottage
2 Beverly Beach Camping;
   Aquaventure; Swiss Fiji Divers
3 Maravu Plantation Resort
4 Taveuni Island Resort
5 Karin's Garden
6 Bibi's Hideaway
7 Margaret Peterson's
8 Camping Ground
9 Coconut Grove Beachfront
   Cottage & Cafe
10 Lomalagi Beachfront Cottage
11 Serre-ni-ika
12 Niranjan's Budget
   Accommodation
13 Lal's Curry Place
15 Audrey's By the Sea
   & Sweet Somethings
16 Little Dolphin Treehouse;
   Pizza Take Away
18 Tovutovu Resort
19 Fiji Forbes Laucala
   Island Resort
20 Matangi Island Resort
21 Qamea Beach Club
24 Garden Island Resort;
   Aqua-Trek; Wathi-po-ee
   Restaurant and
   Cannibal Cafe
27 Kris Back Palace;
   Noks Dive Centre
28 Susie's Plantation;
   Vuna Reef Divers
30 Vatuwiri Farm Resort
31 Vuna Lagoon Lodge
33 Lavena Reception Bure
34 Bouma Reception Bure

OTHER
14 Matei Airport
17 Bhula Bhai Supermarket
22 National Bank; Kool's
   Accommodation;
   Kaba's Motel
23 Government Wharf;
   Korean Wharf; Sunset
   Accommodation
25 Hospital; Police
26 Wairiki Mission
29 Vuna Village Hill Fortification
32 Billyard Sugar Mill

rare palms and native trees such as *evuevu*, *sinu*, *vutu*, *ivi* and *dilo*. Fiji's national flower, the *tagimaucia*, or *Medinilla waterhousei*, grows only at high altitudes. It is found here and on one mountain in Vanua Levu. Its petals are white and its branches are bright red.

Taveuni has many copra plantations. Metal bands are placed around the trunks of the coconut trees in order to stop rats and crabs from climbing up and piercing the coconuts. Vatuwiri Farm Resort at Vuna Point in the south is a good place for viewing fruit bats and for bird-watching.

Bird-Watching Taveuni is one of Fiji's best locations for bird-watching. Over 100 species of birds can be found, partly because the mongoose was never introduced here. Try Des Voeux Peak at dawn for a chance to see the rare orange dove (the male is bright orange with a green head, while the female is mostly green) and the silktail. Another good site is near Qeleni village between Matei and Thurston Point. On the Matei side of the village, follow a 4WD track for 3.5km up the mountain. Here you could see these birds and parrots and fantails, especially between August and September when they are nesting. The deep red feathers of the kula parrot were once an important trade item with the Tongans. The forested Lavena coast is also a good spot to see orange or flame doves, Fiji goshawk, wattled honeyeater, and grey and white heron. Down south you can see and hear magpies, which were introduced to control insects in the copra plantations.

Language
One of the distinctions of the Cakaudrove dialect (common to Taveuni, its offshore islands and eastern Vanua Levu) is the dropped 'k'. The only difference a traveller is likely to notice is with the word *vinaka* (thank you), which is pronounced 'vina'a' or even shortened to 'na'a' or 'na'.

Activities
Diving This area has some fantastic diving. Somosomo Strait (meaning 'good water' in Fijian) has strong tidal currents, which provide a constant flow of nutrients, ideal for soft coral growth and diverse fish life. You are likely to see lots of fish, the occasional shark or turtle, and fantastic coral. In November you may see pilot whales. Taveuni is world-renowned among divers for the spectacular, colourful soft corals at spots such as Rainbow Reef (a fringing reef almost 32km long on the south-west corner of Vanua Levu, but easily accessed from Taveuni), and for drift dives along the Great White Wall. Other sites include Cabbage Patch, Blue Ribbon Eel Reef, The Ledge, The Pinnacle, Yellow Grotto, Annie's Bommie and The Zoo and Vuna Reef off southern Taveuni.

The patch reefs of the Somosomo Strait are fairly shallow (10m to 22m) but have strong tidal currents. The fringing reef in the strait has wall diving (15m to 30m) and larger fish, and is more exposed to weather and surge. The strongest current is actually in the shallow sections over the reefs, lessening with depth. Drift diving is done at some sites. Novice divers may find the currents in the Somosomo Strait challenging, but generally a descent line is used. The area is not just for experienced divers as there are many different sites, and weather conditions vary.

Taveuni Island Resort, Aquaventure and Swiss Fiji Divers are based in Matei, Aqua-Trek at Garden Island Resort in Waiyevo and Vuna Reef Divers and Noks Dive Centre in southern Taveuni. The upmarket resorts on the offshore islands of Matagi, Qamea and Laucala have diving for their guests.

Kayaking From June to September each year, Keni Madden and TC Donovan of Ringgold Reef Kayaking (☎ 880 083) take kayaking/camping tours around Taveuni. They also rent out kayaks during the year; inquire at Beverly Beach Camping. Garden Island Resort at Waiyevo also has ocean kayaks for hire. Some keen kayakers travel the Ravilevu coast.

Hiking Taveuni's Lavena Coastal Walk and Tavoro falls in Bouma National Heritage Park are a must-see for nature lovers. They have marked trails and don't require guides. Keen walkers should consider the Vidawa Forest Walk, also in Bouma, or Des Voeux Peak, or if you are really keen, the trip from Somosomo to Lake Tagimaucia.

Organised Tours
Tatadra Tours at Garden Island Resort (☎ 880 126) in Waiyevo organises group excursions to the island's sights. Taveuni Island Resort and Maravu Plantation Resort, both in Matei, also have organised trips, including bird-watching, rainforest walks, village visits and trips to the Bouma National Heritage Park (F$35) and the Lavena Coastal Walk (F$55).

Accommodation
Taveuni has a good variety of places to stay, ranging from camping and very simple budget places to expensive resorts. Waiyevo has several accommodation options, including the mid-range Kaba's Motel and the more upmarket Garden Island Resort, which also has dorms. While Naqara, next to Somosomo, is not the most picturesque place to stay in Taveuni, it may be convenient for those who have just arrived by boat and want somewhere to crash. Southern Taveuni has budget and mid-range accommodation

and around the airport in Matei there are options to suit all budgets. Eastern Taveuni is a beautiful area and has camping and backpacker accommodation. The upmarket offshore resorts of Qamea, Matagi and Laucala cater mainly to prebooked guests.

Power is by individual generators, which usually run for limited periods.

Some of the mid-range and top-end resorts have dramatically increased their prices since the devaluation of the Fijian dollar in 1998, especially those resorts with ties to America. In general, book in advance, especially in the high season.

Entertainment

Taveuni has many outdoor activities but little to do at night, except perhaps kava drinking. The Meridian Cinema in Wairiki shows movies on Friday, Saturday and Sunday at 7.30 pm.

Shopping

Garden Island Resort in Waiyevo, and Coconut Grove Beachfront Cottage and Maravu Plantation Resort in Matei have the best shops, with local handicrafts.

Getting There & Away

Air The flights to/from Taveuni and Suva or Nadi are stunning – you'll get especially excited if you are a diver! Sunflower Airlines (☎ 880 461) flies to/from Nadi twice daily (F$191 one way, 1½ hours). Air Fiji (☎ 880 062) also flies this route (F$159, at least once daily) and to/from Nausori near Suva (F$114, 55 minutes, two flights daily). Sunflower Airlines flies twice daily to Savusavu and once to Labasa, Vanua Levu (both F$71). Air Fiji has daily flights to Savusavu (F$59).

Matei airport is usually open from 8 am to 4 pm and has a cardphone, kiosk and a toilet block. Margaret Peterson runs the kiosk, selling roti (Indian bread) for F$1.50 as well as scones and other snacks.

Boat The Government Wharf for large vessels, including *Spirit of Free Enterprise (SOFE)* and *Adi Savusavu*, is about 1km north of Waiyevo (towards Matei). Smaller boats depart from the Korean Wharf, a bit farther north. Consort Shipping and Beachcomber Cruises have regular Suva-Savusavu-Taveuni ferries. Prices are competitive. There are also ferry/bus services to Savusavu with Patterson Brothers Shipping and aboard the *Yabula*.

The Patterson Brothers Shipping (☎ 880 036, 880 382) agent is Frank Fong at the Wathi-po-ee Restaurant, near Garden Island Resort in Waiyevo. The trip to Savusavu, on Vanua Levu, involves a ferry across the Somosomo Strait for 1¾ hours to Natuvu, Buca Bay, and then 1½ to two hours on a chartered bus to Savusavu. It can be a long, dusty bus trip, though quite scenic.

Grace (☎ 880 134) departs from the Korean Wharf at 8.30 am daily (except Sunday) for Buca Bay (F$7) and has its own bus to Savusavu for an extra F$7.95. The boat returns at 1 pm. It also does transfers to Rabi at 4 am on Wednesday and Thursday (book by the afternoon before). The only accommodation on Rabi is a guesthouse or camping, and prior permission to visit is required.

The agent for Consort Shipping Line is at the Waiyevo market opposite Garden Island Resort. The MV *SOFE* does twice-weekly Suva-Taveuni voyages via Koro in the Lomaiviti Group and Savusavu (five hours) usually stopping for a couple of hours before proceeding to Suva (another 13 hours).

Beachcomber Cruises' *Adi Savusavu* also does twice-weekly trips to Savusavu and Suva and has better facilities than the *SOFE*. It departs from the Government Wharf. The Taveuni agent is Manoj (☎ 880 591) in Naqara.

Timetables are always changing and the ferries are notorious for delays. The worst thing about the long trips is that the toilets can become disgusting; we recommend that you take your own toilet paper. For more information on services see Ferry in the Getting Around chapter.

Getting Around

A gravel road hugs Taveuni's scenic coast from Lavena in the east to Navakawau in the south. There are also a couple of other inland 4WD tracks. Getting around Taveuni

TAVEUNI

involves a bit of planning, the main disadvantage being the length of time between buses. To get around cheaply and quickly you need to combine buses with walking or hitching, or share taxis with a group.

To/From the Airport From Matei airport expect to pay about F$12 to Waiyevo and F$25 to Vuna (Susie's Plantation) in a taxi. The upmarket resorts provide transfers for guests. See the following entry for information on the local bus service. Matei has many places to stay that are within an easy walk from the airport.

Bus Getting around on the local buses is the best way to meet locals. Pacific Buses (☎ 880 278) has a depot in Naqara, opposite the Taveuni Central Indian School, just south of Somosomo. Monday to Saturday, buses leave for both the north-east (via Matei and Bouma as far as Lavena) and the south-west (via Vuna and Kanacea as far as Navakawau) at 8.30 am, noon and 5 pm. It costs about F$2.50 to travel to the end of the line. The southern bus goes up to Naqarawalu, either on its way to or from Navakawau, depending on how full the bus is. If you wish to continue to Salialevu you will have to walk from Naqarawalu downhill about 8km – the only problem is getting back! It is better to hire a 4WD, taxi or take an organised trip. Beware of getting stranded at the end of the line, as the last buses of the day return the next morning. Lavena has simple accommodation, but Naqarawalu and Navakawau do not. Bus transport on Sunday is restricted to one morning bus from Lavena to Naqara and an afternoon bus from Naqara to Lavena (both one way only). Buses are sometimes full of schoolchildren and it can be frustrating if a bus passes you by and the next one is not for a few hours.

Car Budget Rent a Car (☎ 880 297) has 4WDs. The agent is at the supermarket next to the bakery in Naqara.

Taxi Taxis are readily available in the Matei and Waiyevo areas. It may be wise to book on Sunday. Hiring a taxi for a negotiated fee

and touring most of the island's highlights in a day can be a good idea for a group of people and will probably work out cheaper than hiring a car. For destinations such as Lavena you can go one way by bus and arrange to be picked up at the end at a designated time.

WAIYEVO, SOMOSOMO & AROUND

Waiyevo is the administrative centre of the island. While not a major population centre, it has the island's hospital, police station and representatives of the *SOFE* and Patterson Brothers' ferry services. It is a good base for trips to nearby attractions.

The Government and Korean wharves are both near Lovonivonu, 1km north of Waiyevo (towards Matei). There is a small store on the bend in the road and a school. About 2.5km north of Waiyevo is Naqara, which has Taveuni's main shopping centre and the only bank, and to the north of the river is Somosomo, the island's chiefly village. The influential missionary William Cross is buried here. Naqara and Somosomo have schools, churches and the Great Council of Chiefs' meeting building, built in 1986 for the gathering of important chiefs from all over Fiji.

The 180° meridian passes through Taveuni, about a 10-minute walk south of Waiyevo. There is a sign on the beach side of the road. It's not really very interesting, but the relief map of Taveuni is good for understanding the island's topography. For workability the International Date Line doglegs around Fiji so that everyone is operating on the same time. About 2km south of Waiyevo is Wairiki village, which has a general store, cinema and a beautiful old Catholic Mission on the hill.

Information
Money The only bank on the island is the National Bank at Naqara, just south of Somosomo. The bank will cash travellers cheques but won't do cash advances. The larger supermarkets and top-end resorts accept credit cards, but you may be charged extra. Some resorts will also change travellers cheques.

Post & Communications The post office, on the hill in Waiyevo, is open 8 am to 4 pm (closed for lunch 1 to 2 pm) weekdays. It has a fax service. There are cardphones here and outside the supermarkets in Waiyevo and Naqara.

Emergency Taveuni's health facilities are being upgraded thanks to funding from the Australian and Fijian governments. Its emergency services include a hospital (☎ 880 444) and police (☎ 880 222).

Wairiki Catholic Mission

Wairiki Mission, built in 1907, is about 20 minutes' walk from Waiyevo, past the 180° Meridian sign. The mission overlooks a playing field and the Somosomo Strait. An important canoe battle took place off this beach in the mid-17th century. At the time, Tongan chief Elene Ma'afu had gained control of much of the rest of Fiji. The Taveuni warriors, however, managed to turn back the invading Tongans, who numbered in the thousands. Reportedly, the dead enemies were cooked in *lovo* (feast in which food is cooked in a pit oven) and eaten with *uru* (breadfruit)! The mission was built to thank the French missionary who helped the local warriors with their fighting strategy.

It's worth attending Mass for the fantastic singing (Sunday at 7 am and 9 am); make sure you leave a small donation. The stained glass is thought to have been imported from France, and in the presbytery there is a painting of the famous battle.

Waitavala Waterslide

This natural waterslide is about 25 minutes' walk from Waiyevo supermarket. From the supermarket, with Garden Island Resort on the left, walk north towards Matei and take the first road to the right (about 500m past the resort). At the first fork in the road, keep to the right. Continue up the hill, passing another turn-off to the right, and then past a large shed. Take the next left turn downhill, which leads to a creek and a bridge. The path to the waterslide, or rather waterslides, veers off before the creek following it upstream to the right. It is on the Waitavala estate, which is private land, so if you pass anyone on your way there ask if you can visit. It's probably best to watch a local before attempting a slide as the conditions vary with the water flow and it may be dangerous.

Des Voeux Peak

At 1195m, Des Voeux Peak is Taveuni's second-highest mountain, after Uluigalau at 1241m. The views are great on a clear day and it is possible to see Lake Tagimaucia. Try to make it up there by dawn if you are a keen bird-watcher. To get here take the inland track just before you reach Wairiki Catholic Mission (coming from Waiyevo). Allow three to four hours to walk the 6km up, and at least two to return. It's a steep, arduous climb in the heat, so it's best to go up early. Alternatively, arrange for a trip up and then walk back at your leisure. On weekdays it is sometimes possible to hitch a ride with Telecom or Public Works Department (PWD) workers who go up to service their equipment. Driving requires a 4WD. Hire a vehicle in Naqara (see Getting Around earlier in this chapter) or ask at the travel desk at Garden Island Resort about organised trips.

Lake Tagimaucia

Lake Tagimaucia is in an old volcanic crater, 823m above sea level, in the mountains above Somosomo. Masses of vegetation float on the lake, and the national flower, the rare *tagimaucia* (an epiphytic plant) grows on the lake's shores. This red flower with a white centre blooms from late September to late December and only at this altitude.

It is a difficult walk as it is overgrown and often very muddy. Take lunch and allow eight hours for the round trip. The track starts from Naqara or Somosomo. Hire a guide from the village or ask Garden Island Resort to arrange one for you. Alternatively, the lake can be viewed from Des Voeux Peak.

Activities

Aqua-Trek Taveuni, based at Garden Island Resort, is a well-equipped dive shop with good boats, Nitrox facilities and photo centre. It organises dives at Rainbow Reef

The Legend of the Tagimaucia

One day a young girl was disobedient and her mother lost patience with her. While beating the girl with a bundle of coconut leaves, she told her she never wanted to see her face again. The distraught girl ran away as far as she could until deep in the forest she came upon a large vine-covered *ivi* (Polynesian chestnut) tree. She climbed the tree and became entangled in the vine. She wept and wept and the tears rolling down her face turned to blood, falling onto the vine and becoming beautiful *tagimaucia* flowers. Eventually she managed to escape the forest and returned home, relieved to find her mother had calmed down.

(about 20 minutes by boat). Two dives cost F$165, six dives (three days) F$470 (tanks and belts only). Equipment rental costs F$35/25 for one day/three days or more. Open-water courses cost F$660. The small island of Korolevu, off the resort, has beaches with good snorkelling – trips cost F$10 per person.

Swimming at Waiyevo in front of the Garden Island Resort is possible two hours either side of high tide. Watch the current though and don't swim near Korean Wharf as sharks are sometimes attracted here by fish cleaning.

Places to Stay

Naqara isn't a very interesting place to stay, however, it has a couple of accommodation options. *Kool's Accommodation* (☎ 880 395) is in Naqara. The friendly manager, Chitra Singh, has six very basic rooms in a long block for F$15/22 for singles/doubles. There is electricity from 6 pm to 11 pm, but no fan. Shared facilities include a toilet, shower and a kitchen, where you can cook for yourself, but there is no fridge. Security has reportedly been a problem in the past.

Kaba's Motel (☎ 880 233, postal address: PO Box 4, Somosomo) in Naqara has a guesthouse and a motel block. The guesthouse has four spartan rooms, which share a TV room,

kitchen, two toilets, shower and laundry trough. Rooms have a phone each and cost F$25/30. The newer motel block has six clean, fan-cooled singles/doubles/triples for F$45/55/60. They have tiled floors, TV, telephone, hot water and kitchenettes. Kaba's supermarket is 200m down the road.

Near the Korean wharf at Lovonivonu, south of Naqara, is the very basic *Sunset Accommodation* (☎ 880 229). The basic shack to the side of the small shop has a single and double room opening onto a small sitting area and kitchen for F$15/20. The generator provides electricity between 6 and 10 pm. Theresa will cook you a meal for F$3 or F$4.

Garden Island Resort (☎ 880 286, fax 880 288, ✉ garden@is.com.fj) has good accommodation at mid-range prices. There is no beach, but a pleasant pool and restaurant-bar area looks out to the Somosomo Strait and Vanua Levu beyond. There are some beautiful old flame trees on the site. The double-storey building used to be Travelodge in the 1970s. The rooms have air-con, fans, mosquito screens, sea views and sliding doors to the garden or upstairs to a verandah.

The resort quotes its prices in US$. Rooms cost F$132/168; the optional meal plan is F$75 per person for three meals. Two of the hotel rooms (no air-con) are used as dorms (up to four people in each) for F$30 per person, which is good value.

Places to Eat

Garden Island Resort restaurant has breakfast for under F$10, lunch from F$8 to F$11 and dinner from F$22 to F$27. The food is good quality with a mixture of styles. Happy hour is from 6 to 7 pm. Outsiders are welcome, but order dinner in the afternoon.

Wathi-po-ee Restaurant and Cannibal Cafe next door has cheap Chinese food. It is pretty basic, but its thatched outdoor area overlooking the Somosomo Strait is a pleasant place for a beer.

Directly opposite Garden Island Resort is Waiyevo's small *market*, which has a couple of very basic eateries and takeaway stalls serving Fijian-style food.

In Somosomo, *Jo's Restaurant*, opposite Kaba's Motel, has very simple curries, chop suey or fried rice for F$3.

Waiyevo has a good *supermarket* selling basics, including bread and ice cream. The market sells fresh fish, but it can be difficult to buy fresh fruit and vegetables as the villagers usually grow for their own use. Wairiki has a general store and Kaba's store/supermarket in Somosomo takes credit cards.

SOUTHERN TAVEUNI

The main villages on southern Taveuni are Naqarawalu, in the hills, and, on the southern coast near Vuna Reef, Kanacea, Vuna and Navakawau. The people of Kanacea are descendants of peoples whose island was sold by Tui Cakau to Europeans. Their ancestors were displaced as punishment for siding with the Tongans in a war.

Things to See

The road south from Waiyevo to the Vuna area winds along the rugged coast through beautiful rainforest and dalo and coconut plantations to Vuna and Kanacea villages. About 8km (15 minutes' drive) south of Waiyevo is the **Taveuni Estates** real estate development, previously known as Soqulu Plantation. The initial company went bankrupt, however, it is now under new management. While a few hundred lots have been sold, only about 30 homes were built at the time of writing. Inquire about advance booking of villas for long-term stays. The nine-hole golf course, pool, two tennis courts and a lawn bowls green are, however, open for public use (☎ 880 044): The cost is F$20 for green fees or F$10 per day for tennis. On weekends the bar is a club for locals. The rainforest in this area is excellent for bird-watching.

Also in the area is an ancient **Warrior Burial Cave**. This cave was once used as a hidden cemetery for warriors, so that their death would be kept secret from enemies, for the same reason some chiefs were buried inside their own *bure* (thatched dwelling). The lava tube cave runs for about 360m down to the ocean, but the entrance has been sealed.

At the end of the road past Naqarawalu is Salialevu, a large freehold copra plantation and beef farm, historically important for the remains of **Billyard Sugar Mill** from last century.

Vatuwiri Farm Resort, at Vuna Point, is another farm of interest. In its heyday it was one of the main copra estates on Taveuni. The 800-hectare farm is still one of the biggest on Taveuni (the largest is about 1600 hectares). James Tarte established the estate in 1871 and introduced the magpie into Taveuni to control stick insects. There are some interesting old stone buildings, including tiny cottages and kitchens for the blackbirded (kidnapped and sold into slavery) and indentured labourers who worked here. Economic necessity has driven the Tarte family to diversify into cocoa, vanilla, sugar, cattle, Fijian asparagus, *voy voy* (tree for mats) and tourism. The remains of the old **Vuna village hill fortification**, above the present villages of Vuna and Kanacea and partly on Vatuwiri Farm Resort land, are worth a visit if you are interested in archaeology, although you won't see much if the site is overgrown. The village was built on a strategic point and natural lookout, from where it was possible to survey the Vuna reef for intruding canoes. Large flat areas are linked by crossings over deep defensive ditches. Many stone foundations remain to tell their story: The tallest one would have been the chief's bure, linked to that of his wives; the one with a double base was the temple; and the largest was the meeting bure. Shells, pottery, axes and sea-washed rocks have been found at the site.

The **Blow Hole**, south-east of Vuna village, performs best on a big south-westerly swell. However, don't come down to this end of the island just for this, unless you have never seen a blow hole before.

Activities

Diving and snorkelling on the Vuna Reef is very good; go through Vuna Reef Divers at Susie's Plantation or Noks Dive Centre at Kris Back Palace. You are likely to see big fish, beautiful coral and the occasional shark. Vuna Reef Divers (☎/fax 880 125)

TAVEUNI

has OK dive equipment and dive boats, and lessons are available in English and German. It offers two-tank boat dives for F$95 and open-water courses for F$400, including all equipment. With Noks Dive Centre a two-tank dive, including equipment, costs F$99, or F$22 for a shore dive.

Susie's Plantation offers trips to Namoli Beach (north of Vuna and Kanacea villages) and the blowhole, and horse riding. A four-hour ride through thick rainforest to a volcanic crater costs about F$35 per person.

Vatuwiri Farm Resort offers reef fishing for F$15 per day for a minimum of two people, game fishing and horse riding for F$30/35 per day for guests/nonguests (group of four), trips to the fortified village site or to a volcano crater, cattle mustering, trekking, and fruit bat- and bird-watching. *Lady Vuna,* a 12m catamaran, can be chartered for F$1000 per night or F$750 for a day trip with food and drinks included.

Places to Stay & Eat

The Palms (☎/fax 880 241) has accommodation in a 120-year-old Soqulu Plantation historic home with five bedrooms for rent. Otherwise, southern Taveuni has only budget accommodation. Those wanting contact with Fijian village life should try Salote's *Vuna Lagoon Lodge (☎/fax 880 627,* **@** *bulavakaviti@is.com.fj).* It has simple and clean rooms, two minutes' walk from Vuna village on the edge of Vuna Lagoon. The house has a kitchen, laundry with washing machine, sitting area and verandah. Some rooms have en suite and fans. Electricity is on from 6 to 11 pm. Rooms cost F$30/50 for singles/doubles, or F$12 each in a four-bed dorm. You can cook for yourself with free fruit and vegetables from the garden. Otherwise, home-cooked meals cost F$5 for breakfast, F$3 to F$5 for lunch and F$10 to F$15 for dinner. There is a sandy beach nearby; bring your own (BYO) snorkelling gear. Present a *sevusevu* (gift, such as *yaqona,* the drink made from kava) to the chief upon arrival. Vehicles can be hired from the village for around F$60, or F$5 for a horse. Other activities include fishing, kava sessions and snorkelling.

Susie's Plantation (☎/fax 880 125) was established as a copra plantation in the 1850s. The resort was operational but pretty rundown at the time of writing. There is no beach but the black-lava rock contrasting with the turquoise water is quite beautiful. The large garden has fruit and coconut trees, and orchids. It has camping for F$8.50 per person and beds in a basic 12-bed dorm for F$12 per person. Sharing a double room costs F$15 per person. Don't leave your valuables here, as the dorm building is not far from the road and robberies have been reported. There are basic kitchen facilities, a toilet and a shower, with cold water only. The main house has few rooms of varying size and price, ranging from F$38 to F$55. Across the garden there are three private bure, each with self-catering facilities (no fridge), en suites and mosquito nets. They are fairly rustic but comfortable and cost from F$60 to F$70. Breakfast is F$5.50 for fruit and toast or F$10 for eggs, fruit, toast and cereal. Lunch is F$12 and a three-course dinner is F$16. Kava drinking is the nighttime entertainment. MasterCard and Visa are accepted but incur a 5% charge.

Kris Back Palace (☎ 880 246, fax 880 072), run by friendly Fiji-Indian couple Saviri and Bobby Shankaran, has budget (far from palatial) accommodation. It is fairly isolated, about 7km north of Vuna village, on a rugged section of rocky coastline. There is no beach, but snorkelling is good; it's possible to swim through underwater caves. The dorm, a simple thatched geometric bure, sleeps five people for F$15 per person. Mosquito nets and linen are provided. The double bure costs F$30. It is very basic, with a veranda and concrete floor, and is near the water's edge. The toilets, showers and laundry trough are a bit distant from the bure, so watch you don't sprain an ankle on the rough terrain at night! Camping is F$7 per person. Electricity is available from 6 to 9 pm. The very rustic kitchen hut, right on the water's edge, has a stove and sink but you can also cook at the owner's house across the road. Alternatively, Saviri will provide three meals (Indian and Fijian) for F$18 per day.

Vatuwiri Farm Resort (☎ 880 316, fax 880 314) has a couple of accommodation options for guests. Staying here will give you an insight into life on a plantation from the viewpoint of a part-European family. The three small beachfront cottages cost F$110 per night; each has a double bed and sitting area and a semidetached en suite. One, perched on the water's edge with a porch, also has a kitchen that can take a single bed. A room with en suite in the homestead also costs F$110 per night. A long weatherboard building with a veranda, which used to be the estate workers' quarters and feels a bit like a stable, has been converted into six rooms (up to three people per room) and costs F$30 per person. There are no cooking facilities, but up at the homestead you can get three meals a day, afternoon tea, fruit and snacks for F$60 per person. Solar electricity is available.

The Vuna area has a couple of small *general stores* including one near Vatuwiri Farm, which opens only occasionally. The shop in Kanacea has a limited range. Families grow fruit and vegetables for their own use only, so it is almost impossible to buy fresh produce. There is a local butcher who also sells beer.

Getting There & Away
It's about one hour by car or about two hours by local bus from Matei airport to the Vuna village area, along a winding, mostly rough road that hugs the coast. The section from Waiyevo to Vuna is beautiful and passes through dense, verdant forest and dalo and coconut plantations. See Getting Around earlier in this chapter for more information. Expect to pay F$30/20 from the airport/ferry wharf by taxi to Susie's Plantation and F$35/25 to Vuna village, or F$5/2.60 by bus.

MATEI & AROUND
Matei is a fast-growing residential area around the airport. The freehold land is popular with Americans and other foreigners searching for a piece of tropical paradise. Prince Charles Beach and Beverly Beach are OK for snorkelling. The four small islands

immediately offshore from Naselesele Point have some good snorkelling (the third is known as the local 'Honeymoon Island'). Farther to the east is the larger Viubani.

Diving
The small, reliable dive shop Aquaventure (☎/fax 880 381, ✉ aquaventure@is.com.fj) is based at Beverly Beach, about 1km west of the Matei airport. Dive trips cost F$115 for a two-tank dive, with tanks and weights only (F$20 extra for full equipment). Openwater courses, including full equipment hire (four to five days), cost F$478. Multidive packages and other courses are also available. Aquaventure will also take snorkellers out to the reefs if space is available on the dive boat (maximum six).

Swiss Fiji Divers (☎/fax 880 586, ✉ sfd@is.com.fj) is a new dive shop just north of Beverly Beach Camping that offers high-quality gear, including computer consoles, masks with underwater communication, and scooters. Two-tank dives cost F$180 for tanks and weights only (F$60 a day extra for basic equipment rental). An openwater course including all gear costs F$690.

Taveuni Island Resort has its own dive operation for guests (see Places to Stay – Top End in this section).

Places to Stay – Budget
Margaret Peterson (☎ 880 171), the friendly woman at the airport kiosk, has two double *rooms* in her house, which she rents for F$35/70 for singles/doubles, including three meals. If you can't find her at the kiosk, try her house. It is about a five-minute walk from the airport towards Waiyevo, through a beautiful stretch of forest that was unfortunately butchered during the roadworks. Hers is the drive on the left at the bus stop and her house is up the hill. Margaret is also a good cook.

Bibi's Hideaway (☎ 880 443, 880 365, postal address: PO Box 80, Waiyevo) is owned and run by the amiable James Biba. Unlike most places in the area, James has been able to maintain the same prices here for a decade. He has three self-contained cottages in his large garden in a quiet and convenient location, about seven minutes from the airport towards Waiyevo. Bibi is happy to give guests some of the produce from his garden: bananas, pawpaws, mangoes, pineapples, oranges, coconuts, guavas and kava.

The two simple cottages have spacious sitting rooms and kitchens, and there is a newer bure, built mostly with the rent money obtained when the film crew of *Return to the Blue Lagoon* spent some time there. The oldest cottage costs F$27.50/ 38.50 and can accommodate up to seven people (each extra adult F$10). The other two-bedroom cottage costs F$30 per room, singles or doubles. The self-contained bure, with its cane-lined interior, a large window with a view to the garden and verandah, costs F$50 a single or double. All units have fridges and mosquito nets. It is also possible to camp here for F$10/15 or F$8/12 if you have your own tent.

Karin's Garden (*☎/fax 880 511*), just across the road from Bibi's, is on a long, narrow block of land that ends in a steep cliff. It has a spectacular bird's-eye view of the reef. The one accommodation unit with two bedrooms opens off a tall central kitchen and dining room, and onto a long veranda. It is spacious and comfortable, with plywood lining and timber floors. Each double/twin room has its own en suite, wardrobe, hot water and fan but the generator is turned off at 10 pm. Prices are F$95 per room and a minimum stay of two nights applies.

There are a couple of camping sites southwest of the airport. There is a new *camping ground* on the northernmost point of the island, which has spectacular views from the cliff overlooking the Somosomo Strait. It had good, spacious tents at the time of writing. *Beverly Beach Camping* (*☎ 880 684*) is about 15 minutes' walk from the airport, past Taveuni Island Resort and Maravu Plantation Resort. The camp, squeezed between the road and along the edge of a white-sand beach beneath fantastic, huge, poison-fish trees, is a good place to lay back and relax on the beach. It accommodates a maximum of 12 people. Camp sites cost F$8 per person (with or without tent). The camp

has seen better days; the bure were blown over by Cyclone Gavin and the sealing of the road has encroached on its space. It has very basic facilities including flush toilets, shower and a sheltered area for cooking and dining. The atmosphere can be fun. Bill sometimes brings around fresh fruit and vegetables in the morning. He also provides equipment for snorkelling and fishing.

Another five minutes' walk farther south and across the road from the Prince Charles Beach is *Lisi's Campsite & Cottage* (*☎ 880 194*), Vacala Estate, c/o PA Matei. Unfortunately, the sandy beach, previously the best on Taveuni, was largely washed away by Cyclone Gavin. It offers basic facilities for campers for F$5 per person. There is also a five-bedroom cottage with shared bathroom for F$15/25. Simple meals can be provided.

There are also a couple of budget places east of the airport. *Niranjan's Budget Accommodation* (*☎ 880 406*), c/o PA Matei, is three minutes' walk east of the airport. It has four self-contained, rather shabby rooms with cooking facilities for F$35/45. Children under 10 pay F$8.80. Curry dinners cost F$15. A dorm in the old shop at the front is planned; beds will cost F$15 per person.

Tovutovu Resort (*☎ 880 560, fax 880 722*) is about 20 minutes' walk south-east of Matei airport, past the Bhula Bhai Supermarket towards Naselesele village. It is run by Alan Petersen on the family's copra plantation. The front two self-contained bure have small kitchenettes and cost F$75, sleeping three in each. The two rear bure with private toilet and shower but no cooking facilities cost F$65 for singles or doubles. Bure have mosquito screens, hot water, and fans and power from 5 to 9 pm. The eight-bed dorm on higher ground at the back of the resort is very simple with a wonky floor, but is nevertheless a good option for backpackers. It has a communal kitchen and deck with views and costs F$15 per bed. Bikes can be hired for F$15 per day, and snorkelling trips cost F$10. It also has a restaurant and family chapel on the hill. Farther up past the end of the airport runway is an old village lookout site.

Places to Stay – Mid-Range

It seems that just about everyone in Matei has a cottage or two for rent in their garden, some of which can be shared and are good value for groups or families. There are several houses available for short-term rental – contact Dolores Porter (☎ 880 461, 880 299) at the Sunflower Airlines desk at the airport.

Three minutes' walk east of the airport is *Coconut Grove Beachfront Cottage* (☎/fax 880 328, ✉ coconutgrove@is.com.fj), with two cute beachfront cottages and a guestroom within the restaurant/house. The guestroom has a double bed, en suite, hot water and fan for F$110. The larger freestanding cottage has a double and a single bed, fan, fridge, cooking facilities, woven mats, timber floor and a private open-air shower for F$176 for up to three people. The smaller cosier unit has a double bed, en suite, fan and verandah for F$132. Walk-in rates may apply, especially from January to March. There are nice views across the water to the islets, and access through the garden to a small private beach.

About three minutes' walk farther on is another self-contained apartment, *Lomalagi Beachfront Cottage* (☎ 880 299) c/o PA Matei. It can be rented for F$100 a night for a double (F$5 per extra person, maximum four) or for F$600 per week. Speak to Dolores Porter at the Sunflower Airlines desk at the airport or the caretaker that lives on the property (there is no sign on the gate). The unit has cooking facilities, fridge and solar power. It is joined to the owner's unit by a common deck, which overlooks the beach.

Sere-ni-ika (☎ 880 164), two doors down from Lomalagi Beachfront Cottage, is a large house with spacious kitchen, living area and verandah that overlooks the sea. It costs F$150 a night for a double plus F$10 for each extra guest (maximum six). A laundry service, meals and baby-sitting can be arranged.

American expat Audrey Brown, famous for her home-made biscuits, runs *Audrey's by the Sea* (☎ 880 039), a comfortable self-contained cottage in her garden, costing F$105. Located on a small hill about 10 minutes' walk down the road east of Matei's airport, it is across the road from the sea and close to the local supermarket. The cottage has an open geometric plan like her house, with views to the water through the coconut trees. It has a tizzy plush interior – white and turquoise with lots of cushions and lacy curtains. Children are not allowed.

Little Dolphin Treehouse (☎ 880 130) is in a beautiful spot between Audrey's and Bhula Bhai Supermarket. It has a great view of the ocean and islands, and the unit is good value for F$55 a day. The Treehouse is a cute double-storey building with polished timber floors, a double bed upstairs, and single bed, kitchen and bathroom with hot water downstairs. It has electricity from sunset to 10.30 pm.

Places to Stay – Top End

Well-established *Taveuni Island Resort* (☎ 880 441, fax 880 466, ✉ info@divetaveuni .com) is about 10 minutes' walk from the airport towards Waiyevo, on a spectacular cliff site overlooking the Somosomo Strait. The resort, set in an immaculately maintained garden, has recently undergone renovations, which included the addition of a beautiful cliff-top swimming pool. The deck built out over the cliff is great for watching sunsets. You can walk down to a small, white-sand beach.

The units have covered decks with views, king-size beds, air-con, fans, minibars and outdoor showers in private courtyards. Accommodation costs F$550/660 standard/ luxury per person a night, including meals, transfers and nonalcoholic drinks. Credit cards are accepted. Children under 15 years are not accepted. The majority of guests are on prebooked packages, mostly divers or honeymooners. Meals are a gourmet's delight and dining is on the restaurant deck. The resort's dive operation caters mainly to prebooked guests as well. A two-tank morning dive is F$220 per person, including lunch. It also has snorkelling trips, including lunch. One reader has raved about the operation's excellent planning and the food provided.

On the hill across the road from Taveuni Island Resort is *Maravu Plantation Resort* (☎ *880 555, fax 880 600,* ☎ *maravu@ is.com.fj).* The 22-hectare property is also a working copra plantation. The 10 standard units here have an en suite, ceiling fan, minibar, tea- and coffee-making facilities, and verandah with hammocks. There are also two standard interconnecting rooms. The five deluxe bure have timber cladding, reed lining and parquetry floors; they sleep up to four people. There are three honeymoon bure with private outdoor showers and sundeck. Standard units cost F$340/476/590 for singles/doubles/triples, and deluxe versions cost F$390/558/719, or F$600 a double for honeymoon bure. The resort has a good pool and baby-sitting is available. Prices include three gourmet meals a day and transfers. Organised activities for guests include horse riding, plantation tours, snorkelling trips and trips to sites around the island. Diving is through Swiss Fiji Divers.

Places to Eat

Restaurants & Cafes One of Taveuni's best places to eat is *Coconut Grove Cafe* (☎ *880 328),* just east of the airport terminal. It is the home of Ronna Goldstein and her well-mannered Doberman, Gracy. Dining is on her verandah, overlooking the water, islets and a cute beach. Try the best fresh-fruit shakes on Taveuni for F$3 to F$4. The restaurant offers breakfast from F$3.50 to F$6, including banana bread, and lunch for F$5 to F$10. Dinner mains are in the F$12.50 to F$20 range. The menu is displayed on the front door. Place your dinner order before 4 pm and if Ronna is not at home you can leave a note. The menu includes fresh vegetables, home-made pasta, salads, fish, delicious desserts such as passionfruit cream pie and chocolate fudge cake, and real coffee. There is an 'Island Tunes' and buffet night twice-weekly. Ronna also has a small gift shop with cards, jewellery, T-shirts and woven baskets. The restaurant is usually closed January through to March.

Karin's Garden (☎ *880 511)* serves good European-style food. It is just across the road from Bibi's Hideaway. Cooked breakfasts

cost F$6 to F$10, spaghetti and sandwiches cost F$4 to F$13 and set-menu dinners cost F$20. Dinner is meat or fish and normally doesn't cater for vegetarians. Book for dinner before 3 pm and check what is on the day's menu. The bread and yogurt is homemade and the vegetables come from the garden. Credit cards are not accepted. The view from the cliff farther down the block is spectacular at sunset, and on a clear day you can see large fish and dolphins swimming past.

The restaurant at *Tovutovu Resort* has an outdoor deck overlooking Viubani. The food is good value, with main courses ranging from F$7 to F$15. There is a buffet and music on Friday nights for F$15.

Margaret Peterson, who sells snacks at the airport kiosk, also prepares dinner at her *home* (great food and lots of it) for F$15 per person. Let her know in advance. *Lal's Curry Place* (☎ *880 705),* south-east of the airport on the front porch of a house, has good Indian food. Ideally, order one hour in advance. A meal of rice, roti, curry, chutney and soup costs F$10.

Audrey's Sweet Something's, 10 minutes' walk east of the airport, is a good place for brewed coffee and cake, including sponge torte with jam filling, almond-meringue top, coconut and pineapple cake, chocolate cookies, lime tarts and fudge cake.

Maravu Plantation Resort's restaurant is excellent but pricey at F$30/40 for the set lunch/dinner.

Fast Food The airport *kiosk* opens for plane arrivals and departures and sells roti parcels, muffins and scones.

Local taxi driver Mahabir (☎ 880 545) will deliver *takeaway* Indian curries, mutton or chicken with rice and dhal in the Matei area for around F$8. Give about an hour's advance warning.

Mrs Harry's (☎ 880 404) takeaway curries are good value and popular among campers staying at Beverly Beach. Bansraji (Harry's wife) prepares the meals at her house up on the hill almost opposite Beverly Beach Camping. It is best if you order before 4 pm for dinner, and she will also cook lunch if you order in advance. Curries and vegetarian dishes cost F$3 or F$5 for fish or meat with roti and dhal.

Self-Catering Bhula Bhai Supermarket in Matei (☎ 880 462, fax 880 050) is open from 7 am to 5.30 pm daily (closed Sunday). It sells a range of groceries, film, stationery, clothing and phonecards and accepts Visa and MasterCard (charge 10%, F$90 limit). The local cardphone and bus stop is also here.

Getting There & Away

The island's airport is at Matei (for more information on air services, see the introductory Getting There & Away section earlier in this chapter). Matei is about 45 minutes by bus from Waiyevo (see the introductory Getting Around section earlier in this chapter).

EASTERN TAVEUNI

Eastern Taveuni's beautiful, wild coast and lush rainforest are a magnet for nature lovers. Scenes for the 1991 movie, *Return to the Blue Lagoon,* were filmed at Bouma National Heritage Park's Tavoro Falls, and at Lavena beach. The villagers have rejected logging in favour of ecotourism. The Bouma Environmental Tourism Project is helping to preserve land and sea resources while creating an income from visitors. The project was initiated by landowners and the New Zealand Maruia, Royal Forest and Bird Protection societies. Funding and assistance was received from the Fijian and New Zealand governments. The people of Bouma planned and built the extensive trails.

Bouma National Heritage Park

This national park protects over 80% of Taveuni's total area , covering about 15,000 hectares of rainforest and coastal forest. The park has several kilometres of bush walks and the three beautiful (modest size) **Tavoro Waterfalls**, with natural swimming pools. The walking track begins opposite the reception bure, south of the river in Bouma. The first waterfall is about 24m high. It is only 10 minutes' walk along a flat and easy path, which is well maintained.

There is a screened area for changing and a few picnic tables and BBQ plates.

The second waterfall, a bit smaller than the first, also has a good swimming pool. To reach it continue along the path for another 30 to 40 minutes. Initially the track is quite steep, but has steps, handrails and lookout spots with seats. The view through the coconut trees to the zigzagging reef and the island of Qamea beyond is quite spectacular. Over the hill the track passes through rainforest and along the way a river crossing has a rope to help you jump from stone to stone. Reaching the third fall involves a hike along a less maintained, often muddy path through the forest for an extra 30 minutes. Smaller than the other two (about 10m high), it has a great swimming pool and rocks for jumping off (check for obstructions first!).

The park fee is F$5, or F$7 per person for a guided waterfall tour. Morning and afternoon teas and lunch are available at the reception bure (open 9 am to 4 pm) and there is an area where you can *camp* (☎ 880 390, ✉ *TRCNZ@compuserve.com, postal address: c/o PA Bouma*) with thatched shelters, toilets and baggage storage.

If you are keen walker, try the **Vidawa Forest Walk**. It is a full-day guided walk (it can only be done with guides – you cannot go on your own) that starts at Vidawa village, goes to the historic fortified village sites of Navuga and follows trails into the rainforest (prolific birdlife here), through river streams and down to the waterfalls near Bouma. Book in advance. The trip runs every Friday or by special arrangement for groups (maximum of eight). It costs F$40/60 for children/adults, including pickup and drop-off at resorts around Taveuni, guides, lunch, afternoon tea and park fee.

Getting There & Away By local bus, Bouma park is 45 minutes from Matei, and 1½ hours from Naqara. A taxi (up to five people) will cost F$15 to F$20. See the introductory Getting Around section earlier in this chapter for bus times. A new tourist transport service is being set up by the park administration.

If you are in the mood for a marathon it is possible to catch the early morning bus to Bouma, make a flying visit to all three waterfalls, and catch the early afternoon bus at about 1.40 pm on to Lavena. In a rush you can do the coastal walk before dark and either stay overnight at Lavena or be picked up by a pre-arranged taxi. The early afternoon bus returns to Matei and the late afternoon bus spends the night at Lavena.

Lavena Coastal Walk

Lavena village is at the end of the road and, while it is not easy to get to, it's worth the trouble. The white-sand beach is good for swimming and snorkelling, and there is even surf here, though not consistently. The currents can be strong. The park entry fee of F$5 per person, payable at the reception bure, entitles you to use the beaches and the coastal walk.

The Lavena Coastal Walk is a beautiful hike along the forest edge, with the gorgeous **Wainibau Falls** as a reward at the end. However, you should take care at the falls: Water levels can increase rapidly, as one reader, who visited the falls with friends, found out:

We got caught in a violent flash flood and almost drowned. After talking to many locals we found out that these flash floods develop relatively frequently at these falls, even if it hasn't been raining in the area. Just a few weeks (before) a local teenager got caught and swept away. They found him unconscious halfway down the river...People should stay to the left of the pool at the bottom of the falls...if people swim to the right (where the water looks calmer) they run the danger of getting stuck and drowning.

Ulla Bunz

The 5km of well-marked path is mostly easy; allow at least three hours return. The first 1.5km is parallel to a long, white-sand beach, changing to black volcanic sand beach and becoming increasingly rocky. About halfway are strange pedestal formations caused by the coral base layer being eroded by the sea water, leaving bulbous rock shapes on fine bases. The track continues past a village, across a suspension bridge at Wainisairi Creek (the only stream

to flow out of Lake Tagimaucia) and up the valley of Wainibau Creek. This creek forms the boundary of the Bouma (Wainikeli) and Vuna lands and is also the boundary of the Ravilevu Nature Reserve to the south. To see and reach the falls you have to walk over rocks and swim a short distance through two deep pools, so you'll need a waterproof camera to take shots. Be careful about leaving your gear here, however. Two cascades fall at different angles into a deep pool with sheer walls. There are lots of fish in the creek.

Places to Stay & Eat The *reception bure* (☎ 880 116 801, radio telephone) at Lavena now offers four twin-share rooms with small kitchen, dining area overlooking the beach, and shower and toilet, which overnight guests share with day visitors and office/reception. It costs F$15 per person. It is also possible to camp if you have your own tent for F$7 per person. There is an outdoor table and seats in a cute shaded spot on the point. The village *store* nearby has the usual tinned fish and meat, noodles and eggs, but you may need to buy fresh produce direct from the locals or bring your own. Meals can be provided by local families for under F$10.

Getting There & Away Lavena village is about 15 minutes' drive past Bouma, 35 minutes from Matei. However, by local bus it takes about one hour from Matei or just under two from Waiyevo. On Tuesday and Thursday the early morning bus from Naqara goes on to Lavena. The last bus stays in Lavena and returns to Waiyevo the next morning at 6.15 am, so you may need to arrange in advance for a Matei taxi to pick you up. Expect to pay around F$25 for a taxi to/from Matei. See the introductory Getting Around section earlier in this chapter for information on taxi services and the local bus services from Naqara via Matei. If you have your own mountain bike, allow about 3½ hours of hot, hard work one way. A new tourist transport service to Lavena is being set up by the park administration.

Savulevu Yavonu Falls

The Ravilevu coast is the section from Lavena Point down to Salialevu on the rough, exposed eastern side of Taveuni. It is a straight stretch of coast without any foreshore, but with cliffs and open ocean. About halfway along, the 20m high Savulevu Yavonu waterfall plunges off a cliff into the sea. During WWII, ships used the falls as a fresh water depot, going directly under the flow to refill their water reservoir. Access to the falls is by boat only, and is dependent on the weather as the ocean can get very rough on this side of the island; day trips cost F$80 for a group of three to six. Inquire at Lavena's reception bure.

OFFSHORE ISLANDS

Qamea, Laucala and Matagi are a group of islands just east of Thurston Point across the Tasman Strait from north-eastern Taveuni. Qamea and Laucala are located inside a lagoon formed by a single barrier reef, which wraps around the south-east side, broken only by a passage east of Laucala. The islands have lovely white-sand beaches. The original inhabitants of Qamea and Laucala were displaced by local chiefs in the mid-19th century for siding with Tongan chief Enele Ma'afu during a war. Laucala and Matagi are privately owned. Each island has an upmarket resort, catering mainly to diving and game-fishing enthusiasts. Generally the only travellers who see these beautiful islands are resort visitors, although others may be able to visit Qamea if invited by local villagers. If you are lucky enough to fly over, the view is superb.

Matagi

Stunning horseshoe-shaped Matagi, formed by a submerged volcanic crater, is 10km off Taveuni's coast. The island is only about 100 hectares in area, with steep rainforest sides rising to 130m.

The bay faces north to open sea and there is a fringing reef on the south-west side of the island where the ***Matangi Island Resort*** *(☎ 880 260, fax 880 274, ✉ matangiisland@ is.com.fj)* is situated along a white-sand beach. The Douglas family began this small-scale resort in 1987, catering for a maximum of 32 guests. Children of any age are accepted and baby-sitting is available. All accommodation have en suite, ceiling fan, stocked fridge and tea- and coffee-making facilities. The food here is very good. The generator supplies power 24 hours a day and all bure have gas hot water.

There are eight spacious, circular-plan bure with umbrella-like roofs, which sleep up to four people and an infant. The rooms have an en suite, ceiling fan, stocked fridge and tea- and coffee-making facilities. Rates are usually quoted in US dollars. Rates including all meals and most activities are F$332/610/828 for singles/doubles/triples for standard rectangular bure, and F$436/ 822/1154 for spacious circular bure.

Alternatively, the fantastic 'treehouses' cost F$488. They are perched about 5m up in the tree canopy with views to the beach, Qamea, Taveuni and beyond. Kids would love them but they are reserved for honeymooners and couples only. They have split levels, separate lounge and outdoor decks.

Rates include private picnic lunches in the secluded bay, a day trip to Taveuni, and nonmotorised water sports (windsurfing, snorkelling, kayaking, sailing, paddle boarding). Diving, water-skiing and saltwater fly fishing are also offered. Unlimited shore diving is included in the price, otherwise dive rates are F$180 for two tanks (F$40 for gear hire), or F$580 for an openwater course. Matagi boasts 30 dive spots within 10 to 30 minutes of the island.

Getting There & Away The Matangi Island Resort minibus meets guests at Matei airport. It is a 15-minute drive to Navakacoa village landing, on a volcanic, black-sand beach, followed by a 20-minute boat ride to the island. Return transfers to Taveuni airstrip cost F$80 per adult and are free for children.

Qamea

Qamea is the closest of the three islands to Taveuni, only 2.5km east of Thurston Point. It is also the largest at about 1km in length and between 700m and 5km in width. The island's coast has a number of bays with white-sand beaches and a narrow mangrove inlet on the west side. The interior, especially on the north side, is covered with steep green hills and sloping valleys, with little flat land. Qamea is rich in birdlife and is notable for the *lairo*, the annual migration of land crabs. For a few days from late November to early December, at the start of their breeding season, masses of crabs move together from the mud flats towards the sea.

Qamea has six villages, but the upmarket *Qamea Beach Club* (☎ *880 220, fax 880 092,* @ *qamea@is.com.fj*) is the only place for travellers to stay on the island. Opened in 1982, the resort is on 16 hectares along a lovely white-sand beach. The resort has a fresh spring-water swimming pool, 24-hour power and a lofty entertainment/restaurant bure with an expansive verandah. Children under 13 are not accepted.

Each of the 11 rectangular bure has en suite, sitting area, fan, minibar, hot showers, tea- and coffee-making facilities, ceiling fan, and a hammock on the verandah. Bure can accommodate four at a squeeze. Rates, including meals and transfers, are F$820/1040/1240 for singles/doubles/triples. The new villa is much more spacious and costs F$1200/1400 for doubles/triples.

Dive Qamea charges F$176 for a two-tank dive trip, plus F$33 for full gear hire, or F$594 for an open-water course. There is excellent snorkelling just offshore. Other activities include windsurfing, sailing, outrigger canoeing, nature walks, village visits and fish drives.

Trips can be organised to Tavoro Falls at Bouma (F$45 per person plus F$5 entry fee) and to the Lavena Coastal Walk and Wanibau Falls (F$55 per person plus F$5

entrance fee). A three-hour boat trip around Qamea is F$220 per boat, including picnic lunch, and a trip to Nanuku (a beautiful atoll about 50km away) is F$350. Fishing costs F$25 per hour.

Getting There & Away Guests are picked up by the resort minibus at Matei airport and driven to Navakacoa village landing (15 minutes, about 10km) and taken by speedboat to the island (about 15 minutes, 2.5km).

Laucala

The island of Laucala is about 5km long and 3.5km wide, just 500m east across the strait from Qamea. It is privately owned by the estate of the late US millionaire Malcolm Forbes. Most of the Fijians who live on the island work on the estate's copra plantations or at the upmarket *Fiji Forbes Laucala Island Resort* (☎ *880 077, 719-379 3263 USA, fax 880 099, 379 3266 USA*). With only seven bure, it caters for a maximum of 20 guests, who tend to be mainly Americans, and prices are quoted in US dollars. Rates are F$5000 per person for seven nights plus F$750 per additional night. Children are half-price or free if under two. The resort offers water-skiing, deep-sea fishing and diving for its guests, and all activities, meals and drinks are included in the rate. The bure each have a bedroom, lounge, dining area, kitchen, air-con and a stocked bar. Groups of eight to 12 adults can book out the whole resort.

Getting There & Away Laucala has its own airstrip and most visitors are flown to the island from Nadi.

Making pandanus mats, Kadavu

Kadavu beach

Somosomo Church, Taveuni

Yanuya (front) and Tavua islands, Mamanucas

The Warwick Resort, Coral Coast on Viti Levu

Traditional *bure* at Vatukarasa village on Viti Levu's Coral Coast

Kadavu Group

The Kadavu (pronounced ka**nd**-a-vu) Group is comprised of Kadavu (Fiji's fourth-largest island), Ono, Galoa and a number of smaller islands. The group is about 100km south of Viti Levu. The main island is 411 sq km in area – comparable to Taveuni. It is irregular in shape and the coastline is so deeply indented that it is almost cut in three by deep bays. At 838m, Nabukelevu (Mt Washington) is the highest peak. The rugged island has lush rainforests, especially on the eastern side, and is home to a wide variety of birdlife. The Kadavu honeyeater, Kadavu fantail, velvet fruit dove and the colourful Kadavu musk parrot are all indigenous.

The explorer Dumont d'Urville sailed past the island in 1834 and named the long fringing reef after his ship, the *Astrolabe*. When space at Levuka proved limited, Kadavu's Galoa Harbour was considered as a potential site for the new colonial capital. Otherwise, the group has remained removed from Fiji's major historical events.

Kadavu's population of 12,000 lives in about 72 villages or settlements. The local economy is based on subsistence agriculture and the export of local produce to the mainland. Tourism is slowly expanding, due to the isolation and lack of infrastructure. Each village has its own fishing grounds, and resorts negotiate to use the areas for diving, surfing or fishing. There are few roads on Kadavu and most transportation is by boat.

The prevailing south-easterly winds can batter the exposed south-eastern side of the

island. Expect some rough weather from April to August.

Orientation

The small town of Vunisea is Kadavu's administrative centre, with the island's police station, post office, hospital (all on the top of the hill) and airstrip. It's easy to get around on foot, but Vunisea doesn't have much to interest the traveller. It is on a narrow isthmus with Namalata Bay to the west and North Bay to the east.

Information

Money Most of the resorts are distant from Vunisea. Some resorts do accept credit cards but it is probably best to bring cash with you to Kadavu, as the National Bank at the Vunisea post office doesn't change travellers cheques or handle credit-card transactions.

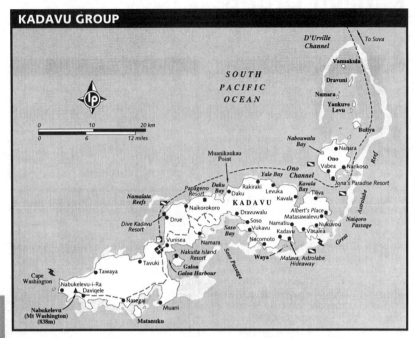

KADAVU GROUP

Post & Communications The Vunisea post and telephone offices are a short walk from the airstrip, on top of the hill. The shop within the post office sells clothes and stationery. Opening hours are 8 am to 4 pm weekdays and 9 am to 1 pm Saturdays. Kadavu's telephone exchange is now automated and has public cardphones. Kavala Bay, at the north-eastern end of the island, also has a post office.

Medical Services Vunisea's hospital, completed in 1996, was jointly funded by Australian aid and the Fijian government. The building works were part of a F$7 million project to improve Kadavu's medical and health services, however, it is reportedly already fairly rundown. Divers suffering from the bends can be transferred to the Fiji Recompression Chamber Facility in Suva by medevac helicopter service. This will be costly unless your travel insurance covers it!

Emergency In the event of an emergency, dial the police on ☎ 336 007 or the hospital on ☎ 336 008.

Dangers & Annoyances

The ferry trip to Kadavu from Suva can be rough and unreliable; fly instead. The small boats used for transfers to/from the airstrip often don't have life jackets or radios.

Activities

Remote and rugged Kadavu is a great place for nature lovers, hikers and bird-watchers. The island is mountainous, especially on the eastern side, and has rainforest, numerous waterfalls and hiking trails (used mainly by school children). Ask locals if the track is clear before heading off. Due to their isolation, the villagers are very traditional here. If visiting a village, ask to speak to the *turaga-ni-koro* first and don't wear a hat or carry things on your shoulders (see Dos & Don'ts in the Facts about Fiji chapter).

There are a few nice beaches and most places to stay have equipment for snorkelling and other water sports. Sometimes there are stingers in the water, which can be uncomfortable for swimmers and snorkellers.

Diving Most travellers are attracted to Kadavu by its reefs, which offer some excellent diving. The famous **Astrolabe Reef** skirts the eastern side of the Kadavu Group. Expect brilliantly coloured soft and hard corals, vertical drop-offs and a wonderful array of marine life, including lots of reef sharks. However, diving on the reef is variable, ranging from terrible to incredible. The weather quite often dictates which sites are suitable to dive, and visibility can range from 15m to 70m. See the Places to Stay section later in this chapter for dive operators' contact details.

Matava, Astrolabe Hideaway dives from the **Soso Passage** to **Naiqoro Passage**, offering cave dives, shark dives and unexplored sites. Albert's Place dives the Naiqoro Passage and, during rough weather, sites on the sheltered side of Ono. Dive Kadavu also dives this area as well as the **Namalata reefs** on the north-western side of the island, which are more sheltered from the prevailing winds than the Astrolabe Reef. See the Facts for the Visitor chapter for more information on diving.

Surfing Vesi Passage, off Matava, Astrolabe Hideaway, has powerful surf averaging 6ft (1.8m). It is only suitable on calm days. There is also surf at **Cape Washington**, on the south-western point of Kadavu. But surfers have a poor reputation here, having offended villagers in the past.

Sea & Dive Kayaking The season for organised kayaking trips is from May to September – contact Tamarillo Sea Kayaking in New Zealand (☎ 04-801 7549, fax 801 7349, @ enquires@tamarillo.co.nz).

Dive Kadavu Resort has diving kayaks for hire with professional instruction available. Matava, Astrolabe Hideaway has two-person kayaks for hire.

Places to Stay
Consider transportation costs when choosing accommodation. The budget places all allow camping.

Places to Stay – Budget
Travellers stranded in Vunisea should consider *Biana Accommodation (☎ 336 010),* which has reasonable rooms for singles or doubles for F$40, including breakfast. Lunch or dinner is F$5. There is also a common lounge area. Biana is on the hill near the Namalata Bay wharf, about 2km north of the airport, and there is a grocery store

The Battle of the Shark & Octopus Gods

Dakuwaqa the Shark God once cruised the Fiji islands challenging other reef guardians. On hearing that a monster in Kadavu waters was reportedly stronger than himself, he sped down to the island

to disprove the rumour. Dakuwaqa came across the giant octopus and adopted his usual battle strategy of charging with his mouth wide open and sharp teeth prepared. The octopus, however, anchored itself to the coral reef and swiftly wrapped its free tentacles around the shark's body and jaws, clasping the shark in a death lock. Dakuwaqa was rendered helpless and had to beg for mercy. In return for lenience, the octopus demanded that his subjects, the people of Kadavu, be forever protected from shark attack. In Kadavu the people now fish without fear and regard the shark as their protector. Most won't eat shark or octopus out of respect for their gods.

nearby. Alternatively, **Thema** (☎ 336 028), who runs the airport kiosk, allows people to stay in her home for F$10 per person. She can arrange visits to a nearby waterfall.

Albert's Place (☎ 336 086) is on a tidal beach on the north-eastern corner of Kadavu, close to Naiqoro Passage. It is run by Albert O'Connor, a Fijian descendent of an Irish beachcomber who came to Kadavu in 1804 and married the daughter of a local chief. Camping is F$5.50 per person and dorm beds are F$6. There are 10 basic *bure* (thatched dwellings), with mosquito nets and woven floors mats but no electricity, which cost F$16/30 for singles/doubles. The toilet blocks have flush toilets and cold showers. At the time of writing, a new dining and entertaining area was being built, which will also have accommodation. The food is simple and costs F$25 per day or F$6/10/13 for breakfast/lunch/dinner. There is also a small shop here, with basic grocery items only. Self-caterers can pay F$3 to use the kitchen or have free use of the wood stove outside.

Snorkelling is quite good in front of the resort at high tide. Diving with Naiqoro Divers is usually good (F$95 for two-tank dives, including all gear), but equipment and boats are very basic. The Astrolabe Reef is a 10-minute boat ride from the resort. Other activities include volleyball, hikes to a village, and waterfall/reef trips for F$15/10 per person with a minimum of four. Day hikes to villages can also be arranged.

Transfers from Vunisea airstrip cost F$60 for one person, F$25 per person for two people or F$23 per person for three or more. The trip takes about 1½ to two hours, depending on the weather, and the boat travels whichever side is calmest.

Within walking distance north of Albert's Place is the newly rebuilt **Waisalima Beach Resort** (☎ 336 018, fax 321 899, @ divekadavu@is.com.fj), on the former site of Nukubalavu Resort which burnt down. It opened in late 1999, though was under construction at the time we came upon it. By appearances it will be a good budget option in Kadavu. At the south-eastern end of Kadavu island it has views of Ono, which is a short boat ride across the channel. It has a long stretch of sandy, tidal beach, which is OK for swimming but is best at high tide. Accommodation in traditional-style bure with private bathrooms costs F$70/50 a single/double per person; in bure with shared facilities it is F$35/25; dorm accommodation is F$10 and camp sites F$5 per person. Three-meal-a-day packages are F$35, or you can pay F$12/12/18 for breakfast/lunch/dinner. Quality diving is provided by Dive Kadavu, which has set up a new dive shop at Waisalima. Two-tank dive excursions cost F$90 per day for up four days, F$85 for five to seven days and F$80 for more than eight days.

Ono, a roughly oval-shaped island in the north-east of the group, has a budget resort at its southern end. **Jona's Paradise Resort** (☎ 307 058, fax 303 860, @ divekadavu@is.com.fj) has been upgraded recently and is run in association with Dive Kadavu. It's ideal for those who want a quiet time in rustic accommodation in a beautiful place. The five very simple thatched bure are spaced along the beachfront. There is a minimum three-night stay and the price per person is F$70/60 for singles/doubles. Dorm beds, with a maximum of four in a bure, are F$50 and it is F$36 per person to camp. Prices include three simple meals, but bring your own snacks as there is no shop. There is an amenities block with flush toilets and hot-water showers and the larger bure has its own bathroom.

The white-sand beach is one of the best in Kadavu, with good snorkelling directly in front of the resort. Diving is with Dive Kadavu and two-tank morning dives cost F$90. Other activities include fishing and scenic boat trips around Ono island. Return transfers from Vunisea airstrip are F$100 per person.

On the northern point of Galoa island, just south-east of Vunisea, is **Nakuita Island Resort** (☎ 336 703, fax 336 097), formerly known as Reece's Place and Galoa Island Resort. Bill Reece loves to tell stories about the history of the island, expound on medicinal plants and show you the point where people once went to die so that their spirits could leave them for the afterlife. There is a large stone fish trap on the point and a beach graveyard where blackbirded labourers who died of smallpox were buried. A whaling station also once operated here.

Things might be a bit unpredictable at Nakuita, however, it is cheap and quite close to Vunisea. Camping is F$5 per person and accommodation in simple bungalows with private bathrooms is F$12/24 for singles/doubles. Meals are F$4/6/8 for breakfast/lunch/dinner. Diving with Dive 2000 Fiji costs F$60 for a two-tank dive and shore dives are F$15. Equipment rental is F$10. Snorkelling trips are F$8 per person. Transfers from Vunisea are F$7 one way in a small open boat, and the trip can be rough.

Places to Stay – Mid-Range

Matava, Astrolabe Hideaway (☎ 336 098, fax 336 099, @ matava@suva.is.com.fj) is managed by four young Australian guys. 'Matava' is named after a battle that took place on this beach between the locals and warriors from Rewa (near Suva) back in the 17th century. The beach at the front of the resort isn't great – the tide goes out a long way, so boat access can be a bit awkward with dive gear. However, a reef links it to a picturesque offshore island, which makes a great snorkelling or kayaking trip. There is a beautiful view from the hill behind the resort. It can be windy and exposed on this side of the island, but the place has a rugged beauty and a sense of remoteness.

The nine bure are rustic but comfortable, with timber floors and verandahs as well as solar-powered lighting. The best accommodation option is the new oceanview bure for F$104 for singles or doubles. Otherwise, the waterfront bure with private facilities cost F$88 for single or doubles. Bure with shared facilities are good value for F$50 singles or doubles. The small dorm at the back (maximum of four) costs F$16 per person. There is spring water, 12V solar electricity and gas hot water for showers. A three-meal package is F$41 and meals are served on the verandah of the big restaurant-bar bure overlooking the water through the trees.

Matava has reasonably good dive equipment, and claims to have a dive site where

you can see manta rays all year round. A two-tank dive is F$104 (tanks and belts only) plus F$22 daily for gear hire; it is F$500 to do the open-water course. Other activities include reef ecology programs, snorkelling, reef surfing, kayaking, organised bushwalking and village visits and a waterfall visit. The boat trip from Vunisea airstrip to Matava (F$27 per person one way, 50 minutes) can be a bit rough.

Places to Stay – Top End

Dive Kadavu Resort (☎ 311 780, fax 303 860, @ divekadavu@is.com.fj) caters mainly to divers. It is on the western side of Kadavu, sheltered from the prevailing south-easterly winds, and conveniently located for travellers arriving by plane. The lovely beach is good for swimming and snorkelling at all tides. Children under 12 are not accepted.

It has two fan-cooled, oceanview rooms at F$260/440 for singles/doubles and seven beachfront rooms at F$300/520 or F$220 per person with four in one room. All rooms have verandahs, insect screening, hot water and are well ventilated. Children under 12 years are not accepted. Rates include three meals and airport transfers. The hillside restaurant-bar has a great view through the coconut palms and thatched bure rooftops across the water to Nabukelevu (Mt Washington). The food is excellent, especially the *lovo* (a feast in which food is cooked in a pit oven). There is a good swap and reference library, with interesting books for divers and naturalists.

Dive Kadavu has an excellent set-up with good equipment and boats. Two-tank morning dive trips cost F$160 and open-water courses are F$660. Up to four dives per day are offered. Snorkelling trips with the divers are F$30 per person and underwater cameras are available for hire. Namalata Reef is about 5km offshore and day trips to the sheltered Ono side of Astrolabe Reef are arranged with a stop for lunch at a village or at Jona's Paradise Resort on Ono. The use of windsurfers, paddle boards and sea kayaks is included in the rates. Other activities are forest walks in the hills, village visits and a weekly lovo. Airport transfers take 15 minutes by boat.

Papageno Resort (☎ *303 355, fax 303 533,* @ *papagenoresort@is.com)*, previously known as Malawai, is 14.5km northeast of Vunisea. It is a quiet, upmarket, family-friendly retreat for up to 10 guests. The three fan-cooled cottages have en suites, hot water and minibars and are spaced along a sandy beach. They are spacious and can comfortably accommodate three people, or four in the larger cottage. Rates are F$300/400 for singles/doubles and include breakfast, dinner, return boat transfers (40 minutes one way) and non-motorised activities. Activities include snorkelling, village visits and waterfall walks. There is fresh water, home-grown fruit and vegies and generator and solar power. Anneliese, the new Californian owner, organises cultural exchanges for school children. The resort is run by Wati and Onisimo – the latter an excellent chef. Meals are served in the plantation house and a local band plays music for guests. A minimum stay of three nights applies.

Places to Eat
There are small stores in Vunisea, Kavala Bay, Albert's Place and near Matava, Astrolabe Hideaway. Most of the resorts are very remote, so even if all your meals are provided it may be an idea to take along snacks.

Getting There & Away
Air Air Fiji has daily return flights from Nadi to Kadavu, via Nausori airport near Suva (1½ hours). Sunflower Airlines has daily flights to Kadavu from Nadi (45 minutes). See the air fares chart in the Getting Around chapter.

It is a beautiful, but sometimes turbulent, flight to Kadavu from either Nadi or Suva over stunning reefs. The approach to Vunisea's Namalata airstrip (☎ 336 042) over Namalata Bay has a spectacular view of Nabukelevu, which rises steeply at the south-western point of Kadavu. The airport has a kiosk. Ideally, have your accommodation and transfers booked in advance, otherwise you could be stranded in Vunisea's (see the Places to Stay section earlier in this chapter).

Ferry Suva to Kadavu on the ferry MV *Bulou-ni-ceva* is F$42 per person one way. This service is mostly for cargo and local use, and it is irregular and unreliable, taking anything from four hours to two days! It visits Vunisea, Kavala Bay and Nabukelevu-i-Ra. The trip can be fine or terrible, depending on the weather you strike. Contact Kadavu Shipping in Suva (☎ 312 428).

Getting Around
Kadavu's few roads are restricted to the Vunisea area. It's easy to walk around the small town or to hitch a ride. Small boats are the group's principal mode of transport. Each resort has its own boat and will pick up guests from Vunisea airstrip; make sure you make arrangements in advance. Boat trips are expensive due to fuel costs and mark-ups. Most boats don't have life jackets or radios. In rough weather it can be a bone-crunching and wet trip to the more remote resorts.

Lau & Moala Groups

The Lau Group is about halfway between the main islands of Fiji, to the west, and the Kingdom of Tonga, to the east. The group has about 57 small islands, scattered over 400km from north to south. Geographically, Lau is subdivided into northern and southern Lau, and the Moala Group lies to the west of southern Lau. Together the island groups are under the administration of the Eastern Division. The climate in this region is drier than in most parts of Fiji.

Most islands of the Lau Group are made of composite materials; some are pure limestone and a few are volcanic. Interrupted periods of uplift permitted coral to grow over the limestone, creating great masses of reefs. Relatively recent volcanic activity is evident by the lava domes on top of the limestone bases of some of the smaller islands.

The islanders of southern Lau are well known for their crafts: Moce, Vatoa, Ono-i-Lau and Namuka produce *masi* (bark cloth) and the artisans of Fulaga are excellent woodcarvers.

History

Because of Lau's proximity to Tonga, the islanders have been greatly influenced by Polynesian people and culture. The southeast trade winds made it easy to sail from Tonga to Fiji, but more difficult to return. A revolution in canoe design facilitated traffic and trade between the island groups. Tongan and Samoan canoe-builders began settling in Fiji in the late 1700s, bringing with them their innovative canoe designs as well as other decorative skills and crafts. They intermarried with Fijians, and the Tongan influence is expressed in names, language, food, decoration, architecture and physical features.

Both Captain Cook and Captain Bligh sighted the Lau Group on their explorations in the late 18th century. The first real contact with Europeans was in 1800 when the American schooner *Argo* was wrecked on Bukatatanoa Reef east of Lakeba. The ship

HIGHLIGHTS

- Snorkel or dive the fantastic coral reefs of this pristine region.
- Visit Lakeba's Oso Nabukete cave.
- Experience the interesting blend of Fijian and Tongan cultures.

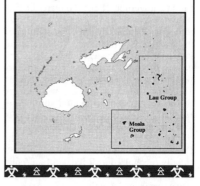

was on its way to deliver supplies to the penal colony of Norfolk Island. Fijians of Oneata looted the wreck for muskets and gunpowder and the sailors lived with the islanders until being killed in disputes. Oliver Slater survived to become influential in Bua, Vanua Levu (see the 'Precious Cargo' boxed text in the Vanua Levu chapter).

The first Christian missionaries entered Fiji via Lau. Two Tahitians from the London Missionary Society (LMS) tried unsuccessfully to set up in Lakeba, and then moved on to establish themselves in Oneata in 1830, where they managed to convert a small number of people. Wesleyan missionaries William Cross and David Cargill settled in Lakeba in 1835. They arrived with an emissary of King George of Tonga and, out of respect for the king, the Tui Nayau (king or prominent chief of Lau) made them welcome. He and his people, however, were not interested in being converted. Cross and Cargill developed a system for written Fijian and produced the first book in that language. The Tui Nayau eventually accepted Christianity in 1849.

Northern Lau was traditionally allied with the Cakaudrove province (eastern Vanua Levu and Taveuni), but by the mid-19th century the region became dominated by Tonga. In 1847 Tongan nobleman Enele Ma'afu, cousin of King Taufa'ahau of Tonga, led an armada of war canoes to Vanua Balavu to investigate the killing of a preacher. Six years later the king appointed Ma'afu governor of the Tongans in Fiji. After the murder of 17 Wesleyans, Ma'afu took Vanua Balavu by force and subjugated its inhabitants. He established Sawana village near Lomaloma as his base. The Tongans assisted in local Fijian wars in return for protection by Chief Cakobau of Bau. By 1855 Ma'afu had become a powerful force in the region and influential throughout much of Fiji. His aim was to conquer all Fiji and convert the people to Christianity.

Ma'afu was one of the signatories to the Deed of Cession to Britain and became officially recognised as Roko Tui Lau (chief of Lau). After his death in 1881, Tongan power weakened, the title passed to the Tui Nayau, and many Tongans returned to their home country. Despite the distance from the rest of Fiji and their relatively small land area, the chiefs of the Lau Group have always been surprisingly influential. Chiefs with the title Tui Nayau include the late Ratu Sukuna and the current president, Ratu Mara.

Diving

The remote Lau Group is still relatively unexplored in terms of diving. The Lau waters are officially protected by the Fijian government, and commercial fishing is prohibited in the area. The upmarket resorts near Vanua Balavu have their own dive operations. Apart from introductory resort courses, however, diving is limited to those with experience.

Nai'a Cruises, an excellent live-aboard operator based at Pacific Harbour on Viti Levu, offers special charters to Lau. *Fiji Aggressor,* based at Savusavu on Vanua Levu (see Savusavu & Around in the Vanua

A Local Delicacy

One week after the full moon in November, the people of Vanua Balavu witness the annual rising of the *balolo* (tiny green and brown sea worms). At sunrise the Susui villagers collect worms by the thousands. The catch is first soaked in fresh water, then packed into baskets and cooked overnight in a *lovo* (underground oven). The fishy-tasting baked worms are considered a delicacy.

Levu chapter for details), and *MV Princess II,* based at Nadi, also visit Lau.

Accommodation

Lakeba and Vanua Balavu have budget accommodation and there are upmarket resorts on Kaibu and on Yanuyanu, just offshore from Vanua Balavu. You can also visit Lau on a live-aboard dive boat (see the Diving section earlier in this chapter).

There is little other infrastructure for travellers and there are no banks.

Getting There & Away

Moala, Vanua Balavu, Cicia, Lakeba and Kaibu have airstrips. Air Fiji flies Suva-Vanua Balavu and Suva-Lakeba.

There are regular cargo and passenger boats to the Lau group (see the Getting There & Away sections later in this chapter and the introductory Getting Around chapter for details).

Yachties require permission to visit the islands. Details are given under Travel Permits in the Facts for the Visitor chapter. Contact the Lau provincial headquarters in Lakeba (see the Lakeba section later in this chapter).

Northern Lau

Northern Lau's largest island is Vanua Balavu. It has an airstrip and an upmarket resort, as does Kaibu to the west. The islands of Naitauba, Kanacea, Mago and Cicia are important for copra production.

VANUA BALAVU & AROUND

Vanua Balavu, together with eight other smaller islands within the same enclosing barrier reef, was named the 'Exploring Isles' by Commodore Wilkes of the US Exploring Expedition, who charted the northern Lau Group in 1840. This beautiful island, roughly a reversed S-shape and averaging about 2km wide, has lots of **sandy beaches** and rugged limestone hills. The **Bay of Islands** at the north-western end of the island is used as a hurricane shelter by yachts. Along the eastern coast there is a road that has occasional passing carriers (small trucks). Taveuni is visible in the distance, 115km to the north-west.

The largest village on the island is **Lomaloma** on the south-east coast. In the mid-19th century Tonga conquered the island and the village of Sawana was built next to Lomaloma. Fifth-generation Tongan descendants still live in Sawana, and the houses with rounded ends show the influence of Tongan architecture. The first of Fiji's ports, Lomaloma was regularly visited by sailing ships trading in the Pacific. In its heyday Lomaloma had many hotels and shops as well as Fiji's first botanical gardens, though little remains of its past grandeur. The Fijian inhabitants of Vanua Balavu trace their ancestry to Tailevu

(south-east Viti Levu) and Cakaudrove (eastern Vanua Levu and Taveuni). Today the people of Vanua Balavu rely largely on copra and bêche-de-mer for their income.

Places to Stay

There are a couple of budget guesthouses on Vanua Balavu and both can organise boat excursions and snorkelling trips. *Moana's Guesthouse (☎ 895 006)* is at Sawana. Built in traditional Tongan style, it has two bedrooms and a living area. Rates are F$30 per person, including three meals.

Nawanawa Estate is the other budget option, and is closer to the airstrip. There is no contact number here, but someone usually meets incoming flights. Accommodation costs F$40, including meals.

The tiny island of Yanuyanu, just offshore from Lomaloma, has the upmarket *Lomaloma Resort (☎ 895 091 or 313 815 in Suva, fax 895 092 or 313 905 in Suva, ✉ lomaloma@suva.is.com.fj)*. Yanuyanu is owned by Ratu Mara, the president of Fiji and the Tui Lau (paramount chief of Lau). The remote resort opened in 1994 and caters for a maximum of 22 guests in seven Tongan-style *bure* (thatched dwellings). Rates are US$245/375 (F$490/750) for singles/doubles, including all meals, beer and soft drinks, and boat transfers from Vanua Balavu. The Great House has a bar, lounge and dining area, and seafood is the focus of the menu.

Activities included in the rates are snorkelling trips, nonmotorised water sports, treks, village tours, *meke* (dance performances that enact stories and legends) and trips to hot springs. Boats can be chartered for game fishing. Guests can snorkel off the beach and around the island, but you need to take a boat trip to Vanua Balavu for decent sandy beaches.

The resort charges F$240 for a two-tank diving trip, plus F$30 for equipment rental. Dive-and-accommodation packages are available, as well as package rates for a nondiving partner. A seven-night, six-day package costs US$1687 (F$3374) per person. Dive sites include the Tonga Express – a fast current in the Tongan Passage – Outer

---

Fatal Attraction

There is a freshwater lake near the village of Mavana, on the north-east corner of Vanua Balavu, which is considered sacred. The people of Mavana gather here annually for a fun ceremony authorised by their traditional priest. Naked except for a leaf skirt, they jump around in the lake to stir up the muddy waters. This provokes the large fish known as *yawa* (a type of mullet usually only found in the sea) to spring into the air. It is believed that the male fish are attracted to the female villagers and thus easily trapped in the nets. Legend has it that the fish were dropped into the lake by a Tongan princess while flying over the island on her way to visit her lover on Taveuni.

Limits and Magic Kingdom, on the protected side of Vanua Balavu. Some dive sites are an hour from the resort and plankton can sometimes reduce visibility to 10m to 20m.

Getting There & Away

Vanua Balavu is 355km east of Nadi, about halfway to Tonga. Air Fiji has twice-weekly flights from Nadi via Suva to Vanua Balavu. See the air fares chart in the Getting Around chapter.

The airstrip is centrally located on the island. Guests of Lomaloma Resort are transferred to the resort by a 10-minute truck ride, followed by a five-minute boat ride.

If you have plenty of time you can also reach the island by cargo/passenger boat. Saliabasaga Shipping and Ika Corporation both have fortnightly trips from Suva to the Lau Group, including Vanua Balavu. See under Boat in the Getting Around chapter for details. A one-way fare with Saliabasaga Shipping is F$66, including meals. Expect to spend about a week on board.

KAIBU & YACATA

Kaibu is a 352-hectare, privately owned island in the northern Lau Group, 55km west of Vanua Balavu. It shares a fringing reef with the larger Yacata island. *Kaimbu Island Resort* (☎ *880 333, fax 880 334* ✉ *kaimbu@ earthlink.net)* is an exclusive resort with only three bure accommodating a maximum of six guests. Each bure has its own beach and costs US$1095 (F$2200) per couple per night. The minimum stay is seven nights. Generally, only couples are accepted unless the whole island is reserved for US$2750 (F$5500) per night, in which case children can stay. Rates include all meals, drinks and activities.

Activities offered include diving on the barrier reef, lagoon snorkelling, sports fishing, sailing, water-skiing, wind surfing, catamaran sailing, trekking, cave visits and picnics on an uninhabited island.

Getting There & Away

The island has its own airstrip and guests reach the resort by charter plane. Return transfers from Suva are F$2170 per couple.

Southern Lau

Lakeba, being the hereditary seat of the Tui Nayau (chief of Lau), is the most important island in southern Lau. It is Fiji's 10th-largest island and the largest of the Lau Group. Southern Lau has 16 other islands, mostly within 100km south-east of Lakeba. Vatoa and Ono-i-Lau are more isolated and farther south.

LAKEBA
pop 2000

Lakeba is a roughly circular-shaped volcanic island, approximately 9km in diameter, with a small peninsula at its southern end. There is a road around its perimeter and several roads across the interior. To the east is a wide **lagoon** enclosed by a barrier reef.

About 2000 people live in the island's eight villages. Yams, coconuts and *kumala* (sweet potatoes) grow well on the fertile coast and the interior is covered with grasslands, pandanus and pine plantations. The former prime minister and current president, Ratu Mara (also the Tui Nayau), comes from Lakeba.

Lakeba was once a meeting place for Fijians and Tongans, and the place where Christian missionaries first entered Fiji via Tonga and Tahiti. It was frequently visited by Europeans before the trading settlement was established at Levuka.

Shark Calling

The villagers of Nasaqalau perform a shark-calling ritual in October or November each year. About a month prior to the ceremony, the spot on the reef where the calling is to take place is marked by a post and a flag of *masi* (bark cloth). A traditional priest ensures no-one goes near the post or fishes in the area. On the designated day the caller, standing neck-high in the water, chants for up to an hour. A school of sharks, led by a white shark, will be drawn to the place. Traditionally, all of the sharks except the white shark are killed and eaten by the villagers.

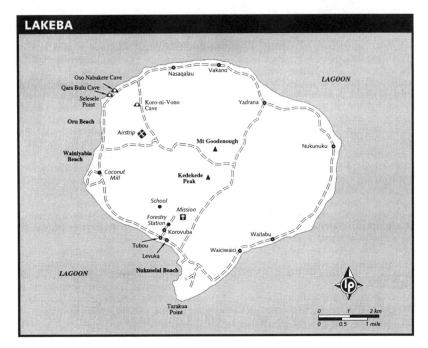

LAKEBA

The island has several caves worth visiting, especially **Oso Nabukete**, which translates as 'too narrow for pregnant women'. Take some *kava* (the roots of the Polynesian pepper shrub) as a *sevusevu* (gift) to Nasaqalau village, where you can arrange a guide for about F$5. Ideally, take your own torch. The island also has the remains of an **old fortification**, where the people retreated in times of war.

The provincial headquarters (☎ 823 035) for the Lau Group is in **Tubou** at the southern end of Lakeba. There is also a police station (☎ 823 043), post office, telephone exchange, hospital (☎ 823 066) and guesthouse here, and some nearby **beaches** that are good for snorkelling. Elene Ma'afu, the once-powerful Tongan chief, is buried here, as is Ratu Sir Lala Sukuna, formerly an influential Tui Lau (see the 'Ratu Sukuna & the Native Lands Trust Board' boxed text in the Suva section of the Viti Levu chapter).

Places to Stay
Call the Lau provincial office (☎ 823 035) to check if you can visit the island and to book accommodation. *Jackson's Resthouse (☎ 823 188)*, run by Kesosoni Qica, can accommodate up to 10 people. It costs F$35 per person, including three meals.

Getting There & Away
Air Fiji has twice-weekly flights from Suva to Lakeba that take 75 minutes one way (see the air fares chart in the Getting Around chapter). There is a bus from the airstrip to Tubou and carriers and buses circle the island.

If you have plenty of time you can also reach the island by boat. Ika Corporation, Saliabasaga Shipping and Taikabara Shipping each have fortnightly trips from Suva to the Lau Group, including Lakeba. See under Boat in the Getting Around chapter for details. A one-way fare including meals is F$66.

LAU & MOALA GROUPS

Moala Group

The three islands of the Moala Group – Moala, Totoya and Matuku – are geographically removed from Lau but administered as part of the Eastern Division. They are about halfway between Kadavu and the southern Lau Group, south-east of the Lomaiviti Group. The islands are the eroded tops of previously submerged volcanic cones that have lifted more than 3km to the sea surface. Totoya's horseshoe shape is the result of a sunken volcano crater forming a land-locked lagoon. The volcano was active 4.9 million years ago. Matuku has rich volcanic soil, steep wooded peaks and a submerged crater on its western side. However, this beautiful island is generally inaccessible to visitors. Each of the islands has villages.

MOALA

Moala is the largest and most northerly of the group. It is about 160km from Suva and 110km from Lakeba. The 65-sq-km island is roughly triangular in shape, with a deeply indented coast. The highest peak reaches 460m and has two small **crater lakes**. It has extremely fertile soil and supports nine villages. The villagers produce copra and bananas, which they send to Suva, a night's sail away. The ancestors of Moala's inhabitants came from Viti Levu.

There is no accommodation here. But don't just turn up uninvited; you need to be invited to stay by a local. In the past, travellers have visited the island for homestays with the Draunidalo family.

Getting There & Away

Air Fiji has flights from Suva to Moala twice weekly. See the air fares chart in the Getting Around chapter.

Khans Shipping has cargo/passenger boats that make the trip most weeks. Khans visits Moala, Matuku, Totoya in the Moala Group as well as Gau and Nairai in the Lomaiviti Group. See under Boat in the Getting Around chapter for details.

Rotuma

Rotuma is an isolated, 30-sq-km volcanic island, 470km north of the Yasawa Group. Its shape resembles a whale, with the larger body of land linked to the small tail end to the west by the Motusa isthmus. It is about 13km long by 5km at its widest point, with extinct volcanic craters rising up to 250m. The smaller islands of Uea, Hatana and Hofliua are 3 to 6km west of Rotuma. Uea is a high, rocky island and the spectacular Hofliua is also known as 'split island' because of its unusual rock formation. These offshore islands are important seabird rookeries. Endemic wildlife includes the Rotuman gecko and the red-and-black Rotuman honeyeater.

Officially Rotuma is a province of Fiji, but – unlike predominantly Melanesian Fiji – its indigenous population of 3000 people is Polynesian. Rotuma's distinct culture has developed over hundreds of years. Tongans invaded Rotuma during the 17th century and the Tongan influence is evident in the language and dance.

In 1791 Europeans on the HMS *Pandora* stopped here to search for mutineers from the *Bounty*. Rotuma became an important port, and the local people were exposed to traders, runaway sailors and convicts. During the mid-19th century, Tongan Wesleyan and Marist Roman Catholic missionaries introduced their versions of Christianity. By the 1870s the religious groups were warring and, in response to the unrest, the Rotuman chiefs decided to cede their home to Britain. Rotuma became joined politically to the Fijian colony in 1881.

Rotuma has a population of about 3000. Most young people leave their remote island home to find work, and about 6500 ethnic Rotumans live on other Fijian islands, mostly in Suva on Viti Levu. Villagers fish and grow fruit (including oranges and bananas), root crops and coconuts in the fertile soil. There is no bank or shopping centre, just a cooperative. Rotuma produces copra, which is processed at the mill near Savusavu

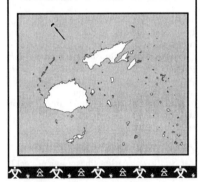

on Vanua Levu. In 1988 Rotumans demonstrated their wish to become independent from Fiji, but the movement was quashed by the Fijian government. In the early 1990s the island hit the news over bad debts and bank-loan scandals.

Things to See & Do

Experience staying with villagers on this remote island. The best **beaches** are at Oinafa and at Vovoe, west of **Sororoa Bluff**. There are good views from this bluff and from **Mt Suelhof** (256m). There are **archaeological sites** at Sisilo (Graveyard of the Kings), Ki ne he'e and Tafea Point (stone walls).

Places to Stay

For many years tourists were decidedly unwelcome and cruise ships have been stopped from visiting the island. However, the Rotuman chiefs have recently decided to allow

ROTUMA

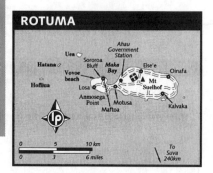

The Origin of Rotuma

Rotumans believe their ancestors came from Samoa. The spot where the island presently lies was nothing but open sea until the arrival of Samoan chief Raho and his favourite grandchild. The little girl was unhappy in her homeland as her cousin was always annoying her. To escape his torment, she convinced her grandfather to take her away to live on another island. For days and nights their entourage sailed westward in an outrigger canoe, but failed to find land. Eventually the chief threw some Samoan soil overboard. The soil grew to form a beautiful, fertile island, which he named Rotuma. Some of the soil scattered, forming the other small islands. Rotumans commemorate this legend in their dance and song.

small numbers of visitors. Make sure you bring cash and that you don't turn up unannounced.

Village stays with **Rotuma Island Backpackers** (☎ *891 290*) in Motusa are F$11 per couple. It is extra for meals and you'll need to bring your own tent.

You could also try to make arrangements with the island's district officer (☎ 891 011), or else inquire with Sunflower Airlines.

Getting There & Away

Air Sunflower Airlines has a twice-weekly flight from Nadi to Suva (Nausori) and on to Rotuma (3¼ hours). See the air fares chart in the Getting Around chapter.

Boat Contact Kadavu Shipping (☎ 312 428, 311 766, Suva) for information on the irregular passenger service on the MV *Bulou-ni-Ceva* (F$90/130 for deck/cabin). The trip takes two days.

Yachts occasionally visit the island, and must obtain permission to anchor from the Ahau government station in Maka Bay, on the northern side of the island.

Language

One of the reasons many visitors from the English-speaking world find Fiji such a congenial place to visit is that they don't have to learn another language – the majority of the local people they come in contact with can speak English, and all signs and official forms are also in English. At the same time, for almost all local people, English is not their mother tongue – indigenous Fijians speak Fijian at home and Fiji Indians speak Fijian Hindi. If you really wish to have a better knowledge of the Fijian people and their culture, it's important that you know something of the Fijian languages – and, no matter how poor your first attempts at communicating, you'll receive much encouragement from Fijians.

FIJIAN

The many regional dialects found in Fiji today all descend, at least partly, from the language spoken by the original inhabitants. They would have come from one of the island groups to the west, either the Solomons or Vanuatu, having left their South-East Asian homeland at least 1000 years previously and spread eastwards by way of Indonesia, the Philippines and Papua New Guinea. From Fiji, groups left to settle the nearby islands of Rotuma, Tonga and Samoa, and from there they spread out to inhabit the rest of Polynesia, including Hawaii in the north, Rapa Nui (Easter Island) in the east, and Aotearoa (New Zealand) in the south. All the people in this vast area speak related languages belonging to the Austronesian language family.

There are some 300 regional varieties (dialects) of Fijian, all belonging to one of two major groupings. All varieties spoken to the west of a line extending north-south, with a couple of kinks, across the centre of Viti Levu belong to the Western Fijian group, while all others are Eastern Fijian.

Fortunately for the language learner there is one variety, based on the eastern varieties of the Bau-Rewa area, which is understood by Fijians throughout the islands. This standard form of Fijian is popularly known as *vosa vakabau* (Bauan), though linguists prefer to call it standard Fijian. It's used in conversation among Fijians from different areas, on the radio and in schools, and is the variety used in this chapter.

In Fijian, there are two ways of saying 'you', 'your', and 'yours'. If you are speaking to someone who is your superior, or an adult stranger, you should use a longer 'polite' form. This form is easy to remember because it always ends in *-nī*. In all other situations, a shorter 'informal' address is used.

Pronunciation

Fijian pronunciation isn't especially difficult for the English speaker, since most of the sounds found in Fijian have similar counterparts in English. The standard Fijian alphabet uses all the English letters, except 'x'. The letters 'h' and 'z' are used for borrowed words only and occur rarely.

Since the Fijian alphabet was devised relatively recently (in the 1830s), and by a missionary who was also a very competent linguist, it is phonetically consistent, ie each letter represents only one sound, and each sound is represented by only one letter.

As with all Pacific languages, the five Fijian vowels are pronounced much as they are in languages such as Spanish, German and Italian:

a	as in 'father'
e	as in 'bet'
i	as in 'machine'
o	as in 'more'
u	as in 'flute'

Vowels have both short or long variants, with the long vowel having a significantly longer sound. In this guide a long sound is indicated by a macron (stroke) above the vowel, eg **ā**. An approximate English equivalent is the difference between the final vowel sound in 'icy' and 'I see'. To convey the correct meaning of a word it's important that vowel length is taken into account in your pronunciation. For example, *mama* means 'a ring', *mamā* means 'chew it', and *māmā* means 'light' (in weight). Note that *māmā* takes about twice as long to pronounce as *mama*.

Most consonants are pronounced as they are in English, but there are a few differences you need to be aware of:

b	pronounced with a preceding nasal consonant as 'mb'
c	as the 'th' in 'this' (not as in 'thick')
d	pronounced with a preceding nasal consonant as 'nd'
g	as the 'ng' in 'sing' (not as in 'angry')
j	as the 'ch' in 'charm' but without a following puff of breath
k	as in 'kick' but without a following puff of breath
p	as in 'pip' but without a following puff of breath
q	as the 'ng' in 'angry' (not as in 'sing')
r	trilled as in Scottish English or Spanish
t	as in 'tap' but without a following puff of breath, often pronounced 'ch' before 'i'
v	pronounced with the lower lip against the upper lip (not against the upper teeth as in English) – somewhere between a 'v' and a 'b'

Occasionally on maps and in tourist publications you'll find a variation on the spelling system used in this guide – it's intended to be easier for English speakers to negotiate. In this alternative system, Yanuca is spelt 'Yanutha', Beqa 'Mbengga', and so on.

Further Reading

A good introduction to the language is Lonely Planet's *Fijian phrasebook*, written by Paul Geraghty, which provides all the

---

'Fijinglish'

Here are a few English words and phrases used in Fijian but with slightly different meanings:

Fijian English	English
grog	kava
bluff	lie, deceive
chow	food, eat
set	OK, ready
step	cut school, wag
Good luck to ...!	It serves ... right!
Not even!	No way!

---

essential words and phrases travellers need, along with grammar and cultural points. Lonely Planet's *South Pacific phrasebook* covers the languages of many South Pacific islands – ideal if you are visiting a few countries in one trip. Those interested in further studies of Fijian will find George Milner's *Fijian Grammar* (Government Press, Suva, 1956) an excellent introduction to the language. Likewise, Albert Schütz's *Spoken Fijian* (University Press of Hawaii, Honolulu, 1979) is a good primer for more advanced studies.

Greetings & Civilities

Hello.	*Bula!*
Hello. (reply)	*Io, bula/Ia, bula.* (more respectful)
Good morning.	*Yadra.*
Goodbye.	*Moce.* (if you don't expect to see them again)
See you later.	*Au sā liu mada.*

You may also hear the following:

Where are you going?
O(nì) lai vei? (used as we ask 'How are you?')
Nowhere special, just wandering around.
Sega, gādē gā. (as with the response to 'How are you' – no need to be specific)
Let's shake hands.
Daru lùlulu mada.

Yes.	*Io.*
No.	*Sega.*
Thank you (very much).	*Vinaka (vakalevu).*
Sorry. (general)	*(Nì) Vosota sara.*
What's your name?	*O cei na yacamu(nì)?*
My name is ...	*O yau o ...*
Pleased to meet you.	*Ia, (nì) bula.*
Where are you from?	*O iko/kemunì mai vei?*
I'm from ...	*O yau mai ...*
How old are you?	*O yabaki vica?*
I'm ... years old.	*Au yabaki ...*
Are you married?	*O(nì) vakawati?*
How many children do you have?	*Lē vica na luvemu(nì)?*
I don't have any children.	*E sega na luvequ.*
I have a daughter/son.	*E dua na luvequ yalewa/tagane.*

Language Difficulties

I don't speak Fijian/English.	*Au sega ni kilā na vosa vakaviti/ vakavālagi.*
Do you speak English?	*O(nì) kilā na vosa vakavālagi?*
I understand.	*Sā macala.*
I don't understand.	*E sega ni macala.*

Getting Around

Where is the ...?	*I vei na ...?*
airport	*rārā ni waqavuka*
(main) bus station	*basten*
bus stop	*ikelekele ni basi*

When does the ... leave/arrive?	*Vica na kaloko e lako/ kele kina na ...?*
bus	*basi*
plane	*waqavuka*
boat	*waqa*

I want to go to ...	*Au via lako i ...*
How do I get to ...?	*I vei na sala i ...?*
Is it far?	*E yawa?*
Can I walk there?	*E rawa niu taubale kina?*
Can you show me (on the map)?	*Vakaraitaka mada (ena mape)?*
Go straight ahead.	*Vakadodonu.*

| Turn left. | *Gole i na imawì.* |
| Turn right. | *Gole i na imatau.* |

Compass bearings (north etc) are never used. Instead you'll hear:

on the sea side of ...	*mai ... i wai*
on the land side of ...	*mai ... i vanua*
the far side of ...	*mai ... i liu*
this side of ...	*mai ... i muri*

Around Town

I'm looking for ...	*Au vāqarā ...*
a church	*na valenilotu*
the ... embassy	*na ebasì/valeni-volavola ni ...*
the market	*na mākete*
the museum	*na vale ni yau māroroi*
the police	*na ovisa*
the post office	*na posi(tōvesi)*
a public toilet	*na valelailai*
the tourist office	*na valenivolavola ni saravanua*

What time does it open/close?	*E dola/sogo ina vica?*
May I take your photo?	*Au tabaki iko mada?*
I'll send you the photo.	*Au na vākauta yani na itaba.*

Accommodation

Where is a ...?	*I vei ...?*
hotel	*dua na ōtela*
cheap hotel	*ōtela saurawarawa*

A note of caution. The term 'guesthouse' and its Fijian equivalent, *dua na bure ni vulagi*, often refer to establishments offering rooms for hire by the hour.

I'm going to stay for...	*Au na ...*
one day	*siga dua*
one week	*mācawa dua*

I'm not sure how long I'm staying.
    Sega ni macala na dedē ni noqu tiko.

Where is the bathroom?
I vei na valenisili?
Where is the toilet?
I vei na valelailai?

Food

restaurant	*valenikana*
Chinese/Indian restaurant	*valenikana ni kai Jaina/Idia*
food vendor	*volitaki kākana*
breakfast	*katalau*
lunch	*vakasigalevu*
dinner	*vakayakavi*

Shopping

How much is it?	*E vica?*
That's too expensive for me.	*Au sega ni rawata.*
I'm just looking.	*Sarasara gā.*
bookshop	*sitoa ni vola*
clothing shop	*sitoa ni sulu*
laundry	*valenisavasava*
market	*mākete*
pharmacy	*kēmesi*

Health

I need a doctor.	*Au via raici vuniwai.*
Where is the hospital?	*I vei na valenibula?*
I'm constipated.	*Au sega ni valelailai rawa.*
I have a stomach-ache.	*E mosi na ketequ.*
I'm diabetic.	*Au tauvi matenisuka.*
I'm epileptic.	*Au manumanusoni.*
I'm allergic to penicillin.	*E dau lako vakacā vei au na penisilini.*
I have my own syringe.	*E tiko na noqu icula.*
I'm on the pill.	*Au gunu vuanikau ni yalani.*

condoms	*rapa, kodom*
contraceptive	*wai ni yalani*
diarrhoea	*coka*
medicine	*wainimate*
nausea	*lomalomacā*
sanitary napkin	*qamuqamu*

Emergencies

Help!	*Oilei!*
Go away!	*Lako tani!*
Call a doctor!	*Qiria na vuniwai!*
Call an ambulance!	*Qiria na lori ni valenibula!*
I've been robbed!	*Butako!*
Call the police!	*Qiria na ovisa!*
I've been raped.	*Au sā kucuvi.*
I'm lost.	*Au sā sese.*
Where are the toilets?	*I vei na valelailai?*

Time & Dates

What time is it?	*Sā vica na kaloko?*
today	*nikua*
tonight	*na bogi nikua*
tomorrow	*nimataka*
yesterday	*nanoa*

Monday	*Mōniti*
Tuesday	*Tùsiti*
Wednesday	*Vukelulu*
Thursday	*Lotulevu*
Friday	*Vakaraubuka*
Saturday	*Vakarauwai*
Sunday	*Sigatabu*

Numbers

0	*saiva*
1	*dua*
2	*rua*
3	*tolu*
4	*vā*
5	*lima*
6	*ono*
7	*vitu*
8	*walu*
9	*ciwa*
10	*tini*
11	*tínikadua*
12	*tínikarua*
20	*rúasagavulu*
21	*rúasagavulukadua*
30	*tólusagavulu*
100	*dua na drau*
1000	*dua na udolu*

FIJIAN HINDI

Fijian Hindi (sometimes called Fiji Hindustani) is the language of all Fiji Indians. It has features of the many regional dialects of Hindi spoken by the Indian indentured labourers who were brought to Fiji from 1879 to 1916. (Some people call Fijian Hindi 'Bhojpuri', but this is the name of just one of the many dialects that contributed to the language.)

Many words from English are found in Fijian Hindi (such as room, towel, book and reef), but some of these have slightly different meanings. For example, the word 'book' in Fijian Hindi includes magazines and pamphlets, and if you refer to a person of the opposite sex as a 'friend', it implies that he/she is your sexual partner.

Fijian Hindi is used in all informal settings, such as in the family and among friends. But the 'Standard Hindi' of India is considered appropriate for formal contexts, such as in public speaking, radio broadcasting and writing. The Hindu majority write in Standard Hindi using the Devanagari script with a large number of words taken from the ancient Sanskrit language. The Muslims use the PersoArabic script and words taken from Persian and Arabic. (This literary style is often considered a separate language, called Urdu.) Fiji Indians have to learn Standard Hindi or Urdu in school along with English, so while they all speak Fijian Hindi informally, not everyone knows the formal varieties.

Some people say that Fijian Hindi is just a 'broken' or 'corrupted' version of standard Hindi. In fact, it is a legitimate dialect with its own grammatical rules and vocabulary unique to Fiji.

Pronunciation

Fijian Hindi is normally written only in guides for foreigners, such as this, and transcribed using the English alphabet. Since there are at least 42 different sounds in Fijian Hindi and only 26 letters in the English alphabet, some adjustments have to be made. The vowels are as follows:

a	as in 'about' or 'sofa'
ā	as in 'father'
e	as in 'bet'
i	as in 'police'
o	as in 'obey'
u	as in 'rule'
ai	as in 'hail'
āi	as in 'aisle'
au	as the 'o' in 'own'
oi	as in 'boil'

Fijian Hindi also has nasalised vowels, as in French words such as *bon* and *sans*. This is shown with a tilde over the vowel (eg **ã**) or with the letter 'n' if there's a following consonant.

The consonants **b, f, g** (as in 'go'), **h, j, k, l, m, n, p, s, v, y, w**, and **z** are similar to those of English. The symbol **č** is used for the 'ch' sound (as in 'chip') and **š** is used for the 'sh' sound (as in 'ship').

Pronunciation of other consonants is a little tricky. Fijian Hindi has two 't' sounds and two 'd' sounds – all different from English. In 't' and 'd' in English, the tip of the tongue touches the ridge behind the upper teeth, but in Fijian Hindi it either touches the back of the front teeth (dental) or is curled back to touch the roof of the mouth (retroflex). The dental consonants are shown as 't̪' and 'd̪' and the retroflex ones as 't̩' and 'd̩', and they're important in distinguishing meaning. For example:

āt̩ā/āt̪ā	coming/flour
t̩ab/t̪ab	then/tub
d̩āl/d̪āl	dhal (lentils)/branch

You can substitute the English 't' and 'd' for the retroflex ones and still be understood. There are also two 'r' sounds different from English. In the first, written as **r**, the tongue touches the ridge above the upper teeth and is flapped quickly forward, similar to the way we say the 't' sound in 'butter' when speaking quickly. In the second, written as **r̩**, the tongue is curled back, touching the roof of the mouth (as in the retroflex sounds) and then flapped forward. You can sometimes substitute English 'rd' for this sound.

Finally, there are 'aspirated' consonants. If you hold your hand in front of your mouth and say 'Peter Piper picked a peck of pickled peppers', you'll feel a puff of air each time you say the 'p' sound – this is called aspiration. When you say 'spade, spill, spit, speak', you don't feel the puff of air, because in these words the 'p' sound is not aspirated. In Fijian Hindi, aspiration is important in distinguishing meaning. Aspiration is indicated by the use of an 'h' after the consonants – for example:

pul/phul	bridge/flower
kālā/khālā	black/valley
ṭāli/ṭhāli	clapping/brass plate

Other aspirated consonants are:

bh	as in 'grab him' said quickly
čh	as in 'church hat' said quickly
ḍh	as in 'mad house'
gh	as in 'slug him'
jh	as in 'bridge house'
ṭh	as in 'out house'

Note that some books use a different system of transcription. For example, 'aa' may be used for ā and 'T', 'D', 'R' for ṭ, ḍ and ṛ.

Greetings & Civilities
There are no exact equivalents for 'hello' and 'goodbye' in Fijian Hindi. The most common greeting is *kaise* (How are you?). The usual reply is *ṭik* (fine). In parting, it's common to say *fir milegā* (We'll meet again).

More formal greetings are: *namaṣṭe* (for Hindus), *salām alaikum* (for Muslims) – the reply to the latter is *alaikum salām*.

There are no equivalents for 'please' and 'thank you'. To be polite in making requests, people use the word *ṭhoṛā* (a little) and a special form of the verb ending in *nā*, eg *ṭhoṛā nimak denā* (Please pass the salt).

They also use the polite form of the word 'you', *āp*, instead of the informal *tum*. Polite and informal modes of address are indicated in this guide by the abbreviations 'pol' and 'inf' respectively.

For 'thanks', people often just say *ačhā* (good). The English 'please' and 'thank you' are also commonly used. The word *ḍhanyavāḍ* is used to thank someone who has done something special for you. It means something like 'blessings be bestowed upon you'.

Yes.	*hã*
No.	*nahī*
Maybe.	*sāyiṭ*
I'm sorry. (for something serious)	*māf karnā*
What's your name?	*āpke/ṭumār nām kā hai?* (pol/inf)
My name is ...	*hamār nām ...*
Where are you from?	*āp/ṭum kahã ke hai?* (pol/inf)
I'm from ...	*ham ... ke hai*
Are you married?	*šāḍi ho gayā?*
How many children do you have?	*kiṭnā laṛkā hai?*
I don't have any children.	*laṛkā nahī hai*
Two boys and three girls.	*ḍui laṛkā aur ṭin laṛki*

Language Difficulties
Do you speak English?	*āp/ṭum English bolṭā?* (pol/inf)
Does anyone here speak English?	*koi English bole?*
I don't understand.	*ham nahī samajhṭā*

Getting Around
Where is the ...?	*... kahã hai?*
shop	*ḍukān*
airport	*eyapoṭ*
(main) bus station	*basṭen*
market	*mākeṭ*
temple	*manḍir*
mosque	*masjiḍ*
church	*čeč*

You can also use the English words hotel, guesthouse, camping ground, toilet, post office, embassy, tourist information office, museum, cafe, restaurant and telephone.

I want to go to ...	*ham ... jāe mangṭā*
Is it near/far?	*nagič/ḍur hai?*

Can I go by foot?	*paiḍar jāe sakṭā?*
Go straight ahead.	*sidhā jāo*
Please write down the address.	*ṭhoṛā eḍres likh denā*

By the ...	*... ke pās*
coconut tree	*nariyal ke peṛ*
mango tree	*ām ke peṛ*
breadfruit tree	*belfuṭ ke peṛ*
sugar-cane field	*gannā kheṭ*

When does the ... leave/arrive?	*kiṭnā baje ... čale/ pahunče?*
ship	*jahāj*
car	*moṭṭar*

You can also use the English words bus, plane, boat.

Food & Drink

to eat, food	*khāna*
to drink	*pinā*
tea	*čā*
yaqona (kava)	*nengonā, grog*
liquor	*ḍāru*
beer	*bia*
water	*pāni*

I don't drink alcohol.	*ham ḍāru nahī piṭā*
I don't eat hot (spicy) food.	*ham ṭiṭā nahī khāṭā*
I don't eat meat.	*ham gos nahī khāṭā*
I eat vegetables.	*ham ṭarkāri khāṭā*
Just a little.	*ṭoṛā ṭhoṛā*
Enough!	*bas!*
very good	*bahuṭačhā*

Health

I'm ...	*hame ...*
diabetic	*čini ke bimāri hai*
epileptic	*mirgi awe*
asthmatic	*sās fule ke bimāri hai*

I'm allergic to penicillin.	*penesilin se ham bimār ho jāi*
I have a stomach-ache.	*hamār peṭ pirāwe*
I feel nauseous.	*hame čhāṇṭ lage*
I'm constipated.	*peṭ kaṛā ho gayā*

Emergencies

Help me!	*hame maḍad karo!*
Go away!	*jāo!*
Call the doctor/ police.	*ḍokṭā ke/pulis ke bulāo*
Where is the hospital?	*āspaṭāl kahã hai?*
I've been robbed.	*čori ho gayā*
I've been raped.	*koi hame reip karis*

condom	*konḍom, raba*
contraceptive	*pariwār niyojan ke dawāi*
medicine	*dawāi*
sanitary napkin	*peḍ, nepkin*
tampon	*ṭampon*

Time & Dates

What time is it?	*kiṭnā baje?*
It's ... o'clock.	*... baje*
When?	*kab?*
today	*āj*
tonight	*āj rāṭke*
tomorrow	*bihān*
yesterday	*kal*

English days of the week are generally used.

Numbers

1		*ek*
2		*ḍui*
3		*ṭin*
4		*čār*
5		*pānč*
6		*čhe*
7		*sāṭ*
8		*āṭh*
9		*nau*
10		*das*
100		*sau*
1000		*hazār*

Note: English numbers are generally used for 20–99.

Glossary

achar – Indian pickles
adi – female chief
arkatis – agents under commission collecting indentured labourers

baigan – eggplant
balabala – tree ferns
bêche-de-mer – a type of sea cucumber with an elongated body, leathery skin and a cluster of tentacles at the mouth; they were gathered by early traders and sold in China and South-East Asia as a delicacy and aphrodisiac
beka – flying fox
bele – leafy green vegetable
bete – priests of the old Fijian religion
bhaji – spinach, or any leafy green vegetable
bhindi – okra
bilibili – bamboo raft
bilo – drinking vessel made from half a coconut shell
breadfruit – a tree of the Pacific Islands, the trunk of which is used for lumber and canoe building; the fruit, which has a texture like bread, is cooked and eaten
bua – frangipani
bula – cheers (literally, 'life')
bula shirt – tapa or floral design shirt
burau – ceremonial *yaqona*-drinking ritual
bure – thatched dwelling
bure bose – meeting house
bure kalou – ancient temple

choro – steal
cibi – death dance
copra – dried coconut kernel, used for making coconut oil

dadakulaci – banded sea krait, Fiji's most common snake
dakua – a tree of the kauri family
dalo – the taro plant, cultivated for its edible root stock
dele – (or *wate*) a dance in which women sexually humiliated enemy corpses and captives
dhaniya – coriander
drua – double-hulled canoe

girmitiya – indentured labourer

ibe – a mat
ibuburau – drinking vessels used in *yaqona* rites
ika – fish
ivi – Polynesian chestnut tree

jalebi – an Indian sweet
jira – cumin

kai colo – hill people
kaihidi – Fiji Indian
kaivalagi – literally, 'people from far away', Europeans
kaiviti – indigenous Fijian
kanikani – scaly skin from excessive *kava* use
kasou – very drunk
kava – the Polynesian pepper shrub *(Piper methysticum),* or a drink prepared from its aromatic roots
kerekere – custom of shared property
kokoda – fish salad
koro – village headed by a hereditary chief
kumala – sweet potato

lagoon – a body of water that is bounded by an encircling reef
liku – the skirt of womanhood, made out of grasses or strips of pandanus leaves – this tradition was phased out by the missionaries
lolo – coconut cream
lovo – feast in which food is cooked in a pit oven

malo – see *masi*
mangrove – a tropical tree that grows in tidal mud flats and extends looping prop roots along the shore
masala – curry powder
masi – (also known as *malo* or *tapa*) bark cloth with designs printed in black and rust; different styles are also made in other regions of the South Pacific
mataqali – extended family or landowning group

meke – a dance performance that enacts stories and legends

nama – an edible seaweed that looks like miniature green grapes
narak – hell
NAUI – National Association of Underwater Instructors

open-water course – a certification diving course run by PADI or NAUI

PADI – Professional Association of Diving Instructors, the world's largest diving association
paidar – on foot
paisa – money
pandanus – a plant common to the tropics whose sword-shaped leaves are used to make mats and baskets
piala – small metal enamel bowl
puri – deep-fried, flat Indian bread

rara – ceremonial ground
ratu – male chief
roti – flat Indian bread (like tortillas)
rourou – taro leaves

saqa – trevally fish
seo – an Indian savoury snack
sevusevu – a presentation of a gift such as *yaqona* or, more powerfully, a *tabua* as a request for certain favours
sulu – skirt or wrapped cloth worn to below the knees

tabu – forbidden or sacred, implying a religious sanction
tabua – the teeth of sperm whales, which have a special ceremonial value for Fijians; they are still used as negotiating tokens to symbolise esteem or atonement
taga yaqona – pounded *kava*
takia – Fijian canoe
talanoa – to chat, to tell stories
tanoa – *yaqona* drinking bowl
tapa – see *masi*
tavioka – cassava, a type of root crop
tevoro – a god of the old Fijian religion
tikina – a group of Fijian villages linked together
trade winds – the near-constant winds that dominate most of the tropics
tui – king
turaga – chief
turaga-ni-koro – hereditary chief

vale – a family house
vale lailai – toilet
vanua – land, region, place
vasu – a system in which a chiefly woman's sons could claim support and ownership over the property of her brothers from other villages
vatu ni bokola – head-chopping stone
veli – a group of little gods
vesi – ironwood, considered a sacred timber
vilavilairevo – fire walking (literally, 'jumping into the oven')
vinaka – thank you
Viti – another name for Fiji

waka – bunch of *kava* roots
wakalou – climbing fern species
wate – see *dele*

yaqona – (also known as *kava*) a mildly narcotic beverage drunk socially
yasana – a province formed by several *tikina*
yavu – bases for housing

Acknowledgments

THANKS

Many thanks to the travellers who used the last edition and wrote to us with helpful hints, useful advice and interesting anecdotes:

A J & E S Bensemann, Abdul Kalaam, Aida & Richard Crimes, Alaisdair Raynham, Alan Bradley, Alan Kendall, Alan Wong, Alexander Erich, Alexander Zumbrunn, Alison Wiseman, Allen Hoppes, Amanda Norman, Amir & Simone Zimmermann, Andrea Cutler, Andrea Lanyon, Andrea Schaefer, Andrea Schuele, Andrew Mitchell, Andy Davis, Andy Ganner, Angie Doyle, Anice Paterson, Anna & Rolf Hedman, Anna Reiss, Annalisa Hounsome, Anne Bowyer, Annie Miskofitidis, Antonia Butler, Aron Wahl, Arthur VD Mast, Assaf Zvuloni, Barb De Filippo, Barnie Jones, Beda Brun del Re, Ben Wright, BJ Skane, Bjorn Fuchtenkord, Bob Kelley, Brad Johnson, Brooke Charles, Bruce Paterson, Cara Ely, Caragh Curran, Carol Ann Prince, Carolyn & Craig Barrack, Cassidy Thomas, Catherine Watkins, Chandrakant N Shah, Charlie Tomberg, Charlott Lobsack, Charlotta Homanen, Chris Souilivaert, Christine Porter, Claire King, Clare Kenny, Clare Mackinlay, Clare Sixsmith, Collin McKenny, Curly Carswell, Dan Fowler, Daniel Munday, Darcy Gimas, Dave Potter, Dave Rasmussen, David & Ceri-Joy Peacock, David B Leventhal, David Moreton, David Owen, Deborah Todd, Derek Bissell, Do Cammick, Donna Roemling, Dr Andreas & Niklas Hau, Dr Irmgard Ehlers, Edward J Benett, Eileen Barrett, Eirik Kavli, Eleanor Swain, Elizabeth Pollard, Ellen Daniell, Emily Levan, Erwin & Diana van Engelen, Eva Cermak, Fabio Barella, Felette Dittmer, Felix Naschold, Francesco Neva, Frank Van Kampen, Fried Hoeben, Frode Nebell, Garath Harper, Gemma Hall, Geoffrey Tickell, George McLelland, Geraldine Hopper, Gordon Reed, Graham Whitehead, H & D Holappa, Hakon Sonneland, Hazel Cameron Johnson, Hazel John, Helen Woodward, Helle Bjerre, Hellmut Golde, Henrik Nyberg, Henrik Sondergaard, Howard Jamieson, Ian Sayer, Impetus Holowillums, Jackie Carver, Jackie Keeble, Jacqueline Merlini, James Gobert, Jane Battersby, Jane Dunn, Jane McKenzie, Janette Denison, Janette Mather, Jean Underwood, Jemma Harris, Jenny Visser, Jeri Solomon, Jim McNamara, Jo Scott, Joan Bayes, Joanne Longbottom, Joe & Helene Tuwai, Joel & Maria Teresa Prades, John & Eleanore Woollard, John & Jean Wheatley Price, John Caldeira, John Donkin, John Fowler, John Turnpenny, Julia Ditrich, Julie Louttit, June Best, K Shield, K Handley, Karen & Paul Keiser, Karyn Steer, Katherine Wharton, Kathy Forsyth, Ken & Margery Nash, Kennerly Clay, Kevin Crampton, Kevin McGarry, Kim Van Dyke, Kirsten Hartshorne, Kirsty Morris, Larry Berkowitz, Lauren Baldoni, Laurence & Jean-Francois Walhin, Leigh & Mike Ackland, Leigh Ann Whyte, Lesley James, Leslie Leung, Lincoln Bramwell, Linda Nawava, Lisa Nowacki, Liz Elmhirst, Louise Curtis, Lynne Mitchell, M & N Nakamura, M Witheu, Marie Boyle, Mark & Anita Voskamp, Mark Capra, Mark Domroese, Mark Patel, Mark Sigman, Martin & Marie Lycett, Martin Kyllo, Matthew Whitaker, Melanie Copland, Melanie Knox, Melissa Hewitt, Michael Coggins, Michael Livni, Michele Taylor, Mike Fee, Mikey Sheahan, Morten Hansen, N Southern, Nathalie Meunier, Neil Griggs, Nerolie & Geoff Stodart, Nicholas Lee, Nick Buckle, Nicola Schaab, Nils Holle, Pat Kirikiti, Paul Cauthorn, Paul D Varady, Paul Francis, Penny Vine, Peter Beer, Peter O'Brien, Phil Dunnington, Philip Bennett, Philip McKernan, Phillip Reineck, Pia & Michael Dowling, Rachel & Brian Dodds, Rachel Lynch, Ramie Blatt, Rebecca Leask, Rich Brantingham, Richelle Letendre, Rob Hulls, Rob Pitts, Rob Stephenson, Robert Saunders, Robin Irwin, Roger Roth, Roger Thiedeman, Ron Eisele, Ron Rosenthal, Rudi Kaur, Rusi Brown, Russell Hall, Sam Williams, Sarah Schnapp, Sasha Hayman, Sean McQuaid, Shannon Boyer, Sharon Wheatly, Simon Anderson, Simon Swift, Simon Taylor, Skadi Heckmueïler, Solveig Michelsen, Srinivas Addanki, Stefan Estermann, Steve & Sarah Williams, Steve Booth, Steve Layton, Steve Preston, Steve Rovai, Stuart Chambers, Stuart Dees, Stuart Norton, Sue & John Smith, Susan Ampleford, Terry & Rae Powell, Tevita & Carolyn Fotofili, Thomas Woltmann, Tina Rich, Tracey McGregor, Ulla Bunz, Valerie & David Box, Vida Gircys, Warren Leonard, Warren Nunn, Wes & Jill Barrett, Wilna van Eyssen.

week #3 June 26 - July 3
Seru/Heather - Big.
Manoa - Book Project Fiji

NubuLevu / Nasivikoso

week #3
July 2 - Return to Nadi

:)

WEEK #4
July 3 - July 10
- Mamanuca Islands, Waya Island,
- Seashell Cove, Suva

Thurs
July 3 - sailing thru Mamanuca Islands
Mystery Island for Lunch

meet Evan
allowances
Fri (TAKE pizzas) Nadi overnight. · Cook at 5am -5:30 return
· 8am Cap Cook -Photos pm

July 4 - travel to Garden of Sleeping Giant
Evan shows up Lautoka + Waya Island [11:30 a.m.]

SAT
July 5 - Waya - am. snorkeling p.m. entertain

Sun July 6 - Waya ..dead day

Mon July 7 - Return to Lautoka, travel
sunrise hike pm MTN Biking
to Seashell Cove.

Tues July 8 - Group splits - surfing, diving,
Natadola Beach + Sigatoka Sand
Dunes.
Seashell Cove overnight.

Julia/SHAYNA

WED July 9 → Travel to Suva. City Day
South Pacific Games

How to Suva Boat/Car — Overnight in Suva (Camping?)
Get to Suva

WEEK 5 (NAKUKU?)

July 10-17 - NAKUKU Village, Seashell
SAVUSAVU to MUMU'S — Cove, Taveuni, Yasawa Islands,
Nasivikoko

Thurs July 10 - Group Splits. <u>Jeff/Michael</u> (west) surfing
- Lindsay/Michelle - Big Fiji (week) — seashell cove
DAVE/MEG - Nasivikoso (week)

Get off at Savu Savu → others in Suva then Savusavu
to NAKUKU (me?) overnight
(week)

WED July 16 — Yasawa Islands
NADI meets with EVAN

WEEK 6 (LAST WEEK)
July - 17-24

Thurs July 17 - Surf/Dive + Nakuku return
to NADI (me?)

FRI July 18 - Nasivikoso for Celebrations

Sat July 19 - Nasivikoso Village

SUN - July 20 -22 - NAVSORI Highlands (?)
TUES

July 23 - return to Nadi - Meet w/
overnight — EVAN

WEEK 7
July 24 - July 31
BFE - TAVEUNI
Community Service - SUVA SAVUSAVU
NAKUKU Village

WEEK 8
July 31 - Aug 7
Nasivikoso, MAMANUCA ISLANDS
Waya ISLAND

WEEK 9
Aug 7 - Aug 14
Big Fiji Explorer

My responsibilities
?'s
- Where is seashell cove, from sea shell cove
- How do we get to suva - boat/carrier?
- ~~Where is NAKUKU~~
- how do we travel back to Nasivikoso from NAKUKU
- CAN I join BFE when we split?
    w/ Michelle + Lindsay

- Jeff - 7:20am on July 23rd
- manoa - bring Alex back
          Thurs, July 10 (Film)
- PACK FOR 2 weeks
- Photos of BIG GROUPS
- Distribute film - tomorrow a.m. → Mike
- double copies

LONELY PLANET

ON THE ROAD

Travel Guides explore cities, regions and countries, and supply information on transport, restaurants and accommodation, covering all budgets. They come with reliable, easy-to-use maps, practical advice, cultural and historical facts and a rundown on attractions both on and off the beaten track. There are over 200 titles in this classic series, covering nearly every country in the world.

 Lonely Planet Upgrades extend the shelf life of existing travel guides by detailing any changes that may affect travel in a region since a book has been published. Upgrades can be downloaded for free from **www.lonelyplanet.com/upgrades**

For travellers with more time than money, **Shoestring** guides offer dependable, first-hand information with hundreds of detailed maps, plus insider tips for stretching money as far as possible. Covering entire continents in most cases, the six-volume shoestring guides are known around the world as 'backpackers bibles'.

For the discerning short-term visitor, **Condensed** guides highlight the best a destination has to offer in a full-colour, pocket-sized format designed for quick access. They include everything from top sights and walking tours to opinionated reviews of where to eat, stay, shop and have fun.

CitySync lets travellers use their Palm™ or Visor™ hand-held computers to guide them through a city with handy tips on transport, history, cultural life, major sights, and shopping and entertainment options. It can also quickly search and sort hundreds of reviews of hotels, restaurants and attractions, and pinpoint their location on scrollable street maps. CitySync can be downloaded from **www.citysync.com**

MAPS & ATLASES

Lonely Planet's **City Maps** feature downtown and metropolitan maps, as well as transit routes and walking tours. The maps come complete with an index of streets, a listing of sights and a plastic coat for extra durability.

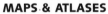

Road Atlases are an essential navigation tool for serious travellers. Cross-referenced with the guidebooks, they also feature distance and climate charts and a complete site index.

LONELY PLANET

ESSENTIALS

Read This First books help new travellers to hit the road with confidence. These invaluable predeparture guides give step-by-step advice on preparing for a trip, budgeting, arranging a visa, planning an itinerary and staying safe while still getting off the beaten track.

Healthy Travel pocket guides offer a regional rundown on disease hot spots and practical advice on predeparture health measures, staying well on the road and what to do in emergencies. The guides come with a user-friendly design and helpful diagrams and tables.

Lonely Planet's **Phrasebooks** cover the essential words and phrases travellers need when they're strangers in a strange land. They come in a pocket-sized format with colour tabs for quick reference, extensive vocabulary lists, easy-to-follow pronunciation keys and two-way dictionaries.

Miffed by blurry photos of the Taj Mahal? Tired of the classic 'top of the head cut off' shot? **Travel Photography: A Guide to Taking Better Pictures** will help you turn ordinary holiday snaps into striking images and give you the know-how to capture every scene, from frenetic festivals to peaceful beach sunrises.

Lonely Planet's **Travel Journal** is a lightweight but sturdy travel diary for jotting down all those on-the-road observations and significant travel moments. It comes with a handy time-zone wheel, a world map and useful travel information.

Lonely Planet's eKno is an all-in-one communication service developed especially for travellers. It offers low-cost international calls and free email and voicemail so that you can keep in touch while on the road. Check it out on **www.ekno.lonelyplanet.com**

FOOD & RESTAURANT GUIDES

Lonely Planet's **Out to Eat** guides recommend the brightest and best places to eat and drink in top international cities. These gourmet companions are arranged by neighbourhood, packed with dependable maps, garnished with scene-setting photos and served with quirky features.

For people who live to eat, drink and travel, **World Food** guides explore the culinary culture of each country. Entertaining and adventurous, each guide is packed with detail on staples and specialities, regional cuisine and local markets, as well as sumptuous recipes, comprehensive culinary dictionaries and lavish photos good enough to eat.

OUTDOOR GUIDES

For those who believe the best way to see the world is on foot, Lonely Planet's **Walking Guides** detail everything from family strolls to difficult treks, with 'when to go and how to do it' advice supplemented by reliable maps and essential travel information.

Cycling Guides map a destination's best bike tours, long and short, in day-by-day detail. They contain all the information a cyclist needs, including advice on bike maintenance, places to eat and stay, innovative maps with detailed cues to the rides, and elevation charts.

The **Watching Wildlife** series is perfect for travellers who want authoritative information but don't want to tote a heavy field guide. Packed with advice on where, when and how to view a region's wildlife, each title features photos of over 300 species and contains engaging comments on the local flora and fauna.

With underwater colour photos throughout, **Pisces Books** explore the world's best diving and snorkelling areas. Each book contains listings of diving services and dive resorts, detailed information on depth, visibility and difficulty of dives, and a roundup of the marine life you're likely to see through your mask.

LONELY PLANET

OFF THE ROAD

Journeys, the travel literature series written by renowned travel authors, capture the spirit of a place or illuminate a culture with a journalist's attention to detail and a novelist's flair for words. These are tales to soak up while you're actually on the road or dip into as an at-home armchair indulgence.

The range of lavishly illustrated **Pictorial** books is just the ticket for both travellers and dreamers. Off-beat tales and vivid photographs bring the adventure of travel to your doorstep long before the journey begins and long after it is over.

Lonely Planet **Videos** encourage the same independent, tough-minded approach as the guidebooks. Currently airing throughout the world, this award-winning series features innovative footage and an original soundtrack.

Yes, we know, work is tough, so do a little bit of deskside dreaming with the spiral-bound Lonely Planet **Diary** or a Lonely Planet **Wall Calendar**, filled with great photos from around the world.

TRAVELLERS NETWORK

Lonely Planet Online. Lonely Planet's award-winning Web site has insider information on hundreds of destinations, from Amsterdam to Zimbabwe, complete with interactive maps and relevant links. The site also offers the latest travel news, recent reports from travellers on the road, guidebook upgrades, a travel links site, an online book-buying option and a lively travellers bulletin board. It can be viewed at **www.lonelyplanet.com** or AOL keyword: lp.

Planet Talk is a quarterly print newsletter, full of gossip, advice, anecdotes and author articles. It provides an antidote to the being-at-home blues and lets you plan and dream for the next trip. Contact the nearest Lonely Planet office for your free copy.

Comet, the free Lonely Planet newsletter, comes via email once a month. It's loaded with travel news, advice, dispatches from authors, travel competitions and letters from readers. To subscribe, click on the Comet subscription link on the front page of the Web site.

Lonely Planet Guides by Region

Lonely Planet is known worldwide for publishing practical, reliable and no-nonsense travel information in our guides and on our Web site. The Lonely Planet list covers just about every accessible part of the world. Currently there are 16 series: Travel guides, Shoestring guides, Condensed guides, Phrasebooks, Read This First, Healthy Travel, Walking guides, Cycling guides, Watching Wildlife guides, Pisces Diving & Snorkeling guides, City Maps, Road Atlases, Out to Eat, World Food, Journeys travel literature and Pictorials.

AFRICA Africa on a shoestring • Botswana • Cairo • Cairo City Map • Cape Town • Cape Town City Map • East Africa • Egypt • Egyptian Arabic phrasebook • Ethiopia, Eritrea & Djibouti • Ethiopian Amharic phrasebook • The Gambia & Senegal • Healthy Travel Africa • Kenya • Malawi • Morocco • Moroccan Arabic phrasebook • Mozambique • Namibia • Read This First: Africa • South Africa, Lesotho & Swaziland • Southern Africa • Southern Africa Road Atlas • Swahili phrasebook • Tanzania, Zanzibar & Pemba • Trekking in East Africa • Tunisia • Watching Wildlife East Africa • Watching Wildlife Southern Africa • West Africa • World Food Morocco • Zambia • Zimbabwe, Botswana & Namibia
Travel Literature: Mali Blues: Traveling to an African Beat • The Rainbird: A Central African Journey • Songs to an African Sunset: A Zimbabwean Story

AUSTRALIA & THE PACIFIC Aboriginal Australia & the Torres Strait Islands •Auckland • Australia • Australian phrasebook • Australia Road Atlas • Cycling Australia • Cycling New Zealand • Fiji • Fijian phrasebook • Healthy Travel Australia, NZ & the Pacific • Islands of Australia's Great Barrier Reef • Melbourne • Melbourne City Map • Micronesia • New Caledonia • New South Wales • New Zealand • Northern Territory • Outback Australia • Out to Eat – Melbourne • Out to Eat – Sydney • Papua New Guinea • Pidgin phrasebook • Queensland • Rarotonga & the Cook Islands • Samoa • Solomon Islands • South Australia • South Pacific • South Pacific phrasebook • Sydney • Sydney City Map • Sydney Condensed • Tahiti & French Polynesia • Tasmania • Tonga • Tramping in New Zealand • Vanuatu • Victoria • Walking in Australia • Watching Wildlife Australia • Western Australia
Travel Literature: Islands in the Clouds: Travels in the Highlands of New Guinea • Kiwi Tracks: A New Zealand Journey • Sean & David's Long Drive

CENTRAL AMERICA & THE CARIBBEAN Bahamas, Turks & Caicos • Baja California • Belize, Guatemala & Yucatán • Bermuda • Central America on a shoestring • Costa Rica • Costa Rica Spanish phrasebook • Cuba • Cycling Cuba • Dominican Republic & Haiti • Eastern Caribbean • Guatemala • Havana • Healthy Travel Central & South America • Jamaica • Mexico • Mexico City • Panama • Puerto Rico • Read This First: Central & South America • Virgin Islands • World Food Caribbean • World Food Mexico • Yucatán
Travel Literature: Green Dreams: Travels in Central America

EUROPE Amsterdam • Amsterdam City Map • Amsterdam Condensed • Andalucía • Athens • Austria • Baltic States phrasebook • Barcelona • Barcelona City Map • Belgium & Luxembourg • Berlin • Berlin City Map • Britain • British phrasebook • Brussels, Bruges & Antwerp • Brussels City Map • Budapest • Budapest City Map • Canary Islands • Catalunya & the Costa Brava • Central Europe • Central Europe phrasebook • Copenhagen • Corfu & the Ionians • Corsica • Crete • Crete Condensed • Croatia • Cycling Britain • Cycling France • Cyprus • Czech & Slovak Republics • Czech phrasebook • Denmark • Dublin • Dublin City Map • Dublin Condensed • Eastern Europe • Eastern Europe phrasebook • Edinburgh • Edinburgh City Map • England • Estonia, Latvia & Lithuania • Europe on a shoestring • Europe phrasebook • Finland • Florence • Florence City Map • France • Frankfurt City Map • Frankfurt Condensed • French phrasebook • Georgia, Armenia & Azerbaijan • Germany • German phrasebook • Greece • Greek Islands • Greek phrasebook • Hungary • Iceland, Greenland & the Faroe Islands • Ireland • Italian phrasebook • Italy • Kraków • Lisbon • The Loire • London • London City Map • London Condensed • Madrid • Madrid City Map • Malta • Mediterranean Europe • Milan, Turin & Genoa • Moscow • Munich • Netherlands • Normandy • Norway • Out to Eat – London • Out to Eat – Paris • Paris • Paris City Map • Paris Condensed • Poland • Polish phrasebook • Portugal • Portuguese phrasebook • Prague • Prague City Map • Provence & the Côte d'Azur • Read This First: Europe • Rhodes & the Dodecanese • Romania & Moldova • Rome • Rome City Map • Rome Condensed • Russia, Ukraine & Belarus • Russian phrasebook • Scandinavian & Baltic Europe • Scandinavian phrasebook • Scotland • Sicily • Slovenia • South-West France • Spain • Spanish phrasebook • Stockholm • St Petersburg • St Petersburg City Map • Sweden • Switzerland • Tuscany • Ukrainian phrasebook • Venice • Vienna • Wales • Walking in Britain • Walking in France • Walking in Ireland • Walking in Italy • Walking in Scotland • Walking in Spain • Walking in Switzerland • Western Europe • World Food France • World Food Greece • World Food Ireland • World Food Italy • World Food Spain **Travel Literature:** After Yugoslavia • Love and War in the Apennines • The Olive Grove: Travels in Greece • On the Shores of the Mediterranean • Round Ireland in Low Gear • A Small Place in Italy

Lonely Planet Mail Order

Lonely Planet products are distributed worldwide. They are also available by mail order from Lonely Planet, so if you have difficulty finding a title please write to us. North and South American residents should write to 150 Linden St, Oakland, CA 94607, USA; European and African residents should write to 10a Spring Place, London NW5 3BH, UK; and residents of other countries to Locked Bag 1, Footscray, Victoria 3011, Australia.

INDIAN SUBCONTINENT & THE INDIAN OCEAN Bangladesh • Bengali phrasebook • Bhutan • Delhi • Goa • Healthy Travel Asia & India • Hindi & Urdu phrasebook • India • India & Bangladesh City Map • Indian Himalaya • Karakoram Highway • Kathmandu City Map • Kerala • Madagascar • Maldives • Mauritius, Réunion & Seychelles • Mumbai (Bombay) • Nepal • Nepali phrasebook • North India • Pakistan • Rajasthan • Read This First: Asia & India • South India • Sri Lanka • Sri Lanka phrasebook • Tibet • Tibetan phrasebook • Trekking in the Indian Himalaya • Trekking in the Karakoram & Hindukush • Trekking in the Nepal Himalaya • World Food India **Travel Literature:** The Age of Kali: Indian Travels and Encounters • Hello Goodnight: A Life of Goa • In Rajasthan • Maverick in Madagascar • A Season in Heaven: True Tales from the Road to Kathmandu • Shopping for Buddhas • A Short Walk in the Hindu Kush • Slowly Down the Ganges

MIDDLE EAST & CENTRAL ASIA Bahrain, Kuwait & Qatar • Central Asia • Central Asia phrasebook • Dubai • Farsi (Persian) phrasebook • Hebrew phrasebook • Iran • Israel & the Palestinian Territories • Istanbul • Istanbul City Map • Istanbul to Cairo • Istanbul to Kathmandu • Jerusalem • Jerusalem City Map • Jordan • Lebanon • Middle East • Oman & the United Arab Emirates • Syria • Turkey • Turkish phrasebook • World Food Turkey • Yemen **Travel Literature:** Black on Black: Iran Revisited • Breaking Ranks: Turbulent Travels in the Promised Land • The Gates of Damascus • Kingdom of the Film Stars: Journey into Jordan

NORTH AMERICA Alaska • Boston • Boston City Map • Boston Condensed • British Columbia • California & Nevada • California Condensed • Canada • Chicago • Chicago City Map • Chicago Condensed • Florida • Georgia & the Carolinas • Great Lakes • Hawaii • Hiking in Alaska • Hiking in the USA • Honolulu & Oahu City Map • Las Vegas • Los Angeles • Los Angeles City Map • Louisiana & the Deep South • Miami • Miami City Map • Montreal • New England • New Orleans • New Orleans City Map • New York City • New York City City Map • New York City Condensed • New York, New Jersey & Pennsylvania • Oahu • Out to Eat – San Francisco • Pacific Northwest • Rocky Mountains • San Diego & Tijuana • San Francisco • San Francisco City Map • Seattle • Seattle City Map • Southwest • Texas • Toronto • USA • USA phrasebook • Vancouver • Vancouver City Map • Virginia & the Capital Region • Washington, DC • Washington, DC City Map • World Food New Orleans **Travel Literature**: Caught Inside: A Surfer's Year on the California Coast • Drive Thru America

NORTH-EAST ASIA Beijing • Beijing City Map • Cantonese phrasebook • China • Hiking in Japan • Hong Kong & Macau • Hong Kong City Map • Hong Kong Condensed • Japan • Japanese phrasebook • Korea • Korean phrasebook • Kyoto • Mandarin phrasebook • Mongolia • Mongolian phrasebook • Seoul • Shanghai • South-West China • Taiwan • Tokyo • Tokyo Condensed • World Food Hong Kong • World Food Japan **Travel Literature:** In Xanadu: A Quest • Lost Japan

SOUTH AMERICA Argentina, Uruguay & Paraguay • Bolivia • Brazil • Brazilian phrasebook • Buenos Aires • Buenos Aires City Map • Chile & Easter Island • Colombia • Ecuador & the Galapagos Islands • Healthy Travel Central & South America • Latin American Spanish phrasebook • Peru • Quechua phrasebook • Read This First: Central & South America • Rio de Janeiro • Rio de Janeiro City Map • Santiago de Chile • South America on a shoestring • Trekking in the Patagonian Andes • Venezuela **Travel Literature**: Full Circle: A South American Journey

SOUTH-EAST ASIA Bali & Lombok • Bangkok • Bangkok City Map • Burmese phrasebook • Cambodia • Cycling Vietnam, Laos & Cambodia • East Timor phrasebook • Hanoi • Healthy Travel Asia & India • Hill Tribes phrasebook • Ho Chi Minh City (Saigon) • Indonesia • Indonesian phrasebook • Indonesia's Eastern Islands • Java • Lao phrasebook • Laos • Malay phrasebook • Malaysia, Singapore & Brunei • Myanmar (Burma) • Philippines • Pilipino (Tagalog) phrasebook • Read This First: Asia & India • Singapore • Singapore City Map • South-East Asia on a shoestring • South-East Asia phrasebook • Thailand • Thailand's Islands & Beaches • Thailand, Vietnam, Laos & Cambodia Road Atlas • Thai phrasebook • Vietnam • Vietnamese phrasebook • World Food Indonesia • World Food Thailand • World Food Vietnam

ALSO AVAILABLE: Antarctica • The Arctic • The Blue Man: Tales of Travel, Love and Coffee • Brief Encounters: Stories of Love, Sex & Travel • Buddhist Stupas in Asia: The Shape of Perfection • Chasing Rickshaws • The Last Grain Race • Lonely Planet ... On the Edge: Adventurous Escapades from Around the World • Lonely Planet Unpacked • Lonely Planet Unpacked Again • Not the Only Planet: Science Fiction Travel Stories • Ports of Call: A Journey by Sea • Sacred India • Travel Photography: A Guide to Taking Better Pictures • Travel with Children • Tuvalu: Portrait of an Island Nation

Index

Text

Bold indicates maps.

Boxed Text

MAP LEGEND

CITY ROUTES

Freeway	Freeway
Highway	Primary Road
Road	Secondary Road
Street	Street
Lane	Lane
	On/Off Ramp

	Unsealed Road
	One Way Street
	Pedestrian Street
	Stepped Street
	Tunnel
	Footbridge

REGIONAL ROUTES

	Tollway, Freeway
	Primary Road
	Secondary Road
	Minor Road

BOUNDARIES

	International
	State
	Disputed
	Fortified Wall

♦HYDROGRAPHY

	River, Creek
	Canal
	Lake

	Dry Lake; Salt Lake
	Spring; Rapids
	Waterfalls

TRANSPORT ROUTES & STATIONS

	Train
	Underground Train
	Metro
	Tramway
	Cable Car, Chairlift

	Ferry
	Walking Trail
	Walking Tour
	Path
	Pier or Jetty

AREA FEATURES

	Building
	Park, Gardens

	Market
	Sports Ground

	Beach
	Cemetery

	Campus
	Plaza

POPULATION SYMBOLS

✪ CAPITAL	National Capital	● CITY	City
☉ CAPITAL	State Capital	● Town	Town

● Village	Village
	Urban Area

MAP SYMBOLS

▪	Place to Stay	▼	Place to Eat	●	Point of Interest

✈	Airfield, Airport	◣ ▣	Dive Site, Snorkelling	⌂	Museum	⚑	Swimming Pool
⚓	Anchorage	⚐	Golf Course	⌑	National Park	⬡	Synagogue
⑄	Bank	Ⓤ	Hindu	Ⓟ	Parking	☎	Telephone
▣	Bus Terminal	✛	Hospital	★	Police Station	▲	Temple
⌂	Caravan Park	☼	Lookout	✉	Post Office	❶	Tourist Information
⌂	Cave	⚱	Monument	⊟	Pub or Bar	○	Toilet
⛪	Church	☪	Mosque	✪	Shopping Centre	▦	Zoo

Note: not all symbols displayed above appear in this book

LONELY PLANET OFFICES

Australia
Locked Bag 1, Footscray, Victoria 3011
☎ 03 8379 8000 fax 03 8379 8111
email: talk2us@lonelyplanet.com.au

UK
10a Spring Place, London NW5 3BH
☎ 020 7428 4800 fax 020 7428 4828
email: go@lonelyplanet.co.uk

USA
150 Linden St, Oakland, CA 94607
☎ 510 893 8555 TOLL FREE: 800 275 8555
fax 510 893 8572
email: info@lonelyplanet.com

France
1 rue du Dahomey, 75011 Paris
☎ 01 55 25 33 00 fax 01 55 25 33 01
email: bip@lonelyplanet.fr
www.lonelyplanet.fr

World Wide Web: www.lonelyplanet.com *or* AOL keyword: lp
Lonely Planet Images: lpi@lonelyplanet.com.au